Microsoft®
Project/Visual Basic®
Reference

PUBLISHED BY
Microsoft Press
A Division of Microsoft Corporation
One Microsoft Way
Redmond, Washington 98052-6399

Copyright © 1996 by Microsoft Press

Library of Congress Cataloging-in-Publication Data
Microsoft project/Visual Basic reference / Microsoft Corporation.
        p.   cm.
    ISBN 1-57231-310-2
    1. Computer software--Dictionaries.   2. Microsoft Project.
3. Microsoft Visual BASIC.   I. Microsoft Corporation.
QA76.752.M53   1996
658.4'04'02855369--dc20   96-6770
                                                               CIP

Printed and bound in the United States of America.

1 2 3 4 5 6 7 8 9 PHOENIX 1 0 9 8 7 6

Distributed to the book trade in Canada by Macmillan of Canada, a division of Canada Publishing
Corporation.

A CIP catalogue record for this book is available from the British Library.

Microsoft Press books are available through booksellers and distributors worldwide. For further
information about international editions, contact your local Microsoft Corporation office. Or contact
Microsoft Press International directly at fax (206) 936-7329.

Acquisitions Editor: Casey D. Doyle
Project Editors: Maureen Williams Zimmerman, Judith Bloch

Introduction

This manual is an alphabetic reference for Visual Basic for Microsoft Project. The reference contains topics for all functions, methods, objects, properties, and statements in the language, and is essentially identical to the information contained in Microsoft Project Visual Basic Help.

Unless otherwise noted, each topic in this manual is applicable to both Microsoft Project 4.0 for Windows 3.1 and Microsoft Project for Windows 95.

Where to Find Information About Microsoft Project

For general information about Microsoft Project, see the *User's Guide for Microsoft Project for Windows 95 and Windows 3.1.*

If you're new to Microsoft Project, or if you prefer a task-oriented approach to learning, you might want to start by reading *Microsoft Project Step by Step*, a self-paced tutorial also available from Microsoft Press.

You can also visit the Microsoft Project forum on The Microsoft Network (Go To MSProject) for more information on Microsoft Project, chat sessions with other users, and more. Or you can visit Microsoft Project on the Internet at http://www.microsoft.com/MSProject.

Tips on How to Learn Visual Basic

The following are suggestions for getting the most from the time you spend learning Visual Basic.

Learn Microsoft Project first

The more you know about Microsoft Project, the better prepared you'll be to venture into Visual Basic. Most macros perform a sequence of actions in Microsoft Project, and most instructions in a macro are equivalent to commands or actions in Microsoft Project. Consequently, working with Visual Basic is a little like working with Microsoft Project without a user interface; instead of commands and dialog boxes, you use Visual Basic instructions. The statements and functions you use to write instructions are much easier to understand if you're familiar with the features they represent in Microsoft Project.

Also, if you know Microsoft Project well, you can better answer the question you're most likely to ask when writing a macro: "What's the best way to do this?" People have been known to write long macros for tasks that could have been handled by a single Microsoft Project command.

Learn what you need, when you need it

Learn what you need for the task at hand. Visual Basic can seem overwhelming at first, particularly if you haven't had experience with a macro programming language. A great way to learn the language is to investigate how to implement a particular macro idea you have. As you gain experience writing different types of macros, you'll cover a lot of ground.

Use the macro recorder

The macro recorder can record the Visual Basic instruction for virtually every action you take in Microsoft Project. You can use the macro recorder to see how actions in Microsoft Project translate into Visual Basic instructions, and vice versa. Also, you'll find that recording part of a macro is often faster and easier than writing out the instructions.

Use Visual Basic Help

Help is a powerful tool for learning Visual Basic. In a Visual Basic module, you can type a Visual Basic keyword and—with the insertion point somewhere in the keyword—press F1 to immediately display Visual Basic Help for that keyword. The Visual Basic Help topic for most keywords includes an example you can copy and paste into your macro. For more information, see "Using Online Help" later in this introduction.

Using Online Help

Microsoft Project provides an extensive Help system for the Visual Basic language, the objects that Microsoft Project supports, and the properties and methods of those objects.

If you clicked Typical when you installed Microsoft Project, you'll need to run Setup again to install Help for Visual Basic for Microsoft Project.

You can access Visual Basic Help in any of the following four ways:

- In a Visual Basic module, place the insertion point anywhere in an object, property, method, function, or other keyword, and then press F1 to get context-sensitive Help.

- On the Help menu, click Microsoft Project Help Topics. You can then either click "Working with Visual Basic" on the Contents tab, look up a specific topic or Visual Basic term on the Index tab, or perform a full-text search from the Find tab.

- On the Help menu, click Microsoft Project Help Topics. You can then ask a question on the Answer Wizard tab and read the topics displayed in the Programming and Language Reference section of the dialog box.
- With a Visual Basic module active, click Object Browser on the View menu, and then click the Element Help button (appears as a question mark below the Objects/Modules box) for information about an object, method, property, or function.

Document Conventions

This book uses the typographic conventions shown in the following table. You might not recognize all the terms or Visual Basic keywords, but you'll learn more about them later.

Example of convention	Description
setup	Words or characters you're instructed to type appear in bold.
Sub, If, ChDir, MsgBox, True, Add, Height, Application, Range, Row	Words in bold with the initial letter capitalized indicate a language-specific term: a property, method, or object name; or another Visual Basic keyword.
Propertyname	In syntax, italic type indicates placeholders for information you supply.
Index	In syntax, bold italic type indicates placeholders for arguments when you can use either positional or named-argument syntax.
[*expressionlist*]	In syntax, items inside square brackets are optional.
{**While|Until**}	In syntax, braces and a vertical bar indicate a mandatory choice between two or more items.
ENTER	Small capital letters are used for the names of keys and key combinations, such as ENTER and CTRL+R.
CTRL+V	A plus sign (+) between key names indicates a combination of keys. For example, CTRL+V means to hold down the CTRL key while pressing the V key.
MyVar	This font is used for example code.

Programming Style

This book uses the following programming style guidelines for code examples.

- The following font is used for code.

```
Sub HelloWorld
    Cells(1,1).Value = "Hello, world!"
End Sub
```

- An apostrophe (') introduces comments in code.

```
' This is a comment; these two lines
' are ignored when the program is running.
```

- Names of macros and user-defined functions appear with initial letters capitalized throughout this book. Note that macro and function names cannot include spaces, so if a name consists of more than one word, the other words in the name also have their initial letters capitalized.

```
' The AuditResult user-defined function is in the Finance module.
Function AuditResult(latestIncome, expenses, taxes, commissions)
```

  Argument and variable names appear with initial letters lowercase (to distinguish them from macro, function, property, method, and object names).

- Keywords appear with initial letters capitalized, whereas built-in constants appear with an initial lowercase "xl" or "vb."

```
' Sub is a keyword.
Sub Title(titleText)
```

```
' xlManual is a built-in constant.
Application.Calculation = xlManual
```

- Control-flow blocks and statements in **Sub** and **Function** procedures are indented within the code that surrounds them.

```
Sub CheckRecordSound
    SoundRecordCapable = Application.CanRecordSounds
    If SoundRecordCapable Then
        Cells(1,1).SoundNote.Record
    End If
End Sub
```

- The line-continuation character—an underscore (_)—indicates that code continued from one line to the next is part of the same logical line. You can type these statements all on one line in the Visual Basic module. You can also divide lines of code and add the line-continuation character yourself.

```
ActiveSheet.Rectangles.Add _
    width:=200, _
    height:=200, _
    left:=50, _
    top:=50
```

Microsoft Product Support Services

Microsoft offers a variety of support options to help you get the most from your Microsoft product. For more information about Microsoft Product Support Services, see the *User's Guide for Microsoft Project for Windows 95 and Windows 3.1.*

Outside the United States, contact Microsoft Product Support Services at the Microsoft subsidiary office that serves your area. Microsoft subsidiary offices and the countries they serve are listed in the *User's Guide for Microsoft Project for Windows 95 and Windows 3.1.*

& Operator

Description   Used to force string concatenation of two expressions.

Syntax   *result = expression1* **&** *expression2*

Elements   The **&** operator syntax has these parts:

Part	Description
result	Any **String** or **Variant** variable.
expression1	Any expression.
expression2	Any expression.

Remarks   Whenever an *expression* is not a string, it is converted to a **String** variant. The data type of *result* is **String** if both expressions are **String** expressions; otherwise, *result* is a **String** variant. If both expressions are **Null**, *result* is also **Null**. However, if only one *expression* is a **Null**, that expression is treated as a zero-length string when concatenated with the other expression. Any expression that is **Empty** is also treated as a zero-length string.

See Also   Operator Precedence.

Example   This example uses the **&** operator to force string concatenation.

```
MyStr = "Hello" & " World"        ' Returns "Hello World".
MyStr = "Check " & 123 & " Check" ' Returns "Check 123 Check".
```

* Operator

Description   Used to multiply two numbers.

Syntax   *result = number1*∗*number2*

Elements   The ∗ operator syntax has these parts:

Part	Description
result	Any numeric variable.
number1	Any numeric expression.
number2	Any numeric expression.

| Remarks | The data type of *result* is usually the same as that of the most precise expression. The order of precision, from least to most precise, is **Integer**, **Long**, **Single**, **Double**, **Currency**. The following are exceptions to this order: |

- When multiplication involves a **Single** and a **Long**, the data type of *result* is converted to a **Double**.
- When the data type of *result* is a **Long**, **Single**, or **Date** variant that overflows its legal range, *result* is converted to a **Variant** containing a **Double**.
- When the data type of *result* is an **Integer** variant that overflows its legal range, *result* is converted to a **Long** variant.

If one or both expressions are **Null** expressions, *result* is a **Null**. If an expression is **Empty**, it is treated as if it were 0.

See Also   Operator Precedence.

Example   This example uses the * operator to multiply two numbers.

```
MyValue = 2 * 2              ' Returns 4.
MyValue = 459.35 * 334.90   ' Returns 153836.315.
```

+ Operator

Description   Used to sum two numbers.

Syntax   *result = expression1+expression2*

Elements   The + operator syntax has these parts:

Part	Description
result	Any numeric variable.
expression1	Any expression.
expression2	Any expression.

Remarks   Although you can also use the + operator to concatenate two character strings, you should use the **&** operator for concatenation to eliminate ambiguity and provide self-documenting code.

When you use the + operator, you may not be able to determine whether addition or string concatenation will occur. If at least one expression is not a **Variant**, the following rules apply:

If	Then
Both expressions are numeric data types (**Boolean, Integer, Long, Single, Double, Date** or **Currency**)	Add.
Both expressions are **String**	Concatenate.
One expression is a numeric data type and the other is any **Variant** (except a **Null**)	Add.
One expression is a **String** and the other is any **Variant** (except a **Null**)	Concatenate.
One expression is an **Empty Variant**	Return the remaining expression unchanged as *result*.
One expression is a numeric data type and the other is a **String**	A Type mismatch error occurs.
Either expression is a **Null**	*result* is a **Null.**

If both expressions are **Variant** expressions, the underlying type of the expressions determines the behavior of the **+** operator in the following way:

If	Then
Both **Variant** expressions are numeric	Add.
Both **Variant** expressions are strings	Concatenate.
One **Variant** expression is numeric and the other is a string	Add.

For simple arithmetic addition involving only expressions of numeric data types, the data type of *result* is usually the same as that of the most precise expression. The order of precision, from least to most precise, is **Integer, Long, Single, Double,** and **Currency**. The following are exceptions to this order:

- When a **Single** and a **Long** are added together, the data type of *result* is converted to a **Double**.

- When the data type of *result* is a **Long, Single,** or **Date** variant that overflows its legal range, *result* is converted to a **Double** variant.

- When the data type of *result* is an **Integer** variant that overflows its legal range, *result* is converted to a **Long** variant.

- When a **Date** is added to any other data type, the data type of *result* is always a **Date**.

If one or both expressions are **Null** expressions, *result* is a **Null**. If both expressions are **Empty**, *result* is an **Integer**. However, if only one expression is **Empty**, the other expression is returned unchanged as *result*.

See Also   Operator Precedence.

Example

This example uses the + operator to sum numbers. The + operator can also be used to concatenate strings but to eliminate ambiguity, you should use the **&** operator instead.

```
MyNumber = 2 + 2              ' Returns 4.
MyNumber = 4257.04 + 98112    ' Returns 102369.04.
Var1 = "34" : Var2 = 6        ' Initialize variables.
MyNumber = Var1 + Var2        ' Returns 40.
Var1 = "34" : Var2 = "6"      ' Initialize variables.
MyNumber = Var1 + Var2          Returns "346" (string concatenation).
```

- Operator

Description

Used to find the difference between two numbers or to indicate the negative value of a numeric expression.

Syntax 1

result = number1-number2

Syntax 2

-number

Elements

The - operator syntax has these parts:

Part	Description
result	Any numeric variable.
number	Any numeric expression.
number1	Any numeric expression.
number2	Any numeric expression.

Remarks

In Syntax 1, the - operator is the arithmetic subtraction operator used to find the difference between two numbers. In Syntax 2, the - operator is used as the unary negation operator to indicate the negative value of an expression.

The data type of *result* is usually the same as that of the most precise expression. The order of precision, from least to most precise, is **Integer**, **Long**, **Single**, **Double**, **Currency**. The following are exceptions to this order:

- When subtraction involves a **Single** and a **Long**, the data type of *result* is converted to a **Double**.

- When the data type of *result* is a **Long, Single,** or **Date** variant that overflows its legal range, *result* is converted to a **Variant** containing a **Double**.

- When the data type of *result* is an **Integer** variant that overflows its legal range, *result* is converted to a **Long** variant.

- When subtraction involves a **Date** and any other data type, the data type of *result* is a **Date**.
- When subtraction involves two **Date** expressions, the data type of *result* is **Double**.

If one or both expressions are **Null** expressions, *result* is a **Null**. If an expression is **Empty**, it is treated as if it were 0.

See Also Operator Precedence.

Example This example uses the - operator to calculate the difference between two numbers.

```
MyResult = 4 - 2          ' Returns 2.
MyResult = 459.35 - 334.90   ' Returns 124.45.
```

/ Operator

Description Used to divide two numbers and return a floating-point result.

Syntax *result = number1/number2*

Elements The / operator syntax has these parts:

Part	Description
result	Any numeric variable.
number1	Any numeric expression.
number2	Any numeric expression.

Remarks The data type of *result* is usually a **Double** or a **Double** variant. The following are exceptions to this rule:

- When both expressions are **Integer** or **Single** expressions, *result* is a **Single** unless it overflows its legal range; in which case, an error occurs.
- When both expressions are **Integer** or **Single** variants, *result* is a **Single** variant unless it overflows its legal range; in which case, *result* is a **Variant** containing a **Double**.

If one or both expressions are **Null** expressions, *result* is a **Null**. Any expression that is **Empty** is treated as 0.

See Also Operator Precedence.

Example

This example uses the / operator to perform floating-point division.

```
MyValue = 10 / 4     ' Returns 2.5.
MyValue = 10 / 3     ' Returns 3.333333.
```

\ Operator

Description

Used to divide two numbers and return an integer result.

Syntax

result = number1\number2

Elements

The \ operator syntax has these parts:

Part	Description
result	Any numeric variable.
number1	Any numeric expression.
number2	Any numeric expression.

Remarks

Before division is performed, the numeric expressions are rounded to **Integer** or **Long** expressions.

Usually, the data type of *result* is an **Integer**, **Integer** variant, **Long**, or **Long** variant, regardless of whether or not *result* is a whole number. Any fractional portion is truncated. However, if any expression is a **Null**, *result* is also a **Null**. Any expression that is **Empty** is treated as 0.

See Also

Operator Precedence.

Example

This example uses the \ operator to perform integer division.

```
MyValue = 11 \ 4     ' Returns 2.
MyValue = 9 \ 3      ' Returns 3.
MyValue = 100 \ 3    ' Returns 33.
```

^ Operator

Description

Used to raise a number to the power of an exponent.

Syntax

result = number^exponent

Elements	The ^ operator syntax has these parts:

Part	Description
result	Any numeric variable.
number	Any numeric expression.
exponent	Any numeric expression.

Remarks

Number can be negative only if *exponent* is an integer value. When more than one exponentiation is performed in a single expression, the ^ operator is evaluated as it is encountered from left to right.

Usually, the data type of *result* is a **Double** or a **Variant** containing a **Double**. However, if either *number* or *exponent* is a **Null** expression, *result* is also a **Null**.

See Also

Operator Precedence.

Example

This example uses the ^ operator to raise a number to the power of an exponent.

```
MyValue = 2 ^ 2      ' Returns 4.
MyValue = 3 ^ 3 ^ 3  ' Returns 19683.
MyValue = (-5) ^ 3   ' Returns -125.
```

About Method

Applies To

Application Object.

Description

Displays the About Microsoft Project dialog box, which lists version, copyright, and license information about Microsoft Project.

Syntax

[*object.*]**HelpAbout**

Elements

The *object* placeholder is an object expression that evaluates to an object in the Applies To list.

Remarks

In Microsoft Project for Microsoft Windows, the **HelpAbout** method has the same effect as the About Microsoft Project command on the Help menu.

In Microsoft Project for the Macintosh, the **HelpAbout** method has the same effect as the About Microsoft Project command on the Apple menu.

See Also

About Method, **GanttChartWizard** Method, **HelpCueCards** Method, **HelpLaunch** Method, **HelpOnlineIndex** Method, **HelpQuickPreview** Method, **HelpSearch** Method, **HelpTechnicalSupport** Method.

Abs Function

Description   Returns the absolute value of a number.

Syntax   **Abs**(*number*)

Elements   The *number* argument can be any valid numeric expression. If *number* contains no valid data, **Null** is returned; if it is an uninitialized variable, **Empty** is returned.

Remarks   The absolute value of a number is its unsigned magnitude. For example, ABS(-1) and ABS(1) both return 1.

See Also   **Sgn** Function.

Example   This example uses the **Abs** function to compute the absolute value of a number.

```
MyNumber = Abs(50.3)    ' Returns 50.3.
MyNumber = Abs(-50.3)   ' Returns 50.3.
```

AccrueAt Property

Applies To   **Resource** Object, **Resources** Collection.

Description   Returns or sets when a task accrues the cost of a resource.

Syntax   *object*.**AccrueAt** [= *value*]

Elements   The **AccrueAt** property syntax has the following parts:

Part	Description
object	An object expression that evaluates to an object in the Applies To list.
value	A constant that specifies when a task accrues the cost of the resource, as shown under Settings.

Settings   The **AccrueAt** property has the following settings:

Setting	Description
pjStart	A task accrues the cost of the resource when the task starts.
pjProrated	A task accrues the cost of the resource as the task progresses.
pjEnd	A task accrues the cost of the resource when the project ends.

See Also	**Cost** Property, **CostPerUse** Property, **OvertimeRate** Property, **StandardRate** Property.
Example	The following example sets the **AccrueAt** property to **pjProrated** for each task in the active project.

```
Sub SetProratedAccrueAt()
    Dim R        ' Resource object used in For Each loop

    ' Cause tasks to accrue the cost of resources during the task.
    For Each R in ActiveProject.Resources
        R.AccrueAt = pjProrated
    Next R
End Sub
```

Activate Method

Applies To	**Pane** Object; **Project** Object, **Projects** Collection; **Window** Object, **Windows** Collection.
Description	Activates a pane, project, or window.
Syntax	*object*.**Activate**
Elements	The *object* placeholder is an object expression that evaluates to an object in the Applies To list.
Example	The following examples activate the next and previous projects, respectively.

```
Sub ProjectNext()
    If ActiveProject.Index < Projects.Count Then
        Projects(ActiveProject.Index + 1).Activate
    Else
        Projects(1).Activate
    End If
End Sub

Sub ProjectPrevious()
    If ActiveProject.Index > 1 Then
        Projects(ActiveProject.Index - 1).Activate
    Else
        Projects(Projects.Count).Activate
    End If
End Sub
```

ActiveCell Property

Applies To	**Application** Object.
Description	Returns the active cell of an application.
Syntax	[*object.*]**ActiveCell**
Elements	The *object* placeholder is an object expression that evaluates to an object in the Applies To list.
See Also	**ActivePane** Property, **ActiveProject** Property, **ActiveSelection** Property, **ActiveWindow** Property, **Cell** Object, **Selection** Object.
Example	The following example displays the name of the resources assigned to the selected task.

```
Sub ResourceNames()
    For each r in ActiveCell.Task.Assignments
        MsgBox r.ResourceName
    Next r
End Sub
```

ActivePane Property

Applies To	**Window** Object, **Windows** Collection.
Description	Returns the active pane of a window.
Syntax	*object.***ActivePane**
Elements	The *object* placeholder is an object expression that evaluates to an object in the Applies To list.
See Also	**ActiveCell** Property, **ActiveProject** Property, **ActiveSelection** Property, **ActiveWindow** Property, **BottomPane** Property, **Pane** Object, **TopPane** Property.

ActiveProject Property

Applies To	**Application** Object.

Description   Returns the active project of an application.

Syntax   [*object*.]**ActiveProject**

Elements   The *object* placeholder is an object expression that evaluates to an object in the
                       Applies To list.

See Also   **ActiveCell** Property; **ActivePane** Property; **ActiveSelection** Property;
                       ActiveWindow Property; **Project** Object, **Projects** Collection; **Projects** Method.

Example   The following example adds the date and time to the notes in the summary
                       information and then saves the project.

```
Sub SaveAndNoteTime()
    Dim NL                       ' Newline characters
    NL = Chr(10) + Chr(13)       ' NL = Linefeed + Carriage Return
    ActiveProject.Notes = ActiveProject.Notes & NL & _
    "This project was last saved on " & Date$ & " at " & Time$ & "."
    FileSave
End Sub
```

ActiveSelection Property

Applies To   **Application** Object.

Description   Returns the active selection of an application.

Syntax   [*object*.]**ActiveSelection**

Elements   The *object* placeholder is an object expression that evaluates to an object in the
                       Applies To list.

See Also   **ActiveCell** Property, **ActivePane** Property, **ActiveProject** Property,
                       ActiveWindow Property, **Cell** Object, **Selection** Object.

Example   The following example displays the name of each selected task in a message box.

```
Sub SelectedTasks()
    If Not (ActiveSelection.Tasks Is Nothing) Then
        For Each t in ActiveSelection.Tasks
            MsgBox t.Name
        Next t
    End If
End Sub
```

ActiveWindow Property

Applies To	**Application** Object.
Description	Returns the active window of an application.
Syntax	[*object*.]**ActiveWindow**
Elements	The *object* placeholder is an object expression that evaluates to an object in the Applies To list.
See Also	**ActiveCell** Property; **ActivePane** Property; **ActiveProject** Property; **ActiveSelection** Property; **Window** Object, **Windows** Collection; **Windows** Method.

ActualCost Property

Applies To	**Assignment** Object, **Assignments** Collection; **Project** Object, **Projects** Collection; **Resource** Object, **Resources** Collection; **Task** Object, **Tasks** Collection.
Description	Returns or sets the actual cost for an assignment, project, resource, or task. Read only for **Project** or **Resource** objects, and **Task** objects with one or more resources.
Syntax	*object*.**ActualCost** [= *value*]
Elements	The **ActualCost** property syntax has these parts:

Part	Description
object	An object expression that evaluates to an object in the Applies To list.
value	A numeric expression of the actual cost of the assignment or task.

See Also	**ActualDuration** Property, **ActualFinish** Property, **ActualStart** Property, **ActualWork** Property, **BaselineCost** Property, **Cost** Property, **CostVariance** Property, **RemainingCost** Property.

Example

The following example prompts the user for actual costs of tasks with no resources in the active project.

```
Sub GetActualCostsForTasks()
    Dim Entry    ' User input
    Dim T        ' Task object used in For Each loop

    ' Count the resources of each task in the active project.
    For Each T in ActiveProject.Tasks

        ' If a task has no resources, then prompt user for actual cost.
        If T.Resources.Count = 0 Then
            Do While 1
                Entry = InputBox("Enter the cost to " & T.Name & ":")

                ' Exit loop if user enters number or presses Cancel.
                If IsNumeric(Entry) Or Entry = Empty Then
                    Exit Do

                ' User didn't enter a number; tell user to try again.
                Else
                    MsgBox("You didn't enter a number; try again.")
                End If
            Loop

            ' If user didn't press Cancel, assign actual cost to task.
            If Not StrComp(Entry, Empty, 1) = 0 Then
                T.ActualCost = Entry
            End If
        End If
    Next T
End Sub
```

ActualDuration Property

Applies To   **Project** Object, **Projects** Collection; **Task** Object, **Tasks** Collection.

Description   Returns or sets the actual duration (in minutes) of an project or task. Read only for **Project** object.

Syntax   *object*.**ActualDuration** [= *value*]

Elements   The **ActualDuration** property syntax has these parts:

Part	Description
object	An object expression that evaluates to an object in the Applies To list.
value	A numeric expression of the duration of the task, in minutes.

See Also

ActualCost Property, **ActualFinish** Property, **ActualStart** Property, **ActualWork** Property, **BaselineDuration** Property, **Duration** Property, **DurationVariance** Property, **RemainingDuration** Property.

Example

The following example marks the tasks in the active project with actual durations that exceed a certain number of minutes.

```
Sub MarkTasksWithLongDurations()
    Dim T                        ' Task object used in For Each loop
    Dim Minutes as Long          ' Duration entered by user

    ' Prompt user for the actual duration, in minutes.
    Minutes = Val(InputBox("Enter the actual duration, in minutes: "))

    ' Don't do anything if the InputBox was cancelled.
    If Minutes = 0 Then Exit Sub

    ' Cycle through the tasks of the active project.
    For Each T in ActiveProject.Tasks

        ' Mark a task, if it exceeds the duration.
        If T.ActualDuration > Minutes Then T.Marked = True
    Next T
End Sub
```

ActualFinish Property

Applies To

Project Object, **Projects** Collection; **Task** Object, **Tasks** Collection.

Description

Returns or sets the actual finish date of a project or task. Read only for **Project** object.

Syntax

object.**ActualFinish** [= *value*]

Elements   The **ActualFinish** property syntax has these parts:

Part	Description
object	An object expression that evaluates to an object in the Applies To list.
value	A date expression of the actual finish date of the task.

See Also   **ActualCost** Property, **ActualDuration** Property, **ActualStart** Property, **ActualWork** Property, **BaselineFinish** Property, **Finish** Property, **FinishVariance** Property.

Example

The following example prompts the user to set the actual finish dates of tasks in the active project.

```
Sub SetActualFinishForTasks ()
    Dim T           ' Task object used in For Each loop
    Dim Entry       ' User's entry

    For Each T in ActiveProject.Tasks

        ' Loop until user enters a date or presses Cancel.
        Do While 1
            Entry = InputBox("Enter the actual finish date for " & _
                    T.Name & ":")
            If IsDate(Entry) Or Entry = Empty Then
                Exit Do
            Else
                MsgBox("You didn't enter a date; try again.")
            End If
        Loop

        'If user didn't press Cancel, set the task's actual finish date.
        If Entry <> Empty Then
            T.ActualFinish = Entry
        End If
    Next T
End Sub
```

ActualStart Property

Applies To   **Project** Object, **Projects** Collection; **Task** Object, **Tasks** Collection.

Description	Returns or sets the actual start date of a project or task. Read only for **Project** object.
Syntax	*object*.**ActualStart** [= *value*]
Elements	The **ActualStart** property syntax has these parts:

Part	Description
object	An object expression that evaluates to an object in the Applies To list.
value	A date expression of the actual start date of the task.

See Also	**ActualCost** Property, **ActualDuration** Property, **ActualFinish** Property, **ActualWork** Property, **BaselineStart** Property, **Start** Property, **StartVariance** Property.

ActualWork Property

Applies To	**Assignment** Object, **Assignments** Collection; **Project** Object, **Projects** Collection; **Resource** Object, **Resources** Collection; **Task** Object, **Tasks** Collection.
Description	Returns or sets the actual work (in minutes) for a assignment, project, resource, or task. Read only for **Project** or **Resource** objects, and **Task** objects with one or more resources.
Syntax	*object*.**ActualWork** [= *value*]
Elements	The **ActualWork** property syntax has these parts:

Part	Description
object	An object expression that evaluates to an object in the Applies To list.
value	A numeric expression of the actual work for the assignment or task, in minutes.

See Also	**ActualCost** Property, **ActualDuration** Property, **ActualFinish** Property, **ActualStart** Property, **BaselineWork** Property, **RemainingWork** Property, **Work** Property, **WorkVariance** Property.

Add Method

Applies To	**DocumentProperties** Collection Object.
Description	Creates a new custom document property. Returns a **DocumentProperty** object.
	To use this method, you should establish a reference to the Microsoft Office 95 Object Library by using the References command (Tools menu).
Syntax	*object*.**Add**(*name, linkToContent, type*[, *value, linkSource*])
Elements	The **Add** method syntax has the following object qualifier and named arguments:

Part	Description
object	The custom **DocumentProperties** collection object. Required.
name	The name of the property. Required.
linkToContent	Specifies whether the property is linked to the content of the container document. If **True**, the *linkSource* argument is required. If **False**, the *value* argument is required. Required.
type	The data type of the property (can be one of **offPropertyTypeBoolean**, **offPropertyTypeDate**, **offPropertyTypeFloat**, **offPropertyTypeString**, or **offPropertyTypeNumber**). Required.
value	The value of the property if it's not linked to the content of the container document. The value is converted to match the data type specified by the *type* argument, if possible; otherwise, an error occurs. If *linkToContent* is **True**, this argument is ignored and the new document property has a default value until linked property values are updated by the container application (usually when the document is saved). Optional.
linkSource	Ignored if *linkToContent* is **False**. The source of the linked property. The container application determines what types of source linking are allowed. Optional.

Remarks	This method cannot be used with the collection of built-in document properties.

Alerts Method

Applies To	**Application** Object.
Description	Determines whether alerts appear when a macro runs.

Syntax	[*object.*]**Alerts** [*show*]
Elements	The **Alerts** method syntax has the following object qualifier and named arguments:

Part	Description
object	An object expression that evaluates to an object in the Applies To list.
show	A Boolean expression that specifies whether to display alerts when the macro runs. By default, the *show* argument is **True**.

Remarks	The **Alerts** method applies only to the macro that contains the method.
See Also	**Macro** Method.

AMText Property

Applies To	**Application** Object.
Description	Returns the text Microsoft Project displays next to morning hours in the 12-hour time format.
Syntax	[*object.*]**AMText**
Elements	The *object* placeholder is an object expression that evaluates to an object in the Applies To list.
Remarks	Microsoft Project for Microsoft Windows sets the **AMText** property equal to the corresponding value in the Regional settings of the Microsoft Windows Control Panel.
	On the Macintosh, using System 7.1 and later, you can use the Date & Time control panel to change this value.
See Also	**PMText** Property, **TimeLeadingZero** Property, **TimeSeparator** Property, **TwelveHourTimeFormat** Property.

And Operator

Description	Used to perform a logical conjunction on two expressions.
Syntax	*result* = *expression1* **And** *expression2*
Elements	The **And** operator syntax has these parts:

Part	Description
result	Any numeric variable.
expression1	Any expression.
expression2	Any expression.

Remarks

If, and only if, both expressions evaluate **True**, *result* is **True**. If either expression evaluates **False**, *result* is **False**. The following table illustrates how *result* is determined:

True	True	True
True	False	False
True	Null	Null
False	True	False
False	False	False
False	Null	False
Null	True	Null
Null	False	False
Null	Null	Null

The **And** operator also performs a bit-wise comparison of identically positioned bits in two numeric expressions and sets the corresponding bit in *result* according to the following truth table:

0	0	0
0	1	0
1	0	0
1	1	1

See Also

Operator Precedence.

Example

This example uses the **And** operator to perform a logical conjunction on two expressions.

```
A = 10: B = 8: C = 6 : D = Null  ' Initialize variables.
MyCheck = A > B And B > C        ' Returns True.
MyCheck = B > A And B > C        ' Returns False.
MyCheck = A > B And B > D        ' Returns Null.
MyCheck = A And B                ' Returns 8 (bit-wise comparison).
```

AppActivate Method

Applies To   **Application** Object.

Description   Activates Microsoft Project or any application you specify.

Syntax   [*object*.]**AppActivate** [*application*]

Elements   The **AppActivate** method syntax has the following object qualifier and named arguments:

Part	Description
object	An object expression that evaluates to an object in the Applies To list. Required.
application	A string expression that specifies the name of an application to activate. This is an application filename or the application's four-letter type. For example, Microsoft Project = MSPJ, Microsoft Excel = XCEL, Microsoft Word = MSWD, Microsoft PowerPoint = PPT3, and Microsoft FoxPro = FOXX. If the argument is not specified, then Microsoft Project will be activated. Optional.

Remarks   This method, along with the **AppLaunch** method, applies to Microsoft Project for the Macintosh. The **AppActivate** method gives focus to an application which is already running. The **AppLaunch** method starts and activates an application. For Microsoft Project for Microsoft Windows, use the **AppExecute** method.

There is also an **AppActivate** statement, which applies to both Microsoft Windows and the Macintosh. You can use the Object Browser to review the **AppActivate** statement. First, choose the Object Browser. From Libraries/Projects, choose VBA. From Classes/Modules, choose Interaction. From Methods/Properties, choose AppActivate. Click the **?** button to get Help on the selection.

You can communicate with another application using OLE automation or dynamic data exchange (DDE).

See Also   **AppExecute** Method.

Example   The following example starts and activates Microsoft Excel.

```
Sub StartMicrosoftExcel()
    AppLaunch Application := "XCEL"
End Sub
```

AppActivate Statement

Description   Activates an application window.

Syntax   **AppActivate** *title* [*,wait*]

Elements   The **AppActivate** statement syntax has these named-argument parts:

Part	Description
title	In Microsoft Windows, the *title* argument is the string in the title bar of the application window you want to activate.
	On the Macintosh (System 7.0 or later), the *title* argument is the application name. You can use the **MacID** function to specify an application's signature instead of the application name. For example,
	`AppActivate MacID("MSWD")`
	In addition, the task ID returned by the **Shell** function can be used, in place of *title*, to activate an application.
wait	Boolean value specifying whether the calling application has the focus before activating another. If **False** (default), the specified application is immediately activated, even if the calling application does not have the focus. If **True**, the calling application waits until it has the focus, then activates the specified application.

Remarks   The **AppActivate** statement changes the focus to the named application or window but does not affect whether it is maximized or minimized. Focus moves from the activated application window when the user takes some action to change the focus or close the window. Use the **Shell** function to start an application and set the window style.

In trying to find the application to activate, a comparison is made to try to find an application whose title string is an exact match with *title*. If unsuccessful, any application's title string that begins with *title* is activated. In Microsoft Windows, if there is more than one instance of the application named by *title*, one is arbitrarily activated.

If you use the **MacID** function with **AppActivate** in Microsoft Windows, an error occurs.

See Also   **MacID** Function, **SendKeys** Statement, **Shell** Function.

Example   This example illustrates various uses of the **AppActivate** statement to activate an application window. On the Macintosh, you can use the **MacID** function to specify the application's signature instead of the application's name. The **AppActivate** statement is available with Macintosh System 7.0 or later.

```
' In Microsoft Windows.
AppActivate "Microsoft Word"                ' Activate Word.
' AppActivate can also use the return value of the Shell function.
MyAppID = Shell("C:\WORD\WINWORD.EXE", 1)   ' Run Microsoft Word.
AppActivate MyAppID                         ' Activate Microsoft Word.

' On the Macintosh.
AppActivate "Microsoft Word"                ' Activate Microsoft Word.
' MacID("MSWD") returns signature for Microsoft Word.
AppActivate MacID("MSWD")                    ' Activate Microsoft Word.
' You can also use the return value of the Shell function.
ReturnValue = Shell("Microsoft Excel")      ' Run Microsoft Excel.
AppActivate ReturnValue                     ' Activate Microsoft Excel.
```

AppExecute Method

Applies To   **Application** Object.

Description   Starts an application.

Syntax   [*object.*]**AppExecute** [*window, command, minimize, activate*]

Elements   The **AppExecute** method syntax has the following object qualifier and named
                    arguments:

Part	Description
object	An object expression that evaluates to an object in the Applies To list. Optional.
window	A string expression that specifies the name of an application to activate. If the application is running, Microsoft Project ignores the *command* argument. Optional.
command	A string expression that specifies the command to start the application. Required if you don't specify the *window* argument.
minimize	A Boolean expression that specifies the main window state of the application.
	True The main window is minimized.
	False The main window is restored to its previous state.
	By default, the *minimize* argument is **False**. Optional.
activate	A Boolean expression that specifies whether to activate the application you specify with the *command* argument. By default, the *activate* argument is **True**. Optional.

Remarks   This method applies to Microsoft Project for Microsoft Windows. For Microsoft
                    Project for the Macintosh, use the **AppLaunch** method. After you start another

application, you can communicate with the application using OLE automation or dynamic data exchange (DDE).

See Also   **AppActivate** Method, **AppLaunch** Method, **AppMaximize** Method, **AppMove** Method, **AppRestore** Method, **AppSize** Method.

Example   The following example starts and activates Microsoft Excel.

```
Sub StartMicrosoftExcel()
    AppExecute Command := "Excel.exe"
End Sub
```

AppLaunch Method

Applies To   **Application** Object.

Description   Activates an application.

Syntax   [*object.*]**AppLaunch** *application*[, *document, activate*]

Elements   The **AppLaunch** method syntax has the following object qualifier and named arguments:

Part	Description
object	An object expression that evaluates to an object in the Applies To list. Optional.
application	A string expression that specifies the name of an application to launch. This is an application filename or the application's four-letter type. For example, Microsoft Project = MSPJ, Microsoft Excel = XCEL, Microsoft Word = MSWD, Microsoft PowerPoint = PPTS, and Microsoft FoxPro = FOXX. If the application is running, Microsoft Project ignores the *application* argument. Required.
document	A string expression that specifies the path of the document to be opened when the application is started. Optional.
activate	A Boolean expression that specifies whether to activate the application you specify. By default, the *activate* argument is **True**. Optional.

Remarks   This method applies to Microsoft Project for the Macintosh. For Microsoft Project for Microsoft Windows, use the **AppExecute** method. After you start another application, you can communicate with the application using OLE automation or dynamic data exchange (DDE).

See Also   **AppExecute** Method.

Example   The following example starts and activates Microsoft Excel.

```
Sub StartMicrosoftExcel()
    AppLaunch Application := "XCEL"
End Sub
```

Application Object

Description   The application that runs the macro or contains a particular object.

Remarks   In Microsoft Project, the **Application** object is the parent of the **Cell**, **Project**, **Selection**, and **Window** objects, and the **Projects** and **Windows** collections.

Properties   **ActiveCell** Property, **ActiveProject** Property, **ActiveSelection** Property, **ActiveWindow** Property, **AMText** Property, **Application** Property, **AskToUpdateLinks** Property, **AutoLevel** Property, **AutoRemoveDelay** Property, **Calculation** Property, **Caption** Property, **CellDragAndDrop** Property, **CopyResourceUsageHeader** Property, **DateOrder** Property, **DateSeparator** Property, **DayLeadingZero** Property, **DecimalSeparator** Property, **DefaultDateFormat** Property, **DefaultView** Property, **DisplayAlerts** Property, **DisplayEntryBar** Property, **DisplayNotesIndicator** Property, **DisplayOLEIndicator** Property, **DisplayPlanningWizard** Property, **DisplayScheduleMessages** Property, **DisplayScrollBars** Property, **DisplayStatusBar** Property, **DisplayWizardErrors** Property, **DisplayWizardScheduling** Property, **DisplayWizardUsage** Property, **Height** Property, **Left** Property, **LevelOrder** Property, **LevelWithinSlack** Property, **ListSeparator** Property, **LoadLastFile** Property, **MailSession** Property, **MailSystem** Property, **MonthLeadingZero** Property, **MoveAfterReturn** Property, **Name** Property, **OperatingSystem** Property, **Parent** Property, **Path** Property, **PathSeparator** Property, **PMText** Property, **PromptForSummaryInfo** Property, **ShowTipOfDay** Property, **ShowToolTips** Property, **ShowWelcome** Property, **StartWeekOn** Property, **StartYearIn** Property, **SupportsMultipleDocuments** Property, **SupportsMultipleWindows** Property, **ThousandsSeparator** Property, **TimeLeadingZero** Property, **TimeSeparator** Property, **Top** Property, **TwelveHourTimeFormat** Property, **UsableHeight** Property, **UsableWidth** Property, **UserName** Property, **Version** Property, **Visible** Property, **Width** Property, **WindowState** Property

Methods   **Alerts** Method, **AppExecute** Method, **AppMaximize** Method, **AppMinimize** Method, **AppMove** Method, **AppRestore** Method, **AppSize** Method, **BarBoxStyles** Method, **BarRounding** Method, **BaseCalendarCreate** Method, **BaseCalendarDelete** Method, **BaseCalendarEditDays** Method,

BaseCalendarRename Method, **BaseCalendarReset** Method, **BaseCalendars** Method, **BaselineSave** Method, **CalculateAll** Method, **CalculateProject** Method, **CalendarBarStyles** Method, **CalendarBarStylesEdit** Method, **CalendarBestFitWeekHeight** Method, **CalendarDateBoxes** Method, **CalendarDateShading** Method, **CalendarDateShadingEdit** Method, **CalendarLayout** Method, **CalendarTaskList** Method, **CalendarTimescale** Method, **CalendarWeekHeadings** Method, **ChangeWorkingTime** Method, **CheckField** Method, **ColumnAlignment** Method, **ColumnBestFit** Method, **ColumnDelete** Method, **ColumnEdit** Method, **ColumnInsert** Method, **ConsolidateProjects** Method, **CreatePublisher** Method, **CustomForms** Method, **DateAdd** Method, **DateDifference** Method, **DateFormat** Method, **DateSubtract** Method, **DDEExecute** Method, **DDEInitiate** Method, **DDELinksUpdate** Method, **DDEPasteLink** Method, **DDETerminate** Method, **DocClose** Method, **DocMaximize** Method, **DocMove** Method, **DocRestore** Method, **DocSize** Method, **DrawingCreate** Method, **DrawingCycleColor** Method, **DrawingMove** Method, **DrawingProperties** Method, **DrawingReshape** Method, **DrawingToolbarShow** Method, **DurationFormat** Method, **DurationValue** Method, **EditClear** Method, **EditClearFormats** Method, **EditCopy** Method, **EditCopyPicture** Method, **EditCut** Method, **EditDelete** Method, **EditGoto** Method, **EditInsert** Method, **EditionStopAll** Method, **EditPaste** Method, **EditPasteSpecial** Method, **EditUndo** Method, **FileClose** Method, **FileCloseAll** Method, **FileExit** Method, **FileLoadLast** Method, **FileNew** Method, **FileOpen** Method, **FilePageSetup** Method, **FilePageSetupCalendar** Method, **FilePageSetupCalendarText** Method, **FilePageSetupFooter** Method, **FilePageSetupFooterText** Method, **FilePageSetupHeader** Method, **FilePageSetupHeaderText** Method, **FilePageSetupLegend** Method, **FilePageSetupLegendText** Method, **FilePageSetupMargins** Method, **FilePageSetupPage** Method, **FilePageSetupView** Method, **FilePrint** Method, **FilePrintPreview** Method, **FilePrintSetup** Method, **FileQuit** Method, **FileSave** Method, **FileSaveAs** Method, **FileSaveWorkspace** Method, **FillDown** Method, **FilterApply** Method, **FilterEdit** Method, **Filters** Method, **Find** Method, **FindFile** Method, **FindNext** Method, **FindPrevious** Method, **Font** Method, **FontBold** Method, **FontItalic** Method, **FontUnderline** Method, **Form** Method, **FormatCopy** Method, **FormatPainter** Method, **FormatPaste** Method, **FormViewShow** Method, **GanttBarFormat** Method, **GanttBarLinks** Method, **GanttBarSize** Method, **GanttBarStyleDelete** Method, **GanttBarStyleEdit** Method, **GanttBarTextDateFormat** Method, **GanttChartWizard** Method, **GanttShowDrawings** Method, **GotoNextOverallocation** Method, **GotoTaskDates** Method, **Gridlines** Method, **GridlinesEdit** Method, **HelpAbout** Method, **HelpContents** Method, **HelpContextHelp** Method, **HelpCueCards** Method, **HelpLaunch** Method, **HelpOnlineIndex** Method, **HelpQuickPreview** Method, **HelpSearch** Method, **HelpTechnicalSupport** Method, **InformationDialog** Method, **InsertNotes** Method, **Layout** Method, **LayoutNow** Method, **LevelingClear** Method, **LevelingOptions** Method, **LevelNow** Method, **LinkTasks** Method, **LinkTasksEdit** Method, **Macro** Method, **MailLogOff**

Method, **MailLogOn** Method, **MailRoutingSlip** Method, **MailSend** Method, **MailSendProjectMail** Method, **MailSendScheduleNote** Method, **MailUpdateProject** Method, **MenuBarApply** Method, **MenuBarEdit** Method, **MenuBars** Method, **Message** Method, **ObjectChangeIcon** Method, **ObjectConvert** Method, **ObjectInsert** Method, **ObjectLinks** Method, **ObjectVerb** Method, **OptionsCalculation** Method, **OptionsCalendar** Method, **OptionsEdit** Method, **OptionsGeneral** Method, **OptionsModuleFormat** Method, **OptionsModuleGeneral** Method, **OptionsPreferences** Method, **OptionsSchedule** Method, **OptionsSpelling** Method, **OptionsView** Method, **Organizer** Method, **OrganizerDeleteItem** Method, **OrganizerMoveItem** Method, **OrganizerRenameItem** Method, **OutlineHideSubtasks** Method, **OutlineIndent** Method, **OutlineOutdent** Method, **OutlineShowAllTasks** Method, **OutlineShowSubtasks** Method, **OutlineSymbolsToggle** Method, **PageBreakRemove** Method, **PageBreakSet** Method, **PageBreaksRemoveAll** Method, **PageBreaksShow** Method, **PaneClose** Method, **PaneCreate** Method, **PaneNext** Method, **PERTBorders** Method, **PERTBoxStyles** Method, **PERTLayout** Method, **PERTSetTask** Method, **PERTShowHideFields** Method, **Projects** Method, **ProjectStatistics** Method, **ProjectSummaryInfo** Method, **PublisherOptions** Method, **Quit** Method, **RecurringTaskInsert** Method, **ReportPrint** Method, **ReportPrintPreview** Method, **Reports** Method, **ResourceAssignment** Method, **ResourceCalendarEditDays** Method, **ResourceCalendarReset** Method, **ResourceCalendars** Method, **ResourceGraphBarStyles** Method, **ResourceSharing** Method, **ResourceSharingPoolAction** Method, **RowClear** Method, **RowDelete** Method, **RowInsert** Method, **SchedulePlusReminderSet** Method, **SelectAll** Method, **SelectBeginning** Method, **SelectCell** Method, **SelectCellDown** Method, **SelectCellLeft** Method, **SelectCellRight** Method, **SelectCellUp** Method, **SelectColumn** Method, **SelectEnd** Method, **SelectionExtend** Method, **SelectRange** Method, **SelectResourceCell** Method, **SelectResourceColumn** Method, **SelectResourceField** Method, **SelectRow** Method, **SelectRowEnd** Method, **SelectRowStart** Method, **SelectSheet** Method, **SelectTaskCell** Method, **SelectTaskColumn** Method, **SelectTaskField** Method, **SetActiveCell** Method, **SetField** Method, **SetMatchingField** Method, **SetResourceField** Method, **SetTaskField** Method, **Sort** Method, **SpellingCheck** Method, **SubscriberOptions** Method, **SubscribeTo** Method, **TableApply** Method, **TableEdit** Method, **Tables** Method, **TextStyles** Method, **Timescale** Method, **TimescaledData** Method, **TimescaleEdit** Method, **TimescaleNonWorking** Method, **TipOfTheDay** Method, **ToolbarCopyToolFace** Method, **ToolbarCustomizeTool** Method, **ToolbarDeleteTool** Method, **ToolbarInsertTool** Method, **ToolbarPasteToolFace** Method, **Toolbars** Method, **ToolbarsCustomize** Method, **UnlinkTasks** Method, **UpdateProject** Method, **UpdateTasks** Method, **ViewApply** Method, **ViewEditCombination** Method, **ViewEditSingle** Method, **Views** Method, **ViewShowAvailability** Method, **ViewShowCost** Method, **ViewShowCumulativeCost** Method, **ViewShowCumulativeWork** Method, **ViewShowNotes** Method, **ViewShowObjects** Method, **ViewShowOverallocation**

Method, **ViewShowPeakUnits** Method, **ViewShowPercentAllocation** Method, **ViewShowPredecessorsSuccessors** Method, **ViewShowResourcesPredecessors** Method, **ViewShowResourcesSuccessors** Method, **ViewShowSchedule** Method, **ViewShowSelectedTasks** Method, **ViewShowWork** Method, **WindowActivate** Method, **WindowArrangeAll** Method, **WindowHide** Method, **WindowMoreWindows** Method, **WindowNewWindow** Method, **WindowNext** Method, **WindowPrev** Method, **Windows** Method, **WindowSplit** Method, **WindowUnhide** Method, **Zoom** Method, **ZoomCalendar** Method, **ZoomIn** Method, **ZoomOut** Method, **ZoomPERT** Method, **ZoomTimescale** Method.

See Also   **Application** Property; **Cell** Object; **Project** Object, **Projects** Collection; **Selection** Object; **Window** Object, **Windows** Collection.

Application Property

Applies To   **Application** Object; **Assignment** Object, **Assignments** Collection; **Calendar** Object, **Calendars** Collection; **Cell** Object; **Day** Object, **Days** Collection; **List** Object; **Month** Object, **Months** Collection; **Pane** Object; **Period** Object; **Project** Object, **Projects** Collection; **Resource** Object, **Resources** Collection; **Selection** Object; **Shift** Object; **Task** Object, **Tasks** Collection; **Weekday** Object, **Weekdays** Collection; **Window** Object, **Windows** Collection; **Year** Object, **Years** Collection.

Description   Returns the application that runs the macro or contains a particular object.

Syntax   [*object.*]**Application**

Elements   The *object* placeholder is an object expression that evaluates to an object in the Applies To list.

See Also   **Application** Object.

AppMaximize Method

Applies To   **Application** Object.

Description   Maximizes the main window of Microsoft Project.

Syntax   [*object.*]**AppMaximize**

Elements   The *object* placeholder is an object expression that evaluates to an object in the Applies To list.

Remarks	This method applies to Microsoft Project for Microsoft Windows.
See Also	**AppExecute** Method, **AppMinimize** Method, **AppMove** Method, **AppRestore** Method, **AppSize** Method, **WindowState** Property.
Example	The following example maximizes the main window of Microsoft Project.

```
Sub MaximizeMainWindow()
    AppMaximize
End Sub
```

AppMinimize Method

Applies To	**Application** Object.
Description	Minimizes the main window of Microsoft Project.
Syntax	[*object*.]**AppMinimize**
Elements	The *object* placeholder is an object expression that evaluates to an object in the Applies To list.
Remarks	This method applies to Microsoft Project for Microsoft Windows.
See Also	**AppExecute** Method, **AppMaximize** Method, **AppMove** Method, **AppRestore** Method, **AppSize** Method, **WindowState** Property.
Example	The following example minimizes the main window of Microsoft Project.

```
Sub MinimizeMainWindow()
    AppMinimize
End Sub
```

AppMove Method

Applies To	**Application** Object.
Description	Moves the main window of Microsoft Project.
Syntax	[*object*.]**AppMove** [*xPosition*, *yPosition*, *points*]
Elements	The **AppMove** method syntax has the following object qualifier and named arguments:

Part	Description
object	An object expression that evaluates to an object in the Applies To list. Optional.
xPosition	A numeric expression that specifies the distance of the main window from the left edge of the screen. Optional.
yPosition	A numeric expression that specifies the distance of the main window from the top edge of the screen. Optional.
points	A Boolean expression that specifies the measurement units.

    True   The positions you specify with the *xPosition* and *yPosition* arguments are measured in points.

    False   The positions you specify with the *xPosition* and *yPosition* arguments are measured in pixels.

By default, the *points* argument is **False**. Optional.

Remarks

This method applies to Microsoft Project for Microsoft Windows.

See Also

AppExecute Method, **AppMaximize** Method, **AppMinimize** Method, **AppRestore** Method, **AppSize** Method, **Left** Property, **Top** Property.

Example

The following example moves the main window of Microsoft Project 9 points to the left.

```
Sub MoveMainWindowToLeft()
    AppMove xPosition := Application.Left - 9, points := True
End Sub
```

AppRestore Method

Applies To

Application Object.

Description

Restores the main window of Microsoft Project to its last nonminimized and nonmaximized state.

Syntax

[*object.*]**AppRestore**

Elements

The *object* placeholder is an object expression that evaluates to an object in the Applies To list.

Remarks

This method applies to Microsoft Project for Microsoft Windows.

See Also

AppExecute Method, **AppMaximize** Method, **AppMinimize** Method, **AppMove** Method, **AppSize** Method, **WindowState** Property.

Example

The following example restores the main window of Microsoft Project to its last nonminimized and nonmaximized state.

```
Sub RestoreMainWindow()
    AppRestore
End Sub
```

AppSize Method

Applies To

Application Object.

Description

Sets the width and height of the main window of Microsoft Project.

Syntax

[*object.*]**AppSize** [*width, height, points*]

Elements

The **AppSize** method syntax has the following object qualifier and named arguments:

Part	Description
object	An object expression that evaluates to an object in the Applies To list. Optional.
width	A numeric expression that specifies the new width of the main window. Optional.
height	A numeric expression that specifies the new height of the main window. Optional.
points	A Boolean expression that specifies the measurement units.

	True	The values you specify with the *width* and *height* arguments are measured in points.
	False	The values you specify with the *width* and *height* arguments are measured in pixels.

By default, the *points* argument is **False**. Optional.

Remarks

This method applies to Microsoft Project for Microsoft Windows.

See Also

AppExecute Method, **AppMaximize** Method, **AppMinimize** Method, **AppMove** Method, **AppRestore** Method, **Height** Property, **UsableHeight** Property, **UsableWidth** Property, **Width** Property.

Example

The following example moves the main window of Microsoft Project to the left half of the screen.

```
Sub MoveMainWindowToLeftHalf()
    AppSize Width := UsableWidth / 2, Height := UsableHeight, _
        points := True
    Application.Left = 0
End Sub
```

Array Function

Description

Returns a **Variant** containing an array.

Syntax

Array(*arglist***)**

Elements

The *arglist* consists of a comma-delimited list of an arbitrary number of values that are assigned to the elements of the array contained within the **Variant**. If no arguments are specified, an array of zero-length is created.

Remarks

Although a **Variant** containing an array is conceptually different from an array whose elements are of type **Variant**, the way the array elements are accessed is the same. The notation used to refer to any element of an array consists of the variable name followed by parentheses containing an index number to the desired element. In the following example, the first statement creates a variable A as a **Variant**. The second statement assigns an array to the variable A. The final statement illustrates how to assign the value contained in the second array element to another variable.

```
Dim A As Variant
A = Array(10,20,30)
B = A(2)
```

The lower bound of an array created using the **Array** function is determined by the lower bound specified with the **Option Base** statement.

See Also

Def*type* Statements, **Dim** Statement, **Let** Statement, **Option Base** Statement.

Example

This example uses the **Array** function to return a **Variant** containing an array.

```
MyWeek = Array("Mon", "Tue", "Wed", "Thu", "Fri", "Sat", "Sun")
' Return values assume lower bound equals 1 (using Option Base).
MyDay = MyWeek(2)    ' Returns "Tue".
MyDay = MyWeek(4)    ' Returns "Thu".
```

Asc Function

Description   Returns the character code corresponding to the first letter in a string.

Syntax   **Asc(*string*)**

Elements   The ***string*** named argument is any valid string expression. If the ***string*** contains no characters, a run-time error occurs.

See Also   **Chr** Function.

Example   This example uses the **Asc** function to return a character code corresponding to the first letter in the string.

```
MyNumber = Asc("A")      ' Returns 65.
MyNumber = Asc("a")      ' Returns 97.
MyNumber = Asc("Apple")  ' Returns 65.
```

AskToUpdateLinks Property

Applies To   **Application** Object.

Description   Returns or sets whether DDE and OLE links are updated automatically.

Syntax   [*object*.]**AskToUpdateLinks** [= *value*]

Elements   The **AskToUpdateLinks** property syntax has the following parts:

Part	Description
object	An object expression that evaluates to an object in the Applies To list.
value	A Boolean expression that specifies whether DDE links are updated automatically.

See Also   **DDEExecute** Method, **DDEInitiate** Method, **DDELinksUpdate** Method, **DDEPasteLink** Method, **DDETerminate** Method, **OptionsEdit** Method.

Assignment Object, Assignments Collection

Description An assignment or the assignments for a task or resource.

Properties **ActualCost** Property, **ActualWork** Property, **Application** Property, **BaselineCost** Property, **BaselineWork** Property, **Cost** Property, **Count** Property, **Delay** Property, **Finish** Property, **Index** Property, **OvertimeWork** Property, **Parent** Property, **ProjectID** Property, **RemainingCost** Property, **RemainingWork** Property, **ResourceID** Property, **ResourceName** Property, **Start** Property, **TaskID** Property, **TaskName** Property, **UniqueID** Property, **Units** Property, **Work** Property

Methods **Add** Method, **Delete** Method, **UniqueID** Method

See Also **Assignments** Method; **Resource** Object, **Resources** Collection; **Task** Object, **Tasks** Collection.

Assignments Method

Applies To **Resource** Object, **Resources** Collection; **Task** Object, **Tasks** Collection.

Description Returns an assignment or the assignments for a task or resource.

Syntax *object*.**Assignments**[(*index*)]

Elements The **Assignments** method syntax has the following object qualifier and named arguments:

Part	Description
object	An object expression that evaluates to an object in the Applies To list.
index	A numeric expression that specifies the index of the *object*.

See Also **Assignment** Object, **Assignments** Collection.

Example   The following example displays the name of the resources assigned to the selected task.

```
Sub ResourceNames()
    For Each r in ActiveCell.Task.Assignments
        MsgBox r.ResourceName
    Next r
End Sub
```

Atn Function

Description   Returns the arctangent of a number.

Syntax   **Atn(*number*)**

Elements   The *number* named argument can be any valid numeric expression.

Remarks   The **Atn** function takes the ratio of two sides of a right triangle (*number*) and returns the corresponding angle in radians. The ratio is the length of the side opposite the angle divided by the length of the side adjacent to the angle.

The range of the result is -pi/2 to pi/2 radians.

To convert degrees to radians, multiply degrees by pi/180. To convert radians to degrees, multiply radians by 180/pi.

Note   Atn is the inverse trigonometric function of Tan, which takes an angle as its argument and returns the ratio of two sides of a right triangle. Do not confuse Atn with the cotangent, which is the simple inverse of a tangent (1/tangent).

See Also   **Cos** Function, Derived Math Functions, **Sin** Function, **Tan** Function.

Example   This example uses the **Atn** function to return the arctangent of a number.

```
Pi = 4 * Atn(1) ' Calculate the value of pi.
```

Author Property

Applies To   **Project** Object, **Projects** Collection.

Description   Returns or sets the name of a project's author.

Syntax	[*object*.]**Author** [= *value*]
Elements	The **Author** property syntax has these parts:

Part	Description
object	An object expression that evaluates to an object in the Applies To list.
value	A string expression that specifies the name of the project's author.

Remarks	By default, the **Author** property equals the **UserName** property.
See Also	**Comments** Property, **Company** Property, **CurrentDate** Property, **Keywords** Property, **Manager** Property, **Notes** Property, **ScheduleFromStart** Property, **Subject** Property, **Template** Property, **Title** Property.

AutoAddResources Property

Applies To	**Project** Object, **Projects** Collection.
Description	Returns or sets whether the Resource Form appears when you create new resources.
Syntax	[*object*.]**AutoAddResources** [= *value*]
Elements	The **AutoAddResources** property syntax has these parts:

Part	Description
object	An object expression that evaluates to an object in the Applies To list.
value	A Boolean expression that specifies whether or not the Resource Form appears when you create new resources, as shown under Settings.

Settings	The **AutoAddResources** property has these settings:

Setting	Description
True	The Resource Form doesn't appear when you create new resources.
False	The Resource Form appears when you create new resources.

See Also	**AutoLinkTasks** Property, **AutoSplitTasks** Property, **AutoTrack** Property.

Example

The following example prompts the user to set the **AutoAddResources**, **AutoCalculate**, **AutoLinkTasks**, **AutoSplitTasks**, and **AutoTrack** properties.

```
Sub PromptForAutoPropertySettings()
    Dim I                   ' Used in For...Next loop
    Dim Prompts(5)          ' Prompts to display on the screen
    Dim Responses(5)        ' User responses to prompts

    ' Set each prompt.
    Prompts(1) = "Automatically add resources (suppress the" & _
        " Resource Form when you choose the Add button on" & _
        " the Resource Assignment dialog box)?"
    Prompts(2) = "Automatically recalculate a project when" & _
        " a value, such as a date or cost, changes?"
    Prompts(3) = "Automatically link tasks that you cut," & _
        " move, or insert?"
    Prompts(4) = "Automatically split tasks into parts for" & _
        " work complete and work remaining?"
    Prompts(5) = "Automatically update the remaining work and" & _
        " cost for a resource when the completion percentage" & _
        " of one of the resource's tasks changes?"

    ' Display each prompt, and store the user's responses.
    For I = 1 To 5
        Response = MsgBox(Prompts(I), 4)
        Responses(I) = (Response = vbYes)
    Next I

    ' Set the automatic properties according to the user's responses.
    ActiveProject.AutoAddResources = Responses(1)
    OptionsCalculation automatic:=Responses(2)
    ActiveProject.AutoLinkTasks = Responses(3)
    ActiveProject.AutoSplitTasks = Responses(4)
    ActiveProject.AutoTrack = Responses(5)
End Sub
```

AutoCorrect Method

Applies To   **Application** Object.

Description   Displays the AutoCorrect dialog.

Syntax   *object*.**AutoCorrect**

Elements   The *object* placeholder is any object expression that evaluates to an object in the Applies To list.

See Also   **SpellingCheck** Method.

AutoLevel Property

Applies To   **Application** Object.

Description   Returns or sets whether resources are automatically leveled.

Syntax   [*object*.]**AutoLevel** [= *value*]

Elements   The **AutoLevel** property syntax has the following parts:

Part	Description
object	An object expression that evaluates to an object in the Applies To list.
value	A Boolean expression that specifies whether resources are automatically leveled.

See Also   **AutoAddResources** Property, **AutoRemoveDelay** Property, **LevelingOptions** Method, **LevelNow** Method.

AutoLinkTasks Property

Applies To   **Project** Object, **Projects** Collection.

Description   Returns or sets whether Microsoft Project automatically links sequential tasks that you cut, move, or insert.

Syntax   [*object*.]**AutoLinkTasks** [= *value*]

Elements   The **AutoLinkTasks** property syntax has these parts:

Part	Description
object	An object expression that evaluates to an object in the Applies To list.
value	A Boolean expression that specifies whether Microsoft Project automatically links sequential tasks that you cut, move, or insert, as shown under Settings.

Settings   The **AutoLinkTasks** property has these settings:

Setting	Description
True	Microsoft Project automatically links sequential tasks that you cut, move, or insert.
False	Microsoft Project does not link sequential tasks that you cut, move, or insert.

See Also   **AutoAddResources** Property, **AutoSplitTasks** Property, **AutoTrack** Property.

AutoRemoveDelay Property

Applies To   **Application** Object.

Description   Returns or sets whether delays are automatically removed from tasks before leveling occurs.

Syntax   [*object.*]**AutoRemoveDelay** [= *value*]

Elements   The **AutoRemoveDelay** property syntax has the following parts:

Part	Description
object	An object expression that evaluates to an object in the Applies To list.
value	A Boolean expression that specifies whether delays are automatically removed from tasks.

See Also   **AutoLevel** Property, **LevelingOptions** Method.

AutoSplitTasks Property

Applies To   **Project** Object, **Projects** Collection.

Description   Returns or sets whether Microsoft Project automatically splits tasks into parts for work complete and work remaining.

Syntax   [*object.*]**AutoSplitTasks** [= *value*]

Elements   The **AutoSplitTasks** property syntax has these parts:

Part	Description
object	An object expression that evaluates to an object in the Applies To list.
value	A Boolean expression that specifies whether Microsoft Project automatically splits tasks, as shown under Settings.

Settings   The **AutoSplitTasks** property has these settings:

Setting	Description
True	Microsoft Project automatically splits tasks into parts for work complete and work remaining.
False	Microsoft Project doesn't automatically split tasks.

See Also   **AutoAddResources** Property, **AutoLinkTasks** Property, **AutoTrack** Property.

AutoTrack Property

Applies To   **Project** Object, **Projects** Collection.

Description   Returns or sets whether Microsoft Project automatically updates the work and costs of a task's resources when the task's percent complete changes.

Syntax   [*object*.]**AutoTrack** [= *value*]

Elements   The **AutoTrack** property syntax has these parts:

Part	Description
object	An object expression that evaluates to an object in the Applies To list.
value	A Boolean expression that specifies whether Microsoft Project automatically updates the work and costs of a task's resources, as shown under Settings.

Settings   The **AutoTrack** property has these settings:

Setting	Description
True	Microsoft Project automatically updates the work and costs of a task's resources when the task's percent complete changes.
False	Microsoft Project doesn't update the work and costs of a task's resources; you must update the work and costs manually.

See Also   **AutoAddResources** Property, **AutoLinkTasks** Property, **AutoSplitTasks** Property.

BarBoxStyles Method

Applies To	**Application** Object.
Description	Displays the Bar Styles or Box Styles dialog box, which prompts the user to specify bar styles (Gantt Chart, Resource Graph, and Calendar) or box styles (PERT Chart) respectively.
Syntax	[*object.*]**BarBoxStyles**
Elements	The *object* placeholder is an object expression that evaluates to an object in the Applies To list.
Remarks	The **BarBoxStyles** method has the same effect as the Bar Styles command (Gantt Chart, Resource Graph, and Calendar view) or the Box Styles (PERT Chart) command on the Format menu.
	The **BarBoxStyles** method has no effect unless the active view is the Gantt Chart, Resource Graph, Calendar, or PERT Chart.
See Also	**CalendarBarStyles** Method, **CalendarBarStylesEdit** Method, **GanttBarStyleDelete** Method, **GanttBarStyleEdit** Method, **PERTBoxStyles** Method.

BarRounding Method

Applies To	**Application** Object.
Description	Turns automatic bar rounding on or off.
Syntax	[*object.*]**BarRounding** [*on*]
Elements	The **BarRounding** method syntax has the following object qualifier and named arguments:

Part	Description
object	An object expression that evaluates to an object in the Applies To list.
on	A Boolean expression that specifies whether bar rounding occurs automatically. By default, the *on* argument is **True**.

See Also	**CalendarBarStyles** Method, **DefaultFinishTime** Property, **DefaultStartTime** Property.

BaseCalendar Property

Applies To	**Calendar** Object, **Calendars** Collection; **Resource** Object, **Resources** Collection.
Description	Returns a base calendar or the base calendar for a resource calendar.
Syntax	*object*.**BaseCalendar**
Elements	The *object* placeholder is an object expression that evaluates to an object in the Applies To list.
See Also	**BaseCalendars** Method; **Calendar** Object, **Calendars** Collection; **Calendar** Property.

BaseCalendarCreate Method

Applies To	**Application** Object.
Description	Creates a base calendar.
Syntax	[*object*.]**BaseCalendarCreate** *name*[*, fromName*]
Elements	The **BaseCalendarCreate** method syntax has the following object qualifier and named arguments:

Part	Description
object	An object expression that evaluates to an object in the Applies To list. Optional.
name	A string expression that specifies the name of the base calendar to create. Required.
fromName	A string expression that specifies the name of the base calendar to copy. Optional.

See Also	**BaseCalendarDelete** Method, **BaseCalendarEditDays** Method, **BaseCalendarRename** Method, **BaseCalendarReset** Method, **BaseCalendars** Method, **ChangeWorkingTime** Method, **ResourceCalendars** Method.
Example	The following example creates a new base calendar called "Base Holiday Calendar."

```
Sub CreateHolidayCalendar()
    BaseCalendarCreate Name := "Base Holiday Calendar"
End Sub
```

BaseCalendarDelete Method

Applies To

Application Object.

Description

Deletes a base calendar.

Syntax

[*object*.]**BaseCalendarDelete** *name*

Elements

The **BaseCalendarDelete** method syntax has the following object qualifier and named arguments:

Part	Description
object	An object expression that evaluates to an object in the Applies To list. Optional.
name	A string expression that specifies the name of the base calendar to delete. Required.

See Also

BaseCalendarCreate Method, **BaseCalendarEditDays** Method, **BaseCalendarRename** Method, **BaseCalendarReset** Method, **BaseCalendars** Method, **ResourceCalendars** Method.

Example

The following example deletes the base calendar entered by the user.

```
Sub DeleteCalendar()
    x = InputBox("Enter name of base calendar to delete")
    BaseCalendarDelete name:=x
End Sub
```

BaseCalendarEditDays Method

Applies To

Application Object.

Description

Changes one or more consecutive days in a base calendar.

Syntax

[*object*.]**BaseCalendarEditDays** *name*[, *startDate, endDate, weekday, working, from1, to1, from2, to2, from3, to3*]

Elements

The **BaseCalendarEditDays** method syntax has the following object qualifier and named arguments:

Part	Description
object	An object expression that evaluates to an object in the Applies To list. Optional.
name	A string expression that specifies the name of the base calendar to change. Required.
startDate	A date expression that specifies the first date to change. Optional.
endDate	A date expression that specifies the last date to change. Optional.
weekDay	A constant that specifies the weekday to change. If you specify values for the *startDate* and *endDate* arguments, the *weekDay* argument is ignored. Optional.
working	A Boolean expression that specifies whether the days are working days. Optional.
from1	A string expression that specifies the start time of the first shift. Optional.
to1	A string expression that specifies the end time of the first shift. Optional.
from2	A string expression that specifies the start time of the second shift. Optional.
to2	A string expression that specifies the end time of the second shift. Optional.
from3	A string expression that specifies the start time of the third shift. Optional.
to3	A string expression that specifies the end time of the third shift. Optional.

The *weekDay* argument has these settings:

pjSunday	1	Sunday
pjMonday	2	Monday
pjTuesday	3	Tuesday
pjWednesday	4	Wednesday
pjThursday	5	Thursday
pjFriday	6	Friday
pjSaturday	7	Saturday

See Also

BaseCalendarCreate Method, **BaseCalendarDelete** Method, **BaseCalendarRename** Method, **BaseCalendarReset** Method, **BaseCalendars** Method, **ResourceCalendars** Method.

Example

The following example makes Wednesday a nonworking day in the Standard calendar.

```
Sub MakeWednesdaysNonWorking()
    BaseCalendarEditDays Name := "Standard", Weekday := pjWednesday, _
        Working := False
End Sub
```

The following example makes the days from 2/10/94 to 2/12/94 nonworking days in the Standard calendar.

```
Sub MakeWednesdaysNonWorking2()
    BaseCalendarEditDays Name := "Standard", startDate := "2/10/94", _
        endDate := "2/12/94", Working := False
End Sub
```

BaseCalendarRename Method

Applies To   **Application** Object.

Description   Renames a base calendar.

Syntax   [*object.*]**BaseCalendarRename** *fromName*, *toName*

Elements   The **BaseCalendarRename** method syntax has the following object qualifier and named arguments:

Part	Description
object	An object expression that evaluates to an object in the Applies To list. Optional.
fromName	A string expression that specifies the base calendar to rename. Required.
toName	A string expression that specifies the new name of the base calendar you specify with the *fromName* argument. Required.

See Also   **BaseCalendarCreate** Method, **BaseCalendarDelete** Method, **BaseCalendarEditDays** Method, **BaseCalendarReset** Method, **BaseCalendars** Method, **ResourceCalendars** Method.

Example   The following example changes the name of the base calendar from Standard to Old Standard.

```
Sub RenameStandardCalendar()
    BaseCalendarRename fromName:="Standard", toName:="Old Standard"
End Sub
```

BaseCalendarReset Method

Applies To   **Application** Object.

Description   Resets a base calendar.

Syntax   [*object*.]**BaseCalendarReset** *name*

Elements   The **BaseCalendarReset** method syntax has the following object qualifier and
                    named arguments:

Part	Description
object	An object expression that evaluates to an object in the Applies To list. Optional.
name	A string expression that specifies the name of the base calendar to reset. Required.

Remarks   Base calendars have the following default characteristics:

- Monday through Friday are working days with two shifts (8 A.M. to 12 P.M. and 1 P.M. to 5 P.M.).

- Saturday and Sunday are nonworking days.

See Also   **BaseCalendarCreate** Method, **BaseCalendarDelete** Method,
                    BaseCalendarEditDays Method, **BaseCalendarRename** Method,
                    BaseCalendars Method, **ResourceCalendars** Method.

Example   The following example resets the Standard base calendar to the default settings.

```
Sub RestoreBaseCalendar()
    BaseCalendarReset name:="Standard"
End Sub
```

BaseCalendars Method

Applies To   **Application** Object; **Project** Object, **Projects** Collection.

Description   Displays the Change Working Time dialog box, which prompts the user to change a
                    calendar (Syntax 1) or returns a base calendar or the base calendars in a project
                    (Syntax 2).

Syntax 1   [*object*.]**BaseCalendars**

| Syntax 2 | [*object.*]**BaseCalendars** [(*index*)] |

Elements

The **BaseCalendars** method syntax has the following object qualifier and named arguments:

Part	Description
object	An object expression that evaluates to an Application object (Syntax 1) or a Project object (Syntax 2). Optional.
index	A numeric expression that specifies the index of the object or a string expression that specifies the name of the window. Optional.

Remarks

The **BaseCalendars** method (Syntax 1) has the same effect as the Change Working Time command on the Tools menu. The *object* argument is required for a Project object.

See Also

BaseCalendarCreate Method, **BaseCalendarDelete** Method, **BaseCalendarEditDays** Method, **BaseCalendarRename** Method, **BaseCalendarReset** Method, **Calendar** Property, **ResourceCalendars** Method.

BaselineCost Property

Applies To

Assignment Object, **Assignments** Collection; **Project** Object, **Projects** Collection; **Resource** Object, **Resources** Collection; **Task** Object, Tasks Collection.

Description

Returns or sets the baseline cost for an assignment, project, resource, or task. Read only for **Project** or **Resource** objects, and **Task** objects with one or more resources.

Syntax

*object.***BaselineCost** [= *value*]

Elements

The **BaselineCost** property syntax has these parts:

Part	Description
object	An object expression that evaluates to an object in the Applies To list.
value	A numeric expression of the baseline cost for the assignment or task.

See Also

ActualCost Property, **BaselineDuration** Property, **BaselineFinish** Property, **BaselineStart** Property, **BaselineWork** Property, **Cost** Property, **CostVariance** Property, **RemainingCost** Property.

BaselineDuration Property

Applies To   **Project** Object, **Projects** Collection; **Task** Object, **Tasks** Collection.

Description   Returns or sets the baseline duration (in minutes) of a project or task. Read only for **Project** object.

Syntax   *object*.**BaselineDuration** [= *value*]

Elements   The **BaselineDuration** property syntax has these parts:

Part	Description
object	An object expression that evaluates to an object in the Applies To list.
value	A numeric expression of the baseline duration of the task, in minutes.

See Also   **ActualDuration** Property, **BaselineCost** Property, **BaselineFinish** Property, **BaselineStart** Property, **BaselineWork** Property, **Duration** Property, **DurationVariance** Property, **RemainingDuration** Property.

BaselineFinish Property

Applies To   **Project** Object, **Projects** Collection; **Task** Object, **Tasks** Collection.

Description   Returns or sets the baseline finish date of a project or task. Read only for **Project** object.

Syntax   *object*.**BaselineFinish** [= *value*]

Elements   The **BaselineFinish** property syntax has these parts:

Part	Description
object	An object expression that evaluates to an object in the Applies To list.
value	A date expression of the baseline finish date of the task.

See Also   **ActualFinish** Property, **BaselineCost** Property, **BaselineDuration** Property, **BaselineStart** Property, **BaselineWork** Property, **Finish** Property, **FinishVariance** Property.

BaselineSave Method

Applies To   **Application** Object.

Description   Creates a baseline plan.

Syntax   [*object*.]**BaselineSave** [*all*, *copy*, *into*]

Elements   The **BaselineSave** method syntax has the following object qualifier and named arguments:

Part	Description
object	An object expression that evaluates to an object in the Applies To list. Optional.
all	A Boolean expression that specifies whether to set the baseline plan for all tasks. By default, the *all* argument is **True**. Optional. The *all* argument has these settings:
	True Sets the baseline plan for all tasks.
	False Sets the baseline plan for the selected tasks.
copy	A constant that specifies the field to copy. Optional.
into	A constant that specifies where to copy the field. Optional.

The *copy* argument has these settings:

pjCopyCurrent	0	All scheduling information from the current project
pjCopyBaseline	1	The baseline start and baseline finish dates for the task
pjCopyStart_Finish1	2	The dates in the Start1 and Finish1 custom fields
pjCopyStart_Finish2	3	The dates in the Start2 and Finish2 custom fields
pjCopyStart_Finish3	4	The dates in the Start3 and Finish3 custom fields
pjCopyStart_Finish4	5	The dates in the Start4 and Finish4 custom fields
pjCopyStart_Finish5	6	The dates in the Start5 and Finish5 custom fields

The *into* argument has these settings:

pjIntoBaseline	0	All baseline information in the current project
pjIntoStart_Finish1	1	The dates in the Start1 and Finish1 custom fields of the task
pjIntoStart_Finish2	2	The dates in the Start2 and Finish2 custom fields of the task
pjIntoStart_Finish3	3	The dates in the Start3 and Finish3 custom fields of the task
pjIntoStart_Finish4	4	The dates in the Start4 and Finish4 custom fields of the task
pjIntoStart_Finish5	5	The dates in the Start5 and Finish5 custom fields of the task

See Also

BaselineFinish Property, **BaselineStart** Property, **Finish** Property, **Start** Property.

Example

The following example ages a baseline by copying it into subsequent Start and Finish fields. The Baseline Start and Baseline Finish fields will hold the most recent baseline information, while the Start5 and Finish5 fields will hold the oldest baseline information.

```
Sub AgingBaseline()
    BaselineSave copy:=pjCopyStart_Finish4, into:=pjIntoStart_Finish5
    BaselineSave copy:=pjCopyStart_Finish3, into:=pjIntoStart_Finish4
    BaselineSave copy:=pjCopyStart_Finish2, into:=pjIntoStart_Finish3
    BaselineSave copy:=pjCopyStart_Finish1, into:=pjIntoStart_Finish2
    BaselineSave copy:=pjCopyBaseline, into:=pjIntoStart_Finish1
    BaselineSave copy:=pjCopyCurrent, into:=pjIntoBaseline
End Sub
```

BaselineStart Property

Applies To

Project Object, **Projects** Collection; **Task** Object, **Tasks** Collection.

Description

Returns or sets the baseline start date of a project or task. Read only for **Project** object.

Syntax

object.**BaselineStart** [= *value*]

Elements

The **BaselineStart** property syntax has these parts:

Part	Description
object	An object expression that evaluates to an object in the Applies To list.
value	A date expression of the baseline start of the task.

See Also   **ActualStart** Property, **BaselineCost** Property, **BaselineDuration** Property, **BaselineFinish** Property, **BaselineWork** Property, **Start** Property, **StartVariance** Property.

BaselineWork Property

Applies To   **Assignment** Object, **Assignments** Collection; **Project** Object, **Projects** Collection; **Resource** Object, **Resources** Collection; **Task** Object, **Tasks** Collection.

Description   Returns or sets the baseline work (in minutes) for an assignment, project, resource, or task. Read only for **Project** or **Resource**, and **Task** objects with one or more resources.

Syntax   *object*.**BaselineWork** [= *value*]

Elements   The **BaselineWork** property syntax has these parts:

Part	Description
object	An object expression that evaluates to an object in the Applies To list.
value	A numeric expression of the baseline work for the assignment or task, in minutes.

See Also   **ActualWork** Property, **BaselineCost** Property, **BaselineDuration** Property, **BaselineFinish** Property, **BaselineStart** Property, **RemainingWork** Property, **Work** Property, **WorkVariance** Property.

BCWP Property

Applies To   **Project** Object, **Projects** Collection; **Task** Object, **Tasks** Collection.

Description   Returns the BCWP for a task.

Syntax   *object*.**BCWP**

Elements	The *object* placeholder is an object expression that evaluates to an object in the Applies To list.
See Also	**BaselineCost** Property, **Cost** Property, **CostVariance** Property, **CV** Property, **SV** Property.

BCWS Property

Applies To	**Project** Object, **Projects** Collection; **Task** Object, **Tasks** Collection.
Description	Returns the BCWS for a task.
Syntax	*object***.BCWS**
Elements	The *object* placeholder is an object expression that evaluates to an object in the Applies To list.
See Also	**BaselineCost** Property, **BCWP** Property, **Cost** Property, **CostVariance** Property, **CV** Property, **SV** Property.

Beep Statement

Description	Sounds a tone through the computer's speaker.
Syntax	**Beep**
Remarks	The frequency and duration of the beep depends on hardware, which may vary among computers.
Example	This example uses the **Beep** statement to sound three consecutive tones through the computer's speaker.

```
For I = 1 to 3      ' Loop 3 times.
    Beep            ' Sound a tone.
Next I
```

Boolean Data Type

Description   **Boolean** variables are stored as 16-bit (2-byte) numbers, but they can only be **True** or **False**. **Boolean** variables display as either True or False (when **Print** is used) or #TRUE# or #FALSE# (when **Write #** is used). Use the keywords **True** and **False** to assign one of the two states to **Boolean** variables.

When other numeric data types are converted to **Boolean** values, 0 becomes **False** while all other values become **True**. When **Boolean** values are converted to other data types, **False** becomes 0 while **True** becomes -1.

See Also   **CBool** Function, Data Type Summary, **Def***type* Statements, **Integer** Data Type.

BottomPane Property

Applies To   **Window** Object, **Windows** Collection.

Description   Returns the bottom pane of a window.

Syntax   *object*.**BottomPane**

Elements   The *object* placeholder is an object expression that evaluates to an object in the Applies To list.

See Also   **ActivePane** Property, **Pane** Object, **TopPane** Property.

BuiltinDocumentProperties Property

Applies To   **Project** Object, **Projects** Collection.

Description   Returns the built-in properties of the document.

Syntax   *object*.**BuiltinDocumentProperties**

Elements   The *object* placeholder is an object expression that evaluates to an object in the Applies To list.

Remarks   To use this property, you should establish a reference to the Microsoft Office 95 Object Library by using the References command from the Tools menu. The Object

Library contains definitions for the Visual Basic objects, properties, methods, and constants used to manipulate document properties.

This property returns the entire collection of built-in document properties. Use the **Item** method to return a single member of the collection (a **DocumentProperty** object) by specifying either the name of the property or the collection index (as a number).

Because the **Item** method is the default method for the **DocumentProperties** collection object, the following statements are identical:

```
BuiltinDocumentProperties.Item(1)
BuiltinDocumentProperties(1)
```

Use the **CustomDocumentProperties** property to return the collection of custom document properties.

See Also   **CustomDocumentProperties** Property, **FileProperties** Method, **Project** Property.

CalculateAll Method

Applies To   **Application** Object.

Description   Calculates all open projects.

Syntax   [*object*.]**CalculateAll**

Elements   The *object* placeholder is an object expression that evaluates to an object in the Applies To list.

See Also   **CalculateProject** Method, **Calculation** Property, **OptionsCalculation** Method.

CalculateProject Method

Applies To   **Application** Object.

Description   Calculates the active project.

Syntax   [*object*.]**CalculateProject**

Elements   The *object* placeholder is an object expression that evaluates to an object in the Applies To list.

See Also   **CalculateAll** Method, **Calculation** Property, **OptionsCalculation** Method.

Calculation Property

Applies To   **Application** Object.

Description   Returns or sets whether the calculation mode is automatic or manual.

Syntax   [*object.*]**Calculation** [= *value*]

Elements   The **Calculation** property syntax has these parts:

Part	Description
object	An object expression that evaluates to an object in the Applies To list.
value	A constant that specifies the calculation mode, as shown under Settings.

Settings   The **Calculation** property has these settings:

pjAutomatic	**True**	The calculation mode is automatic.
pjManual	**False**	The calculation mode is manual.

See Also   **CalculateAll** Method, **CalculateProject** Method.

Calendar Object, Calendars Collection

The calendar or a calendar for a resource or project.

Remarks   In Microsoft Project, **Calendar** objects are parents of **Weekdays** collections, **Years** collections, and **Period** objects.

Properties   **Application** Property, **BaseCalendar** Property, **Count** Property, **Index** Property, **Name** Property, **Parent** Property.

Methods   **Delete** Method, **Period** Method, **Reset** Method, **Weekdays** Method, **Years** Method

See Also   **BaseCalendars** Method; **Calendar** Property; **Period** Object; **Project** Object, **Projects** Collection; **Resource** Object, **Resources** Collection; **Weekday** Object, **Weekdays** Collection; **Year** Object, **Years** Collection.

Calendar Property

Applies To	**Calendar** Object, **Calendars** Collection; **Resource** Object, **Resources** Collection.
Description	Returns a base calendar or the base calendar for a resource calendar.
Syntax	*object*.**BaseCalendar**
Elements	The *object* placeholder is an object expression that evaluates to an object in the Applies To list.
See Also	**BaseCalendars** Method; **Calendar** Object, **Calendars** Collection; **Calendar** Property.

CalendarBarStyles Method

Applies To	**Application** Object.
Description	Turns bar rounding on or off in the Calendar.
Syntax	[*object*.]**CalendarBarStyles**[*barRounding*]
Elements	The **CalendarBarStyles** method syntax has the following object qualifier and named arguments:

Part	Description
object	An object expression that evaluates to an object in the Applies To list.
barRounding	A Boolean expression that specifies whether to round bars in the Calendar to midnight if their start times are less than or equal to the default start time, or if their end times are greater than or equal to the default end time.

Remarks	The **CalendarBarStyles** method has no effect unless the Calendar is the active view.
	You can set the default start and default end times with the **OptionsCalendar** method.
See Also	**CalendarBarStylesEdit** Method, **CalendarBestFitWeekHeight** Method, **CalendarDateBoxes** Method, **CalendarDateShading** Method, **CalendarDateShadingEdit** Method, **CalendarLayout** Method,

CalendarTaskList Method, **CalendarTimescale** Method, **CalendarWeekHeadings** Method, **ZoomCalendar** Method.

Example

The following example turns on bar rounding in the Calendar view.

```
Sub CalendarBarRounding()
    CalendarBarStyles barRounding:=True
End Sub
```

CalendarBarStylesEdit Method

Applies To

Application Object.

Description

Changes the style of a bar in the Calendar.

Syntax

[*object*.]**CalendarBarStylesEdit** *item*[, *bar*, *pattern*, *color*, *align*, *wrap*, *shadow*, *field1*, *field2*, *field3*, *field4*, *field5*]

Elements

The **CalendarBarStylesEdit** method syntax has the following object qualifier and named arguments:

Part	Description
object	An object expression that evaluates to an object in the Applies To list. Optional.
item	A constant that specifies which calendar bar to edit. Required.
bar	A constant that specifies the bar type. Optional.
pattern	A constant that specifies the bar pattern. Optional.
color	A constant that specifies the bar color. Optional.
align	A constant that specifies the justification of text in the bar. Optional.
wrap	A Boolean expression that specifies whether to wrap the text in the bar. Optional.
shadow	A Boolean expression that specifies whether the bar has a shadow. Optional.
field1	A string expression that specifies the first field to display in the bar. Optional.
field2	A string expression that specifies the second field to display in the bar. Optional.
field3	A string expression that specifies the third field to display in the bar. Optional.

Part	Description
field4	A string expression that specifies the fourth field to display in the bar. Optional.
field5	A string expression that specifies the fifth field to display in the bar. Optional.

The *item* argument has these settings:

pjBarNoncritical	0	Calendar bars for noncritical tasks
pjBarCritical	1	Calendar bars for critical tasks
pjBarSummary	2	Calendar bars for summary tasks
pjBarMilestone	3	Calendar bars for milestone tasks
pjBarMarked	5	Calendar bars for marked tasks
pjBarHighlighted	6	Calendar bars for highlighted tasks
pjBarProjectSummary	7	Calendar bars for project summary tasks

The *bar* argument has these settings:

pjNormalBar	0	Rectangular bar
pjLineBar	1	Line bar
pjNoBar	2	No bar

The *pattern* argument has these settings:

pjHollow	0	Hollow
pjSolid	1	Solid
pjLightFill	2	Light fill
pjMediumFill	3	Medium fill
pjDarkFill	4	Dark fill
pjDiagonalLeft	5	Diagonal left
pjDiagonalRight	6	Diagonal right
pjDiagonalCross	7	Diagonal cross
pjLineVertical	8	Vertical line
pjLineHorizontal	9	Horizontal line
pjLineCross	10	Crossed line

The *color* argument has these settings:

pjBlack	0	Black
pjRed	1	Red
pjYellow	2	Yellow
pjLime	3	Lime
pjAqua	4	Aqua
pjBlue	5	Blue
pjFuchsia	6	Fuchsia
pjWhite	7	White
pjMaroon	8	Maroon
pjGreen	9	Green
pjOlive	10	Olive
pjNavy	11	Navy
pjPurple	12	Purple
pjTeal	13	Teal
pjGray	14	Gray
pjSilver	15	Silver

The *align* argument has these settings:

pjLeft	0	Align left.
pjCenter	1	Align center.
pjRight	2	Align right.

Remarks

If you specify a string expression for one of the arguments *field1* through *field5*, you must specify string expressions for any preceding field. For example, if you specify *field2*, you must also specify *field1*.

See Also

CalendarBarStyles Method, **CalendarBestFitWeekHeight** Method, **CalendarDateBoxes** Method, **CalendarDateShading** Method, **CalendarDateShadingEdit** Method, **CalendarLayout** Method, **CalendarTaskList** Method, **CalendarTimescale** Method, **CalendarWeekHeadings** Method.

CalendarBestFitWeekHeight Method

Applies To	**Application** Object.
Description	Changes the height of the active calendar box to display all task bars.
Syntax	[*object*.]**CalendarBestFitWeekHeight**
Elements	The *object* placeholder is an object expression that evaluates to an object in the Applies To list.
See Also	**CalendarBarStyles** Method, **CalendarBarStylesEdit** Method, **CalendarDateBoxes** Method, **CalendarDateShading** Method, **CalendarDateShadingEdit** Method, **CalendarLayout** Method, **CalendarTaskList** Method, **CalendarTimescale** Method, **CalendarWeekHeadings** Method.

CalendarDateBoxes Method

Applies To	**Application** Object.
Description	Customizes the date boxes in the Calendar.
Syntax	[*object*.]**CalendarDateBoxes** [*topLeft*, *topRight*, *bottomLeft*, *bottomRight*, *topColor*, *bottomColor*, *topPattern*, *bottomPattern*]
Elements	The **CalendarDateBoxes** method syntax has the following object qualifier and named arguments:

Part	Description
object	An object expression that evaluates to an object in the Applies To list. Optional.
topLeft	A constant that specifies the format for dates in the upper-left corner of each date box. Optional.
topRight	A constant that specifies the format for dates in the upper-right corner of each date box. Optional.
bottomLeft	A constant that specifies the format for dates in the lower-left corner of each date box. Optional.
bottomRight	A constant that specifies the format for dates in the lower-right corner of each date box. Optional.

Part	Description
topColor	A constant that specifies the color of the top band in each date box. Optional.
bottomColor	A constant that specifies the color of the bottom band in each date box. Optional.
topPattern	A constant that specifies the pattern of the top band in each date box. Optional.
bottomPattern	A constant that specifies the pattern of the bottom band in each date box. Optional.

The *topLeft*, *topRight*, *bottomLeft*, and *bottomRight* arguments have these settings:

pjDay_mm_dd	27	1/31, 2/1
pjDay_mm_dd_yy	26	1/31/94, 2/1/94
pjDay_m_dd	115	J 31, F1
pjDay_mmm_dd	25	Jan 31, Feb 1
pjDay_mmm_dd_yyy	24	Jan 31, '94; Feb 1, '94
pjDay_di	20	M, T
pjDay_di_mm_dd	110	M 1/31, T 2/1
pjDay_di_dd	107	M 31, T 1
pjDay_di_m_dd	114	M J 31, T F 1
pjDay_didd	121	M31, T1
pjDay_ddi	119	Mo, Tu
pjDay_ddi_mm_dd	109	Mo 1/31, Tu 2/1
pjDay_ddi_dd	106	Mo 31, Tu 1
pjDay_ddi_m_dd	113	Mo J 31, Tu F 1
pjDay_ddd	19	Mon, Tue
pjDay_ddd_mm_dd	108	Mon 1/31, Tue 2/1
pjDay_ddd_mm_dd_yy	52	Mon 1/31/94; Tue 2/1/94
pjDay_ddd_dd	105	Mon 31, Tue 1
pjDay_ddd_m_dd	112	Mon J 31, Tue F 1
pjDay_ddd_mmm_dd	23	Mon Jan 31, Tue Feb 1
pjDay_ddd_mmm_dd_yyy	22	Mon Jan 31, '94; Tue Feb 1, '94
pjDay_ddd_mmmm_dd	111	Mon January 31, Tue February 1
pjDay_dddd	18	Monday, Tuesday
pjDayFromEnd_dd	54	4, 3 (the day from the end date of the project)

pjDayFromEnd_Ddd	53	D4, D3 (the day from the end date of the project)
pjDayFromEnd_Day_dd	41	Day 4, Day 3 (the day from the end date of the project)
pjDayFromStart_dd	56	1, 2 (the day from the start date of the project)
pjDayFromStart_Ddd	55	D1, D2 (the day from the start date of the project)
pjDayFromStart_Day_dd	40	Day 1, Day 2 (the day from the start date of the project)
pjDayOfMonth_dd	21	31, 1 (the day of the month)
pjDayOfYear_dd	118	31, 32 (the day of the year)
pjDayOfYear_dd_yyyy	117	31 1994, 32 1994 (the day of the year followed by the year)
pjDayOfYear_dd_yyy	116	31 '94, 32 '94 (the day of the year followed by the year)
pjNoDateFormat	35	No date is displayed.
pjOverflowIndicator	122	The overflow indicator is displayed.

The *topColor* and *bottomColor* arguments have these settings:

pjBlack	0	Black
pjRed	1	Red
pjYellow	2	Yellow
pjLime	3	Lime
pjAqua	4	Aqua
pjBlue	5	Blue
pjFuchsia	6	Fuchsia
pjWhite	7	White
pjMaroon	8	Maroon
pjGreen	9	Green
pjOlive	10	Olive
pjNavy	11	Navy
pjPurple	12	Purple
pjTeal	13	Teal
pjGray	14	Gray
pjSilver	15	Silver

The *topPattern* and *bottomPattern* arguments have these settings:

pjHollow	0	Hollow
pjSolid	1	Solid
pjLightFill	2	Light fill
pjMediumFill	3	Medium fill
pjDarkFill	4	Dark fill
pjDiagonalLeft	5	Diagonal left
pjDiagonalRight	6	Diagonal right
pjDiagonalCross	7	Diagonal cross
pjLineVertical	8	Vertical line
pjLineHorizontal	9	Horizontal line
pjLineCross	10	Crossed line

Remarks

The **CalendarDateBoxes** method has no effect unless the Calendar is the active view.

See Also

CalendarBarStyles Method, **CalendarBarStylesEdit** Method, **CalendarBestFitWeekHeight** Method, **CalendarDateShading** Method, **CalendarDateShadingEdit** Method, **CalendarLayout** Method, **CalendarTaskList** Method, **CalendarTimescale** Method, **CalendarWeekHeadings** Method, **ZoomCalendar** Method.

Example

The following example displays the day of the week (for example, Monday) in the upper-left corner of the calendar date boxes and the month and date (for example, Jan 31) in the upper-right corner of the calendar date boxes.

```
Sub FormatCalendarDays()
    CalendarDateBoxes topleft:=pjDay_dddd, topRight:=pjDay_mmm_dd
End Sub
```

CalendarDateShading Method

Applies To

Application Object.

Description

Determines which calendar is displayed.

Syntax

[*object*.]**CalendarDateShading**[*baseCalendarName, resourceUniqueID, projectIndex*]

Elements

The **CalendarDateShading** method syntax has the following object qualifier and named arguments:

Part	Description
object	An object expression that evaluates to an object in the Applies To list. Optional.
baseCalendarName	A string expression that specifies the name of a base calendar to use for shading. Optional.
resourceUniqueID	A numeric expression that specifies the unique identification number of a resource. (The corresponding resource calendar is used for shading.) Optional.
projectIndex	A numeric expression that specifies the index of the calendar to use. Use the *projectIndex* argument to distinguish between two calendars with the same name (consolidated projects only). Optional.

Remarks   You must specify either the *baseCalendarName* argument or the *resourceUniqueID* argument, but you cannot specify both arguments. The *projectIndex* argument is required for a consolidated project. The **CalendarDateShading** method has no effect unless the Calendar is the active view.

See Also   **CalendarBarStyles** Method, **CalendarBarStylesEdit** Method, **CalendarBestFitWeekHeight** Method, **CalendarDateBoxes** Method, **CalendarDateShadingEdit** Method, **CalendarLayout** Method, **CalendarTaskList** Method, **CalendarTimescale** Method, **CalendarWeekHeadings** Method, **ZoomCalendar** Method.

CalendarDateShadingEdit Method

Applies To   **Application** Object.

Description   Changes box shading in the Calendar.

Syntax   [*object*.]**CalendarDateShadingEdit** *item*[, *pattern*, *color*]

Elements   The **CalendarDateShadingEdit** method syntax has the following object qualifier and named arguments:

Part	Description
object	An object expression that evaluates to an object in the Applies To list. Optional.
item	A constant that specifies the type of calendar exception to change. Required.

Part	Description
pattern	A constant that specifies a pattern for the type of date box you specify with the *item* argument. Optional.
color	A constant that specifies a color for the type of date box you specify with the *item* argument. Optional.

The *item* argument has these settings:

pjBaseWorking	0	Working days in a base calendar
pjBaseNonWorking	1	Nonworking days in a base calendar
pjBaseNonDefaultWorking	2	In a base calendar, working days for which the working hours are different from the default working hours
pjResourceWorking	3	Working days in a resource calendar
pjResourceNonWorking	4	Nonworking days in a resource calendar

The *pattern* argument has these settings:

pjHollow	0	Hollow
pjSolid	1	Solid
pjLightFill	2	Light fill
pjMediumFill	3	Medium fill
pjDarkFill	4	Dark fill
pjDiagonalLeft	5	Diagonal left
pjDiagonalRight	6	Diagonal right
pjDiagonalCross	7	Diagonal cross
pjLineVertical	8	Vertical line
pjLineHorizontal	9	Horizontal line
pjLineCross	10	Crossed line

The *color* argument has these settings:

pjBlack	0	Black
pjRed	1	Red
pjYellow	2	Yellow
pjLime	3	Lime
pjAqua	4	Aqua
pjBlue	5	Blue
pjFuchsia	6	Fuchsia
pjWhite	7	White
pjMaroon	8	Maroon
pjGreen	9	Green
pjOlive	10	Olive
pjNavy	11	Navy
pjPurple	12	Purple
pjTeal	13	Teal
pjGray	14	Gray
pjSilver	15	Silver

Remarks

The **CalendarDateShadingEdit** method has no effect unless the Calendar is the active view.

See Also

CalendarBarStyles Method, **CalendarBarStylesEdit** Method, **CalendarBestFitWeekHeight** Method, **CalendarDateBoxes** Method, **CalendarDateShading** Method, **CalendarLayout** Method, **CalendarTaskList** Method, **CalendarTimescale** Method, **CalendarWeekHeadings** Method, **ZoomCalendar** Method.

CalendarLayout Method

Applies To

Application Object.

Description

Changes how task bars are arranged on the Calendar.

Syntax

[*object*.]**CalendarLayout** [*sortOrder, autoLayout*]

Elements

The **CalendarLayout** method syntax has the following object qualifier and named arguments:

Part	Description
object	An object expression that evaluates to an object in the Applies To list. Optional.
sortOrder	A Boolean expression that specifies whether to display tasks in the Calendar using the current sort order. By default, the *sortOrder* argument is **True**. Optional. The *sortOrder* argument has these settings:

	True	Displays tasks using the current sort order.
	False	Changes the sort order to display as many tasks as possible.

Part	Description
autoLayout	A Boolean expression that specifies whether to automatically change the Calendar view to reflect task changes. Optional.

Remarks

Use the **Sort** method to set the current sort order.

The **CalendarLayout** method has no effect unless the Calendar is the active view.

See Also

Layout Method, **LayoutNow** Method, **PERTLayout** Method.

CalendarTaskList Method

Applies To

Application Object.

Description

Displays the list of tasks for a specific date.

Syntax

[*object*.]**CalendarTaskList** [*date*]

Elements

The **CalendarTaskList** method syntax has the following object qualifier and named arguments:

Part	Description
object	An object expression that evaluates to an object in the Applies To list.
date	A string expression that specifies a date.

Remarks

The **CalendarTaskList** method has no effect unless the Calendar is the active view.

See Also

CalendarBarStyles Method, **CalendarBarStylesEdit** Method, **CalendarBestFitWeekHeight** Method, **CalendarDateBoxes** Method, **CalendarDateShading** Method, **CalendarDateShadingEdit** Method, **CalendarLayout** Method, **CalendarTimescale** Method, **CalendarWeekHeadings** Method, **ZoomCalendar** Method.

CalendarTimescale Method

Applies To   **Application** Object.

Description   Displays the Timescale box, which allows the user to customize the Calendar view.

Syntax   [*object*.]**CalendarTimescale**

Elements   The *object* placeholder is an object expression that evaluates to an object in the Applies To list.

Remarks   The **CalendarTimescale** method has the same effect as the Timescale command on the Format menu.

The **CalendarTimescale** method has no effect unless the Calendar is the active view.

See Also   **CalendarBarStyles** Method, **CalendarBarStylesEdit** Method, **CalendarBestFitWeekHeight** Method, **CalendarDateBoxes** Method, **CalendarDateShading** Method, **CalendarDateShadingEdit** Method, **CalendarLayout** Method, **CalendarTaskList** Method, **CalendarWeekHeadings** Method, **ZoomCalendar** Method.

CalendarWeekHeadings Method

Applies To   **Application** Object.

Description   Customizes headings in the Calendar.

Syntax   [*object*.]**CalendarWeekHeadings** [*monthTitle, weekTitle, dayTitle, showPreview, daysPerWeek*]

Elements   The **CalendarWeekHeadings** method syntax has the following object qualifier and named arguments:

Part	Description
object	An object expression that evaluates to an object in the Applies To list. Optional.
monthTitle	A constant that specifies the format of the month title. Optional.
weekTitle	A constant that specifies the format of week titles. Optional.

Part	Description
dayTitle	A constant that specifies the format of day titles. Optional.
showPreview	A Boolean expression that specifies whether to show previews of the next and previous months. Optional.
daysPerWeek	A numeric expression that specifies the number of days per week to display. You can set the *daysPerWeek* argument to 5 or 7. Optional.

The *monthTitle* argument has these settings:

Constant	Examples of the date format
pjMonth_mm	1, 2
pjMonth_mm_yy	1/94, 2/94
pjMonth_mm_yyy	1 '94, 2 '94
pjMonth_m	J, F
pjMonth_mmm	Jan, Feb
pjMonth_mmm_yyy	Jan '94, Feb '94
pjMonth_mmmm	January, February
pjMonth_mmmm_yyyy	January 1994, February 1994
pjMonth_FromEnd_mm	5, 4 (months from end date of project)
pjMonthFromEnd_Mmm	M5, M4 (months from end date of project)
pjMonthFromEnd_Month_mm	Month5, Month4 (months from end date of project)
pjMonthFromStart_mm	1, 2 (months from start date of project)
pjMonthFromStart_Mmm	M1, M2 (months from start date of project)
pjMonthFromStart_Month_mm	Month1, Month2 (months from start date of project)
pjNoDateFormat	No date is displayed.

The *weekTitle* argument has these settings:

Constant	Examples of the date format
pjWeek_mm_dd	1/31, 2/7
pjWeek_mm_dd_yy	1/31/94, 2/7/94
pjWeek_m_dd	J 31, F 7
pjWeek_mmm_dd	Jan 31, Feb 7
pjWeek_mmm_dd_yyy	Jan 31, '94
pjWeek_mmmm_dd	January 31, February 7
pjWeek_mmmm_dd_yyyy	January 31, 1994; February 7, 1994

Constant	Examples of the date format
pjWeek_di_mm_dd	M 1/31, M 2/7
pjWeek_di_m_dd	M J 31, M F 7
pjWeek_di_mmm_dd	M Jan 31, M February 7
pjWeek_ddi_mm_dd	Mo 1/31, Mo 2/7
pjWeek_ddi_m_dd	Mo J 31, Mo F 7
pjWeek_ddi_mmm_dd	Mo Jan 31, Mo Feb 7
pjWeek_ddd_mm_dd	Mon 1/31, Mon 2/7
pjWeek_ddd_mm_dd_yy	Mon 1/31/94, Mon 2/7/94
pjWeek_ddd_dd	Mon 31, Mon 7
pjWeek_ddd_ww	Mon 5, Mon 6 (number of week in year)
pjWeek_ddd_m_dd	Mon J 31, Mon F 7
pjWeek_ddd_mmm_dd	Mon Jan 31, Mon Feb 7
pjWeek_ddd_mmm_dd_yyy	Mon Jan 31, '94; Mon Feb 7, '94
pjWeek_ddd_mmmm_dd	Mon January 31, Mon February 7
pjWeek_ddd_mmmm_dd_yyy	Mon January 31, '94; Mon February 7, '94
pjNoDateFormat	No date is displayed.

The *dayTitle* argument has these settings:

Constant	Description
pjDay_di	M, T, etc.
pjDay_ddi	Mo, Tu, etc.
pjDay_ddd	Mon, Tue, etc.
pjDay_dddd	Monday, Tuesday, etc.
pjNoDateFormat	No date is displayed.

Remarks

The **CalendarWeekHeadings** method has no effect unless the Calendar is the active view.

See Also

CalendarBarStyles Method, **CalendarBarStylesEdit** Method, **CalendarBestFitWeekHeight** Method, **CalendarDateBoxes** Method, **CalendarDateShading** Method, **CalendarDateShadingEdit** Method, **CalendarLayout** Method, **CalendarTaskList** Method, **CalendarTimescale** Method, **ZoomCalendar** Method.

Call Statement

Description

Transfers control to a **Sub** procedure, **Function** procedure, dynamic-link library (DLL) procedure, or a Macintosh code resource procedure.

Syntax

[**Call**] *name* [*argumentlist*]

Elements

The **Call** statement syntax has these parts:

Part	Description
Call	Optional keyword; if specified, you must enclose *argumentlist* in parentheses. For example:
	`Call MyProc(0)`
name	Name of the procedure to call.
argumentlist	Comma-delimited list of variables, arrays, or expressions to pass to the procedure. Components of *argumentlist* may include the keywords **ByVal** or **ByRef** to describe how the arguments are to be treated by the called procedure. However, **ByVal** and **ByRef** can be used with **Call** only when making a call to a DLL procedure or a Macintosh code resource.

Remarks

You are never required to use the **Call** keyword when calling a procedure. However, if you use the **Call** keyword to call a procedure that requires arguments, *argumentlist* must be enclosed in parentheses. If you omit the **Call** keyword, you also must omit the parentheses around *argumentlist*. If you use either **Call** syntax to call any intrinsic or user-defined function, the function's return value is discarded.

To pass a whole array to a procedure, use the array name followed by empty parentheses.

See Also

Declare Statement.

Example

This example illustrates how the **Call** statement is used to transfer control to a **Sub** procedure, an intrinsic function, a dynamic-link library (DLL) procedure and a procedure in a Macintosh code resource.

```
' Call a Sub procedure.
Call PrintToDebugWindow("Hello World")
' The above statement causes control to be passed to the following
' Sub procedure.
Sub PrintToDebugWindow(AnyString)
    Debug.Print AnyString    ' Print to Debug window.
End Sub

' Call an intrinsic function. The return value of the function is
' discarded.
Call Shell(AppName, 1)   ' AppName contains the path of the executable.

' Call a Microsoft Windows DLL procedure.
Declare Sub MessageBeep Lib "User" (ByVal N As Integer)
Sub CallMyDll()
    Call MessageBeep(0) ' Call Windows DLL procedure.
    MessageBeep 0       ' Call again without Call keyword.
End Sub

' Call a Macintosh Code Resource.
Declare Sub MessageAlert Lib "MyHd:MyAlert" Alias "MyAlert" (ByVal N _
As Integer)
Sub CallMyCodeResource()
    Call MessageAlert(0)' Call Macintosh code resource.
    MessageAlert 0       ' Call again without Call keyword.
End Sub
```

Caption Property

Applies To   **Application** Object; **Window** Object, **Windows** Collection.

Description   Returns or sets the text in the title bar of the main window (**Application** object) or
                    a project window (**Window** object).

Syntax   *object*.**Caption** [= *value*]

Elements   The **Caption** property syntax has these parts:

Part	Description
object	An object expression that evaluates to an object in the Applies To list.
value	A string expression that specifies the text in the title bar, or **Empty**. If you set the **Caption** property to **Empty**, the title bar displays a default caption.

Remarks   When the active window is maximized, the title bar displays the caption for both
                    the main and active windows, separating the captions with a hyphen. For example,
                    if the caption for the main window is "Microsoft Project" and the caption for the
                    active window is "Project1," then the title bar displays "Microsoft Project -
                    Project1" when the active window is maximized.

The default caption for the main window is "Microsoft Project."

In a project with one window, the default caption for the window is the filename of the project.

In a project with multiple windows, the default caption for each window is "*name:n,*" where *name* is the filename of the project and *n* is a unique number for the window.

For Microsoft Project for the Macintosh, this property is supported read-only for the **Application** object.

See Also   **Height** Property, **Left** Property, **Top** Property, **UsableHeight** Property, **UsableWidth** Property, **Visible** Property, **Width** Property, **WindowState** Property.

Example   The following example prompts the user to change the caption for the active window.

```
Sub ChangeWindowCaption()
    Dim Entry    ' Caption entered by user

    ' Prompt user for a new caption.
    Entry = InputBox("Enter a new caption for the active window" & _
        " (enter 'reset' to set the caption to its default).")

    ' If user chooses the Cancel button, exit Sub procedure.
    If Entry = Empty Then Exit Sub

    ' Set or reset the caption.
    If Entry = "reset" Then
        ActiveWindow.Caption = Empty
    Else
        ActiveWindow.Caption = Entry
    End If
End Sub
```

CBool Function

Description   Converts an expression to a **Boolean**.

Syntax   **CBool**(*expression*)

Elements   The *expression* argument is any valid numeric expression.

Remarks   If *expression* is zero, **False** is returned; otherwise, **True** is returned. If *expression* can't be interpreted as a numeric value, a run-time error occurs.

See Also   Data Type Summary.

Example   This example uses the **CBool** function to convert an expression to a **Boolean**. If the expression evaluates to a nonzero value, **CBool** returns **True**; otherwise, it returns **False**.

```
A = 5 : B = 5          ' Define variables.
Check = CBool(A = B)' Check contains True.
A = 0                  ' Define variable.
Check = CBool(A)       ' Check contains False.
```

CCur Function

Description   Converts an expression to a **Currency**.

Syntax   **CCur**(*expression*)

Elements   The *expression* argument is any valid numeric or string expression.

Remarks   In general, you can document your code using the data type conversion functions to show that the result of some operation should be expressed as a particular data type rather than the default data type. For example, use **CCur** to force currency arithmetic in cases where single-precision, double-precision, or integer arithmetic normally would occur.

You should use the **CCur** function instead of **Val** to provide internationally-aware conversions from any other data type to a **Currency**. For example, different decimal separators are properly recognized depending on the locale setting of your computer, as are different thousand separators and various currency options.

If *expression* lies outside the acceptable range for the **Currency** data type, an error occurs.

See Also   Data Type Summary.

Example   This example uses the **CCur** function to convert an expression to a **Currency**.

```
MyDouble = 543.214588        ' MyDouble is a Double.
MyCurr = CCur(MyDouble * 2) ' Convert result (1086.4292) to Currency.
```

CDate Function

Description	Converts an expression to a **Date**.
Syntax	**CDate**(*date*)
Elements	The *date* argument is any valid date expression.
Remarks	Use the **IsDate** function to determine if *date* can be converted to a date or time. **CDate** recognizes date and time literals as well as some numbers that fall within the range of acceptable dates. When converting a number to a date, the whole number portion is converted to a date. Any fractional part of the number is converted to a time of day, starting at midnight.

CDate recognizes date formats according to the international settings of your system. The correct order of day, month, and year may not be determined if it is provided in a format other than one of the recognized date settings. In addition, a long date format is not recognized if it also contains the day-of-the-week string.

Note A **CVDate** function is also provided for compatibility with previous versions of Visual Basic. However, since there is now an intrinsic **Date** type, there is no further need for **CVDate**. The syntax of the **CVDate** function is identical to the **CDate** function. The difference is that it returns a **Variant** whose subtype is Date instead of an actual **Date** type. The same effect can be achieved by converting an expression to a **Date** and then assigning it to a **Variant**. This technique is consistent with the conversion of all other intrinsic types to their equivalent **Variant** subtypes.

See Also	Data Type Summary, **IsDate** Function.
Example	This example uses the **CDate** function to convert a string to a **Date**. In general, it is bad programming practice to hard code dates/times as strings as shown in this example. Use date literals instead.

```
MyDate = "February 12, 1969"    ' Define date.
MyShortDate = CDate(MyDate)     ' Convert to Date data type.
MyTime = "4:35:47 PM"           ' Define time.
MyShortTime = CDate(MyTime)     ' Convert to Date data type.
```

CDbl Function

Description   Converts an expression to a **Double**.

Syntax   **CDbl**(*expression*)

Elements   The *expression* argument is any valid numeric or string expression.

Remarks   In general, you can document your code using the data type conversion functions to show that the result of some operation should be expressed as a particular data type rather than the default data type. For example, use **CDbl** or **CSng** to force double- or single-precision arithmetic in cases where currency or integer arithmetic normally would occur.

You should use the **CDbl** function instead of **Val** to provide internationally-aware conversions from any other data type to a **Double**. For example, different decimal separators and thousands separators are properly recognized depending on the locale setting of your system.

See Also   Data Type Summary.

Example   This example uses the **CDbl** function to convert an expression to a **Double**.

```
MyCurr = CCur(234.456784)            ' MyCurr is a Currency.
MyDouble = CDbl(MyCurr * 8.2 * 0.01) ' Convert result to Double.
```

Cell Object

Description   The active cell.

Properties   **Application** Property, **FieldID** Property, **FieldName** Property, **Parent** Property, **Resource** Property, **Task** Property

See Also   **ActiveCell** Property, **Application** Object.

CellDragAndDrop Property

Applies To   **Application** Object.

Description	Returns or sets whether you can move and copy cells by dragging and dropping them.
Syntax	[*object*.]**CellDragAndDrop** [= *value*]
Elements	The **CellDragAndDrop** property syntax has these parts:

Part	Description
object	An object expression that evaluates to an object in the Applies To list.
value	A Boolean expression that specifies whether you can move and copy cells by dragging and dropping them, as shown under Settings.

Settings   The **CellDragAndDrop** property has these settings:

Setting	Description
True	You can move and copy cells by dragging and dropping them.
False	You can move and copy cells only by cutting or copying and then pasting them.

See Also   **DisplayAlerts** Property, **DisplayEntryBar** Property, **DisplayScrollBars** Property, **DisplayStatusBar** Property.

Example   The following example changes the **CellDragAndDrop** property.

```
Sub ChangeCellDragAndDrop()
    CellDragAndDrop = Not CellDragAndDrop
End Sub
```

ChangeWorkingTime Method

Applies To	**Application** Object.
Description	Displays the Change Working Time dialog box, which prompts the user to change a calendar.
Syntax	[*object*.]**ChangeWorkingTime**
Elements	The *object* placeholder is an object expression that evaluates to an object in the Applies To list.
Remarks	The **ChangeWorkingTime** method has the same effect as the Change Working Time command on the Format menu.
See Also	**BaseCalendarEditDays** Method, **BaseCalendarReset** Method, **BaseCalendars** Method.

ChDir Statement

Description   Changes the current directory or folder.

Syntax   **ChDir** *path*

Elements   The *path* named argument is a string expression that identifies which directory or folder becomes the new default directory or folder—may include drive. If no drive is specified, **ChDir** changes the default directory or folder on the current drive.

Remarks   In Microsoft Windows, the **ChDir** statement changes the default directory but not the default drive. For example, if the default drive is C, the following statement changes the default directory on drive D, but C remains the default drive:

```
ChDir "D:\TMP"
```

On the Macintosh, the default drive always changes to whatever drive is specified in *path*.

See Also   **ChDrive** Statement, **CurDir** Function, **Dir** Function, **MkDir** Statement, **RmDir** Statement.

Example   This example uses the **ChDir** statement to change the current directory or folder.

```
' Change current directory or folder to "MYDIR".
ChDir "MYDIR"

' In Microsoft Windows.
' Assume "C:" is the current drive.  The following statement changes
' the default directory on drive "D:".  "C:" remains the current drive.
ChDir "D:\WINDOWS\SYSTEM"

' On the Macintosh.
' Changes default folder and default drive.
ChDir "HD:MY FOLDER"
```

ChDrive Statement

Description   Changes the current drive.

Syntax   **ChDrive** *drive*

Elements   The *drive* named argument is a string expression that specifies an existing drive. If you supply a zero-length argument (""), the current drive doesn't change. In Microsoft Windows, if the argument *drive* is a multiple-character string, **ChDrive**

uses only the first letter. On the Macintosh, **ChDrive** changes the current folder to the root folder of the specifed drive.

See Also

ChDir Statement, **CurDir** Function, **MkDir** Statement, **RmDir** Statement.

Example

This example uses the **ChDrive** statement to change the current drive.

```
' In Microsoft Windows.
ChDrive "D" ' Make "D" the current drive.

' On the Macintosh.
' Make "MY DRIVE" the current drive
ChDrive "MY DRIVE:"
' Make "MY DRIVE" the current drive and current folder since its the
' root.
ChDrive "MY DRIVE:MY FOLDER"
```

CheckField Method

Applies To

Application Object.

Description

Returns a value indicating whether the selected tasks or resources meet the criteria you specify.

Syntax

[*object*.]**CheckField** *field*, *value*[, *test*, *op*, *field2*, *value2*, *test2*]

Elements

The **CheckField** method syntax has the following object qualifier and named arguments:

Part	Description
object	An object expression that evaluates to an object in the Applies To list. Optional.
field	A string expression that specifies the name of the field to search. Required.
value	A string expression that specifies the value you want to compare to the value in each field. Required.
test	A string expression that specifies how to compare values, as shown in the table below. By default, the *test* argument is "equals". Optional.
op	A string expression that specifies how the criteria you establish with the *fieldName*, *test*, and *value* arguments relate to the second criteria. You can set the *op* argument to "And" or "Or". Optional.
field2	A string expression that specifies a second field to search. Optional.

Part	Description
value2	A string expression that specifies the value you want to compare to the value in each second field. Optional.
test2	A string expression that specifies how to compare values involving the second criteria, as shown in the table below. Optional.

The *test* and *test2* arguments have these settings:

Setting	Search the field you specify with the *field* argument for a value that
"equals"	Equals the value you specify with the *value* argument.
"not equals"	Does not equal the value you specify with the *value* argument.
"greater"	Is greater than the value you specify with the *value* argument.
"gtr or equal"	Is greater than or equal to the value you specify with the *value* argument.
"less"	Is less than the value you specify with the *value* argument.
"less or equal"	Is less than or equal to the value you specify with the *value* argument.
"within"	Is within the value you specify with the *value* argument.
"not within"	Is not within the value you specify with the *value* argument.
"contains"	Contains the value you specify with the *value* argument.
"doesn't contain"	Does not contain the value you specify with the *value* argument.
"contains exactly"	Exactly contains the value you specify with the *value* argument.

Return Values   Returns **True** if the selected tasks or resources meet the criteria you specify; otherwise, returns **False**.

See Also   **FilterApply** Method, **FilterEdit** Method, **Filters** Method, **Sort** Method.

Chr Function

Description   Returns the character associated with the specified character code.

Syntax   **Chr(*charcode*)**

Elements   The ***charcode*** named argument is a number in the range 0 to 255, inclusive, that identifies a character.

Remarks   Numbers from 0 to 31 are the same as standard, nonprintable ASCII codes. For example, **Chr**(10) returns a linefeed character.

See Also   **Asc** Function, **Str** Function.

Example   This example uses the **Chr** function to return the character associated with the specified character code.

```
MyChar = Chr(65)    ' Returns A.
MyChar = Chr(97)    ' Returns a.
MyChar = Chr(62)    ' Returns >.
MyChar = Chr(37)    ' Returns %.
```

CInt Function

Description   Converts an expression to an **Integer**.

Syntax   **CInt**(*expression*)

Elements   The *expression* argument is any valid numeric or string expression.

Remarks   In general, you can document your code using the data type conversion functions to show that the result of some operation should be expressed as a particular data type rather than the default data type. For example, use **CInt** or **CLng** to force integer arithmetic in cases where currency, single-precision, or double-precision arithmetic normally would occur.

You should use the **CInt** function instead of **Val** to provide internationally-aware conversions from any other data type to an **Integer**. For example, different decimal separators are properly recognized depending on the locale setting of your system, as are different thousand separators.

If *expression* lies outside the acceptable range for the **Integer** data type, an error occurs.

Note **CInt** differs from the **Fix** and **Int** functions that truncate, rather than round, the fractional part of a number. When the fractional part is exactly 0.5, the **CInt** function always rounds it to the nearest even number. For example, 0.5 rounds to 0, and 1.5 rounds to 2.

See Also   Data Type Summary; **Int** Function, **Fix** Function.

Example   This example uses the **CInt** function to convert a value to an **Integer**.

```
MyDouble = 2345.5678    ' MyDouble is a Double.
MyInt = CInt(MyDouble)  ' MyInt contains 2346.
```

Clear Method

Applies To	**Application** Object.
Description	Clears the active cells.
Syntax	[*object*.]**EditClear** [*contents, formats, notes*]
Elements	The **EditClear** method syntax has the following object qualifier and named arguments:

Part	Description
object	An object expression that evaluates to an object in the Applies To list. Optional.
contents	A Boolean expression that specifies whether to clear the contents of the active cells. By default, the *contents* argument is **True**. Optional.
formats	A Boolean expression that specifies whether to clear the formats of the active cells. By default, the *formats* argument is **False**. Optional.
notes	A Boolean expression that specifies whether to clear the notes of the active cells. By default, the *notes* argument is **False**. Optional.

See Also	**EditClearFormats** Method, **EditCopy** Method, **EditCut** Method, **EditDelete** Method, **RowClear** Method.
Example	The following example clears the contents, formats, and notes of the active cells.

```
Sub ClearAll()
    EditClear True, True, True
End Sub
```

ClipboardShow Method

Applies To	**Application** Object.
Description	Displays the contents of the Clipboard. The Clipboard contains the information you last cut or copied with the Cut, Copy, or Copy Picture command.
Syntax	[*object*.]**ClipboardShow**
Elements	The *object* placeholder is an object expression that evaluates to an object in the Applies To list.
Remarks	This method applies to Microsoft Project for the Macintosh.

See Also   **EditCopy** Method, **EditCopyPicture** Method, **EditCut** Method, **EditPaste** Method.

Example   The following example displays the Clipboard.

```
Sub ClipboardShow()
    ClipboardShow
End Sub
```

CLng Function

Description   Converts an expression to a **Long**.

Syntax   **CLng**(*expression*)

Elements   The *expression* argument is any valid numeric or string expression.

Remarks   In general, you can document your code using the data type conversion functions to show that the result of some operation should be expressed as a particular data type rather than the default data type. For example, use **CInt** or **CLng** to force integer arithmetic in cases where currency, single-precision, or double-precision arithmetic normally would occur.

You should use the **CLng** function instead of **Val** to provide internationally-aware conversions from any other data type to a **Long**. For example, different decimal separators are properly recognized depending on the locale setting of your system, as are different thousand separators.

If *expression* lies outside the acceptable range for the **Long** data type, an error occurs.

Note **CLng** differs from the **Fix** and **Int** functions that truncate, rather than round, the fractional part of a number. When the fractional part is exactly 0.5, the **CLng** function always rounds it to the nearest even number. For example, 0.5 rounds to 0, and 1.5 rounds to 2.

See Also   Data Type Summary; **Int** Function, **Fix** Function.

Example   This example uses the **CLng** function to convert a value to a **Long**.

```
MyVal1 = 25427.45 : MyVal2 = 25427.55    ' MyVal1, MyVal2 are Doubles.
MyLong1 = CLng(MyVal1)                   ' MyLong1 contains 25427.
MyLong2 = CLng(MyVal2)                   ' MyLong2 contains 25428.
```

Close Method

Applies To	**Application** Object.
Description	Closes the active project.
Syntax	[*object*.]**DocClose**
Elements	The *object* placeholder is an object expression that evaluates to an object in the Applies To list.
See Also	**DocMaximize** Method, **DocMove** Method, **DocRestore** Method, **DocSize** Method.

Close Statement

Description	Concludes input/output (I/O) to a file opened using the **Open** statement.
Syntax	**Close** [*filenumberlist*]
Elements	The *filenumberlist* argument can be one or more file numbers using the following syntax, where *filenumber* is any valid file number:
	[#]*filenumber*][,[#]*filenumber*] ...
Remarks	If you omit *filenumberlist*, all active files opened by the **Open** statement are closed.
	When you close files that were opened for **Output** or **Append**, the final buffer of output is written to the operating system buffer for that file. All buffer space associated with the closed file is released.
	When the **Close** statement executes, the association of a file with its file number ends.
See Also	**End** Statement, **Open** Statement, **Reset** Statement, **Stop** Statement.
Example	This example uses the **Close** statement to close all three files opened for **Output**.

```
For I = 1 To 3                     ' Loop 3 times.
    FileName = "TEST" & I          ' Create file name.
    Open FileName For Output As #I ' Open file.
    Print #I, "This is a test."    ' Write string to file.
Next I
Close                              ' Close all 3 open files.
```

Code Property

Applies To   **Resource** Object, **Resources** Collection.

Description   Returns or sets the code of a resource.

Syntax   *object*.**Code** [= *value*]

Elements   The **Code** property syntax has the following parts:

Part	Description
object	An object expression that evaluates to an object in the Applies To list.
value	A string expression that specifies the code of a resource.

See Also   **Group** Property, **Initials** Property, **Name** Property, **Notes** Property, **Textn** Properties.

ColumnAlignment Method

Applies To   **Application** Object.

Description   Sets the alignment of text in the active columns.

Syntax   [*object*.]**ColumnAlignment** *align*

Elements   The **ColumnAlignment** method syntax has the following object qualifier and named arguments:

Part	Description
object	An object expression that evaluates to an object in the Applies To list. Optional.
align	A constant that specifies the alignment of text in the active columns. Required.

The *align* argument has these settings:

pjLeft	0	Align left.
pjCenter	1	Align center.
pjRight	2	Align right.

See Also   **ColumnBestFit** Method, **ColumnDelete** Method, **ColumnEdit** Method, **ColumnInsert** Method.

ColumnBestFit Method

Applies To   **Application** Object.

Description   Sets the width of a column to the width of its widest item.

Syntax   [*object.*]**ColumnBestFit** [*column*]

Elements   The **ColumnBestFit** method syntax has the following object qualifier and named argument:

Part	Description
object	An object expression that evaluates to an object in the Applies To list.
value	A numeric expression that specifies the column to adjust. Columns are numbered from left to right, starting with 1. If you omit the *column* argument, Microsoft Project adjusts the width of the column that contains the active cell.

See Also   **ColumnDelete** Method, **ColumnInsert** Method, **RowDelete** Method, **RowInsert** Method.

Example   The following example adjusts the widths of the first five columns in the active table.

```
Sub BestFitFirstFiveCols()
    Dim I        ' Index used in For...Next loop.
    For I = 1 To 5
        ColumnBestFit Column := I
    Next I
End Sub
```

ColumnDelete Method

Applies To   **Application** Object.

Description   Deletes the active column or the column containing the active cell.

Syntax   [*object.*]**ColumnDelete**

Elements	The *object* placeholder is an object expression that evaluates to an object in the Applies To list.
See Also	**ColumnAlignment** Method, **ColumnBestFit** Method, **ColumnEdit** Method, **ColumnInsert** Method, **TableApply** Method, **TableEdit** Method, **Tables** Method.

ColumnEdit Method

Applies To	**Application** Object.
Description	Edits the active column or the column containing the active cell.
Syntax	[*object*.]**ColumnEdit** [*column*]
Elements	The **ColumnEdit** method syntax has the following object qualifier and named arguments:

Part	Description
object	An object expression that evaluates to an object in the Applies To list.
column	A numeric expression that specifies the number of the column to change. By default, the *column* argument equals the number of the active column.

See Also	**ColumnAlignment** Method, **ColumnBestFit** Method, **ColumnDelete** Method, **ColumnInsert** Method, **TableApply** Method, **TableEdit** Method, **Tables** Method.

ColumnInsert Method

Applies To	**Application** Object.
Description	Inserts a column to the left of the active column, and then displays the Column Definition box.
Syntax	[*object*.]**ColumnInsert**
Elements	The *object* placeholder is an object expression that evaluates to an object in the Applies To list.
See Also	**ColumnBestFit** Method, **ColumnDelete** Method, **RowDelete** Method, **RowInsert** Method.

Comments Property

Applies To	**Project** Object, **Projects** Collection.
Description	Returns or sets comments for a project.
Syntax	*object*.**Comments** [= *value*]
Elements	The **Comments** property syntax has these parts:

Part	Description
object	An object expression that evaluates to an object in the Applies To list.
value	A string expression that specifies the comments for the project.

Remarks	The **Comments** property is the same as the **Notes** property. For example, if you assign a value to the **Comments** property, you can retrieve the value with the **Notes** property; if you assign a value to the **Notes** property, you can retrieve the value with the **Comments** property.
See Also	**Author** Property, **Company** Property, **CurrentDate** Property, **Keywords** Property, **Manager** Property, **Notes** Property, **ScheduleFromStart** Property, **Subject** Property, **Template** Property, **Title** Property.

Company Property

Applies To	**Project** Object, **Projects** Collection.
Description	Returns or sets the company name associated with a project.
Syntax	*object*.**Company** [= *value*]
Elements	The **Company** property syntax has these parts:

Part	Description
object	An object expression that evaluates to an object in the Applies To list.
value	A string expression of the company name associated with the project.

See Also	**Author** Property, **Comments** Property, **CurrentDate** Property, **Keywords** Property, **Manager** Property, **Notes** Property, **ScheduleFromStart** Property, **Subject** Property, **Template** Property, **Title** Property.

Comparison Operators

Description

Used to compare expressions.

Syntax

result = expression1 comparisonoperator expression2
result = object1 **Is** *object2*
result = string **Like** *pattern*

Elements

Comparison operators have these parts:

Part	Description
result	Any numeric variable.
expression	Any expression.
comparisonoperator	Any comparison operator.
object	Any object name.
string	Any string expression.
pattern	Any string expression or range of characters.

Remarks

The **Is** and **Like** operators have specific comparison functionality that differs from the operators in the following table. The following table contains a list of the comparison operators and the conditions that determine whether *result* is **True**, **False**, or **Null**:

<	Less than	*expression1 < expression2*	*expression1 >= expression2*	*expression1* or *expression2* = **Null**
<=	Less than or equal to	*expression1 <= expression2*	*expression1 > expression2*	*expression1* or *expression2* = **Null**
>	Greater than	*expression1 > expression2*	*expression1 <= expression2*	*expression1* or *expression2* = **Null**
>=	Greater than or equal to	*expression1 >= expression2*	*expression1 < expression2*	*expression1* or *expression2* = **Null**
=	Equal to	*expression1 = expression2*	*expression1 <> expression2*	*expression1* or *expression2* = **Null**
<>	Not equal to	*expression1 <> expression2*	*expression1 = expression2*	*expression1* or *expression2* = **Null**

When comparing two expressions, you may not be able to easily determine whether the expressions are being compared as numbers or as strings. The following table shows how the expressions are compared or what results when either expression is not a **Variant**:

If	Then
Both expressions are numeric data types (**Integer**, **Long**, **Single**, **Double**, or **Currency**)	Perform a numeric comparison.
Both expressions are **String**	Perform a string comparison.
One expression is a numeric data type and the other is a **Variant** that is, or can be, a number	Perform a numeric comparison.
One expression is a numeric data type and the other is a string **Variant** that can't be converted to a number	A `Type Mismatch` error occurs.
One expression is a **String** and the other is any **Variant** (except a **Null**)	Perform a string comparison.
One expression is **Empty** and the other is a numeric data type	Perform a numeric comparison, using 0 as the **Empty** expression.
One expression is **Empty** and the other is a **String**	Perform a string comparison, using a zero-length string as the **Empty** expression.

If *expression1* and *expression2* are both **Variant** expressions, their underlying type determines how they are compared. The following table shows how the expressions are compared or what results from the comparison, depending on the underlying type of the **Variant**:

If	Then
Both **Variant** expressions are numeric	Perform a numeric comparison.
Both **Variant** expressions are strings	Perform a string comparison.
One **Variant** expression is numeric and the other is a string	The numeric expression is less than the string expression.
One **Variant** expression is **Empty** and the other is numeric	Perform a numeric comparison, using 0 as the **Empty** expression.
One **Variant** expression is **Empty** and the other is a string	Perform a string comparison, using a zero-length string as the **Empty** expression.
Both **Variant** expressions are **Empty**	The expressions are equal.

Note If a **Currency** is compared with a **Single** or **Double**, the **Single** or **Double** is converted to a **Currency**. This causes any fractional part of the **Single** or **Double** value less than 0.0001 to be lost and may cause two values to compare as equal when they are not. When a **Single** is compared to a **Double**, the **Double** is rounded to the precision of the **Single**.

See Also

Is Operator, **Like** Operator, Operator Precedence, **Option Compare** Statement.

Example

This example shows various uses of comparison operators, which you use to compare expressions.

```
MyResult = (45 < 35)       ' Returns False.
MyResult = (45 = 45)       ' Returns True.
MyResult = (4 <> 3)        ' Returns True.
MyResult = ("5" > "4")     ' Returns True.
Var1 = "5" : Var2 = 4      ' Initialize variables.
MyResult = (Var1 > Var2)   ' Returns True.
Var1 = 5 : Var2 = Empty
MyResult = (Var1 > Var2)   ' Returns True.
Var1 = 0 : Var2 = Empty
MyResult = (Var1 = Var2)   ' Returns True.
```

Confirmed Property

Applies To

Project Object, **Projects** Collection; **Task** Object, **Tasks** Collection.

Description

Returns whether the resources of a project or task have accepted the task assignments specified in a Microsoft Project mail message.

Syntax

object.**Confirmed**

Elements

The *object* placeholder is an object expression that evaluates to an object in the Applies To list.

Remarks

This method applies to Microsoft Project for Microsoft Windows.

See Also

MailSendProjectMail Method, **UpdateNeeded** Property.

ConsolidateProjects Method

Applies To

Application Object.

Description

Displays the data from one or more projects in a single window.

Syntax	[*object.*]**ConsolidateProjects** [*filenames, newWindow, attachToSources, poolResources, hideSubtasks*]
Elements	The **ConsolidateProjects** method syntax has the following object qualifier and named arguments:

Part	Description
object	An object expression that evaluates to an object in the Applies To list. Optional.
filenames	A string expression that specifies one or more filenames of projects to consolidate. Optional.
newWindow	A Boolean expression that specifies whether to create a new window for the projects you specify with the *filenames* argument. The *newWindow* argument is ignored unless the active project is a consolidated project. Optional.
attachToSources	A Boolean expression that specifies whether changes in the consolidated project affect source projects. Optional.
poolResources	A Boolean expression that specifies whether to pool the resources of the projects you specify with the *filenames* argument. Optional.
hideSubtasks	A Boolean expression that specifies whether to hide the subtasks of the projects you specify with the *filenames* argument. Optional.

See Also	**FileOpen** Method, **ViewEditCombination** Method.
Example	The following example creates a consolidated project, prints a report, and closes the consolidated project without saving it.

```
Sub ConsolidatedReport()
    ConsolidateProjects Filenames := "project1.mpp,project2.mpp"
    ReportPrint Name:="Critical Tasks"
    FileClose save := pjDoNotSave
End Sub
```

Const Statement

Description	Declares constants for use in place of literal values.
Syntax	[**Public**	**Private**] **Const** *constname* [**As** *type*] = *expression*
Elements	The **Const** statement syntax has these parts:

Part	Description
Public	Used at module level to declare constants that are available to all procedures in all modules. Not allowed in procedures.
Private	Used at module level to declare constants that are available only within the module where the declaration is made. Not allowed in procedures.
constname	Name of the constant; follows standard variable naming conventions.
type	Data type of the constant; may be **Boolean**, **Integer**, **Long**, **Currency**, **Single**, **Double**, **Date**, **String**, or **Variant**. Use a separate **As** *type* clause for each constant being declared.
expression	Literal, other constant, or any combination including arithmetic or logical operators except **Is**.

Remarks

If not explicitly specified using either **Public** or **Private**, constants are **Private** by default.

Several constant declarations can be combined on the same line by separating each constant assignment with a comma. If constant declarations are combined in this way, the **Public** or **Private** keywords, if used, apply to all of them.

You can't use string concatenation, variables, user-defined or intrinsic functions (such as **Chr**) in expressions assigned to constants.

If you don't explicitly declare the constant type (using **As** *type*), the constant is given a data type that is most appropriate for the expression provided.

Constants declared in **Sub**, **Function**, or **Property** procedures are local to that procedure. A constant declared outside a procedure is defined throughout the module in which it is declared. You can use constants anywhere you would use an expression.

See Also

Def*type* Statements, **Let** Statement.

Example

This example uses the **Const** statement to declare constants for use in place of literal values.

```
' Constants are Private by default.
Const MyVar = 459

' Declare Public constant.
Public Const MyString = "HELP"

' Declare Private Integer constant.
Private Const MyInt As Integer = 5

' Declare multiple constants on same line.
Const MyStr = "Hello", MyDouble As Double = 3.4567
```

ConstraintDate Property

Applies To   **Project** Object, **Projects** Collection; **Task** Object, **Tasks** Collection.

Description   Returns or sets a constraint date for a task.

Syntax   *object*.**ConstraintDate** [= *value*]

Elements   The **ConstraintDate** property syntax has these parts:

Part	Description
object	An object expression that evaluates to an object in the Applies To list.
value	A date expression that specifies the constraint date for the task.

Remarks   Microsoft Project uses the constraint date only when you set a constraint on a task. To set a constraint on a task, use the **ConstraintType** property.

See Also   **ConstraintType** Property.

Example   The following example sets the constraint type to SNET and the constraint date to the current date for tasks in the active project without constraint types.

```
Sub SetConstraintDate()
    Dim T               ' Task object used in For Each loop

    ' Set the constraint type and date for tasks without constraints.
    For Each T in ActiveProject.Tasks
        If T.ConstraintType = pjASAP Then
            T.ConstraintDate = CurrentDate
            T.ConstraintType = pjSNET
        End If
    Next T
End Sub
```

ConstraintType Property

Applies To   **Project** Object, **Projects** Collection; **Task** Object, **Tasks** Collection.

Description   Returns or sets a constraint type for a task.

Syntax   *object*.**ConstraintType** [= *value*]

Elements   The **ConstraintType** property syntax has these parts:

Part	Description
object	An object expression that evaluates to an object in the Applies To list.
value	A constant that specifies a constraint type, as shown under Settings.

Settings

The **ConstraintType** property has these settings:

pjALAP	As Late As Possible	The task occurs as late as possible in the schedule without delaying subsequent tasks.
pjASAP	As Soon As Possible	The task occurs as soon as possible in the schedule. This is the default constraint type for tasks.
pjFNET	Finish No Earlier Than	The task finishes on or after the constraint date.
pjFNLT	Finish No Later Than	The task finishes on or before the constraint date.
pjMFO	Must Finish On	The task finishes on the constraint date.
pjMSO	Must Start On	The task starts on the constraint date.
pjSNET	Start No Earlier Than	The task starts on or after the constraint date.
pjSNLT	Start No Later Than	The task starts on or before the constraint date.

Remarks

If you set the **ConstraintType** property to **pjFNET**, **pjFNLT**, **pjMFO**, **pjMSO**, **pjSNET**, or **pjSNLT**, Microsoft Project uses the constraint date for the task. To set the constraint date, use the **ConstraintDate** property.

See Also

ConstraintDate Property.

Example

The following example changes the constraint type of tasks from MSO and MFO to SNET and FNLT.

```
Sub ChangeConstraintTypes()
    Dim T       ' Task object used in For Each loop

    ' Change constraint types from MSO and MFO to SNET and FNLT.
    For Each T in ActiveProject.Tasks
        If T.ConstraintType = pjMSO Then
            T.ConstraintType = pjSNET
        ElseIf T.ConstraintType = pjMFO Then
            T.ConstraintType = pjFNLT
        End If
    Next T
End Sub
```

Contact Property

Applies To   **Project** Object, **Projects** Collection; **Task** Object, **Tasks** Collection.

Description   The electronic mail address of the person who is responsible for a project or task.

Syntax   *object*.**Contact** [= *value*]

Elements   The **Contact** property syntax has the following parts:

Part	Description
object	An object expression that evaluates to an object in the Applies To list.
value	A string expression that specifies the electronic mail address of the person responsible for the project or task.

Remarks   This method applies to Microsoft Project for Microsoft Windows.

See Also   **EMailAddress** Property, **MailRoutingSlip** Method, **MailSend** Method, **MailSendProjectMail** Method.

CopyResourceUsageHeader Property

Applies To   **Application** Object.

Description   Returns or sets whether header information is copied in the Resource Usage view.

Syntax   [*object*.]**CopyResourceUsageHeader**

Elements   The *object* placeholder is an object expression that evaluates to an object in the Applies To list.

See Also   **AskToUpdateLinks** Property, **CellDragAndDrop** Property, **MoveAfterReturn** Property, **OptionsEdit** Method.

Cos Function

Description   Returns the cosine of an angle.

Syntax   **Cos(*number*)**

Elements The *number* named argument can be any valid numeric expression that expresses an angle in radians.

Remarks The **Cos** function takes an angle and returns the ratio of two sides of a right triangle. The ratio is the length of the side adjacent to the angle divided by the length of the hypotenuse.

The result lies in the range -1 to 1.

To convert degrees to radians, multiply degrees by pi/180. To convert radians to degrees, multiply radians by 180/pi.

See Also **Atn** Function, Derived Math Functions, **Sin** Function, **Tan** Function.

Example This example uses the **Cos** function to return the cosine of an angle.

```
MyAngle = 1.3              ' Define angle in radians.
MySecant = 1 / Cos(MyAngle) ' Calculate secant.
```

Cost*n* Property

Applies To **Project** Object, **Projects** Collection; **Task** Object, **Tasks** Collection.

Description Returns or sets the value in an additional cost field for a task or project.

Syntax *object*.**Cost***n* [= *value*]

Elements The **Cost***n* property syntaxes have the following parts:

Part	Description
object	An object expression that evaluates to an object in the Applies To list.
n	A number from 1 to 3.
value	A numeric expression that specifies the value for the additional cost field.

See Also **ActualCost** Property, **BaselineCost** Property, **Cost** Property.

CostPerUse Property

Applies To **Resource** Object, **Resources** Collection.

Description Returns the cost per use of a resource.

Syntax	*object*.**CostPerUse** [= *value*]
Elements	The **CostPerUse** property syntax has the following parts:

Part	Description
object	An object expression that evaluates to an object in the Applies To list.
value	A numeric expression that specifies the cost per use of the resource.

See Also   **AccrueAt** Property, **Cost** Property, **OvertimeRate** Property, **StandardRate** Property.

Example   The following example displays the sum of the cost per use of each resource in the active project.

```
Sub TotalCostPerUse()
    Dim R              ' Resource object used in For Each loop
    Dim TotalCostPerUse ' The total cost per use

    ' Add up the cost per use of each resource.
    For Each R in ActiveProject.Resources
        TotalCostPerUse = TotalCostPerUse + R.CostPerUse
    Next R

    ' Display the total cost per use.
    MsgBox("Sum of the cost per use of each resource in this" & _
        " project: " & TotalCostPerUse)
End Sub
```

CostVariance Property

Applies To   **Project** Object, **Projects** Collection; **Resource** Object, **Resources** Collection; **Task** Object, **Tasks** Collection.

Description   Returns the variance between the baseline cost and the cost of a project or task.

Syntax   *object*.**CostVariance**

Elements   The *object* placeholder is an object expression that evaluates to an object in the Applies To list.

See Also   **ActualCost** Property, **BaselineCost** Property, **Cost** Property, **DurationVariance** Property, **FinishVariance** Property, **FixedCost** Property, **RemainingCost** Property, **StartVariance** Property, **WorkVariance** Property.

Count Property

Applies To **Assignment** Object, **Assignments** Collection; **Calendar** Object, **Calendars** Collection; **Day** Object, **Days** Collection; **List** Object; **Month** Object, **Months** Collection; **Period** Object; **Project** Object, **Projects** Collection; **Resource** Object, **Resources** Collection; **Task** Object, **Tasks** Collection; **Weekday** Object, **Weekdays** Collection; **Window** Object, **Windows** Collection; **Year** Object, **Years** Collection.

Description Returns the number of objects in a collection or the number of days in a month, period, or year. Returns 1 when applied to the **Day** object.

Syntax *object*.**Count**

Elements The *object* placeholder is any object expression that evaluates to an object in the Applies To list.

See Also **Add** Method, **Delete** Method, **Index** Property, **NumberOfResources** Property, **NumberOfTasks** Property.

Example The following example prompts the user for the name of a resource, and then assigns that resource to tasks without any resources.

```
Sub AssignResource()
    Dim T              ' Task object used in For Each loop
    Dim R              ' Resource object used in For Each loop
    Dim RName          ' Resource name
    Dim RID            ' Resource ID

    RID = 0
    RName = InputBox("Enter the name of a resource: ")

    For Each R in ActiveProject.Resources
        If R.Name = RName Then
            RID = R.ID
            Exit For
        End If
    Next R
```

```
                         If RID <> 0 Then
                             ' Assign the resource to tasks without any resources.
                             For Each T In ActiveProject.Tasks
                                 If T.Assignments.Count = 0 Then
                                     T.Assignments.Add T.ID, RID
                                 End If
                             Next T
                         Else
                             MsgBox Prompt:=RName & " is not a resource in this project.", _
                                 buttons:=vbExclamation
                         End If
                 End Sub
```

Created Property

Applies To	**Project** Object, **Projects** Collection; **Task** Object, **Tasks** Collection.
Description	The date a project or task was created.
Syntax	*object*.**Created** [= *value*]
Elements	The **Created** property syntax has the following parts:

Part	Description
object	An object expression that evaluates to an object in the Applies To list.
value	A date expression that specifies when the task or project was created.

See Also	**CurrentDate** Property.

CreatePublisher Method

Applies To	**Application** Object.
Description	Publishes selected items.
Syntax	[*object*.]**CreatePublisher** (*Edition, Contains*)
Elements	The **CreatePublisher** method has the following object qualifier and named arguments:

Part	Description
object	An object expression that evaluates to an object in the Applies To list. Optional.
Edition	The path name and file name of the new edition. If omitted, a default of current path + default edition name is used. Optional.
Contains	A constant that specifies the material to be published. The default is **pjAll**. Optional.

The *Contains* argument has these settings:

pjAll	0	All.
pjPictureOnly	1	Picture only.

Remarks This method applies to Microsoft Project for the Macintosh.

See Also **PublisherOptions** Method, **SubscribeTo** Method.

CreationDate Property

Applies To **Project** Object, **Projects** Collection.

Description Returns the creation date of a project.

Syntax *object*.**CreationDate**

Elements The *object* placeholder is an object expression that evaluates to an object in the Applies To list.

See Also **LastSaveDate** Property.

Example The following example adds the creation date of the active project to its notes.

```
Sub AddCreationDateToNotes()
    Dim NL As String    ' Newline characters
    NL = Chr(13) + Chr(10)   ' NL = Carriage Return + Linefeed

    ' Add the creation date to the notes of the active project.
    ActiveProject.Notes = ActiveProject.Notes & NL & "This project" & _
        " was created on " & ActiveProject.CreationDate
End Sub
```

Critical Property

Applies To	**Project** Object, **Projects** Collection; **Task** Object, **Tasks** Collection.
Description	Returns a value that indicates whether a task is on the critical path.
Syntax	*object*.**Critical**
Elements	The *object* placeholder is an object expression that evaluates to an object in the Applies To list.
Settings	The **Critical** property has the following settings:

Setting	Description
True	The task is on the critical path.
False	The task is not on the critical path.

See Also	**Delay** Property, **FreeSlack** Property, **TotalSlack** Property.
Example	The following example sets the highest priority for critical tasks in the active project.

```
Sub MakeCriticalTasksHighestPriority()
    Dim T As Task    ' Task object used in For Each loop

    ' Look for critical tasks in the active project.
    For Each T In ActiveProject.Tasks
        If T.Critical Then T.Priority = pjPriorityHighest
    Next T
End Sub
```

CSng Function

Description	Converts an expression to a **Single**.
Syntax	**CSng**(*expression*)
Elements	The *expression* argument is any valid numeric or string expression.
Remarks	In general, you can document your code using the data type conversion functions to show that the result of some operation should be expressed as a particular data type rather than the default data type. For example, use **CDbl** or **CSng** to force double-

or single-precision arithmetic in cases where currency or integer arithmetic normally would occur.

You should use the **CSng** function instead of **Val** to provide internationally-aware conversions from any other data type to a **Single**. For example, different decimal separators are properly recognized depending on the locale setting of your system, as are different thousand separators.

If *expression* lies outside the acceptable range for the **Single** data type, an error occurs.

See Also	Data Type Summary.
Example	This example uses the **CSng** function to convert a value to a **Single**.

```
' MyDouble1, MyDouble2 are Doubles.
MyDouble1 = 75.3421115 : MyDouble2 = 75.3421555
MySingle1 = CSng(MyDouble1) ' MySingle1 contains 75.34211.
MySingle2 = CSng(MyDouble2) ' MySingle2 contains 75.34216.
```

CStr Function

Description	Converts an expression to a **String**.
Syntax	**CStr**(*expression*)
Elements	The *expression* argument is any valid numeric or string expression.
Remarks	In general, you can document your code using the data type conversion functions to show that the result of some operation should be expressed as a particular data type rather than the default data type. For example, use **CStr** to force the result to be expressed as a **String**.

You should use the **CStr** function instead of **Str** to provide internationally-aware conversions from any other data type to a **String**. For example, different decimal separators are properly recognized depending on the locale setting of your system.

The data in *expression* determines what is returned according to the following table:

If *expression* is	CStr returns
Boolean	**String** containing **True** or **False** (translated as appropriate for locale).
Date	**String** containing a date in the short-date format of your system.
Null	A run-time error.

If *expression* is	CStr returns
Empty	A zero-length **String** ("").
Error	A **String** containing the word **Error** (translated as appropriate for locale) followed by the error number.
Other Numeric	A **String** containing the number.

See Also   Data Type Summary, **Str** Function.

Example   This example uses the **CStr** function to convert a numeric value to a **String**.

```
MyDouble = 437.324        ' MyDouble is a Double.
MyString = CStr(MyDouble)  ' MyString contains "437.324".
```

CurDir Function

Description   Returns the current path.

Syntax   **CurDir**[(*drive*)]

Elements   The *drive* argument is a string expression that specifies an existing drive. In Microsoft Windows, if no drive is specified or if *drive* is zero-length (""), **CurDir** returns the path for the current drive. On the Macintosh, **CurDir** ignores any *drive* specified and simply returns the path for the current drive.

See Also   **ChDir** Statement, **ChDrive** Statement, **MkDir** Statement, **RmDir** Statement.

Example   This example uses the **CurDir** function to return the current path.

```
' In Microsoft Windows.
' Assume current path on C Drive is  "C:\WINDOWS\SYSTEM".
' Assume current path on D Drive is "D:\EXCEL".
' Assume C is the current drive.
MyPath = CurDir         ' Returns "C:\WINDOWS\SYSTEM".
MyPath = CurDir("C")    ' Returns "C:\WINDOWS\SYSTEM".
MyPath = CurDir("D")    ' Returns "D:\EXCEL".

' On the Macintosh.
' Drive letters are ignored. Path for current drive is returned.
' Assume current path on HD Drive is  "HD:MY FOLDER".
' Assume HD is the current drive. Drive MD also exists on the machine.
MyPath = CurDir         ' Returns "HD:MY FOLDER".
MyPath = CurDir("HD")   ' Returns "HD:MY FOLDER".
MyPath = CurDir("MD")   ' Returns "HD:MY FOLDER".
```

Currency Data Type

Description

Currency variables are stored as 64-bit (8-byte) numbers in an integer format, scaled by 10,000 to give a fixed-point number with 15 digits to the left of the decimal point and 4 digits to the right. This representation provides a range of -922,337,203,685,477.5808 to 922,337,203,685,477.5807. The type-declaration character for **Currency** is @ (character code 64).

The **Currency** data type is useful for calculations involving money and for fixed-point calculations in which accuracy is particularly important.

See Also

CCur Function, Data Type Summary, **Def***type* Statements, **Long** Data Type.

CurrencyDigits Property

Applies To

Project Object, **Projects** Collection.

Description

Sets or returns the number of digits following the decimal separator character, in currency values.

Syntax

object.**CurrencyDigits** [= *value*]

Elements

The **CurrencyDigits** property syntax has these parts:

Object	Description
object	An object expression that evaluates to an object in the Applies To list.
value	A numeric expression that specifies the number of digits following the decimal separator character, in currency values.

Remarks

Microsoft Project for Microsoft Windows sets the **CurrencyDigits** property equal to the corresponding value in theRegional settings of the Microsoft Windows Control Panel.

On the Macintosh, using System 7.1 and later, you can use the Numbers control panel to change this value.

See Also

CurrencySymbol Property, **CurrencySymbolPosition** Property.

CurrencySymbol Property

Applies To   **Project** Object, **Projects** Collection.

Description   Returns or sets the characters that denote currency values.

Syntax   *object*.**CurrencySymbol** [= *value*]

Elements   The **CurrencySymbol** property syntax has these parts:

Object	Description
object	An object expression that evaluates to an object in the Applies To list.
value	A string expression of the characters that denote currency values.

Remarks   Microsoft Project for Microsoft Windows sets the **CurrencySymbol** property equal to the corresponding value in theRegional settings of the Microsoft Windows Control Panel.

On the Macintosh, using System 7.1 and later, you can use the Numbers control panel to change this value.

See Also   **CurrencyDigits** Property, **CurrencySymbolPosition** Property.

Example   The following example formats currency values in the active project according to the country specified by the user.

```
Sub FormatCurrency()
    Dim Country      As String

    ' Prompt the user to enter the name of a country.
    ' Specify the possible countries in dialog box?
    Country = UCase(InputBox("Enter the name of a country: ", _
        "Format Currency By Country"))
    Select Case Country
        Case "US", "United States", "USA", "United States of America"
            ActiveProject.CurrencySymbol = "$"
            ActiveProject.CurrencySymbolPosition = pjBefore
        Case "FRANCE"
            ActiveProject.CurrencySymbol = "F"
            ActiveProject.CurrencySymbolPosition = pjAfterWithSpace
        Case "ENGLAND"
            ActiveProject.CurrencySymbol = Chr(163)
            ActiveProject.CurrencySymbolPosition = pjBefore
        Case "GERMANY"
            ActiveProject.CurrencySymbol = "DM"
            ActiveProject.CurrencySymbolPosition = pjAfterWithSpace
```

```
                         Case "SWEDEN"
                             ActiveProject.CurrencySymbol = "kr"
                             ActiveProject.CurrencySymbolPosition = pjAfterWithSpace
                         ' Warn user if the currency format is not known.
                         Case Else
                             MsgBox("I don't know the currency format for that country.")
                     End Select
                 End Sub
```

CurrencySymbolPosition Property

Applies To	**Project** Object, **Projects** Collection.
Description	Returns or sets the location of the currency symbol.
Syntax	*object*.**CurrencySymbolPosition** [= *value*]
Elements	The **CurrencySymbolPosition** property syntax has these parts:

Object	Description
object	An object expression that evaluates to an object in the Applies To list.
value	A constant that specifies the location of the currency symbol.

Settings The **CurrencySymbolPosition** property has these settings:

pjBefore	0	The currency symbol appears before currency values.
pjAfter	1	The currency symbol appears after currency values.
pjBeforeWithSpace	2	The currency symbol and a space appear before currency values.
pjAfterWithSpace	3	A space and the currency symbol appear after currency values.

Remarks Microsoft Project for Microsoft Windows sets the **CurrencySymbolPosition** property equal to the corresponding value in the Regional settings of the Microsoft Windows Control Panel.

On the Macintosh, using System 7.1 and later, you can use the Numbers control panel to change this value.

See Also **CurrencyDigits** Property, **CurrencySymbol** Property.

CurrentDate Property

Applies To   **Project** Object, **Projects** Collection.

Description   Returns or sets the current date for a project.

Syntax   *object*.**CurrentDate** [= *value*]

Elements   The **CurrentDate** property syntax has these parts:

Part	Description
object	An object expression that evaluates to an object in the Applies To list.
value	A date expression of the current date for the project.

Remarks   When a project opens, Microsoft Project automatically sets the project's current date equal to the system date.

See Also   **Author** Property, **Comments** Property, **Company** Property, **Keywords** Property, **Manager** Property, **Notes** Property, **ScheduleFromStart** Property, **Subject** Property, **Template** Property, **Title** Property.

Example   The following example sets the current date of the active project to the previous Monday.

```
Sub SetCurrentDateToPreviousMonday()
    Dim I    ' Index used in For loop

    ' Loop while the current date is not Monday.
    Do While Weekday(ActiveProject.CurrentDate) <> pjMonday

        ' Subtract one day from the current date.
        ActiveProject.CurrentDate = _
            DateSerial(Year(ActiveProject.CurrentDate), _
            Month(ActiveProject.CurrentDate), _
            Day(ActiveProject.CurrentDate - 1))
    Loop
End Sub
```

CurrentFilter Property

Applies To   **Project** Object, **Projects** Collection.

Description   Returns the name of the current filter for a project.

Syntax	*object*.**CurrentFilter**
Elements	The *object* placeholder is an object expression that evaluates to an object in the Applies To list.
See Also	**CurrentTable** Property, **CurrentView** Property, **ResourceFilterList** Method, **TaskFilterList** Method.
Example	The following example displays the name of the current view, table, and filter in a dialog box.

```
Sub ViewDetails()
    NL = Chr$(13) & Chr$(10)
    strTemp = "View: " & ActiveProject.CurrentView & NL
    strTemp = strTemp & "Table:" & ActiveProject.CurrentTable & NL
    strTemp = strTemp & "Filter: " & ActiveProject.CurrentFilter
    MsgBox strTemp
End Sub
```

CurrentTable Property

Applies To	**Project** Object, **Projects** Collection.
Description	Returns the name of the current table for a project.
Syntax	*object*.**CurrentTable**
Elements	The *object* placeholder is an object expression that evaluates to an object in the Applies To list.
See Also	**CurrentFilter** Property, **CurrentView** Property, **ResourceTableList** Method, **TaskTableList** Method.
Example	The following example displays the name of the current view, table, and filter in a dialog box.

```
Sub ViewDetails()
    NL = Chr$(13) & Chr$(10)
    strTemp = "View: " & ActiveProject.CurrentView & NL
    strTemp = strTemp & "Table: " & ActiveProject.CurrentTable & NL
    strTemp = strTemp & "Filter: " & ActiveProject.CurrentFilter
    MsgBox strTemp
End Sub
```

CurrentView Property

Applies To	**Project** Object, **Projects** Collection.
Description	Returns the name of the current view for a project.
Syntax	*object*.**CurrentView**
Elements	The *object* placeholder is an object expression that evaluates to an object in the Applies To list.
See Also	**CurrentFilter** Property, **CurrentTable** Property, **ResourceViewList** Method, **TaskViewList** Method, **ViewList** Method.
Example	The following example displays the name of the current view, table, and filter in a dialog box.

```
Sub ViewDetails()
    NL = Chr$(13) & Chr$(10)
    strTemp = "View: " & ActiveProject.CurrentView & NL
    strTemp = strTemp & "Table: " & ActiveProject.CurrentTable & NL
    strTemp = strTemp & "Filter: " & ActiveProject.CurrentFilter
    MsgBox strTemp
End Sub
```

CustomDocumentProperties Property

Applies To	**Project** Object, **Projects** Collection.
Description	Returns the custom properties of the document.
Syntax	*object*.**CustomDocumentProperties**
Elements	The *object* placeholder is an object expression that evaluates to an object in the Applies To list.
Remarks	To use this property, you should establish a reference to the Microsoft Office 95 Object Library by using the References command from the Tools menu. The Object Library contains definitions for the Visual Basic objects, properties, methods, and constants used to manipulate document properties.
	This property returns the entire collection of custom document properties. Use the **Item** method to return a single member of the collection (a **DocumentProperty**

object) by specifying either the name of the property or the collection index as a number.

Because the **Item** method is the default method for the **DocumentProperties** collection object, the following statements are identical:

```
CustomDocumentProperties.Item("Complete")
CustomDocumentProperties("Complete")
```

Use the **BuiltinDocumentProperties** property to return the collection of built-in document properties.

See Also   **BuiltinDocumentProperties** Property, **FileProperties** Method.

CustomForms Method

Applies To   **Application** Object.

Description   Displays the Custom Forms dialog box, which prompts the user to manage custom forms.

Syntax   [*object*.]**CustomForms**

Elements   The *object* placeholder is an object expression that evaluates to an object in the Applies To list.

Remarks   The **CustomForms** method has the same effect as the Forms command on the Customize submenu, which is available from the Tools menu.

See Also   **Form** Method.

CV Property

Applies To   **Project** Object, **Projects** Collection; **Task** Object, **Tasks** Collection.

Description   Returns the CV for a task or project.

Syntax   *object*.**CV**

Elements   The *object* placeholder is an object expression that evaluates to an object in the Applies To list.

See Also   **BCWP** Property, **SV** Property.

CVar Function

Description	Converts an expression to a **Variant**.
Syntax	**CVar**(*expression*)
Elements	The *expression* argument is any valid numeric or string expression.
Remarks	In general, you can document your code using the data type conversion functions to show that the result of some operation should be expressed as a particular data type rather than the default data type. For example, use **CVar** to force the result to be expressed as a **Variant**.
See Also	Data Type Summary.
Example	This example uses the **CVar** function to convert an expression to a **Variant**.

```
MyInt = 4534              ' MyInt is an Integer.
MyVar = CVar(MyInt & "000") ' MyVar contains 4534000.
```

CVErr Function

Description	Returns a **Variant** of subtype **Error** containing an error number specified by the user.
Syntax	**CVErr**(*errornumber*)
Elements	The *errornumber* argument is any valid error number.
Remarks	Use the **CVErr** function to create user-defined errors in user-created procedures. For example, if you create a function that accepts several arguments and normally returns a string, you can have your function evaluate the input arguments to ensure they are within acceptable range. If they are not, it is likely that your function will not return what you expect. In this event, **CVErr** allows you to return an error number that tells you what action to take.
	Note that implicit conversion of an **Error** is not allowed. For example, you can't directly assign the return value of **CVErr** to a non-**Variant** variable. However, you can perform an explicit conversion (using **CInt**, **CDbl**, and so on) of the value returned by **CVErr** and assign that to a variable of the appropriate data type.
See Also	Data Type Summary, **IsError** Function.

Example

This example uses the **CVErr** function to return an Error **Variant**. The user-defined function `CalculateDouble` returns an error if the argument passed to it isn't a number. **CVErr** is useful for returning user-defined errors from user-defined procedures. Use the **IsError** function to test if the value is an error.

```
' Define CalculateDouble Function procedure.
Function CalculateDouble(Number)
    If IsNumeric(Number) Then
        CalculateDouble = Number * 2     ' Return result.
    Else
        CalculateDouble = CVErr(2001)    ' Return a user-defined error
    End If  ' number.
End Function
```

Data Type Summary

Description

The following table shows the supported data types, including their storage sizes and ranges.

Boolean	2 bytes	**True** or **False**.
Integer	2 bytes	-32,768 to 32,767.
Long (long integer)	4 bytes	-2,147,483,648 to 2,147,483,647.
Single (single-precision floating-point)	4 bytes	-3.402823E38 to -1.401298E-45 for negative values; 1.401298E-45 to 3.402823E38 for positive values.
Double (double-precision floating-point)	8 bytes	-1.79769313486232E308 to -4.94065645841247E-324 for negative values; 4.94065645841247E-324 to 1.79769313486232E308 for positive values.
Currency (scaled integer)	8 bytes	-922,337,203,685,477.5808 to 922,337,203,685,477.5807.
Date	8 bytes	January 1, 100 to December 31, 9999.
Object	4 bytes	Any **Object** reference.
String	1 byte per character	0 to approximately 2 billion (approximately 65,535 for Microsoft Windows version 3.1 and earlier).
Variant	16 bytes + 1 byte for each character	Any numeric value up to the range of a **Double** or any character text.
User-defined (using Type)	Number required by elements	The range of each element is the same as the range of its data type.

See Also   **Boolean** Data Type, **Currency** Data Type, **Date** Data Type, **Def***type* Statements, **Double** Data Type, **Integer** Data Type, **Long** Data Type, **Object** Data Type, **Single** Data Type, **String** Data Type, **Type** Statement, **Variant** Data Type.

Date Data Type

Description   **Date** variables are stored as 64-bit (8-byte) numbers that represent dates ranging from 1 January 100 to 31 December 9999 and times from 0:00:00 to 23:59:59. Any recognizable literal date values can be assigned to **Date** variables. Literal dates must be enclosed within number sign characters (#). For example, #January 1, 1993# or #1 Jan 93#.

Date variables display dates according to the short date format recognized by your computer. Times display according to the time format (either 12- or 24-hour) recognized by your computer.

When other numeric data types are converted to **Date**, values to the left of the decimal represent date information while values to the right of the decimal represent time. Midnight is 0 and midday is .5. Negative whole numbers represent dates before 30 December 1899. When **Date** variables are converted to other numeric data types, they appear only as numbers.

See Also   **CDate** Function, Data Type Summary, **Def***type* Statements, **Double** Data Type, **Variant** Data Type.

Date Function

Description   Converts an expression to a **Date**.

Syntax   **CDate**(*date*)

Elements   The *date* argument is any valid date expression.

Remarks   Use the **IsDate** function to determine if *date* can be converted to a date or time. **CDate** recognizes date and time literals as well as some numbers that fall within the range of acceptable dates. When converting a number to a date, the whole number portion is converted to a date. Any fractional part of the number is converted to a time of day, starting at midnight.

CDate recognizes date formats according to the international settings of your system. The correct order of day, month, and year may not be determined if it is provided in a format other than one of the recognized date settings. In addition, a long date format is not recognized if it also contains the day-of-the-week string.

Note   A **CVDate** function is also provided for compatibility with previous versions of Visual Basic. However, since there is now an intrinsic **Date** type, there is no further need for **CVDate**. The syntax of the **CVDate** function is identical to the **CDate** function. The difference is that it returns a **Variant** whose subtype is Date instead of an actual **Date** type. The same effect can be achieved by converting an expression to a **Date** and then assigning it to a **Variant**. This technique is consistent with the conversion of all other intrinsic types to their equivalent **Variant** subtypes.

See Also   Data Type Summary, **IsDate** Function.

Example   This example uses the **Date** function to return the current system date.

```
MyDate = Date        ' MyDate contains current system date.
```

Date Statement

Description   Sets the current system date.

Syntax   **Date** = *date*

Elements   For MS-DOS computers, the *date* argument must be a date from January 1, 1980 through December 31, 2099, or an error occurs. For the Macintosh, *date* must be a date from January 1, 1904 through December 31, 2040. For all other systems, *date* is limited to dates from January 1, 100 through December 31, 9999.

Remarks
Note   If you use the **Date** statement to set the date on computers using versions of MS-DOS earlier than version 3.3, the change remains in effect only until you change it again or turn off your computer. Many computers have a battery-powered CMOS RAM that retains date and time information when the computer is turned off. However, to permanently change the date on computers running earlier versions of MS-DOS, you may have to use your Setup disk or perform some equivalent action. Refer to the documentation for your particular system.

See Also   **Date** Function, **Time** Function, **Time** Statement.

Example   This example uses the **Date** statement to set the computer system date.

```
' In the development environment, the date literal will display in short
' format using the locale settings of your code.
MyDate = #February 12, 1985#     ' Assign a date.
Date = MyDate                    ' Change system date.
```

DateAdd Method

Applies To   **Application** Object.

Description   Returns the date that follows another date by a specified duration.

Syntax   [*object*.]**DateAdd** (*startDate*, *duration*[, *calendar*])

Elements   The **DateAdd** method syntax has the following object qualifier and named arguments:

Part	Description
object	An object expression that evaluates to an object in the Applies To list. Optional.
startDate	A string expression or date expression that specifies the start date. Required.
duration	A string expression that specifies the duration or a numeric expression that specifies the duration in minutes to add to the start date. Required.
calendar	An object expression that evaluates to a base calendar object or a resource calendar. By default, the *calendar* argument equals the calendar of the active project. Optional.

See Also   **DateDifference** Method, **DateFormat** Method, **DateSubtract** Method.

Example   The following example displays the finish date of a three-day task that begins on 7/11/94 at 8 A.M.

```
Sub FindFinishDate()
    MsgBox DateAdd(StartDate := "7/11/94 8:00 AM", Duration := "3d")
End Sub
```

DateDifference Method

Applies To   **Application** Object.

Description	Returns the duration between two dates in minutes.
Syntax	[*object*.]**DateDifference** (*startDate*, *finishDate*[, *calendar*])
Elements	The **DateDifference** method syntax has the following object qualifier and named arguments:

Part	Description
object	An object expression that evaluates to an object in the Applies To list. Optional.
startDate	A string expression or date expression that specifies the start date. Required.
finishDate	A string expression or date expression that specifies the finish date. Required.
calendar	An object expression that evaluates to a base calendar object or a resource calendar. By default, the *calendar* argument equals the calendar of the active project. Optional.

See Also	**DateAdd** Method, **DateFormat** Method, **DateSubtract** Method.
Example	The following example displays the duration of a task that begins on 7/11/94 at 8 A.M. and ends on 7/13/94 at 5:00 P.M.

```
Sub FindDuration()
    MsgBox DateDifference ("7/11/94 8:00 AM", "7/13/94 5:00 PM")
End Sub
```

DateFormat Method

Applies To	**Application** Object.
Description	Sets the date format for text around bars on the Gantt Chart.
Syntax	[*object*.]**GanttBarTextDateFormat** [*dateFormat*]
Elements	The **GanttBarTextDateFormat** method syntax has the following object qualifier and named arguments:

Part	Description
object	An object expression that evaluates to an object in the Applies To list.
dateFormat	A constant that specifies the format of dates in the Gantt bar text.

The *dateFormat* argument has these settings:

pjDateDefault	-1	The default format, as specified on the View tab of the Options dialog box. (To display the Options dialog box, choose Options from the Tools menu.)
pjDate_mm_dd_yy_hh_mmAM	0	1/31/94 12:33 PM
pjDate_mm_dd_yy	1	1/31/94
pjDate_mmmm_dd_yyyy_hh_mmAM	2	January 31, 1994 12:33 PM
pjDate_mmmm_dd_yyyy	3	January 31, 1994
pjDate_mmm_dd_hh_mmAM	4	Jan 31 12:33 PM
pjDate_mmm_dd_yyy	5	Jan 31 '94
pjDate_mmmm_dd	6	January 31
pjDate_mmm_dd	7	Jan 31
pjDate_ddd_mm_dd_yy_hh_mmAM	8	Mon 1/31/94 12:33 PM
pjDate_ddd_mm_dd_yy	9	Mon 1/31/94
pjDate_ddd_mmm_dd_yyy	10	Mon Jan 31, '94
pjDate_ddd_hh_mmAM	11	Mon 12:33 PM
pjDate_mm_dd	12	1/31
pjDate_dd	13	31
pjDate_hh_mmAM	14	12:33 PM
pjDate_ddd_mmm_dd	15	Mon Jan 31
pjDate_ddd_mm_dd	16	Mon 1/31
pjDate_ddd_dd	17	Mon 31
pjDate_Www_dd	18	W05/1
pjDate_Www_dd_yy_hh_mmAM	19	W05/1/94 12:33 PM

See Also   **GanttBarFormat** Method, **GanttBarLinks** Method, **GanttBarSize** Method, **GanttBarStyleDelete** Method, **GanttBarStyleEdit** Method, **GanttChartWizard** Method, **GanttShowDrawings** Method.

DateOrder Property

Applies To   **Application** Object.

Description   Returns the order in date values of the day, month, and year.

Syntax	[*object*.]**DateOrder**
Elements	The *object* placeholder is an object expression that evaluates to an object in the Applies To list.
Settings	The **DateOrder** property has these settings:

pjDayMonthYear	0	In dates, the day appears first, the month appears second, and the year appears last. In this format, dates appear as 22/03/93 or 22 March, 1993.
pjMonthDayYear	1	In dates, the month appears first, the day appears second, and the year appears last. In this format, dates appear as 03/22/93 or March 22, 1993.
pjYearMonthDay	2	In dates, the year appears first, the month appears second, and the year appears last. In this format, dates appear as 93/03/22 or 1993 March, 22.

Remarks	Microsoft Project for Microsoft Windows sets the **DateOrder** property equal to the corresponding value in the Regional settings of the Microsoft Windows Control Panel.
	On the Macintosh, using System 7.1 and later, you can use the Date & Time control panel to change this value.
See Also	**DateFormat** Method, **DateSeparator** Property, **DayLeadingZero** Property, **MonthLeadingZero** Property.

DateSeparator Property

Applies To	**Application** Object.
Description	Returns the date separator character.
Syntax	[*object*.]**DateSeparator**
Elements	The *object* placeholder is an object expression that evaluates to an object in the Applies To list.
Remarks	Microsoft Project for Microsoft Windows sets the **DateSeparator** property equal to the corresponding value in the Regional settings of the Microsoft Windows Control Panel.

On the Macintosh, using System 7.1 and later, you can use the Date & Time control panel to change this value.

See Also   **DateFormat** Method, **DateOrder** Property, **DayLeadingZero** Property, **MonthLeadingZero** Property.

DateSerial Function

Description   Returns a date for a specified year, month, and day.

Syntax   **DateSerial(*year*, *month*, *day*)**

Elements   The **DateSerial** function syntax has these named-argument parts:

Part	Description
year	Number between 100 and 9999, inclusive, or a numeric expression.
month	Number between 1 and 12, inclusive, or a numeric expression.
day	Number between 1 and 31, inclusive, or a numeric expression.

Remarks   To specify a date, such as December 31, 1991, the range of numbers for each **DateSerial** argument should be in the normally accepted range for the unit; that is; 1-31 for days and 1-12 for months. However, you can also specify relative dates for each argument using any numeric expression that represents some number of days, months, or years before or after a certain date.

The following example uses numeric expressions instead of absolute date numbers. Here the **DateSerial** function returns a date that is the day before the first day (1 - 1) of two months before August (8 - 2) of 10 years before 1990 (1990 - 10); in other words, May, 31, 1980.

```
DateSerial(1990 - 10, 8 - 2, 1 - 1)
```

For the *year* argument, values between 0 and 99, inclusive, are interpreted as the years 1900-1999. For all other *year* arguments, use a complete four-digit year (for example, 1800).

If the date specified by the three arguments, either directly or by expression, falls outside the acceptable range of dates, an error occurs.

See Also   **Date** Function, **Date** Statement, **DateValue** Function, **Day** Function, **Month** Function, **Now** Function, **TimeSerial** Function, **TimeValue** Function, **Weekday** Function, **Year** Function.

Example   This example uses the **DateSerial** function to return the date for the specified year, month and day.

```
' MyDate contains the date for February 12, 1969.
MyDate = DateSerial(1969, 2, 12) ' Return a date.
```

DateSubtract Method

Applies To   **Application** Object.

Description   Returns the date that precedes another date by a specified duration.

Syntax   [*object.*]**DateSubtract** (*finishDate*, *duration*[, *calendar*])

Elements   The **DateSubtract** method syntax has the following object qualifier and named arguments:

Part	Description
object	An object expression that evaluates to an object in the Applies To list. Optional.
finishDate	A string expression or date expression that specifies the finish date. Required.
duration	A string expression or numeric expression that specifies the duration to subtract from the finish date. Required.
calendar	An object expression that evaluates to a base calendar object or a resource calendar. By default, the *calendar* argument equals the calendar of the active project. Optional.

See Also   **DateAdd** Method, **DateDifference** Method, **DateFormat** Method.

Example   The following example displays the start date of a task that lasts three days and ends on 7/13/94 at 5:00 P.M.

```
Sub FindDuration()
    MsgBox DateSubtract("7/13/94 5:00 PM", "3d")
End Sub
```

DateValue Function

Description   Returns a date.

Syntax   **DateValue**(*date*)

Elements   The *date* named argument is normally a string expression representing a date from January 1, 100 through December 31, 9999. However, *date* can also be any expression that can represent a date, a time, or both a date and time, in that range.

Remarks   If the *date* argument includes time information, **DateValue** doesn't return it. However, if *date* includes invalid time information (such as "89:98"), an error occurs.

If *date* is a string that includes only numbers separated by valid date separators, **DateValue** recognizes the order for month, day, and year according to the Short Date format you specified for your system. **DateValue** also recognizes unambiguous dates that contain month names, either in long or abbreviated form. For example, in addition to recognizing 12/30/1991 and 12/30/91, **DateValue** also recognizes December 30, 1991 and Dec 30, 1991.

If the year part of *date* is omitted, **DateValue** uses the current year from your computer's system date.

See Also   **CDate** Function, **Date** Function, **Date** Statement, **DateSerial** Function, **Day** Function, **Month** Function, **Now** Function, **TimeSerial** Function, **TimeValue** Function, **Weekday** Function, **Year** Function.

Example   This example uses the **DateValue** function to convert a string to a date. In general, it is bad programming practice to hard code dates/times as strings as shown in this example. Use date literals instead.

```
MyDate = DateValue("February 12, 1969")  ' Return a date.
```

Day Function

Description   Returns a whole number between 1 and 31, inclusive, representing the day of the month.

Syntax   **Day(*date*)**

Elements   The *date* named argument is limited to a date or numbers and strings, in any combination, that can represent a date. If *date* contains no valid data, **Null** is returned.

See Also   **Date** Function, **Date** Statement, **Hour** Function, **Minute** Function, **Month** Function, **Now** Function, **Second** Function, **Weekday** Function, **Year** Function.

Example   This example uses the **Day** function to obtain the day of the month from a specified date.

```
' In the development environment, the date literal will display in short
' format using the locale settings of your code.
MyDate = #February 12, 1969# ' Assign a date.
MyDay = Day(MyDate)              ' MyDay contains 12.
```

Day Object, Days Collection

Description   A day or the days in a month.

Remarks   In Microsoft Project, **Day** objects are parents of **Shift** objects.

Properties   **Application** Property, **Calendar** Property, **Count** Property, **Index** Property, **Name** Property, **Parent** Property, **Shiftn** Property, **Working** Property

Methods   **Default** Method

See Also   **Days** Method; **Month** Object, **Months** Collection; **Shift** Object.

DayLeadingZero Property

Applies To   **Application** Object.

Description   Returns **True** if Microsoft Project displays zeroes before single-digit days in dates; returns **False** otherwise.

Syntax   [*object*.]**DayLeadingZero**

Elements   The *object* placeholder is an object expression that evaluates to an object in the Applies To list.

Remarks   Microsoft Project for Microsoft Windows sets the **DayLeadingZero** property equal to the corresponding value in the Regional settings of the Microsoft Windows Control Panel.

On the Macintosh, using System 7.1 and later, you can use the Date & Time control panel to change this value.

See Also   **DateFormat** Method, **DateOrder** Property, **DateSeparator** Property, **MonthLeadingZero** Property.

Days Method

Applies To	**Application** Object.
Description	Changes one or more consecutive days in a base calendar.
Syntax	[*object.*]**BaseCalendarEditDays** *name*[, *startDate*, *endDate*, *weekday*, *working*, *from1*, *to1*, *from2*, *to2*, *from3*, *to3*]
Elements	The **BaseCalendarEditDays** method syntax has the following object qualifier and named arguments:

Part	Description
object	An object expression that evaluates to an object in the Applies To list. Optional.
name	A string expression that specifies the name of the base calendar to change. Required.
startDate	A date expression that specifies the first date to change. Optional.
endDate	A date expression that specifies the last date to change. Optional.
weekDay	A constant that specifies the weekday to change. If you specify values for the *startDate* and *endDate* arguments, the *weekDay* argument is ignored. Optional.
working	A Boolean expression that specifies whether the days are working days. Optional.
from1	A string expression that specifies the start time of the first shift. Optional.
to1	A string expression that specifies the end time of the first shift. Optional.
from2	A string expression that specifies the start time of the second shift. Optional.
to2	A string expression that specifies the end time of the second shift. Optional.
from3	A string expression that specifies the start time of the third shift. Optional.
to3	A string expression that specifies the end time of the third shift. Optional.

The *weekDay* argument has these settings:

pjSunday	1	Sunday
pjMonday	2	Monday

pjTuesday	3	Tuesday
pjWednesday	4	Wednesday
pjThursday	5	Thursday
pjFriday	6	Friday
pjSaturday	7	Saturday

See Also   **BaseCalendarCreate** Method, **BaseCalendarDelete** Method, **BaseCalendarRename** Method, **BaseCalendarReset** Method, **BaseCalendars** Method, **ResourceCalendars** Method.

Example   The following example makes Wednesday a nonworking day in the Standard calendar.

```
Sub MakeWednesdaysNonWorking1()
    BaseCalendarEditDays Name := "Standard", Weekday := pjWednesday, _
        Working := False
End Sub
```

The following example makes the days from 2/10/94 to 2/12/94 nonworking days in the Standard calendar.

```
Sub MakeWednesdaysNonWorking2()
    BaseCalendarEditDays Name := "Standard", startDate := "2/10/94", _
        endDate := "2/12/94", Working := False
End Sub
```

DDEExecute Method

Applies To   **Application** Object.

Description   Performs actions or runs commands in another application by using dynamic data exchange (DDE).

Syntax   [*object*.]**DDEExecute** *command*[, *timeout*]

Elements   The **DDEExecute** method syntax has the following object qualifier and named arguments:

Part	Description
object	An object expression that evaluates to an object in the Applies To list.
command	A string expression of the command you want to carry out in another application.
timeout	A numeric expression that specifies the number of seconds to wait for the other application to execute the command you specify with the *command* argument. By default, the *timeout* argument is 5.

Remarks

For information about what commands you can send to an application that supports DDE, consult the documentation for the application.

If your macro displays a dialog box in another application, you may need to increase the default value for the *timeout* argument.

See Also

DDEInitiate Method, **DDETerminate** Method.

Example

This example creates a new worksheet in Microsoft Excel.

```
Sub CreateNewMSExcelBook()
    DDEInitiate "Excel", "System"
    DDEExecute Command := "[NEW(1)]"
    DDETerminate
End Sub
```

DDEInitiate Method

Applies To

Application Object.

Description

Opens a dynamic data exchange (DDE) channel to an application.

Syntax

[*object*.]**DDEInitiate** *app*, *topic*

Elements

The **DDEInitiate Method** syntax has the following object qualifier and named arguments:

Part	Description
object	An object expression that evaluates to an object in the Applies To list.
app	A string expression that specifies the name of the application to which you want to send commands. Required.
topic	A string expression that specifies a document in the application to which you want to send commands.

See Also

DDEExecute Method, **DDETerminate** Method.

Example

This example creates a new worksheet in Microsoft Excel.

```
Sub CreateNewMSExcelBook()
    DDEInitiate "Excel", "System"
    DDEExecute Command := "[NEW(1)]"
    DDETerminate
End Sub
```

DDELinksUpdate Method

Applies To   **Application** Object.

Description   Updates DDE links.

Syntax   [*object*.]**DDELinksUpdate**

Elements   The *object* placeholder is an object expression that evaluates to an object in the Applies To list.

See Also   **DDEExecute** Method, **DDEInitiate** Method, **DDEPasteLink** Method, **DDETerminate** Method.

DDEPasteLink Method

Applies To   **Application** Object.

Description   Pastes the contents of the Clipboard into the active selection, establishing a link with the application that supplies the information.

Syntax   [*object*.]**DDEPasteLink**

Elements   The *object* placeholder is an object expression that evaluates to an object in the Applies To list.

See Also   **EditCopy** Method, **EditPaste** Method, **EditPasteSpecial** Method.

DDETerminate Method

Applies To   **Application** Object.

Description   Ends a dynamic data exchange (DDE) session.

Syntax	[*object*.]**DDETerminate**
Elements	The *object* placeholder is an object expression that evaluates to an object in the Applies To list.
See Also	**DDEExecute** Method, **DDEInitiate** Method, **DDELinksUpdate** Method.
Example	This example creates a new worksheet in Microsoft Excel.

```
Sub CreateNewMSExcelBook()
    DDEInitiate "Excel", "System"
    DDEExecute Command := "[NEW(1)]"
    DDETerminate
End Sub
```

Debug Object

Description	The **Debug** object is accessed with the keyword **Debug**, and is used to send output to the Debug window at run time.
Methods	**Print** Method

DecimalSeparator Property

Applies To	**Application** Object.
Description	Returns the character that separates the whole and fractional parts of a number.
Syntax	[*object*.]**DecimalSeparator**
Elements	The *object* placeholder is an object expression that evaluates to an object in the Applies To list.
Remarks	Microsoft Project for Microsoft Windows sets the **DecimalSeparator** property equal to the corresponding value in the Regional settings of the Microsoft Windows Control Panel.
	On the Macintosh, using System 7.1 and later, you can use the Numbers control panel to change this value.
See Also	**ThousandsSeparator** Property.

Declare Statement

Description

Used at module level to declare references to external procedures in a dynamic-link library (DLL) or Macintosh code resource.

Syntax 1

[**Public** | **Private**] **Declare Sub** *name* [**CDecl**] **Lib** *"libname"* [**Alias** *"aliasname"*][([*arglist*])]

Syntax 2

[**Public** | **Private**] **Declare Function** *name* [**CDecl**] **Lib** *"libname"* [**Alias** *"aliasname"*] [([*arglist*])][**As** *type*]

Elements

The **Declare** statement syntax has these parts:

Part	Description
Public	Used to declare procedures that are available to all other procedures in all modules.
Private	Used to declare procedures that are available only within the module where the declaration is made.
Sub	Indicates that the procedure doesn't return a value.
Function	Indicates that the procedure returns a value that can be used in an expression.
name	Any valid procedure name.
CDecl	For the Macintosh only. Indicates that the procedure uses C language argument order, naming conventions, and calling conventions.
Lib	Indicates that a DLL or code resource contains the procedure being declared. The **Lib** clause is required for all declarations.
libname	Name of the DLL or code resource that contains the declared procedure.
Alias	Indicates that the procedure being called has another name in the DLL or is in a Macintosh code resource. This is useful when the external procedure name is the same as a keyword. You can also use **Alias** when a DLL procedure has the same name as a **Public** variable or constant or any other procedure in the same scope. **Alias** is also useful if any characters in the DLL procedure name aren't allowed in names.
aliasname	Name of the procedure in the DLL or code resource.
	In Microsoft Windows, if the first character is not a #, *aliasname* is the name of the procedure's entry point in the DLL. If # is the first character, all characters that follow must indicate the ordinal number of the procedure's entry point. (continued)

Part	Description
	On the Macintosh, the syntax to specify the code resource type is as follows:
	"[*resourcetype*]$[*resourcename*]"
	The *resourcetype* is any valid 4-character constant. If omitted, the default *resourcetype* is CODE. The *resourcename* is the procedure name in the code resource. If *resourcename* is omitted, it is assumed to be the same as *name*.
arglist	List of variables representing arguments that are passed to the procedure when it is called.
type	Data type of the value returned by a **Function** procedure; may be **Boolean**, **Integer**, **Long**, **Currency**, **Single**, **Double**, **Date**, **String** (variable length only), **Object**, **Variant**, a user-defined type, or an object type.

The *arglist* argument has the following syntax and parts:

[**Optional**][**ByVal** | **ByRef**][**ParamArray**] *varname*[( )][**As** *type*]

Part	Description
Optional	Indicates that an argument is not required. If used, all subsequent arguments in *arglist* must also be optional and declared using the **Optional** keyword. All **Optional** arguments must be **Variant**. **Optional** can't be used for any argument if **ParamArray** is used.
ByVal	Indicates that the argument is passed by value.
ByRef	Indicates that the argument is passed by reference.
ParamArray	Used only as the last argument in *arglist* to indicate that the final argument is an **Optional** array of **Variant** elements. The **ParamArray** keyword allows you to provide an arbitrary number of arguments. May not be used with **ByVal**, **ByRef**, or **Optional**.
varname	Name of the variable representing the argument being passed to the procedure; follows standard variable naming conventions.
type	Data type of the argument passed to the procedure; may be **Boolean**, **Integer**, **Long**, **Currency**, **Single**, **Double**, **Date**, **String** (variable length only), **Object**, **Variant**, a user-defined type, or an object type.

Remarks

For **Function** procedures, the data type of the procedure determines the data type it returns. You can use an **As** clause following the *arglist* to specify the return type of the function. Within *arglist* you can use an **As** clause to specify the data type of any of the arguments passed to the procedure. In addition to specifying any of the standard data types, you can specify **As Any** in the *arglist* to inhibit type checking and allow any data type to be passed to the procedure.

Empty parentheses indicate that the **Sub** or **Function** procedure has no arguments and that arguments should be checked to ensure that none are passed. In the following example, First takes no arguments. If you use arguments in a call to First, an error occurs:

```
Declare Sub First Lib "MyLib" ()
```

If you include an argument list, the number and type of arguments are checked each time the procedure is called. In the following example, First takes one **Long** argument:

```
Declare Sub First Lib "MyLib" (X As Long)
```

Note You can't have fixed-length strings in the argument list of a Declare statement because only variable-length strings can be passed to procedures. Fixed-length strings can appear as procedure arguments, but they are converted to variable-length strings before being passed.

See Also	**Call** Statement.
Example	This example shows how the **Declare** statement is used at the module level to declare a reference to an external procedure in a dynamic-link library (DLL) or Macintosh code resource.

```
' In Microsoft Windows.
Declare Sub MessageBeep Lib "User" (ByVal N As Integer)

' On the Macintosh.
Declare Sub MessageAlert Lib "MyHd:MyAlert" Alias "MyAlert" (ByVal N _
As Integer)
```

Default Method

Applies To	**Day** Object, **Days** Collection; **Month** Object, **Months** Collection; **Period** Object; **Weekday** Object, **Weekdays** Collection; **Year** Object, **Years** Collection.
Description	Resets the properties of a resource calendar, such as start and finish dates, to the values in the corresponding base calendar.
Syntax	*object*.**Default**
Elements	The *object* placeholder is an object expression that evaluates to an object in the Applies To list.
See Also	**Clear** Method, **Finish** Property, **Reset** Method, **Start** Property, **Working** Property.

DefaultDateFormat Property

Applies To   **Application** Object.

Description   Returns or sets the default date format.

Syntax   [*object.*]**DefaultDateFormat** [= *value*]

Elements   The **DefaultDateFormat** property syntax has the following parts:

Part	Description
object	An object expression that evaluates to an object in the Applies To list.
value	A constant that specifies the default date format.

The *value* argument has these settings:

pjDate_mm_dd_yy_hh_mmAM	0	1/31/94 12:33 PM
pjDate_mm_dd_yy	1	1/31/94
pjDate_mmmm_dd_yyyy_hh_mmAM	2	January 31, 1994 12:33 PM
pjDate_mmmm_dd_yyyy	3	January 31, 1994
pjDate_mmm_dd_hh_mmAM	4	Jan 31 12:33 PM
pjDate_mmm_dd_yyy	5	Jan 31 '94
pjDate_mmmm_dd	6	January 31
pjDate_mmm_dd	7	Jan 31
pjDate_ddd_mm_dd_yy_mmAM	8	Mon 1/31/94 12:33 PM
pjDate_ddd_mm_dd_yy	9	Mon 1/31/94
pjDate_ddd_mmm_dd_yyy	10	Mon Jan 31, '94
pjDate_ddd_hh_mmAM	11	Mon 12:33 PM
pjDate_mm_dd	12	1/31
pjDate_dd	13	31
pjDate_hh_mmAM	14	12:33 PM
pjDate_ddd_mmm_dd	15	Mon Jan 31
pjDate_ddd_mm_dd	16	Mon 1/31
pjDate_ddd_dd	17	Mon 31
pjDate_Www_dd	18	W05/1
pjDate_Www_dd_yy_hh_mmAM	19	W05/1/94 12:33 PM

GanttBarTextDateFormat Method, **OptionsView** Method, **PERTBoxStyles** Method, **TableEdit** Method.

DefaultDurationUnits Property

Applies To   **Project** Object, **Projects** Collection.

Description   Returns or sets the default duration units.

Syntax   [*object.*]**DefaultDurationUnits** [= *value*]

Elements   The **DefaultDurationUnits** property syntax has these parts:

Part	Description
object	An object expression that evaluates to an object in the Applies To list.
value	A constant that specifies the default duration units, as shown under Settings.

Elements   The **DefaultDurationUnits** property has these settings:

Setting	Description
pjMinutes	The default duration units are minutes.
pjHours	The default duration units are hours.
pjDays	The default duration units are days.
pjWeeks	The default duration units are weeks.

See Also   **DefaultFixedDuration** Property, **DefaultResourceOvertimeRate** Property, **DefaultResourceStandardRate** Property, **DefaultView** Property, **DefaultWorkUnits** Property.

DefaultFinishTime Property

Applies To   **Project** Object, **Projects** Collection.

Description   Returns or sets the default finish time.

Syntax   *object.***DefaultFinishTime** [= *value*]

Elements   The **DefaultFinishTime** property syntax has the following parts:

Part	Description
object	An object expression that evaluates to an object in the Applies To list.
value	A date expression that specifies the default finish time.

See Also   **DefaultDateFormat** Property, **DefaultStartTime** Property, **DefaultView** Property.

DefaultFixedDuration Property

Applies To   **Project** Object, **Projects** Collection.

Description   Returns or sets whether or not new tasks in a project have fixed durations.

Syntax   [*object*.]**DefaultFixedDuration** [= *value*]

Elements   The **DefaultFixedDuration** property syntax has these parts:

Part	Description
object	An object expression that evaluates to an object in the Applies To list.
value	A Boolean expression that specifies whether or not new tasks in the project have fixed durations.

See Also   **DefaultDurationUnits** Property, **DefaultResourceOvertimeRate** Property, **DefaultResourceStandardRate** Property, **DefaultView** Property, **DefaultWorkUnits** Property.

DefaultResourceOvertimeRate Property

Applies To   **Project** Object, **Projects** Collection.

Description   Returns or sets the default overtime rate of pay for resources.

Syntax   [*object*.]**DefaultResourceOvertimeRate** [= *value*]

Elements   The **DefaultResourceOvertimeRate** property syntax has these parts:

Part	Description
object	An object expression that evaluates to an object in the Applies To list.
value	A string expression that specifies the default rate of pay for resources.

See Also

See Also	**DefaultDurationUnits** Property, **DefaultFixedDuration** Property, **DefaultResourceStandardRate** Property, **DefaultView** Property, **DefaultWorkUnits** Property.

DefaultResourceStandardRate Property

Applies To   **Project** Object, **Projects** Collection.

Description   Returns or sets the default standard rate of pay for resources.

Syntax   [*object*.]**DefaultResourceStandardRate** [= *value*]

Elements   The **DefaultResourceStandardRate** property syntax has these parts:

Part	Description
object	An object expression that evaluates to an object in the Applies To list.
value	A string expression that specifies the default standard rate of pay for resources.

See Also   **DefaultDurationUnits** Property, **DefaultFixedDuration** Property, **DefaultResourceOvertimeRate** Property, **DefaultView** Property, **DefaultWorkUnits** Property.

DefaultStartTime Property

Applies To   **Project** Object, **Projects** Collection.

Description   Returns or sets the default time for start fields in Microsoft Project.

Syntax   [*object*.]**DefaultStartTime** [= *value*]

Elements   The **DefaultStartTime** property syntax has these parts:

Object	Description
object	An object expression that evaluates to an object in the Applies To list.
value	A string expression that specifies the default start time for date fields in Microsoft Project.

See Also   **DefaultDurationUnits** Property, **DefaultFinishTime** Property, **DefaultResourceOvertimeRate** Property, **DefaultResourceStandardRate** Property, **DefaultView** Property, **DefaultWorkUnits** Property.

DefaultView Property

Applies To **Application** Object.

Description Returns or sets the view that appears when you start Microsoft Project.

Syntax [*object.*]**DefaultView** [= *value*]

Elements The **DefaultView** property syntax has these parts:

Part	Description
object	An object expression that evaluates to an object in the Applies To list.
value	A string expression that specifies which view appears when you start Microsoft Project, as shown under Settings.

Settings The **DefaultView** property syntax has these settings:

Setting	Description
"Calendar"	The default view is the Calendar view.
"Gantt Chart"	The default view is the Gantt Chart.
"PERT Chart"	The default view is the PERT Chart.
"Resource Form"	The default view is the Resource Form.
"Resource Graph"	The default view is the Resource Graph.
"Resource Sheet"	The default view is the Resource Sheet.
"Resource Usage"	The default view is the Resource Usage view.
"Task Entry"	The default view is the Task Entry view.
"Task Form"	The default view is the Task Form.
"Task PERT"	The default view is the Task PERT Chart.
"Task Sheet"	The default view is the Task Sheet.

See Also **DefaultDurationUnits** Property, **DefaultFixedDuration** Property, **DefaultResourceOvertimeRate** Property, **DefaultResourceStandardRate** Property, **DefaultWorkUnits** Property.

DefaultWorkUnits Property

Applies To **Project** Object, **Projects** Collection.

Description	Returns or sets the default work units.
Syntax	[*object.*]**DefaultWorkUnits** [= *value*]
Elements	The **DefaultWorkUnits** property syntax has these parts:

Part	Description
object	An object expression that evaluates to an object in the Applies To list.
value	A constant that specifies the default work units, as shown under Settings.

Settings	The **DefaultWorkUnits** property has these settings:

Setting	Description
pjMinutes	The default work units are minutes.
pjHours	The default work units are hours.
pjDays	The default work units are days.
pjWeeks	The default work units are weeks.

See Also	**DefaultDurationUnits** Property, **DefaultFixedDuration** Property, **DefaultResourceOvertimeRate** Property, **DefaultResourceStandardRate** Property, **DefaultView** Property.

Def*type* Statements

Description	Used at module level to set the default data type for variables and **Function** procedures whose names start with the specified characters.
Syntax	**DefBool** *letterrange*[,*letterrange*] . . .
	DefInt *letterrange*[,*letterrange*] . . .
	DefLng *letterrange*[,*letterrange*] . . .
	DefCur *letterrange*[,*letterrange*] . . .
	DefSng *letterrange*[,*letterrange*] . . .
	DefDbl *letterrange*[,*letterrange*] . . .
	DefDate *letterrange*[,*letterrange*] . . .
	DefStr *letterrange*[,*letterrange*] . . .

DefObj *letterrange*[,*letterrange*] **. . .**

DefVar *letterrange*[,*letterrange*] **. . .**

Elements   The argument *letterrange* has the following syntax:

letter1[-*letter2*]

The arguments *letter1* and *letter2* specify the name range for which you can set a default data type. Each argument represents the first letter of the variable or **Function** procedure name and can be any letter of the alphabet. The case of letters in *letterrange* isn't significant.

Remarks   The statement name determines the data type:

Statement	Data Type
DefBool	**Boolean**
DefInt	**Integer**
DefLng	**Long**
DefCur	**Currency**
DefSng	**Single**
DefDbl	**Double**
DefDate	**Date**
DefStr	**String**
DefObj	**Object**
DefVar	**Variant**

For example, in the following program fragment, Message is a string variable:

```
DefStr A-Q
. . .
Message = "Out of stack space."
```

A **Def***type* statement affects only the module where it is used. For example, a **DefInt** statement in one module affects only the default data type of variables and **Function** procedures declared in that module; the default data type of variables in other modules is unaffected. If not explicitly declared with a **Def***type* statement, the default data type for all variables and all **Function** procedures is **Variant**.

When you specify a letter range, it usually defines the data type for variables that begin with letters in the lower 128 characters of the character set. However, when you specify the letter range A-Z, you set the default to the specified data type for all variables, including any that begin with international characters from the extended part of the character set (128-255).

Once the range A-Z has been specified, you can't further redefine any subranges of variables using **Def**type statements. In fact, once a range has been specified, if you include a previously defined letter in another **Def**type statement, an error occurs. However, you can explicitly specify the data type of any variable, defined or not, using a **Dim** statement with an **As** type clause. For example, you can use the following code at module level to define a variable as a **Double** even though the default data type is **Integer**:

```
DefInt A-Z
Dim TaxRate As Double
```

Deftype statements don't affect elements of user-defined types since they must be explicitly declared.

See Also

Let Statement.

Example

This example shows various uses of the **Def**type statements to set default data types of variables and function procedures whose names start with specified characters. The default data type can be overridden only by explicit assignment using the **Dim** statement. **Def**type statements can only be used at the module-level.

```
' Variable names beginning with A through K default to Integer.
DefInt A-K
' Variable names beginning with L through Z default to String.
DefStr L-Z
CalcVar = 4                    ' Initialize Integer.
StringVar = "Hello there"      ' Initialize String.
AnyVar = "Hello"               ' Causes "Type mismatch" error.
Dim Calc As Double             ' Explicitly set the type to Double.
Calc = 2.3455                  ' Assign a Double.

' Deftype statements also apply to function procedures.
CalcNum = ATestFunction(4)   ' Call user-defined function.

' ATestFunction function procedure definition.
Function ATestFunction(INumber)
    ATestFunction = INumber * 2 ' Return value is an integer.
End Function
```

Delay Property

Applies To

Application Object.

Description

Returns or sets whether delays are automatically removed from tasks before leveling occurs.

Syntax

[object.]**AutoRemoveDelay** [= value]

Elements

The **AutoRemoveDelay** property syntax has the following parts:

Part	Description
object	An object expression that evaluates to an object in the Applies To list.
value	A Boolean expression that specifies whether delays are automatically removed from tasks.

See Also   **AutoLevel** Property, **LevelingOptions** Method.

Delete Method

Applies To   **Application** Object.

Description   Deletes the active row or the row that contains the active cell.

Syntax   [*object.*]**RowDelete**

Elements   The *object* placeholder is an object expression that evaluates to an object in the Applies To list.

See Also   **ColumnBestFit** Method, **ColumnDelete** Method, **ColumnInsert** Method, **RowInsert** Method.

Derived Math Functions

Description   The following is a list of nonintrinsic math functions that can be derived from the intrinsic math functions:

Function	Derived equivalents
Secant	Sec(X) = 1 / Cos(X)
Cosecant	Cosec(X) = 1 / Sin(X)
Cotangent	Cotan((X) = 1 / Tan(X)
Inverse Sine	Arcsin(X) = Atn(X / Sqr(-X * X + 1))
Inverse Cosine	Arccos(X) = Atn(-X / Sqr(-X * X + 1)) + 1.5708
Inverse Secant	Arcsec(X) = Atn(X / Sqr(X * X - 1)) + Sgn((X) -1) * 1.5708
Inverse Cosecant	Arccosec(X) = Atn(X / Sqr(X * X - 1)) + (Sgn(X) - 1) * 1.5708
Inverse Cotangent	Arccotan(X) = Atn(X) + 1.5708
Hyperbolic Sine	HSin(X) = (Exp(X) - Exp(-X)) / 2

Function	Derived equivalents
Hyperbolic Cosine	$HCos(X) = (Exp(X) + Exp(-X)) / 2$
Hyperbolic Tangent	$HTan(X) = (Exp(X) - Exp(-X)) / (Exp(X) + Exp(-X))$
Hyperbolic Secant	$HSec(X) = 2 / (Exp(X) + Exp(-X))$
Hyperbolic Cosecant	$HCosec(X) = 2 / (Exp(X) - Exp(-X))$
Hyperbolic Cotangent	$HCotan(X) = (Exp(X) + Exp(-X)) / (Exp(X) - Exp(-X))$
Inverse Hyperbolic Sine	$HArcsin(X) = Log(X + Sqr(X * X + 1))$
Inverse Hyperbolic Cosine	$HArccos(X) = Log(X + Sqr(X * X - 1))$
Inverse Hyperbolic Tangent	$HArctan(X) = Log((1 + X) / (1 - X)) / 2$
Inverse Hyperbolic Secant	$HArcsec(X) = Log((Sqr(-X * X + 1) + 1) / X)$
Inverse Hyperbolic Cosecant	$HArccosec(X) = Log((Sgn(X) * Sqr(X * X + 1) +1) / X)$
Inverse Hyperbolic Cotangent	$HArccotan(X) = Log((X + 1) / (X - 1)) / 2$
Logarithm to base N	$LogN(X) = Log(X) / Log(N)$

See Also **Atn** Function, **Cos** Function, **Exp** Function, **Log** Function, **Sin** Function, **Sqr** Function, **Tan** Function.

Dim Statement

Description Declares variables and allocates storage space.

Syntax **Dim** *varname*[([*subscripts*])][**As** *type*][,*varname*[([*subscripts*])][**As** *type*]] **. . .**

Elements The **Dim** statement syntax has these parts:

Part	Description
varname	Name of the variable; follows standard variable naming conventions.
subscripts	Dimensions of an array variable; up to 60 multiple dimensions may be declared. The *subscripts* argument uses the following syntax:
	[*lower* **To**] *upper* [,[*lower* **To**] *upper*] **. . .**
type	Data type of the variable; may be **Boolean**, **Integer**, **Long**, **Currency**, **Single**, **Double**, **Date**, **String** (for variable-length strings), **String** * *length* (for fixed-length strings), **Object**, **Variant**, a user-defined type, or an object type. Use a separate **As** *type* clause for each variable you declare.

Remarks Variables declared with **Dim** at the module level are available to all procedures within the module. At the procedure level, variables are available only within the procedure.

Use the **Dim** statement at module or procedure level to declare the data type or object type of a variable. For example, the following statement declares a variable as an **Integer**.

```
Dim NumberOfEmployees As Integer
```

If you do not specify a data type or object type, and there is no **Def***type* statement in the module, the variable is **Variant** by default.

When variables are initialized, a numeric variable is initialized to 0, a variable-length string is initialized to a zero-length string, and a fixed-length string is filled with zeros. **Variant** variables are initialized to **Empty**. Each element of a user-defined type variable is initialized as if it was a separate variable. A variable that refers to an object must be assigned an existing object using the **Set** statement before it can be used. Until it is assigned an object, the declared object variable has the special value **Nothing**, which indicates that it does not refer to any particular instance of an object.

You can also use the **Dim** statement with empty parentheses to declare dynamic arrays. After declaring a dynamic array, use the **ReDim** statement within a procedure to define the number of dimensions and elements in the array. If you try to redeclare a dimension for an array variable whose size was explicitly specified in a **Private**, **Public** or **Dim** statement, an error occurs.

Tip When you use the Dim statement in a procedure, it is a generally accepted programming practice to put the Dim statement at the beginning of the procedure.

See Also

Array Function, **Option Base** Statement, **Private** Statement, **Public** Statement, **ReDim** Statement, **Set** Statement, **Static** Statement, **Type** Statement.

Example

This example shows various uses of the **Dim** statement to declare variables. The **Dim** statement is also used to declare arrays. The default lower bound for array subscripts is 0 and can be overridden at the module level using the **Option Base** statement.

```
' AnyValue and MyValue are declared as Variant by default with values
' set to Empty.
Dim AnyValue, MyValue

' Explicitly declare a variable of type Integer.
Dim Number As Integer

' Multiple declarations on a single line. AnotherVar is of type Variant
' since its type is omitted.
Dim AnotherVar, Choice As Boolean, BirthDate As Date

' DayArray is an array of Variants with 51 elements indexed,
' starting at 0 thru 50, assuming Option Base is set to 0 (default) for
' the current module.
Dim DayArray(50)
```

```
' Matrix is a two-dimensional array of integers.
Dim Matrix(3,4) As Integer

' MyMatrix is a three-dimensional array of doubles with explicit
' bounds.
Dim MyMatrix(1 To 5,  4 To 9,  3 To 5) As Double

' BirthDay is an array of dates with indexes from 1 to 10.
Dim BirthDay(1 To 10) As Date

' MyArray is a dynamic array.
Dim MyArray()
```

Dir Function

Description   Returns the current path.

Syntax   **CurDir**[(*drive*)]

Elements   The *drive* argument is a string expression that specifies an existing drive. In Microsoft Windows, if no drive is specified or if *drive* is zero-length (""), **CurDir** returns the path for the current drive. On the Macintosh, **CurDir** ignores any *drive* specified and simply returns the path for the current drive.

See Also   **ChDir** Statement, **ChDrive** Statement, **MkDir** Statement, **RmDir** Statement.

Example   This example uses the **Dir** function to check if certain files and directories exist. The **MacID** function may be used on the Macintosh to specify the file type.

```
' In Microsoft Windows.
' Returns "WIN.INI" if it exists.
MyFile = Dir("C:\WINDOWS\WIN.INI")

' Returns file name with specified extension. If more than one *.ini
' file exists, the first file name found is returned.
MyFile = Dir("C:\WINDOWS\*.ini")

' Call Dir again without arguments to return the next *.ini file in the
' same directory.
MyFile = Dir

' Return first *.txt file with a set hidden attribute.
MyFile = Dir("*.TXT", vbHidden)



' On the Macintosh.
' Use the MacID function to specify file type.
' The following statement returns the first "TEXT" file found in the
' specified directory or folder.
MyFile = Dir("HD:MyFolder:", MacID("TEXT"))
```

DisplayAlerts Property

Applies To   **Application** Object.

Description   Returns or sets whether Microsoft Project displays error messages when a macro
runs.

Syntax   [*object.*]**DisplayAlerts** [= *value*]

Elements   The **DisplayAlerts** property syntax has these parts:

Part	Description
object	An object expression that evaluates to an object in the Applies To list.
value	A Boolean expression that specifies whether Microsoft Project displays error messages when a macro runs, as shown under Settings.

Settings   The **DisplayAlerts** property has these settings:

Setting	Description
True	Microsoft Project displays error messages when a macro runs.
False	Microsoft Project does not display error messages when a macro runs.

See Also   **CellDragAndDrop** Property, **DisplayEntryBar** Property, **DisplayScrollBars**
Property, **DisplayStatusBar** Property.

DisplayEntryBar Property

Applies To   **Application** Object.

Description   Returns or sets whether the entry bar is visible.

Syntax   [*object.*]**DisplayEntryBar** [= *value*]

Elements   The **DisplayEntryBar** property syntax has these parts:

Part	Description
object	An object expression that evaluates to an object in the Applies To list.
value	A Boolean expression that displays or hides the entry bar.

Settings	The **DisplayEntryBar** property has these settings:

Setting	Description
True	The entry bar is visible.
False	The entry bar is not visible.

See Also   **CellDragAndDrop** Property, **DisplayAlerts** Property, **DisplayScrollBars** Property, **DisplayStatusBar** Property.

DisplayNotesIndicator Property

Applies To   **Application** Object.

Description   Returns or sets whether an indicator appears in cells to show which tasks or resources have notes.

Syntax   [*object*.]**DisplayNotesIndicator** [= *value*]

Elements   The **DisplayNotesIndicator** property syntax has the following parts:

Part	Description
object	An object expression that evaluates to an object in the Applies To list.
value	A Boolean expression that specifies whether to display an indicator in cells to show which tasks or resources have notes.

See Also   **DisplayAlerts** Property, **DisplayEntryBar** Property, **DisplayOLEIndicator** Property, **DisplayPlanningWizard** Property, **DisplayProjectSummaryTask** Property, **DisplayScheduleMessages** Property, **DisplayScrollBars** Property, **DisplayStatusBar** Property, **DisplayWizardErrors** Property, **DisplayWizardScheduling** Property, **DisplayWizardUsage** Property.

DisplayOLEIndicator Property

Applies To   **Application** Object.

Description   Returns or sets whether an indicator appears in cells used for OLE.

Syntax	[*object*.]**DisplayOLEIndicator** [= *value*]
Elements	The **DisplayOLEIndicator** property syntax has the following parts:

Part	Description
object	An object expression that evaluates to an object in the Applies To list.
value	A Boolean expression that specifies whether to display an indicator in cells used for OLE.

See Also   **DisplayAlerts** Property, **DisplayEntryBar** Property, **DisplayNotesIndicator** Property, **DisplayPlanningWizard** Property, **DisplayProjectSummaryTask** Property, **DisplayScheduleMessages** Property, **DisplayScrollBars** Property, **DisplayStatusBar** Property, **DisplayWizardErrors** Property, **DisplayWizardScheduling** Property, **DisplayWizardUsage** Property.

DisplayPlanningWizard Property

Applies To	**Application** Object.
Description	Returns or sets whether the PlanningWizard is active.
Syntax	[*object*.]**DisplayPlanningWizard** [= *value*]
Elements	The **DisplayPlanningWizard** property syntax has the following parts:

Part	Description
object	An object expression that evaluates to an object in the Applies To list.
value	A Boolean expression that specifies whether the PlanningWizard is running.

See Also   **DisplayAlerts** Property, **DisplayEntryBar** Property, **DisplayNotesIndicator** Property, **DisplayOLEIndicator** Property, **DisplayProjectSummaryTask** Property, **DisplayScheduleMessages** Property, **DisplayScrollBars** Property, **DisplayStatusBar** Property, **DisplayWizardErrors** Property, **DisplayWizardScheduling** Property, **DisplayWizardUsage** Property.

Example

The following example resets the PlanningWizard.

```
Sub ResetWizard()
    Application.DisplayPlanningWizard = True
    Application.DisplayWizardErrors = True
    Application.DisplayWizardScheduling = True
    Application.DisplayWizardUsage = True
End Sub
```

DisplayProjectSummaryTask Property

Applies To   **Project** Object, **Projects** Collection.

Description   Returns or sets whether the summary task for a project is visible.

Syntax   *object*.**DisplayProjectSummaryTask** [= *value*]

Elements   The **DisplayProjectSummaryTask** property syntax has the following parts:

Part	Description
object	An object expression that evaluates to an object in the Applies To list.
value	A Boolean expression that specifies whether the project summary task is visible.

See Also   **OptionsView** Method.

Example   The following example creates a new project and displays its summary task.

```
Sub NewProject()
    FileNew
    ActiveProject.DisplayProjectSummaryTask = True
End Sub
```

DisplayScheduleMessages Property

Applies To   **Application** Object.

Description   Returns whether or not scheduling messages are displayed.

Syntax   [*object*.]**DisplayScheduleMessages** [= *value*]

Elements   The **DisplayScheduleMessages** property syntax has the following parts:

Part	Description
object	An object expression that evaluates to an object in the Applies To list.
value	A Boolean expression that specifies whether messages appear when scheduling problems occur.

Remarks   This method applies to Microsoft Project for Microsoft Windows.

See Also   **DisplayAlerts** Property, **DisplayEntryBar** Property, **DisplayNotesIndicator** Property, **DisplayOLEIndicator** Property, **DisplayPlanningWizard** Property, **DisplayProjectSummaryTask** Property, **DisplayScrollBars** Property, **DisplayStatusBar** Property, **DisplayWizardErrors** Property, **DisplayWizardScheduling** Property, **DisplayWizardUsage** Property.

DisplayScrollBars Property

Applies To   **Application** Object.

Description   Returns or sets whether the scroll bars are visible.

Syntax   [*object*.]**DisplayScrollBars** [= *value*]

Elements   The **DisplayScrollBars** property syntax has these parts:

Part	Description
object	An object expression that evaluates to an object in the Applies To list.
value	A Boolean expression that displays or hides the scroll bars.

Settings   The **DisplayScrollBars** property has these settings:

Setting	Description
True	The scroll bars are visible.
False	The scroll bars are not visible.

See Also   **CellDragAndDrop** Property, **DisplayAlerts** Property, **DisplayEntryBar** Property, **DisplayStatusBar** Property.

Example   The following example changes the setting of the **DisplayScrollBars** property.

```
Sub ChangeDisplayScrollBars
    DisplayScrollBars = Not DisplayScrollBars
End Sub
```

DisplayStatusBar Property

Applies To	**Application** Object.
Description	Returns or sets whether the status bar is visible.
Syntax	[*object*.]**DisplayStatusBar** [= *value*]
Elements	The **DisplayStatusBar** property syntax has these parts:

Part	Description
object	An object expression that evaluates to an object in the Applies To list.
value	A Boolean expression that displays or hides the status bar.

Settings   The **DisplayStatusBar** property has these settings:

Setting	Description
True	The status bar is visible.
False	The status bar is not visible.

See Also   **CellDragAndDrop** Property, **DisplayAlerts** Property, **DisplayEntryBar** Property, **DisplayScrollBars** Property.

DisplayWizardErrors Property

Applies To	**Application** Object.
Description	Returns or sets whether the PlanningWizard displays messages about errors.
Syntax	[*object*.]**DisplayWizardErrors** [= *value*]
Elements	The **DisplayWizardErrors** property syntax has the following parts:

Part	Description
object	An object expression that evaluates to an object in the Applies To list.
value	A Boolean expression that specifies whether the PlanningWizard displays messages about errors.

See Also	**DisplayAlerts** Property, **DisplayEntryBar** Property, **DisplayNotesIndicator** Property, **DisplayOLEIndicator** Property, **DisplayPlanningWizard** Property, **DisplayProjectSummaryTask** Property, **DisplayScheduleMessages** Property, **DisplayScrollBars** Property, **DisplayStatusBar** Property, **DisplayWizardScheduling** Property, **DisplayWizardUsage** Property.
Example	The following example resets the PlanningWizard.

```
Sub ResetWizard()
    Application.DisplayPlanningWizard = True
    Application.DisplayWizardErrors = True
    Application.DisplayWizardScheduling = True
    Application.DisplayWizardUsage = True
End Sub
```

DisplayWizardScheduling Property

Applies To	**Application** Object.
Description	Returns or sets whether the PlanningWizard displays messages about scheduling problems.
Syntax	[*object*.]**DisplayWizardScheduling** [= *value*]
Elements	The **DisplayWizardScheduling** property syntax has the following parts:

Part	Description
object	An object expression that evaluates to an object in the Applies To list.
value	A Boolean expression that specifies whether the PlanningWizard displays messages about scheduling problems.

See Also	**DisplayAlerts** Property, **DisplayEntryBar** Property, **DisplayNotesIndicator** Property, **DisplayOLEIndicator** Property, **DisplayPlanningWizard** Property, **DisplayProjectSummaryTask** Property, **DisplayScheduleMessages** Property, **DisplayScrollBars** Property, **DisplayStatusBar** Property, **DisplayWizardErrors** Property, **DisplayWizardUsage** Property.
Example	The following example resets the PlanningWizard.

```
Sub ResetWizard()
    Application.DisplayPlanningWizard = True
    Application.DisplayWizardErrors = True
    Application.DisplayWizardScheduling = True
    Application.DisplayWizardUsage = True
End Sub
```

DisplayWizardUsage Property

Applies To   **Application** Object.

Description   Returns or sets whether the PlanningWizard displays tips about using Microsoft Project more effectively.

Syntax   [*object.*]**DisplayWizardUsage** [= *value*]

Elements   The **DisplayWizardUsage** property syntax has the following parts:

Part	Description
object	An object expression that evaluates to an object in the Applies To list.
value	A Boolean expression that specifies whether the PlanningWizard displays tips about using Microsoft Project more effectively.

See Also   **DisplayAlerts** Property, **DisplayEntryBar** Property, **DisplayNotesIndicator** Property, **DisplayOLEIndicator** Property, **DisplayPlanningWizard** Property, **DisplayProjectSummaryTask** Property, **DisplayScheduleMessages** Property, **DisplayScrollBars** Property, **DisplayStatusBar** Property, **DisplayWizardErrors** Property, **DisplayWizardScheduling** Property.

Example   The following example resets the PlanningWizard.

```
Sub ResetWizard()
    Application.DisplayPlanningWizard = True
    Application.DisplayWizardErrors = True
    Application.DisplayWizardScheduling = True
    Application.DisplayWizardUsage = True
End Sub
```

Do...Loop Statement

Description   Repeats a block of statements while a condition is **True** or until a condition becomes **True**.

Syntax 1   **Do** [{**While** | **Until**} *condition*]
　　　　　　　[*statements*]
　　　　　　　[**Exit Do**]
　　　　　　　[*statements*]
　　　　　　Loop

| Syntax 2 | **Do**
    [*statements*]
    [**Exit Do**]
    [*statements*]
Loop [{**While** | **Until**}*condition*] |

Elements

The **Do...Loop** statement syntax has these parts:

Part	Description
condition	Expression that is **True** or **False**.
statements	One or more statements that are repeated while or until *condition* is **True**.

Remarks

The **Exit Do** can only be used within a **Do...Loop** control structure to provide an alternate way to exit a **Do...Loop**. Any number of **Exit Do** statements may be placed anywhere in the **Do...Loop**. Often used with the evaluation of some condition (for example, **If...Then**), **Exit Do** transfers control to the statement immediately following the **Loop**.

When used within nested **Do...Loop** statements, **Exit Do** transfers control to the loop that is one nested level above the loop where it occurs.

See Also

Exit Statement, **For...Next** Statement, **While...Wend** Statement.

Example

This example shows how **Do...Loop** statements can be used. The inner **Do...Loop** statement loops 10 times, sets the value of the flag to **False**, and exits prematurely using the **Exit Do** statement. The outer loop exits immediately upon checking the value of the flag.

```
Check = True : Counter = 0        ' Initialize variables.
Do   ' Outer Loop.
    Do While Counter < 20         ' Inner Loop.
        Counter = Counter + 1     ' Increment Counter.
        If Counter = 10 Then      ' If condition is true.
            Check = False         ' Set value of flag to False.
            Exit Do               ' Exit inner loop.
        End If
    Loop
Loop Until Check = False          ' Exit outer loop immediately.
```

DocClose Method

Applies To

Application Object.

Description

Closes the active project.

Syntax

[*object.*]**DocClose**

Elements	The *object* placeholder is an object expression that evaluates to an object in the Applies To list.
See Also	**DocMaximize** Method, **DocMove** Method, **DocRestore** Method, **DocSize** Method.

DocMaximize Method

Applies To	**Application** Object.
Description	Maximizes the window of the active project.
Syntax	[*object*.]**DocMaximize**
Elements	The *object* placeholder is an object expression that evaluates to an object in the Applies To list.
Remarks	For Microsoft Project for the Macintosh, this method toggles between the maximized and restored windows states.
See Also	**DocClose** Method, **DocMaximize** Method, **DocMove** Method, **DocRestore** Method, **DocSize** Method, **WindowState** Property.

DocMove Method

Applies To	**Application** Object.
Description	Moves the active window.
Syntax	[*object*.]**DocMove** [*xPosition*, *yPosition*, *points*]
Elements	The **DocMove** method syntax has the following object qualifier and named arguments:

Part	Description
object	An object expression that evaluates to an object in the Applies To list. Optional.
xPosition	A numeric expression that specifies the distance of the active window from the left edge of the screen. Optional.

Part	Description
yPosition	A numeric expression that specifies the distance of the active window from the top edge of the screen. Optional.
points	A Boolean expression that specifies the measurement units.

True	The positions you specify with the *xPosition* and *yPosition* arguments are measured in points.
False	The positions you specify with the *xPosition* and *yPosition* arguments are measured in pixels.

By default, the *points* argument is **False**. Optional.

Remarks

The positions specified are taken from the top, left corner of the usable area of the main screen. The usable area is the area left after taking out the menu bar and toolbars.

See Also

DocClose Method, **DocMaximize** Method, **DocRestore** Method, **DocSize** Method, **Left** Property, **Top** Property.

Example

The following example moves the window of the active project to the upper-left corner of the main window.

```
Sub MoveProjectWindowToCorner()
    DocMove xPosition := 0, yPosition := 0
End Sub
```

DocRestore Method

Applies To

Application Object.

Description

Sets the active window to its last nonmaximized state.

Syntax

[*object.*]**DocRestore**

Elements

The *object* placeholder is an object expression that evaluates to an object in the Applies To list.

See Also

DocClose Method, **DocMaximize** Method, **DocMove** Method, **DocSize** Method, **WindowState** Property.

DocSize Method

Applies To

Application Object.

Description	Sets the width and height of the active window.
Syntax	[*object.*]**DocSize** [*width, height, points*]
Elements	The **DocSize** method syntax has the following object qualifier and named arguments:

Part	Description
object	An object expression that evaluates to an object in the Applies To list. Optional.
width	A numeric expression that specifies the new width of the active window. Optional.
height	A numeric expression that specifies the new height of the active window. Optional.
points	A Boolean expression that specifies the measurement units.

	True	The values you specify with the *width* and *height* arguments are measured in points.
	False	The values you specify with the *width* and *height* arguments are measured in pixels.

By default, the *points* argument is **False**. Optional.

See Also	**DocClose** Method, **DocMaximize** Method, **DocMove** Method, **DocRestore** Method, **Height** Property, **Top** Property.
Example	The following example tiles the windows of open projects vertically within the main window of Microsoft Project.

```
Sub TileProjectWindowsVertically()
    Dim I          ' Index used in For...Next loop
    For I = 1 To Application.Windows.Count
        Windows(I).Activate
        DocSize Width := UsableWidth / Windows.Count, _
            Height := UsableHeight
        DocMove xPosition := (I - 1) * UsableWidth / Windows.Count, _
            yPosition := 0
    Next I
End Sub
```

DoEvents Statement

Description	Yields execution so that the operating system can process other events.
Syntax	**DoEvents**

Remarks   **DoEvents** passes control to the operating system. Control is not returned until the operating system has finished processing the events in its queue and, for Microsoft Windows only, all keys in the **SendKeys** queue have been sent.

If parts of your code take up too much processor time, use **DoEvents** periodically to relinquish control to the operating system so that events, such as keyboard input and mouse clicks, can be processed without significant delay.

Caution   Make sure the procedure that has given up control with **DoEvents** is not executed again from a different part of your code before the first **DoEvents** call returns; this could cause unpredictable results. In addition, do not use **DoEvents** if other applications could possibly interact with your procedure in unforeseen ways during the time you have yielded control.

Example   This example uses the **DoEvents** Statement to cause execution to yield to the operating system once every 1000 iterations of the loop.

```
For I = 1 To 150000          ' Start loop.
    If I Mod 1000 = 0 Then   ' If loop has repeated 1000 times.
        DoEvents             ' Yield to operating system.
    End If
Next I                       ' Increment loop counter.
```

Double Data Type

Description   **Double** (double-precision floating-point) variables are stored as 64-bit (8-byte) numbers ranging in value from -1.79769313486232E308 to -4.94065645841247E-324 for negative values and from 4.94065645841247E-324 to 1.79769313486232E308 for positive values. The type-declaration character for **Double** is # (character code 35).

See Also   **CDbl** Function, Data Type Summary, **Def**_type_ Statements, **Single** Data Type.

DrawingCreate Method

Applies To   **Application** Object.

Description   Creates a drawing.

Syntax   [*object*.]**DrawingCreate** *type*[, *behind*]

Elements

The **DrawingCreate** method syntax has the following object qualifier and named arguments:

Part	Description
object	An object expression that evaluates to an object in the Applies To list. Optional.
type	A constant that specifies the type of drawing to create. Required.
behind	A Boolean expression that specifies whether the drawing is created behind task bars. By default, the *behind* argument is **False**. Optional.

The *type* argument has these settings:

pjOLEObject	1	OLE Object
pjLine	2	Line
pjArrow	3	Arrow
pjRectangle	4	Rectangle
pjEllipse	5	Ellipse
pjArc	6	Arc
pjPolygon	7	Polygon
pjTextBox	8	Text box

See Also

DrawingCycleColor Method, **DrawingMove** Method, **DrawingProperties** Method, **DrawingReshape** Method, **DrawingToolbarShow** Method.

DrawingCycleColor Method

Applies To	**Application** Object.
Description	Changes the color of the active drawing object.
Syntax	[*object*.]**DrawingCycleColor**
Elements	The *object* placeholder is an object expression that evaluates to an object in the Applies To list.
Remarks	The **DrawingCycleColor** method has the same effect as the Cycle Color button on the Drawing toolbar.
See Also	**DrawingMove** Method, **DrawingProperties** Method, **DrawingReshape** Method, **DrawingToolbarShow** Method.

DrawingMove Method

Applies To   **Application** Object.

Description   Moves the active drawing object forward or backward in the drawing layers.

Syntax   [*object*.]**DrawingMove** *forward, full*

Elements   The **DrawingMove** method syntax has the following object qualifier and named arguments:

Part	Description
object	An object expression that evaluates to an object in the Applies To list. Optional.
forward	A Boolean expression that specifies whether to move the active drawing object forward or backward. By default, the *forward* argument is **False**. Optional. The *forward* argument has these settings:

True	Moves the object forward in the drawing layers.
False	Moves the object backward in the drawing layers.

Part	Description
full	A Boolean expression that specifies whether to move the object to the back (when the *forward* argument is **False**) or the front (when the *forward* argument is **True**) of the drawing layers. By default, the *full* argument is **False**. Optional. The *full* argument has these settings:

True	Moves the object to the front or back of the drawing layers.
False	Moves the object forward or backward one drawing layer.

See Also   **DrawingCycleColor** Method, **DrawingProperties** Method, **DrawingReshape** Method, **DrawingToolbarShow** Method.

DrawingProperties Method

Applies To   **Application** Object.

Description   Displays the Format Drawing dialog box, which prompts the user to customize the active drawing object.

Syntax   [*object*.]**DrawingProperties** [*sizePositionTab*]

Elements

The **DrawingProperties** method syntax has the following object qualifier and named arguments:

Part	Description
object	An object expression that evaluates to an object in the Applies To list. Optional.
sizePositionTab	A Boolean expression that specifies whether to display the Size And Position tab of the Drawing Properties dialog box.

Remarks

The **DrawingProperties** method has no effect unless a drawing object is active.

The **DrawingProperties** method has the same effect as the Properties command on the Drawing submenu, which is on the Format menu.

See Also

DrawingCycleColor Method, **DrawingMove** Method, **DrawingReshape** Method, **DrawingToolbarShow** Method.

DrawingReshape Method

Applies To

Application Object.

Description

Changes the drawing mode to resize if the current mode is reshape; changes the drawing mode to reshape if the current mode is resize.

Syntax

[*object*.]**DrawingReshape**

Elements

The *object* placeholder is an object expression that evaluates to an object in the Applies To list.

Remarks

The **DrawingReshape** method has the same effect as the Reshape button on the Drawing toolbar.

See Also

DrawingCycleColor Method, **DrawingMove** Method, **DrawingProperties** Method, **DrawingToolbarShow** Method.

DrawingToolbarShow Method

Applies To

Application Object.

Description

Displays the Drawing toolbar, if it is not visible. When the Drawing Toolbar is displayed, this method will change it to a floating toolbar from a docked toolbar.

Syntax	[*object.*]**DrawingToolbarShow**
Elements	The *object* placeholder is an object expression that evaluates to an object in the Applies To list.
See Also	**DrawingCycleColor** Method, **DrawingMove** Method, **DrawingProperties** Method, **DrawingReshape** Method, **Toolbars** Method.

Duration Property

Applies To	**Project** Object, **Projects** Collection; **Task** Object, **Tasks** Collection.
Description	Returns or sets the actual duration (in minutes) of an project or task. Read only for **Project** object.
Syntax	*object.***ActualDuration** [= *value*]
Elements	The **ActualDuration** property syntax has these parts:

Part	Description
object	An object expression that evaluates to an object in the Applies To list.
value	A numeric expression of the duration of the task, in minutes.

See Also	**ActualCost** Property, **ActualFinish** Property, **ActualStart** Property, **ActualWork** Property, **BaselineDuration** Property, **Duration** Property, **DurationVariance** Property, **RemainingDuration** Property.
Example	The following example marks the tasks in the active project with actual durations that exceed a certain number of minutes.

```
Sub MarkTasksWithLongDurations()
    Dim T                ' Task object used in For Each loop
    Dim Minutes as Long       ' Duration entered by user

    ' Prompt user for the actual duration, in minutes.
    Minutes = Val(InputBox("Enter the actual duration, in minutes: "))

    ' Don't do anything if the InputBox was cancelled.
    If Minutes = 0 Then Exit Sub

    ' Cycle through the tasks of the active project.
    For Each T in ActiveProject.Tasks
```

```
                     ' Mark a task, if it exceeds the duration.
                     If T.ActualDuration > Minutes Then T.Marked = True
               Next T
         End Sub
```

DurationFormat Method

Applies To   **Application** Object.

Description   Returns a duration in the specified units.

Syntax   [*object*.]**DurationFormat** (*duration*, *units*)

Elements   The **DurationFormat** method syntax has the following object qualifier and named arguments:

Part	Description
object	An object expression that evaluates to an object in the Applies To list. Optional.
duration	A string expression that specifies the duration or a numeric expression that specifies the duration in minutes. Required.
units	A constant that specifies the units. Required.

The *units* argument has these settings:

pjMinutes	0	Minutes
pjHours	1	Hours
pjDays	2	Days
pjWeeks	3	Weeks
pjElapsedMinutes	4	Elapsed minutes
pjElapsedHours	5	Elapsed hours
pjElapsedDays	6	Elapsed days
pjElapsedWeeks	7	Elapsed weeks

Return Values   Returns the duration in the specified units.

Remarks   For example, if you specify "2w" for the duration argument, and **pjDays** for the units argument, the **DurationFormat** method returns "14d".

See Also   **ActualDuration** Property, **BaselineDuration** Property, **Duration** Property, **Durationn** Property, **DurationValue** Method.

Example   The following example displays the duration of the selected task in weeks.

```
Sub DurationInWeeks()
    MsgBox DurationFormat(ActiveCell.Task.Duration, pjWeeks)
End Sub
```

Duration*n* Property

Applies To   **Project** Object, **Projects** Collection; **Task** Object, **Tasks** Collection.

Description   Returns or sets the value of an additional duration field for a project or task.

Syntax   *object*.**Duration***n* [= *value*]

Elements   The **Duration***n* property syntaxes have the following parts:

Part	Description
object	An object expression that evaluates to an object in the Applies To list.
n	A number from 1 to 3.
value	A string expression that specifies the duration or a numeric expression that specifies the duration in minutes for the additional duration field.

See Also   **ActualDuration** Property, **BaselineDuration** Property, **Duration** Property, **DurationFormat** Method, **DurationValue** Method.

DurationValue Method

Applies To   **Application** Object.

Description   Returns the number of minutes in a duration.

Syntax   [*object*.]**DurationValue** (*duration*)

Elements   The **DurationValue** method syntax has the following object qualifier and named arguments:

Part	Description
object	An object expression that evaluates to an object in the Applies To list. Optional.
duration	A string expression that specifies the duration. Required.

See Also	**ActualDuration** Property, **BaselineDuration** Property, **Duration** Property, **DurationFormat** Method, **Durationn** Property.
Example	The following example adds the entered value to the duration of the selected task.

```
Sub DurationAdder()
    x = DurationValue(InputBox("Enter amount by which to increase" & _
        " the duration"))
    ActiveCell.Task.Duration = ActiveCell.Task.Duration + x
End Sub
```

DurationVariance Property

Applies To	**Project** Object, **Projects** Collection; **Task** Object, **Tasks** Collection.
Description	Returns the variance, in minutes, between the planned duration and the duration of a project or task.
Syntax	*object*.**DurationVariance**
Elements	The *object* placeholder is an object expression that evaluates to an object in the Applies To list.
See Also	**ActualDuration** Property, **BaselineDuration** Property, **CostVariance** Property, **Duration** Property, **FinishVariance** Property, **RemainingDuration** Property, **StartVariance** Property, **WorkVariance** Property.

EarlyFinish Property

Applies To	**Project** Object, **Projects** Collection; **Task** Object, **Tasks** Collection.
Description	Returns the earliest date on which a task can finish.
Syntax	*object*.**EarlyFinish**
Elements	The *object* placeholder is an object expression that evaluates to an object in the Applies To list.
See Also	**EarlyStart** Property, **LateFinish** Property, **LateStart** Property.

EarlyStart Property

Applies To	**Project** Object, **Projects** Collection; **Task** Object, **Tasks** Collection.
Description	Returns the earliest date on which a task can start.
Syntax	*object*.**EarlyStart**
Elements	The *object* placeholder is an object expression that evaluates to an object in the Applies To list.
See Also	**EarlyFinish** Property, **LateFinish** Property, **LateStart** Property.

EditClear Method

Applies To	**Application** Object.
Description	Clears the active cells.
Syntax	[*object*.]**EditClear** [*contents*, *formats*, *notes*]
Elements	The **EditClear** method syntax has the following object qualifier and named arguments:

Part	Description
object	An object expression that evaluates to an object in the Applies To list. Optional.
contents	A Boolean expression that specifies whether to clear the contents of the active cells. By default, the *contents* argument is **True**. Optional.
formats	A Boolean expression that specifies whether to clear the formats of the active cells. By default, the *formats* argument is **False**. Optional.
notes	A Boolean expression that specifies whether to clear the notes of the active cells. By default, the *notes* argument is **False**. Optional.

See Also	**EditClearFormats** Method, **EditCopy** Method, **EditCut** Method, **EditDelete** Method, **RowClear** Method.
Example	The following example clears the contents, formats, and notes of the active cells.

```
Sub ClearAll()
    EditClear True, True, True
End Sub
```

EditClearFormats Method

Applies To	**Application** Object.
Description	Clears the format of the active cells.
Syntax	[*object*.]**EditClearFormats**
Elements	The *object* placeholder is an object expression that evaluates to an object in the Applies To list.
Remarks	The **EditClearFormats** method has the same effect as the Clear Formats command on the Edit menu.
See Also	**EditClear** Method, **EditCut** Method, **EditDelete** Method, **EditUndo** Method.

EditCopy Method

Applies To	**Application** Object.
Description	Copies data.
Syntax	[*object*.]**EditCopy** [*fromDate, toDate, includeTable, includeTimescale, tableOnly*]
Elements	The **EditCopy** method syntax has the following object qualifier and named arguments:

Part	Description
object	An object expression that evaluates to an object in the Applies To list. Optional.
fromDate	A date expression that specifies the first date to copy. By default, the *fromDate* argument equals the first date in the timescale portion of the Resource Usage view. The *fromDate* argument is ignored unless the active view is the Resource Usage view. Optional.
toDate	A date expression that specifies the last date to copy. By default, the *toDate* argument equals the last date in the timescale portion of the Resource Usage view. The *toDate* argument is ignored unless the active view is the Resource Usage view. Optional.

Part	Description
includeTable	A Boolean expression that specifies whether to include table information. By default, the *includeTable* argument is **False**. Optional. Applies to Microsoft Windows.
includeTimescale	A Boolean expression that specifies whether to include timescale information. By default, the *includeTimescale* argument is **False**. Optional. Applies to Microsoft Windows.
tableOnly	A Boolean expression that specifies whether to include table information. Optional. Applies to the Macintosh.

See Also   **DDEPasteLink** Method, **EditClear** Method, **EditCopyPicture** Method, **EditCut** Method, **EditDelete** Method, **EditPaste** Method.

Example   The following example copies table information for the year 1994.

```
Sub CopyOneYear()
    EditCopy "01/01/94", "12/31/94"
End Sub
```

EditCopyPicture Method

Applies To   **Application** Object.

Description   Copies the view as a picture or an OLE object.

Syntax   [*object.*]**EditCopyPicture** [*object, forPrinter*]

Elements   The **EditCopyPicture** method syntax has the following object qualifier and named arguments:

Part	Description
object	An object expression that evaluates to an object in the Applies To list. Optional.
object	A Boolean expression that specifies whether the view should be copied as an OLE object or as a picture. By default, the *object* argument is **False**. Optional.
	True Copies the view as an OLE object. **False** Copies the view as a picture.
forPrinter	A Boolean expression that specifies whether to copy the view for the screen or the printer. By default, the *forPrinter* argument is **False**. Optional.
	True Copies the view for the printer. **False** Copies the view for the screen.

See Also	**DDEPasteLink** Method, **EditClear** Method, **EditClearFormats** Method, **EditCopy** Method, **EditCut** Method, **EditDelete** Method, **EditInsert** Method, **EditPaste** Method, **EditPasteSpecial** Method, **EditUndo** Method.

EditCut Method

Applies To	**Application** Object.
Description	Cuts the active items.
Syntax	[*object*.]**EditCut**
Elements	The *object* placeholder is an object expression that evaluates to an object in the Applies To list.
See Also	**EditClear** Method, **EditCopy** Method, **EditDelete** Method, **EditPaste** Method.

EditDelete Method

Applies To	**Application** Object.
Description	Deletes the active row, active column, or row containing the active cell.
Syntax	[*object*.]**EditDelete**
Elements	The *object* placeholder is an object expression that evaluates to an object in the Applies To list.
See Also	**ColumnDelete** Method, **ColumnInsert** Method, **EditClear** Method, **EditCopy** Method, **EditCut** Method, **RowClear** Method, **RowDelete** Method, **RowInsert** Method.

EditGoto Method

Applies To	**Application** Object.
Description	Scrolls to a resource, task, or date.
Syntax	[*object*.]**EditGoto** [*id, date*]

Elements   The **EditGoto** method syntax has the following object qualifier and named arguments:

Part	Description
object	An object expression that evaluates to an object in the Applies To list. Optional.
id	A numeric expression that specifies the identification number of the task or resource to display in the active pane. Optional.
date	A date expression that specifies the first date to display in the active pane. Optional.

See Also   **Find** Method.

Example   The following example prompts the user for a date, or a task or resource id number, and then scrolls to that resource or date in the active pane.

```
Sub PromptUserForEditGotoArguments()
    Dim Entry    ' Name of resource or date entered by user

    ' Prompt the user for a date, or a task or resource id.
    Entry = InputBox("Enter a date, or a task or resource" & _
        " id to which you want to scroll in the active pane.")

    ' If user enters a date, then scroll to a date in the active pane.
    If IsDate(Entry) Then
        EditGoto date := Entry

    ' Otherwise, scroll to a resource in the active pane.
    Else
        EditGoto id := ActiveProject.Resources(Entry).ID
    End If
End Sub
```

EditInsert Method

Applies To   **Application** Object.

Description   Inserts a new column to the left of the active column, or inserts a new row above the active row or the row containing the active cell.

Syntax   [*object*.]**EditInsert**

Elements   The *object* placeholder is an object expression that evaluates to an object in the Applies To list.

See Also	**ColumnDelete** Method, **ColumnInsert** Method, **EditDelete** Method, **RowDelete** Method, **RowInsert** Method.

EditionStopAll Method

Applies To	**Application** Object.
Description	Temporarily suspends all edition updates.
Syntax	[*object*.]**EditionStopAll** (*Stop*)
Elements	The **EditionStopAll** method has the following object qualifier and named arguments:

Part	Description
object	An object expression that evaluates to an object in the Applies To list. Optional.
Stop	A Boolean expression that specifies whether to suspend the edition or not. By default, *Stop* = **TRUE**. Optional.

Remarks	This method applies to Microsoft Project for the Macintosh.
See Also	**CreatePublisher** Method, **SubscribeTo** Method.

EditPaste Method

Applies To	**Application** Object.
Description	Pastes the contents of the Clipboard into the active selection.
Syntax	[*object*.]**EditPaste**
Elements	The *object* placeholder is an object expression that evaluates to an object in the Applies To list.
See Also	**DDEPasteLink** Method, **EditCopy** Method, **EditCut** Method.

EditPasteSpecial Method

Applies To   **Application** Object.

Description   Copies or links data from the Clipboard into the active selection.

Syntax   [*object*.]**EditPasteSpecial** [*link*], *type, DisplayAsIcon*

Elements   The **EditPasteSpecial** Method syntax has the following object qualifier and named arguments:

Part	Description
bject	An object expression that evaluates to an object in the Applies To list.
link	Any valid Boolean expression that specifies whether to link the data to its source application.
type	Can have the following values: 0 = Embed Object; 1 = Picture; 2 = Text Data; 3 = Project Data
DisplayAsIcon	A Boolean expression that, if True, displays the object as an icon.

See Also   **DDEPasteLink** Method, **EditCopy** Method, **EditCopyPicture** Method, **EditCut** Method, **EditPaste** Method, **EditUndo** Method.

EditUndo Method

Applies To   **Application** Object.

Description   Undoes the most recent command, if possible.

Syntax   [*object*.]**EditUndo**

Elements   The *object* placeholder is an object expression that evaluates to an object in the Applies To list.

See Also   **DDEPasteLink** Method, **EditClear** Method, **EditCopy** Method, **EditCut** Method, **EditDelete** Method, **EditPaste** Method.

Else Statement

Description Conditionally executes a group of statements, depending on the value of an expression.

Syntax 1 **If** *condition* **Then** *statements* [**Else** *elsestatements*]

Syntax 2 **If** *condition* **Then**
    [*statements*]
[**ElseIf** *condition-n* **Then**
    [*elseifstatements*]] . . .
[**Else**
    [*elsestatements*]]
End If

Elements Syntax 1 has these parts:

Part	Description
condition	Numeric or string expression that evaluates **True** or **False**.
statements	One or more statements separated by colons; executed if *condition* is **True**.
elsestatements	One or more statements separated by colons; executed if *condition* is **False**.

Syntax 2 has these parts:

Part	Description
condition	Expression that is **True** or **False**.
statements	One or more statements executed if *condition* is **True**.
condition-n	Numeric or string expression that evaluates **True** or **False**.
elseifstatements	One or more statements executed if associated *condition-n* is **True**.
elsestatements	One or more statements executed if no previous *condition-n* expressions are **True**.

Remarks You can use the single-line form (Syntax 1) for short, simple tests. However, the block form (Syntax 2) provides more structure and flexibility than the single-line form and is usually easier to read, maintain, and debug.

Note   With Syntax 1 it is possible to have multiple statements executed as the result of an **If...Then** decision, but they must all be on the same line and separated by colons, as in the following statement:

```
If A > 10 Then A = A + 1 : B = B + A : C = C + B
```

When executing a block **If** (Syntax 2), *condition* is tested. If *condition* is **True**, the statements following **Then** are executed. If *condition* is **False**, each **ElseIf** condition (if any) is evaluated in turn. When a **True** condition is found, the statements immediately following the associated **Then** are executed. If none of the **ElseIf** conditions are **True** (or if there are no **ElseIf** clauses), the statements following **Else** are executed. After executing the statements following **Then** or **Else**, execution continues with the statement following **End If**.

The **Else** and **ElseIf** clauses are both optional. You can have as many **ElseIf** clauses as you want in a block **If**, but none can appear after an **Else** clause. Block **If** statements can be nested; that is, contained within one another.

What follows the **Then** keyword is examined to determine whether or not a statement is a block **If**. If anything other than a comment appears after **Then** on the same line, the statement is treated as a single-line **If** statement.

A block **If** statement must be the first statement on a line. The **Else**, **ElseIf**, and **End If** parts of the statement can have only a line number or line label preceding them. The block **If** must end with an **End If** statement.

Tip   **Select Case** may be more useful when evaluating a single expression that has several possible actions.

See Also   **Select Case** Statement.

EMailAddress Property

Applies To   **Resource** Object, **Resources** Collection.

Description   Returns or sets the electronic mail address of a resource.

Syntax   *object*.**EMailAddress** [= *value*]

Elements   The **EMailAddress** property syntax has the following parts:

Part	Description
object	An object expression that evaluates to an object in the Applies To list.
value	A string expression that specifies the electronic mail address.

Remarks   This method applies to Microsoft Project for Microsoft Windows.

See Also   **MailRoutingSlip** Method, **MailSend** Method, **MailSendProjectMail** Method, **MailSendScheduleNote** Method.

End Statement

Description   Ends a procedure or block.

Syntax   **End**

   End Function

   End If

   End Property

   End Select

   End Sub

   End Type

   End With

Elements   The **End** statement syntax has these forms:

Statement	Description
End	Terminates procedure execution. Never required by itself but may be placed anywhere in a procedure to close files opened with the **Open** statement and to clear variables.
End Function	Required to end a **Function** statement.
End If	Required to end a block **If...Then...Else** statement.
End Property	Required to end a **Property Let**, **Property Get**, or **Property Set** procedure.
End Select	Required to end a **Select Case** statement.
End Sub	Required to end a **Sub** statement.
End Type	Required to end a user-defined type definition (**Type** statement).
End With	Required to end a **With** statement.

Remarks

Note   When executed, the **End** statement resets all module-level variables and all static local variables in all modules. If you need to preserve the value of these variables, use **Stop** instead. You can then resume execution while preserving the value of those variables.

See Also

Exit Statement, **Function** Statement, **If...Then...Else** Statement, **Property Get** Statement, **Property Let** Statement, **Property Set** Statement, **Select Case** Statement, **Stop** Statement, **Sub** Statement, **Type** Statement, **With** Statement.

Example

This example uses the **End** Statement to end code execution, a **Select Case** block, and a **Sub** procedure.

```
Sub EndStatementDemo()
    For Number = 1 To 2                 ' Loop 2 times.
        Select Case Number              ' Evaluate Number.
            Case 1                      ' If Number equals 1.
                Debug.Print Number      ' Print value to Debug window.
            Case Else                   ' If Number does not equal 1.
                End                     ' Terminate procedure execution.
        End Select                      ' End of Select Case Statement.
    Next Number
End Sub                                 ' End of Sub procedure.
```

EOF Function

Description   Returns a value that indicates whether the end of a file has been reached.

Syntax   **EOF(***filenumber***)**

Elements   The *filenumber* named argument is any valid file number.

Remarks   Use **EOF** to avoid an error when attempting to get input past the end of a file.

False is returned unless the end of the file has been reached; then **True** is returned. When used with files opened for **Random** or **Binary** access, **EOF** returns **False** unless the last executed **Get** statement is unable to read an entire record; then **True** is returned.

See Also   **Loc** Function, **LOF** Function, **Open** Statement.

Example   This example uses the **EOF** function to detect the end of a file. For purposes of this example, assume that MyFile is a text file with a few lines of text.

```
Open "MyFile" For Input As #1       ' Open file for input.
Do While Not EOF(1)                 ' Check for end of file.
    Line Input #1, InputData        ' Read line of data.
    Debug.Print InputData           ' Print to Debug window.
Loop
Close #1                            ' Close file.
```

Eqv Operator

Description	Used to perform a logical equivalence on two expressions.
Syntax	*result = expression1* **Eqv** *expression2*
Elements	The **Eqv** operator syntax has these parts:

Part	Description
result	Any numeric variable.
expression1	Any expression.
expression2	Any expression.

Remarks

If either expression is a **Null**, *result* is also a **Null**. When neither expression is a **Null**, *result* is determined according to the following table:

True	**True**	**True**
True	**False**	**False**
False	**True**	**False**
False	**False**	**True**

The **Eqv** operator performs a bit-wise comparison of identically positioned bits in two numeric expressions and sets the corresponding bit in *result* according to the following truth table:

0	0	1
0	1	0
1	0	0
1	1	1

See Also

Operator Precedence.

Example

This example uses the **Eqv** operator to perform logical equivalence on two expressions.

```
A = 10: B = 8: C = 6 : D = Null  ' Initialize variables.
MyCheck = A > B Eqv B > C         ' Returns True.
MyCheck = B > A Eqv B > C         ' Returns False.
MyCheck = A > B Eqv B > D         ' Returns Null.
MyCheck = A Eqv B                 ' Returns -3 (bit-wise comparison).
```

Erase Statement

Description   Reinitializes the elements of fixed-size arrays and deallocates dynamic-array storage space.

Syntax   **Erase** *arraylist*

Elements   The *arraylist* argument is one or more comma-delimited array variables to be erased.

Remarks   It is important to know whether an array is fixed-size (ordinary) or dynamic because **Erase** behaves differently depending on the type of array. No memory is recovered for fixed-size arrays. **Erase** sets the elements of a fixed array as follows:

Type of array	Effect of Erase on fixed-array elements
Fixed numeric array	Sets each element to zero.
Fixed string array (variable length)	Sets each element to zero-length ("").
Fixed string array (fixed length)	Sets each element to zero.
Fixed **Variant** array	Sets each element to **Empty**.
Array of user-defined types	Sets each element as if it were a separate variable.
Array of objects	Sets each element to the special value **Nothing**.

Erase frees the memory used by dynamic arrays. Before your program can refer to the dynamic array again, it must redeclare the array variable's dimensions using a **ReDim** statement.

See Also   **Array** Function, **Dim** Statement, **Private** Statement, **Public** Statement, **ReDim** Statement, **Static** Statement.

Example   This example uses the **Erase** statement to reinitialize the elements of fixed-size arrays and deallocate dynamic-array storage space.

```
' Declare array variables.
Dim NumArray(10) As Integer          ' Integer array.
Dim StrVarArray(10) As String        ' Variable-string array.
Dim StrFixArray(10) As String * 10   ' Fixed-string array.
Dim VarArray(10) As Variant          ' Variant array.
Dim DynamicArray() As Integer        ' Dynamic array.
ReDim DynamicArray(10)               ' Allocate storage space.
Erase NumArray                       ' Each element set to 0.
Erase StrVarArray                    ' Each element set to "".
Erase StrFixArray                    ' Each element set to 0.
Erase VarArray                       ' Each element set to Empty.
Erase DynamicArray                   ' Free memory used by array.
```

Err Function

Description   Returns a **Variant** of subtype **Error** containing an error number specified by the user.

Syntax   **CVErr**(*errornumber*)

Elements   The *errornumber* argument is any valid error number.

Remarks   Use the **CVErr** function to create user-defined errors in user-created procedures. For example, if you create a function that accepts several arguments and normally returns a string, you can have your function evaluate the input arguments to ensure they are within acceptable range. If they are not, it is likely that your function will not return what you expect. In this event, **CVErr** allows you to return an error number that tells you what action to take.

Note that implicit conversion of an **Error** is not allowed. For example, you can't directly assign the return value of **CVErr** to a non-**Variant** variable. However, you can perform an explicit conversion (using **CInt**, **CDbl**, and so on) of the value returned by **CVErr** and assign that to a variable of the appropriate data type.

See Also   Data Type Summary, **IsError** Function.

Err Statement

Description   Sets **Err** to a specific value.

Syntax   **Err** = *errornumber*

Elements   The *errornumber* argument can be any valid error number or 0, which means no run-time error occurred.

Remarks   **Err** is used to record whether a run-time error has occurred and identifies the error. Use the **Err** statement to set **Err** to a nonzero, whole number to communicate error information between procedures. For example, you might use one of the unassigned run-time error numbers as an application-specific error number. To determine which error numbers are being used, use the **Error** function, the **Error** statement, or both. To avoid conflict with existing error numbers, create user-defined errors by defining your first error at 65,535 and work down from there.

You can also set **Err** to 0 using any form of the **Resume** or **On Error** statement or by executing an **Exit Sub**, **Exit Function** or **Exit Property** statement within an error handler. In addition, the **Error** statement can set **Err** to any value to simulate any run-time error.

See Also   **Err**, **Erl** Functions; **Error** Function; **Error** Statement.

Example   This example shows how the **Err** statement is used to clear an error by setting **Err** to 0. Error number 55 is generated to illustrate its usage.

```
On Error Resume Next          ' Enable error handling.
Open "TESTFILE" For Output as #1 ' Open file for output.
Kill "TESTFILE"               ' Attempt to delete open file.
Select Case Err               ' Evaluate Error Number.
   Case 55                    ' "File already open" error.
      Close #1                ' Close open file.
      Kill "TESTFILE"         ' Delete file.
      Err = 0                 ' Reset Err to 0.
   Case Else
      ' Handle other situations here...
End Select
```

Err, Erl Functions

Description   Returns error status.

Syntax   **Err**

Erl

Remarks .   After an error occurs, the **Err** function returns a number that is the run-time error number, identifying the error. The **Erl** function returns a number that is the line number of the line in which the error occurred, or the numbered line most closely preceding it.

Because **Err** and **Erl** return meaningful values only after an error has occurred, they are usually used in error-handling routines to determine the error and corrective action. Both **Err** and **Erl** are reset to 0 after any form of the **Resume** or **On Error** statement and after an **Exit Sub** or **Exit Function** statement within an error-handling routine.

Caution If you set up an error handler using **On Error GoTo** and that error handler calls another procedure, the value of **Err** and **Erl** may be reset to 0. To make sure that the value doesn't change, assign the values of **Err** or **Erl** to variables before calling another procedure or before executing **Resume, On Error, Exit Sub, Exit Function**, or **Exit Property**.

You can directly set the value returned by the **Err** function using the **Err** statement. You can set values for both **Err** and **Erl** indirectly using the **Error** statement.

The **Erl** function returns only a line number, not a line label, located at or before the line producing the error. Line numbers greater than 65,529 are treated as line labels and can't be returned by **Erl**. If your procedure has no line numbers, or if there is no line number before the point at which an error occurs, **Erl** returns 0.

See Also   **Err** Statement, **Error** Function, **Error** Statement, **On Error** Statement, **Resume** Statement.

Example   This example shows an error-handling routine which uses the **Err** and **Erl** functions. If there are no additional errors, **Err** returns error number 11 and **Erl** returns line 1030.

```
Sub ErrDemo()
1010  On Error GoTo ErrorHandler ' Set up an error handler.
1020  B = 1: C = 0               ' Initialize variables.
1030  A = B \ C                  ' Cause a "Division by zero" error.
1040  Exit Sub
ErrorHandler:                    ' Error handler.
    ErrorNumber = Err            ' Get run-time error number.
    ErrorLine = Erl              ' Get line number.
    Resume Next                  ' Resume execution at next line.
End Sub
```

Error Function

Description   Returns the error message that corresponds to a given error number.

Syntax   **Error**[(*errornumber*)]

Elements   The *errornumber* argument can be any valid error number. If *errornumber* is not defined, an error occurs. If omitted, the message corresponding to the most recent run-time error is returned. If no run-time error has occurred, **Error** returns a zero-length string (**""**).

Remarks   Use the **Err** function to return the error number for the most recent run-time error.

See Also   **Err**, **Erl** Functions; **Error** Statement.

Example   This example uses the **Error** function to print error messages that correspond to the specified error numbers.

```
For ErrorNumber = 61 To 64       ' Loop through values 61 - 64.
    Debug.Print Error(ErrorNumber)  ' Print error to Debug window.
Next ErrorNumber
```

Error Statement

Description	Simulates the occurrence of an error.
Syntax	**Error** *errornumber*
Elements	The *errornumber* can be any valid error number.
Remarks	If *errornumber* is defined, the **Error** statement simulates the occurrence of that error; that is, it sets the value of **Err** to *errornumber*.

To define your own error numbers, use a number greater than any of the standard error numbers. To avoid conflict with existing error numbers, create user-defined errors by defining your first error at 65,535 and work down from there.

If an **Error** statement is executed when no error-handling routine is enabled, an error message is displayed and execution stops. If the **Error** statement specifies an error number that is not used, an error message is displayed.

See Also	**Err**, **Erl** Functions; **Error** Function; **On Error** Statement; **Resume** Statement.
Example	This example uses the **Error** statement to simulate error 11.

```
On Error Resume Next' Enable error handling.
Error 11            ' Simulate the "Division by zero" error.
```

Exit Statement

Description	Exits a block of **Do...Loop**, **For...Next**, **Function**, **Sub**, or **Property** code.
Syntax	**Exit Do**
	Exit For
	Exit Function
	Exit Property
	Exit Sub
Elements	The **Exit** statement syntax has these forms:

Statement	Description
Exit Do	Provides a way to exit a **Do...Loop** statement. It can be used only inside a **Do...Loop** statement. **Exit Do** transfers control to the statement following the **Loop** statement. When used within nested **Do...Loop** statements, **Exit Do** transfers control to the loop that is one nested level above the loop where it occurs.
Exit For	Provides a way to exit a **For** loop. It can be used only in a **For...Next** or **For Each...Next** loop. **Exit For** transfers control to the statement following the **Next** statement. When used within nested **For** loops, **Exit For** transfers control to the loop that is one nested level above the loop where it occurs.
Exit Function	Immediately exits the **Function** procedure in which it appears. Execution continues with the statement following the statement that called the **Function**.
Exit Property	Immediately exits the **Property** procedure in which it appears. Execution continues with the statement following the statement that called the **Property** procedure.
Exit Sub	Immediately exits the **Sub** procedure in which it appears. Execution continues with the statement following the statement that called the **Sub**.

Remarks

Do not confuse **Exit** statements with **End** statements. **Exit** does not define the end of a structure.

See Also

Do...Loop Statement, **End** Statement, **For...Next** Statement, **Function** Statement, **Property Get** Statement, **Property Let** Statement, **Property Set** Statement, **Stop** Statement, **Sub** Statement.

Example

This example uses the **Exit** statement to exit a **For...Next** loop, a **Do...Loop**, and a **Sub** procedure.

```
Sub ExitStatementDemo()
    Do                              ' Set up infinite loop.
    For I = 1 To 1000               ' Loop 1000 times.
    MyNum = Int(Rnd * 1000)         ' Generate random numbers.
    Select Case MyNum               ' Evaluate random number.
    Case 7: Exit For                ' If 7, exit For...Next.
    Case 29: Exit Do                ' If 29, exit Do...Loop.
    Case 54: Exit Sub               ' If 54, exit Sub procedure.
    End Select
    Next I
    Loop
End Sub
```

Exp Function

Description   Returns *e* (the base of natural logarithms) raised to a power.

Syntax   **Exp(*number*)**

Elements   The ***number*** named argument can be any valid numeric expression.

Remarks   If the value of ***number*** exceeds 709.782712893, an error occurs. The constant *e* is approximately 2.718282.

Note The Exp function complements the action of the Log function and is sometimes referred to as the antilogarithm.

See Also   Derived Math Functions, **Log** Function.

Example   This example uses the **Exp** function to return *e* raised to a power.

```
' Define angle in radians.
MyAngle = 1.3
' Calculate hyperbolic sine.
MyHSin = (Exp(MyAngle) - Exp(- 1 * MyAngle)) / 2
```

FieldID Property

Applies To   **Cell** Object.

Description   Returns the identification number of the task or resource field in the active cell.

Syntax   *object*.**FieldID**

Elements   The **FieldID** property syntax has the following parts:

Part	Description
object	An object expression that evaluates to an object in the Applies To list.
FieldID	A constant that specifies the returned field.

The *FieldID* property has these settings:

pjTaskActualCost	7	Actual Cost
pjTaskActualDuration	28	Actual Duration

pjTaskActualFinish	42	Actual Finish
pjTaskActualStart	41	Actual Start
pjTaskActualWork	2	Actual Work
pjTaskBaselineCost	6	Baseline Cost
pjTaskBaselineDuration	27	Baseline Duration
pjTaskBaselineFinish	44	Baseline Finish
pjTaskBaselineStart	43	Baseline Start
pjTaskBaselineWork	1	Baseline Work
pjTaskBCWP	11	BCWP
pjTaskBCWS	12	BCWS
pjTaskConfirmed	110	Confirmed
pjTaskConstraintDate	18	Constraint Date
pjTaskConstraintType	17	Constraint Type
pjTaskContact	112	Contact
pjTaskCost	5	Cost
pjTaskCost1	106	Cost1
pjTaskCost2	107	Cost2
pjTaskCost3	108	Cost3
pjTaskCostVariance	9	Cost Variance
pjTaskCreated	93	Created
pjTaskCritical	19	Critical
pjTaskCV	83	CV
pjTaskDelay	20	Delay
pjTaskDuration	29	Duration
pjTaskDuration1	103	Duration1
pjTaskDuration2	104	Duration2
pjTaskDuration3	105	Duration3
pjTaskDurationVariance	30	Duration Variance
pjTaskEarlyFinish	38	Early Finish
pjTaskEarlyStart	37	Early Start
pjTaskFinish	36	Finish
pjTaskFinish1	53	Finish1
pjTaskFinish2	56	Finish2
pjTaskFinish3	59	Finish3
pjTaskFinish4	62	Finish4
pjTaskFinish5	65	Finish5

pjTaskFinishVariance	46	Finish Variance
pjTaskFixedCost	8	Fixed Cost
pjTaskFixedDuration	34	Fixed (Duration)
pjTaskFlag1	72	Flag1
pjTaskFlag10	81	Flag10
pjTaskFlag2	73	Flag2
pjTaskFlag3	74	Flag3
pjTaskFlag4	75	Flag4
pjTaskFlag5	76	Flag5
pjTaskFlag6	77	Flag6
pjTaskFlag7	78	Flag7
pjTaskFlag8	79	Flag8
pjTaskFlag9	80	Flag9
pjTaskFreeSlack	21	Free Slack
pjTaskHideBar	109	Hide Bar
pjTaskID	23	ID
pjTaskLateFinish	40	Late Finish
pjTaskLateStart	39	Late Start
pjTaskLinkedFields	98	Linked Fields
pjTaskMarked	71	Marked
pjTaskMilestone	24	Milestone
pjTaskName	14	Name
pjTaskNotes	15	Notes
pjTaskNumber1	87	Number1
pjTaskNumber2	88	Number2
pjTaskNumber3	89	Number3
pjTaskNumber4	90	Number4
pjTaskNumber5	91	Number5
pjTaskObjects	97	Objects
pjTaskOutlineLevel	85	Outline Level
pjTaskOutlineNumber	102	Outline Number
pjTaskPercentComplete	32	% Complete
pjTaskPercentWorkComplete	33	% Work Complete
pjTaskPredecessors	47	Predecessors
pjTaskPriority	25	Priority
pjTaskProject	84	Project

pjTaskRemainingCost	10	Remaining Cost
pjTaskRemainingDuration	31	Remaining Duration
pjTaskRemainingWork	4	Remaining Work
pjTaskResourceGroup	113	Resource Group
pjTaskResourceInitials	50	Resource Initials
pjTaskResourceNames	49	Resource Names
pjTaskResume	99	Resume
pjTaskResumeNoEarlierThan	101	Resume No Earlier Than
pjTaskRollup	82	Rollup
pjTaskSheetNotes	94	Sheet Notes
pjTaskStart	35	Start
pjTaskStart1	52	Start1
pjTaskStart2	55	Start2
pjTaskStart3	58	Start3
pjTaskStart4	61	Start4
pjTaskStart5	64	Start5
pjTaskStartVariance	45	Start Variance
pjTaskStop	100	Stop
pjTaskSubproject	26	Subproject File
pjTaskSuccessors	48	Successors
pjTaskSummary	92	Summary
pjTaskSV	13	SV
pjTaskText1	51	Text1
pjTaskText10	70	Text10
pjTaskText2	54	Text2
pjTaskText3	57	Text3
pjTaskText4	60	Text4
pjTaskText5	63	Text5
pjTaskText6	66	Text6
pjTaskText7	67	Text7
pjTaskText8	68	Text8
pjTaskText9	69	Text9
pjTaskTotalSlack	22	Total Slack
pjTaskUniqueID	86	Unique ID
pjTaskUniquePredecessors	95	Unique ID Predecessors
pjTaskUniqueSuccessors	96	Unique ID Successors

pjTaskUpdateNeeded	111	Update Needed
pjTaskWBS	16	WBS
pjTaskWork	0	Work
pjTaskWorkVariance	3	Work Variance
pjResourceAccrueAt	19	Accrue At
pjResourceActualCost	11	Actual Cost
pjResourceActualWork	14	Actual Work
pjResourceBaseCalendar	5	Base Calendar
pjResourceBaselineCost	17	Baseline Cost
pjResourceBaselineWork	15	Baseline Work
pjResourceCode	10	Code
pjResourceCost	12	Cost
pjResourceCostPerUse	18	Cost Per Use
pjResourceCostVariance	24	Cost Variance
pjResourceEMailAddress	35	Email address
pjResourceGroup	3	Group
pjResourceID	0	ID
pjResourceInitials	2	Initials
pjResourceLinkedFields	34	Linked Fields
pjResourceMaxUnits	4	Max Units
pjResourceName	1	Name
pjResourceNotes	20	Notes
pjResourceObjects	33	Objects
pjResourceOverallocated	25	Overallocated
pjResourceOvertimeRate	7	Overtime Rate
pjResourceOvertimeWork	16	Overtime Work
pjResourcePeakUnits	26	Peak
pjResourcePercentWorkComplete	29	% Work Complete
pjResourceRemainingCost	21	Remaining Cost
pjReosurceRemainingWork	22	Remaining Work
pjResourceSheetNotes	28	Sheet Notes
pjResourceStandardRate	6	Standard Rate
pjResourceText1	8	Text1
pjResourceText2	9	Text2
pjResourceText3	30	Text3
pjResourceText4	31	Text4

pjResourceText5	32	Text5
pjResourceUniqueID	27	Unique ID
pjResourceWork	13	Work
pjResourceWorkVariance	23	Work Variance

See Also   **FieldIDList** Method, **FieldName** Property, **FieldNameList** Method, **GetField** Method, **SetField** Method.

FieldIDList Method

Applies To   **Selection** Object.

Description   Returns a field identification number or all field identification numbers for the selected fields.

Syntax   *object*.**FieldIDList**[(*index*)]

Elements   The **FieldIDList** method syntax has the following object qualifier and named arguments:

Part	Description
bject	An object expression that evaluates to an object in the Applies To list.
index	A numeric expression that specifies the index of the *object*.

See Also   **ActiveCell** Property, **ActiveSelection** Property, **FieldID** Property, **GetField** Method, **List** Object, **SetField** Method.

FieldName Property

Applies To   **Cell** Object.

Description   Returns the name of the field in the active cell.

Syntax   *object*.**FieldName**

Elements   The *object* placeholder is an object expression that evaluates to an object in the Applies To list.

See Also   **FieldID** Property, **FieldIDList** Method.

FieldNameList Method

Applies To   **Selection** Object.

Description   Returns the field names for all selected fields.

Syntax   *object*.**FieldNameList**

Elements   The *object* placeholder is an object expression that evaluates to an object in the Applies To list.

See Also   **ActiveCell** Property, **ActiveSelection** Property, **FieldName** Property, **List** Object.

FileAttr Function

Description   Returns file mode or operating system file handle information for files opened using the **Open** statement.

Syntax   **FileAttr(*filenumber,returnType*)**

Elements   The **FileAttr** function syntax has these named-argument parts:

Part	Description
filenumber	Any valid file number.
returnType	Number indicating the type of information to return: specify **1** to return a value indicating the file mode; specify **2** to return the operating system file handle.

Return Values   When the *returnType* argument is 1, the following return values indicate the file mode:

Value	File Mode
1	Input
2	Output
4	Random
8	Append
32	Binary

See Also   **GetAttr** Function, **Open** Statement, **SetAttr** Statement.

Example

This example uses the **FileAttr** function to return the file mode and file handle of an open file.

```
FileNum = 1                          ' Assign file number.
Open "TESTFILE" For Append As FileNum    ' Open file.
Handle = FileAttr(FileNum, 1)        ' Returns 8 (Append file mode).
Mode = FileAttr(FileNum, 2)          ' Returns file handle.
Close FileNum                        ' Close file.
```

FileClose Method

Applies To

Application Object.

Description

Closes the active project.

Syntax

[*object*.]**FileClose** [*save, noAuto*]

Elements

The **FileClose** method syntax has the following object qualifier and named arguments:

Part	Description
object	An object expression that evaluates to an object in the Applies To list.
save	A constant that specifies whether to save the active project before closing it. If you omit the *save* argument, Microsoft Project prompts the user to save the project.
noAuto	A Boolean expression that specifies whether to run the Auto_Close macro if it exists. By default, the *noAuto* value is **False**. Optional.

The *save* argument has these settings:

pjDoNotSave	0	Changes to the file are not saved.
pjSave	1	Changes to the file are saved.
pjPromptSave	2	The user is prompted to save changes to the file.

See Also

FileCloseAll Method, **FileOpen** Method.

Example

The following example saves and closes the active project.

```
Sub SaveAndCloseActiveProject()
    FileClose(1)
End Sub
```

FileCloseAll Method

Applies To	**Application** Object.
Description	Closes all projects.
Syntax	[*object.*]**FileCloseAll** [*save*]
Elements	The **FileCloseAll** method syntax has the following object qualifier and named arguments:

Part	Description
object	An object expression that evaluates to an object in the Applies To list.
save	A constant that specifies whether to save all project files before closing them. If you omit the *save* argument, Microsoft Project prompts the user to save each file.

The *save* argument has these settings:

pjDoNotSave	0	Changes to the open files are not saved.
pjSave	1	Changes to the open files are saved.
pjPromptSave	2	The user is prompted to save changes to each file.

See Also	**FileClose** Method, **FileOpen** Method.
Example	The following example closes all open projects, saving them if necessary.

```
Sub CloseAndSaveOpenProjects()
    FileCloseAll(1)
End Sub
```

FileCopy Statement

Description	Copies a file.
Syntax	**FileCopy** *source*, *destination*
Elements	The **FileCopy** statement syntax has these named argument parts:

Part	Description
source	String expression that specifies the name of the file to be copied—may include directory or folder, and drive.
destination	String expression that specifies the target file name—may include directory or folder, and drive.

Remarks Open files can only be copied for read-only access.

See Also Kill Statement, Name Statement.

Example This example uses the **FileCopy** statement to copy one file to another. For purposes of this example, assume that SRCFILE is a file containing some data.

```
SourceFile = "SRCFILE"              ' Define source file name.
DestinationFile = "DESTFILE"        ' Define target file name.
FileCopy SourceFile, DestinationFile ' Copy source to target.
```

FileDateTime Function

Description Returns a date that indicates the date and time when a file was created or last modified .

Syntax **FileDateTime(*pathname*)**

Elements The *pathname* named argument is a string expression that specifies a file name—may include directory or folder, and drive.

See Also **FileLen** Function, **GetAttr** Function.

Example This example uses the **FileDateTime** function to get the date and time when a file was created or last modified. The format of the date and time displayed is based on the locale settings of your system.

```
' Assume TESTFILE was last modified on February 12 1993 at 4:35:47 PM.
' Assume United States/English locale settings.
MyStamp = FileDateTime("TESTFILE")   ' Returns "2/12/93 4:35:47 PM".
```

FileExit Method

Applies To **Application** Object.

Description Quits Microsoft Project.

Syntax [*object.*]**FileExit** [*save*]

Elements	The **FileExit** method syntax has the following object qualifier and named arguments:

Part	Description
object	An object expression that evaluates to an object in the Applies To list.
save	A constant that specifies whether to save open project files before quitting Microsoft Project. If you omit the *save* argument, Microsoft Project prompts the user to save each file.

The *save* argument has these settings:

pjDoNotSave	0	Changes to open files are not saved.
pjSave	1	Changes to open files are saved.
pjPromptSave	2	The user is prompted to save changes to open files.

Remarks	This method applies to Microsoft Project for Microsoft Windows.
See Also	**FileClose** Method, **FileCloseAll** Method.
Example	The following example quits Microsoft Project after prompting the user to save each open project.

```
Sub QuitProject()
    FileExit 2
End Sub
```

FileLen Function

Description	Returns the length of a file in bytes.
Syntax	**FileLen(*pathname*)**
Elements	The *pathname* named argument is a string expression that specifies a file name— may include directory or folder, and drive.
Remarks	If the specified file is open when the **FileLen** function is called, the value returned represents the last saved disk size of the file.
	To obtain the length of an open file, use the **LOF** function.
See Also	**FileDateTime** Function, **GetAttr** Function, **LOF** Function.
Example	This example uses the **FileLen** function to return the length of a file in bytes. For purposes of this example, assume that TESTFILE is a file containing some data.

```
MySize = FileLen("TESTFILE") ' Returns file length (bytes).
```

FileLoadLast Method

Applies To	**Application** Object.
Description	Opens one of the last four most recently used files.
Syntax	[*object*.]**FileLoadLast** [*number*]
Elements	The **FileLoadLast** method syntax has the following object qualifier and named arguments:

Part	Description
object	An object expression that evaluates to an object in the Applies To list.
number	A numeric expression from 1 to 4 that specifies which of the last four most recently used files to open.

See Also	**FileOpen** Method.
Example	The following example opens the four most recently used files.

```
Sub OpenThe4MRUFiles()
    Dim I        ' Index used in For...Next loop
    For I = 1 to 4
        FileLoadLast(I)
    Next I
End Sub
```

FileNew Method

Applies To	**Application** Object.
Description	Creates a new project.
Syntax	[*object*.]**FileNew** [*summaryInfo*]
Elements	The **FileNew** method syntax has the following object qualifier and named arguments:

Part	Description
object	An object expression that evaluates to an object in the Applies To list. Optional.
summaryInfo	A Boolean expression that specifies whether to display the Summary Info box when creating the project. By default, the *summaryInfo* argument equals the corresponding setting in the General section of the Options dialog box. Optional.

See Also   **FileOpen** Method.

FileOpen Method

Applies To   **Application** Object.

Description   Opens a project.

Syntax   [*object*.]**FileOpen** *name*[, *readOnly*, *merge*, *taskInformation*, *table*, *sheet*, *noAuto*]

Elements   The **FileOpen** method syntax has the following object qualifier and named arguments:

Part	Description
object	An object expression that evaluates to an object in the Applies To list. Optional.
name	A string expression that specifies the name of the project file to open. Required.
readOnly	A Boolean expression that specifies whether to open the file as a read-only project. Optional.
merge	A constant that specifies whether to automatically merge the file with the active project. By default, the *merge* argument is **pjDoNotMerge**. Optional.
taskInformation	A Boolean expression that specifies whether the file contains information on tasks or resources (for a project saved under a non-Microsoft Project file format). By default, the *taskInformation* argument is **True** if the active view is a task view and **False** otherwise. Optional.
table	A string expression that specifies the name of a table in which to place the resource or task information (for a project saved under a non-Microsoft Project file format). By default, the *table* argument equals the name of the active table. Optional.

Part	Description
sheet	A string expression that specifies which sheet to read when opening a workbook created in Microsoft Excel version 5.0 or later.
noAuto	A Boolean expression that specifies whether to run the Auto_Open macro if it exists. By default, the *noAuto* value is **False**. Optional.

The *merge* argument has these settings:

pjDoNotMerge	0	Don't merge.
pjMerge	1	Merge.
pjPrompt	2	Prompt user to merge.

See Also   **FileClose** Method, **FileCloseAll** Method, **FileExit** Method, **FileLoadLast** Method, **FileNew** Method, **FilePageSetup** Method, **FilePrint** Method, **FilePrintPreview** Method, **FilePrintSetup** Method, **FileSave** Method, **FileSaveAs** Method, **FileSaveWorkspace** Method.

FilePageSetup Method

Applies To   **Application** Object.

Description   Displays the Page Setup dialog box. Equivalent to choosing Page Setup from the File menu.

Syntax   [*object*.]**FilePageSetup** [*name*]

Elements   The **FilePageSetup** method syntax has the following object qualifier and named arguments:

Part	Description
bject	An object expression that evaluates to an object in the Applies To list. Optional.
name	A string expression that specifies the name of the file to be used. By default, the *name* argument equals the active file. Optional.

See Also   **FilePrintPreview** Method, **FilePrintSetup** Method, **Reports** Method.

FilePageSetupCalendar Method

Description   Sets up the Calendar for printing.

Syntax   [*object*.]**FilePageSetupCalendar** [*name, monthsPerPage, weeksPerPage, screenWeekHeight, onlyDaysInMonth, onlyWeeksInMonth, monthPreviews, monthTitle, additionalTasks, groupAdditionalTasks, printNotes*]

Elements   The **FilePageSetupCalendar** method syntax has the following object qualifier and named arguments:

Part	Description
object	An object expression that evaluates to an object in the Applies To list. Optional.
name	A string expression that specifies the name of the view or report to edit. Optional.
monthsPerPage	A numeric expression that specifies the number of months (1 or 2) to print on each page. Optional.
weeksPerPage	A numeric expression that specifies the number of weeks to print on each page. Optional.
screenWeekHeight	A Boolean expression that specifies whether to use the week height displayed on screen for the printout. Optional.
onlyDaysInMonth	A Boolean expression that specifies whether to print only days in the month. The *onlyDaysInMonth* argument is ignored unless you specify a value for the *monthsPerPage* argument. Optional.
	True Prints only days in the month. **False** Prints the days at the end of the previous month and at the start of the next month in addition to the days in the month.
onlyWeeksInMonth	A Boolean expression that specifies whether to print only the weeks that are fully contained in the month. The *onlyWeeksInMonth* argument is ignored unless you specify a value for the *monthsPerPage* argument. Optional.
	True Prints only weeks that are fully contained in the month. **False** Prints weeks that have one or more days in the month.

Part	Description
monthPreviews	A Boolean expression that specifies whether to print the preview calendars for the previous and next months. Optional.
monthTitle	A Boolean expression that specifies whether to print the month title. Optional.
additionalTasks	A Boolean expression that specifies whether to print tasks that do not fit on the Calendar. (Additional tasks appear at the end of the printout.) Optional.
groupAdditionalTasks	A Boolean expression that specifies whether to group additional tasks by day. Optional.
printNotes	A Boolean expression that specifies whether to print the notes associated with each task. Optional.

See Also **FilePageSetup** Method, **FilePageSetupCalendarText** Method, **FilePageSetupFooter** Method, **FilePageSetupFooterText** Method, **FilePageSetupHeader** Method, **FilePageSetupHeaderText** Method, **FilePageSetupLegend** Method, **FilePageSetupLegendText** Method, **FilePageSetupMargins** Method, **FilePageSetupPage** Method, **FilePageSetupView** Method.

FilePageSetupCalendarText Method

Applies To **Application** Object.

Description Formats calendar text for printing.

Syntax [*object*.]**FilePageSetupCalendarText** [*name, item, font, size, bold, italic, underline, color*]

Elements The **FilePageSetupCalendarText** method syntax has the following object qualifier and named arguments:

Part	Description
object	An object expression that evaluates to an object in the Applies To list. Optional.
name	A string expression that specifies the name of the view or report to edit. Optional.
item	A constant that specifies the text item to format. Optional.
font	A string expression that specifies the font name. Optional.
size	A numeric expression that specifies the font size. Optional.

Part	Description
object	An object expression that evaluates to an object in the Applies To list. Optional.
bold	A Boolean expression that specifies whether the text is bold. Optional.
italic	A Boolean expression that specifies whether the text is italic. Optional.
underline	A Boolean expression that specifies whether the text is underlined. Optional.
color	A constant that specifies the color of the text. Optional.

The *item* argument has these settings:

pjAll	0	All
pjMonthlyTitles	1	Monthly titles
pjPreviousNextMonths	2	Previous and next months
pjAdditionalTasks	3	Additional tasks

The *color* argument has these settings:

pjBlack	0	Black
pjRed	1	Red
pjYellow	2	Yellow
pjLime	3	Lime
pjAqua	4	Aqua
pjBlue	5	Blue
pjFuchsia	6	Fuchsia
pjWhite	7	White
pjMaroon	8	Maroon
pjGreen	9	Green
pjOlive	10	Olive
pjNavy	11	Navy
pjPurple	12	Purple
pjTeal	13	Teal
pjGray	14	Gray
pjSilver	15	Silver

See Also   **FilePageSetup** Method, **FilePageSetupCalendar** Method, **FilePageSetupFooter** Method, **FilePageSetupFooterText** Method, **FilePageSetupHeader** Method, **FilePageSetupHeaderText** Method, **FilePageSetupLegend** Method, **FilePageSetupLegendText** Method, **FilePageSetupMargins** Method, **FilePageSetupPage** Method, **FilePageSetupView** Method.

FilePageSetupFooter Method

Description   Sets up footers for printing.

Syntax   [*object*.]**FilePageSetupFooter**[*name*, *left*, *center*, *right*]

Elements   The **FilePageSetupFooter** method syntax has the following object qualifier and named arguments:

Part	Description
object	An object expression that evaluates to an object in the Applies To list. Optional.
name	A string expression that specifies the name of the view or report for which to set up footers for printing. Optional.
left	A string expression that specifies the text to display in the left footer. Optional.
center	A string expression that specifies the text to display in the center footer. Optional.
right	A string expression that specifies the text to display in the right footer. Optional.

See Also   **FilePageSetup** Method, **FilePageSetupCalendar** Method, **FilePageSetupCalendarText** Method, **FilePageSetupFooterText** Method, **FilePageSetupHeader** Method, **FilePageSetupHeaderText** Method, **FilePageSetupLegend** Method, **FilePageSetupLegendText** Method, **FilePageSetupMargins** Method, **FilePageSetupPage** Method, **FilePageSetupView** Method.

FilePageSetupFooterText Method

Applies To
    Application Object.

Description
    Formats footer text for printing.

Syntax
    [*object*.]**FilePageSetupFooterText** [*name, alignment, item, font, size, bold, italic, underline, color*]

Elements
    The **FilePageSetupFooterText** method syntax has the following object qualifier and named arguments:

Part	Description
object	An object expression that evaluates to an object in the Applies To list. Optional.
name	A string expression that specifies the name of the view or report for which to format footer text. Optional.
alignment	A constant that specifies which footer text to format. Optional.
item	A constant that specifies the text item to format. Optional.
font	A string expression that specifies the font name. Optional.
size	A numeric expression that specifies the font size. Optional.
bold	A Boolean expression that specifies whether the text is bold. By default, the *bold* argument is **False**. Optional.
italic	A Boolean expression that specifies whether the text is italic. By default, the *italic* argument is **False**. Optional.
underline	A Boolean expression that specifies whether the text is underlined. By default, the *underline* argument is **False**. Optional.
color	A constant that specifies the text color. Optional.

The *alignment* argument has these settings:

pjLeft	0	Align left.
pjCenter	1	Align center.
pjRight	2	Align right.

The *item* argument has these settings:

pjAll	0	Formats all footer lines.
pjLine1	1	Formats the first line of the footer.

The *color* argument has these settings:

pjBlack	0	Black
pjRed	1	Red
pjYellow	2	Yellow
pjLime	3	Lime
pjAqua	4	Aqua
pjBlue	5	Blue
pjFuchsia	6	Fuchsia
pjWhite	7	White
pjMaroon	8	Maroon
pjGreen	9	Green
pjOlive	10	Olive
pjNavy	11	Navy
pjPurple	12	Purple
pjTeal	13	Teal
pjGray	14	Gray
pjSilver	15	Silver

See Also

FilePageSetup Method, **FilePageSetupCalendar** Method, **FilePageSetupCalendarText** Method, **FilePageSetupFooter** Method, **FilePageSetupHeader** Method, **FilePageSetupHeaderText** Method, **FilePageSetupLegend** Method, **FilePageSetupLegendText** Method, **FilePageSetupMargins** Method, **FilePageSetupPage** Method, **FilePageSetupView** Method.

FilePageSetupHeader Method

Description   Sets up headers for printing.

Syntax   [*object.*]**FilePageSetupHeader** [*name*, *left*, *center*, *right*]

pjGray	14	Gray
pjSilver	15	Silver

See Also   **FilePageSetup** Method, **FilePageSetupCalendar** Method, **FilePageSetupCalendarText** Method, **FilePageSetupFooter** Method, **FilePageSetupFooterText** Method, **FilePageSetupHeader** Method, **FilePageSetupLegend** Method, **FilePageSetupLegendText** Method, **FilePageSetupMargins** Method, **FilePageSetupPage** Method, **FilePageSetupView** Method.

FilePageSetupLegend Method

Description   Sets up legends for printing.

Syntax   [*object.*]**FilePageSetupLegend** [*name, left, center, right, textWidth, legendOn*]

Elements   The **FilePageSetupLegend** method syntax has the following object qualifier and named arguments:

Part	Description
object	An object expression that evaluates to an object in the Applies To list. Optional.
name	A string expression that specifies the name of the view or report for which to set up legend text for printing. Optional.
left	A string expression that specifies the text to display in the left legend. Optional.
center	A string expression that specifies the text to display in the center legend. Optional.
right	A string expression that specifies the text to display in the right legend. Optional.
textWidth	A numeric expression that specifies the width of the text, in inches or centimeters. Optional.
legendOn	A constant that specifies on which pages the legend appears. Optional.

The *legendOn* argument has these settings:

pjNone	0	Don't print legend.
pjAfterLastPage	1	Print legend after last page.
pjOnEveryPage	2	Print legend on every page.

See Also

FilePageSetup Method, **FilePageSetupCalendar** Method, **FilePageSetupCalendarText** Method, **FilePageSetupFooter** Method, **FilePageSetupFooterText** Method, **FilePageSetupHeader** Method, **FilePageSetupHeaderText** Method, **FilePageSetupLegendText** Method, **FilePageSetupMargins** Method, **FilePageSetupPage** Method, **FilePageSetupView** Method.

FilePageSetupLegendText Method

Applies To   **Application** Object.

Description   Formats legend text for printing.

Syntax   [*object*.]**FilePageSetupLegendText** [*name, alignment, item, font, size, bold, italic, underline, color*]

Elements   The **FilePageSetupLegendText** method syntax has the following object qualifier and named arguments:

Part	Description
object	An object expression that evaluates to an object in the Applies To list. Optional.
name	A string expression that specifies the name of the view or report for which to set up legend text for printing. Optional.
alignment	A constant that specifies which legend text to format. Optional.
item	A constant that specifies the text item to format. Optional.
font	A string expression that specifies the font name. Optional.
size	A numeric expression that specifies the font size. Optional.
bold	A Boolean expression that specifies whether the text is bold. Optional.
italic	A Boolean expression that specifies whether the text is italic. Optional.
underline	A Boolean expression that specifies whether the text is underlined. Optional.

Part	Description
color	A constant that specifies the text color. Optional.

The *alignment* argument has these settings:

pjLeft	0	Align left.
pjCenter	1	Align center.
pjRight	2	Align right.

The *item* argument has these settings:

pjAll	0	Formats all legend lines.
pjLine1	1	Formats the first line of the legend.
pjLine2	2	Formats the second line of the legend.
pjLine3	3	Formats the third line of the legend.

The *color* argument has these settings:

pjBlack	0	Black
pjRed	1	Red
pjYellow	2	Yellow
pjLime	3	Lime
pjAqua	4	Aqua
pjBlue	5	Blue
pjFuchsia	6	Fuchsia
pjWhite	7	White
pjMaroon	8	Maroon
pjGreen	9	Green
pjOlive	10	Olive
pjNavy	11	Navy
pjPurple	12	Purple
pjTeal	13	Teal
pjGray	14	Gray
pjSilver	15	Silver

See Also

FilePageSetup Method, **FilePageSetupCalendar** Method,
FilePageSetupCalendarText Method, **FilePageSetupFooter** Method,
FilePageSetupFooterText Method, **FilePageSetupHeader** Method,
FilePageSetupHeaderText Method, **FilePageSetupLegend** Method,
FilePageSetupMargins Method, **FilePageSetupPage** Method,
FilePageSetupView Method.

FilePageSetupMargins Method

Applies To   **Application** Object.

Description   Sets up margins for printing.

Syntax   [*object*.]**FilePageSetupMargins** [*name, top, bottom, left, right, borders*]

Elements   The **FilePageSetupMargins** method syntax has the following object qualifier and
named arguments:

Part	Description
object	An object expression that evaluates to an object in the Applies To list. Optional.
name	A string expression that specifies the name of the view or report for which to set up margins for printing. Optional.
top	A numeric expression that specifies the top margin, in inches or centimeters. Optional.
bottom	A numeric expression that specifies the bottom margin, in inches or centimeters. Optional.
left	A numeric expression that specifies the left margin, in inches or centimeters. Optional.
right	A numeric expression that specifies the right margin, in inches or centimeters. Optional.
borders	A constant that specifies where to print borders. Optional.

The *borders* argument has these settings:

pjNone	0	Don't print borders.
pjAroundEveryPage	1	Print borders on every page.
pjOutsidePages	2	Print borders around outside pages.

See Also   **FilePageSetup** Method, **FilePageSetupCalendar** Method,
FilePageSetupCalendarText Method, **FilePageSetupFooter** Method,
FilePageSetupFooterText Method, **FilePageSetupHeader** Method,
FilePageSetupHeaderText Method, **FilePageSetupLegend** Method,
FilePageSetupLegendText Method, **FilePageSetupPage** Method,
FilePageSetupView Method.

FilePageSetupPage Method

Applies To   **Application** Object.

Description   Sets up pages for printing.

Syntax   [*object.*]**FilePageSetupPage** [*name, portrait, percentScale, pagesTall,
pagesWide*]

Elements   The **FilePageSetupPage** method syntax has the following object qualifier and
named arguments:

Part	Description
object	An object expression that evaluates to an object in the Applies To list. Optional.
name	A string expression that specifies the name of the view or report for which to set up pages for printing. Optional.
portrait	A Boolean expression that specifies whether to print with portrait or landscape orientation. Optional.
percentScale	A numeric expression that specifies the scaling factor. Optional.
pagesTall	A numeric expression that specifies the height of the printout, in pages. Optional.
pagesWide	A numeric expression that specifies the width of the printout, in pages. Optional.

See Also   **FilePageSetup** Method, **FilePageSetupCalendar** Method,
FilePageSetupCalendarText Method, **FilePageSetupFooter** Method,
FilePageSetupFooterText Method, **FilePageSetupHeader** Method,
FilePageSetupHeaderText Method, **FilePageSetupLegend** Method,
FilePageSetupLegendText Method, **FilePageSetupMargins** Method,
FilePageSetupView Method.

FilePageSetupView Method

Applies To   **Application** Object.

Description   Sets up pages for printing.

Syntax   [*object.*]**FilePageSetupView** [*name, allSheetColumns, repeatColumns, printNotes, printBlankPages, bestPageFitTimescale*]

Elements   The **FilePageSetupView** method syntax has the following object qualifier and named arguments:

Part	Description
object	An object expression that evaluates to an object in the Applies To list. Optional.
name	A string expression that specifies the view or report for which to set up pages for printing. Optional.
allSheetColumns	A Boolean expression that specifies whether to print all table columns or visible table columns. Optional.
repeatColumns	A numeric expression that specifies the number of table columns to print on each page. Optional.
printNotes	A Boolean expression that specifies whether to print notes. Optional.
printBlankPages	A Boolean expression that specifies whether to print blank pages. Optional.
bestPageFitTimescale	A Boolean expression that specifies whether to adjust the timescale to exactly fill the last page. Optional.

See Also   **FilePageSetup** Method, **FilePageSetupCalendar** Method, **FilePageSetupCalendarText** Method, **FilePageSetupFooter** Method, **FilePageSetupFooterText** Method, **FilePageSetupHeader** Method, **FilePageSetupHeaderText** Method, **FilePageSetupLegend** Method, **FilePageSetupLegendText** Method, **FilePageSetupMargins** Method, **FilePageSetupPage** Method.

FilePrint Method

Applies To   **Application** Object.

Description	Prints the active view.
Syntax	[*object.*]**FilePrint** [*fromPage, toPage, pageBreaks, draft, copies, fromDate, toDate, onePageWide, preview, color*]
Elements	The **FilePrint** method syntax has the following object qualifier and named arguments:

Part	Description
bject	An object expression that evaluates to an object in the Applies To list. Optional.
fromPage	A numeric expression that specifies the first page to print. Optional.
toPage	A numeric expression that specifies the last page to print. Optional.
pageBreaks	A Boolean expression that specifies whether to use (**True**) or ignore (**False**) manual page breaks when printing. If you omit the *pageBreaks* argument, Microsoft Project uses manual page breaks. Optional.
draft	A Boolean expression that specifies whether to print the active view in draft mode. By default, the *draft* argument is **False**. Optional. This parameter applies to Microsoft Project for Microsoft Windows.
copies	A numeric expression that specifies the number of copies to print. Optional.
fromDate	A date expression that specifies the first date to print. Optional.
toDate	A date expression that specifies the last date to print. Optional.
onePageWide	A Boolean expression that specifies whether to print only the leftmost columns of the active view. By default, the *onePageWide* argument is **False**. Optional.
preview	A Boolean expression that specifies whether to preview or print the active view. By default, Microsoft Project prints the active view. Optional.
color	A Boolean expression that specifies whether to print the active view in color (**True**) or black and white (**False**). If you omit the *color* argument, Microsoft Project prints the active view in black and white.

See Also	**FilePageSetup** Method, **FilePrintPreview** Method, **FilePrintSetup** Method, **Reports** Method.
Example	The following example prints the active view without using manual page breaks.

```
Sub PrintViewWithoutPageBreaks()
    FilePrint pageBreaks := False
End Sub
```

FilePrintPreview Method

Applies To   **Application** Object.

Description   Provides a print preview of the active project.

Syntax   [*object*.]**FilePrintPreview**

Elements   The *object* placeholder is an object expression that evaluates to an object in the Applies To list.

Remarks   The **FilePrintPreview** method has the same effect as the Print Preview command on the File menu.

See Also   **FilePrint** Method, **FilePrintSetup** Method, **ReportPrint** Method, **ReportPrintPreview** Method.

FilePrintSetup Method

Applies To   **Application** Object.

Description   Specifies the active printer.

Syntax   [*object*.]**FilePrintSetup** [*printer*]

Elements   The **FilePrintSetup** method syntax has the following object qualifier and named argument:

Part	Description
object	An object expression that evaluates to an object in the Applies To list.
printer	A string expression that specifies the full name or port name of the active printer.

Remarks   This method applies to Microsoft Project for Microsoft Windows.

See Also   **FilePageSetup** Method, **FilePrint** Method, **FilePrintPreview** Method, **Reports** Method.

Example   The following example sets the active printer to the printer on the LPT1 port.

```
Sub SetActivePrinterToLPT1()
    FilePrintSetup("LPT1:")
End Sub
```

FileProperties Method

Applies To	**Application** Object.
Description	Displays the Properties dialog for the current project file.
Syntax	*object*.**FileProperties**
Elements	The *object* placeholder is any object expression that evaluates to an object in the Applies To list.
Remarks	See the appropriate VBA properties of the Project object which can be used to manipulate the values of these properties.
See Also	**BuiltinDocumentProperties** Property, **CustomDocumentProperties** Property, **Project** Property.

FileQuit Method

Applies To	**Application** Object.
Description	Quits Microsoft Project.
Syntax	[*object*.]**FileQuit** [*save*]
Elements	The **FileQuit** method syntax has the following object qualifier and named arguments:

Part	Description
object	An object expression that evaluates to an object in the Applies To list.
save	A constant that specifies whether to save open project files before quitting Microsoft Project. If you omit the *save* argument, Microsoft Project prompts the user to save each file.

The *save* argument has these settings:

pjDoNotSave	0	Changes to open files are not saved.
pjSave	1	Changes to open files are saved.
pjPromptSave	2	The user is prompted to save changes to open files.

Remarks	This method applies to Microsoft Project for the Macintosh.
See Also	**FileClose** Method, **FileCloseAll** Method.
Example	The following example quits Microsoft Project after prompting the user to save each open project.

```
Sub QuitProject()
    FileQuit() Save: = pjPromptSave
End Sub
```

FileSave Method

Applies To	**Application** Object.
Description	Saves the active project.
Syntax	[*object*.]**FileSave**
Elements	The *object* placeholder is an object expression that evaluates to an object in the Applies To list.
See Also	**FileNew** Method, **FileOpen** Method, **FileSaveAs** Method.

FileSaveAs Method

Applies To	**Application** Object.
Description	Saves the active project under a new filename and specifies save options.
Syntax	[*object*.]**FileSaveAs** *name*[, *format, backup, readOnly, taskInformation, filtered, table*]
Elements	The **FileSaveAs** method syntax has the following object qualifier and named arguments:

Part	Description
object	An object expression that evaluates to an object in the Applies To list. Optional.
name	A string expression that specifies the filename under which to save the active project. Required.
format	A constant that specifies the format of the file. By default, the *format* argument is **pjMPP**. Optional.

Part	Description
backup	A Boolean expression that specifies whether to create a backup of the file. Optional.
readOnly	A Boolean expression that specifies whether to prompt the user to open the file as a read-only project. By default, the *readOnly* argument is **False**. Optional.
taskInformation	A Boolean expression that specifies whether the file should contain information on tasks or resources (for a project saved under a non-Microsoft Project format). By default, the *taskInformation* argument is **True** if the active view is a task view and **False** otherwise. Optional.
filtered	A Boolean expression that specifies whether to save all tasks or resources or the filtered tasks or resources. By default, the *filtered* argument is **False**. Optional.
table	A string expression that specifies the name of the table containing the task or resource information (for a project saved under a non-Microsoft Project format). By default, the *table* argument equals the name of the active table. Optional.

The *format* argument has these settings:

pjMPP	0	Microsoft Project
pjMPX1	1	MPX 1.0
pjMPX3	2	MPX 3.0
pjTXT	3	Text
pjCSV	4	CSV
pjXLS	5	Microsoft Excel
pjWKS	6	Lotus 1-2-3. Applies to Microsoft Project for Microsoft Windows.
pjWK1	7	Lotus 1-2-3. Applies to Microsoft Project for Microsoft Windows.
pjWK3	8	Lotus 1-2-3. Applies to Microsoft Project for Microsoft Windows.
pjDB3	9	dBase 3. Applies to Microsoft Project for Microsoft Windows.
pjDB4	10	dBase 4. Applies to Microsoft Project for Microsoft Windows.
pjMPT	11	Template
pjMPX4	12	MPX 4.0
pjFOX	13	Microsoft FoxPro

See Also	**FileClose** Method, **FileCloseAll** Method, **FileExit** Method, **FileLoadLast** Method, **FileNew** Method, **FileOpen** Method, **FilePageSetup** Method, **FilePrint** Method, **FilePrintPreview** Method, **FilePrintSetup** Method, **FileSave** Method, **FileSaveWorkspace** Method.

FileSaveWorkspace Method

Applies To	**Application** Object.
Description	Saves a list of open files and the current settings in the Options dialog box.
Syntax	[*object.*]**FileSaveWorkspace** [*name*]
Elements	The **FileSaveWorkspace** method syntax has the following object qualifier and named arguments:

Part	Description
object	An object expression that evaluates to an object in the Applies To list.
name	A string expression that specifies the name of the file to create. If you omit the *name* argument, Microsoft Project prompts the user for the name of the file.

See Also	**FileSave** Method, **FileSaveAs** Method.
Example	The following example saves the workspace based upon the name of the first project file.

```
Sub SaveWorkspaceByProjectName()
    Dim WSName As String
    If InStr(Projects(1).Name, ".") Then
        WSName = Left$(Projects(1).Name, _
            Len(Projects(1).Name - 1)) + "W"
    Else
        WSName = Projects(1).Name + ".MPW"
    End If
    FileSaveWorkspace WSName
End Sub
```

FillDown Method

Applies To	**Application** Object.

Description	Fills the active cells with the values in the top row of the selection.
Syntax	[*object*.]**FillDown**
Elements	The *object* placeholder is an object expression that evaluates to an object in the Applies To list.
See Also	**EditCopy** Method, **EditPaste** Method.

FilterApply Method

Applies To	**Application** Object.
Description	Sets the current filter.
Syntax	[*object*.]**FilterApply** *name*[, *highlight*, *value1*, *value2*]
Elements	The **FilterApply** method syntax has the following object qualifier and named arguments:

Part	Description
object	An object expression that evaluates to an object in the Applies To list. Optional.
name	A string expression that specifies the name of the filter to use. Required.
highlight	A Boolean expression that specifies whether to highlight rows (**True**) or apply the filter (**False**). By default, the *highlight* argument is **False**. Optional.
value1	A string expression that specifies the first value to use when applying an interactive filter. Optional.
value2	A string expression that specifies the second value to use when applying an interactive filter. Optional.

See Also	**FilterEdit** Method, **Filters** Method, **OrganizerDeleteItem** Method.
Example	The following example highlights filtered items.

```
Sub HighlightCriticalTasks()
    FilterApply Name := "Critical", highlight := True
End Sub
```

FilterEdit Method

Applies To **Application** Object.

Description Edits a filter.

Syntax [*object.*]**FilterEdit** *name, taskFilter, test*[, *create, overwriteExisting, newName, fieldName, newFieldName, value, operation, showInMenu, showSummaryTasks*]

Elements The **FilterEdit** method syntax has the following object qualifier and named arguments:

Part	Description
object	An object expression that evaluates to an object in the Applies To list. Optional.
name	A string expression that specifies the name of a filter to edit, create, or copy. Required.
taskFilter	A Boolean expression that specifies whether the filter you specify with the *name* argument contains task or resource information. Required.
test	A string expression that specifies the filter criteria. Required.
create	A Boolean expression that specifies whether to create a new filter. By default, the *create* argument is **False**. Optional. The *create* argument has these settings:
	True A new filter is created. If the *newName* argument is **Empty**, the new filter is given the name you specify with the *name* argument. Otherwise, the new filter is a copy of the filter you specify with the *name* argument, and the new filter is given the name you specify with the *newName* argument.
	False A new filter is not created.
overwriteExisting	A Boolean expression that specifies whether to overwrite the existing filter with a new filter. By default, the *overwriteExisting* argument is **False**. Optional.

Part	Description
newName	A string expression that specifies a new name for the filter you specify with the *name* argument (*create* argument is **False**) or a name for the new filter you create (*create* argument is **True**). By default, the *newName* argument is **Empty**. If the *newName* argument is **Empty** and the *create* argument is **False**, the filter you specify with the *name* argument retains its current name. Optional.
fieldName	A string expression that specifies the name of a field to change. Optional.
newFieldName	A string expression that specifies a new name for the field you specify with the *fieldName* argument. Optional.
value	A string expression that specifies the value to compare with the value in the field you specify with the *fieldName* argument. Optional.
operation	A string expression that specifies how the criteria you establish with the *fieldName*, *test*, and *value* arguments relate to other criteria in the filter. You can set the *operation* argument to "And" or "Or". Optional.
showInMenu	A Boolean expression that specifies whether to display the filter in the Filters menu. (The Filters menu appears when you choose Filters from the Tools menu.) By default, the *showInMenu* argument is **False**. Optional.
showSummaryTasks	A Boolean expression that specifies whether to display the summary tasks of the filtered tasks. By default, the *showSummaryTasks* argument is **False**. Optional.

The *test* argument has these settings:

Setting	Filter tasks when the value you specify with the *fieldName* argument
"equals"	Equals the value you specify with the *value* argument.
"not equals"	Does not equal the value you specify with the *value* argument.
"greater"	Is greater than the value you specify with the *value* argument.
"gtr or equal"	Is greater than or equal to the value you specify with the *value* argument.
"less"	Is less than the value you specify with the *value* argument.
"less or equal"	Is less than or equal to the value you specify with the *value* argument.
"within"	Is within the value you specify with the *value* argument.
"not within"	Is not within the value you specify with the *value* argument.
"contains"	Contains the value you specify with the *value* argument.

Setting	Filter tasks when the value you specify with the *fieldName* argument
"doesn't contain"	Does not contain the value you specify with the **value** argument.
"contains exactly"	Exactly contains the value you specify with the **value** argument.

See Also

FilterApply Method, **Filters** Method, **Find** Method.

Example

The following example creates a filter for tasks with the highest priority (if one doesn't exist), and then applies the filter.

```
Sub CreateAndApplyHighestPriorityFilter()
    Dim TaskName      ' Index for For Each loop
    Dim Found         ' Whether or not the filter exists.

    Found = False     ' Assume the filter doesn't exist.

    ' Look for filter.
    For Each TaskName In ActiveProject.TaskFilterList
        If TaskName = "Highest Priority" Then
            Found = True
            Exit For
        End If
    Next TaskName

    ' If filter doesn't exist, create it.
    If Not Found Then FilterEdit Name:="Highest Priority", _
        create:=True, taskFilter:=True, FieldName:="Priority", _
        test:="equals", value:="Highest"

    ' Apply the filter.
    FilterApply "Highest Priority"
End Sub
```

Filters Method

Applies To   **Application** Object.

Description   Displays the More Filters dialog box, which prompts the user to use a filter.

Syntax   [*object*.]**Filters**

Elements   The *object* placeholder is an object expression that evaluates to an object in the Applies To list.

Remarks   The **Filters** method is equivalent to the More Filters command on the Filtered For submenu, which is available on the Tools menu.

See Also   **FilterApply** Method, **FilterEdit** Method, **Find** Method, **OrganizerDeleteItem** Method.

Find Method

Applies To   **Application** Object.

Description   Finds a value in the active table.

Syntax   [*object.*]**Find** *field*, *test*, *value*[, *next*]

Elements   The **Find Method** syntax has the following object qualifier and named arguments:

Part	Description
object	An object expression that evaluates to an object in the Applies To list. Optional.
field	A string expression that specifies the name of the field to search. Required.
test	A string expression that specifies the search criteria. Required.
value	A string expression that specifies the value to compare with the value in the field you specify with the *field* argument. Required.
next	A Boolean expression that specifies whether to search for the next or previous occurrence of items matching the search criteria. By default, the *next* argument is **True**. Optional. The *next* argument has these settings:

True	Search for the next occurrence of items matching the search criteria.
False	Search for the previous occurrence of items matching the search criteria.

The *test* argument has these settings:

Setting	Search the field you specify with the *field* argument for a value that
"equals"	Equals the value you specify with the *value* argument.
"not equals"	Does not equal the value you specify with the *value* argument.
"greater"	Is greater than the value you specify with the *value* argument.
"gtr or equal"	Is greater than or equal to the value you specify with the *value* argument.

Setting	Search the field you specify with the *field* argument for a value that
"less"	Is less than the value you specify with the *value* argument.
"less or equal"	Is less than or equal to the value you specify with the *value* argument.
"within"	Is within the value you specify with the *value* argument.
"not within"	Is not within the value you specify with the *value* argument.
"contains"	Contains the value you specify with the *value* argument.
"doesn't contain"	Does not contain the value you specify with the *value* argument.
"contains exactly"	Exactly contains the value you specify with the *value* argument.

Return Values Returns **True** if a match is found; otherwise returns **False**.

See Also **EditGoto** Method, **FilterApply** Method, **FilterEdit** Method, **Filters** Method, **GotoNextOverallocation** Method, **GotoTaskDates** Method.

Example The following example finds the next task with highest priority.

```
Sub FindFirstID
    Find field:="Priority", test:="equals", value:="Highest"
End Sub
```

FindFile Method

Applies To **Application** Object.

Description Displays the File Open dialog box, which allows the user to search for a file.

Syntax [*object*.]**FindFile**

Elements The *object* placeholder is an object expression that evaluates to an object in the Applies To list.

Remarks This method applies to Microsoft Project for Microsoft Windows.

See Also **FileOpen** Method, **Find** Method.

FindNext Method

Applies To	**Application** Object.
Description	Repeats the last search, going forward.
Syntax	[*object.*]**FindNext**
Elements	The *object* placeholder is an object expression that evaluates to an object in the Applies To list.
Return Values	Returns **True** if the search succeeds; otherwise returns **False**.
See Also	**EditGoto** Method, **FilterApply** Method, **FilterEdit** Method, **Filters** Method, **Find** Method, **FindPrevious** Method, **GotoNextOverallocation** Method, **GotoTaskDates** Method.

FindPrevious Method

Applies To	**Application** Object.
Description	Repeats the last search, going backward.
Syntax	[*object.*]**FindPrevious**
Elements	The *object* placeholder is an object expression that evaluates to an object in the Applies To list.
Return Values	Returns **True** if the search succeeds; otherwise returns **False**.
See Also	**EditGoto** Method, **FilterApply** Method, **FilterEdit** Method, **Filters** Method, **Find** Method, **FindNext** Method, **GotoNextOverallocation** Method, **GotoTaskDates** Method.

Finish Property

Applies To	**Project** Object, **Projects** Collection; **Task** Object, **Tasks** Collection.
Description	Returns the earliest date on which a task can finish.

Syntax	*object*.**EarlyFinish**
Elements	The *object* placeholder is an object expression that evaluates to an object in the Applies To list.
See Also	**EarlyStart** Property, **LateFinish** Property, **LateStart** Property.

Finish*n* Property

Applies To	**Project** Object, **Projects** Collection; **Task** Object, **Tasks** Collection.
Description	Returns or sets the value of an additional finish date field for a project or task.
Syntax	*object*.**Finish***n* [= *value*]
Elements	The **Finish***n* property syntaxes have the following parts:

Part	Description
object	An object expression that evaluates to an object in the Applies To list.
n	A number from 1 to 5.
value	A date expression that specifies the finish date.

See Also	**ActualFinish** Property, **BaselineFinish** Property, **Finish** Property, **Start***n* Property.

FinishVariance Property

Applies To	**Project** Object, **Projects** Collection; **Task** Object, **Tasks** Collection.
Description	Returns the variance, in minutes, between the baseline finish date and the finish date of a project or task.
Syntax	*object*.**FinishVariance**
Elements	The *object* placeholder is an object expression that evaluates to an object in the Applies To list.
See Also	**ActualFinish** Property, **BaselineFinish** Property, **CostVariance** Property, **DurationVariance** Property, **Finish** Property, **StartVariance** Property, **WorkVariance** Property.

FixedCost Property

Applies To   **Project** Object, **Projects** Collection; **Task** Object, **Tasks** Collection.

Description   Returns or sets a fixed cost for a task.

Syntax   *object*.**FixedCost** [= *value*]

Elements   The **FixedCost** property syntax has the following parts:

Part	Description
object	An object expression that evaluates to an object in the Applies To list.
value	A numeric expression that specifies a fixed cost for the task.

See Also   **ActualCost** Property, **BaselineCost** Property, **Cost** Property, **CostVariance** Property, **RemainingCost** Property.

Example   The following example increases the fixed costs of marked tasks by an amount specified by the user.

```
Sub IncreaseFixedCosts()
    Dim T        ' Task object used in For Each loop
    Dim Entry

    ' Prompt user for the increase amount.
    Entry = InputBox("Increase the fixed costs of marked tasks" & _
        " by what amount?")

    ' If entry is invalid, display error message and exit Sub procedure.
    If Not IsNumeric(Entry) Then
        MsgBox("You didn't enter a numeric value!")
        Exit Sub
    End If

    ' Increase the fixed costs of marked tasks by the specified amount.
    For Each T in ActiveProject.Tasks
        If T.Marked Then
            T.FixedCost = T.FixedCost + Entry
        End If
    Next T
End Sub
```

FixedDuration Property

Applies To	**Project** Object, **Projects** Collection.
Description	Returns or sets whether or not new tasks in a project have fixed durations.
Syntax	[*object*.]**DefaultFixedDuration** [= *value*]
Elements	The **DefaultFixedDuration** property syntax has these parts:

Part	Description
object	An object expression that evaluates to an object in the Applies To list.
value	A Boolean expression that specifies whether or not new tasks in the project have fixed durations.

See Also	**DefaultDurationUnits** Property, **DefaultResourceOvertimeRate** Property, **DefaultResourceStandardRate** Property, **DefaultView** Property, **DefaultWorkUnits** Property.

Flagn Properties

Applies To	**Project** Object, **Projects** Collection; **Task** Object, **Tasks** Collection.
Description	Returns or sets a flag associated with a project or task.
Syntax	*object*.**Flag***n* [= *value*]
Elements	The **Flag***n* property syntaxes have the following parts:

Part	Description
object	An object expression that evaluates to an object in the Applies To list.
n	A number from 1 to 10.
value	A Boolean expression that sets or unsets the flag, as shown under Settings.

Settings	The **Flag***n* properties have the following settings:

Setting	Description
True	The flag is set.
False	The flag is not set.

See Also   **Notes** Property, **Numbern** Properties, **Summary** Property, **Textn** Properties.

Example   The following example deletes tasks in the active project with their **Flag1** properties set to **True**.

```
Sub DeleteNonEssentialTasks()
    Dim T    ' Task object used in For Each loop

    ' Delete nonessential tasks in the active project.
    For Each T In ActiveProject.Tasks
        If Not (T Is Nothing) Then
            If T.Flag1 = True Then T.Delete
        End If
    Next T
End Sub
```

Font Method

Applies To   **Application** Object.

Description   Sets the font for the text in the active cells.

Syntax   [*object.*]**Font** [*name, size, bold, italic, underline, color, reset*]

Elements   The **Font** method syntax has the following object qualifier and named arguments:

Part	Description
object	An object expression that evaluates to an object in the Applies To list. Optional.
name	A string expression that specifies the name of the font. Optional.
size	A numeric expression that specifies the size of the font. Optional.
bold	A Boolean expression that specifies whether the font is bold. Optional.
italic	A Boolean expression that specifies whether the font is italic. Optional.
underline	A Boolean expression that specifies whether the font is underlined. Optional.

Part	Description
color	A constant that specifies the color of the font. Optional.
reset	A Boolean expression that specifies whether to reset the font to its default characteristics. If you set the *reset* argument to **True**, all other arguments are ignored. By default, the *reset* argument is **False**. Optional.

The *color* argument has these settings:

pjBlack	0	Black
pjRed	1	Red
pjYellow	2	Yellow
pjLime	3	Lime
pjAqua	4	Aqua
pjBlue	5	Blue
pjFuchsia	6	Fuchsia
pjWhite	7	White
pjMaroon	8	Maroon
pjGreen	9	Green
pjOlive	10	Olive
pjNavy	11	Navy
pjPurple	12	Purple
pjTeal	13	Teal
pjGray	14	Gray
pjSilver	15	Silver

See Also

FontBold Method, **FontItalic** Method, **FontUnderline** Method, **FormatCopy** Method, **FormatPainter** Method, **FormatPaste** Method, **TextStyles** Method.

Example

The following example formats selected text using 16-point Geneva.

```
Sub FormatGeneva16()
    Font name:="Geneva", size:=16, bold:=False, italic:=False, _
        underline:=False, color:=pjBlack
End Sub
```

FontBold Method

Applies To	**Application** Object.
Description	Applies or removes bold formatting from the selected text.
Syntax	[*object*.]**FontBold** [*set*]
Elements	The **FontBold** method syntax has the following object qualifier and named arguments:

Part	Description
object	An object expression that evaluates to an object in the Applies To list.
set	A Boolean expression that specifies whether to apply or remove bold formatting from the selected task. By default, the *set* argument is **False** if the selected text is bold and **True** otherwise.

See Also	**Font** Method, **FontItalic** Method, **FontUnderline** Method.

FontItalic Method

Applies To	**Application** Object.
Description	Applies or removes italic formatting from the selected text.
Syntax	[*object*.]**FontItalic** [*set*]
Elements	The **FontItalic** method syntax has the following object qualifier and named arguments:

Part	Description
object	An object expression that evaluates to an object in the Applies To list.
set	A Boolean expression that specifies whether to apply or remove italic formatting from the selected text. By default, the *set* argument is **False** if the selected text is italic and **True** otherwise.

See Also	**Font** Method, **FontBold** Method, **FontUnderline** Method.

FontUnderline Method

Applies To	**Application** Object.
Description	Applies or removes underlining from the selected text.
Syntax	[*object*.]**FontUnderline** [*set*]
Elements	The **FontUnderline** method syntax has the following object qualifier and named arguments:

Part	Description
object	An object expression that evaluates to an object in the Applies To list.
set	A Boolean expression that specifies whether to clear or remove underlining from the selected text. By default, the *set* argument is **False** if the selected text is underlined and **True** otherwise.

See Also	**Font** Method, **FontBold** Method, **FontItalic** Method.

For Each...Next Statement

Description	Repeats a group of statements for each element in an array or collection.
Syntax	**For Each** *element* **In** *group* [*statements*] [**Exit For**] [*statements*] **Next** [*element*]
Elements	The **For Each...Next** statement syntax has these parts:

Part	Description
element	Variable used to iterate through the elements of the collection or array. For collections, *element* can only be a **Variant** variable, a generic **Object** variable, or any specific OLE Automation object variable. For arrays, *element* can only be a **Variant** variable.
group	Name of an object collection or array (except an array of user-defined types).
statements	One or more statements that are executed on each item in *collection*.

Important When using **For Each... Next** with arrays, you can only read the value contained in the array elements indicated by the control variable *element*. You cannot set the value by assigning a value to *element*.

Remarks

The **For Each** block is entered if there is at least one element in *group*. Once the loop has been entered, all the statements in the loop are executed for the first element in *group*. Then, as long as there are more elements in *group*, the statements in the loop continue to execute for each element. When there are no more elements in *group*, the loop is exited and execution continues with the statement following the **Next** statement.

The **Exit For** can only be used within a **For Each...Next** or **For...Next** control structure to provide an alternate way to exit. Any number of **Exit For** statements may be placed anywhere in the loop. The **Exit For** is often used with the evaluation of some condition (for example, **If...Then**), and transfers control to the statement immediately following **Next**.

You can nest **For Each...Next** loops by placing one **For Each...Next** loop within another. However, each loop *element* must be unique.

Note If you omit *element* in a **Next** statement, execution continues as if you had included it. If a **Next** statement is encountered before its corresponding **For** statement, an error occurs.

You can't use the **For Each...Next** statement with an array of user-defined types because a **Variant** can't contain a user-defined type.

See Also

Do...Loop Statement, **Exit** Statement, **For...Next** Statement, **While...Wend** Statement.

Example

This example uses the **For Each...Next** statement to search the Text property of all elements in a collection for the existence of the string "Hello". In the example, MyObject is a text-related object and is an element of the collection MyCollection. Both are generic names used for illustration purposes only.

```
Found = False                        ' Initialize variable.
For Each MyObject In MyCollection     ' Iterate through each element.
    If MyObject.Text = "Hello" Then   ' If Text equals "Hello".
        Found = True                  ' Set Found to True.
        Exit For                      ' Exit loop.
    End If
Next
```

For...Next Statement

Description   Repeats a group of statements a specified number of times.

Syntax   **For** *counter* = *start* **To** *end* [**Step** *step*]
     [*statements*]
     [**Exit For**]
     [*statements*]
Next [*counter*]

Elements   The **For...Next** statement syntax has these parts:

Part	Description
counter	Numeric variable used as a loop counter. The variable can't be any array element or any element of a user-defined type.
start	Initial value of *counter*.
end	Final value of *counter*.
step	Amount *counter* is changed each time through the loop. If not specified, *step* defaults to one.
statements	One or more statements between **For** and **Next** that are executed the specified number of times.

Remarks   The *step* argument can be either positive or negative. The value of the *step* argument determines loop processing as follows:

Value	Loop executes if
Positive or 0	*counter* <= *end*
Negative	*counter* >= *end*

Once the loop starts and all statements in the loop have executed, *step* is added to *counter*. At this point, either the statements in the loop execute again (based on the same test that caused the loop to execute initially), or the loop is exited and execution continues with the statement following the **Next** statement.

Tip   Changing the value of *counter* while inside a loop can make it more difficult to read and debug.

The **Exit For** can only be used within a **For Each...Next** or **For...Next** control structure to provide an alternate way to exit. Any number of **Exit For** statements may be placed anywhere in the loop. The **Exit For** is often used with the evaluation of some condition (for example, **If...Then**), and transfers control to the statement immediately following **Next**.

You can nest **For...Next** loops by placing one **For...Next** loop within another. Give each loop a unique variable name as its *counter*. The following construction is correct:

```
For I = 1 To 10
    For J = 1 To 10
        For K = 1 To 10
            . . .
        Next K
    Next J
Next I
```

Note   If you omit *counter* in a **Next** statement, execution continues as if you had included it. If a **Next** statement is encountered before its corresponding **For** statement, an error occurs.

See Also   **Do...Loop** Statement, **Exit** Statement, **For Each...Next** Statement, **While...Wend** Statement.

Example   This example uses the **For...Next** statement to create a string that contains 10 instances of the numbers 0 through 9, each string separated from the other by a single space. The outer loop uses a loop counter variable that is decremented each time through the loop.

```
For Words = 10 To 1 Step -1          ' Set up 10 repetitions.
    For Chars = 0 To 9               ' Set up 10 repetitions.
        MyString = MyString & Chars  ' Append number to string.
    Next Chars
    MyString = MyString & " "        ' Append a space.
Next Words
```

Form Method

Applies To   **Application** Object.

Description   Displays a custom form.

Syntax   [*object.*]**Form** [*name*]

Elements   The **Form** method syntax has the following object qualifier and named arguments:

Part	Description
object	An object expression that evaluates to an object in the Applies To list.
name	A string expression that specifies the name of a custom form. By default, the **Form** method displays Task or Resource Form.

Remarks   The **Form** method produces an error if you specify the name of a resource form when the active view is a Task view, or if you specify the name of a task form when the active view is a Resource view.

See Also   **CustomForms** Method.

Example   The following example displays the Cost Tracking form.

```
Sub DisplayCostTrackingForm
    Form("Cost Tracking")
End Sub
```

Format Function

Description   Formats an expression according to instructions contained in a format expression.

Syntax   **Format**(*expression*[,*format*])

Elements   The **Format** function syntax has these parts:

Part	Description
expression	Any valid *expression*.
format	A valid named or user-defined format expression.

Remarks

To Format These	Do This
Numbers	Use predefined named numeric formats or create user-defined numeric formats.
Dates and times	Use predefined named date/time formats or create user-defined date/time formats.
Date and time serial numbers	Use date and time formats or numeric formats.
Strings	Create your own user-defined string formats.

If you try to format a number without specifying *format*, **Format** provides the same functionality as the **Str** function. However, positive numbers formatted as strings using **Format** lack the leading space reserved for displaying the sign of the value; whereas, those converted using **Str** retain the leading space.

Example

This example shows various uses of the **Format** function to format values using both named and user-defined formats. For the date separator (/), time separator (:) and AM/ PM literal, the actual formatted output displayed by your system depends on the settings at the time. When times and dates are listed back in the development environment, the short time and short date formats of the code locale are used. When displayed by running code, the short time and short date formats of the system locale are used, which may be different from the code locale. For this example, English - US is assumed.

```
' MyTime and MyDate will be displayed in the development environment
' using current system short time and short date settings.
MyTime = #17:04:23#
MyDate = #January 27, 1993#

' Returns current system time in the system-defined long time format.
MyStr = Format(Time, "Long Time")

' Returns current system date in the system-defined long date format.
MyStr = Format(Date, "Long Date")

MyStr = Format(MyTime, "h:m:s")            ' Returns "17:4:23".
MyStr = Format(MyTime, "hh:mm:ss AMPM")    ' Returns "05:04:23 PM".
MyStr = Format(MyDate, "dddd, mmm d yyyy") ' Returns
                                           '"Wednesday, Jan 27 1993".
' If format is not supplied, a string is returned.
MyStr = Format(23)                         ' Returns "23".

' User-defined formats.
MyStr = Format(5459.4, "##,##0.00")        ' Returns "5,459.40".
MyStr = Format(334.9, "###0.00")           ' Returns "334.90".
MyStr = Format(5, "0.00%")                 ' Returns "500.00%".
MyStr = Format("HELLO", "<")               ' Returns "hello".
MyStr = Format("This is it", ">")          ' Returns "THIS IS IT".
```

Different Formats for Different Numeric Values

A format expression for numbers can have from one to four sections separated by semicolons. (If the *format* argument contains one of the predefined formats, only one section is allowed.)

If you use	The result is
One section only	The format expression applies to all values.
Two sections	The first section applies to positive values and zeros, the second to negative values.
Three sections	The first section applies to positive values, the second to negative values, and the third to zeros.
Four sections	The first section applies to positive values, the second to negative values, the third to zeros, and the fourth to **Null** values.

The following example has two sections: the first defines the format for positive values and zeros; the second section defines the format for negative values.

```
"$#,##0;($#,##0)"
```

If you include semicolons with nothing between them, the missing section is printed using the format of the positive value. For example, the following format displays positive and negative values using the format in the first section and displays "Zero" if the value is zero.

```
"$#,##0;;\Z\e\r\o"
```

Different Formats for Different String Values

A format expression for strings can have one section, or two sections separated by a semicolon.

If you use	The result is
One section only	The format applies to all string data.
Two sections	The first section applies to string data, the second to **Null** values and zero-length strings.

Named Date/Time Formats

The following table identifies the predefined date and time format names:

Format Name	Description
General Date	Display a date and/or time. For real numbers, display a date and time (for example, 4/3/93 05:34 PM); if there is no fractional part, display only a date (for example, 4/3/93); if there is no integer part, display time only (for example, 05:34 PM). Date display is determined by your system settings.
Long Date	Display a date according to your system's long date format.
Medium Date	Display a date using the medium date format appropriate for the language version of the host application.
Short Date	Display a date using your system's short date format.
Long Time	Display a time using your system's long time format: includes hours, minutes, seconds.
Medium Time	Display time in 12-hour format using hours and minutes and the AM/PM designator.
Short Time	Display a time using the 24-hour format (for example, 17:45).

Named Numeric Formats

The following table identifies the predefined numeric format names:

Format Name	Description
General Number	Display number as is, with no thousand separators.
Currency	Display number with thousand separator, if appropriate; display negative numbers enclosed in parentheses; display two digits to the right of the decimal separator. Note that output is based on system settings.
Fixed	Display at least one digit to the left and two digits to the right of the decimal separator.
Standard	Display number with thousands separator, at least one digit to the left and two digits to the right of the decimal separator.
Percent	Display number multiplied by 100 with a percent sign (%) appended to the right; always displays two digits to the right of the decimal separator.
Scientific	Use standard scientific notation.
Yes/No	Display No if number is 0; otherwise, display Yes.
True/False	Display **False** if number is 0; otherwise, display **True**.
On/Off	Display Off if number is 0; otherwise, display On.

User-Defined Date/Time Formats

The following table identifies characters you can use to create user-defined date/time formats:

Character	Description
:	Time separator. In some locales, other characters may be used to represent the time separator. The time separator separates hours, minutes, and seconds when time values are formatted. The actual character used as the time separator in formatted output is determined by your system settings.
/	Date separator. In some locales, other characters may be used to represent the date separator. The date separator separates the day, month, and year when date values are formatted. The actual character used as the date separator in formatted output is determined by your system settings.
c	Display the date as ddddd and display the time as t t t t t, in that order. Display only date information if there is no fractional part to the date serial number; display only time information if there is no integer portion.
d	Display the day as a number without a leading zero (1-31).
dd	Display the day as a number with a leading zero (01-31).
ddd	Display the day as an abbreviation (Sun-Sat).
dddd	Display the day as a full name (SundaySaturday).
ddddd	Display a date as a complete date (including day, month, and year), formatted according to your system's short date format setting. For Microsoft Windows, the default short date format is m/d/yy.
dddddd	Display a date serial number as a complete date (including day, month, and year) formatted according to the long date setting recognized by your system. For Microsoft Windows, the default long date format is mmmm dd, yyyy.
w	Display the day of the week as a number (1 for Sunday through 7 for Saturday).
ww	Display the week of the year as a number (1-53).
m	Display the month as a number without a leading zero (1-12). If m immediately follows h or hh, the minute rather than the month is displayed.
mm	Display the month as a number with a leading zero (01-12). If m immediately follows h or hh, the minute rather than the month is displayed.

Character	Description
mmm	Display the month as an abbreviation (Jan-Dec).
mmmm	Display the month as a full month name (January-December).
q	Display the quarter of the year as a number (1-4).
y	Display the day of the year as a number (1-366).
yy	Display the year as a 2-digit number (00-99).
yyyy	Display the year as a 4-digit number (100-9999).
h	Display the hour as a number without leading zeros (0-23).
hh	Display the hour as a number with leading zeros (00-23).
n	Display the minute as a number without leading zeros (0-59).
nn	Display the minute as a number with leading zeros (00-59).
s	Display the second as a number without leading zeros (0-59).
ss	Display the second as a number with leading zeros (00-59).
ttttt	Display a time as a complete time (including hour, minute, and second), formatted using the time separator defined by the time format recognized by your system. A leading zero is displayed if the leading zero option is selected and the time is before 10:00 A.M. or P.M. The default time format is h:mm:ss.
AM/PM	Use the 12-hour clock and display an uppercase AM with any hour before noon; display an uppercase PM with any hour between noon and 11:59 P.M.
am/pm	Use the 12-hour clock and display a lowercase AM with any hour before noon; display a lowercase PM with any hour between noon and 11:59 P.M.
A/P	Use the 12-hour clock and display an uppercase A with any hour before noon; display an uppercase P with any hour between noon and 11:59 P.M.
a/p	Use the 12-hour clock and display a lowercase A with any hour before noon; display a lowercase P with any hour between noon and 11:59 P.M.
AMPM	Use the 12-hour clock and display the AM string literal as defined by your system with any hour before noon; display the PM string literal as defined by your system with any hour between noon and 11:59 P.M. AMPM can be either uppercase or lowercase, but the case of the string displayed matches the string as defined by your system settings. For Microsoft Windows, the default format is AM/PM.

Examples   The following are examples of user-defined date and time formats for December 7, 1958:

Format	Display
m/d/yy	12/7/58
d-mm	7-Dec
d-mmmm-yy	7-December-58
d-mmmm	7 December
mmmm-yy	December 58
hh:mm AM/PM	08:50 PM
h:mm:ss a/p	8:50:35 p
h:mm	20:50
h:mm:ss	20:50:35
m/d/yy h:mm	12/7/58 20:50

User-Defined Numeric Formats

The following table identifies characters you can use to create user-defined number formats:

Character	Description
None	**No formatting**
	Display the number with no formatting.
0	**Digit placeholder**
	Display a digit or a zero. If the expression has a digit in the position where the 0 appears in the format string, display it; otherwise, display a zero in that position.
	If the number has fewer digits than there are zeros (on either side of the decimal) in the format expression, display leading or trailing zeros. If the number has more digits to the right of the decimal separator than there are zeros to the right of the decimal separator in the format expression, round the number to as many decimal places as there are zeros. If the number has more digits to the left of the decimal separator than there are zeros to the left of the decimal separator in the format expression, display the extra digits without modification.
#	**Digit placeholder**
	Display a digit or nothing. If the expression has a digit in the position where the # appears in the format string, display it; otherwise, display nothing in that position.
	This symbol works like the 0 digit placeholder, except that leading and trailing zeros aren't displayed if the number has the same or fewer digits than there are # characters on either side of the decimal separator in the format expression.

Character	Description
.	**Decimal placeholder**
	In some locales, a comma is used as the decimal separator. The decimal placeholder determines how many digits are displayed to the left and right of the decimal separator. If the format expression contains only number signs to the left of this symbol, numbers smaller than 1 begin with a decimal separator. If you always want a leading zero displayed with fractional numbers, use 0 as the first digit placeholder to the left of the decimal separator instead. The actual character used as a decimal placeholder in the formatted output depends on the Number Format recognized by your system.
%	**Percentage placeholder**
	The expression is multiplied by 100. The percent character (%) is inserted in the position where it appears in the format string.
,	**Thousand separator**
	In some locales, a period is used as a thousand separator. The thousand separator separates thousands from hundreds within a number that has four or more places to the left of the decimal separator. Standard use of the thousand separator is specified if the format contains a thousand separator surrounded by digit placeholders (0 or #). Two adjacent thousand separators or a thousand separator immediately to the left of the decimal separator (whether or not a decimal is specified) means "scale the number by dividing it by 1000, rounding as needed." You can scale large numbers using this technique. For example, you can use the format string "##0,," to represent 100 million as 100. Numbers smaller than 1 million are displayed as 0. Two adjacent thousand separators in any position other than immediately to the left of the decimal separator are treated simply as specifying the use of a thousand separator. The actual character used as the thousand separator in the formatted output depends on the Number Format recognized by your system.
:	**Time separator**
	In some locales, other characters may be used to represent the time separator. The time separator separates hours, minutes, and seconds when time values are formatted. The actual character used as the time separator in formatted output is determined by your system settings.
/	**Date separator**
	In some locales, other characters may be used to represent the date separator. The date separator separates the day, month, and year when date values are formatted. The actual character used as the date separator in formatted output is determined by your system settings.

Character	Description
E- E+ e- e+	**Scientific format**
	If the format expression contains at least one digit placeholder (0 or #) to the right of E-, E+, e-, or e+, the number is displayed in scientific format and E or e is inserted between the number and its exponent. The number of digit placeholders to the right determines the number of digits in the exponent. Use E- or e- to place a minus sign next to negative exponents. Use E+ or e+ to place a minus sign next to negative exponents and a plus sign next to positive exponents.
- + $ ( ) space	**Display a literal character**
	To display a character other than one of those listed, precede it with a backslash (\) or enclose it in double quotation marks (" ").
****	**Display the next character in the format string**
	Many characters in the format expression have a special meaning and can't be displayed as literal characters unless they are preceded by a backslash. The backslash itself isn't displayed. Using a backslash is the same as enclosing the next character in double quotation marks. To display a backslash, use two backslashes (\\).
	Examples of characters that can't be displayed as literal characters are the date- and time-formatting characters (a, c, d, h, m, n, p, q, s, t, w, y, and /:), the numeric-formatting characters (#, 0, %, E, e, comma, and period), and the string-formatting characters (@, &, <, >, and !).
"ABC"	**Display the string inside the double quotation marks**
	To include a string in *format* from within code, you must use **Chr**(34) to enclose the text (34 is the character code for a double quotation mark).

Example

Some sample format expressions for numbers are shown below. (These examples all assume that your system's locale setting is English-US.) The first column contains the format strings. The other columns contain the output that results if the formatted data has the value given in the column headings.

Format (*format*)	Positive 5	Negative 5	Decimal .5	Null
Zero-length string	5	-5	0.5	
0	5	-5	1	
0.00	5.00	-5.00	0.50	
#,##0	5	-5	1	
#,##0.00;;;Nil	5.00	-5.00	0.50	Nil
$#,##0;($#,##0)	$5	($5)	$1	
$#,##0.00;($#,##0.00)	$5.00	($5.00)	$0.50	

Format (*format*)	Positive 5	Negative 5	Decimal .5	Null
0%	500%	-500%	50%	
0.00%	500.00%	-500.00%	50.00%	
0.00E+00	5.00E+00	-5.00E+00	5.00E-01	
0.00E-00	5.00E00	-5.00E00	5.00E-01	

User-Defined String Formats

You can use any of the following characters to create a format expression for strings:

Character	Description
@	**Character placeholder**
	Display a character or a space. If the string has a character in the position where the @ appears in the format string, display it; otherwise, display a space in that position. Placeholders are filled from right to left unless there is an ! character in the format string. See below.
&	**Character placeholder**
	Display a character or nothing. If the string has a character in the position where the & appears, display it; otherwise, display nothing. Placeholders are filled from right to left unless there is an ! character in the format string. See below.
<	**Force lowercase**
	Display all characters in lowercase format.
>	**Force uppercase**
	Display all characters in uppercase format.
!	**Force left to right fill of placeholders**
	The default is to fill from right to left.

FormatCopy Method

Applies To   **Application** Object.

Description   Copies the formats of the active cells.

Syntax   [*object*.]**FormatCopy**

Elements	The *object* placeholder is an object expression that evaluates to an object in the Applies To list.
See Also	**Font** Method, **FormatPainter** Method, **FormatPaste** Method, **TextStyles** Method.

FormatPainter Method

Applies To	**Application** Object.
Description	Paints the formatting of the selected object onto another object.
Syntax	[*object*.]**FormatPainter**
Elements	The *object* placeholder is anis an object expression that evaluates to an object in the Applies To list.
See Also	**FormatCopy** Method, **FormatPaste** Method.

FormatPaste Method

Applies To	**Application** Object.
Description	Pastes formats—copied with the **FormatCopy** method—into the active cells.
Syntax	[*object*.]**FormatPaste**
Elements	The *object* placeholder is an object expression that evaluates to an object in the Applies To list.
See Also	**Font** Method, **FormatCopy** Method, **FormatPainter** Method, **TextStyles** Method.

FormViewShow Method

Applies To	**Application** Object.
Description	Shows or hides the Form view in the lower pane.
Syntax	[*object*.]**FormViewShow**

Elements   The *object* placeholder is an object expression that evaluates to an object in the Applies To list.

See Also   **ViewApply** Method, **WindowSplit** Method.

FreeFile Function

Description   Returns the next file number available for use by the **Open** statement.

Syntax   **FreeFile**[(*rangenumber*)]

Elements   The *rangenumber* argument specifies the range from which the next free file number is to be returned. Specify a **0** (default) to return a file number in the range 1 to 255, inclusive. Specify a **1** to return a file number in the range 256 to 511.

Remarks   Use **FreeFile** when you need to supply a file number and you want to make sure the file number is not already in use.

See Also   **Open** Statement.

Example   This example uses the **FreeFile** function to return the next available file number. Five files are opened for output within the loop and some sample data is written to each.

```
For MyIndex = 1 to 5                           ' Loop 5 times.
    FileNumber = FreeFile                      ' Get unused file number.
    Open "TEST" & MyIndex For Output As #FileNumber  ' Create file name.
    Write #FileNumber, "This is a sample"       ' Output text.
    Close #FileNumber                          ' Close file.
Next MyIndex
```

FreeSlack Property

Applies To   **Project** Object, **Projects** Collection; **Task** Object, **Tasks** Collection.

Description   Returns the free slack for a task, in minutes.

Syntax   *object*.**FreeSlack**

Elements   The *object* placeholder is an object expression that evaluates to an object in the Applies To list.

See Also   **Critical** Property, **Delay** Property, **TotalSlack** Property.

Example

The following example eliminates free slack in the active project by changing the start dates of tasks with free slack.

```
Sub EliminateFreeSlack()
    Dim T As Task    ' Task object used in For Each loop
    For Each T In ActiveProject.Tasks
        If T.FreeSlack > 0 Then
            T.Start = DateAdd(T.Start, T.FreeSlack)
        End If
    Next T
End Sub
```

FullName Property

Applies To

Project Object, **Projects** Collection.

Description

Returns the pathname of a project, followed by the path separator character and the name of the project.

Syntax

object.**FullName**

Elements

The *object* placeholder is an object expression that evaluates to an object in the Applies To list.

Remarks

The **FullName** property returns **Empty** for an unsaved project.

In Microsoft Windows, the **FullName** property returns "C:\WINPROJ\LITWARE.MPP" for a project named LITWARE.MPP in the WINPROJ folder of the C: drive or "\\APP\PROJECT\LITWARE.MPP" for a project named LITWARE.MPP in the PROJECT share of the APP network drive.

On the Macintosh, the **FullName** property returns "MINE:WINPROJ:LITWARE" for a project named LITWARE in the WINPROJ folder on the drive named MINE.

See Also

CreationDate Property, **HasPassword** Property, **LastSaveDate** Property, **LastSavedBy** Property, **Name** Property, **Path** Property, **ReadOnly** Property, **ReadOnlyRecommended** Property, **RevisionNumber** Property, **Saved** Property, **WriteReserved** Property.

Example

The following example prompts the user for the full name of a file and then closes the file.

```
Sub CloseFile()
    Dim P             ' Project object used in For Each loop
    Dim FileName      ' Full name of a file

    ' Prompt user for the full name of a file.
    FileName = InputBox("Close which file? Include its path: ")
```

```
        ' Search the open projects for the file.
        For Each P in Application.Projects
            ' If the file is found, close it.
            If P.FullName = FileName Then
                P.Activate
                FileClose
                Exit Sub
            End If
        Next P

        ' Inform user if the file is not found.
        MsgBox("Could not find the file " & FileName)
    End Sub
```

Function Statement

Description   Declares the name, arguments, and code that form the body of a **Function** procedure.

Syntax   [**Public** | **Private**][**Static**] **Function** *name* [(*arglist*)][**As** *type*]
    [*statements*]
    [*name* = *expression*]
    [**Exit Function**]
    [*statements*]
    [*name* = *expression*]
End Function

Elements   The **Function** statement syntax has these parts:

Part	Description
Public	Indicates that the **Function** procedure is accessible to all other procedures in all modules. If used in a private module (one that contains an **Option Private** statement) the procedure is not available outside the project.
Private	Indicates that the **Function** procedure is accessible only to other procedures in the module where it is declared.
Static	Indicates that the **Function** procedure's local variables are preserved between calls. The **Static** attribute doesn't affect variables that are declared outside the **Function**, even if they are used in the procedure.
name	Name of the **Function**; follows standard variable naming conventions.
arglist	List of variables representing arguments that are passed to the **Function** procedure when it is called. Multiple variables are separated by commas.

Part	Description
type	Data type of the value returned by the **Function** procedure; may be **Boolean**, **Integer**, **Long**, **Currency**, **Single**, **Double**, **Date**, **String** (except fixed length), **Object**, **Variant** or any user-defined type. Arrays of any type can't be returned, but a **Variant** containing an array can.
statements	Any group of statements to be executed within the body of the **Function** procedure.
expression	Return value of the **Function**.

The *arglist* argument has the following syntax and parts:

[Optional][ByVal | ByRef][ParamArray] *varname*[( )][**As** *type*]

Part	Description
Optional	Indicates that an argument is not required. If used, all subsequent arguments in *arglist* must also be optional and declared using the **Optional** keyword. All **Optional** arguments must be **Variant**. **Optional** can't be used for any argument if **ParamArray** is used.
ByVal	Indicates that the argument is passed by value.
ByRef	Indicates that the argument is passed by reference.
ParamArray	Used only as the last argument in *arglist* to indicate that the final argument is an **Optional** array of **Variant** elements. The **ParamArray** keyword allows you to provide an arbitrary number of arguments. May not be used with **ByVal**, **ByRef**, or **Optional**.
varname	Name of the variable representing the argument; follows standard variable naming conventions.
type	Data type of the argument passed to the procedure; may be **Boolean**, **Integer**, **Long**, **Currency**, **Single**, **Double**, **Date**, **String** (variable length only), **Object**, **Variant**, a user-defined type, or an object type.

Remarks

If not explicitly specified using either **Public** or **Private**, **Function** procedures are **Public** by default. If **Static** is not used, the value of local variables is not preserved between calls.

All executable code must be in procedures. You can't define a **Function** procedure inside another **Function**, **Sub**, or **Property** procedure.

The **Exit Function** keywords cause an immediate exit from a **Function** procedure. Program execution continues with the statement following the statement that called the **Function** procedure. Any number of **Exit Function** statements can appear anywhere in a **Function** procedure.

Like a **Sub** procedure, a **Function** procedure is a separate procedure that can take arguments, perform a series of statements, and change the values of its arguments. However, unlike a **Sub** procedure, a **Function** procedure can be used on the right hand side of an expression in the same way you use any intrinsic function, such as **Sqr**, **Cos**, or **Chr**, when you want to use the value returned by the function.

You call a **Function** procedure using the function name, followed by the argument list in parentheses, in an expression. If the function has no arguments, you still must include the parentheses. See the **Call** statement for specific information on how to call **Function** procedures.

Caution   Function procedures can be recursive; that is, they can call themselves to perform a given task. However, recursion can lead to stack overflow. The Static keyword is usually not used with recursive Function procedures.

To return a value from a function, assign the value to the function name. Any number of such assignments can appear anywhere within the procedure. If no value is assigned to *name*, the procedure returns a default value: a numeric function returns 0, a string function returns a zero-length string (""), and a **Variant** function returns **Empty**. A function that returns an object reference returns **Nothing** if no object reference is assigned to *name* (using **Set**) within the **Function**.

The following example shows how to assign a return value to a function named BinarySearch. In this case, **False** is assigned to the name to indicate that some value was not found.

```
Function BinarySearch(. . .) As Boolean
. . .
    ' Value not found. Return a value of False.
    If lower > upper Then
        BinarySearch = False
        Exit Function
    End If
. . .
End Function
```

Variables used in **Function** procedures fall into two categories: those that are explicitly declared within the procedure and those that are not. Variables that are explicitly declared in a procedure (using **Dim** or the equivalent) are always local to the procedure. Other variables used but not explicitly declared in a procedure are also local unless they are explicitly declared at some higher level outside the procedure.

Caution A procedure can use a variable that is not explicitly declared in the procedure, but a name conflict can occur if anything you have defined at the module level has the same name. If your procedure refers to an undeclared variable that has the same name as another procedure, constant or variable, it is assumed that your procedure is referring to that module-level name. Explicitly declare variables to avoid this kind of conflict. You can use an Option Explicit statement to force explicit declaration of variables.

Caution Arithmetic expressions may be rearranged to increase internal efficiency. Avoid using a Function procedure in an arithmetic expression when the function changes the value of variables in the same expression.

See Also

Call Statement, **Dim** Statement, **Option Explicit** Statement, **Property Get** Statement, **Property Let** Statement, **Property Set** Statement, **Set** Statement, **Static** Statement, **Sub** Statement.

Example

This example uses the **Function** statement to declare the name, arguments and code that form the body of a **Function** procedure.

```
' The following user-defined function returns the square root of the
' argument passed to it.
Function CalculateSquareRoot(NumberArg As Double) As Double
    If NumberArg < 0 Then      ' Evaluate argument.
        Exit Function          ' Exit to calling procedure.
    Else
        CalculateSquareRoot = Sqr(NumberArg) ' Return square root.
    EndIf
End Function

' Using the ParamArray keyword enables a function to accept a variable
' number of arguments. In the following definition, FirstArg is passed
' by value.
Function CalcSum(ByVal FirstArg As Integer, ParamArray OtherArgs())
' If the function is invoked as...
ReturnValue = CalcSum(4,3,2,1)
' Local variables get the following values: FirstArg=4, OtherArgs(1)=3,
' OtherArgs(2) = 2 and so on, assuming default lower bound for
' arrays = 1.

' If a function's arguments are defined as...
Function MyFunc(MyStr As String, Optional MyArg1, Optional MyArg2)
' It can be invoked in the following ways.
RetVal = MyFunc("Hello", 2, "World") ' All 3 arguments supplied.
RetVal = MyFunc("Test", , 5)         ' Second argument omitted.
RetVal = MyFunc("Test")              ' First argument only.
```

GanttBarFormat Method

Applies To	**Application** Object.
Description	Formats Gantt bars.
Syntax	[*object.*]**GanttBarFormat**(*taskID, ganttStyle, startShape, startType, startColor, middleShape, middlePattern, middleColor, endShape, endType, endColor, leftText, rightText, topText, bottomText, insideText, reset*)
Elements	The **GanttBarFormat** method syntax has the following object qualifier and named arguments:

Part	Description
object	An object expression that evaluates to an object in the Applies To list. Optional.
taskID	A numeric expression that specifies the identification number of the task represented by the Gantt bar to change. By default, the **GanttBarFormat** method applies to the selected tasks. Optional.
ganttStyle	A numeric expression that specifies the style applied to the Gantt bar to be formatted. The value for the *ganttStyle* argument is based on the position of the bar style in the list. For example, the value "3" returns the third bar style in the list. Optional.
startShape	A constant that specifies the start shape of the Gantt bar. Optional.
startType	A constant that specifies the start type of the Gantt bar. Optional.
startColor	A constant that specifies the start color of the Gantt bar. Optional.
middleShape	A constant that specifies the middle shape of the Gantt bar. Optional.
middlePattern	A constant that specifies the middle pattern of the Gantt bar. Optional.
middleColor	A constant that specifies the middle color of the Gantt bar. Optional.
endShape	A constant that specifies the end shape of the Gantt bar. Optional.
endType	A constant that specifies the end type of the Gantt bar. Optional.
endColor	A constant that specifies the end color of the Gantt bar. Optional.

Part	Description
leftText	A string expression that specifies a task field to display to the left of the Gantt bar. Optional.
rightText	A string expression that specifies a task field to display to the right of the Gantt bar. Optional.
topText	A string expression that specifies a task field to display above the Gantt bar. Optional.
bottomText	A string expression that specifies a task field to display below the Gantt bar. Optional.
insideText	A string expression that specifies a task field to display inside the Gantt bar. Optional.
reset	A Boolean expression that specifies whether to reset the bar formatting to the formatting of the style. By default, reset is False. Optional.

The *startShape* and *endShape* arguments have these settings:

pjNone	0	None
pjHouseUp	1	House
pjHouseDown	2	Upside-down house
pjDiamond	3	Diamond
pjTriangleUp	4	Triangle pointing up
pjTriangleDown	5	Triangle pointing down
pjTriangleRight	6	Triangle pointing right
pjTriangleLeft	7	Triangle pointing left
pjArrowUp	8	Arrow pointing up
pjCaretDownTop	9	Caret pointing down on the top half of the bar
pjCaretUpBottom	10	Caret pointing up on the bottom half of the bar
pjLineShape	11	Line
pjSquare	12	Square
pjCircleDiamond	13	Circled diamond
pjArrowDown	14	Arrow pointing down
pjCircleTriangleUp	15	Circled triangle pointing up
pjCircleTriangleDown	16	Circled triangle pointing down
pjCircleArrowUp	17	Circled arrow pointing up
pjCircleArrowDown	18	Circled arrow pointing down

pjCircle	19	Circle
pjStar	20	Star

The *startType* and *endType* arguments have these settings:

pjSolid	0	Solid
pjFramed	1	Framed
pjDashed	2	Dashed

The *startColor*, *middleColor*, and *endColor* arguments have these settings:

pjBlack	0	Black
pjRed	1	Red
pjYellow	2	Yellow
pjLime	3	Lime
pjAqua	4	Aqua
pjBlue	5	Blue
pjFuchsia	6	Fuchsia
pjWhite	7	White
pjMaroon	8	Maroon
pjGreen	9	Green
pjOlive	10	Olive
pjNavy	11	Navy
pjPurple	12	Purple
pjTeal	13	Teal
pjGray	14	Gray
pjSilver	15	Silver

The *middleShape* argument has these settings:

pjNone	0	None
pjRectangleBar	1	Rectangle
pjRectangleTop	2	Rectangle in top third of available space
pjRectangleMiddle	3	Rectangle in middle third of available space
pjRectangleBottom	4	Rectangle in bottom third of available space
pjLineTop	5	Line in top third of available space
pjLineMiddle	6	Line in middle third of available space
pjLineBottom	7	Line in bottom third of available space

The *middlePattern* argument has these settings:

pjHollow	0	Hollow
pjSolidFill	1	Solid
pjLightFill	2	Light fill
pjMediumFill	3	Medium fill
pjDarkFill	4	Dark fill
pjDiagonalLeft	5	Diagonal left
pjDiagonalRight	6	Diagonal right
pjDiagonalCross	7	Diagonal cross
pjLineVertical	8	Vertical line
pjLineHorizontal	9	Horizontal line
pjLineCross	10	Crossed line

Remarks   Use the **GanttBarFormat** method to change the formatting of Gantt bars from their default styles. To define the default styles, use the **GanttBarStyleEdit** method.

See Also   **GanttBarLinks** Method, **GanttBarSize** Method, **GanttBarStyleDelete** Method, **GanttBarStyleEdit** Method.

GanttBarLinks Method

Applies To   **Application** Object.

Description   Shows or hides links on the Gantt Chart.

Syntax   [*object*.]**GanttBarLinks** [*display*]

Elements   The **GanttBarLinks** method syntax has the following object qualifier and named arguments:

Part	Description
object	An object expression that evaluates to an object in the Applies To list.
display	A constant that specifies which links to show.

The *display* argument has these settings:

pjNone	0	Don't draw links.
pjToTop	1	Draw links from end to top.
pjToEnd	2	Draw links from end to end.

See Also   **GanttBarFormat** Method, **GanttBarSize** Method, **GanttBarStyleDelete** Method, **GanttBarStyleEdit** Method, **GanttBarTextDateFormat** Method, **GanttChartWizard** Method, **GanttShowDrawings** Method.

GanttBarSize Method

Applies To   **Application** Object.

Description   Sets the width, in points, of the Gantt bars in the active Gantt Chart.

Syntax   [*object.*]**GanttBarSize** *size*

Elements   The **GanttBarSize** method syntax has the following object qualifier and named arguments:

Part	Description
object	An object expression that evaluates to an object in the Applies To list. Optional.
size	A constant that specifies the width, in points, of the Gantt bars in the active Gantt Chart. Required.

The *size* argument has these settings:

pjBarSize6	6	The width of the Gantt bars is 6 points.
pjBarSize8	8	The width of the Gantt bars is 8 points.
pjBarSize10	10	The width of the Gantt bars is 10 points.
pjBarSize12	12	The width of the Gantt bars is 12 points.
pjBarSize14	14	The width of the Gantt bars is 14 points.
pjBarSize18	18	The width of the Gantt bars is 18 points.
pjBarSize24	24	The width of the Gantt bars is 24 points.

See Also   **GanttBarFormat** Method, **GanttBarLinks** Method, **GanttBarStyleDelete** Method, **GanttBarStyleEdit** Method, **GanttBarTextDateFormat** Method, **GanttChartWizard** Method, **GanttShowDrawings** Method.

GanttBarStyleDelete Method

Applies To   **Application** Object.

Description   Deletes a Gantt bar style from the active Gantt Chart.

Syntax   [*object.*]**GanttBarStyleDelete** *item*

Elements   The **GanttBarStyleDelete** method syntax has the following object qualifier and named arguments:

Part	Description
object	An object expression that evaluates to an object in the Applies To list. Optional.
item	A string expression that specifies the name or row number of the Gantt bar to delete from the Bar Styles dialog box. (The Bar Styles dialog box appears when you choose Bar Styles from the Format menu.) Required.

See Also   **GanttBarLinks** Method, **GanttBarSize** Method, **GanttBarStyleEdit** Method, **GanttBarTextDateFormat** Method, **GanttChartWizard** Method, **GanttShowDrawings** Method.

GanttBarStyleEdit Method

Applies To   **Application** Object.

Description   Changes or creates a Gantt bar style.

Syntax   [*object.*]**GanttBarStyleEdit** *item*, *create*[, *name*, *startShape*, *startType*, *startColor*, *middleShape*, *middleColor*, *middlePattern*, *endShape*, *endType*, *endColor*, *showFor*, *row*, *from*, *to*, *bottomText*, *topText*, *leftText*, *rightText*, *insideText*]

Elements   The **GanttBarStyleEdit** method syntax has the following object qualifier and named arguments:

Part	Description
object	An object expression that evaluates to an object in the Applies To list. Optional.
item	A string expression that specifies the name or row number of the Gantt bar style to change in the Bar Styles dialog box. (The Bar Styles box appears when you choose Bar Styles from the Format menu.) Required.
create	A Boolean expression that specifies whether to create a new Gantt bar style. If you set the *create* argument to **True**, a new Gantt bar style is inserted in the Bar Styles dialog box before the Gantt bar style you specify with the *item* argument. If the *item* argument is "-1", then the new Gantt bar style is added to the end of the list of styles. By default, the *create* argument is **False**. Required.
name	A string expression that specifies a new name for the Gantt bar. Optional.
startShape	A constant that specifies the start shape of the Gantt bar. Optional.
startType	A constant that specifies the start type of the Gantt bar. Optional.
startColor	A constant that specifies the start color of the Gantt bar. Optional.
middleShape	A constant that specifies the middle shape of the Gantt bar. Optional.
middleColor	A constant that specifies the middle color of the Gantt bar. Optional.
middlePattern	A constant that specifies the middle pattern of the Gantt bar. Optional.
endShape	A constant that specifies the end shape of the Gantt bar. Optional.
endType	A constant that specifies the end type of the Gantt bar. Optional.
endColor	A constant that specifies the end color of the Gantt bar. Optional.
showFor	A string expression that specifies one or more task types, separated by the list separator character. Optional.
row	A numeric expression from 1 to 4 that specifies the row in which the Gantt bar appears. Optional.
from	A string expression that specifies the date field for the start of the Gantt bar. Optional.
to	A string expression that specifies the date field for the end of the Gantt bar. Optional.

Part	Description
bottomText	A string expression that specifies a task field to display below the Gantt bar. Optional.
topText	A string expression that specifies a task field to display above the Gantt bar. Optional.
leftText	A string expression that specifies a task field to display to the left of the Gantt bar. Optional.
rightText	A string expression that specifies a task field to display to the right of the Gantt bar. Optional.
insideText	A string expression that specifies a task field to display inside the Gantt bar. Optional.

The *startShape* and *endShape* arguments have these settings:

pjNone	0	None
pjHouseUp	1	House
pjHouseDown	2	Upside-down house
pjDiamond	3	Diamond
pjCircleDiamond	4	Circled diamond
pjTriangleUp	5	Triangle pointing up
pjTriangleDown	6	Triangle pointing down
pjTriangleRight	7	Triangle pointing right
pjTriangleLeft	8	Triangle pointing left
pjCircleTriangleUp	9	Circled triangle pointing up
pjCircleTriangleDown	10	Circled triangle pointing down
pjArrowUp	11	Arrow pointing up
pjArrowDown	12	Arrow pointing down
pjCircleArrowUp	13	Circled arrow pointing up
pjCircleArrowDown	14	Circled arrow pointing down
pjCaretDownTop	15	Caret pointing down on the top half of the bar
pjCaretUpBottom	16	Caret pointing up on the bottom half of the bar
pjLine	17	Line
pjSquare	18	Square
pjCircle	19	Circle
pjStar	20	Star

The *startType* and *endType* arguments have these settings:

pjDashed	0	Dashed
pjFramed	1	Framed
pjSolid	2	Solid

The *startColor*, *middleColor*, and *endColor* arguments have these settings:

pjBlack	0	Black
pjRed	1	Red
pjYellow	2	Yellow
pjLime	3	Lime
pjAqua	4	Aqua
pjBlue	5	Blue
pjFuchsia	6	Fuchsia
pjWhite	7	White
pjMaroon	8	Maroon
pjGreen	9	Green
pjOlive	10	Olive
pjNavy	11	Navy
pjPurple	12	Purple
pjTeal	13	Teal
pjGray	14	Gray
pjSilver	15	Silver

The *middleShape* argument has these settings:

pjNone	0	None
pjRectangle	1	Rectangle
pjRectangleTop	2	Rectangle in top third of available space
pjRectangleMiddle	3	Rectangle in middle third of available space
pjRectangleBottom	4	Rectangle in bottom third of available space
pjLineTop	5	Line in top third of available space
pjLineMiddle	6	Line in middle third of available space
pjLineBottom	7	Line in bottom third of available space

The *middlePattern* argument has these settings:

pjHollow	0	Hollow
pjSolid	1	Solid
pjLightFill	2	Light fill
pjMediumFill	3	Medium fill
pjDarkFill	4	Dark fill
pjDiagonalLeft	5	Diagonal left
pjDiagonalRight	6	Diagonal right
pjDiagonalCross	7	Diagonal cross
pjLineVertical	8	Vertical line
pjLineHorizontal	9	Horizontal line
pjLineCross	10	Crossed line

Remarks

The Bar Styles dialog box can contain up to 20 style entries.

See Also

GanttBarFormat Method, **GanttBarLinks** Method, **GanttBarSize** Method, **GanttBarStyleDelete** Method, **GanttBarTextDateFormat** Method, **GanttChartWizard** Method, **GanttShowDrawings** Method.

Example

The following example creates a new bar style that consists of a light green color and ends with a star shape.

```
Sub ModifyGanttBar()
    GanttBarStyleEdit item:=-1, create:=True, Name:="Kris' Bar Style", _
        middleColor:=3, endShape:=20
End Sub
```

GanttBarTextDateFormat Method

Applies To

Application Object.

Description

Sets the date format for text around bars on the Gantt Chart.

Syntax

[*object*.]**GanttBarTextDateFormat** [*dateFormat*]

Elements

The **GanttBarTextDateFormat** method syntax has the following object qualifier and named arguments:

Part	Description
object	An object expression that evaluates to an object in the Applies To list.
dateFormat	A constant that specifies the format of dates in the Gantt bar text.

The *dateFormat* argument has these settings:

pjDateDefault	-1	The default format, as specified on the View tab of the Options dialog box. (To display the Options dialog box, choose Options from the Tools menu.)
pjDate_mm_dd_yy_hh_mmAM	0	1/31/94 12:33 PM
pjDate_mm_dd_yy	1	1/31/94
pjDate_mmmm_dd_yyyy_hh_mmAM	2	January 31, 1994 12:33 PM
pjDate_mmmm_dd_yyyy	3	January 31, 1994
pjDate_mmm_dd_hh_mmAM	4	Jan 31 12:33 PM
pjDate_mmm_dd_yyy	5	Jan 31 '94
pjDate_mmmm_dd	6	January 31
pjDate_mmm_dd	7	Jan 31
pjDate_ddd_mm_dd_yy_hh_mmAM	8	Mon 1/31/94 12:33 PM
pjDate_ddd_mm_dd_yy	9	Mon 1/31/94
pjDate_ddd_mmm_dd_yyy	10	Mon Jan 31, '94
pjDate_ddd_hh_mmAM	11	Mon 12:33 PM
pjDate_mm_dd	12	1/31
pjDate_dd	13	31
pjDate_hh_mmAM	14	12:33 PM
pjDate_ddd_mmm_dd	15	Mon Jan 31
pjDate_ddd_mm_dd	16	Mon 1/31
pjDate_ddd_dd	17	Mon 31
pjDate_Www_dd	18	W05/1
pjDate_Www_dd_yy_hh_mmAM	19	W05/1/94 12:33 PM

See Also   **GanttBarFormat** Method, **GanttBarLinks** Method, **GanttBarSize** Method, **GanttBarStyleDelete** Method, **GanttBarStyleEdit** Method, **GanttChartWizard** Method, **GanttShowDrawings** Method.

GanttChartWizard Method

Applies To   **Application** Object.

Description   Starts the GanttChartWizard.

Syntax   [*object*.]**GanttChartWizard**

Elements   The *object* placeholder is an object expression that evaluates to an object in the Applies To list.

See Also   **GanttBarFormat** Method, **HelpAbout** Method, **HelpCueCards** Method, **HelpLaunch** Method, **HelpOnlineIndex** Method, **HelpQuickPreview** Method, **HelpSearch** Method, **HelpTechnicalSupport** Method.

GanttShowDrawings Method

Applies To   **Application** Object.

Description   Hides or shows drawings on the Gantt Chart.

Syntax   [*object*.]**GanttShowDrawings** [*display*]

Elements   The **GanttShowDrawings** method syntax has the following object qualifier and named arguments:

Part	Description
object	An object expression that evaluates to an object in the Applies To list.
display	A Boolean expression that specifies whether to show drawings on the Gantt Chart. By default, the *display* argument is **True**.

See Also   **GanttBarFormat** Method, **GanttBarLinks** Method, **GanttBarSize** Method, **GanttBarStyleDelete** Method, **GanttBarStyleEdit** Method, **GanttBarTextDateFormat** Method, **GanttChartWizard** Method.

Get Statement

Description   Declares the name, arguments, and code that form the body of a **Property** procedure, which gets the value of a property.

Syntax   [**Public** | **Private**][**Static**] **Property Get** *name* [(*arglist*)][**As** *type*]
    [*statements*]
    [*name* = *expression*]
    [**Exit Property**]
    [*statements*]
    [*name* = *expression*]
    End Property

Elements   The **Property Get** statement syntax has these parts:

Part	Description
Public	Indicates that the **Property Get** procedure is accessible to all other procedures in all modules. If used in a private module (one that contains an **Option Private** statement) the procedure is not available outside the project.
Private	Indicates that the **Property Get** procedure is accessible only to other procedures in the module where it is declared.
Static	Indicates that the **Property Get** procedure's local variables are preserved between calls. The **Static** attribute doesn't affect variables that are declared outside the **Property Get** procedure, even if they are used in the procedure.
name	Name of the **Property Get** procedure; follows standard variable naming conventions, except that the name can be the same as a **Property Let** or **Property Set** procedure in the same module.
arglist	List of variables representing arguments that are passed to the **Property Get** procedure when it is called. Multiple variables are separated by commas.
type	Data type of the value returned by the **Property Get** procedure; may be **Boolean**, **Integer**, **Long**, **Currency**, **Single**, **Double**, **Date**, **String** (except fixed length), **Object**, or **Variant**. Arrays of any type can't be returned, but a **Variant** containing an array can.
statements	Any group of statements to be executed within the body of the **Property Get** procedure.
expression	Value of the property returned by the procedure defined by the **Property Get** statement.

The *arglist* argument has the following syntax and parts:

[**Optional**][**ByVal** | **ByRef**] *varname*[( )][**As** *type*]

Part	Description
Optional	Indicates that an argument is not required. If used, all subsequent arguments in *arglist* must also be optional and declared using the **Optional** keyword. All **Optional** arguments must be **Variant**.
ByVal	Indicates that the argument is passed by value.
ByRef	Indicates that the argument is passed by reference.
varname	Name of the variable representing the argument; follows standard variable naming conventions.
type	Data type of the argument passed to the **Property Get** procedure; may be **Boolean**, **Integer**, **Long**, **Currency**, **Single**, **Double**, **Date**, **String** (variable length only), **Object**, **Variant**, a user-defined type, or an object type.

Remarks

If not explicitly specified using either **Public** or **Private**, **Property** procedures are **Public** by default. If **Static** is not used, the value of local variables is not preserved between calls.

All executable code must be in procedures. You can't define a **Property Get** procedure inside another **Sub**, **Function**, or **Property** procedure.

The **Exit Property** keywords cause an immediate exit from a **Property Get** procedure. Program execution continues with the statement following the statement that called the **Property Get** procedure. Any number of **Exit Property** statements can appear anywhere in a **Property Get** procedure.

Like a **Sub** and **Property Let** procedure, a **Property Get** procedure is a separate procedure that can take arguments, perform a series of statements, and change the values of its arguments. However, unlike a **Sub** or **Property Let** procedure, a **Property Get** procedure can be used on the right-hand side of an expression in the same way you use a **Function** or a property name when you want to return the value of a property.

See Also

Function Statement, **Property Let** Statement, **Property Set** Statement, **Sub** Statement.

Example

This example uses the **Get** statement to read data from a disk file into a variable. For purposes of this example, assume that TESTFILE is a file containing five records of the user-defined type Record.

```
Type Record ' Define user-defined type.
    ID As Integer
    Name As String * 20
End Type

Dim MyRecord As Record        ' Declare variable.
' Open sample file for random access.
Open "TESTFILE" For Random As #1 Len = Len(MyRecord)
' Read the sample file using the Get statement.
Position = 3                  ' Define record number.
Get #1, Position, MyRecord    ' Read third record.
Close #1                      ' Close file.
```

GetAttr Function

Description   Returns a number representing the attributes of a file, directory or folder, or volume label.

Syntax   **GetAttr(*pathname*)**

Elements   The ***pathname*** named argument is a string expression that specifies a file name—may include directory or folder, and drive.

Return Values   The value returned by **GetAttr** is the sum of the following attribute values:

0	vbNormal	Normal.
1	vbReadonly	Read-only.
2	vbHidden	Hidden.
4	vbSystem	System file—not available on the Macintosh.
8	vbVolume	Volume label—not available on the Macintosh.
16	vbDirectory	Directory or folder.
32	vbArchive	File has changed since last backup—not available on the Macintosh.

Note These constants are specified by Visual Basic. As a result, the names can be used anywhere in your code in place of the actual values.

Remarks

To determine which attributes are set, use the **And** operator to perform a bit-wise comparison of the value returned by the **GetAttr** function and the value of the individual file attribute you want. If the result is not zero, that attribute is set for the named file. For example, the return value of the following **And** expression is zero if the Archive attribute is not set:

```
Result = GetAttr(FName) And vbArchive
```

A nonzero value is returned if the Archive attribute is set.

See Also

FileAttr Function, **SetAttr** Statement.

Example

This example uses the **GetAttr** statement to determine the attributes of a file and directory or folder.

```
' Assume file TESTFILE has hidden attribute set.
MyAttr = GetAttr("TESTFILE") ' Returns 2.

' Assume file TESTFILE has hidden and read-only attributes set.
MyAttr = GetAttr("TESTFILE") ' Returns 3.

' Assume MYDIR is a directory or folder.
MyAttr = GetAttr("MYDIR")    ' Returns 16.
```

GetField Method

Applies To

Resource Object, **Resources** Collection; **Task** Object, **Tasks** Collection.

Description

Returns the value in a field.

Syntax

object.**GetField** (*fieldID*)

Elements

The **GetField** method syntax has the following object qualifier and named arguments:

Part	Description
object	An object expression that evaluates to an object in the Applies To list.
fieldID	A constant that specifies the field to get.

The *fieldID* argument has these settings:

pjTaskActualCost	7	Actual Cost
pjTaskActualDuration	28	Actual Duration
pjTaskActualFinish	42	Actual Finish
pjTaskActualStart	41	Actual Start

pjTaskActualWork	2	Actual Work
pjTaskBaselineCost	6	Baseline Cost
pjTaskBaselineDuration	27	Baseline Duration
pjTaskBaselineFinish	44	Baseline Finish
pjTaskBaselineStart	43	Baseline Start
pjTaskBaselineWork	1	Baseline Work
pjTaskBCWP	11	BCWP
pjTaskBCWS	12	BCWS
pjTaskConfirmed	110	Confirmed
pjTaskConstraintDate	18	Constraint Date
pjTaskConstraintType	17	Constraint Type
pjTaskContact	112	Contact
pjTaskCost	5	Cost
pjTaskCost1	106	Cost1
pjTaskCost2	107	Cost2
pjTaskCost3	108	Cost3
pjTaskCostVariance	9	Cost Variance
pjTaskCreated	93	Created
pjTaskCritical	19	Critical
pjTaskCV	83	CV
pjTaskDelay	20	Delay
pjTaskDuration	29	Duration
pjTaskDuration1	103	Duration1
pjTaskDuration2	104	Duration2
pjTaskDuration3	105	Duration3
pjTaskDurationVariance	30	Duration Variance
pjTaskEarlyFinish	38	Early Finish
pjTaskEarlyStart	37	Early Start
pjTaskFinish	36	Finish
pjTaskFinish1	53	Finish1
pjTaskFinish2	56	Finish2
pjTaskFinish3	59	Finish3
pjTaskFinish4	62	Finish4
pjTaskFinish5	65	Finish5
pjTaskFinishVariance	46	Finish Variance
pjTaskFixedCost	8	Fixed Cost

pjTaskFixedDuration	34	Fixed (Duration)
pjTaskFlag1	72	Flag1
pjTaskFlag10	81	Flag10
pjTaskFlag2	73	Flag2
pjTaskFlag3	74	Flag3
pjTaskFlag4	75	Flag4
pjTaskFlag5	76	Flag5
pjTaskFlag6	77	Flag6
pjTaskFlag7	78	Flag7
pjTaskFlag8	79	Flag8
pjTaskFlag9	80	Flag9
pjTaskFreeSlack	21	Free Slack
pjTaskHideBar	109	Hide Bar
pjTaskID	23	ID
pjTaskLateFinish	40	Late Finish
pjTaskLateStart	39	Late Start
pjTaskLinkedFields	98	Linked Fields
pjTaskMarked	71	Marked
pjTaskMilestone	24	Milestone
pjTaskName	14	Name
pjTaskNotes	15	Notes
pjTaskNumber1	87	Number1
pjTaskNumber2	88	Number2
pjTaskNumber3	89	Number3
pjTaskNumber4	90	Number4
pjTaskNumber5	91	Number5
pjTaskObjects	97	Objects
pjTaskOutlineLevel	85	Outline Level
pjTaskOutlineNumber	102	Outline Number
pjTaskPercentComplete	32	% Complete
pjTaskPercentWorkComplete	33	% Work Complete
pjTaskPredecessors	47	Predecessors
pjTaskPriority	25	Priority
pjTaskProject	84	Project
pjTaskRemainingCost	10	Remaining Cost
pjTaskRemainingDuration	31	Remaining Duration

pjTaskRemainingWork	4	Remaining Work
pjTaskResourceGroup	113	Resource Group
pjTaskResourceInitials	50	Resource Initials
pjTaskResourceNames	49	Resource Names
pjTaskResume	99	Resume
pjTaskResumeNoEarlierThan	101	Resume No Earlier Than
pjTaskRollup	82	Rollup
pjTaskSheetNotes	94	Sheet Notes
pjTaskStart	35	Start
pjTaskStart1	52	Start1
pjTaskStart2	55	Start2
pjTaskStart3	58	Start3
pjTaskStart4	61	Start4
pjTaskStart5	64	Start5
pjTaskStartVariance	45	Start Variance
pjTaskStop	100	Stop
pjTaskSubproject	26	Subproject File
pjTaskSuccessors	48	Successors
pjTaskSummary	92	Summary
pjTaskSV	13	SV
pjTaskText1	51	Text1
pjTaskText10	70	Text10
pjTaskText2	54	Text2
pjTaskText3	57	Text3
pjTaskText4	60	Text4
pjTaskText5	63	Text5
pjTaskText6	66	Text6
pjTaskText7	67	Text7
pjTaskText8	68	Text8
pjTaskText9	69	Text9
pjTaskTotalSlack	22	Total Slack
pjTaskUniqueID	86	Unique ID
pjTaskUniquePredecessors	95	Unique ID Predecessors
pjTaskUniqueSuccessors	96	Unique ID Successors
pjTaskUpdateNeeded	111	Update Needed
pjTaskWBS	16	WBS

pjTaskWork	0	Work
pjTaskWorkVariance	3	Work Variance
pjResourceAccrueAt	19	Accrue At
pjResourceActualCost	11	Actual Cost
pjResourceActualWork	14	Actual Work
pjResourceBaseCalendar	5	Base Calendar
pjResourceBaselineCost	17	Baseline Cost
pjResourceBaselineWork	15	Baseline Work
pjResourceCode	10	Code
pjResourceCost	12	Cost
pjResourceCostPerUse	18	Cost Per Use
pjResourceCostVariance	24	Cost Variance
pjResourceEMailAddress	35	Email address
pjResourceGroup	3	Group
pjResourceID	0	ID
pjResourceInitials	2	Initials
pjResourceLinkedFields	34	Linked Fields
pjResourceMaxUnits	4	Max Units
pjResourceName	1	Name
pjResourceNotes	20	Notes
pjResourceObjects	33	Objects
pjResourceOverallocated	25	Overallocated
pjResourceOvertimeRate	7	Overtime Rate
pjResourceOvertimeWork	16	Overtime Work
pjResourcePeakUnits	26	Peak
pjResourcePercentWorkComplete	29	% Work Complete
pjResourceRemainingCost	21	Remaining Cost
pjReosurceRemainingWork	22	Remaining Work
pjResourceSheetNotes	28	Sheet Notes
pjResourceStandardRate	6	Standard Rate
pjResourceText1	8	Text1
pjResourceText2	9	Text2
pjResourceText3	30	Text3
pjResourceText4	31	Text4
pjResourceText5	32	Text5

pjResourceUniqueID	27	Unique ID
pjResourceWork	13	Work
pjResourceWorkVariance	23	Work Variance

See Also   **FieldID** Property, **FieldIDList** Method, **SetField** Method.

Example   The following example displays the value entered by the user in the field.

```
Sub DisplayField()
    strTemp = InputBox("Enter the name of the field you want to see")
    strTemp = LCase (strTemp)
    Select Case strTemp
        Case "name"
            intFieldID = pjResourceName
        Case "initials"
            intFieldID = pjResourceInitials
        Case "standard rate"
            intFieldID = pjResourceStandardRate
        Case ""
            End
        Case Else
            MsgBox "You entered a field I don't understand"
            End
    End Select
    MsgBox(ActiveCell.Resource.GetField(FieldID:=intFieldID))
Done:
End Sub
```

GoSub...Return Statement

Description   Branch to and return from a subroutine within a procedure.

Syntax   **GoSub** *line*

...

line

...

Return

Elements   The *line* argument can be any line label or line number.

Remarks   You can use **GoSub** and **Return** anywhere in a procedure, but **GoSub** and the corresponding **Return** must be in the same procedure. A subroutine can contain more than one **Return** statement, but the first **Return** statement encountered causes the flow of execution to branch back to the statement immediately following the most recently executed **GoSub** statement.

Note You can't enter or exit **Sub** procedures with **GoSub...Return**.

Tip Creating separate procedures which you can call may provide a more structured alternative to using **GoSub...Return**.

See Also **End** Statement; **GoTo** Statement; **On...GoSub**, **On...GoTo** Statements; **Sub** Statement.

Example This example uses **GoSub** to call a subroutine within a **Sub** procedure. The **Return** statement causes the execution to resume at the statement immediately following the **Gosub** statement. The **Exit Sub** statement is used to prevent control from accidentally flowing into the subroutine.

```
Sub GosubDemo()
    Num = 10                ' Initialize variable.
    GoSub MyRoutine         ' Branch to subroutine.
    Debug.Print Num         ' Print value upon return.
    Exit Sub                ' Exit Sub procedure.
MyRoutine:                  ' Start of subroutine.
    Num = Num \ 2           ' Halve the value.
    Return                  ' Return from subroutine.
End Sub
```

GoTo Statement

Description Branches unconditionally to a specified line within a procedure.

Syntax **GoTo** *line*

Elements The *line* argument can be any line label or line number.

Remarks **GoTo** can branch only to lines within the procedure where it appears.

Note Too many **GoTo** statements can be difficult to read and debug. Use structured control statements (**Do...Loop**, **For...Next**, **If...Then...Else**, **Select Case**) whenever possible.

See Also **Do...Loop** Statement, **For...Next** Statement, **GoSub...Return** Statement, **If...Then...Else** Statement, **Select Case** Statement.

Example This example uses the **GoTo** statement to branch to line labels within a procedure.

```
Sub GotoStatementDemo()
    Number = 1              ' Initialize variable.
    ' Evaluate Number and branch to appropriate label.
    If Number = 1 Then GoTo Line1 Else GoTo Line2

Line1:
    MyString = "Number equals 1"
    GoTo LastLine           ' Go to LastLine.
Line2:
    ' The following statement never gets executed.
    MyString = "Number equals 2"
LastLine:
    Debug.Print MyString    ' Print 1 in Debug window.
End Sub
```

GotoNextOverallocation Method

Applies To   **Application** Object.

Description   Scrolls a timescale view to display the next overallocated resource.

Syntax   [*object*.]**GotoNextOverallocation**

Elements   The *object* placeholder is an object expression that evaluates to an object in the Applies To list.

See Also   **EditGoto** Method, **GotoTaskDates** Method.

GotoTaskDates Method

Applies To   **Application** Object.

Description   Scrolls the Gantt Chart to display the starting date of the active task.

Syntax   [*object*.]**GotoTaskDates**

Elements   The *object* placeholder is an object expression that evaluates to an object in the Applies To list.

See Also   **GotoNextOverallocation** Method.

Gridlines Method

Applies To	**Application** Object.
Description	Displays the Gridlines dialog box.
Syntax	[*object*.]**Gridlines**
Elements	The *object* placeholder is an object expression that evaluates to an object in the Applies To list.
See Also	**GridlinesEdit** Method.

GridlinesEdit Method

Applies To	**Application** Object.
Description	Edits gridlines.
Syntax	[*object*.]**GridlinesEdit** *item*, *normalType*, *normalColor*, *interval*, *intervalType*, *intervalColor*
Elements	The **GridlinesEdit** method syntax has the following object qualifier and named arguments:

Part	Description
object	An object expression that evaluates to an object in the Applies To list. Optional.
item	A constant that specifies the gridline to edit. Required.
normalType	A constant that specifies the type for normal gridlines. Optional.
normalColor	A constant that specifies the color for normal gridlines. Optional.
interval	A numeric expression from 0 to 99 that specifies the interval between gridlines. Optional.
intervalType	A constant that specifies the type for secondary gridlines. Optional.
intervalColor	A constant that specifies the color for secondary gridlines. Optional.

The *item* argument has these settings for the Gantt Chart:

pjBarRows	1	Bar rows
pjMajorColumns	2	Major columns
pjMinorColumns	3	Minor columns
pjGanttCurrentDate	4	Current date
pjGanttSheetRows	5	Sheet rows
pjGanttSheetColumns	6	Sheet columns
pjGanttTitleVertical	7	Vertical title
pjGanttTitleHorizontal	8	Horizontal title
pjGanttPageBreaks	9	Page breaks
pjGanttProjectStart	10	Project start
pjGanttProjectFinish	11	Project finish

The *item* argument has these settings for the Calendar:

pjCalendarDays	0	Days
pjCalendarWeeks	1	Weeks
pjCalendarTitleVertical	2	Vertical title
pjCalendarTitleHorizontal	3	Horizontal title
pjDateBoxTop	4	Top of date box
pjDateBoxBottom	5	Bottom of date box

The *item* argument has these settings for the Resource Graph:

pjMinorVertical	1	Minor vertical headings
pjHorizontal	2	Horizontal headings
pjGraphCurrentDate	3	Current date
pjGraphTitleVertical	4	Vertical title
pjGraphTitleHorizontal	5	Horizontal title
pjGraphProjectStart	6	Project start
pjGraphProjectFinish	7	Project finish

The *item* argument has these settings for the Task and Resource Sheets:

pjSheetColumns	1	Sheet columns
pjSheetTitleVertical	2	Vertical title
pjSheetTitleHorizontal	3	Horizontal title
pjSheetPageBreaks	4	Page breaks

The *item* argument has these settings for the Resource Usage view:

pjUsageMajorColumns	1	Major columns
pjUsageMinorColumns	2	Minor columns
pjUsageSheetRows	3	Sheet rows
pjUsageSheetColumns	4	Sheet columns
pjUsageTitleVertical	5	Vertical title
pjUsageTitleHorizontal	6	Horizontal title
pjUsagePageBreaks	7	Page breaks
pjUsageProjectStart	8	Project start
pjUsageProjectFinish	9	Project finish

The *normalType* and *intervalType* arguments have these settings:

pjNone	0	None
pjContinuous	1	Solid
pjCloseDot	2	Close-dotted
pjDot	3	Dotted
pjDash	4	Dashed

The *normalColor* and *intervalColor* arguments have these settings:

pjBlack	0	Black
pjRed	1	Red
pjYellow	2	Yellow
pjLime	3	Lime
pjAqua	4	Aqua
pjBlue	5	Blue
pjFuchsia	6	Fuchsia
pjWhite	7	White
pjMaroon	8	Maroon
pjGreen	9	Green
pjOlive	10	Olive
pjNavy	11	Navy
pjPurple	12	Purple
pjTeal	13	Teal
pjGray	14	Gray
pjSilver	15	Silver

Group Property

Applies To	**Project** Object, **Projects** Collection; **Task** Object, **Tasks** Collection.
Description	The names of groups associated with the resources for a task.
Syntax	*object*.**ResourceGroup**
Elements	The *object* placeholder is an object expression that evaluates to an object in the Applies To list.
Remarks	For example, if Bob's group is "Writers" and Greg's group is "Editors", and Greg and Bob are assigned to the same task, then the **ResourceGroup** property for that task returns "Writers,Editors".

Note This example assumes that the list separator character is the comma (,). You can set the list separator character with the **ListSeparator** property.

See Also	**Group** Property, **ResourceInitials** Property, **ResourceNames** Property, **ResourcePoolName** Property.

HasPassword Property

Applies To	**Project** Object, **Projects** Collection.
Description	Returns whether a project has a password.
Syntax	*object*.**HasPassword**
Elements	The *object* placeholder is an object expression that evaluates to an object in the Applies To list.
Settings	The **HasPassword** property has these settings:

Setting	Description
True	The project has a password.
False	The project does not have a password.

See Also   **CreationDate** Property, **FullName** Property, **LastSaveDate** Property, **LastSavedBy** Property, **Name** Property, **Path** Property, **ReadOnly** Property, **ReadOnlyRecommended** Property, **RevisionNumber** Property, **Saved** Property, **WriteReserved** Property.

Example   The following example displays a list of open projects that have passwords.

```
Sub ListProjectsWithPasswords()
    Dim P                       ' Project object used in For Each loop
    Dim NameList                ' Names of projects with passwords
    Dim NL                      ' Newline characters
    NL = Chr(13) & Chr(10)      ' NL = Carriage Return + Linefeed

    ' Check each open project for passwords.
    For Each P in Application.Projects

        ' If a project has a password, add its name to the list.
        If P.HasPassword Then
            NameList = NameList & P.Name & NL
        End If
    Next

    ' Display information about projects with passwords.
    If NameList = "" Then
        MsgBox("No open projects have passwords.")
    Else
        MsgBox("The following open projects have passwords: " & _
            NL & NL & NameList)
    End If
End Sub
```

Height Property

Applies To   **Application** Object; **Window** Object, **Windows** Collection.

Description   Returns or sets the height of the main window (**Application** object) or a project window (**Window** object).

Syntax   *object*.**Height** [= *value*]

Elements   The **Height** property syntax has these parts:

Part	Description
object	An object expression that evaluates to an object in the Applies To list.
value	A numeric expression that specifies the height of the window, in points.

Remarks A window changes its height by moving its bottom corners. For Microsoft Project for the Macintosh, this property is supported read-only for the **Application** object.

See Also **Caption** Property, **Left** Property, **Top** Property, **UsableHeight** Property, **UsableWidth** Property, **Visible** Property, **Width** Property, **WindowState** Property.

Example The following example places the main window in the lower half of the screen.

```
Sub PlaceProjectInLowerScreenHalf()
    Application.WindowState = pjMaximized
    Application.Height = Application.Height / 2
    Application.Top = Application.Height
End Sub
```

HelpAbout Method

Applies To **Application** Object.

Description Displays the About Microsoft Project dialog box, which lists version, copyright, and license information about Microsoft Project.

Syntax [*object.*]**HelpAbout**

Elements The *object* placeholder is an object expression that evaluates to an object in the Applies To list.

Remarks In Microsoft Project for Microsoft Windows, the **HelpAbout** method has the same effect as the About Microsoft Project command on the Help menu.

In Microsoft Project for the Macintosh, the **HelpAbout** method has the same effect as the About Microsoft Project command on the Apple menu.

See Also **About** Method, **GanttChartWizard** Method, **HelpCueCards** Method, **HelpLaunch** Method, **HelpOnlineIndex** Method, **HelpQuickPreview** Method, **HelpSearch** Method, **HelpTechnicalSupport** Method.

HelpAnswerWizard Method

Applies To **Application** Object.

Description	Displays the Help Topics dialog with the AnswerWizard tab on top. The difference between this method and the HelpTopics method is that the HelpTopics method remembers which tab was last active while the HelpAnswerWizard method always places the AnswerWizard on top.
Syntax	[*object.*]**HelpAnswerWizard**
Elements	The *object* placeholder is an object expression that evaluates to an object in the Applies To list
Remarks	Available in all views.
See Also	**HelpAnswerWizard** Method, **HelpSearch** Method.

HelpContents Method

Applies To	**Application** Object.
Description	Displays the Microsoft Project Help Topics dialog with the Contents tab on top.
Syntax	[*object.*]**HelpContents**
Elements	The *object* placeholder is an object expression that evaluates to an object in the Applies To list.
Remarks	In Microsoft Windows 95, the **HelpContents** method has the same effect as the Microsoft Project Help Topics command on the Help menu.
	On the Macintosh, the **HelpContents** method has the same effect as the Microsoft Project Help command on the ? menu.
See Also	**HelpAbout** Method.

HelpContextHelp Method

Applies To	**Application** Object.
Description	Invokes the ScreenTip cursor. Clicking a context displays a ScreenTip popup..
Syntax	[*object.*]**HelpContextHelp**

Elements   The *object* placeholder is an object expression that evaluates to an object in the Applies To list.

See Also   **HelpAbout** Method, **HelpContents** Method, **HelpContextHelp** Method, **HelpCueCards** Method, **HelpLaunch** Method, **HelpOnlineIndex** Method, **HelpQuickPreview** Method, **HelpSearch** Method, **HelpTechnicalSupport** Method.

HelpCueCards Method

Applies To   **Application** Object.

Description   Starts Cue Cards.

Syntax   [*object.*]**HelpCueCards** [*fileName, contextNumber*]

Elements   The **HelpCueCards** method syntax has the following object qualifier and named arguments:

Part	Description
object	An object expression that evaluates to an object in the Applies To list. Optional.
fileName	A string expression that specifies the filename of the Cue Cards to start. Optional. If *filename* is not specified, the Help Topics dialog is displayed with the Contents tab on top.
contextNumber	A numeric expression that specifies the context number of a topic to display. Optional.

Remarks   There are no Cue Cards in Microsoft Project 4.1. This method is supported for Microsoft Project 4.0.

See Also   **GanttChartWizard** Method, **HelpAbout** Method, **HelpLaunch** Method, **HelpOnlineIndex** Method, **HelpQuickPreview** Method, **HelpSearch** Method, **HelpTechnicalSupport** Method.

HelpKeywordHelp Method

Applies To   **Application** Object.

Description   Displays the Help topic for the VBA keyword selected in the VBA code window.

Syntax	[*object*.]**HelpKeywordHelp**
Elements	The *object* placeholder is an object expression that evaluates to an object in the Applies To list
Remarks	Available in the Module Editor view only. This method does not work when run from a macro. You must define a toolbar button or menu item to run this method.
See Also	**HelpAnswerWizard** Method, **HelpSearch** Method.

HelpLaunch Method

Applies To	**Application** Object.
Description	Starts a Help file.
Syntax	[*object*.]**HelpLaunch** [*fileName*, *contextNumber*, *search*, *searchKey*]
Elements	The **HelpLaunch** method syntax has the following object qualifier and named arguments:

Part	Description
object	An object expression that evaluates to an object in the Applies To list. Optional.
fileName	A string expression that specifies the name of the Help file to start. Optional.
contextNumber	A numeric expression that specifies the context number of a topic to display. Optional.
search	A Boolean expression that specifies whether to display the Help Topics dialog with the Index tab on top, which allows the user to search for a particular topic. If you set the *search* argument to **True**, the *contextNumber* argument is ignored. By default, the *search* argument is **False**. Optional.
searchKey	A string expression that specifies a keyword for the Index tab to search on. Optional.

See Also	**GanttChartWizard** Method, **HelpAbout** Method, **HelpCueCards** Method, **HelpOnlineIndex** Method, **HelpQuickPreview** Method, **HelpSearch** Method, **HelpTechnicalSupport** Method.

Example

The following example displays the topic or list of topics, if the keyword has a match. If there is no match, it displays the Microsoft Project Help Topics dialog with the Index tab on top with "task" entered as the search word.

```
Sub SearchHelp()
    HelpLaunch search:=True, searchKey:="task"
End Sub
```

HelpMicrosoftNetwork Method

Applies To   **Application** Object.

Description   Displays a dialog which lists shortcuts to areas on the Microsoft Network.

Syntax   [*object*.]**HelpMicrosoftNetwork**

Elements   The *object* placeholder is an object expression that evaluates to an object in the Applies To list

Remarks   Available in all views when you have an account on, and are connected to, the Microsoft Network.

See Also   **HelpAnswerWizard** Method, **HelpSearch** Method.

HelpOnlineIndex Method

Applies To   **Application** Object.

Description   Displays the Microsoft Project Help Topics dialog.

Syntax   [*object*.]**HelpOnlineIndex**

Elements   The *object* placeholder is an object expression that evaluates to an object in the Applies To list.

Remarks   The **HelpOnlineIndex** method has the same effect as the **HelpTopics** method for Microsoft Project 4.1.

See Also   **GanttChartWizard** Method, **HelpAbout** Method, **HelpCueCards** Method, **HelpLaunch** Method, **HelpQuickPreview** Method, **HelpSearch** Method, **HelpTechnicalSupport** Method.

HelpQuickPreview Method

Applies To	**Application** Object.
Description	Starts the Quick Preview of Microsoft Project.
Syntax	[*object*.]**HelpQuickPreview**
Elements	The *object* placeholder is an object expression that evaluates to an object in the Applies To list.
See Also	**HelpAbout** Method, **HelpContents** Method, **HelpCueCards** Method, **HelpLaunch** Method, **HelpOnlineIndex** Method, **HelpSearch** Method, **HelpTechnicalSupport** Method.

HelpSearch Method

Applies To	**Application** Object.
Description	Displays the Microsoft Project Help Topics dialog.
Syntax	[*object*.]**HelpSearch**
Elements	The *object* placeholder is an object expression that evaluates to an object in the Applies To list.
Remarks	The **HelpSearch** method has the same effect as the **HelpTopics** method for Microsoft Project 4.1.
See Also	**GanttChartWizard** Method, **HelpAbout** Method, **HelpCueCards** Method, **HelpLaunch** Method, **HelpOnlineIndex** Method, **HelpQuickPreview** Method, **HelpTechnicalSupport** Method.

HelpTechnicalSupport Method

Applies To	**Application** Object.
Description	Displays information about obtaining technical support for Microsoft Project.
Syntax	[*object*.]**HelpTechnicalSupport**

Elements   The *object* placeholder is an object expression that evaluates to an object in the Applies To list.

Remarks   The **HelpTechnicalSupport** method has the same effect as selecting Product Support from Help Contents for Microsoft Windows 95 or the ? menu for the Macintosh.

See Also   **GanttChartWizard** Method, **HelpAbout** Method, **HelpCueCards** Method, **HelpLaunch** Method, **HelpOnlineIndex** Method, **HelpQuickPreview** Method, **HelpSearch** Method.

HelpTopics Method

Applies To   **Application** Object.

Description   Launches Help with the Microsoft Project Help file displaying the Help Topics dialog.

Syntax   [*object*.]**HelpTopics**

Elements   The *object* placeholder is any object expression that evaluates to an object in the Applies To list.

Remarks   Available in all views or when there is no open project.

See Also   **HelpAnswerWizard** Method, **HelpSearch** Method.

Hex Function

Description   Returns a string representing the hexadecimal value of a number.

Syntax   **Hex(*number*)**

Elements   The *number* named argument is any valid numeric expression.

Remarks   If *number* is not already a whole number, it is rounded to the nearest whole number before being evaluated.

If *number* is	Hex returns
Null	An error.
Empty	Zero (0).
Any other number	Up to eight hexadecimal characters.

You can represent hexadecimal numbers directly by preceding numbers in the proper range with `&H`. For example, `&H10` represents decimal 16 in hexadecimal notation.

See Also   **Oct** Function.

Example   This example uses the **Hex** function to return the hexadecimal value of a number.

```
MyHex = Hex(5)        ' Returns 5.
MyHex = Hex(10)       ' Returns A.
MyHex = Hex(459)      ' Returns 1CB.
```

HideBar Property

Applies To   **Project** Object, **Projects** Collection; **Task** Object, **Tasks** Collection.

Description   Returns or sets whether a task bar appears on the Gantt Chart or Calendar.

Syntax   *object*.**HideBar** [= *value*]

Elements   The **HideBar** property syntax has the following parts:

Part	Description
object	An object expression that evaluates to an object in the Applies To list.
value	A Boolean expression that specifies whether the task bar appears on the Gantt Chart or Calendar.

See Also   **Rollup** Property, **Summary** Property.

Hour Function

Description   Returns a whole number between 0 and 23, inclusive, representing the hour of the day.

Syntax	**Hour**(*time*)
Elements	The *time* named argument is limited to a time or numbers and strings, in any combination, that can represent a time. If *time* contains no valid data, **Null** is returned.
See Also	**Day** Function, **Minute** Function, **Now** Function, **Second** Function, **Time** Function, **Time** Statement.
Example	This example uses the **Hour** function to obtain the hour from a specified time.

```
' In the development environment, the time (date literal) will display
' in short format using the locale settings of your code.
MyTime = #4:35:17 PM#    ' Assign a time.
MyHour = Hour(MyTime)    ' MyHour contains 16.
```

HoursPerDay Property

Applies To	**Project** Object, **Projects** Collection.
Description	Returns or sets the number of hours per day for a project.
Syntax	*object*.**HoursPerDay** [= *value*]
Elements	The **HoursPerDay** property syntax has the following parts:

Part	Description
object	An object expression that evaluates to an object in the Applies To list.
value	A numeric expression that specifies the default hours per day for the project.

See Also	**HoursPerWeek** Property.

HoursPerWeek Property

Applies To	**Project** Object, **Projects** Collection.
Description	Returns or sets the number of hours per week for a project.
Syntax	*object*.**HoursPerWeek** [= *value*]
Elements	The **HoursPerWeek** property syntax has the following parts:

Part	Description
object	An object expression that evaluates to an object in the Applies To list.
value	A numeric expression that specifies the default hours per week for the project.

See Also   **HoursPerDay** Property.

ID Property

Applies To   **Project** Object, **Projects** Collection, **Resource** Object, **Resources** Collection, **Task** Object, **Tasks** Collection.

Description   Returns the identification number of the task or resource.

Syntax   *object*.**ID**

Elements   The *object* placeholder is any object expression that evaluates to an object in the Applies To list.

Remarks   The **ID** property changes when a task or resource moves to a new location on a Task Sheet or Resource Sheet. Use the **UniqueID** property if you want a constant reference to a task or resource.

If...Then...Else Statement

Conditionally executes a group of statements, depending on the value of an expression.

Syntax 1   **If** *condition* **Then** *statements* [**Else** *elsestatements*]

Syntax 2   **If** *condition* **Then**
    [*statements*]
[**ElseIf** *condition-n* **Then**
    [*elseifstatements*]] . . .
[**Else**
    [*elsestatements*]]
End If

Elements

Syntax 1 has these parts:

Part	Description
condition	Numeric or string expression that evaluates **True** or **False**.
statements	One or more statements separated by colons; executed if *condition* is **True**.
elsestatements	One or more statements separated by colons; executed if *condition* is **False**.

Syntax 2 has these parts:

Part	Description
condition	Expression that is **True** or **False**.
statements	One or more statements executed if *condition* is **True**.
condition-n	Numeric or string expression that evaluates **True** or **False**.
elseifstatements	One or more statements executed if associated *condition-n* is **True**.
elsestatements	One or more statements executed if no previous *condition-n* expressions are **True**.

Remarks

You can use the single-line form (Syntax 1) for short, simple tests. However, the block form (Syntax 2) provides more structure and flexibility than the single-line form and is usually easier to read, maintain, and debug.

Note With Syntax 1 it is possible to have multiple statements executed as the result of an **If...Then** decision, but they must all be on the same line and separated by colons, as in the following statement:

```
If A > 10 Then A = A + 1 : B = B + A : C = C + B
```

When executing a block **If** (Syntax 2), *condition* is tested. If *condition* is **True**, the statements following **Then** are executed. If *condition* is **False**, each **ElseIf** condition (if any) is evaluated in turn. When a **True** condition is found, the statements immediately following the associated **Then** are executed. If none of the **ElseIf** conditions are **True** (or if there are no **ElseIf** clauses), the statements following **Else** are executed. After executing the statements following **Then** or **Else**, execution continues with the statement following **End If**.

The **Else** and **ElseIf** clauses are both optional. You can have as many **ElseIf** clauses as you want in a block **If**, but none can appear after an **Else** clause. Block **If** statements can be nested; that is, contained within one another.

What follows the **Then** keyword is examined to determine whether or not a statement is a block **If**. If anything other than a comment appears after **Then** on the same line, the statement is treated as a single-line **If** statement.

A block **If** statement must be the first statement on a line. The **Else**, **ElseIf**, and **End If** parts of the statement can have only a line number or line label preceding them. The block **If** must end with an **End If** statement.

Tip **Select Case** may be more useful when evaluating a single expression that has several possible actions.

See Also

Select Case Statement.

Example

This example shows uses of the **If...Then...Else** statement.

```
Number = 53 ' Initialize variable.
If Number < 10 Then
    Digits = 1
ElseIf Number < 100 Then
' Condition evaluates to True so the next statement is executed.
    Digits = 2
Else
    Digits = 3
End If
' Assign a value using the single line form of syntax.
If Digits = 1 Then MyString = "One" Else MyString = "More than one"
```

Imp Operator

Description

Used to perform a logical implication on two expressions.

Syntax

result = *expression1* **Imp** *expression2*

Elements

The **Imp** operator syntax has these parts:

Part	Description
result	Any numeric variable.
expression1	Any expression.
expression2	Any expression.

Remarks

The following table illustrates how *result* is determined:

True	**True**	**True**
True	**False**	**False**
True	**Null**	**Null**
False	**True**	**True**
False	**False**	**True**
False	**Null**	**True**
Null	**True**	**True**
Null	**False**	**Null**
Null	**Null**	**Null**

The **Imp** operator performs a bit-wise comparison of identically positioned bits in two numeric expressions and sets the corresponding bit in *result* according to the following truth table:

0	0	1
0	1	1
1	0	0
1	1	1

See Also

Operator Precedence.

Example

This example uses the **Imp** Operator to perform logical implication on two expressions.

```
A = 10: B = 8: C = 6 : D = Null   ' Initialize variables.
MyCheck = A > B Imp B > C          ' Returns True.
MyCheck = A > B Imp C > B          ' Returns False.
MyCheck = B > A Imp C > B          ' Returns True.
MyCheck = B > A Imp C > D          ' Returns True.
MyCheck = C > D Imp B > A          ' Returns Null.
MyCheck = B Imp A                  ' Returns -1 (bit-wise comparison).
```

Index Property

Applies To

Assignment Object, **Assignments** Collection; **Calendar** Object, **Calendars** Collection; **Day** Object, **Days** Collection; **Month** Object, **Months** Collection; **Pane** Object; **Project** Object, **Projects** Collection; **Resource** Object, **Resources** Collection; **Shift** Object; **Task** Object, **Tasks** Collection; **Weekday** Object, **Weekdays** Collection; **Window** Object, **Windows** Collection; **Year** Object, **Years** Collection.

Description	Returns the index of an object in its containing collection.
Syntax	*object*.**Index**
Elements	The *object* placeholder is any object expression that evaluates to an object in the Applies To list.
Remarks	For the **Shift** object, the **Index** property returns a shift number (1, 2, or 3). For the **Pane** object, the **Index** property returns 1 for an upper pane or 2 for a lower pane.
See Also	**Add** Method, **Count** Property, **Delete** Method.
Example	The following example switches to a window in the next project with the same index as the active window. This macro can help you compare information between projects that have a similar window arrangement.

For example, if you always put a Gantt Chart in the same index of a project's **Windows** collection, you can display a Gantt Chart in one project, and then use this macro to easily switch to the Gantt Charts of your other projects.

```
Sub ActivateSameWindowInNextProject()

    ' Check for a next project.
    If ActiveProject.Index = Application.Projects.Count Then
        MsgBox("No more open projects")

    ' Check for an equivalent window in the next project.
    ElseIf ActiveProject.Windows.ActiveWindow.Index > _
        Projects(ActiveProject.Index + 1).Windows.Count Then
            MsgBox("No equivalent window in the next project")

    ' If everything's okay, switch to the window in the next project.
    Else
        Projects(ActiveProject.Index + 1). _
            Windows(ActiveWindow.Index).Activate
    End If
End Sub
```

InformationDialog Method

Applies To	**Application** Object.
Description	Displays the Task Information dialog box in task views and the Resource Information dialog box in resource views. These dialog boxes allow the user to view information about the selected tasks or resources.
Syntax	[*object*.]**InformationDialog** [*tab*]

Elements

The **InformationDialog** method syntax has the following object qualifier and named arguments:

Part	Description
object	An object expression that evaluates to an object in the Applies To list.
tab	A constant that specifies the tab to display in the Task Information dialog box. By default, the tab argument is **pjGeneralTab**.

The *tab* argument has these settings:

pjGeneralTab	0	General tab
pjPredecessorsTab	1	Predecessors tab
pjResourcesTab	2	Resources tab
pjAdvancedTab	3	Advanced tab
pjNotesTab	4	Notes tab

See Also

CustomForms Method, **Form** Method.

Initials Property

Applies To

Task Object, **Tasks** Collection.

Description

Returns the initials of the resources assigned to a task.

Syntax

object.**ResourceInitials**

Elements

The *object* placeholder is an object expression that evaluates to an object in the Applies To list.

Remarks

The **ResourceInitials** property returns "KI,TI,KD,AT,RS,BB" if the initials of the resources assigned to the task you specify are KI, TI, KD, AT, RS, and BB respectively.

Note This example assumes that the list separator character is the comma (,). You can determine the list separator character with the **ListSeparator** property.

See Also

ResourceGroup Property, **ResourceID** Property, **ResourceNames** Property, **TaskID** Property.

Input # Statement

Description   Reads data from an open sequential file and assigns the data to variables.

Syntax   **Input #***filenumber,varlist*

Elements   The **Input #** statement syntax has these parts:

Part	Description
filenumber	Any valid file number.
varlist	Comma-delimited list of variables that are assigned values read from the file: can't be an array or object variable. However, variables that describe an element of an array or user-defined type may be used.

Remarks   When read, standard string or numeric data is assigned to variables as is. The following table illustrates how other input data is treated:

Data	Value assigned to variable
Delimiting comma or blank line	**Empty**.
#NULL#	**Null**.
#TRUE# or #FALSE#	**True** or **False.**
#*yyyy-mm-dd hh:mm:ss*#	The date and/or time represented by the expression.
#ERROR *errornumber*#	*errornumber* (variable is a **Variant** tagged as an error).

Double quotation marks (**"**) within input data are ignored.

Data items in a file must appear in the same order as the variables in *varlist* and be matched with variables of the same data type. If a variable is numeric and the data is not, zero is assigned to the variable.

If the end of the file is reached while a data item is being input, the input is terminated and an error occurs.

Note In order to correctly read data from a file into variables, you should always use the **Write #** statement instead of the **Print #** statement to write the data to the files. Using **Write #** ensures that each separate data field is properly delimited.

See Also   **Input** Function, **Write #** Statement.

Example

This example uses the **Input #** statement to read data from a file into two variables. For purposes of this example, assume that TESTFILE is a file with a few lines of data written to it using the **Write #** statement; that is, each line contains a string in quotations and a number separated by a comma, for example, ("Hello", 234).

```
Open "TESTFILE" For Input As #1      ' Open file for input.
Do While Not EOF(1)                  ' Loop until end of file.
    Input #1, MyString, MyNumber     ' Read data into variables.
    Debug.Print MyString, MyNumber   ' Print data to Debug window.
Loop
Close #1                             ' Close file.
```

Input Function

Description

Returns characters (bytes) from an open sequential file.

Syntax

Input(*number*,[#]*filenumber*)

Elements

The **Input** function syntax has these parts:

Part	Description
number	Any valid numeric expression specifying the number of characters to return.
filenumber	Any valid file number.

Remarks

Use this function only with files opened in **Input** or **Binary** mode.

Unlike the **Input #** statement, the **Input** function returns all of the characters it reads including commas, carriage returns, linefeeds, quotation marks, and leading spaces.

Note   Another function (**InputB**) is provided for use with the double-byte character sets (DBCS) used in some Asian locales. Instead of specifying the number of characters to return, *number* specifies the number of bytes. In areas where DBCS is not used, **InputB** behaves the same as **Input**.

See Also

Input # Statement.

Example

This example uses the **Input** function to read one character at a time from a file and print it to the Debug window. For purposes of this example, assume that TESTFILE is a text file with a few lines of sample data.

```
Open "TESTFILE" For Input As #1    ' Open file.
Do While Not EOF(1)                ' Loop until end of file.
    MyChar = Input(1, #1)          ' Get one character.
    Debug.Print MyChar             ' Print to Debug window.
Loop
Close #1                           ' Close file.
```

InputBox Function

Description   Displays a prompt in a dialog box, waits for the user to input text or choose a button, and returns the contents of the text box.

Syntax   **InputBox(***prompt*[,*title*][,*default*][,*xpos*][,*ypos*][,*helpfile,context*]**)**

Elements   The **InputBox** function syntax has these named-argument parts:

Part	Description
prompt	String expression displayed as the message in the dialog box. The maximum length of *prompt* is approximately 1024 characters, depending on the width of the characters used. If *prompt* consists of more than one line, be sure to include a carriage return (character code 13), or carriage return linefeed (character code 10) between each line.
title	String expression displayed in the title bar of the dialog box. If you omit *title*, nothing is placed in the title bar.
default	String expression displayed in the text box as the default response if no other input is provided. If you omit *default*, the text box is displayed empty.
xpos	Numeric expression that specifies, in twips, the horizontal distance of the left edge of the dialog box from the left edge of the screen. If *xpos* is omitted, the dialog box is horizontally centered.
ypos	Numeric expression that specifies, in twips, the vertical distance of the upper edge of the dialog box from the top of the screen. If *ypos* is omitted, the dialog box is vertically positioned approximately one-third of the way down the screen.
helpfile	String expression that identifies the Help file to use to provide context-sensitive Help for the dialog box. If *helpfile* is provided, *context* must also be provided.
context	Numeric expression that is the Help context number the Help author assigned to the appropriate Help topic. If *context* is provided, *helpfile* must also be provided.

Remarks	When both *helpfile* and *context* are supplied, a Help button is automatically added to the dialog box.
	If the user chooses OK or presses Enter, the **InputBox** function returns whatever is in the text box. If the user chooses Cancel, the function returns a zero-length string ("").
See Also	**MsgBox** Function.
Example	This example shows various ways to use the **InputBox** function to prompt the user to enter a value. If the x and y positions are omitted, the dialog is automatically centered for the respective axes. The variable MyValue contains the value entered by the user if the user chooses OK or presses ENTER. If the user chooses Cancel, a zero-length string is returned.

```
Message = "Enter a value between 1 and 3"    ' Set prompt.
Title = "InputBox Demo"                      ' Set title.
Default = "1"                                ' Set default.
' Display message, title, and default value.
MyValue = InputBox(Message, Title, Default)

' Use helpfile and context. The help button is added automatically.
MyValue = InputBox(Message, Title, , , , "DEMO.HLP", 10)

' Display dialog at position 100,100
MyValue = InputBox(Message, Title, Default, 100, 100)
```

InsertNotes Method

Applies To	**Application** Object.
Description	Prompts the user to enter notes for the active task or resource. If a task or resource is not active, Microsoft Project creates a new task (when a task view is active) or resource (when a resource view is active).
Syntax	[*object.*]**InsertNotes**
Elements	The *object* placeholder is an object expression that evaluates to an object in the Applies To list.
See Also	**Notes** Property.

InStr Function

Description	Returns the position of the first occurrence of one string within another.

Syntax	**InStr**([*start,*]*string1,string2*[*,compare*])
Elements	The **InStr** function syntax has these parts:

Part	Description
start	Numeric expression that sets the starting position for each search. If omitted, search begins at the first character position. If *start* contains no valid data, an error occurs. *Start* is required if *compare* is specified.
string1	String expression being searched. If *string1* contains no valid data, **Null** is returned.
string2	String expression sought. If *string2* contains no valid data, **Null** is returned.
compare	Number specifying the type of string comparison. Specify **1** to perform a textual case-insensitive comparison. Specify **0** (default) to perform a binary comparison. If *compare* is **Null**, an error occurs. *Start* is required if *compare* is specified. If *compare* is omitted, the setting of **Option Compare** is used to determine the type of comparison.

Return Values

Value	Description
0	*string1* is zero-length.
start	*string2* is zero-length.
0	*string2* not found.
Position at which match is found	*string2* is found within *string1*.
0	*start* > *string2*.

Remarks

> Note   When Option Compare Text is specified, comparisons are textual and case-insensitive. When Option Compare Binary is specified, comparisons are strictly binary.

> Note   Another function (InStrB) is provided for use with the double-byte character sets (DBCS) used in some Asian locales. Instead of returning the character position of the first occurence of one string within another, InStrB returns the byte position. In areas where DBCS is not used, InStrB behaves the same as InStr.

See Also	**Option Compare** Statement.
Example	This example uses the **InStr** function to return the position of the first occurrence of one string within another.

```
SearchString ="XXpXXpXXPXXP"     ' String to search in.
SearchChar = "P"                 ' Search for "P".

' A textual comparison starting at position 4. Returns 6.
MyPos = InStr(4, SearchString, SearchChar, 1)

' A binary comparison starting at position 1. Returns 9.
MyPos = InStr(1, SearchString, SearchChar, 0)

' Comparison is binary by default (if last argument is omitted).
MyPos = InStr(SearchString, SearchChar)  ' Returns 9.
MyPos = InStr(1, SearchString, "W")      ' Returns 0.
```

Int Function, Fix Function

Description

Returns the integer portion of a number.

Syntax

Int(*number*)
Fix(*number*)

Elements

The *number* argument can be any valid numeric expression. If *number* contains no valid data, **Null** is returned.

Remarks

Both **Int** and **Fix** remove the fractional part of *number* and return the resulting integer value.

The difference between **Int** and **Fix** is that if *number* is negative, **Int** returns the first negative integer less than or equal to *number,* whereas **Fix** returns the first negative integer greater than or equal to *number.* For example, **Int** converts -8.4 to -9, and **Fix** converts -8.4 to -8.

Fix(*number*) is equivalent to:

```
Sgn(number) * Int(Abs(number))
```

See Also

CInt Function.

Example

This example illustrates how the **Int** and **Fix** functions return integer portions of numbers. In the case of a negative number argument, the **Int** function returns the the first negative integer less than or equal to the number; whereas, the **Fix** function returns the first negative integer greater than or equal to the number.

```
MyNumber = Int(99.8)     ' Returns 99.
MyNumber = Fix(99.2)     ' Returns 99.
MyNumber = Int(-99.8)    ' Returns -100.
MyNumber = Fix(-99.8)    ' Returns -99.
MyNumber = Int(-99.2)    ' Returns -100.
MyNumber = Fix(-99.2)    ' Returns -99.
```

Integer Data Type

Description   **Integer** variables are stored as 16-bit (2-byte) numbers ranging in value from -32,768 to 32,767. The type-declaration character for **Integer** is % (character code 37).

You can also use **Integer** variables to represent enumerated values. An enumerated value can contain a finite set of unique whole numbers, each of which has special meaning in the context in which it is used. Enumerated values provide a convenient way to select among a known number of choices. For example, when asking the user to select a color from a list, you could have 0 = black, 1 = white, and so on. It is good programming practice to define constants using the **Const** statement for each enumerated value.

See Also   **CInt** Function, Data Type Summary, **Def***type* Statements, **Long** Data Type, **Variant** Data Type.

Is Operator

Description   Used to compare two object reference variables.

Syntax   *result* = *object1* **Is** *object2*

Elements   The **Is** operator syntax has these parts:

Part	Description
result	Any numeric variable.
object1	Any object name.
object2	Any object name.

Remarks   If *object1* and *object2* both refer to the same object, *result* is **True**; if they do not, *result* is **False**. Two variables can be made to refer to the same object in several ways.

In the following example, A has been set to refer to the same object as B:

```
Set A = B
```

The following example makes A and B refer to the same object as C:

```
Set A = C
Set B = C
```

See Also   Comparison Operators, Operator Precedence, **Set** Statement.

Example   This example uses the **Is** operator to compare two object references. All the object variables used here are generic names and for illustration purposes only.

```
Set YourObject = MyObject            ' Assign object references.
Set ThisObject = MyObject
Set ThatObject = OtherObject
MyCheck = YourObject Is ThisObject   ' Returns True.
MyCheck = ThatObject Is ThisObject   ' Returns False.
' Assume MyObject <> OtherObject
MyCheck = MyObject Is ThatObject     ' Returns False.
```

IsArray Function

Description   Returns a value indicating whether a variable is an array.

Syntax   **IsArray(*varname*)**

Elements   The ***varname*** named argument can be any variable.

Remarks   **IsArray** returns **True** if the variable is an array; otherwise, it returns **False**.

See Also   **Array** Function, **IsDate** Function, **IsEmpty** Function, **IsError** Function, **IsMissing** Function, **IsNull** Function, **IsNumeric** Function, **IsObject** Function, **TypeName** Function, **Variant** Data Type, **VarType** Function.

Example   This example uses the **IsArray** function to check if a variable is an array.

```
Dim MyArray(1 To 5) As Integer   ' Declare array variable.
YourArray = Array(1, 2, 3)       ' Use Array function.
MyCheck = IsArray(MyArray)       ' Returns True.
MyCheck = IsArray(YourArray)     ' Returns True.
```

IsDate Function

Description   Returns a value indicating whether an expression can be converted to a date.

Syntax	**IsDate**(*expression*)
Elements	The *expression* named argument can be any date or string expression recognizable as a date or time.
Remarks	**IsDate** returns **True** if the expression is a date or can legally be converted to a date; otherwise, it returns **False**. The range of valid dates is January 1, 100 A.D. through December 31, 9999 A.D.
See Also	**CDate** Function, **Date** Data Type, **IsArray** Function, **IsEmpty** Function, **IsError** Function, **IsMissing** Function, **IsNull** Function, **IsNumeric** Function, **IsObject** Function, **TypeName** Function, **Variant** Data Type, **VarType** Function.
Example	This example uses the **IsDate** function to determine if an expression can be converted to a date.

```
MyDate = "February 12, 1969" : YourDate = #2/12/69# : NoDate = "Hello"
MyCheck = IsDate(MyDate)      ' Returns True.
MyCheck = IsDate(YourDate)    ' Returns True.
MyCheck = IsDate(NoDate)      ' Returns False.
```

IsEmpty Function

Description	Returns a value indicating whether a variable has been initialized.
Syntax	**IsEmpty**(*expression*)
Elements	The *expression* named argument can be any numeric or string expression. However, because **IsEmpty** is used to determine if individual variables are initialized, the *expression* argument is most often a single variable name.
Remarks	**IsEmpty** returns **True** if the variable is **Empty**; otherwise, it returns **False**. **False** is always returned if *expression* contains more than one variable.
See Also	**IsArray** Function, **IsDate** Function, **IsError** Function, **IsMissing** Function, **IsNull** Function, **IsNumeric** Function, **IsObject** Function, **TypeName** Function, **Variant** Data Type, **VarType** Function.
Example	This example uses the **IsEmpty** function to determine whether or not a variable has been initialized.

```
MyCheck = IsEmpty(MyVar)      ' Returns True.
MyVar = Null                  ' Assign Null.
MyCheck = IsEmpty(MyVar)      ' Returns False.
MyVar = Empty                 ' Assign Empty.
MyCheck = IsEmpty(MyVar)      ' Returns True.
```

IsError Function

Description   Returns a value indicating whether an expression is an error value.

Syntax   **IsError**(*expression*)

Elements   The *expression* named argument can be any numeric expression used to indicate an error value.

Remarks   Error values are created by converting real numbers to error values using the **CVErr** function. The **IsError** function is used to determine if a numeric expression represents an error. **IsError** returns **True** if the *expression* argument indicates an error; otherwise, it returns **False**.

See Also   **CVErr** Function, **IsArray** Function, **IsDate** Function, **IsEmpty** Function, **IsMissing** Function, **IsNull** Function, **IsNumeric** Function, **IsObject** Function, **TypeName** Function, **Variant** Data Type, **VarType** Function.

Example   This example uses the **IsError** function to check if a numeric expression is an error value. The **CVErr** function is used to return an **Error Variant** from a user-defined function.

```
' Assume UserFunction is a user-defined function
' procedure that returns an error value; e.g., return
' value assigned with the statement UserFunction =
' CVErr(32767) where 32767 is a user-defined number.
ReturnVal = UserFunction()
MyCheck = IsError(ReturnVal) ' Returns True.
```

IsMissing Function

Description   Returns a value indicating whether an optional argument has been passed to a procedure.

Syntax   **IsMissing**(*argname*)

Elements   The *argname* named argument is the name of an optional procedure argument.

Remarks   The **IsMissing** function is used in a procedure that has optional arguments, including **ParamArray** arguments, to determine whether an argument has been passed to the procedure. **IsMissing** returns **True** if no value has been passed for the specified argument; otherwise, it returns **False**.

See Also   **Function** Statement, **IsArray** Function, **IsDate** Function, **IsEmpty** Function, **IsError** Function, **IsNull** Function, **IsNumeric** Function, **IsObject** Function, **Property Get** Statement, **Property Let** Statement, **Property Set** Statement, **Sub** Statement, **TypeName** Function, **Variant** Data Type, **VarType** Function.

Example   This example uses the **IsMissing** function to check if an optional argument has been passed to a user-defined procedure.

```
' The following statements call the user-defined function procedure.
ReturnValue = ReturnTwice()  ' Returns Null.
ReturnValue = ReturnTwice(2) ' Returns 4.

' Function procedure definition.
Function ReturnTwice(Optional A)
    If IsMissing(A) Then
        ' If argument is missing, return a Null.
        ReturnTwice = Null
    Else
        ' If argument is present, return twice the value.
        ReturnTwice = A * 2
    End If
End Function
```

IsNull Function

Description   Returns a value that indicates whether an expression contains no valid data (**Null**).

Syntax   **IsNull**(*expression*)

Elements   The *expression* named argument can be any numeric or string expression.

Remarks   **IsNull** returns **True** if *expression* is **Null**, that is, it contains no valid data; otherwise, **IsNull** returns **False**. If *expression* consists of more than one variable, **Null** in any variable causes **True** to be returned for the entire expression.

The **Null** value indicates that the **Variant** contains no valid data. **Null** is not the same as **Empty**, which indicates that a variable has not yet been initialized. It is also not the same as a zero-length string, which is sometimes referred to as a null string.

Important Use the **IsNull** function to determine whether an expression contains a **Null** value. Expressions that you might expect to evaluate **True** under some circumstances, such as `If Var = Null` and `If Var <> Null`, are always **False**. This is because any expression containing a **Null** is itself **Null** and therefore **False**.

See Also

IsArray Function, **IsDate** Function, **IsEmpty** Function, **IsError** Function, **IsMissing** Function, **IsNumeric** Function, **IsObject** Function, **TypeName** Function, **Variant** Data Type, **VarType** Function.

Example

This example uses the **IsNull** function to determine if a variable contains a **Null**.

```
MyCheck = IsNull(MyVar) ' Returns False.
MyVar = ""
MyCheck = IsNull(MyVar) ' Returns False.
MyVar = Null
MyCheck = IsNull(MyVar) ' Returns True.
```

IsNumeric Function

Description

Returns a value indicating whether an expression can be evaluated as a number.

Syntax

IsNumeric(*expression*)

Elements

The *expression* named argument can be any numeric or string expression.

Remarks

IsNumeric returns **True** if the entire *expression* is recognized as a number; otherwise, it returns **False**.

IsNumeric returns **False** if *expression* is a date expression.

See Also

IsArray Function, **IsDate** Function, **IsEmpty** Function, **IsError** Function, **IsMissing** Function, **IsNull** Function, **IsObject** Function, **TypeName** Function, **Variant** Data Type, **VarType** Function.

Example

This example uses the **IsNumeric** function to determine if a variable can be evaluated as a number.

```
MyVar = "53"                     ' Assign value.
MyCheck = IsNumeric(MyVar)       ' Returns True.
MyVar = "459.95"                 ' Assign value.
MyCheck = IsNumeric(MyVar)       ' Returns True.
MyVar = "45 Help"                ' Assign value.
MyCheck = IsNumeric(MyVar)       ' Returns False.
```

IsObject Function

Description

Returns a value indicating whether an expression references a valid OLE Automation object.

Syntax	**IsObject**(*expression*)
Elements	The *expression* named argument can be any expression.
Remarks	**IsObject** returns **True** if *expression* is a valid reference to an actual object; otherwise, it returns **False**.
See Also	**IsArray** Function, **IsDate** Function, **IsEmpty** Function, **IsError** Function, **IsMissing** Function, **IsNull** Function, **IsNumeric** Function, **Object** Data Type, **Set** Statement, **TypeName** Function, **Variant** Data Type, **VarType** Function.
Example	This example uses the **IsObject** function to determine if a variable references a valid object. MyObject and YourObject are object variables of the same type. They are generic names used here for illustration purposes only.

```
Dim MyInt As Integer              ' Declare variable.
Set YourObject = MyObject         ' Assign an object reference.
MyCheck = IsObject(YourObject)    ' Returns True.
MyCheck = IsObject(MyInt)         ' Returns False.
```

Keywords Property

Applies To	**Project** Object, **Projects** Collection
Description	Returns or sets the keywords associated with a project.
Syntax	*object*.**Keywords** [= *value*]
Elements	The **Keywords** property syntax has the following parts:

Part	Description
object	An object expression that evaluates to an object in the Applies To list.
Value	A string expression that specifies the keywords associated with the project.

See Also	**Author** Property, **Comments** Property, **Subject** Property, **Title** Property.

Kill Statement

Description	Deletes files from a disk.
Syntax	**Kill** *pathname*

Elements   The *pathname* named argument is a string expression that specifies one or more file names to be deleted—may include directory or folder, and drive.

Remarks   **Kill** supports the use of '*' (multiple character) and '?' (single character) wildcards to specify multiple files. However, on the Macintosh, these characters are treated as valid file name characters and can't be used as wildcards to specify multiple files.

Since the Macintosh does not support wildcards, use the file type to identify groups of files to delete. You can use the **MacID** function to specify file type instead of repeating the command with separate file names. For example, the following statement deletes all 'TEXT' files in the current folder.

```
Kill MacID("TEXT")
```

If you use the **MacID** function with **Kill** in Microsoft Windows, an error occurs.

An error occurs if you try to use **Kill** to delete an open file.

To delete directories, use the **RmDir** statement.

See Also   **MacID** Function, **RmDir** Statement.

Example   This example uses the **Kill** statement to delete a file from a disk. Since the Macintosh does not support wildcards, you can use the **MacID** function to specify the file type instead of the file name.

```
' Assume TESTFILE is a file containing some data.
Kill "TestFile"     ' Delete file.

' In Microsoft Windows.
' Delete all *.txt files in current directory.
Kill "*.txt"

' On the Macintosh.
' Use the MacID function to delete all PICT files in current folder
Kill MacID("PICT")
```

LastPrintedDate Property

Applies To   **Project** Object, **Projects** Collection.

Description   Returns the date a project was last printed.

Syntax   *object*.**LastPrintedDate**

Elements   The *object* placeholder is an object expression that evaluates to an object in the Applies To list.

See Also   Cost Property, **Duration** Property, **Finish** Property, **Index** Property, **PercentComplete** Property, **PercentWorkComplete** Property, **Start** Property, **Work** Property.

LastSaveDate Property

Applies To   **Project** Object, **Projects** Collection.

Description   Returns the date a project was last saved.

Syntax   *object*.**LastSaveDate**

Elements   The *object* placeholder is an object expression that evaluates to an object in the Applies To list.

See Also   **CreationDate** Property.

LastSavedBy Property

Applies To   **Project** Object, **Projects** Collection.

Description   Returns the name of the user who last saved a project.

Syntax   *object*.**LastSavedBy**

Elements   The *object* placeholder is an object expression that evaluates to an object in the Applies To list.

See Also   **Saved** Property.

Example   The following example adds to the notes of the active project the date the active project was last saved and the name of the user who last saved it.

```
Sub AddSaveInfoToNotes()
    Dim NL  As String      ' Newline characters
    NL = Chr(13) + Chr(10)  ' NL = Carriage Return + Linefeed

    ' Add the save information to the project's notes.
    ActiveProject.Notes = ActiveProject.Notes & NL & "This project" & _
        " was last saved on " & CStr(ActiveProject.LastSaveDate) & _
        " by " & ActiveProject.LastSavedBy
End Sub
```

LateFinish Property

Applies To	**Project** Object, **Projects** Collection; **Task** Object, **Tasks** Collection.
Description	Returns the latest date on which a task or project can finish.
Syntax	*object*.**LateFinish**
Elements	The *object* placeholder is an object expression that evaluates to an object in the Applies To list.
See Also	**EarlyFinish** Property, **EarlyStart** Property, **LateStart** Property.

LateStart Property

Applies To	**Project** Object, **Projects** Collection; **Task** Object, **Tasks** Collection.
Description	Returns the latest date on which a task can start.
Syntax	*object*.**LateStart**
Elements	The *object* placeholder is an object expression that evaluates to act in the Applies To list.
See Also	**EarlyFinish** Property, **EarlyStart** Property, **LateFinish** Property.

Layout Method

Applies To	**Application** Object.
Description	Displays the Layout dialog box, which allows the user to set layout options for the current view.
Syntax	[*object*.]**Layout**
Elements	The *object* placeholder is an object expression that evaluates to an object in the Applies To list.

LayoutNow Method

Applies To	**Application** Object.
Description	Lays out the current view according to its layout options.
Syntax	[*object*.]**LayoutNow**
Elements	The *object* placeholder is an object expression that evaluates to an object in the Applies To list.
Remarks	You can set layout options with the **Layout** method.
See Also	**CalendarLayout** Method, **Layout** Method, **PERTLayout** Method.

LBound Function

Description	Returns the smallest available subscript for the indicated dimension of an array.
Syntax	**LBound**(*arrayname*[,*dimension*])
Elements	The **LBound** statement syntax has these parts:

Part	Description
arrayname	Name of the array variable; follows standard variable naming conventions.
dimension	Whole number indicating which dimension's lower bound is returned. Use 1 for the first dimension, 2 for the second, and so on. If *dimension* is omitted, 1 is assumed.

Remarks   The **LBound** function is used with the **UBound** function to determine the size of an array. Use the **UBound** function to find the upper limit of an array dimension.

LBound returns the values listed in the table below for an array with the following dimensions:

```
Dim A(1 To 100, 0 To 3, -3 To 4)
```

Statement	Return Value
LBound(A, 1)	1
LBound(A, 2)	0
LBound(A, 3)	-3

The default lower bound for any dimension is either 0 or 1, depending on the setting of the **Option Base** statement.

Arrays for which dimensions are set using the **To** clause in a **Dim**, **Private**, **Public**, **ReDim**, or **Static** statement can have any integer value as a lower bound.

See Also
Dim Statement, **Option Base** Statement, **Private** Statement, **Public** Statement, **ReDim** Statement, **Static** Statement, **UBound** Function.

Example
This example uses the **LBound** function to determine the smallest available subscript for the indicated dimension of an array. Use the **Option Base** statement to override the default base array subscript value of 0.

```
Dim MyArray(1 To 10, 5 To 15, 10 To 20)  ' Declare array variables.
Dim AnyArray(10)
Lower = LBound(MyArray, 1)   ' Returns 1.
Lower = LBound(MyArray, 3)   ' Returns 10.
Lower = LBound(AnyArray)     ' Returns 0 or 1, depending
                             ' on setting of Option Base.
```

LCase Function

Description
Returns a string that has been converted to lowercase.

Syntax
LCase(*string*)

Elements
The *string* named argument is any valid string expression. If *string* contains no valid data, **Null** is returned.

Remarks
Only uppercase letters are converted to lowercase; all lowercase letters and nonletter characters remain unchanged.

See Also
UCase Function.

Example
This example uses the **LCase** function to return a lowercase version of a string.

```
Uppercase = "Hello World 1234"  ' String to convert.
Lowercase = LCase(UpperCase)    ' Returns "hello world 1234".
```

Left Function

Description	Returns a specified number of characters from the left side of a string.
Syntax	**Left**(*string*,*length*)
Elements	The **Left** function syntax has these named-argument parts:

Part	Description
string	String expression from which the leftmost characters are returned. If *string* contains no valid data, **Null** is returned.
length	Numeric expression indicating how many characters to return. If 0, a zero-length string is returned. If greater than or equal to the number of characters in *string*, the entire string is returned.

Remarks	To determine the number of characters in *string*, use the **Len** function.

Note   Another function (LeftB) is provided for use with the double-byte character sets (DBCS) used in some Asian locales. Instead of specifying the number of characters to return, *length* specifies the number of bytes. In areas where DBCS is not used, LeftB behaves the same as Left.

See Also	**Len** Function, **Mid** Function, **Right** Function.
Example	This example uses the **Left** function to return a specified number of characters from the left side of a string.

```
AnyString = "Hello World"   ' Define string.
MyStr = Left(AnyString, 1)  ' Returns "H".
MyStr = Left(AnyString, 7)  ' Returns "Hello W".
MyStr = Left(AnyString, 20) ' Returns "Hello World".
```

Left Property

Applies To	Application Object; Window Object, Windows Collection.
Description	Returns or sets the distance of the main window from the left edge of the screen (**Application** object), or the distance of a project window from the left edge of the main window (**Window** object).

Syntax	*object*.**Left** [= *value*]
Elements	The **Left** property syntax has these parts:

Part	Description
object	An object expression that evaluates to an object in the Applies To list.
value	A numeric expression that specifies the distance, in points, of the main window from the left edge of the screen or the distance, in points, of a document window from the left edge of the main window.

Remarks	For Microsoft Project for the Macintosh, this property is supported read-only for the **Application** object.
See Also	**Caption** Property, **Height** Property, **Top** Property, **UsableHeight** Property, **UsableWidth** Property, **Visible** Property, **Width** Property, **WindowState** Property.

Len Function

Description	Returns the length of a file in bytes.
Syntax	**FileLen(*pathname*)**
Elements	The ***pathname*** named argument is a string expression that specifies a file name— may include directory or folder, and drive.
Remarks	If the specified file is open when the **FileLen** function is called, the value returned represents the last saved disk size of the file. To obtain the length of an open file, use the **LOF** function.
See Also	**FileDateTime** Function, **GetAttr** Function, **LOF** Function.
Example	This example uses the **Len** function to return the number of characters in a string or the number of bytes required to store a variable.

```
Type CustomerRecord   ' Define user-defined type.
    ID As Integer
    Name As String * 10
    Address As String * 30
End Type
Dim Customer As CustomerRecord   ' Declare variables.
Dim MyInt As Integer, MyCur As Currency
MyString = "Hello World"         ' Initialize.
MyLen = Len(MyInt)               ' Returns 2.
MyLen = Len(Customer)            ' Returns 42.
MyLen = Len(MyString)            ' Returns 11.
MyLen = Len(MyCur)               ' Returns 8.
```

Let Statement

Description   Assigns the value of an expression to a variable or property.

Syntax   [**Let**] *varname* = *expression*

Elements   The **Let** statement syntax has these parts:

Part	Description
varname	Name of the variable or property; follows standard variable naming conventions.
expression	Value assigned to the variable.

Remarks   In order to simplify Basic code, the optional **Let** keyword is most often omitted.

A value expression can be assigned to a variable only if it is of a data type that is compatible with the variable. You can't assign string expressions to numeric variables, and you can't assign numeric expressions to string variables. If you do, an error occurs at compile time.

Variant variables can be assigned either string or numeric expressions. However, the reverse is not always true. Any **Variant** except a **Null** can be assigned to a string variable, but only a **Variant** whose value can be interpreted as a number can be assigned to a numeric variable. Use the **IsNumeric** function to determine if the **Variant** can be converted to a number.

Caution   Assigning an expression of one numeric data type to a variable of a different numeric data type coerces the value of the expression into the data type of the resulting variable.

Let statements can be used to assign one record variable to another only when both variables are of the same user-defined type. Use the **LSet** statement to assign record variables of different user-defined types. Use the **Set** statement to assign object references to variables.

See Also   **Const** Statement, Data Type Summary, **IsNumeric** Function, **LSet** Statement, **Set** Statement, **Variant** Data Type.

Example   This example uses statements with and without the **Let** statement to assign the value of an expression to a variable.

```
' The following variable assignments use the Let statement.
Let MyStr = "Hello World"
Let MyInt = 5
' The following are the same assignments without the Let statement.
MyStr = "Hello World"
MyInt = 5
```

Level Method

Applies To	**Resource** Object, **Resources** Collection.
Description	Levels a resource.
Syntax	*object*.**Level**
Elements	The *object* placeholder is an object expression that evaluates to an object in the Applies To list.
See Also	**Overallocated** Property.
Example	The following example levels the resources of the selected tasks.

```
Sub LevelResourcesInSelectedTasks()
    Dim T        ' Task object used in For Each loop
    Dim A        ' Assignment object used in For Each loop

    ' Level the resources of the selected tasks.
    For Each T In ActiveSelection.Tasks
        For Each A in T.Assignments
            If ActiveProject.Resources(A.ResourceID).Overallocated Then
                ActiveProject.Resources(A.ResourceID).Level
            End If
        Next A
    Next T
End Sub
```

LevelingClear Method

Applies To	**Application** Object.
Description	Removes the effect of leveling.
Syntax	[*object*.]**LevelingClear** [*all*]
Elements	The **LevelingClear** method syntax has the following object qualifier and named arguments:

Part	Description
object	An object expression that evaluates to an object in the Applies To list.
all	A Boolean expression that specifies whether to remove delays from all tasks. By default, the *all* argument is **True**. The *all* argument has these settings:

True	Remove delays from all tasks.
False	Remove delays from active tasks.

See Also   **Delay** Property, **Level** Method, **LevelingOptions** Method, **LevelNow** Method.

LevelingOptions Method

Applies To   **Application** Object.

Description   Specifies leveling options for the active project.

Syntax   [*object*.]**LevelingOptions** [*automatic, delayInSlack, removeDelay, order*]

Elements   The **LevelingOptions** method syntax has the following object qualifier and named arguments:

Part	Description
object	An object expression that evaluates to an object in the Applies To list. Optional.
automatic	A Boolean expression that specifies whether Microsoft Project automatically levels tasks in the active project. Optional.
delayInSlack	A Boolean expression that specifies whether the active project can be delayed beyond the slack time available. Optional.
removeDelay	A Boolean expression that specifies whether to remove delays on tasks before leveling them in the active project. Optional.
order	A constant that specifies how Microsoft Project should resolve resource conflicts when leveling tasks. Optional.

The *order* argument has these settings:

pjLevelID	0	Microsoft Project uses identification numbers only to resolve resource conflicts.
pjLevelStandard	1	Microsoft Project uses predecessors relationships, slack time, dates, priority, and task constraints to resolve resource conflicts.
pjLevelPriority	2	Microsoft Project considers priority first when resolving resource conflicts.

See Also	**Level** Method, **LevelingClear** Method, **LevelNow** Method.
Example	The following example levels resources in the application using priority to resolve conflicts.

```
Sub LevelOverallocatedResources()
    LevelingOptions order := pjLevelPriority
    LevelNow
End Sub
```

LevelNow Method

Applies To	**Application** Object.
Description	Levels overallocated resources.
Syntax	[*object*.]**LevelNow** [*all*]
Elements	The **LevelNow** method syntax has the following object qualifier and named arguments:

Part	Description
object	An object expression that evaluates to an object in the Applies To list.
all	A Boolean expression that specifies whether to level all resources or selected resources. By default, the *all* argument is **True**.

See Also	**LevelingClear** Method, **LevelingOptions** Method.

LevelOrder Property

Applies To	**Application** Object.
Description	Returns or sets the order in which tasks with overallocations will be delayed.
Syntax	[*object*.]**LevelOrder** [= *value*]
Elements	The **LevelOrder** property syntax has the following parts:

Part	Description
object	An object expression that evaluates to an object in the Applies To list.
value	A constant that specifies the order in which resource leveling occurs.

The *value* argument has these settings:

pjLevelID	0	Identification numbers
pjLevelStandard	1	Standard order
pjLevelPriority	2	Priority

See Also   **LevelingOptions** Method, **LevelNow** Method, **LevelWithinSlack** Property.

LevelWithinSlack Property

Applies To   **Application** Object.

Description   Returns or sets whether leveling must occur within total slack.

Syntax   [*object.*]**LevelWithinSlack** [= *value*]

Elements   The **LevelWithinSlack** property syntax has the following parts:

Part	Description
object	An object expression that evaluates to an object in the Applies To list.
value	A Boolean expression that specifies whether leveling must occur within total slack.

See Also   **LevelingOptions** Method, **LevelNow** Method, **LevelOrder** Property.

Like Operator

Description   Used to compare two strings.

Syntax   *result* = *string* **Like** *pattern*

Elements   The **Like** operator syntax has these parts:

Part	Description
result	Any numeric variable.
string	Any string expression.
pattern	Any string expression conforming to the pattern-matching conventions described in the following section.

Remarks   If *string* matches *pattern*, *result* is **True**; if there is no match, *result* is **False**; and if either *string* or *pattern* is a **Null**, *result* is also a **Null**.

The behavior of the **Like** operator depends on the **Option Compare** statement. Unless otherwise specified, the default string-comparison method for each module is **Option Compare Binary**.

Option Compare Binary results in string comparisons based on a sort order derived from the internal binary representations of the characters. In Microsoft Windows, sort order is determined by the code page. On the Macintosh, sort order is determined by the character set. In the following example, a typical binary sort order is shown:

$$A < B < E < Z < a < b < e\ < z < À < Ê < Ø < à < ê < ø$$

Option Compare Text results in string comparisons based on a case-insensitive textual sort order determined by your system's locale. The same characters shown above, when sorted using **Option Compare Text**, produce the following text sort order:

$$(A=a)\ < (\ À=à) < (B=b) < (E=e) < (Ê=ê) < (Z=z) < (Ø=ø)$$

Built-in pattern matching provides a versatile tool for string comparisons. The pattern-matching features allow you to use wildcard characters, character lists, or character ranges, in any combination, to match strings. The following table shows the characters allowed in *pattern* and what they match:

Character(s) in *pattern*	Matches in *string*
?	Any single character.
*	Zero or more characters.
#	Any single digit (0-9).
[*charlist*]	Any single character in *charlist*.
[!*charlist*]	Any single character not in *charlist*.

A group of one or more characters (*charlist*) enclosed in brackets ([ ]) can be used to match any single character in *string* and can include almost any character code, including digits.

Note The special characters left bracket ([), question mark (?), number sign (#), and asterisk (*) can be used to match themselves directly only by enclosing them in brackets. The right bracket (]) can't be used within a group to match itself, but it can be used outside a group as an individual character.

In addition to a simple list of characters enclosed in brackets, *charlist* can specify a range of characters by using a hyphen (-) to separate the upper and lower bounds of the range. For example, [A-Z] in *pattern* results in a match if the corresponding character position in *string* contains any of the uppercase letters in the range A through Z. Multiple ranges are included within the brackets without any delimiters.

The meaning of a specified range depends on the character ordering valid at run time (as determined by **Option Compare** and the locale setting of the system the code is running on). Using the same example shown above with **Option Compare Binary**, the range [A-E] matches A, B and E. With **Option Compare Text**, [A-E] matches A, a, À, à, B, b, E, e. Note that it does not match Ê or ê because accented characters fall after unaccented characters in the sort order.

Other important rules for pattern matching include the following:

- An exclamation point (!) at the beginning of *charlist* means that a match is made if any character except the ones in *charlist* are found in *string*. When used outside brackets, the exclamation point matches itself.

- The hyphen (-) can appear either at the beginning (after an exclamation mark if one is used) or at the end of *charlist* to match itself. In any other location, the hyphen is used to identify a range of characters.

- When a range of characters is specified, they must appear in ascending sort order (from lowest to highest). [A-Z] is a valid pattern, but [Z-A] is not.

- The character sequence [ ] is ignored; it is considered a zero-length string.

See Also   Comparison Operators, **InStr** Function, Operator Precedence, **Option Compare** Statement, **StrComp** Function.

Example   This example uses the **Like** operator to compare a string to a pattern.

```
MyCheck = "aBBBa" Like "a*a"              ' Returns True.
MyCheck = "F" Like "[A-Z]"                ' Returns True.
MyCheck = "F" Like "[!A-Z]"               ' Returns False.
MyCheck = "a2a" Like "a#a"                ' Returns True.
MyCheck = "aM5b" Like "a[L-P]#[!c-e]"     ' Returns True.
MyCheck = "BAT123khg" Like "B?T*"         ' Returns True.
MyCheck = "CAT123khg" Like "B?T*"         ' Returns False.
```

Line Input # Statement

Description   Reads a line from an open sequential file and assigns it to a string variable.

Syntax   **Line Input #***filenumber*,*varname*

Elements	The **Line Input #** statement syntax has these parts:

Part	Description
filenumber	Any valid file number.
varname	Valid string variable name.

Remarks   The **Line Input #** statement reads from a file one character at a time until it encounters a carriage return (**Chr**(13)) or carriage return-linefeed sequence. Carriage return-linefeed sequences are skipped rather than appended to the character string.

See Also   **Input #** Statement.

Example   This example uses the **Line Input #** statement to read a line from a sequential file and assign it to a variable. For purposes of this example, assume that TESTFILE is a text file with a few lines of sample data.

```
Open "TESTFILE" For Input As #1    ' Open file.
Do While Not EOF(1)                ' Loop until end of file.
    Line Input #1, TextLine        ' Read line into variable.
        Debug.Print TextLine       ' Print to Debug window.
Loop
Close #1                           ' Close file.
```

LinkedFields Property

Applies To   **Project** Object, **Projects** Collection; **Resource** Object, **Resources** Collection; **Task** Object, **Tasks** Collection.

Description   Returns whether the task or resource contains fields that are linked.

Syntax   *object*.**LinkedFields**

Elements   The *object* placeholder is an object expression that evaluates to an object in the Applies To list.

See Also   **Flagn** Properties, **Marked** Property, **Objects** Property.

LinkPredecessors Method

Applies To   **Task** Object, **Tasks** Collection.

Description   Adds predecessors to one or more tasks.

Syntax	*object*.**LinkPredecessors** *tasks*[, *type*, *lag*]
Elements	The **LinkPredecessors** method syntax has the following object expression and named arguments:

Part	Description
object	An object expression that evaluates to an object in the Applies To list. Required.
tasks	A **Task** object. The tasks you specify with the *tasks* argument become predecessors of the tasks you specify with the object expression. Required.
type	A constant that specifies the relationship between tasks that become linked. If you omit the *type* argument, the tasks receive a finish-to-start relationship. Optional.
lag	A string expression that specifies the duration of lag time between linked tasks. To specify lead time between tasks, use a string expression for the *lag* argument that evaluates to a negative value. Optional.

The *type* argument has these constants:

Constant	Relationship Between Linked Tasks
pjFinishToStart	Finish-to-start
pjStartToFinish	Start-to-finish
pjStartToStart	Start-to-start
pjFinishToFinish	Finish-to-finish

See Also	**LinkSuccessors** Method, **UnlinkPredecessors** Method.
Example	The following example prompts the user for the name of a task and then makes the task a predecessor of the selected tasks.

```
Sub LinkTasksFromPredecessor()
    Dim Entry    ' Task name entered by user
    Dim T        ' Task object used in For Each loop
    Dim Exists   ' Whether or not the resource exists

    ' Prompt the user for the name of a task to turn into a predecessor.
    Entry = InputBox("Enter the name of a task:")

    Exists = False          ' Assume task doesn't exist.
```

```
        ' Search active project for the specified task.
        For Each T in ActiveProject.Tasks
            If T.Name = Entry Then
                Exists = True
                ' Make the task a predecessor of the selected tasks.
                For i = 1 to ActiveSelection.Tasks.Count
                    ActiveSelection.Tasks(i).LinkPredecessors _
                        Tasks := T
                Next i
            End If
        Next T

        ' If task doesn't exist, display error and quit Sub procedure.
        If Not Exists Then
            MsgBox("Task not found.")
            Exit Sub
        End If
End Sub
```

LinkSuccessors Method

Applies To   **Task** Object, **Tasks** Collection.

Description   Adds successors to one or more tasks.

Syntax   *object*.**LinkSuccessors** *task*[, *type*, *lag*]

Elements   The **LinkSuccessors** method syntax has the following object expression and named arguments:

Part	Description
object	An object expression that evaluates to an object in the Applies To list. Required.
task	A **Task** object or **Tasks** collection. The task you specify with the *task* argument becomes a successor to the tasks you specify with the object expression. Required.
type	A constant that specifies the relationship between tasks that become linked. If you omit the *type* argument, the tasks receive a finish-to-start relationship. Optional.
lag	A string expression that specifies the duration of lag time between linked tasks. To specify lead time between tasks, use a string expression for the *lag* argument that evaluates to a negative value. Optional.

The *type* argument has these constants:

Constant	Relationship between linked tasks
pjFinishToStart	Finish-to-start
pjStartToFinish	Start-to-finish
pjStartToStart	Start-to-start
pjFinishToFinish	Finish-to-finish

See Also   **LinkPredecessors** Method, **UnlinkSuccessors** Method.

Example   The following example prompts the user for the name of a task and then makes the task a successor to the selected tasks.

```
Sub LinkTasksToSuccessor()
    Dim Entry    ' Task name entered by the user
    Dim T        ' Task object used in For Each loop
    Dim Exists   ' Whether or not the resource exists

    ' Prompt the user for the name of a task to turn into a successor.
    Entry = InputBox("Enter the name of a task:")

    Exists = False   ' Assume task doesn't exist.

    ' Search active project for the specified task.
    For Each T in ActiveProject.Tasks
        If T.Name = Entry Then
            Exists = True
            ' Make task a successor to the selected tasks.
            For I = 1 To ActiveSelection.Tasks.Count
                ActiveSelection.Tasks(I).LinkSuccessors _
                    Tasks:=T
            Next I
        End If
    Next T

    ' If task doesn't exist, display error and quit Sub procedure.
    If Not Exists Then
        MsgBox("Task not found.")
        Exit Sub
    End If
End Sub
```

LinkTasksEdit Method

Applies To   **Application** Object.

Description   Edits links.

Syntax   [*object*.]**LinkTasksEdit** *from*, *to*[, *delete*, *type*, *lag*]

Elements   The **LinkTasksEdit** method syntax has the following object qualifier and named arguments:

Part	Description
object	An object expression that evaluates to an object in the Applies To list. Optional.
from	A numeric expression that specifies the identification number of a predecessor task. Required.
to	A numeric expression that specifies the identification number of a successor task. Required.
delete	A Boolean expression that specifies whether to delete the link you specify with the *from* and *to* arguments. Optional.
type	A constant that specifies the relationship between tasks that become linked. If you omit the *type* argument, the tasks receive a finish-to-start relationship. Optional.
lag	A string expression that specifies the duration between linked tasks, or a numeric expression that specifies the duration between linked tasks, in default units. To specify lead time between tasks, use a negative value. Optional.

The *type* argument has these constants:

pjFinishToFinish	0	Finish-to-finish
pjFinishToStart	1	Finish-to-start
pjStartToFinish	2	Start-to-finish
pjStartToStart	3	Start-to-start

See Also   **LinkTasks** Method, **UnlinkTasks** Method.

Example

The following example prompts the user for a range of task identification numbers, and then links the tasks in the range from finish to finish.

```
Sub LinkByFinishDate()
    Dim FirstID     ' The ID number of the first task
    Dim LastID      ' The ID number of the last task.
    FirstID = InputBox("Enter the ID number of the first task to link:")
    If FirstID = Empty Then Exit Sub
    LastID = InputBox("Enter the ID number of the last task to link:")
    If LastID = Empty Then Exit Sub
    LinkTasksEdit from:=FirstID, to:=LastID, type:=pjFinishToFinish
End Sub
```

LinkTasks Method

Applies To   **Application** Object.

Description   Links the selected tasks.

Syntax   [*object*.]**LinkTasks**

Elements   The *object* placeholder is an object expression that evaluates to an object in the Applies To list.

See Also   **LinkTasksEdit** Method, **UnlinkTasks** Method.

List Object

Description   A collection of strings or numbers that contain field identification numbers, field names, resource filters, resource tables, resource views, task filters, task tables, or task views.

Properties   **Application** Property, **Count** Property, **Parent** Property

See Also   **Selection** Object.

ListSeparator Property

Applies To   **Application** Object.

Description   Returns the character that separates items in lists.

Syntax   [*object*.]**ListSeparator**

Elements   The *object* placeholder is an object expression that evaluates to an object in the
                      Applies To list.

Remarks   To set the list separator character in Microsoft Windows, use the Microsoft
                      Windows Control Panel.

See Also   **MoveAfterReturn** Property, **Name** Property, **OperatingSystem** Property,
                      SupportsMultipleDocuments Property, **SupportsMultipleWindows** Property,
                      Version Property.

LoadLastFile Property

Applies To   **Application** Object.

Description   Returns or sets whether or not the file last opened opens automatically when
                      Microsoft Project is started.

Syntax   [*object*.]**LoadLastFile** [= *value*]

Elements   The **LoadLastFile** property syntax has the following parts:

Part	Description
object	An object expression that evaluates to an object in the Applies To list.
value	A Boolean expression that specifies whether the file last opened opens automatically when Microsoft Project is started.

See Also   **FileLoadLast** Method, **FileOpen** Method, **OptionsGeneral** Method,
                      PromptForSummaryInfo Property, **ShowTipOfDay** Property, **ShowWelcome**
                      Property.

Loc Function

Description   Returns the current read/write position within an open file.

Syntax   **Loc**(*filenumber*)

Elements   The *filenumber* named argument is any valid file number.

Remarks   The following describes the return value for each file access mode:

File Access	Return Value
Random	Number of the last record read from or written to the file.
Sequential	Current byte position in the file divided by 128.
Binary	Position of the last byte read or written.

See Also   **EOF** Function, **LOF** Function, **Open** Statement.

Example   This example uses the **Loc** function to return the current read/write position within an open file. For purposes of this example, assume that TESTFILE is a text file with a few lines of sample data.

```
Open "TESTFILE" For Input As #1      ' Open file just created.
Do While Not EOF(1)                  ' Loop until end of file.
    Line Input #1, MyLine            ' Read line into variable.
    MyLocation = Loc(1)              ' Get current position within file.
    ' Print to Debug window.
    Debug.Print MyLine; Tab; MyLocation
Loop
```

Lock...Unlock Statements

Description   Controls access by other processes to all or part of a file opened using the **Open** statement.

Syntax   **Lock** [#]*filenumber*[,*recordrange*]

. . .

Unlock [#]*filenumber*[,*recordrange*]

Elements

The **Lock** and **Unlock** statement syntax has these parts:

Part	Description
filenumber	Any valid file number.
recordrange	The range of records to lock or unlock.

The *recordrange* argument has the following syntax and parts:

recnumber | [*start*] **To** *end*

Part	Description
recnumber	Record number (**Random** mode files) or byte number (**Binary** mode files) at which locking or unlocking begins.
start	Number of the first record or byte to lock or unlock.
end	Number of the last record or byte to lock or unlock.

Remarks

The **Lock** and **Unlock** statements are used in environments where several processes might need access to the same file.

Lock and **Unlock** statements are always used in pairs. The arguments to **Lock** and **Unlock** must match exactly.

The first record/byte in a file is at position 1, the second record/byte is at position 2, and so on. If you specify just one record, then only that record is locked or unlocked. If you specify a range of records and omit a starting record (*start*), all records from the first record to the end of the range (*end*) are locked or unlocked. Using **Lock** without *recnumber* locks the entire file; using **Unlock** without *recnumber* unlocks the entire file.

If the file has been opened for sequential input or output, **Lock** and **Unlock** affect the entire file, regardless of the range specified by *start* and *end*.

Caution Be sure to remove all locks with an **Unlock** statement before closing a file or terminating your program. Failure to remove locks produces unpredictable results.

See Also

Open Statement.

Example

This example illustrates the use of the **Lock** and **Unlock** statements. While a record is being modified, access by other processes to the record is denied. For purposes of this example, assume that TESTFILE is a file containing five records of the user-defined type Record.

```
Type Record ' Define user-defined type.
    ID As Integer
    Name As String * 20
End Type

Dim MyRecord As Record          ' Declare variable.
' Open sample file for random access.
Open "TESTFILE" For Random Shared As #1 Len = Len(MyRecord)
RecordNumber = 4                ' Define record number.
Lock #1, RecordNumber           ' Lock record.
Get #1, RecordNumber, MyRecord  ' Read record.
MyRecord.ID = 234               ' Modify record.
MyRecord.Name = "John Smith"
Put #1, RecordNumber, MyRecord  ' Write modified record.
Unlock #1, RecordNumber         ' Unlock current record.
Close #1                        ' Close file.
```

LOF Function

Description Returns the size, in bytes, of a file opened using the **Open** statement.

Syntax **LOF(*filenumber*)**

Elements The *filenumber* named argument is any valid file number.

Remarks To obtain the length of a file that is not open, use the **FileLen** function.

See Also **EOF** Function, **FileLen** Function, **Loc** Function, **Open** Statement.

Example This example uses the **LOF** function to determine the size of an open disk file. For purposes of this example, assume that TESTFILE is a text file containing sample data.

```
Open "TESTFILE" For Input As #1 ' Open file.
FileLength = LOF(1)             ' Get length of file.
Close #1                        ' Close file.
```

Log Function

Description Returns the natural logarithm of a number.

Syntax **Log(*number*)**

Elements   The *number* named argument can be any valid numeric expression greater than 0.

Remarks   The natural logarithm is the logarithm to the base *e*. The constant *e* is approximately 2.718282.

You can calculate base-*n* logarithms for any number *x* by dividing the natural logarithm of *x* by the natural logarithm of *n* as follows:

$$\text{Log}n(x) = \textbf{Log}(x) / \textbf{Log}(n)$$

The following example illustrates a custom **Function** that calculates base-10 logarithms:

```
Static Function Log10(X)
    Log10 = Log(X) / Log(10#)
End Function
```

See Also   Derived Math Functions, **Exp** Function.

Example   This example uses the **Log** function to return the natural logarithm of a number.

```
' Define angle in radians.
MyAngle = 1.3
' Calculate inverse hyperbolic sine.
MyLog = Log(MyAngle + Sqr(MyAngle * MyAngle + 1))
```

Long Data Type

Description   **Long** (long integer) variables are stored as signed 32-bit (4-byte) numbers ranging in value from -2,147,483,648 to 2,147,483,647. The type-declaration character for **Long** is **&** (character code 38).

See Also   **CLng** Function, Data Type Summary, **Def***type* Statements, **Integer** Data Type.

LSet Statement

Description   Left aligns a string within a string variable, or copies a variable of one user-defined type to another variable of a different user-defined type.

Syntax   **LSet** *stringvar* = *string*

LSet *varname1* = *varname2*

Elements	The **LSet** statement syntax has these parts:

Part	Description
stringvar	Name of string variable.
string	String expression to be left aligned within *stringvar*.
varname1	Variable name of the user-defined type being copied to.
varname2	Variable name of the user-defined type being copied from.

Remarks

LSet replaces any leftover characters in *stringvar* with spaces.

If *string* is longer than *stringvar*, **LSet** places only the leftmost characters, up to the length of the *stringvar,* in *stringvar*.

Only user-defined types containing **Integer**, **Long**, **Double**, **Single**, **String** (fixed-length), or **Currency** types may be copied. The following example copies the contents of RecTwo (a user-defined type variable) to RecOne (a variable of another user-defined type):

```
Type TwoString
    StrFld As String * 2
End Type
Type ThreeString
    StrFld As String * 3
End Type
Dim RecOne As TwoString, RecTwo As ThreeString
LSet RecOne = RecTwo
```

Because RecOne is 2 bytes long, only 2 bytes are copied from RecTwo. **LSet** copies only the number of bytes in the shorter of the two user-defined type variables.

See Also

RSet Statement.

Example

This example uses the **LSet** statement to left align a string within a string variable and to copy a variable of one user-defined type to another variable of a different user-defined type.

```
MyString = "0123456789" ' Initialize string.
LSet MyString = "<-Left" ' MyString contains "<-Left    ".

' LSet is also used to copy a variable of one user-defined
' type to another variable of a different user-defined type.
' Module level.
Type AType  ' Define types.
    AName As String * 10
    AAdd As String * 10
End Type
Type BType
    BName As String * 5
    BAdd As String * 5
End Type

' Procedure level.
Dim AVar As AType, BVar As Btype    ' Declare variables.
AVar.AName = "John Smith"           ' Define fields.
AVar.AAdd = "Rodeo Drv."
LSet BVar = AVar                    ' Copy variables.
' After copying, values are truncated.
Debug.Print BVar.BName             ' Prints "John ".
Debug.Print BVar.BAdd              ' Prints "Smith".
```

LTrim, RTrim, and Trim Functions

Description   Returns a copy of a string without leading spaces (**LTrim**), trailing spaces (**RTrim**), or both leading and trailing spaces (**Trim**).

Syntax   **LTrim(*string*)**

                    RTrim(*string*)

                    Trim(*string*)

Elements   The *string* named argument is any valid string expression. If *string* contains no valid data, **Null** is returned.

See Also   **Left** Function, **Right** Function.

Example   This example uses the **LTrim** and **RTrim** functions to strip leading and trailing spaces from a string variable. Using the **Trim** function alone achieves the same result.

```
MyString = "  <-Trim->  "              ' Initialize.
TrimString = LTrim(MyString)           ' TrimString = "<-Trim->  ".
TrimString = RTrim(MyString)           ' TrimString = "  <-Trim->".
TrimString = LTrim(RTrim(MyString))    ' TrimString = "<-Trim->".
' Using the Trim function alone achieves the same result.
TrimString = Trim(MyString)            ' TrimString = "<-Trim->".
```

MacID Function

Description   Used only on the Macintosh to convert a four-character constant to a value that may be used by **Dir**, **Kill**, **Shell**, and **AppActivate**.

Syntax   **MacID**(*constant*)

Elements   The *constant* named argument consists of four-characters used to specify a resource type, file type, application signature, or Apple Event. For example, TEXT, OBIN, MSWD (Microsoft Word), XCEL (Microsoft Excel), and so on.

Remarks   **MacID** is used with **Dir** and **Kill** to specify a Macintosh file type. Since the Macintosh does not support '*' and '?' as wildcards, you can use a four-character constant instead to identify groups of files. For example, the following statement returns 'TEXT' type files from the current folder:

```
Dir("", MacID("TEXT"))
```

MacID is used with **Shell** and **AppActivate** to specify an application using the application's unique signature.

See Also   **AppActivate** Statement, **Dir** Function, **Kill** Statement, **Shell** Function.

Example   This example shows various uses of the **MacID** function. The **MacID** function is not available in Microsoft Windows.

```
' Return the first text file in folder HD:My Folder.
FileName = Dir("HD:My Folder:", MacID("TEXT"))

' Deletes all "TEXT" files in the current folder.
Kill MacID("TEXT")

' Run Microsoft Excel.
ReturnValue = Shell(MacID("XCEL"))

' Activate Microsoft Word.
AppActivate MacID("MSWD")
```

Macro Method

Applies To	**Application** Object.
Description	Runs a macro.
Syntax	[*object*.]**Macro** [*name*]
Elements	The **Macro** method syntax has the following object qualifier and named arguments:

Part	Description
object	An object expression that evaluates to an object in the Applies To list.
Name	A string expression that specifies the name of the macro to run. By default, the Macros dialog box appears, which prompts the user to manage macros.

Example	The following example runs a macro named Auto_Exec.

```
Sub RunMacro()
    Macro "Auto_Exec"
End Sub
```

MailLogoff Method

Applies To	**Application** Object.
Description	Closes an established MAPI mail session.
Syntax	[*object*.]**MailLogoff**
Elements	The *object* placeholder is an object expression that evaluates to an object in the Applies To list.
Remarks	This method applies to Microsoft Project for Microsoft Windows.
See Also	**MailLogOn** Method, **MailRoutingSlip** Method, **MailSend** Method, **MailSendProjectMail** Method, **MailSendScheduleNote** Method, **MailSession** Property, **MailSystem** Property, **MailUpdateProject** Method.

| **Example** | ```
Sub LogoffFromMail()
    If Not IsNull(Application.MailSession) Then
        MsgBox "Logging off from mail session:" + _
            Application.MailSession
        Application.MailLogoff
    Else
        MsgBox "Logging on to Mail now."
        Application.MailLogon DownloadNewMail := False
        MsgBox "Logging off from mail session:" + _
            Application.MailSession
        Application.MailLogoff
    End If
``` |

MailLogon Method

Applies To	**Application** Object.
Description	Logs into a MAPI Mail and establishes a mail session. A mail session must be established before mail or document routing methods can be used.
Syntax	[*object.*]**MailLogon**(*name*, *password*, *downloadNewMail*)
Elements	The **MailLogon** statement syntax has the following object qualifier and named arguments:

Part	Description
object	An object expression that evaluates to an object in the Applies To list. Optional.
name	A string expression that specifies the mail account name. Optional.
password	A string expression that specifies the mail account password. Optional.
downloadNewMail	A Boolean expression that specifies whether to download new mail immediately. Optional.

Remarks	This method applies to Microsoft Project for Microsoft Windows.

Previously established mail sessions are logged off before an attempt is made to establish the new session.

Omit both the *name* and *password* arguments to use the default mail session for the system. |
```

See Also   **MailLogOff** Method, **MailRoutingSlip** Method, **MailSend** Method, **MailSendProjectMail** Method, **MailSendScheduleNote** Method, **MailSession** Property, **MailSystem** Property, **MailUpdateProject** Method.

Example
```
Sub SessionLogon()
    If IsNull(Application.MailSession) Then
        Application.MailLogon "oscarx", "mypassword", True
    End If
End Sub
```

MailOpen Method

Applies To   **Application** Object.

Description   Reads documents from a Microsoft Mail server.

Syntax   [*object*.]**MailOpen** *(Any)*

Elements   The **MailOpen** method syntax has the following object qualifier and named arguments:

Part	Description
object	An object expression that evaluates to an object in the Applies To list. Optional.
Any	A Boolean expression that specifies whether to open any mail. By default, the *any* argument is **FALSE**. Optional.

Remarks   This method applies to Microsoft Project for the Macintosh.

See Also   **MailSend** Method.

MailPostDocument Method

Applies To   **Application** Object.

Description   Displays the dialog to post a document to Microsoft Exchange.

Syntax   [*object*.]**MailPostDocument**

Elements	The *object* placeholder is any object expression that evaluates to an object in the Applies To list.
Remarks	Available in all views. This method is only supported when a mail system has a Microsoft Exchange server.
See Also	**MailProjectMailCustomize** Method, **MailRoutingSlip** Method, **MailSendProjectMail** Method, **MailSystem** Property, **MailUpdateProject** Method.

MailProjectMailCustomize Method

Applies To	**Application** Object.
Description	Customizes workgroup messages programatically instead of by using the dialog. Available in all views or when no projects are open.
Syntax	[*object*.]**MailProjectMailCustomize** *action*[, *position, fieldID, title, includeInTeamStatus, Editable*]
Elements	The **MailProjectMailCustomize** method has the following object qualifier and named arguments:

Part	Description
object	An object expression that evaluates to an object in the Applies To list. Optional.
action	A constant that specifies the type of action taken. Required.
position	A numeric expression that specifies the number of fields or the position of a particular field. If *Action* = 1, this is the number of fields. Because there are fields which must be included, this number must be greater than 6. If *Action* = 2, this is the position of the particular field Optional. Required if *Action* = 1 or 2.
fieldID	A constant that specifies the id of the field to be included in the message. This is a subset of the list used by the *FieldID* for the **SetField** method with the addition of Workgroup specific fields. Optional. Required if *Action* = 2..
title	A string expression that specifies the title of the field presented to the user. If omitted or blank, the field name is used for the title string Optional.

Part	Description
IncludeInTeamStatus	A Boolean expression that specifies what fields are to be included in the TeamAssign and TeamStatus messages. Optional. Required if *Action* = 2.
Editable	A Boolean expression that specifies whether or not the field is editable by a resource. Optional. Required if *Action* = 2.

The *Action* argument has these settings:

pjMailEndFields	0	End of field definitions.
pjMailStartFields	1	Number of fields.
pjMailDefineField	2	Field definition.

The *FieldID* argument has these settings:

pjMailActualWork	32773	Actual Work field for workgroup messages.
pjMailComments	32769	Comments field for workgroup messages.
pjMailFinish	32771	Finish field for workgroup messages.
pjMailStart	32770	Start field for workgroup messages.
pjMailWork	32772	Work field for workgroup messages.
pjTaskContact	112	Contact field.
pjTaskCost1	106	Cost1 field.
pjTaskCost2	107	Cost2 field.
pjTaskCost3	108	Cost3 field.
pjTaskCritical	19	Critical field.
pjTaskDuration1	103	Duration1 field.
pjTaskDuration2	104	Duration2 field.
pjTaskDuration3	105	Duration3 field.
pjTaskEarlyFinish	38	Early Finish field.
pjTaskEarlyStart	37	Early Start field.
pjTaskFinish1	53	Finish1 field.
pjTaskFinish2	56	Finish2 field.
pjTaskFinish3	59	Finish3 field.
pjTaskFinish4	62	Finish4 field.
pjTaskFinish5	65	Finish5 field.
pjTaskFixedCost	8	Fixed Cost field.
pjTaskFlag1	72	Flag1 field.

pjTaskFlag2	73	Flag2 field.
pjTaskFlag3	74	Flag3 field.
pjTaskFlag4	75	Flag4 field.
pjTaskFlag5	76	Flag5 field.
pjTaskFlag6	77	Flag6 field.
pjTaskFlag7	78	Flag7 field.
pjTaskFlag8	79	Flag8 field.
pjTaskFlag9	80	Flag9 field.
pjTaskFlag0	81	Flag0 field.
pjTaskFreeSlack	21	Free Slack field.
pjTaskLateFinish	40	Late Finish field.
pjTaskLateStart	39	Late Start field.
pjTaskMarked	71	Marked field.
pjTaskName	14	Name field.
pjTaskNumber1	87	Number1 field.
pjTaskNumber2	88	Number2 field.
pjTaskNumber3	89	Number3 field.
pjTaskNumber4	90	Number4 field.
pjTaskNumber5	91	Number5 field.
pjTaskPercentComplete	32	Percent Complete field.
pjTaskPercentWorkComplete	33	Percent Work Complete field.
pjTaskPriority	25	Priority field.
pjTaskProject	84	Project field.
pjTaskResourceNames	49	Resource Names field.
pjTaskStart1	52	Start1 field.
pjTaskStart2	55	Start2 field.
pjTaskStart3	58	Start3 field.
pjTaskStart4	61	Start4 field.
pjTaskStart5	64	Start5 field.
pjTaskText1	51	Text1 field.
pjTaskText2	54	Text2 field.
pjTaskText3	57	Text3 field.
pjTaskText4	60	Text4 field.
pjTaskText5	63	Text5 field.
pjTaskText6	66	Text6 field.
pjTaskText7	67	Text7 field.

pjTaskText8	68	Text8 field.
pjTaskText9	69	Text9 field.
pjTaskText10	70	Text10 field.
pjTaskTotalSlack	22	Total Slack field.
pjTaskWBS	16	WBS field.

See Also **MailRoutingSlip** Method, **MailSendProjectMail** Method, **MailSystem** Property, **MailUpdateProject** Method.

Example The following example first sets up how many fields will be defined (Action=pjMailStartFields). The next set of lines define each field (Action=pjMailDefineField). You must include the definitions of the default fields with the same values for the IncludeInTeamStatus and Editable arguments. The last line indicates that the definitions are complete (Action=pjMailEndFields). It will check for the existence of the default fields and give a run-time error if they are not given.

Note that the default fields (Name, Work, Start, Finished, Completed and Remaining Work, and Comments) must be included in every workgroup message. The order of these fields can change, but their basic definition (Editable, IncludeInTeamStatus) must remain the same as the default.

```
Sub MailProjectMailCustomize()
    ActiveProject.MailProjectMailCustomize Action=pjMailStartFields, _
        Position=(number of fields)
    MailProjectMailCustomize Action=pjMailDefineField, Position=1, _
        FieldID=n, Title="My Title"
        ...
    MailProjectMailCustomize Action=pjMailDefineField, Position=n, _
        FieldID=n, Title="Another Title"
    MailProjectMailCustomize Action=pjMailEndFields
End Sub
```

MailRoutingSlip Method

Applies To **Application** Object.

Description Adds a mail routing slip to the current project.

Syntax

[*object*.]**MailRoutingSlip** [*to, subject, body, allAtOnce, returnWhenDone, trackStatus, clear, sendNow*]

Elements

The **MailRoutingSlip** method syntax has the following object qualifier and named arguments:

Part	Description
object	An object expression that evaluates to an object in the Applies To list. Optional.
to	A string expression that specifies the user names of the primary recipients of the mail, separated by semicolons. Optional.
subject	A string expression that specifies the subject of the mail. Optional.
body	A string expression that specifies the main body of the mail. Optional.
allAtOnce	A Boolean expression that specifies whether to send the mail to all users at the same time or to route the mail from one user to the next. By default, the *allAtOnce* argument is **False**. Optional.
returnWhenDone	A Boolean expression that specifies whether to return the mail to you after it reaches the last recipient. By default, the *returnWhenDone* argument is **True**. Optional.
trackStatus	A Boolean expression that specifies whether to track the location of the mail. By default, the *trackStatus* argument is **True**. Optional.
clear	A Boolean expression that specifies whether to clear the list of user names in the Routing Slip dialog box. By default, the *clear* argument is **False**. Optional.
sendNow	A Boolean expression that specifies whether you want to send the project or edit the mail slip. By default, the *sendNow* argument is **False**. Optional. The *sendNow* argument has these settings:

True	Sends the project now.
False	Edits the mail slip without sending the project.

Remarks

This method applies to Microsoft Project for Microsoft Windows.

See Also

MailLogOff Method, **MailLogOn** Method, **MailSend** Method, **MailSendProjectMail** Method, **MailSendScheduleNote** Method, **MailSession** Property, **MailSystem** Property, **MailUpdateProject** Method.

Example

The following example sends the current schedule to Julie Rogers and then to Michael Edwards.

```
Sub PlanApproval()
  MailRoutingSlip to:= "Julie Rogers;Michael Edwards", _
      subject:="Project Plan Approval", _
      body:="Please review the following plan for approval.", _
      allAtOnce:=False, returnWhenDone:=True, _
      trackStatus:=True, sendNow:=True
End Sub
```

MailSend Method

Applies To   **Application** Object.

Description   Sends a mail message.

Syntax   [*object.*]**MailSend** [*to, cc, subject, body, enclosures, includeDocument, returnReceipt, Bcc, urgent, saveCopy, addRecipient*]

Elements   The **MailSend** method syntax has the following object qualifier and named arguments:

Part	Description
object	An object expression that evaluates to an object in the Applies To list. Optional.
to	A string expression that specifies the user names of the primary recipients of the mail, separated by semicolons. Optional.
cc	A string expression that specifies the user names of the secondary recipients of the mail, separated by semicolons. Optional.
subject	A string expression that specifies the subject of the mail. Optional.
body	A string expression that specifies the main body of the mail. Optional.
enclosures	A string expression that specifies one or more filenames to include with the mail. Use the list separator character to separate multiple filenames. Do not add space between the list separator and the filename. Optional.
includeDocument	A Boolean expression that specifies whether to include the active project in the mail. By default, the *includeDocument* argument is **True**. Optional.

Part	Description
returnReceipt	A Boolean expression that specifies whether a message is sent to the sender when the recipient opens the mail.. By default, the *returnReceipt* argument is **False**. Optional.
Bcc	A string expression that specifies the user names of the mail recipients which will not be displayed, separated by semicolons. Optional.
urgent	A boolean expression that specifies the priority of the mail. Optional.
saveCopy	A boolean expression that specifies whether a copy of the mail is saved in the Sent Mail folder. Optional.
addRecipient	A boolean expression that specifies whether the mail recipients are added to a personal address book. Optional.

Remarks   MAPI support is available in Microsoft Project for Microsoft Windows.

See Also   **MailLogOff** Method, **MailLogOn** Method, **MailRoutingSlip** Method, **MailSendProjectMail** Method, **MailSendScheduleNote** Method, **MailSession** Property, **MailSystem** Property, **MailUpdateProject** Method.

MailSendProjectMail Method

Applies To   **Application** Object.

Description   Sends mail about the active project.

Syntax   [*object.*]**MailSendProjectMail** [*messageType, subject, body, fields, updateAsOf, showDialog, installationMessage*]

Elements   The **MailSendProjectMail** method syntax has the following object qualifier and named arguments:

Part	Description
object	An object expression that evaluates to an object in the Applies To list. Optional.

Part	Description
messageType	A string expression that specifies the type of message to send. By default, the *messageType* argument is "TaskRequest". Optional. The *messageType* argument has these settings:

"Custom"	Sends custom project information to resources assigned to selected tasks.
"TaskRequest"	Sends a message about task assignments.
"TaskUpdates"	Notifies resources of changes in assigned tasks.
"UpdateRequest"	Sends a message requesting status on selected tasks.

Part	Description
subject	A string expression that specifies the subject of the mail. Optional.
body	A string expression that specifies the main text of the mail. Optional.
fields	A string expression that specifies the names of one or more project fields to send in the mail. Use the list separator character to separate multiple project fields. To specify a title for a field, enclose the title in brackets immediately after the field name. Optional.
updateAsOf	A date expression that specifies the date through which a resource is asked to update status in response to an update request message. Optional.
showDialog	A Boolean expression that specifies whether the dialog box will be displayed.
installationMessage	A string expression that specifies the message that appears to users who do not have the message handler installed. If specified, the *installationMessage* argument replaces the default Microsoft Project message. Optional.

Remarks   This method applies to Microsoft Windows.

See Also   **MailLogOff** Method, **MailLogOn** Method, **MailRoutingSlip** Method, **MailSend** Method, **MailSendScheduleNote** Method, **MailSession** Property, **MailSystem** Property, **MailUpdateProject** Method.

MailSendScheduleNote Method

Applies To   **Application** Object.

Description	Sends a schedule note in mail.
Syntax	[*object.*]**MailSendScheduleNote** [*manager, taskContacts, resources, selection, includeDocument, includePicture, body, subject*]
Elements	The **MailSendScheduleNote** method syntax has the following object qualifier and named arguments:

Part	Description
object	An object expression that evaluates to an object in the Applies To list. Optional.
manager	A Boolean expression that specifies whether to send the note to the manager of the active project. By default, the *manager* argument is **True**. Optional.
taskContacts	A Boolean expression that specifies whether to send the note to the contacts for the active project. By default, the *taskContacts* argument is **False**. Optional.
resources	A Boolean expression that specifies whether to send the note to the resources for the active project. By default, the *resources* argument is **True**. Optional.
selection	A Boolean expression that specifies the recipients for the note.
	True Sends the note to the selected resource. **False** Sends the note to all resources.
	By default, the *selection* argument is **True**. Optional.
includeDocument	A Boolean expression that specifies whether to include the active project in the note. By default, the *includeDocument* argument is **False**. Optional.
includePicture	A Boolean expression that specifies whether to include a picture of the active project in the note. By default, the *includePicture* argument is **True**. Optional.
body	A string expression that specifies the main text of the note. Optional.
subject	A string expression that specifies the subject of the note. Optional.

Remarks	This method applies to Microsoft Project for Microsoft Windows. In a task view, the *selection* argument specifies only resources that are assigned to tasks.
See Also	**MailLogOff** Method, **MailLogOn** Method, **MailRoutingSlip** Method, **MailSend** Method, **MailSendProjectMail** Method, **MailSession** Property, **MailSystem** Property, **MailUpdateProject** Method.

MailSession Property

Applies To	**Application** Object.
Description	Returns the MAPI mail session number as a hexadecimal string (if there is an active session), or **Null** if there is no session.
Syntax	[*object*.]**MailSession**
Elements	The *object* placeholder is an object expression that evaluates to an object in the Applies To list.
Remarks	This property applies to Microsoft Project for Microsoft Windows.
See Also	**MailLogOff** Method, **MailLogOn** Method, **MailRoutingSlip** Method, **MailSend** Method, **MailSendProjectMail** Method, **MailSendScheduleNote** Method, **MailSystem** Property, **MailUpdateProject** Method.
Example	The following example logs off of mail if the application is logged onto mail.

```
Sub SessionNumber()
    If Not IsNull(Application.MailSession) Then
        Application.MailLogoff
    End If
End Sub
```

MailSystem Property

Applies To	**Application** Object.
Description	Returns the type of mail system installed on the host machine, as shown under Settings.
Syntax	[*object*.]**MailSystem**
Elements	The *object* placeholder is an object expression that evaluates to an object in the Applies To list.

Settings	The **MailSystem** property has these settings:

pjNoMailSystem	0	Unrecognized or missing e-mail system
pjMAPI	1	Microsoft Mail
pjMAPICompatible	3	Mail system that is compatible with MAPI.
pjMacMail	4	Microsoft Mail for the Apple Macintosh.

Remarks   MAPI is available in Microsoft Project for Microsoft Windows.

See Also   **MailLogOff** Method, **MailLogOn** Method, **MailRoutingSlip** Method, **MailSend** Method, **MailSendProjectMail** Method, **MailSendScheduleNote** Method, **MailSession** Property, **MailUpdateProject** Method.

Example   The following example sends the project file if the host machine is using MAPI.

```
Sub SendMAPI()
    If Application.MailSystem = pjMAPI Then
        MailSend To := "Jean Selva", Subject := "Sample Subject"
    End If
End Sub
```

MailUpdateProject Method

Applies To   **Application** Object.

Description   Uses feedback from Microsoft Project mail to update a project.

Syntax   *object*.**MailUpdateProject** [*dataFile*]

Elements   The **MailUpdateProject** property syntax has the following parts:

Part	Description
object	An object expression that evaluates to an object in the Applies To list. Required.
dataFile	A string expression that specifies the name of the file on which to base the update. Optional.

Remarks   This method applies to Microsoft Project for Microsoft Windows.

See Also

MailLogOff Method, MailLogOn Method, MailRoutingSlip Method, MailSend Method, MailSendProjectMail Method, MailSendScheduleNote Method, MailSession Property, MailSystem Property.

Manager Property

Applies To

Project Object, **Projects** Collection.

Description

Returns or sets the name of the manager for a project.

Syntax

object.**Manager** [= *value*]

Elements

The **Manager** property syntax has these parts:

Part	Description
object	An object expression that evaluates to an object in the Applies To list.
value	A string expression of the name of the project's manager.

See Also

Author Property, **Comments** Property, **Company** Property, **CurrentDate** Property, **Keywords** Property, **Notes** Property, **ScheduleFromStart** Property, **Subject** Property, **Template** Property, **Title** Property.

Marked Property

Applies To

Project Object, **Projects** Collection; **Task** Object, **Tasks** Collection.

Description

Returns or sets whether a task is marked or unmarked.

Syntax

object.**Marked** [= *value*]

Elements

The **Marked** property syntax has these parts:

Part	Description
object	An object expression that evaluates to an object in the Applies To list.
value	A Boolean expression that marks or unmarks the task, as shown under Settings.

Settings

The **Marked** property has these settings:

Setting	Description
True	The task is marked.
False	The task is unmarked.

See Also   **Milestone** Property, **Rollup** Property.

MaxUnits Property

Applies To   **Resource** Object, **Resources** Collection.

Description   Sets or returns the maximum number of units of a resource.

Syntax   *object*.**MaxUnits** [= *value*]

Elements   The **MaxUnits** property syntax has the following parts:

Part	Description
object	An object expression that evaluates to an object in the Applies To list.
value	A numeric expression that specifies the maximum number of units of the resource.

See Also   **Units** Property.

Example   The following example sets the maximum units of each resource in the active project to a number specified by the user.

```
Sub SetDefaultMaxUnits()
    Dim Entry    ' Maximum units specified by user
    Dim R        ' Resource object used in loop

    ' Prompt the user for the default maximum units for each resource.
    Entry = InputBox("Enter the default maximum units" & _
            " for each resource.")

    If IsNumeric(Entry) Then
        For Each R in ActiveProject.Resources
            R.MaxUnits = Entry
        Next R

    ' Display error message if user didn't enter a numeric value.
    Else
        MsgBox("You didn't enter a numeric value!")
    End If
End Sub
```

MenuBarApply Method

Applies To	**Application** Object.
Description	Sets the current or default menu bar.
Syntax	[*object*.]**MenuBarApply** *name*[, *default, noFiles*]
Elements	The **MenuBarApply** method syntax has the following object qualifier and named arguments:

Part	Description
object	An object expression that evaluates to an object in the Applies To list. Optional.
name	A string expression that specifies the name of the menu bar to display. Required.
default	A Boolean expression that specifies whether the menu bar is the default menu bar. By default, the *default* argument is **False**. Optional.
noFiles	A Boolean expression that specifies whether the menu bar appears when no projects are open. By default, the *noFiles* argument is **False**. Optional.

See Also	**MenuBarEdit** Method, **MenuBars** Method.

MenuBarEdit Method

Applies To	**Application** Object.
Description	Creates, copies, or allows the user to edit a menu bar.
Syntax	[*object*.]**MenuBarEdit** [*copy, create, name, newName*]
Elements	The **MenuBarEdit** method syntax has the following object qualifier and named arguments:

Part	Description
object	An object expression that evaluates to an object in the Applies To list. Optional.
copy	A Boolean expression that specifies whether to create a copy of the menu bar you specify with the *name* argument. Optional.
create	A Boolean expression that specifies whether to create a new menu bar or allow the user to edit an existing menu bar. The *create* argument has no effect if the *copy* argument is **True**. Optional.
name	A string expression that specifies the name of the menu bar to create, copy, or allow the user to edit. Optional.
newName	A string expression that specifies the new name of the menu bar you specify with the *name* argument (*create* argument is **False**), or the name of the new menu bar you create (*create* argument is **True**). Optional.

See Also   **MenuBarApply** Method, **MenuBars** Method, **Organizer** Method.

Example   The following example creates a copy of the menu bar called "Standard". The copy is called "Corporate".

```
Sub CopyMenuBar()
    MenuBarEdit copy:=True, name:="Standard", newName:="Corporate"
End Sub
```

MenuBars Method

Applies To   **Application** Object.

Description   Displays the Menu Bars dialog box.

Syntax   [*object*.]**MenuBars**

Elements   The *object* placeholder is an object expression that evaluates to an object in the Applies To list.

See Also   **MenuBarApply** Method, **MenuBarEdit** Method, **OrganizerDeleteItem** Method.

Message Method

Applies To   **Application** Object.

Description   Displays a message in a message box.

Syntax   *object*.**Message** *message*[*, type, yesText, noText*]

Elements   The **Message** method syntax has the following object qualifier and named
                      arguments:

Part	Description
object	An object expression that evaluates to an object in the Applies To list. Required.
message	A string expression containing the message to be displayed in the dialog box. Required.
type	A constant specifying the buttons to include in the dialog box. Default is pjOKOnly. Optional.
yesText	A string expression containing the text to be displayed on the Yes button. Only valid if *type* is pjYesNo or pjYesNoCancel. Default is "Yes". Optional.
noText	A string expression containing the text to be displayed on the No button. Only valid if *type* is pjYesNo or pjYesNoCancel. Default is "No". Optional.

The *type* named argument has these values:

pjOKOnly	0	OK button only
pjOKCancel	1	OK and Cancel buttons
pjYesNo	2	Yes and No buttons
pjYesNoCancel	3	Yes, No, and Cancel buttons

Remarks   The **Message** method is provided for compatibility with the macro language used in
                      Microsoft Project version 3.*x*.

Mid Function

Description   Returns a specified number of characters from a string.

Syntax   **Mid**(*string*, *start*[, *length*])

Elements   The **Mid** function syntax has these parts:

Part	Description
string	String expression from which characters are returned. If *string* contains no valid data, **Null** is returned.
start	Character position in *string* at which the part to be taken begins. If *start* is greater than the number of characters in *string*, **Mid** returns a zero-length string.
length	Number of characters to return. If omitted or if there are fewer than *length* characters in the text (including the character at *start*), all characters from the *start* position to the end of the string are returned.

Remarks   To determine the number of characters in *string*, use the **Len** function.

Note   Another function (MidB) is provided for use with the double-byte character sets (DBCS) used in some Asian locales. Instead of specifying the number of characters to return, *length* specifies the number of bytes. In areas where DBCS is not used, MidB behaves the same as Mid.

See Also   **Left** Function; **Len** Function; **LTrim**, **RTrim**, and **Trim** Functions; **Mid** Statement; **Right** Function.

Example   This example uses the **Mid** function to return a specified number of characters from a string.

```
MyString = "Mid Function Demo"   ' Create text string.
FirstWord = Mid(MyString, 1, 3)  ' Returns "Mid".
LastWord = Mid(MyString, 14, 4)  ' Returns "Demo".
MidWords = Mid(MyString, 5)      ' Returns "Function Demo".
```

Mid Statement

Description   Replaces a specified number of characters in a string variable with characters from another string.

Syntax   **Mid**(*stringvar*, *start*[, *length*])=*string*

Elements   The **Mid** statement syntax has these parts:

Part	Description
stringvar	Name of string variable to modify.
start	Character position in *stringvar* where the replacement of text begins.
length	Number of characters to replace. If omitted, all of *string* is used.
string	String expression that replaces part of *stringvar*.

Remarks   The number of characters replaced is always less than or equal to the number of characters in *stringvar*.

See Also   **Mid** Function.

Example   This example uses the **Mid** statement to replace a specified number of characters in a string variable with characters from another string.

```
MyString = "The dog jumps"              ' Initialize string.
Mid(MyString, 5, 3) = "fox"             ' MyString = "The fox jumps".
Mid(MyString, 5) = "cow"                ' MyString = "The cow jumps".
Mid(MyString, 5) = "cow jumped over"    ' MyString = "The cow jumpe".
Mid(MyString, 5, 3) = "duck"            ' MyString = "The duck jumps".
```

Milestone Property

Applies To   **Project** Object, **Projects** Collection; **Task** Object, **Tasks** Collection.

Description   Returns or sets whether a task is a milestone.

Syntax   *object*.**Milestone** [= *value*]

Elements   The **Milestone** property syntax has these parts:

Part	Description
object	An object expression that evaluates to an object in the Applies To list.
value	A Boolean expression that specifies whether the task is normal or a milestone, as shown under Settings.

Settings   The **Milestone** property has these settings:

Setting	Description
True	The task is a milestone.
False	The task is not a milestone.

See Also   **Marked** Property, **Rollup** Property.

Example   The following example marks as milestones any tasks in the active project with names that begin with the word "Inspection."

```
Sub MarkInspectionTasks()
    Dim T As Task    ' Task object used in For Each loop

    MilestoneName = "Inspection"
    NameLength = Len(MilestoneName)
    ' Check each task for a name that begins with "Inspection."
    For Each T in ActiveProject.Tasks

        ' If the task's name begins with Inspection, it's a milestone.
        If UCase(Left(T.Name, NameLength)) = UCase(MilestoneName) Then
            T.Milestone = True
        End If
    Next T
End Sub
```

Minute Function

Description   Returns a whole number between 0 and 59, inclusive, representing the minute of the hour.

Syntax   **Minute(*time*)**

Elements	The *time* named argument is limited to a time or numbers and strings, in any combination, that can represent a time. If *time* contains no valid data, **Null** is returned.
See Also	**Day** Function, **Hour** Function, **Now** Function, **Second** Function, **Time** Function, **Time** Statement.
Example	This example uses the **Minute** function to obtain the minute of the hour from a specified time.

```
' In the development environment, the time (date literal) will display
' in short format using the locale settings of your code.
MyTime = #4:35:17 PM#        ' Assign a time.
MyMinute = Minute(MyTime)    ' MyMinute contains 35.
```

MkDir Statement

Description	Creates a new directory or folder.
Syntax	**MkDir** *path*
Elements	The *path* named argument is a string expression that identifies the directory or folder to be created—may include drive. If no drive is specified, **MkDir** creates the new directory or folder on the current drive.
Remarks	In Microsoft Windows, if you use **MkDir** to create a directory whose name contains an embedded space, you may be able to access it with some applications, but you can't remove it using standard operating system commands. To remove such a directory, use the **RmDir** statement.
See Also	**ChDir** Statement, **CurDir** Function, **RmDir** Statement.
Example	This example uses the **MkDir** statement to create a directory or folder. If the drive is not specified, the new directory or folder is created on the current drive.

```
MkDir "MYDIR"    ' Make new directory or folder.
```

Mod Operator

Description   Divides two numbers and returns only the remainder.

Syntax   *result* = *number1* **Mod** *number2*

Elements   The **Mod** operator syntax has these parts:

Part	Description
result	Any numeric variable.
number1	Any numeric expression.
number2	Any numeric expression.

Remarks   The modulus, or remainder, operator divides *number1* by *number2* (rounding floating-point numbers to integers) and returns only the remainder as *result*. For example, in the following expression, A (which is *result*) equals 5.

```
A = 19 Mod 6.7
```

Usually, the data type of *result* is an **Integer**, **Integer** variant, **Long**, or **Variant** containing a **Long**, regardless of whether or not *result* is a whole number. Any fractional portion is truncated. However, if any expression is a **Null**, *result* is also a **Null**. Any expression that is **Empty** is treated as 0.

See Also   Operator Precedence.

Example   This example uses the **Mod** operator to divide two numbers and return only the remainder. If either number is a floating-point number, it is first rounded to an integer.

```
MyResult = 10 Mod 5      ' Returns 0.
MyResult = 10 Mod 3      ' Returns 1.
MyResult = 12 Mod 4.3    ' Returns 0.
MyResult = 12.6 Mod 5    ' Returns 3.
```

Month Function

Description   Returns a whole number between 1 and 12, inclusive, representing the month of the year.

Syntax   **Month(*date*)**

Elements   The *date* named argument is limited to a date or numbers and strings, in any combination, that can represent a date. If *date* contains no valid data, **Null** is returned.

See Also   **Date** Function, **Date** Statement, **Day** Function, **Now** Function, **Weekday** Function, **Year** Function.

Example   This example uses the **Month** function to obtain the month from a specified date.

```
' In the development environment, the date literal will display in short
' format using the locale settings of your code.
MyDate = #February 12, 1969#     ' Assign a date.
MyMonth = Month(MyDate)          ' MyMonth contains 2.
```

Month Object, Months Collection

Description   A month or the months in a year.

Remarks   In Microsoft Project, **Month** objects are parents of **Day** and **Shift** objects.

Properties   **Application** Property, **Calendar** Property, **Count** Property, **Index** Property, **Name** Property, **Parent** Property, **Shiftn** Property, **Working** Property

Methods   **Days** Method, **Default** Method

See Also   **Day** Object, **Days** Collection; **Months** Method; **Shift** Object; **Year** Object, **Years** Collection.

MonthLeadingZero Property

Applies To	**Application** Object.
Description	Returns **True** if Microsoft Project displays zeroes before single-digit months in dates; returns **False** otherwise.
Syntax	[*object*.]**MonthLeadingZero**
Elements	The *object* placeholder is an object expression that evaluates to an object in the Applies To list.
Remarks	Microsoft Project for Microsoft Windows sets the **MonthLeadingZero** property equal to the corresponding value in the Regionall settings of the Microsoft Windows Control Panel.
	On the Macintosh, using System 7.1 and later, you can use the Date & Time control panel to change this value.
See Also	**DateFormat** Method, **DateOrder** Property, **DateSeparator** Property, **DayLeadingZero** Property.

Months Method

Applies To	**Year** Object, **Years** Collection.
Description	Returns a month or the months in a year.
Syntax	*object*.**Months**[(***index***)]
Elements	The **Months** method syntax has the following object qualifier and named arguments:

Part	Description
object	An object expression that evaluates to an object in the Applies To list.
index	A numeric expression that specifies the index of the *object* (1–12).

See Also	**Calendar** Object, **Calendars** Collection; **Month** Object, **Months** Collection; **Years** Method.
Example	The following example makes January 1 of every year a nonworking day.

```
Sub NewYearsDayOff()
    For each y in ActiveProject.Calendar.Years
        y.Months(1).Days(1).Working = False
    Next y
End Sub
```

MoveAfterReturn Property

Applies To   **Application** Object.

Description   Returns or sets whether the active field stays active, or the field below the active field becomes active, when you press ENTER.

Syntax   [*object.*]**MoveAfterReturn** [= *value*]

Elements   The **MoveAfterReturn** property syntax has these parts:

Part	Description
object	An object expression that evaluates to an object in the Applies To list.
value	A Boolean expression that specifies whether the active field stays active, or the field below the active field becomes active, when you press ENTER.

Settings   The **MoveAfterReturn** property has these settings:

Setting	Description
True	The active field stays active when you press ENTER.
False	The field below the active field becomes active when you press ENTER.

See Also   **Name** Property, **OperatingSystem** Property, **SupportsMultipleDocuments** Property, **SupportsMultipleWindows** Property, **Version** Property.

MsgBox Function

Description   Displays a message in a dialog box, waits for the user to choose a button, and returns a value indicating which button the user has chosen.

Syntax   **MsgBox(***prompt*[,*buttons*][,*title*][,*helpfile*,*context*]**)**

Elements   The **MsgBox** function syntax has these named-argument parts:

Part	Description
prompt	String expression displayed as the message in the dialog box. The maximum length of *prompt* is approximately 1024 characters, depending on the width of the characters used. If *prompt* consists of more than one line, be sure to include a carriage return (character code 13) or carriage return linefeed (character code 10) between each line.
buttons	Numeric expression that is the sum of values specifying the number and type of buttons to display, the icon style to use, the identity of the default button, and the modality. If omitted, the default value for *buttons* is 0.
title	String expression displayed in the title bar of the dialog box. If you omit *title*, nothing is placed in the title bar.
helpfile	String expression that identifies the Help file to use to provide context-sensitive Help for the dialog box. If *helpfile* is provided, *context* must also be provided.
context	Numeric expression that is the Help context number the Help author assigned to the appropriate Help topic. If *context* is provided, *helpfile* must also be provided.

The *buttons* named argument has these values:

vbOKOnly	0	Display OK button only.
vbOKCancel	1	Display OK and Cancel buttons.
vbAbortRetryIgnore	2	Display Abort, Retry, and Ignore buttons.
vbYesNoCancel	3	Display Yes, No, and Cancel buttons.
vbYesNo	4	Display Yes and No buttons.
vbRetryCancel	5	Display Retry and Cancel buttons.
vbCritical	16	Display Critical Message icon.
vbQuestion	32	Display Warning Query icon.
vbExclamation	48	Display Warning Message icon.
vbInformation	64	Display Information Message icon.
vbDefaultButton1	0	First button is default.
vbDefaultButton2	256	Second button is default.
vbDefaultButton3	512	Third button is default.

vbApplicationModal	0	Application modal; the user must respond to the message box before continuing work in the current application.
vbSystemModal	4096	System modal; all applications are suspended until the user responds to the message box.

The first group of values (0-5) describes the number and type of buttons displayed in the dialog box; the second group (16, 32, 48, 64) describes the icon style; the third group (0, 256, 512) determines which button is the default, and the fourth group (0, 4096) determines the modality of the message box. When adding numbers to create a final value for the argument *buttons*, use only one number from each group.

Note   These constants are specified by Visual Basic. As a result, the names can be used anywhere in your code in place of the actual values.

Return Values

vbOK	1	OK
vbCancel	2	Cancel
vbAbort	3	Abort
vbRetry	4	Retry
vbIgnore	5	Ignore
vbYes	6	Yes
vbNo	7	No

Remarks

When both *helpfile* and *context* are provided, a Help button is automatically added to the dialog box.

If the dialog box displays a Cancel button, pressing the ESC key has the same effect as choosing Cancel. If the dialog box contains a Help button, context-sensitive Help is provided for the dialog box. However, no value is returned until one of the other buttons is chosen.

See Also

InputBox Function.

Example

The example uses the **MsgBox** function to display a critical-error message in a dialog box with Yes and No buttons. The No button is specified as the default response. The value returned by the **MsgBox** function depends on the button chosen by the user. For purposes of this example, assume that DEMO.HLP is a Help file that contains a topic with context number equal to 1000.

```
    Msg = "Do you want to continue ?"                    ' Define message.
Style = vbYesNo + vbCritical + vbDefaultButton2  ' Define buttons.
Title = "MsgBox Demonstration"                     ' Define title.
Help = "DEMO.HLP"                                ' Define help file.
Ctxt = 1000                                   ' Define topic
context.' Display message.
Response = MsgBox(Msg, Style, Title, Help, Ctxt)
If Response = vbYES Then    ' User chose Yes button. MyString = "Yes"
        ' Perform some action.
Else                        ' User chose No button.
    MyString = "No"            ' Perform some action.
End If
```

Name Property

Applies To	**Application** Object.
Description	Returns or sets the name of the user.
Syntax	[*object*.]**UserName** [= *value*]
Elements	The **UserName** property syntax has these parts:

Part	Description
object	An object expression that evaluates to an object in the Applies To list.
value	A string expression that specifies the name of the current user.

Remarks

Use the **UserName** property to customize Microsoft Project options or macros for a particular user.

Suppose you have written a macro called PrintReport that prints the report MINE.MPP when you press Ctrl+R, but another user wants to use the same shortcut keys to print the report YOURS.MPP. You can edit the PrintReport macro so it checks the Username property, prints MINE.MPP if you are the current user, and prints YOURS.MPP otherwise.

See Also

Calculation Property, **ListSeparator** Property, **ShowCriticalSlack** Property, **StartOnCurrentDate** Property, **StartYearIn** Property.

Example

The following example sets preferences in Microsoft Project according to the name of the current user.

```
Sub GetUserName()

    ' Prompt user for his or her name.
    UserName = InputBox("What's your name?", , UserName)

    ' If user is Tamara, then set certain preferences.
    If UserName = "Tamara" Then
        DisplayScheduleMessages = False
        BarRounding On:=False
        Calculation = True

    ' If user is not Tamara, then set default preferences.
    Else
        DisplayScheduleMessages = True
        BarRounding On:=True
        Calculation = False
    End If
End Sub
```

Name Statement

Description   Renames a disk file, directory, or folder.

Syntax   **Name** *oldpathname* **As** *newpathname*

Elements   The **Name** statement syntax has these parts:

Part	Description
oldpathname	String expression that specifies the existing file name and location—may include directory or folder, and drive.
newpathname	String expression that specifies the new file name and location —may include directory or folder, and drive. The file specified by *newpathname* can't already exist.

Remarks   Both *newpathname* and *oldpathname* must be on the same drive. If the path in *newpathname* exists and is different from the path in *oldpathname*, the **Name** statement moves the file to the new directory or folder and renames the file, if necessary. If *newpathname* and *oldpathname* have different paths and the same file name, **Name** moves the file to the new location and leaves the file name unchanged. Using **Name**, you can move a file from one directory or folder to another, but you can't move a directory or folder.

Name supports the use of '*' (multiple character) and '?' (single character) wildcards. However, on the Macintosh, these characters are treated as valid file name characters and can't be used as wildcards to specify multiple files.

Using **Name** on an open file produces an error. You must close an open file before renaming it.

See Also

Kill Statement.

Example

This example uses the **Name** statement to rename a file. For purposes of this example, assume that the directories or folders that are specified already exist.

```
OldName = "OLDFILE" : NewName = "NEWFILE"     ' Define file names.
Name OldName As NewName                        ' Rename file.

' In Microsoft Windows.
OldName = "C:\MYDIR\OLDFILE" : NewName = "C:\YOURDIR\NEWFILE"
Name OldName As NewName ' Move and rename file.

' On the Macintosh.
OldName = "HD:MY FOLDER:OLDFILE" : NewName = "HD:YOUR FOLDER:NEWFILE"
Name OldName As NewName ' Move and rename file.
```

Not Operator

Description

Used to perform logical negation on an expression.

Syntax

result = **Not** *expression*

Elements

The **Not** operator syntax has these parts:

Part	Description
result	Any numeric variable.
expression	Any expression.

Remarks

The following table illustrates how *result* is determined:

If expression is	Then result is
True	**False**
False	**True**
Null	**Null**

In addition, the **Not** operator inverts the bit values of any variable and sets the corresponding bit in *result* according to the following truth table:

Bit in expression	Bit in result
0	1
1	0

See Also

Operator Precedence.

Example

This example uses the **Not** operator to perform logical negation on an expression.

```
A = 10: B = 8: C = 6 : D = Null  ' Initialize variables.
MyCheck = Not(A > B)          ' Returns False.
MyCheck = Not(B > A)          ' Returns True.
MyCheck = Not(C > D)          ' Returns Null.
MyCheck = Not A          ' Returns -11 (bit-wise comparison).
```

Notes Property

Applies To

Project Object, **Projects** Collection; **Resource** Object, **Resources** Collection; **Task** Object, **Tasks** Collection.

Description

Returns or sets the notes for a project, resource, or task.

Syntax

object.**Notes** [= *value*]

Elements

The **Notes** property syntax has these parts:

Part	Description
object	An object expression that evaluates to an object in the Applies To list.
value	A string expression of notes for the project, resource, or task.

Remarks

The **Notes** property is the same as the **Comments** property. For example, if you assign a value to the **Notes** property, you can retrieve the value with the **Comments** property; and if you assign a value to the **Comments** property, you can retrieve the value with the **Notes** property.

See Also

Author Property, **Comments** Property, **Company** Property, **CurrentDate** Property, **Keywords** Property, **Manager** Property, **ScheduleFromStart** Property, **Subject** Property, **Template** Property, **Title** Property.

Example

The following example adds the date and time to the notes of the active project and then saves the project.

```
Sub SaveAndNoteTime()
    Dim NL                  ' Newline characters
    NL = Chr(13) & Chr(10)  ' NL = Carriage Return + Linefeed
    phrase = "This project was last saved on "
    ActiveProject.Notes = ActiveProject.Notes & NL & NL & phrase & _
        Date$ & " at " & Time$ & "."
    FileSave
End Sub
```

Now Function

Description

Returns the current date and time according to the setting of your computer's system date and time.

Syntax

Now

Remarks

Note When displayed directly, the **Now** function's return value is displayed as a string using the short date and time formats you specified for your system.

See Also

Date Function, **Date** Statement, **Day** Function, **Hour** Function, **Minute** Function, **Month** Function, **Second** Function, **Time** Function, **Time** Statement, **Weekday** Function, **Year** Function.

Example

This example uses the **Now** function to return the current system date and time.

```
Today = Now ' Get current system date and time.
```

Numbern Properties

Applies To

Project Object, **Projects** Collection; **Task** Object, **Tasks** Collection.

Description

Returns or sets a number associated with a task.

Syntax

object.**Number***n* [= *value*]

Elements	The **Number***n* property syntaxes have the following parts:

Part	Description
object	An object expression that evaluates to an object in the Applies To list.
n	A number from 1 to 5.
value	A numeric expression that specifies the number associated with the task.

See Also	**Flag***n* Properties, **Notes** Property, **Summary** Property, **Text***n* Properties.

NumberOfResources Property

Applies To	**Project** Object, **Projects** Collection.
Description	Returns the number of resources in a project, not including blank entries.
Syntax	*object***.NumberOfResources**
Elements	The *object* placeholder is an object expression that evaluates to an object in the Applies To list.
See Also	**Count** Property; **NumberOfTasks** Property; **Resource** Object, **Resources** Collection.

NumberOfTasks Property

Applies To	**Project** Object, **Projects** Collection.
Description	Returns the number of tasks in a project, not including blank entries.
Syntax	*object***.NumberOfTasks**
Elements	The *object* placeholder is an object expression that evaluates to an object in the Applies To list.
See Also	**Count** Property; **NumberOfResources** Property; **Resource** Object, **Resources** Collection.

Object Data Type

Description   **Object** variables are stored as 32-bit (4-byte) addresses that refer to objects within an application. A variable declared as an **Object** is one that can subsequently be assigned (using the **Set** statement) to refer to any object produced by the application.

See Also   Data Type Summary, **Deftype** Statements, **IsObject** Function, **Variant** Data Type.

ObjectChangeIcon Method

Applies To   **Application** Object.

Description   Changes the icon of the active object.

Syntax   [*object*.]**ObjectChangeIcon**

Elements   The *object* placeholder is an object expression that evaluates to the server name of the selected object in the Applies To list.

Remarks   This method applies to Microsoft Project for Microsoft Windows. The **ObjectChangeIcon** method has the same effect as the Change Icon command, which is available as a button on the Convert dialog box. (The Convert dialog box appears when you choose Object from the Edit menu, and then choose Convert.)

See Also   **ObjectConvert** Method, **ObjectInsert** Method, **ObjectVerb** Method.

ObjectConvert Method

Applies To   **Application** Object.

Description   Displays the Convert dialog box, which prompts the user to convert the active object to a new format.

Syntax   [*object*.]**ObjectConvert**

Elements   The object placeholder is an object expression that evaluates to the server name of the selected object in the Applies To list.

Remarks	The **ObjectConvert** method has the same effect as the Convert command on the Object submenu, which is available from the Edit menu.
See Also	**ObjectChangeIcon** Method, **ObjectInsert** Method, **ObjectVerb** Method.

ObjectInsert Method

Applies To	**Application** Object.
Description	Displays the Insert Object dialog box, which prompts the user to insert an object.
Syntax	[*object.*]**ObjectInsert**
Elements	The *object* placeholder is an object expression that evaluates to an object in the Applies To list.
Remarks	The **ObjectInsert** method has no effect if the active view is a combination view, PERT Chart, Task PERT Chart, or Resource Graph. In addition to these views, the **ObjectInsert** method has no effect if a non-null task or resource is not selected in the Task or Resource Sheet views. It is also disabled from the Calendar view.
See Also	**ObjectChangeIcon** Method, **ObjectConvert** Method, **ObjectVerb** Method.

ObjectLinks Method

Applies To	**Application** Object.
Description	Displays the Links dialog box, which prompts the user to edit links in the active project.
Syntax	[*object.*]**ObjectLinks**
Elements	The *object* placeholder is an object expression that evaluates to an object in the Applies To list.
Remarks	The **ObjectLinks** method has no effect if the project has no links.
	The **ObjectLinks** method has the same effect as the Links command on the Edit menu.
See Also	**DDEPasteLink** Method, **EditCopy** Method, **EditCopyPicture** Method, **EditCut** Method, **EditUndo** Method, **ObjectChangeIcon** Method, **ObjectConvert** Method, **ObjectInsert** Method, **ObjectVerb** Method.

Objects Property

Applies To	**Project** Object, **Projects** Collection; **Resource** Object, **Resources** Collection; **Task** Object, **Tasks** Collection.
Description	Returns whether the task or resource contains any OLE objects.
Syntax	*object*.**Objects**
Elements	The *object* placeholder is an object expression that evaluates to an object in the Applies To list.
See Also	**Flagn** Properties, **LinkedFields** Property, **Marked** Property.

ObjectVerb Method

Applies To	**Application** Object.
Description	Instructs the active object to perform an action.
Syntax	[*object*.]**ObjectVerb** [*verb*]
Elements	The **ObjectVerb** method syntax has the following object qualifier and named arguments:

Part	Description
object	An object expression that evaluates to an object in the Applies To list.
verb	A numeric expression that specifies an action for the active object to perform.

Remarks	For a list of the actions an object can perform, select the object, and then choose Object from the Edit menu.
	In Microsoft Windows 95, to determine the number associated with a particular action, run the command "regedit /v" by using the Run command from the Start button.. The file REGEDIT.EXE is in your Windows folder.
See Also	**ObjectChangeIcon** Method, **ObjectConvert** Method, **ObjectInsert** Method.

Oct Function

Description   Returns a string representing the octal value of a number.

Syntax   **Oct**(*number*)

Elements   The ***number*** named argument is any valid numeric expression.

Remarks   If ***number*** is not already a whole number, it is rounded to the nearest whole number before being evaluated.

If *number* is	Oct returns
Null	An error.
Empty	Zero (0).
Any other number	Up to 11 octal characters.

You can represent octal numbers directly by preceding numbers in the proper range with &O. For example, &O10 is the octal notation for decimal 8.

See Also   **Hex** Function.

Example   This example uses the **Oct** function to return the octal value of a number.

```
MyOct = Oct(4)   ' Returns 4.
MyOct = Oct(8)   ' Returns 10.
MyOct = Oct(459)' Returns 713.
```

On Error Statement

Description   Enables an error-handling routine and specifies the location of the routine within a procedure; can also be used to disable an error-handling routine.

Syntax   **On Error GoTo** *line*

On Error Resume Next

On Error GoTo 0

Elements

The **On Error** statement syntax can have any of the following forms:

Statement	Description
On Error GoTo *line*	Enables the error-handling routine that starts at *line*, which is any line label or line number. Thereafter, if a run-time error occurs, control branches to *line*. The specified *line* must be in the same procedure as the **On Error** statement. If it isn't, a compile-time error occurs.
On Error Resume Next	Specifies that when a run-time error occurs, control goes to the statement immediately following the statement where the error occurred. In other words, execution continues.
On Error GoTo 0	Disables any enabled error handler in the current procedure.

Remarks

If you don't use an **On Error** statement, any run-time error that occurs is fatal; that is, an error message is generated and execution stops.

If an error occurs while an error handler is active (between the occurrence of the error and a **Resume, Exit Sub, Exit Function**, or **Exit Property** statement), the current procedure's error handler can't handle the error. If the calling procedure has an enabled error handler, control is returned to the calling procedure and its error handler is activated to handle the error. If the calling procedure's error handler is also active, control is passed back through any previous calling procedures until an inactive error handler is found. If no inactive error handler is found, the error is fatal at the point at which it actually occurred. Each time the error handler passes control back to the calling procedure, that procedure becomes the current procedure. Once an error is handled by an error handler in any procedure, execution resumes in the current procedure at the point designated by the **Resume** statement.

Notice that an error-handling routine is not a **Sub** or **Function** procedure. It is a block of code marked by a line label or line number.

Error-handling routines rely on the value in **Err** to determine the cause of the error. The error-handling routine should test or save this value before any other error can occur or before a procedure that could cause an error is called. The value in **Err** reflects only the most recent error. You can use the **Error** function to return the error message associated with any given run-time error number returned by **Err**.

On Error Resume Next causes execution to continue with the statement immediately following the statement that caused the run-time error, or with the statement immediately following the most recent call out of the procedure containing the error-handling routine. This allows execution to continue despite a run-time error. You can then build the error-handling routine in line with the procedure rather than transferring control to another location within the procedure.

On Error GoTo 0 disables error handling in the current procedure. It doesn't specify line 0 as the start of the error-handling code, even if the procedure contains a line numbered 0. Without an **On Error GoTo 0** statement, an error handler is automatically disabled when a procedure is exited.

To prevent error-handling code from running when no error has occurred, place an **Exit Sub, Exit Function**, or **Exit Property** statement, as appropriate, immediately ahead of the error-handling routine, as in the following example:

```
Sub InitializeMatrix(Var1, Var2, Var3, Var4)
    On Error GoTo ErrorHandler
    . . .
    Exit Sub
ErrorHandler:
    . . .
    Resume Next
End Sub
```

Here, the error-handling code follows the **Exit Sub** statement and precedes the **End Sub** statement to separate it from the normal procedure flow. This is only one possible solution; error-handling code can be placed anywhere in a procedure.

See Also

Err Function; **Error** Function; **Resume** Statement.

Example

This example uses the **On Error GoTo** statement to specify the location of an error-handling routine within a procedure. Attempting to delete an open file generates error number 55. The error is handled in the error-handling routine and control is then returned to the statement that caused it.

```
Sub OnErrorStatementDemo()
    On Error GoTo ErrorHandler    ' Enable error-handling routine.
    Open "TESTFILE" For Output as #1 ' Open file for output.
    Kill "TESTFILE"               ' Attempt to delete open file.
    Exit Sub                    ' Exit Sub before error handler.
ErrorHandler:                   ' Error-handling routine.
    Select Case Err             ' Evaluate Error Number.
        Case 55                 ' "File already open" error.
            Close #1            ' Close open file.
        Case Else
            ' Handle other situations here...
    End Select
    Resume        ' Resume execution at same line
                  ' that caused the error.
End Sub
```

On...GoSub, On...GoTo Statements

Description   Branch to one of several specified lines, depending on the value of an expression.

Syntax   **On** *expression* **GoSub** *destinationlist*

On *expression* **GoTo** *destinationlist*

Elements   The **On...GoSub** and **On...GoTo** statement syntax has these parts:

Part	Description
expression	Any numeric expression that evaluates to a whole number between 0 and 255, inclusive. If *expression* is any number other than a whole number, it is rounded before it is evaluated.
destinationlist	List of line numbers or line labels separated by commas.

Remarks   The value of *expression* determines which line in *destinationlist* is branched to. If the value of *expression* is less than 1 or greater than the number of items in the list, one of the following results occurs:

If expression is:	Then
Equal to 0	Control drops to the statement following **On...GoSub** or **On...GoTo**.
Greater than number of items in list	Control drops to the statement following **On...GoSub** or **On...GoTo**.
Negative	An error occurs.
Greater than 255	An error occurs.

You can mix line numbers and line labels in the same list. There is no practical limit to the number of line labels and line numbers you can use with **On...GoSub** and **On...GoTo**. However, if you use more labels or numbers than will fit on a single line, you must use the line-continuation character to continue the logical line onto the next physical line.

Tip **Select Case** provides a more structured and flexible way to perform multiple branching.

See Also   **GoSub...Return** Statement, **GoTo** Statement, **Select Case** Statement.

Example

This example uses the **On...GoSub** and **On...GoTo** statements to branch to subroutines and line labels respectively.

```
Sub OnGosubGotoDemo()
    Number = 2                 ' Initialize variable.
    ' Branch to Sub2.
    On Number GoSub Sub1, Sub2  ' Execution resumes here after
    ' On...GoSub.
    On Number GoTo Line1, Line2 ' Branch to Line2.
    ' Execution does not resume here after On...GoTo.
    Exit Sub
Sub1:
    MyString = "In Sub1" : Return
Sub2:
    MyString = "In Sub2" : Return
Line1:
    MyString = "In Line1"
Line2:
    MyString = "In Line2"
End Sub
```

Open Statement

Description

Enables input/output (I/O) to a file.

Syntax

Open *pathname* [**For** *mode*] [**Access** *access*] [*lock*] **As** [#]*filenumber* [**Len**=*reclength*]

Elements

The **Open** statement syntax has these parts:

Part	Description
pathname	String expression that specifies a file name—may include directory or folder, and drive.
mode	Keyword specifying the file mode: **Append**, **Binary**, **Input**, **Output**, or **Random**.
access	Keyword specifying the operations permitted on the open file: **Read**, **Write**, or **Read Write**.
lock	Keyword specifying the operations permitted on the open file by other processes: **Shared**, **Lock Read**, **Lock Write**, **Lock Read Write**.
filenumber	A valid file number in the range 1 to 511, inclusive. Use the **FreeFile** function to obtain the next available file number.
reclength	Number less than or equal to 32,767 (bytes). For files opened for random access, this value is the record length. For sequential files, this value is the number of characters buffered.

Remarks

You must open a file before any I/O operation can be performed on it. **Open** allocates a buffer for I/O to the file and determines the mode of access to use with the buffer.

If the file specified by *pathname* doesn't exist, it is created when a file is opened for **Append**, **Binary**, **Output**, or **Random** modes.

If the file is already opened by another process and the specified type of access is not allowed, the **Open** operation fails and an error occurs.

The **Len** clause is ignored if *mode* is **Binary**.

Important In **Binary**, **Input**, and **Random** modes, you can open a file using a different file number without first closing the file. In **Append** and **Output** modes, you must close a file before opening it with a different file number.

On the Macintosh, the file mode specified in the **Open** statement determines the initial **Creator** and **Type** property settings:

Output	????	TEXT
Append	????	TEXT
Random	????	OBIN
Binary	????	OBIN
Unspecified	????	OBIN

See Also

Close Statement, **FreeFile** Function.

Example

This example illustrates various uses of the **Open** statement to enable input/output to a file.

```
' Open in sequential-input mode.
Open "TESTFILE" For Input As #1

' Open in binary-file mode for writing operations only.
Open "TESTFILE" For Binary Access Write As #1

' Open file in random-access mode. The file contains records of the
' user-defined type Record.
Type Record ' Define user-defined type.
    ID As Integer
    Name As String * 20
End Type

Dim MyRecord As Record   ' Declare variable.
Open "TESTFILE" For Random As #1 Len = Len(MyRecord)
```

```
' Open for sequential output; any process can read/write to file.
Open "TESTFILE" For Output Shared As #1

' Open in binary-file mode for reading; other processes can't read
' file.
Open "TESTFILE" For Binary Access Read Lock Read As #1
```

OperatingSystem Property

Applies To   **Application** Object.

Description   Returns the name and version of the operating system.

Syntax   [*object*.]**OperatingSystem**

Elements   The *object* placeholder is an object expression that evaluates to an object in the
                    Applies To list.

Remarks   In Microsoft Windows 95, the **OperatingSystem** property returns "Windows 95".

                    On the Macintosh running System 7, the **OperatingSystem** property returns
                    "Macintosh 7.00".

See Also   **MoveAfterReturn** Property, **Name** Property, **SupportsMultipleDocuments**
                    Property, **SupportsMultipleWindows** Property, **Version** Property.

Operator Precedence

Description   When several operations occur in an expression, each part is evaluated and resolved
                    in a predetermined order. That order is known as operator precedence. Parentheses
                    can be used to override the order of precedence and force some parts of an
                    expression to be evaluated before others. Operations within parentheses are always
                    performed before those outside. Within parentheses, however, normal operator
                    precedence is maintained.

When expressions contain operators from more than one category, arithmetic operators are evaluated first, comparison operators are evaluated next, and logical operators are evaluated last. Comparison operators all have equal precedence; that is, they are evaluated in the left to right order in which they appear. Arithmetic and logical operators are evaluated in the following order of precedence:

Exponentiation (^)	Equality (=)	**Not**
Negation (-)	Inequality (<>)	**And**
Multiplication and division (*,/)	Less than (<)	**Or**
Integer division (\)	Greater than (>)	**Xor**
Modulo arithmetic (**Mod**)	Less than or Equal to (<=)	**Eqv**
Addition and subtraction (+,-)	Greater than or Equal to (>=)	**Imp**
String concatenation (**&**)	**Like**	**Is**

When multiplication and division occur together in an expression, each operation is evaluated as it occurs from left to right. Likewise, when addition and subtraction occur together in an expression, each operation is evaluated in order of appearance from left to right.

The string concatenation operator (**&**) is not really an arithmetic operator, but in precedence it does fall after all arithmetic operators and before all comparison operators. Similarly, the **Like** operator, while equal in precedence to all comparison operators, is actually a pattern-matching operator. The **Is** operator is an object reference comparison operator. It does not compare objects or their values; it checks only to determine if two object references refer to the same object.

Arithmetic Operators

^ Operator

* Operator

/ Operator

\ Operator

Mod Operator

+ Operator

- Operator

Concatenation Operators

& Operator

+ Operator

Logical Operators	**And** Operator
	Eqv Operator
	Imp Operator
	Not Operator
	Or Operator
	Xor Operator

Option Base Statement

Description Used at module level to declare the default lower bound for array subscripts.

Syntax **Option Base {0 | 1}**

Remarks If used, the **Option Base** statement must appear in a module before any statements that declare variables or define constants.

Since the default base is **0**, the **Option Base** statement is never required. However, if used, it can appear only once in a module and must precede array declarations that include dimensions.

The **Option Base** statement has no effect on arrays within user-defined types for which the lower bound is always 0.

Tip The To clause in the Dim, Private, Public, ReDim, and Static statements provides a more flexible way to control the range of an array's subscripts. However, if you don't explicitly set the lower bound with a To clause, you can use Option Base to change the default lower bound to 1.

The **Option Base** statement only affects the lower bound of arrays in the module where the statement is located.

See Also **Dim** Statement, **LBound** Function, **Option** Compare Statement**, Option Explicit** Statement, **Option Private** Statement, **Private** Statement, **Public** Statement, **ReDim** Statement, **Static** Statement.

Example This example uses the **Option Base** statement to override the default base array subscript value of 0. The **LBound** function returns the smallest available subscript for the indicated dimension of an array. The **Option Base** statement is used at the module-level only.

```
                       ' Set default array subscripts to 1.
                       Option Base 1

                       im MyArray(20), TwoDArray(3,4)   ' Declare array variables.
                       Dim ZeroArray(0 To 5)            ' Override default base subscript.
                       ' Use LBound function to test lower bounds of arrays.
                       Lower = LBound(MyArray)          ' Returns 1.
                       Lower = LBound(TwoDArray, 2)     ' Returns 1.
                       Lower = LBound(ZeroArray)        ' Returns 0.
```

Option Compare Statement

Description   Used at module level to declare the default comparison mode to use when string data is compared.

Syntax   **Option Compare {Binary | Text}**

Remarks   If used, the **Option Compare** statement must appear in a module before any statements that declare variables or define constants.

The **Option Compare** statement specifies the string comparison method (**Binary** or **Text**) for a module. If a module doesn't include an **Option Compare** statement, the default text comparison method is **Binary**.

Option Compare Binary results in string comparisons based on a sort order derived from the internal binary representations of the characters. In Microsoft Windows, sort order is determined by the code page. On the Macintosh, sort order is determined by the character set. In the following example, a typical binary sort order is shown:

```
A < B < E < Z < a < b < e  < z < À < Ê < Ø < à < ê < ø
```

Option Compare Text results in string comparisons based on a case-insensitive textual sort order determined by your system's locale. The same characters shown above, when sorted using **Option Compare Text**, produce the following text sort order:

```
(A=a) < ( À=à) < (B=b) < (E=e) < (Ê=ê) < (Z=z) < (Ø=ø)
```

See Also	Comparison Operators, **InStr** Function, **Option Base** Statement, **Option Explicit** Statement, **Option Private** Statement, **StrComp** Function.
Example	This example uses the **Option Compare** statement to set the default string comparison mode. The **Option Compare** statement is used at the module-level only.

```
' Set the string comparison method to Binary.
Option Compare Binary    ' i.e. "AAA" less than "aaa"
' Set the string comparison method to Text.
Option Compare Text      ' i.e. "AAA" equal to "aaa".
```

Option Explicit Statement

Description	Used at module level to force explicit declaration of all variables in that module.
Syntax	**Option Explicit**
Remarks	If used, the **Option Explicit** statement must appear in a module before any statements that declare variables or define constants.
	If you don't use the **Option Explicit** statement, all undeclared variables are **Variant** unless the default type is otherwise specified with a **Def**_type_ statement.
	When you use the **Option Explicit** statement, you must explicitly declare all variables using the **Dim**, **Private**, **Public**, **ReDim**, or **Static** statements. If you attempt to use an undeclared variable name, an error occurs at compile time.

Tip   Use Option Explicit to avoid incorrectly typing the name of an existing variable or to avoid risking confusion in code where the scope of the variable is not clear.

See Also	**Const** Statement, **Deftype** Statements, **Dim** Statement, **Function** Statement, **Option Base** Statement, **Option Compare** Statement, **Option Private** Statement, **Private** Statement, **Public** Statement, **ReDim** Statement, **Static** Statement, **Sub** Statement.
Example	This example uses the **Option Explicit** statement to force you to explicitly declare all variables. Attempting to use an undeclared variable gives you an error at compile time. The **Option Explicit** statement is used at the module-level only.

```
    Option Explicit ' Force explicit variable declaration.
    Dim MyVar       ' Declare variable.
    MyInt = 10      ' Undeclared variable generates error.
    MyVar = 10      ' Will not generate error.
```

Option Private Statement

Description   Used at module level to indicate that an entire module is **Private**.

Syntax   **Option Private Module**

Remarks   If used, the **Option Private** statement must appear in a module before any statements that declare variables or define constants.

The public parts (variables, objects, and user-defined types declared at module level) of modules declared **Private** using the **Option Private** statement are still available within the project containing the module, but they are not available to other applications or projects.

See Also   **Option Base** Statement, **Option Compare** Statement, **Option Explicit** Statement, **Private** Statement.

Example   This **Option Private** statement is used at the module-level to indicate that the entire module is private.

```
    Option Private Module    ' Indicate that module is private.
```

OptionsCalculation Method

Applies To   **Application** Object.

Description   Sets the calculation mode to manual or automatic.

Syntax   [*object*.]**OptionsCalculation** [*automatic*]

Elements   The **OptionsCalculation** method syntax has the following object qualifier and named arguments:

Part	Description
object	An object expression that evaluates to an object in the Applies To list.
automatic	A Boolean expression that specifies whether the calculation mode is automatic or manual. By default, the Calculation section of the Options dialog box appears, which prompts the user to set the calculation mode. The ***automatic*** argument has these settings:

True   Sets the calculation mode to automatic.
False   Sets the calculation mode to manual.

See Also   **CalculateAll** Method, **CalculateProject** Method, **Calculation** Property.

Example   The following example sets calculation mode to automatic.

```
Sub ToggleCalculationMode()
    OptionsCalculation (True)
End Sub
```

OptionsCalendar Method

Applies To   **Application** Object.

Description   Sets options for the calendar of the active project.

Syntax   [*object*.]**OptionsCalendar** [*startWeekOnMonday, startYearIn, startTime, finishTime, hoursPerDay, hoursPerWeek, setDefaults*]

Elements   The **OptionsCalendar** method syntax has the following object qualifier and named arguments:

Part	Description
object	An object expression that evaluates to an object in the Applies To list. Optional.
startWeekOnMonday	A Boolean expression that specifies whether calendar weeks start on Monday. Optional. The *startWeekOnMonday* argument has these settings:

True   Calendar weeks start on Monday.
False   Calendar weeks start on Sunday.

startYearIn	A constant that specifies the first month of the fiscal year. Optional.

Part	Description
startTime	A string expression that specifies the default start time for days. Optional.
finishTime	A string expression that specifies the default finish time for days. Optional.
hoursPerDay	A numeric expression that specifies the default number of hours per day. Optional.
hoursPerWeek	A numeric expression that specifies the default number of hours per week. Optional.
setDefaults	A Boolean expression that specifies whether the values you specify with the *startTime*, *finishTime*, *hoursPerDay*, and *hoursPerWeek* arguments become the default values for new projects. By default, the *setDefaults* argument is **False**. Optional.

The *startYearIn* argument has these settings:

pjJanuary	1	January
pjFebruary	2	February
pjMarch	3	March
pjApril	4	April
pjMay	5	May
pjJune	6	June
pjJuly	7	July
pjAugust	8	August
pjSeptember	9	September
pjOctober	10	October
pjNovember	11	November
pjDecember	12	December

See Also   **DefaultFinishTime** Property, **DefaultStartTime** Property, **HoursPerDay** Property, **HoursPerWeek** Property, **OptionsCalculation** Method, **OptionsEdit** Method, **OptionsGeneral** Method, **OptionsModuleFormat** Method, **OptionsModuleGeneral** Method, **OptionsSchedule** Method, **OptionsView** Method.

OptionsEdit Method

Applies To   **Application** Object.

Description   Sets editing options.

Syntax   [*object.*]**OptionsEdit** [*moveAfterReturn, dragAndDrop, updateLinks, copyResourceUsageheade*]

Elements   The **OptionsEdit** method syntax has the following object qualifier and named arguments:

Part	Description
object	An object expression that evaluates to an object in the Applies To list. Optional.
moveAfterReturn	A Boolean expression that specifies whether the next cell or field becomes active when you press ENTER. Optional.
dragAndDrop	A Boolean expression that specifies whether dragging and dropping is allowed. Optional.
updateLinks	A Boolean expression that specifies whether object linking and embedding (OLE) links are updated automatically when the relevant information changes. Optional.
copyResourceUsageHeader	Includes the column headings from the Resource Usage view. Optional.

See Also   **CellDragAndDrop** Property, **DDELinksUpdate** Method, **MoveAfterReturn** Property, **OptionsCalculation** Method, **OptionsCalendar** Method, **OptionsGeneral** Method, **OptionsModuleFormat** Method, **OptionsModuleGeneral** Method, **OptionsSchedule** Method, **OptionsView** Method.

OptionsGeneral Method

Applies To   **Application** Object.

Description   Sets general options.

Syntax

[*object.*]**OptionsGeneral** [*planningWizard, wizardUsage, wizardErrors, wizardScheduling, showTipOfDay, autoAddResources, standardRate, overtimeRate, lastFile, summaryInfo, userName, setDefaults, showWelcome, showToolTips*]

Elements

The **OptionsGeneral** method syntax has the following object qualifier and named arguments:

Part	Description
object	An object expression that evaluates to an object in the Applies To list. Optional.
planningWizard	A Boolean expression that specifies whether to display advice about errors, scheduling, and using Microsoft Project. Optional.
wizardUsage	A Boolean expression that specifies whether to display advice about using Microsoft Project. Optional.
wizardErrors	A Boolean expression that specifies whether to display advice about errors. Optional.
wizardScheduling	A Boolean expression that specifies whether to display advice about scheduling. Optional.
showTipOfDay	A Boolean expression that specifies whether the Tip of the Day appears when you start Microsoft Project. Optional.
autoAddResources	A Boolean expression that specifies whether resources are automatically added to the resource pool. Optional.
standardRate	A string expression that specifies the standard rate for resources. Optional.
overtimeRate	A string expression that specifies the overtime rate for resources. Optional.
lastFile	A Boolean expression that specifies whether the last open file is automatically opened when Microsoft Project starts. Optional.
summaryInfo	A Boolean expression that specifies whether the Project Info dialog box appears when new projects are created. Optional.
userName	A string expression that specifies the name of the current user. Optional.
setDefaults	A Boolean expression that specifies whether to use the values of the *autoAddResources*, *standardRate*, and *overtimeRate* arguments as default values for new projects. Optional.

Part	Description
showWelcome	A Boolean expression that specifies whether to display the Welcome dialog box when Microsoft Project starts. Optional.
showToolTips	A Boolean expression that specifies whether to show ToolTips. Optional.

See Also **OptionsCalculation** Method, **OptionsCalendar** Method, **OptionsEdit** Method, **OptionsModuleFormat** Method, **OptionsModuleGeneral** Method, **OptionsSchedule** Method, **OptionsView** Method, **SpellingCheck** Method.

OptionsModuleFormat Method

Applies To **Application** Object.

Description Displays the Module Format tab in the Options dialog box, which prompts the user to set module format options.

Syntax [*object*.]**OptionsModuleFormat**

Elements The *object* placeholder is an object expression that evaluates to an object in the Applies To list.

See Also **OptionsCalculation** Method, **OptionsCalendar** Method, **OptionsEdit** Method, **OptionsGeneral** Method, **OptionsModuleGeneral** Method, **OptionsSchedule** Method, **OptionsView** Method.

OptionsModuleGeneral Method

Applies To **Application** Object.

Description Displays the Module General tab in the Options dialog box, which prompts the user to set general module options.

Syntax [*object*.]**OptionsModuleGeneral**

Elements The *object* placeholder is an object expression that evaluates to an object in the Applies To list.

See Also	**OptionsCalculation** Method, **OptionsCalendar** Method, **OptionsEdit** Method, **OptionsGeneral** Method, **OptionsModuleFormat** Method, **OptionsSchedule** Method, **OptionsView** Method.

OptionsPreferences Method

Applies To	**Application** Object.
Description	Sets options in Microsoft Project.
Syntax	[*object*.]**OptionsPreferences**
Elements	The *object* placeholder is an object expression that evaluates to an object in the Applies To list.
Remarks	This method is provided for compatibility with the macro language used in Microsoft Project version 3.*x*.
See Also	**OptionsCalculation** Method, **OptionsCalendar** Method, **OptionsEdit** Method, **OptionsGeneral** Method, **OptionsModuleFormat** Method, **OptionsModuleGeneral** Method, **OptionsSchedule** Method, **OptionsSpelling** Method, **OptionsView** Method.

OptionsSchedule Method

Applies To	**Application** Object.
Description	Sets scheduling options.
Syntax	[*object*.]**OptionsSchedule** [*scheduleMessages*, *startOnCurrentDate*, *autoLink*, *autoSplit*, *criticalSlack*, *fixedDuration*, *durationUnits*, *workUnits*, *autoTrack*, *setDefaults*]
Elements	The **OptionsSchedule** method syntax has the following object qualifier and named arguments:

Part	Description
object	An object expression that evaluates to an object in the Applies To list. Optional.
scheduleMessages	A Boolean expression that specifies whether to display messages when scheduling problems occur. Optional.

Part	Description
startOnCurrentDate	A Boolean expression that specifies whether new tasks start on the current date. Optional.
autoLink	A Boolean expression that specifies whether to automatically link tasks. Optional.
autoSplit	A Boolean expression that specifies whether to automatically split tasks in progress. Optional.
criticalSlack	A numeric expression that specifies the maximum amount of slack allowed for critical tasks. Optional.
fixedDuration	A Boolean expression that specifies whether tasks have a fixed duration by default. Optional.
durationUnits	A constant that specifies the default duration units for tasks. Optional.
workUnits	A constant that specifies the default work units for resource assignments. Optional.
autoTrack	A Boolean expression that specifies whether to automatically track resources. Optional.
setDefaults	A Boolean expression that specifies whether the values you specify for the arguments (except for the *scheduleMessages* argument) are the default values for new projects. Optional.

The *durationUnits* and *workUnits* arguments have these settings:

pjMinutes	0	Minutes
pjHours	1	Hours
pjDays	2	Days
pjWeeks	3	Weeks

See Also

AutoLinkTasks Property, **AutoSplitTasks** Property, **AutoTrack** Property, **DefaultDurationUnits** Property, **DefaultFixedDuration** Property, **DefaultWorkUnits** Property, **OptionsCalculation** Method, **OptionsCalendar** Method, **OptionsEdit** Method, **OptionsGeneral** Method, **OptionsModuleFormat** Method, **OptionsModuleGeneral** Method, **OptionsView** Method, **StartOnCurrentDate** Property.

OptionsSpelling Method

Applies To   **Application** Object.

Description   Sets options for the spelling checker.

Syntax   [*object*.]**OptionsSpelling** [*taskName, taskNotes, taskText1, taskText2, taskText3, taskText4, taskText5, taskText6, taskText7, taskText8, taskText9, taskText10, resourceCode, resourceName, resourceNotes, resourceGroup, resourceText1, resourceText2, resourceText3, resourceText4, resourceText5, projectComments, ignoreUppercase, ignoreNumberWords, alwaysSuggest, useCustomDictionary*]

Elements   The **OptionsSpelling** method syntax has the following object qualifier and named arguments:

Part	Description
object	An object expression that evaluates to an object in the Applies To list. Optional.
taskName	A Boolean expression that specifies whether to check the spelling of task names. Optional.
taskNotes	A Boolean expression that specifies whether to check the spelling of task notes. Optional.
taskText1	A Boolean expression that specifies whether to check the spelling in the Text1 fields of tasks. Optional.
taskText2	A Boolean expression that specifies whether to check the spelling in the Text2 fields of tasks. Optional.
taskText3	A Boolean expression that specifies whether to check the spelling in the Text3 fields of tasks. Optional.
taskText4	A Boolean expression that specifies whether to check the spelling in the Text4 fields of tasks. Optional.
taskText5	A Boolean expression that specifies whether to check the spelling in the Text5 fields of tasks. Optional.
taskText6	A Boolean expression that specifies whether to check the spelling in the Text6 fields of tasks. Optional.
taskText7	A Boolean expression that specifies whether to check the spelling in the Text7 fields of tasks. Optional.
taskText8	A Boolean expression that specifies whether to check the spelling in the Text8 fields of tasks. Optional.

Part	Description
taskText9	A Boolean expression that specifies whether to check the spelling in the Text9 fields of tasks. Optional.
taskText10	A Boolean expression that specifies whether to check the spelling in the Text10 fields of tasks. Optional.
resourceCode	A Boolean expression that specifies whether to check the spelling of resource codes. Optional.
resourceName	A Boolean expression that specifies whether to check the spelling of resource names. Optional.
resourceNotes	A Boolean expression that specifies whether to check the spelling of resource notes. Optional.
resourceGroup	A Boolean expression that specifies whether to check the spelling of resource groups. Optional.
resourceText1	A Boolean expression that specifies whether to check the spelling in the Text1 fields of resources. Optional.
resourceText2	A Boolean expression that specifies whether to check the spelling in the Text2 fields of resources. Optional.
resourceText3	A Boolean expression that specifies whether to check the spelling in the Text3 fields of resources. Optional.
resourceText4	A Boolean expression that specifies whether to check the spelling in the Text4 fields of resources. Optional.
resourceText5	A Boolean expression that specifies whether to check the spelling in the Text5 fields of resources. Optional.
projectComments	A Boolean expression that specifies whether to check the spelling of the comments in the Project Information dialog box. Optional.
ignoreUppercase	A Boolean expression that specifies whether to ignore words consisting entirely of uppercase letters. Optional.
ignoreNumberWords	A Boolean expression that specifies whether to ignore words that contain numbers. Optional.
alwaysSuggest	A Boolean expression that specifies whether to always suggest alternate spellings. Optional.
useCustomDictionary	A Boolean expression that specifies whether to use the custom dictionary. Optional.

OptionsCalculation Method, **OptionsCalendar** Method, **OptionsEdit** Method, **OptionsGeneral** Method, **OptionsModuleFormat** Method, **OptionsModuleGeneral** Method, **OptionsSchedule** Method, **OptionsView** Method, **SpellingCheck** Method.

OptionsView Method

Applies To   **Application** Object.

Description   Sets view options.

Syntax   [*object.*]**OptionsView** [*defaultView*, *dateFormat*, *projectSummary*, *displayStatusBar*, *displayEntryBar*, *displayScrollBars*, *currencySymbol*, *symbolPlacement*, *currencyDigits*, *displayOutlineNumber*, *displayOutlineSymbols*, *displayNameIndent*, *displaySummaryTasks*, *displayNotesIndicator*, *setDefaults*, *displayOLEIndicator*]

Elements   The **OptionsView** method syntax has the following object qualifier and named arguments:

Part	Description
object	An object expression that evaluates to an object in the Applies To list. Optional.
defaultView	A string expression that specifies the default view. Optional.
dateFormat	A constant that specifies the date format. Optional.
projectSummary	A Boolean expression that specifies whether the Project Info dialog box appears when a new project is created. It controls whether or not the Project Summary Task is visible. Optional.
displayStatusBar	A Boolean expression that specifies whether to display the status bar. Optional.
displayEntryBar	A Boolean expression that specifies whether to display the entry bar. Optional.
displayScrollBars	A Boolean expression that specifies whether to display scroll bars. Optional.
currencySymbol	A string expression that specifies the symbol for currency values. Optional.
symbolPlacement	A constant that specifies the location of the currency symbol. Optional.

False	Null	Null
Null	True	True
Null	False	Null
Null	Null	Null

The **Or** operator also performs a bit-wise comparison of identically positioned bits in two numeric expressions and sets the corresponding bit in *result* according to the following truth table:

0	0	0
0	1	1
1	0	1
1	1	1

See Also   Operator Precedence.

Example   This example uses the **Or** operator to perform logical disjunction on two expressions.

```
A = 10: B = 8: C = 6 : D = Null  ' Initialize variables.
MyCheck = A > B Or B > C          ' Returns True.
MyCheck = B > A Or B > C          ' Returns True.
MyCheck = A > B Or B > D          ' Returns True.
MyCheck = B > D Or B > A          ' Returns Null.
MyCheck = A Or B             ' Returns 10 (bit-wise comparison).
```

Organizer Method

Applies To   **Application** Object.

Description   Displays the Organizer dialog box, which prompts the user to manage calendars, views, toolbars, menu bars, forms, tables, filters, reports, and modules.

Syntax   [*object*.]**Organizer** [*type, task*]

Elements   The **Organizer** method syntax has the following object qualifier and named arguments:

Part	Description
object	An object expression that evaluates to an object in the Applies To list. Optional.
type	A constant that specifies the type of item to manage. By default, the *type* argument is **pjViews**. Optional.
task	A Boolean expression that specifies whether the item applies to tasks or resources. By default, the *task* argument is **True**. Optional.

The *type* argument has these settings:

pjViews	0	View
pjTables	1	Table
pjFilters	2	Filter
pjModules	3	Module
pjReports	4	Report
pjCalendars	5	Calendar
pjMenuBars	6	Menu bar
pjToolbars	7	Toolbar
pjForms	8	Form

See Also   **OrganizerDeleteItem** Method, **OrganizerMoveItem** Method, **OrganizerRenameItem** Method.

OrganizerDeleteItem Method

Applies To   **Application** Object.

Description   Deletes an item from the Organizer.

Syntax   [*object*.]**OrganizerDeleteItem** *type*, *fileName*, *name*[, *task*]

Elements   The **OrganizerDeleteItem** method syntax has the following object qualifier and named arguments:

Part	Description
object	An object expression that evaluates to an object in the Applies To list. Optional.
type	A constant that specifies the type of item to delete. Required.
fileName	A string expression that specifies the name of the file containing the item to delete. Required.

Part	Description
name	A string expression that specifies the item to delete. Required.
task	A Boolean expression that specifies whether the item applies to tasks or resources. By default, the *task* argument is **True**. Optional.

The *type* argument has these settings:

pjViews	0	View
pjTables	1	Table
pjFilters	2	Filter
pjModules	3	Module
pjReports	4	Report
pjCalendars	5	Calendar
pjMenuBars	6	Menu bar
pjToolbars	7	Toolbar
pjForms	8	Form

See Also   **Organizer** Method, **OrganizerMoveItem** Method, **OrganizerRenameItem** Method.

OrganizerMoveltem Method

Applies To   **Application** Object.

Description   Moves an item in the Organizer.

Syntax   [*object*.]**OrganizerMoveItem** *type*, *fileName*, *toFilename*[, *name*, *task*]

Elements   The **OrganizerMoveItem** method syntax has the following object qualifier and named arguments:

Part	Description
object	An object expression that evaluates to an object in the Applies To list. Optional.
type	A constant that specifies the type of item to move. Required.
fileName	A string expression that specifies the name of the file containing the item to move. Required.
toFilename	A string expression that specifies the name of the new file to contain the item. Required.

Part	Description
name	A string expression that specifies the name of the item to move. By default, all items are moved between the files you specify with the *fileName* and *toFilename* arguments. Optional.
task	A Boolean expression that specifies whether the item applies to tasks or resources. By default, the *task* argument is **True**. Optional.

The *type* argument has these settings:

pjViews	0	View
pjTables	1	Table
pjFilters	2	Filter
pjModules	3	Module
pjReports	4	Report
pjCalendars	5	Calendar
pjMenuBars	6	Menu Bar
pjToolbars	7	Toolbar
pjForms	8	Form

See Also   **Organizer** Method, **OrganizerDeleteItem** Method, **OrganizerRenameItem** Method.

OrganizerRenameItem Method

Applies To   **Application** Object.

Description   Renames an item in the Organizer.

Syntax   [*object*.]**OrganizerRenameItem** *type, fileName, name, newName*[, *task*]

Elements   The **OrganizerRenameItem** method syntax has the following object qualifier and named arguments:

Part	Description
object	An object expression that evaluates to an object in the Applies To list. Optional.
type	A constant that specifies the type of item to rename. Required.
filename	A string expression that specifies the name of the file containing the item to rename. Required.
name	A string expression that specifies the name of the item to rename. Required.
newName	A string expression that specifies a new name for the item you specify with the *name* argument. Required.
task	A Boolean expression that specifies whether the item applies to tasks or resources. By default, the *task* argument is **True**. Optional.

The *type* argument has these settings:

pjViews	0	View
pjTables	1	Table
pjFilters	2	Filter
pjModules	3	Module
pjReports	4	Report
pjCalendars	5	Calendar
pjMenuBars	6	Menu bar
pjToolbars	7	Toolbar
pjForms	8	Form

See Also   **Organizer** Method, **OrganizerDeleteItem** Method, **OrganizerMoveItem** Method.

OutlineChildren Method

Applies To   **Project** Object, **Projects** Collection; **Task** Object, **Tasks** Collection.

Description   Returns a child or the children of a task in the outline.

Syntax   *object*.**OutlineChildren**[(*index*)]

Elements   The **Objects** property syntax has the following object qualifier and named arguments:

Part	Description
object	An object expression that evaluates to an object in the Applies To list.
index	A numeric expression that specifies the index of the *object*.

See Also

OutlineHideSubtasks Method, **OutlineIndent** Method, **OutlineLevel** Property, **OutlineNumber** Property, **OutlineOutdent** Method, **OutlineParent** Property, **OutlineShowAllTasks** Method, **OutlineShowSubtasks** Method.

Example

The following example displays the names of all tasks at the same outline level as the selected task.

```
Sub Siblings()
    Set objParent = ActiveCell.Task.OutlineParent
    For Each objTemp In objParent.OutlineChildren
        strTemp = objTemp.Name & ListSeparator & strTemp
    Next objTemp
    'Remove the last ListSeparator
    strTemp = Left$(strTemp,Len(strTemp)-Len(ListSeparator))
    MsgBox strTemp
End Sub
```

OutlineHideSubtasks Method

Applies To

Application Object; **Task** Object, **Tasks** Collection.

Description

Hides the subtasks of the active tasks.

Syntax

[*object*.]**OutlineHideSubtasks**

Elements

The *object* placeholder represents an object expression that evaluates to an object in the Applies To list.

See Also

OutlineIndent Method, **OutlineLevel** Property, **OutlineOutdent** Method, **OutlineShowAllTasks** Method, **OutlineShowSubtasks** Method.

Example

The following example collapses the entire outline of the first task.

```
Sub OutlineHideAllSubtasks()
    ActiveProject.Tasks(1).OutlineHideSubtasks
End Sub
```

OutlineIndent Method

Applies To   **Application** Object; **Task** Object, **Tasks** Collection.

Description   Indents the active tasks in the outline.

Syntax   *object*.**OutlineIndent** [*levels*]

Elements   The **OutlineIndent** method syntax has the following object qualifier and named arguments:

Part	Description
object	An object expression that evaluates to an object in the Applies To list. Optional.
levels	A numeric expression that specifies the number of levels to indent the active tasks. By default, the *levels* argument is 1. Optional.

See Also   **OutlineHideSubtasks** Method, **OutlineLevel** Property, **OutlineOutdent** Method, **OutlineShowAllTasks** Method, **OutlineShowSubtasks** Method.

Example   The following example demotes the tasks between two selected tasks.

```
Sub DemoteTasksBelowActiveSelection()
    Dim I     ' Index used in For loop

    ' If user hasn't selected exactly two tasks, inform user and quit.
    If ActiveSelection.Tasks.Count <> 2 Then
        MsgBox("Demote failed. Select exactly two tasks and try again.")
        Exit Sub
    End If

    ' Demote the tasks with indexes between the selected tasks.
    For I = ActiveSelection.Tasks(1).Index To _
    ActiveSelection.Tasks(2).Index
        ActiveProject.Tasks.UniqueID(I).OutlineIndent
    Next I
End Sub
```

OutlineLevel Property

Applies To	**Project** Object, **Projects** Collection; **Task** Object, **Tasks** Collection.
Description	Returns the outline level of a task.
Syntax	*object*.**OutlineLevel**
Elements	The *object* placeholder is an object expression that evaluates to an object in the Applies To list.
See Also	**OutlineHideSubtasks** Method, **OutlineIndent** Method, **OutlineNumber** Property, **OutlineOutdent** Method, **OutlineShowAllTasks** Method, **OutlineShowSubtasks** Method.

OutlineNumber Property

Applies To	**Project** Object, **Projects** Collection; **Task** Object, **Tasks** Collection.
Description	Returns the outline number of a task.
Syntax	*object*.**OutlineNumber**
Elements	The *object* placeholder is an object expression that evaluates to an object in the Applies To list.
See Also	**OutlineHideSubtasks** Method, **OutlineIndent** Method, **OutlineLevel** Property, **OutlineOutdent** Method, **OutlineShowAllTasks** Method, **OutlineShowSubtasks** Method.

OutlineOutdent Method

Applies To   **Application** Object; **Task** Object, **Tasks** Collection.

Description   Promotes a task in the outline.

Syntax   *object*.**OutlineOutdent**

Elements   The *object* placeholder is an object expression that evaluates to an object in the Applies To list.

See Also   **OutlineHideSubtasks** Method, **OutlineIndent** Method, **OutlineShowSubtasks** Method.

Example   The following example promotes the tasks between two selected tasks.

```
Sub DemoteTasksBelowActiveSelection()
    Dim I    ' Index used in For loop

    ' If user hasn't selected exactly two tasks, inform user and quit.
    If ActiveSelection.Tasks.Count <> 2 Then
        MsgBox("Demote failed. Select exactly two tasks and try again.")
        Exit Sub
    End If

    ' Demote the tasks with indexes between the selected tasks.
    For I = ActiveSelection.Tasks(1).Index To _
    ActiveSelection.Tasks(2).Index
        ActiveProject.Tasks.UniqueID(I).OutlineOutdent
    Next I
End Sub
```

OutlineParent Property

Applies To   **Task** Object, **Tasks** Collection.

Description   Returns the parent of a task in the outline.

Syntax	*object*.**OutlineParent**
Elements	The *object* placeholder is an object expression that evaluates to an object in the Applies To list.
See Also	**OutlineChildren** Method, **OutlineHideSubtasks** Method, **OutlineIndent** Method, **OutlineLevel** Property, **OutlineNumber** Property, **OutlineOutdent** Method, **OutlineShowAllTasks** Method, **OutlineShowSubtasks** Method.
Example	The following example displays the names of all tasks at the same outline level as the selected task.

```
Sub Siblings()
    Set objParent = ActiveCell.Task.OutlineParent
    For Each objTemp In objParent.OutlineChildren
        strTemp = objTemp.Name & ListSeparator & strTemp
    Next objTemp
    'Remove the last ListSeparator
    strTemp = Left$(strTemp,Len(strTemp)-Len(ListSeparator))
    MsgBox strTemp
End Sub
```

OutlineShowAllTasks Method

Applies To	**Application** Object; **Task** Object, **Tasks** Collection.
Description	Expands all summary tasks in the project.
Syntax	*object*.**OutlineShowAllTasks**
Elements	The *object* placeholder is an object expression that evaluates to an object in the Applies To list.
See Also	**OutlineHideSubtasks** Method, **OutlineIndent** Method, **OutlineLevel** Property, **OutlineNumber** Property, **OutlineOutdent** Method, **OutlineShowSubtasks** Method.
Example	The following example expands all summary tasks in the active project.

```
Sub ShowAllSubtasksSummaryTasks()
   OutlineShowAllTasks
End Sub
```

OutlineShowSubtasks Method

Applies To   **Application** Object; **Task** Object, **Tasks** Collection.

Description   Shows the subtasks of the active tasks.

Syntax   [*object*.]**OutlineShowSubtasks**

Elements   The *object* placeholder is an object expression that evaluates to an object in the Applies To list.

See Also   **OutlineHideSubtasks** Method, **OutlineIndent** Method, **OutlineLevel** Property, **OutlineOutdent** Method, **OutlineShowAllTasks** Method.

OutlineSymbolsToggle Method

Applies To   **Application** Object.

Description   Shows the outline symbols, if they are hidden; hides the outline symbols, if they are visible.

Syntax   [*object*.]**OutlineSymbolsToggle** [*show*]

Elements   The **OutlineSymbolsToggle** method syntax has the following object qualifier and named arguments:

Part	Description
object	An object expression that evaluates to an object in the Applies To list.
show	A Boolean expression that specifies whether to show or hide outline symbols. By default, the *show* argument is **True** if the outline symbols are hidden and **False** if the outline symbols are visible.

See Also   **OutlineHideSubtasks** Method, **OutlineIndent** Method, **OutlineOutdent** Method, **OutlineShowAllTasks** Method, **OutlineShowSubtasks** Method.

Overallocated Property

Applies To	**Resource** Object, **Resources** Collection.
Description	Returns a value that indicates whether a resource is overallocated.
Syntax	*object*.**Overallocated**
Elements	The *object* placeholder is an object expression that evaluates to an object in the Applies To list.
Settings	The **Overallocated** property has the following settings:

Settings	Description
True	The resource is overallocated.
False	The resource is not overallocated.

See Also	**Level** Method, **MaxUnits** Property, **PeakUnits** Property.
Example	The following example displays the percentage of resources in the active project that are overallocated.

```
Sub DisplayOverallocatedPercentage()
    Dim R              ' Resource object used in For Each loop
    Dim NOverallocated  ' Number of overallocated resources

    For Each R in ActiveProject.Resources
        If R.Overallocated Then NOverallocated = NOverallocated + 1
    Next R

    MsgBox(Str(NOverallocated/ActiveProject.Resources.Count * 100) & _
            " percent (" & Str(NOverallocated) & "/" & _
            ActiveProject.Resources.Count & ")" & _
            " of the resources in this project are overallocated.")
End Sub
```

OvertimeRate Property

Applies To	**Project** Object, **Projects** Collection.

Description	Returns or sets the default overtime rate of pay for resources.
Syntax	[*object*.]**DefaultResourceOvertimeRate** [= *value*]
Elements	The **DefaultResourceOvertimeRate** property syntax has these parts:

Part	Description
object	An object expression that evaluates to an object in the Applies To list.
value	A string expression that specifies the default rate of pay for resources.

See Also	**DefaultDurationUnits** Property, **DefaultFixedDuration** Property, **DefaultResourceStandardRate** Property, **DefaultView** Property, **DefaultWorkUnits** Property.

OvertimeWork Property

Applies To	**Assignment** Object, **Assignments** Collection; **Resource** Object, **Resources** Collection.
Description	Returns or sets the overtime work for an assignment. Returns the overtime work for a resource.
Syntax	*object*.**OvertimeWork** [= *value*]
Elements	The **OvertimeWork** property syntax has the following parts:

Part	Description
object	An object expression that evaluates to an object in the Applies To list.
value	A numeric expression that specifies the duration of overtime work for the resource.

See Also	**ActualWork** Property, **BaselineWork** Property, **OvertimeRate** Property, **Work** Property.

PageBreakRemove Method

Applies To	**Application** Object.
Description	Removes a manual page break from the active row.
Syntax	[*object*.]**PageBreakRemove**

Elements	The *object* placeholder is an object expression that evaluates to an object in the Applies To list.
See Also	**PageBreakSet** Method, **PageBreaksRemoveAll** Method.

PageBreakSet Method

Applies To	**Application** Object.
Description	Sets a page break in the active row.
Syntax	[*object*.]**PageBreakSet**
Elements	The *object* placeholder is an object expression that evaluates to an object in the Applies To list.
See Also	**PageBreakRemove** Method, **PageBreaksRemoveAll** Method.

PageBreaksRemoveAll Method

Applies To	**Application** Object.
Description	Removes all manual page breaks in the active project.
Syntax	[*object*.]**PageBreaksRemoveAll**
Elements	The *object* placeholder is an object expression that evaluates to an object in the Applies To list.
See Also	**PageBreakRemove** Method, **PageBreakSet** Method.

PageBreaksShow Method

Applies To	**Application** Object.
Description	Shows or hides page breaks on the PERT Chart.
Syntax	[*object*.]**PageBreaksShow** [*show*]
Elements	The **PageBreaksShow** method syntax has the following object qualifier and named arguments:

Part	Description
object	An object expression that evaluates to an object in the Applies To list.
show	A Boolean expression that specifies whether to show page breaks.

See Also   **PageBreakRemove** Method, **PageBreakSet** Method, **PageBreaksRemoveAll** Method.

Pane Object

Description   A pane of a window.

Properties   **Application** Property, **Index** Property, **Parent** Property

Methods   **Activate** Method, **Close** Method

See Also   **ActivePane** Property; **BottomPane** Property; **TopPane** Property; **Window** Object, **Windows** Collection.

PaneClose Method

Applies To   **Application** Object.

Description   Closes the lower pane of the active window.

Syntax   [*object*.]**PaneClose**

Elements   The *object* placeholder is an object expression that evaluates to an object in the Applies To list.

See Also   **Close** Method, **PaneCreate** Method, **PaneNext** Method.

PaneCreate Method

Applies To   **Application** Object.

Description   Creates a lower pane for the active window. The new pane contains the Task Form or Resource Form, depending on the contents of the upper pane.

Syntax	[*object.*]**PaneCreate**
Elements	The *object* placeholder is an object expression that evaluates to an object in the Applies To list.
See Also	**PaneClose** Method, **PaneNext** Method.

PaneNext Method

Applies To	**Application** Object.
Description	Activates the lower pane if the upper pane is active; activates the upper pane if the lower pane is active.
Syntax	[*object.*]**PaneNext**
Elements	The *object* placeholder is an object expression that evaluates to an object in the Applies To list.
See Also	**PaneClose** Method, **PaneCreate** Method.

Parent Property

Applies To	**Task** Object, **Tasks** Collection.
Description	Returns the parent of a task in the outline.
Syntax	*object.***OutlineParent**
Elements	The *object* placeholder is an object expression that evaluates to an object in the Applies To list.
See Also	**OutlineChildren** Method, **OutlineHideSubtasks** Method, **OutlineIndent** Method, **OutlineLevel** Property, **OutlineNumber** Property, **OutlineOutdent** Method, **OutlineShowAllTasks** Method, **OutlineShowSubtasks** Method.
Example	The following example displays the names of all tasks at the same outline level as the selected task.

```
Sub Siblings()
  Set objParent = ActiveCell.Task.OutlineParent
  For Each objTemp In objParent.OutlineChildren
      strTemp = objTemp.Name & ListSeparator & strTemp
  Next objTemp
  'Remove the last ListSeparator
  strTemp = Left$(strTemp,Len(strTemp)-Len(ListSeparator))
  MsgBox strTemp
End Sub
```

Path Property

Applies To   **Application** Object; **Project** Object, **Projects** Collection.

Description   Returns the pathname of Microsoft Project or an open project.

Syntax   *object*.**Path**

Elements   The *object* placeholder is an object expression that evaluates to an object in the Applies To list.

Remarks   The **Path** property returns **Empty** for an unsaved project.

In Microsoft Windows, if the object is in the WINPROJ folder of the C: drive, the **Path** property returns "C:\WINPROJ" or if the object is in the PROJECT share of the APP network drive, the **Path** property returns "\\APP\PROJECT".

On the Macintosh, if the object is in the WINPROJ folder of a drive called MINE, the **Path** property returns "MINE:WINPROJ".

See Also   **CreationDate** Property, **FullName** Property, **HasPassword** Property, **LastSaveDate** Property, **LastSavedBy** Property, **Name** Property, **ReadOnly** Property, **ReadOnlyRecommended** Property, **RevisionNumber** Property, **Saved** Property, **WriteReserved** Property.

PathSeparator Property

Applies To   **Application** Object.

Description   Returns the character that separates the components of a path name.

Syntax	[*object.*]**PathSeparator**
Elements	The *object* placeholder is an object expression that evaluates to an object in the Applies To list.
Remarks	In Microsoft Windows, the path name separator is the backslash character (\). On the Macintosh, the path name separator is the colon (:).
See Also	**Path** Property.

PeakUnits Property

Applies To	**Resource** Object, **Resources** Collection.
Description	Returns the largest number of units of a resource used at one time.
Syntax	*object.***PeakUnits**
Elements	The *object* placeholder is an object expression that evaluates to an object in the Applies To list.
See Also	**Units** Property.

PercentComplete Property

Applies To	**Project** Object, **Projects** Collection; **Task** Object, **Tasks** Collection.
Description	Returns or sets the percent complete of a task.
Syntax	*object.***PercentComplete** [= *value*]
Elements	The **PercentComplete** property syntax has the following parts:

Part	Description
object	An object expression that evaluates to an object in the Applies To list.
value	A numeric expression that specifies the percent complete of the task. The percent complete ranges from 0 to 100.

See Also	**PercentWorkComplete** Property.
Example	The following example removes a resource from tasks in the active project that have two or more resources and are 85 percent complete.

```
Sub ReallocateResource()
    Dim Entry    ' The name of the resource to remove
    Dim T        ' The task object used in For loop
    Dim RA       ' The resource assignment object to the task

    ' Prompt the user for the name of the resource to remove.
    Entry = InputBox("Enter a resource name:")

    ' Remove the resource from 85% complete tasks with 2+ resources.
    For Each T In ActiveProject.Tasks
        If T.PercentComplete >= 85 And T.Resources.Count > 2 Then
            For Each RA In T.Assignments
                If UCase(Entry) = UCase(RA.ResourceName) Then
                    RA.Delete
                End If
            Next
        End If
    Next T
End Sub
```

PercentWorkComplete Property

Applies To

Project Object, **Projects** Collection; **Resource** Object, **Resources** Collection; **Task** Object, **Tasks** Collection.

Description

Returns or sets the percent of work complete for a project, resource, or task. Read only for **Project** and **Resource** objects.

Syntax

object.**PercentWorkComplete** [= *value*]

Elements

The **PercentWorkComplete** property syntax has the following parts:

Part	Description
object	An object expression that evaluates to an object in the Applies To list.
value	A numeric expression from 1 to 100 that specifies the percent of work complete for the task.

See Also

ActualWork Property, **BaselineWork** Property, **PercentComplete** Property, **RemainingWork** Property, **Work** Property, **WorkVariance** Property.

Example

The following example sets the **Marked** property to **True** for each task in the active project with a percent of work complete that exceeds the percent specified by the user.

```
Sub MarkTasks()
   Dim T As Task    ' Task object used in For Each loop
   Dim Entry    ' Percentage entered by user

   ' Prompt user for a percentage.
   Entry = InputBox("Mark tasks that exceed what percent" + _
           " of work complete? (0-100)")

   ' If user's entry is invalid, display error message and exit.
   If Not IsNumeric(Entry) Then
       MsgBox ("Please enter a number only.")
       Exit Sub
   End If
   If Entry < 0 Or Entry > 100 Then
       MsgBox ("You did not enter a percentage from 0 to 100.")
       Exit Sub
   End If

   ' Mark tasks with percent of work complete greater than user entry.
   For Each T In ActiveProject.Tasks
       If Val(T.PercentWorkComplete) > Val(Entry) Then
           T.Marked = True
       Else
           T.Marked = False
       End If
   Next T
End Sub
```

Period Method

Applies To   **Calendar** Object, **Calendars** Collection.

Description   Returns a period in a calendar.

Syntax   *object*.**Period**(*startDate*, [*finishDate*])

Elements   The **Period** method syntax has the following object qualifier and named arguments:

Part	Description
object	An object expression that evaluates to an object in the Applies To list. Required.
startDate	A string expression that specifies the start date of the period. Required.
finishDate	A string expression that specifies the finish date of the period. By default, the *finishDate* argument equals the *startDate* argument. Optional.

See Also   **BaseCalendars** Method, **Calendar** Property, **Days** Method, **Months** Method, **Period** Object, **Years** Method.

Example   The following example sets a winter holiday for the active project.

```
Sub SetWinterHoliday()
    ActiveProject.Calendar.Period("12/20/93", "12/31/93"). _
        Working = False
End Sub
```

Period Object

Description   A period in a calendar.

Remarks   In Microsoft Project, **Period** objects are parents of **Shift** object.

Properties   **Application** Property, **Calendar** Property, **Count** Property, **Parent** Property, **Shiftn** Property, **Working** Property

Methods   **Default** Method

See Also   **Calendar** Object, **Calendars** Collection; **Period** Method; **Shift** Object.

PERTBorders Method

Applies To   **Application** Object.

Description   Sets the style and color of box borders on the PERT Chart.

Syntax

[*object*.]**PERTBorders** [*criticalStyle, criticalColor, noncriticalStyle, noncriticalColor, criticalMilestoneStyle, criticalMilestoneColor, noncriticalMilestoneStyle, noncriticalMilestoneColor, criticalSummaryStyle, criticalSummaryColor, noncriticalSummaryStyle, noncriticalSummaryColor, criticalSubprojectStyle, criticalSubprojectColor, noncriticalSubprojectStyle, noncriticalSubprojectColor, criticalMarkedStyle, criticalMarkedColor, noncriticalMarkedStyle, noncriticalMarkedColor*]

Elements

The **PERTBorders** method syntax has the following object qualifier and named arguments:

Part	Description
object	An object expression that evaluates to an object in the Applies To list. Optional.
criticalStyle	A constant that specifies the style of box borders for critical tasks. Optional.
criticalColor	A constant that specifies the color of box borders for critical tasks. Optional.
noncriticalStyle	A constant that specifies the style of box borders for noncritical tasks. Optional.
noncriticalColor	A constant that specifies the color of box borders for noncritical tasks. Optional.
criticalMilestoneStyle	A constant that specifies the style of box borders for critical milestone tasks. Optional.
criticalMilestoneColor	A constant that specifies the color of box borders for critical milestone tasks. Optional.
noncriticalMilestoneStyle	A constant that specifies the style of box borders for noncritical milestone tasks. Optional.
noncriticalMilestoneColor	A constant that specifies the color of box borders for noncritical milestone tasks. Optional.
criticalSummaryStyle	A constant that specifies the style of box borders for critical summary tasks. Optional.
criticalSummaryColor	A constant that specifies the color of box borders for critical summary tasks. Optional.
noncriticalSummaryStyle	A constant that specifies the style of box borders for noncritical summary tasks. Optional.
noncriticalSummaryColor	A constant that specifies the color of box borders for noncritical summary tasks. Optional.
criticalSubprojectStyle	A constant that specifies the style of box borders for critical subproject tasks. Optional.

Part	Description
criticalSubprojectColor	A constant that specifies the color of box borders for critical subproject tasks. Optional.
noncriticalSubprojectStyle	A constant that specifies the style of box borders for noncritical subproject tasks. Optional.
noncriticalSubprojectColor	A constant that specifies the color of box borders for noncritical subproject tasks. Optional.
criticalMarkedStyle	A constant that specifies the style of box borders for critical marked tasks. Optional.
criticalMarkedColor	A constant that specifies the color of box borders for critical marked tasks. Optional.
noncriticalMarkedStyle	A constant that specifies the style of box borders for noncritical marked tasks. Optional.
noncriticalMarkedColor	A constant that specifies the color of box borders for noncritical marked tasks. Optional.

The *criticalStyle*, *noncriticalStyle*, *criticalMilestoneStyle*, *noncriticalMilestoneStyle*, *criticalSummaryStyle*, *noncriticalSummaryStyle*, *criticalSubprojectStyle*, *noncriticalSubprojectStyle*, *criticalMarkedStyle*, and *noncriticalMarkedStyle* arguments have these settings:

pjPlainBox	0	Plain
pjThickBox	1	Thick
pjShadowBox	2	Shadow
pjDottedBox	3	Dotted
pjFrame	4	Frame
pjGrayFrame	5	Gray frame
pjPatternFrame	6	Pattern frame
pjMarquee	7	Marquee

The *criticalColor*, *noncriticalColor*, *criticalMilestoneColor*, *noncriticalMilestoneColor*, *criticalSummaryColor*, *nonCriticalSummaryColor*, *criticalSubprojectColor*, *noncriticalSubprojectColor*, *criticalMarkedColor*, and *noncriticalMarkedColor* arguments have these settings:

pjBlack	0	Black
pjRed	1	Red
pjYellow	2	Yellow
pjLime	3	Lime
pjAqua	4	Aqua
pjBlue	5	Blue
pjFuchsia	6	Fuchsia
pjWhite	7	White
pjMaroon	8	Maroon
pjGreen	9	Green
pjOlive	10	Olive
pjNavy	11	Navy
pjPurple	12	Purple
pjTeal	13	Teal
pjGray	14	Gray
pjSilver	15	Silver

See Also   **PERTBoxStyles** Method, **PERTLayout** Method, **PERTSetTask** Method.

PERTBoxStyles Method

Applies To   **Application** Object.

Description   Sets the style of boxes on the PERT Chart.

Syntax   [*object*.]**PERTBoxStyles** [*size, dateFormat, gridlines, crossMarks, field1, field2, field3, field4, field5*]

Elements   The **PERTBoxStyles** method syntax has the following object qualifier and named arguments:

Part	Description
object	An object expression that evaluates to an object in the Applies To list. Optional.
size	A constant that specifies the size of boxes. Optional.
dateFormat	A constant that specifies the date format for boxes. Optional.
gridlines	A Boolean expression that specifies whether gridlines separate the fields in boxes. Optional.

Part	Description
crossMarks	A Boolean expression that specifies whether crossmarks appear in boxes to show finished and ongoing tasks. Optional.
field1	A constant that specifies the name of the first field in boxes. Optional.
field2	A constant that specifies the name of the second field in boxes. Optional.
field3	A constant that specifies the name of the third field in boxes. Optional.
field4	A constant that specifies the name of the fourth field in boxes. Optional.
field5	A constant that specifies the name of the fifth field in boxes. Optional.

The *size* argument has these settings:

pjIDOnly	0	Smallest (contains identification numbers only)
pjSmall	1	Small
pjMedium	2	Medium
pjLarge	3	Large

The *dateFormat* argument has these settings:

pjDateDefault	-1	The default format, as specified on the View tab of the Options dialog box. (To display the Options dialog box, choose Options from the Tools menu.)
pjDate_mm_dd_yy_hh_mmAM	0	1/31/94 12:33 PM
pjDate_mm_dd_yy	1	1/31/94
pjDate_mmmm_dd_yyyy_hh_mmAM	2	January 31, 1994 12:33 PM
pjDate_mmmm_dd_yyyy	3	January 31, 1994
pjDate_mmm_dd_hh_mmAM	4	Jan 31 12:33 PM
pjDate_mmm_dd_yyy	5	Jan 31 '94
pjDate_mmmm_dd	6	January 31
pjDate_mmm_dd	7	Jan 31
pjDate_ddd_mm_dd_yy_mmAM	8	Mon 1/31/94 12:33 PM
pjDate_ddd_mm_dd_yy	9	Mon 1/31/94
pjDate_ddd_mmm_dd_yyy	10	Mon Jan 31, '94
pjDate_ddd_hh_mmAM	11	Mon 12:33 PM

pjDate_mm_dd	12	1/31
pjDate_dd	13	31
pjDate_hh_mmAM	14	12:33 PM
pjDate_ddd_mmm_dd	15	Mon Jan 31
pjDate_ddd_mm_dd	16	Mon 1/31
pjDate_ddd_dd	17	Mon 31
pjDate_Www_dd	18	W05/1
pjDate_Www_dd_yy_hh_mmAM	19	W05/1/94 12:33 PM

The *field1, field2, field3, field4, and field5* arguments have these settings:

pjTaskActualCost	7	Actual Cost
pjTaskActualDuration	28	Actual Duration
pjTaskActualFinish	42	Actual Finish
pjTaskActualStart	41	Actual Start
pjTaskActualWork	2	Actual Work
pjTaskBaselineCost	6	Baseline Cost
pjTaskBaselineDuration	27	Baseline Duration
pjTaskBaselineFinish	44	Baseline Finish
pjTaskBaselineStart	43	Baseline Start
pjTaskBaselineWork	1	Baseline Work
pjTaskBCWP	11	BCWP
pjTaskBCWS	12	BCWS
pjTaskConfirmed	110	Confirmed
pjTaskConstraintDate	18	Constraint Date
pjTaskConstraintType	17	Constraint Type
pjTaskContact	112	Contact
pjTaskCost	5	Cost
pjTaskCost1	106	Cost1
pjTaskCost2	107	Cost2
pjTaskCost3	108	Cost3
pjTaskCostVariance	9	Cost Variance
pjTaskCreated	93	Created
pjTaskCritical	19	Critical
pjTaskCV	83	CV
pjTaskDelay	20	Delay
pjTaskDuration	29	Duration

pjTaskDuration1	103	Duration1
pjTaskDuration2	104	Duration2
pjTaskDuration3	105	Duration3
pjTaskDurationVariance	30	Duration Variance
pjTaskEarlyFinish	38	Early Finish
pjTaskEarlyStart	37	Early Start
pjTaskFinish	36	Finish
pjTaskFinish1	53	Finish1
pjTaskFinish2	56	Finish2
pjTaskFinish3	59	Finish3
pjTaskFinish4	62	Finish4
pjTaskFinish5	65	Finish5
pjTaskFinishVariance	46	Finish Variance
pjTaskFixedCost	8	Fixed Cost
pjTaskFixedDuration	34	Fixed (Duration)
pjTaskFlag1	72	Flag1
pjTaskFlag10	81	Flag10
pjTaskFlag2	73	Flag2
pjTaskFlag3	74	Flag3
pjTaskFlag4	75	Flag4
pjTaskFlag5	76	Flag5
pjTaskFlag6	77	Flag6
pjTaskFlag7	78	Flag7
pjTaskFlag8	79	Flag8
pjTaskFlag9	80	Flag9
pjTaskFreeSlack	21	Free Slack
pjTaskHideBar	109	Hide Bar
pjTaskID	23	ID
pjTaskLateFinish	40	Late Finish
pjTaskLateStart	39	Late Start
pjTaskLinkedFields	98	Linked Fields
pjTaskMarked	71	Marked
pjTaskMilestone	24	Milestone
pjTaskName	14	Name
pjTaskNotes	15	Notes
pjTaskNumber1	87	Number1

pjTaskNumber2	88	Number2
pjTaskNumber3	89	Number3
pjTaskNumber4	90	Number4
pjTaskNumber5	91	Number5
pjTaskObjects	97	Objects
pjTaskOutlineLevel	85	Outline Level
pjTaskOutlineNumber	102	Outline Number
pjTaskPercentComplete	32	% Complete
pjTaskPercentWorkComplete	33	% Work Complete
pjTaskPredecessors	47	Predecessors
pjTaskPriority	25	Priority
pjTaskProject	84	Project
pjTaskRemainingCost	10	Remaining Cost
pjTaskRemainingDuration	31	Remaining Duration
pjTaskRemainingWork	4	Remaining Work
pjTaskResourceGroup	113	Resource Group
pjTaskResourceInitials	50	Resource Initials
pjTaskResourceNames	49	Resource Names
pjTaskResume	99	Resume
pjTaskResumeNoEarlierThan	101	Resume No Earlier Than
pjTaskRollup	82	Rollup
pjTaskSheetNotes	94	Sheet Notes
pjTaskStart	35	Start
pjTaskStart1	52	Start1
pjTaskStart2	55	Start2
pjTaskStart3	58	Start3
pjTaskStart4	61	Start4
pjTaskStart5	64	Start5
pjTaskStartVariance	45	Start Variance
pjTaskStop	100	Stop
pjTaskSubproject	26	Subproject File
pjTaskSuccessors	48	Successors
pjTaskSummary	92	Summary
pjTaskSV	13	SV
pjTaskText1	51	Text1
pjTaskText10	70	Text10

pjTaskText2	54	Text2
pjTaskText3	57	Text3
pjTaskText4	60	Text4
pjTaskText5	63	Text5
pjTaskText6	66	Text6
pjTaskText7	67	Text7
pjTaskText8	68	Text8
pjTaskText9	69	Text9
pjTaskTotalSlack	22	Total Slack
pjTaskUniqueID	86	Unique ID
pjTaskUniquePredecessors	95	Unique ID Predecessors
pjTaskUniqueSuccessors	96	Unique ID Successors
pjTaskUpdateNeeded	111	Update Needed
pjTaskWBS	16	WBS
pjTaskWork	0	Work
pjTaskWorkVariance	3	Work Variance

See Also   **PERTBorders** Method, **PERTLayout** Method, **PERTSetTask** Method.

PERTLayout Method

Applies To   **Application** Object.

Description   Controls the layout of the active PERT Chart.

Syntax   [*object.*]**PERTLayout** [*straight, displayArrows, adjustForPageBreaks, displayPageBreaks*]

Elements   The **PERTLayout** method syntax has the following object qualifier and named arguments:

Part	Description
object	An object expression that evaluates to an object in the Applies To list. Optional.
straight	A Boolean expression that specifies whether the lines connecting the nodes of the active PERT Chart are straight. By default, the *straight* argument is **True**. Optional. The *straight* argument has these settings:

	True	The lines connecting the nodes of the active PERT Chart are straight.
	False	The lines connecting the nodes of the active PERT Chart form right angles.

Part	Description
displayArrows	A Boolean expression that specifies whether arrows connect the nodes of a PERT Chart. By default, the *displayArrows* argument is **True**. Optional.
adjustForPageBreaks	A Boolean expression that specifies whether to adjust the nodes of a PERT Chart around page breaks. By default, the *adjustForPageBreaks* argument is **True**. Optional.
displayPageBreaks	A Boolean expression that specifies whether to display page breaks. By default, the *displayPageBreaks* argument is **True**. Optional.

Remarks

The value you specify for the *adjustForPageBreaks* argument has no effect until you use the **PERTLayout** or **LayoutNow** method.

See Also

CalendarLayout Method, **LayoutNow** Method.

Example

The following example changes PERT Chart link line formatting to straight with arrows.

```
Sub DisplayStraightArrows()
    PERTLayout Straight := True, DisplayArrows := True
End Sub
```

PERTSetTask Method

Applies To   **Application** Object.

Description   Creates, selects, or moves a task on the PERT Chart.

Syntax   [*object*.]**PERTSetTask** [*create, move, taskID, xPosition, yPosition*]

Elements	The **PERTSetTask** method syntax has the following object qualifier and named arguments:

Part	Description
object	An object expression that evaluates to an object in the Applies To list. Optional.
create	A Boolean expression that specifies whether to create a new task. By default, the *create* argument is **False**. Optional.
move	A Boolean expression that specifies whether to move or select the task. By default, the *move* argument is **False**. Optional.
taskID	A numeric expression that specifies the identification number of the task. Optional.
xPosition	A numeric expression that specifies the horizontal position (*create* argument is **True**) or the relative horizontal position (*move* argument is **True**) of the task. Optional.
yPosition	A numeric expression that specifies the vertical position (*create* argument is **True**) or the relative vertical position (*move* argument is **True**) of the task. Optional.

See Also	**PERTBorders** Method, **PERTBoxStyles** Method, **PERTLayout** Method.

PERTShowHideFields Method

Applies To	**Application** Object.
Description	Shows or hides the fields of the active PERT Chart.
Syntax	[*object.*]**PERTShowHideFields** [*show*]
Elements	The **PERTShowHideFields** method syntax has the following object qualifier and named arguments:

Part	Description
object	An object expression that evaluates to an object in the Applies To list.
show	A Boolean expression that specifies whether to show or hide the fields of the PERT boxes in the active PERT Chart. By default, the *show* argument is **True** if the active PERT Chart is showing fields; otherwise the *show* argument is **False**.

See Also	**ZoomIn** Method, **ZoomOut** Method, **ZoomPERT** Method.

PMText Property

Applies To	**Application** Object.
Description	Returns the text Microsoft Project displays next to evening hours in the 12-hour time format.
Syntax	[*object*.]**PMText**
Elements	The *object* placeholder is an object expression that evaluates to an object in the Applies To list.
Remarks	Microsoft Project for Microsoft Windows sets the **PMText** property equal to the corresponding value in the Regional settings of the Microsoft Windows Control Panel.
	On the Macintosh, using System 7.1 and later, you can use the Date & Time control panel to change this value.
See Also	**AMText** Property, **TimeLeadingZero** Property, **TimeSeparator** Property, **TwelveHourTimeFormat** Property.

Predecessors Property

Applies To	**Task** Object, **Tasks** Collection.
Description	Returns the unique identification numbers of the predecessors of a task.
Syntax	*object*.**UniqueIDPredecessors**
Elements	The *object* placeholder is an object expression that evaluates to an object in the Applies To list.
Remarks	For example, the **UniqueIDPredecessors** property returns "5,4,1" if the unique identification numbers of the predecessor tasks are 5, 4, and 1.
	Note This example assumes that the list separator character is the comma (,). You can determine the list separator character with the **ListSeparator** property.
See Also	**PredecessorTasks** Method, **UniqueID** Property, **UniqueIDSuccessors** Property.

PredecessorTasks Method

Applies To   **Task** Object, **Tasks** Collection.

Description   Returns a task or the tasks that are predecessors of a task.

Syntax   *object*.**PredecessorTasks**[(*index*)]

Elements   The **PredecessorTasks** method syntax has the following object qualifier and named arguments:

Part	Description
object	An object expression that evaluates to an object in the Applies To list.
index	A numeric expression that specifies the index of the *object*.

See Also   **LinkPredecessors** Method, **Predecessors** Property, **SuccessorTasks** Method, **Tasks** Method.

Print Method

Applies To   **Debug** Object.

Description   Prints text in the Immediate pane of the Debug window.

Syntax   [*object*.]**Print** [*outputlist*]

Elements
The **Print** method syntax has these parts:

Part	Description
object	Object expression that evaluates to the Debug object.
outputlist	Expression or list of expressions to print. If omitted, a blank line is printed.

The *outputlist* argument has the following syntax and parts:

[{**Spc**(*n*) | **Tab**[(*n*)]}][*expression*][*charpos*]

Part	Description
Spc(*n*)	Used to insert space characters in the output, where *n* is the number of space characters to insert.
Tab(*n*)	Used to position the insertion point to an absolute column number, where *n* is the column number. Use **Tab** with no argument to position the insertion point at the beginning of the next print zone.
expression	Numeric or string expressions to print.
charpos	Specifies the insertion point for the next character. Use a semicolon to specify the insertion point to be immediately after the last character displayed. Use **Tab**(*n*) to position the insertion point to an absolute column number. Use **Tab** with no argument to position the insertion point at the beginning of the next print zone. If *charpos* is omitted, the next character is printed on the next line.

Remarks

Multiple expressions can be separated with either a space or a semicolon. A space has the same effect as a semicolon.

All data printed to the Immediate pane is internationally aware; that is, the data is properly formatted (using the appropriate decimal separator) and the keywords are output in the language appropriate for the international locale specified for your system.

For **Boolean** data, either `True` or `False` is printed. The **True** and **False** keywords are translated, as appropriate, according to the locale setting specified for your system.

Date data is written using the standard short date format recognized by your system. When either the date or the time component is missing or zero, only the data provided gets written.

Nothing is written if *outputlist* data is **Empty**. However, if *outputlist* data is **Null**, `Null` is output. Again, the **Null** keyword is translated, as appropriate, when output.

For error data, the output appears as `Error errorcode`. The **Error** keyword is translated, as appropriate, when output.

Note Because the **Print** method normally prints with proportionally-spaced characters, it is important to remember that there is no correlation between the number of characters printed and the number of fixed-width columns those characters occupy. For example, a wide letter, such as a "W", occupies more than one fixed-width column, whereas a narrow letter, such as an "i", occupies less. To account for cases where wider than average characters are used, you must ensure that your tabular columns are positioned far enough apart. Alternatively, you can print using a fixed-pitch font (such as Courier) to ensure that each character uses only one column.

See Also   **Debug** Object, **Print** # Statement, **Spc** Function, **Tab** Function.

Example   This example uses the **Print** method to output text to the **Debug** object; that is, display text in the Debug window.

```
For I = 11 To 20 ' Loop 10 times.
    ' Print each value on a new line.
    Debug.Print I
Next I

For I = 11 To 20 ' Loop 10 times.
    ' Print values on the same line, next to each other.
    Debug.Print I;
Next I

Debug.Print Spc(10) ; "Hello there"      ' Print 10 spaces before.
Debug.Print Tab(20) ; "This is a test"   ' Print at column 20.
Debug.Print "Hello"; Tab; Tab; "There"   ' Print 2 print zones apart.
```

Print # Statement

Description   Writes display-formatted data to a sequential file.

Syntax   **Print #***filenumber,*[*outputlist*]

Elements   The **Print #** statement syntax has these parts:

Part	Description
filenumber	Any valid file number.
outputlist	Expression or list of expressions to print.

The *outputlist* argument has the following syntax and parts:

[{**Spc**(*n*) | **Tab**[(*n*)]}][*expression*][*charpos*]

Part	Description
Spc(*n*)	Used to insert space characters in the output, where *n* is the number of space characters to insert.
Tab(*n*)	Used to position the insertion point to an absolute column number, where *n* is the column number. Use **Tab** with no argument to position the insertion point at the beginning of the next print zone.

Part	Description
expression	Numeric or string expressions to print.
charpos	Specifies the insertion point for the next character. Use a semicolon to specify the insertion point to be immediately after the last character displayed. Use **Tab**(*n*) to position the insertion point to an absolute column number. Use **Tab** with no argument to position the insertion point at the beginning of the next print zone. If *charpos* is omitted, the next character is printed on the next line.

Remarks

If you omit *outputlist* and include only a list separator after *filenumber*, a blank line prints to the file. Multiple expressions can be separated with either a space or a semicolon. A space has the same effect as a semicolon.

All data written to the file using **Print #** is internationally aware; that is, the data is properly formatted (using the appropriate decimal separator) and the keywords are output in the language appropriate for the international locale specified for your system.

For **Boolean** data, either True or False is printed. The **True** and **False** keywords are translated, as appropriate, according to the locale setting specified for your system.

Date data is written to the file using the standard short date format recognized by your system. When either the date or the time component is missing or zero, only the provided part gets written to the file.

Nothing is written to the file if *outputlist* data is **Empty**. However, if *outputlist* data is **Null**, Null is written to the file. Again, the **Null** keyword is translated, as appropriate.

For error data, the output appears as Error errorcode. The **Error** keyword is translated, as appropriate, when written to the file.

Because **Print #** writes an image of the data to the file, you must delimit the data so it prints correctly. If you use **Tab** with no arguments to move the print position to the next print zone, **Print #** also writes the spaces between print fields to the file.

Note If, at some future time, you want to read the data from a file using the **Input #** statement, use the **Write #** statement instead of the **Print #** statement to write the data to the file. Using **Write #** ensures the integrity of each separate data field by properly delimiting it, so that it can be read back in using **Input #**. Using **Write #** also ensures that it can be correctly read in any locale.

See Also

Open Statement, **Print** Method, **Spc** Function, **Tab** Function, **Write #** Statement.

Example

This example uses the **Print #** statement to write data to a file.

```
    Open "TESTFILE" For Output As #1        ' Open file for output.
Print #1, "This is a test"                 ' Print text to file.
Print #1,                            ' Print blank line to file.
Print #1, "Zone 1"; Tab ; "Zone 2"        ' Print in two print zones.
Print #1, "Hello" ; " " ; "World"         ' Separate strings with space.
Print #1, Spc(5) ; "5 leading spaces "    ' Print 5 leading spaces.
Print #1, Tab(10) ; "Hello"               ' Print word at col 10.

' Assign Boolean, Date, Null and Error values.
MyBool = False : MyDate = #February 12, 1969# : MyNull = Null
MyError = CVErr(32767)
' True, False, Null and Error are translated using locale settings of
' your system. Date literals are written using standard short date
' format.
Print #1, MyBool ; " is a Boolean value"
Print #1, MyDate ; " is a date"
Print #1, MyNull ; " is a null value"
Print #1, MyError ; " is an error value"
Close #1     ' Close file.
```

Priority Property

Applies To   **Project** Object, **Projects** Collection; **Task** Object, **Tasks** Collection.

Description   Returns or sets the priority of a task.

Syntax   *object*.**Priority** [= *value*]

Elements   The **Priority** property syntax has these parts:

Part	Description
object	An object expression that evaluates to an object in the Applies To list.
value	A constant that specifies a priority, as shown under Settings.

Settings   The **Priority** property has these settings:

Setting	Description
pjPriorityDoNotLevel	Microsoft Project does not level the resources assigned to the task.
pjPriorityHighest	The task has the highest priority.
pjPriorityVeryHigh	The task has a very high priority.
pjPriorityHigher	The task has a higher priority.
pjPriorityHigh	The task has a high priority.

pjPriorityMedium	The task has a medium priority.
pjPriorityLow	The task has a low priority.
pjPriorityLower	The task has a lower priority.
pjPriorityVeryLow	The task has a very low priority.
pjPriorityLowest	The task has the lowest priority.

Remarks   Microsoft Project uses the priorities of tasks when leveling resources.

See Also   **ConstraintDate** Property, **ConstraintType** Property, **Flagn** Properties, **Name** Property, **Notes** Property, **Numbern** Properties, **SubProject** Property, **Summary** Property, **Textn** Properties.

Example   The following example sets the tasks on the critical path to the highest priority in the active project.

```
Sub SetPriorityOfCriticalTasks()
    Dim T As Task    ' Task object used in For Each loop

    ' Look for tasks on the critical path.
    For Each T In ActiveProject.Tasks

        ' If it is on critical path, set the task's priority to highest.
        If T.Critical Then
            T.Priority = pjPriorityHighest
        End If
    Next T

End Sub
```

Private Statement

Description   Used at module level to indicate that an entire module is **Private**.

Syntax   **Option Private Module**

Remarks   If used, the **Option Private** statement must appear in a module before any statements that declare variables or define constants.

The public parts (variables, objects, and user-defined types declared at module level) of modules declared **Private** using the **Option Private** statement are still available within the project containing the module, but they are not available to other applications or projects.

See Also   **Option** Base Statement**,** Option Compare Statement, Option Explicit Statement, **Private** Statement.

Example   This **Private** statement is used at the module-level to declare variables as private; that is, they are available only to the module in which they are declared.

```
Private Number As Integer                ' Private integer variable.
Private NameArray(1 To 5) As String      ' Private array variable.
Private MyVar, YourVar, ThisVar As Integer   ' Multiple declarations.
```

Project Object, Projects Collection

Description   An open project or all open projects.

Remarks   In Microsoft Project, **Project** objects are parents of **Windows**, **Tasks**, **Resources**, and **Calendars** collections.

Properties   **ActualCost** Property, **ActualDuration** Property, **ActualFinish** Property, **ActualStart** Property, **ActualWork** Property, **Application** Property, **Author** Property, **AutoAddResources** Property, **AutoLinkTasks** Property, **AutoSplitTasks** Property, **AutoTrack** Property, **BaselineCost** Property, **BaselineDuration** Property, **BaselineFinish** Property, **BaselineStart** Property, **BaselineWork** Property, **BCWP** Property, **Calendar** Property, **Comments** Property, **Company** Property, **Confirmed** Property, **ConstraintDate** Property, **ConstraintType** Property, **Contact** Property, **Cost** Property, **Costn** Property, **CostVariance** Property, **Count** Property, **Created** Property, **CreationDate** Property, **Critical** Property, **CurrencyDigits** Property, **CurrencySymbol** Property, **CurrencySymbolPosition** Property, **CurrentDate** Property, **CurrentFilter** Property, **CurrentTable** Property, **CurrentView** Property, **CV** Property, **DefaultDurationUnits** Property, **DefaultFinishTime** Property, **DefaultFixedDuration** Property, **DefaultResourceOvertimeRate** Property, **DefaultResourceStandardRate** Property, **DefaultStartTime** Property, **DefaultWorkUnits** Property, **Delay** Property, **DisplayProjectSummaryTask** Property, **Duration** Property, **Durationn** Property, **DurationVariance** Property, **EarlyFinish** Property, **EarlyStart** Property, **Finish** Property, **Finishn** Property, **FinishVariance** Property, **FixedCost** Property, **FixedDuration** Property, **Flagn** Properties, **FreeSlack** Property, **FullName** Property, **HasPassword** Property, **HideBar** Property, **HoursPerDay** Property, **HoursPerWeek** Property, **ID** Property, **Index** Property, **Keywords** Property, **LastPrintedDate** Property, **LastSaveDate** Property, **LastSavedBy** Property, **LateFinish** Property, **LateStart** Property, **LinkedFields** Property, **Manager** Property, **Marked** Property, **Milestone** Property, **Name** Property, **Notes** Property, **Numbern** Properties,

NumberOfResources Property, **NumberOfTasks** Property, **Objects** Property, **OutlineLevel** Property, **OutlineNumber** Property, **Parent** Property, **Path** Property, **PercentComplete** Property, **PercentWorkComplete** Property, **Priority** Property, **Project** Property, **ProjectFinish** Property, **ProjectNotes** Property, **ProjectStart** Property, **ReadOnly** Property, **ReadOnlyRecommended** Property, **RemainingCost** Property, **RemainingDuration** Property, **RemainingWork** Property, **ResourceGroup** Property, **ResourceInitials** Property, **ResourceNames** Property, **ResourcePoolName** Property, **Resume** Property, **ResumeNoEarlierThan** Property, **RevisionNumber** Property, **Rollup** Property, **Saved** Property, **ScheduleFromStart** Property, **ShowCriticalSlack** Property, **Start** Property, **Startn** Property, **StartOnCurrentDate** Property, **StartVariance** Property, **Stop** Property, **Subject** Property, **Summary** Property, **SV** Property, **Template** Property, **Textn** Properties, **Title** Property, **TotalSlack** Property, **UniqueID** Property, **UpdateNeeded** Property, **Work** Property, **WorkVariance** Property, **WriteReserved** Property.

Methods

Activate Method, **BaseCalendars** Method, **ReportList** Method, **ResourceFilterList** Method, **Resources** Method, **ResourceTableList** Method, **ResourceViewList** Method, **TaskFilterList** Method, **Tasks** Method, **TaskTableList** Method, **TaskViewList** Method, **ViewList** Method, **Windows** Method

See Also

ActiveProject Property; **Calendar** Object, **Calendars** Collection; **Project** Property; **Projects** Method; **Resource** Object, **Resources** Collection; **Task** Object, **Tasks** Collection; **Window** Object, **Windows** Collection.

Project Property

Applies To

Task Object, **Tasks** Collection.

Description

Returns or sets the subproject for a task.

Syntax

object.**SubProject** [= *value*]

Elements

The **SubProject** property syntax has the following parts:

Part	Description
object	An object expression that evaluates to an object in the Applies To list.
value	A string expression that specifies the filename of a subproject for the task.

See Also

ConstraintType Property, **Priority** Property.

Example

The following example sets a subproject for specified tasks in open projects.

```
Sub SetSubProject()
    Dim TaskName      ' The task name entered by the user
    Dim SubPName      ' The subproject filename entered by the user
    Dim P As Project     ' Project object used in For Each loop
    Dim T As Task        ' Task object used in For Each loop

    ' Prompt the user for a subproject filename and task name.
    TaskName = InputBox("Enter the name of a task.")
    SubPName = InputBox("Enter the filename of a subproject" + _
            " for the task.")

    ' Set the subproject for each instance of the task in open projects.
    For Each P In Projects
        For Each T In P.Tasks
            If T.Name = TaskName Then T.SubProject = SubPName
        Next T
    Next P
End Sub
```

ProjectFinish Property

Applies To   **Project** Object, **Projects** Collection.

Description   Returns or sets the finish date for a project.

Syntax   *object*.**ProjectFinish** [= *value*]

Elements   The **ProjectFinish** property syntax has the following parts:

Part	Description
object	An object expression that evaluates to an object in the Applies To list.
value	A date expression that specifies the finish date for the project.

See Also   **Finish** Property, **ProjectStart** Property.

ProjectID Property

Applies To   **Assignment** Object, **Assignments** Collection.

Description   Returns the identification number for the project to which an assignment belongs.

Syntax	*object*.**ProjectID**
Elements	The *object* placeholder is an object expression that evaluates to an object in the Applies To list.
See Also	**ID** Property, **ResourceID** Property, **ResourceName** Property, **TaskID** Property, **TaskName** Property.

ProjectNotes Property

Applies To	**Project** Object, **Projects** Collection.
Description	Returns the notes for the project.
Syntax	*object*.**ProjectNotes**
Elements	The *object* placeholder is an object expression that evaluates to an object in the Applies To list.
Remarks	The notes are the same as the Comments for a project.
See Also	**Comments** Property, **Notes** Property, **ProjectSummaryInfo** Method.
Example	The following example adds the date and time to the notes in the summary info and then saves the project.

```
Sub SaveAndNoteTime()
    Dim NL                ' Newline characters
    NL = Chr(13) + Chr(10)   ' NL = Carriage return + Linefeed
    Projects(1).ProjectNotes = Projects(1).ProjectNotes & _
        NL & NL & "This project was last saved on " & _
        Date$ & " at " & Time$ & "."
    FileSave
End Sub
```

Projects Method

Applies To	**Application** Object.
Description	Displays the data from one or more projects in a single window.

Syntax	[*object*.]**ConsolidateProjects** [*filenames*, *newWindow*, *attachToSources*, *poolResources*, *hideSubtasks*]
Elements	The **ConsolidateProjects** method syntax has the following object qualifier and named arguments:

Part	Description
object	An object expression that evaluates to an object in the Applies To list. Optional.
filenames	A string expression that specifies one or more filenames of projects to consolidate. Optional.
newWindow	A Boolean expression that specifies whether to create a new window for the projects you specify with the *filenames* argument. The *newWindow* argument is ignored unless the active project is a consolidated project. Optional.
attachToSources	A Boolean expression that specifies whether changes in the consolidated project affect source projects. Optional.
poolResources	A Boolean expression that specifies whether to pool the resources of the projects you specify with the *filenames* argument. Optional.
hideSubtasks	A Boolean expression that specifies whether to hide the subtasks of the projects you specify with the *filenames* argument. Optional.

See Also	**FileOpen** Method, **ViewEditCombination** Method.
Example	The following example creates a consolidated project, prints a report, and closes the consolidated project without saving it.

```
Sub ConsolidatedReport()
    ConsolidateProjects Filenames := "project1.mpp,project2.mpp"
    ReportPrint Name:="Critical Tasks"
    FileClose save := pjDoNotSave
End Sub
```

ProjectStart Property

Applies To	**Project** Object, **Projects** Collection.
Description	Returns or sets the start date for a project.

Syntax	*object*.**ProjectStart** [= *value*]
Elements	The **ProjectStart** property syntax has the following parts:

Part	Description
object	An object expression that evaluates to an object in the Applies To list.
value	A date expression that specifies the start date for the project.

See Also	**ProjectFinish** Property, **Start** Property.

ProjectStatistics Method

Applies To	**Application** Object.
Description	Displays the Project Statistics dialog box.
Syntax	[*object*.]**ProjectStatistics** [*project*]
Elements	The **ProjectStatistics** method syntax has the following object qualifier and named arguments:

Part	Description
object	An object expression that evaluates to an object in the Applies To list. Optional.
project	A string expression that specifies a project. Optional.

Remarks	The **ProjectStatistics** method has the same effect as choosing Project Info from the File menu and then choosing the Statistics button.
See Also	**Cost** Property, **Duration** Property, **Finish** Property, **Start** Property, **Work** Property.

ProjectSummaryInfo Method

Applies To	**Application** Object.
Description	Sets information about a project.
Syntax	[*object*.]**ProjectSummaryInfo** [*project, title, subject, author, company, manager, keywords, comments, start, finish, scheduleFrom, currentDate, calendar*]

Elements

The **ProjectSummary** method syntax has the following object qualifier and named arguments:

Part	Description
object	An object expression that evaluates to an object in the Applies To list. Optional.
project	A string expression that specifies the filename of the project for which you would like to edit the project information. Optional.
title	A string expression that specifies the title of the project. Optional.
subject	A string expression that specifies the subject of the project. Optional.
author	A string expression that specifies the author of the project. Optional.
company	A string expression that specifies the company associated with the project. Optional.
manager	A string expression that specifies the manager of the project. Optional.
keywords	A string expression that specifies the keywords associated with the project. Optional.
comments	A string expression that specifies comments associated with the project. Optional.
start	A string expression that specifies when the project starts. Optional.
finish	A string expression that specifies when the project ends. The *finish* argument is ignored if the *scheduleFrom* argument is **pjProjectStart**. Optional.
scheduleFrom	A Boolean expression that specifies whether to schedule projects from the start date or finish date. Optional.
currentDate	A string expression that specifies the current date for the project. Optional.
calendar	A string expression that specifies the name of the base calendar for the project. Optional.

The *scheduleFrom* argument has these settings:

pjProjectStart	1	Schedules the project from the start date.
pjProjectFinish	2	Schedules the project from the finish date.

See Also

ProjectStatistics Method.

PromptForSummaryInfo Property

Applies To	**Application** Object.
Description	Sets or returns whether a dialog box prompts the user to display the Summary Info dialog box when a new project is created.
Syntax	[*object*.]**PromptForSummaryInfo** [= *value*]
Elements	The **PromptForSummaryInfo** property syntax has the following parts:

Part	Description
object	An object expression that evaluates to an object in the Applies To list.
value	A Boolean expression that specifies whether a dialog box prompts the user to display the Summary Info dialog box when a new project is created.

See Also	**LoadLastFile** Property, **OptionsGeneral** Method, **ShowTipOfDay** Property, **ShowWelcome** Property.

Property Get Statement

Description	Declares the name, arguments, and code that form the body of a **Property** procedure, which gets the value of a property.

Syntax	[**Public** | **Private**][**Static**] **Property Get** *name* [(*arglist*)][**As** *type*]
	    [*statements*]
	    [*name* = *expression*]
	    [**Exit Property**]
	    [*statements*]
	    [*name* = *expression*]
	End Property

Elements	The **Property Get** statement syntax has these parts:

Part	Description
Public	Indicates that the **Property Get** procedure is accessible to all other procedures in all modules. If used in a private module (one that contains an **Option Private** statement) the procedure is not available outside the project.
Private	Indicates that the **Property Get** procedure is accessible only to other procedures in the module where it is declared.
Static	Indicates that the **Property Get** procedure's local variables are preserved between calls. The **Static** attribute doesn't affect variables that are declared outside the **Property Get** procedure, even if they are used in the procedure.
name	Name of the **Property Get** procedure; follows standard variable naming conventions, except that the name can be the same as a **Property Let** or **Property Set** procedure in the same module.
arglist	List of variables representing arguments that are passed to the **Property Get** procedure when it is called. Multiple variables are separated by commas.
type	Data type of the value returned by the **Property Get** procedure; may be **Boolean**, **Integer**, **Long**, **Currency**, **Single**, **Double**, **Date**, **String** (except fixed length), **Object**, or **Variant**. Arrays of any type can't be returned, but a **Variant** containing an array can.
statements	Any group of statements to be executed within the body of the **Property Get** procedure.
expression	Value of the property returned by the procedure defined by the **Property Get** statement.

The *arglist* argument has the following syntax and parts:

[Optional][ByVal | ByRef] *varname*[( )]**[As** *type*]

Part	Description
Optional	Indicates that an argument is not required. If used, all subsequent arguments in *arglist* must also be optional and declared using the **Optional** keyword. All **Optional** arguments must be **Variant**.
ByVal	Indicates that the argument is passed by value.
ByRef	Indicates that the argument is passed by reference.
varname	Name of the variable representing the argument; follows standard variable naming conventions.
type	Data type of the argument passed to the **Property Get** procedure; may be **Boolean**, **Integer**, **Long**, **Currency**, **Single**, **Double**, **Date**, **String** (variable length only), **Object**, **Variant**, a user-defined type, or an object type.

Remarks

If not explicitly specified using either **Public** or **Private**, **Property** procedures are **Public** by default. If **Static** is not used, the value of local variables is not preserved between calls.

All executable code must be in procedures. You can't define a **Property Get** procedure inside another **Sub**, **Function**, or **Property** procedure.

The **Exit Property** keywords cause an immediate exit from a **Property Get** procedure. Program execution continues with the statement following the statement that called the **Property Get** procedure. Any number of **Exit Property** statements can appear anywhere in a **Property Get** procedure.

Like a **Sub** and **Property Let** procedure, a **Property Get** procedure is a separate procedure that can take arguments, perform a series of statements, and change the values of its arguments. However, unlike a **Sub** or **Property Let** procedure, a **Property Get** procedure can be used on the right-hand side of an expression in the same way you use a **Function** or a property name when you want to return the value of a property.

See Also

Function Statement, **Property Let** Statement, **Property Set** Statement, **Sub** Statement.

Example

This example uses the **Property Get** Statement to define a property procedure that gets the value of a property that identifies, as a string, the current color of a pen in a drawing package:

```
Dim CurrentColor As Integer
Const BLACK = 0, RED = 1, GREEN = 2, BLUE = 3

' Returns the current color of the pen as a string
Property Get PenColor() As String
    Select Case CurrentColor
        Case RED
            PenColor = "Red"
        Case GREEN
            PenColor = "Green"
        Case BLUE
            PenColor = "Blue"
    End Select
End Property


' The following line gets the color of the pen
' calling the Property Get procedure.
ColorName = PenColor()
```

Property Let Statement

Description   Declares the name, arguments, and code that form the body of a **Property Let** procedure, which assigns a value to a property.

Syntax   [**Public** | **Private**][**Static**] **Property Let** *name* [(*arglist*)]
    [*statements*]
    [**Exit Property**]
    [*statements*]
End Property

Elements   The **Property Let** statement syntax has these parts:

Part	Description
Public	Indicates that the **Property Let** procedure is accessible to all other procedures in all modules. If used in a private module (one that contains an **Option Private** statement), the procedure is not available outside the project.
Private	Indicates that the **Property Let** procedure is accessible only to other procedures in the module where it is declared.
Static	Indicates that the **Property Let** procedure's local variables are preserved between calls. The **Static** attribute doesn't affect variables that are declared outside the **Property Let** procedure, even if they are used in the procedure.
name	Name of the **Property Let** procedure; follows standard variable naming conventions, except that the name can be the same as a **Property Get** or **Property Set** procedure in the same module.
arglist	List of variables representing arguments that are passed to the **Property Let** procedure when it is called. Multiple variables are separated by commas. The last argument is the value assigned to the property on the right-hand side of an expression.
statements	Any group of statements to be executed within the body of the **Property Let** procedure.

The *arglist* argument has the following syntax and parts:

[**ByVal** | **ByRef**] *varname*[( )][**As** *type*]

Part	Description
ByVal	Indicates that the argument is passed by value.
ByRef	Indicates that the argument is passed by reference.
varname	Name of the variable representing the argument; follows standard variable naming conventions.
type	Data type of the argument passed to the **Property Let** procedure; may be **Boolean, Integer, Long, Currency, Single, Double, Date, String** (variable length only), **Object, Variant**, a user-defined type, or an object type.

Note Every Property Let statement must define at least one argument for the procedure it defines. That argument (or the last argument if there is more than one) will contain the actual value to be assigned to the property when the procedure defined by the Property Let statement is invoked.

Remarks

If not explicitly specified using either **Public** or **Private**, **Property** procedures are **Public** by default. If **Static** is not used, the value of local variables is not preserved between calls.

All executable code must be in procedures. You can't define a **Property Let** procedure inside another **Sub**, **Function**, or **Property** procedure.

The **Exit Property** keywords cause an immediate exit from a **Property Let** procedure. Program execution continues with the statement following the statement that called the **Property Let** procedure. Any number of **Exit Property** statements can appear anywhere in a **Property Let** procedure.

Like a **Function** and **Property Get** procedure, a **Property Let** procedure is a separate procedure that can take arguments, perform a series of statements, and change the value of its arguments. However, unlike a **Function** and **Property Get** procedure, both of which return a value, a **Property Let** procedure can only be used on the left side of a property assignment expression or **Let** statement.

See Also

Function Statement, **Let** Statement, **Property Get** Statement, **Property Set** Statement, **Sub** Statement.

Example

This example uses the **Property Let** statement to define a procedure that assigns a value to a property that identifies the pen color for a drawing package.

```
      Dim CurrentColor As Integer
Const BLACK = 0, RED = 1, GREEN = 2, BLUE = 3

' Sets the pen color property for a Drawing package.
' The module level variable 'CurrentColor' is set to
' a numeric value that identifies the color used for drawing.
Property Let PenColor(ColorName as String)
    Select Case ColorName        ' Check color name string.
        Case "Red"
            CurrentColor = RED   ' Assign value for Red.
        Case "Green"
            CurrentColor = GREEN ' Assign value for Green.
        Case "Blue"
            CurrentColor = BLUE  ' Assign value for Blue.
        Case Else
            CurrentColor = BLACK ' Assign default value.
    End Select
End Property

' The following line sets the PenColor property for a drawing package
' by calling the Property Let procedure.

PenColor() = "Red"
```

Property Set Statement

Description

Declares the name, arguments, and code that form the body of a **Property** procedure, which sets a reference to an object.

Syntax

[Public | Private][Static] Property Set *name* [(*arglist*)]

> [*statements*]
> **[Exit Property]**
> [*statements*]
> **End Property**

Elements

The **Property Set** statement syntax has these parts:

Part	Description
Public	Indicates that the **Property Set** procedure is accessible to all other procedures in all modules. If used in a private module (one that contains an **Option Private** statement), the procedure is not available outside the project.
Private	Indicates that the **Property Set** procedure is accessible only to other procedures in the module where it is declared.

Part	Description
Static	Indicates that the **Property Set** procedure's local variables are preserved between calls. The **Static** attribute doesn't affect variables that are declared outside the **Property Set** procedure, even if they are used in the procedure.
name	Name of the **Property Set** procedure; follows standard variable naming conventions, except that the name can be the same as a **Property Get** or **Property Let** procedure in the same module.
arglist	List of variables representing arguments that are passed to the **Property Set** procedure when it is called. Multiple variables are separated by commas. The last argument is the object reference used on the right-hand side of an object reference assignment.
statements	Any group of statements to be executed within the body of the **Property** procedure.

The *arglist* argument has the following syntax and parts:

[**ByVal** | **ByRef**] *varname*[( )][**As** *type*]

Part	Description
ByVal	Indicates that the argument is passed by value.
ByRef	Indicates that the argument is passed by reference.
varname	Name of the variable representing the argument; follows standard variable naming conventions.
type	Data type of the argument passed to the **Property Set** procedure; may be **Boolean**, **Integer**, **Long**, **Currency**, **Single**, **Double**, **Date**, **String** (variable length only), **Object**, **Variant**, a user-defined type, or an object type.

Note Every Property Set statement must define at least one argument for the procedure it defines. That argument (or the last argument if there is more than one) will contain the actual object reference for the property when the procedure defined by the Property Set statement is invoked.

Remarks

If not explicitly specified using either **Public** or **Private**, **Property** procedures are **Public** by default. If **Static** is not used, the value of local variables is not preserved between calls.

All executable code must be in procedures. You can't define a **Property Set** procedure inside another **Sub**, **Function**, or **Property** procedure.

The **Exit Property** keywords cause an immediate exit from a **Property Set** procedure. Program execution continues with the statement following the statement that called the **Property Set** procedure. Any number of **Exit Property** statements can appear anywhere in a **Property Set** procedure.

Like a **Function** and **Property Get** procedure, a **Property Set** procedure is a separate procedure that can take arguments, perform a series of statements, and change the value of its arguments. However, unlike a **Function** and **Property Get** procedure, both of which return a value, a **Property Set** procedure can only be used on the left side of an object reference assignment (**Set** statement).

See Also   **Function** Statement, **Property Get** Statement, **Property Let** Statement, **Sub** Statement.

Example   This example uses the **Property Set** statement to declare a property procedure which sets a reference to an object.

```
' The Pen property may be set to different Pen implementations.
Property Set Pen(P As Object)
    Set CurrentPen = P   ' Assign Pen to object.
End Property
```

Public Statement

Description   Used at module level to declare public variables and allocate storage space.

Syntax   **Public** *varname*[([*subscripts*])][**As** *type*][,*varname*[([*subscripts*])][**As** *type*]] . . .

Elements   The **Public** statement syntax has these parts:

Part	Description
varname	Name of the variable; follows standard variable naming conventions.
subscripts	Dimensions of an array variable; up to 60 multiple dimensions may be declared. The argument *subscripts* uses the following syntax:
	[*lower* **To**] *upper* [,[*lower* **To**] *upper*] . . .
type	Data type of the variable; may be **Boolean**, **Integer**, **Long**, **Currency**, **Single**, **Double**, **Date**, **String** (for variable-length strings), **String** * *length* (for fixed-length strings), **Object**, **Variant**, a user-defined type, or an object type. Use a separate **As** *type* clause for each variable being defined.

Remarks

Variables declared using the **Public** statement are available to all procedures in all modules in all applications unless **Option Private Module** is in effect; in which case, the variables are **Public** only within the project in which they reside.

Use the **Public** statement to declare the data type or object type of a variable. For example, the following statement declares a variable as an **Integer**:

```
Public NumberOfEmployees As Integer
```

If you do not specify a data type or object type and there is no **Def***type* statement in the module, the variable is **Variant** by default.

When variables are initialized, a numeric variable is initialized to 0, a variable-length string is initialized to a zero-length string, and a fixed-length string is filled with zeros. **Variant** variables are initialized to **Empty**. Each element of a user-defined type variable is initialized as if it was a separate variable. A variable that refers to an object must be assigned an existing object using the **Set** statement before it can be used. Until it is assigned an object, the declared object variable has the special value **Nothing**, which indicates that it does not refer to any particular instance of an object.

You can also use the **Public** statement with empty parentheses to declare dynamic arrays. After declaring a dynamic array, use the **ReDim** statement within a procedure to define the number of dimensions and elements in the array. If you try to redeclare a dimension for an array variable whose size was explicitly specified in a **Private**, **Public** or **Dim** statement, an error occurs.

See Also

Array Function, **Const** Statement, **Dim** Statement, **Option Base** Statement, **Option Private** Statement, **Private** Statement, **ReDim** Statement, **Static** Statement, **Type** Statement.

Example

The **Public** statement is used at the module-level to declare variables as public; that is, they are available to all procedures in all modules in all applications unless **Option Private Module** is in effect.

```
Public Number As Integer              ' Public integer variable.
Public NameArray(1 To 5) As String    ' Public array variable.
Public MyVar, YourVar, ThisVar As Integer  ' Multiple declarations.
```

PublisherOptions Method

Applies To   **Application** Object.

Description   Sets options for publishers.

Syntax   [*object.*]**PublisherOptions** *Name, View, IsTask, UniqueID, Field, OnSave,*
Action

Elements   The **PublisherOptions** method has the following object qualifier and named
arguments:

Part	Description
object	An object expression that evaluates to an object in the Applies To list. Optional.
Name	The file name of the edition to be created. If omitted, the user must specify **IsTask**, **UniqueID**, and **Field** parameters.. Optional.
View	A string expression that refers to the view to be published.
IsTask	A Boolean expression that returns a value indicating whether an expression references a task. By default, *IsTask* = **TRUE**. Optional.
UniqueID	A list of the unique IDs of the tasks or resources to be published. The list is separated by the list separator character. Optional.
Field	The field name or MPX field number that is to be published. Required.
OnSave	A constant that specifies whether to save automatically or manually. Optional.
Action	A constant that specifies whether to cancel or send the publisher. Optional.

The *OnSave* argument has these settings:

pjAutomaticUpdate	4	Updates automatically.
pjManualUpdate	5	Updates manually.

The *Action* argument has these settings:

pjCancel	1	Cancels the publisher.
pjSendPublisher	2	Sends the publisher.

Remarks	This method applies to Microsoft Project for the Macintosh.
See Also	**CreatePublisher** Method, **EditionStopAll** Method, **SubscriberOptions** Method.

Put Statement

Description	Writes from a variable to a disk file.
Syntax	**Put** [#]*filenumber*,[*recnumber*],*varname*
Elements	The **Put** statement syntax has these parts:

Part	Description
filenumber	Any valid file number.
recnumber	Record number (**Random** mode files) or byte number (**Binary** mode files) at which writing begins.
varname	Name of variable containing data to be written to disk.

Remarks

The first record/byte in a file is at position 1, the second record/byte is at position 2, and so on. If you omit *recnumber*, the next record or byte (the one after the last **Get** or **Put** statement or the one pointed to by the last **Seek** function) is written. You must include delimiting commas, for example:

```
Put #4,,FileBuffer
```

For files opened in **Random** mode, the following rules apply:

- If the length of the data being written is less than the length specified in the **Len** clause of the **Open** statement, **Put** still writes subsequent records on record-length boundaries. The space between the end of one record and the beginning of the next record is padded with the existing contents of the file buffer. Because the amount of padding data can't be determined with any certainty, it is generally a good idea to have the record length match the length of the data being written.

- If the variable being written is a variable-length string, **Put** writes a 2-byte descriptor containing the string length and then the variable. The record length specified by the **Len** clause in the **Open** statement must be at least 2 bytes greater than the actual length of the string.

- If the variable being written is a **Variant** of a numeric type, **Put** writes 2 bytes identifying the **VarType** of the **Variant** and then the variable. For example, when writing a **Variant** of **VarType** 3, **Put** writes 6 bytes: 2 bytes identifying the **Variant** as **VarType** 3 (**Long**) and 4 bytes containing the **Long** data. The record length specified by the **Len** clause in the **Open** statement must be at least 2 bytes greater than the actual number of bytes required to store the variable.

- If the variable being written is a **String Variant** (**VarType** 8), **Put** writes 2 bytes identifying the **VarType**, 2 bytes indicating the length of the string, and then the string data. The record length specified by the **Len** clause in the **Open** statement must be at least 4 bytes greater than the actual length of the string.

- If the variable being written is any other type of variable (not a variable-length string and not a **Variant**), **Put** writes only the variable data. The record length specified by the **Len** clause in the **Open** statement must be greater than or equal to the length of the data being written.

- **Put** writes elements of user-defined types as if each were written individually, except there is no padding between elements. The record length specified by the **Len** clause in the **Open** statement must be greater than or equal to the sum of all the bytes required to write the individual elements.

For files opened in **Binary** mode, all of the **Random** rules apply except that:

- The **Len** clause in the **Open** statement has no effect. **Put** writes all variables to disk contiguously; that is, with no padding between records.

- **Put** writes variable-length strings that are not elements of user-defined types without the 2-byte length descriptor. The number of bytes written equals the number of characters in the string. For example, the following statements write 10 bytes to file number 1:

```
VarString$ = String$(10," ")
Put #1,,VarString$
```

See Also

Get Statement, **Open** Statement, **VarType** Function.

Example

This example uses the **Put** statement to write data to a disk file. Five records of the user-defined type Record are written to the file.

```
                       ' Define user-defined type.
                   Type Record
                       ID As Integer
                       Name As String * 20
                   End Type

                   Dim MyRecord As Record                   ' Declare variable.
                   ' Open file for random access.
                   Open "TESTFILE" For Random As #1 Len = Len(MyRecord)
                   For RecordNumber = 1 To 5                 ' Loop 5 times.
                       MyRecord.ID = RecordNumber            ' Define ID.
                       MyRecord.Name = "My Name" & RecordNumber ' Create a string.
                       Put #1, RecordNumber, MyRecord        ' Write record to file.
                   Next RecordNumber
                   Close #1                                  ' Close file.
```

Quit Method

Applies To   **Application** Object.

Description   Closes Microsoft Project.

Syntax   [*object.*]**Quit** [*saveChanges*]

Elements   The **Quit** method has the following object qualifier and named arguments:

Part	Description
object	An object expression that evaluates to an object in the Applies To list.
saveChanges	A constant that specifies whether to save changes to open project files before quitting Microsoft Project. If you omit the *saveChanges* argument, Microsoft Project prompts the user to save new project files and files that have changed since the last time they were saved.

The *saveChanges* argument has these settings:

pjDoNotSave	0	Changes to open files are not saved.
pjSave	1	Changes to open files are saved.
pjPromptSave	2	The user is prompted to save changes to each open file.

See Also   **FileNew** Method, **FileOpen** Method, **FileSave** Method, **FileSaveAs** Method.

Example   The following example saves all open projects and then quits Microsoft Project.

```
Sub SaveChangesAndQuit()
    Quit SaveChanges := pjSave
End Sub
```

Randomize Statement

Description	Initializes the random-number generator.
Syntax	**Randomize** [*number*]
Elements	The *number* named argument can be any valid numeric expression.
Remarks	**Randomize** uses *number* to initialize a random-number generator, giving it a new seed value. If you omit *number,* the value returned by the **Timer** function is used as the new seed value.
	If **Randomize** is not used, the same initial seed is always used to start the sequence.
	Use the **Randomize** statement without an argument to provide a random seed based on the system timer to initialize the random-number generator before **Rnd** is called.
See Also	**Rnd** Function, **Timer** Function.
Example	This example uses the **Randomize** statement to initialize the random-number generator. Because the number argument has been omitted, **Randomize** uses the return value from the **Timer** function as the new seed value.

```
' Initialize random-number generator.
Randomize
' Generate random value between 1 and 6.
MyAngle = Int((6 * Rnd) + 1)
```

ReadOnly Property

Applies To	**Project** Object, **Projects** Collection.
Description	Returns whether a project has read-only or read-write access.
Syntax	*object*.**ReadOnly**

Elements   The *object* placeholder is an object expression that evaluates to an object in the Applies To list.

Settings   The **ReadOnly** property has these settings:

Setting	Description
True	The project has read-only access.
False	The project has read-write access.

See Also   **CreationDate** Property, **FullName** Property, **HasPassword** Property, **LastSaveDate** Property, **LastSavedBy** Property, **Name** Property, **Path** Property, **ReadOnlyRecommended** Property, **RevisionNumber** Property, **Saved** Property, **WriteReserved** Property.

Example

The following example copies projects with read-only access into new files with read-write access.

```
Sub CopyReadOnlyFiles()
    Dim P             ' Project object used in loop
    Dim OldName       ' Name of project
    Dim Path          ' File path to project
    Dim NewName       ' New name of project

    ' Check each open project for Read only access.
    For Each P in Application.Projects

        If P.ReadOnly Then      ' If project has Read only access then
            OldName = P.Name    ' Store its name.
            Path = P.Path       ' Store its path.

            ' Create a new name for file.
            NewName = Left(OldName, Len(OldName) - 4) & ".MRW"
            ' Activate the project.
            P.Activate
            ' Save the project under the new name.
            FileSaveAs Path & PathSeparator & NewName
        End If
    Next P
End Sub
```

ReadOnlyRecommended Property

Applies To	**Project** Object, **Projects** Collection.
Description	Returns a value that specifies whether or not a project should be opened with read-only access.
Syntax	*object*.**ReadOnlyRecommended**
Elements	The *object* placeholder is an object expression that evaluates to an object in the Applies To list.
Settings	The **ReadOnlyRecommended** property has these settings:

Setting	Description
True	The project should be opened with read-only access.
False	The project has no recommended access type.

Remarks	To assign a new value to the **ReadOnlyRecommended** property, use the **FileSaveAs** method.
See Also	**CreationDate** Property, **FullName** Property, **HasPassword** Property, **LastSaveDate** Property, **LastSavedBy** Property, **Name** Property, **Path** Property, **ReadOnly** Property, **RevisionNumber** Property, **Saved** Property, **WriteReserved** Property.
Example	The following example displays the recommend access type for the active project.

```
Sub DisplayAccessType()

    If ActiveProject.ReadOnlyRecommended Then
            MsgBox "Read-only access is recommended for this project."
        Else
            MsgBox "Read-write access is allowed for this project."
        End If

End Sub
```

RecurringTaskInsert Method

Applies To	**Application** Object.
Description	Displays the Recurring Task Information dialog box, which prompts the user to insert a recurring task.
Syntax	[*object.*]**RecurringTaskInsert**
Elements	The *object* placeholder is an object expression that evaluates to an object in the Applies To list.
See Also	**InformationDialog** Method.

ReDim Statement

Description	Used at the procedure level to declare dynamic-array variables and allocate or reallocate storage space.
Syntax	**ReDim** [**Preserve**] *varname*(*subscripts*) [**As** *type*][,*varname*(*subscripts*) [**As** *type*]] . . .
Elements	The **ReDim** statement syntax has these parts:

Part	Description
Preserve	Preserves the data in an existing array when you change the size of the last dimension.
varname	Name of the variable; follows standard variable naming conventions.
subscripts	Dimensions of an array variable; up to 60 multiple dimensions may be declared. The *subscripts* argument uses the following syntax: [*lower* **To**] *upper* [,[*lower* **To**] *upper*] . . .
type	Data type of the variable; may be **Boolean**, **Integer**, **Long**, **Currency**, **Single**, **Double**, **Date**, **String** (for variable-length strings), **String** * *length* (for fixed-length strings), **Object**, **Variant**, a user-defined type, or an object type. Use a separate **As** *type* clause for each variable being defined. For a **Variant** containing an array, *type* describes the type of each element of the array, but does not change the **Variant** to some other type.

Remarks   The R...

RemainingCost Property

Applies To   **Assignment** Object, **Assignments** Collection; **Project** Object, **Projects** Collection; **Resource** Object, **Resources** Collection; **Task** Object, **Tasks** Collection.

Description   Returns or sets the remaining cost for an assignment, project, resource, or task. Read only for **Project** or **Resource**, and **Task** objects with one or more resources.

Syntax   *object*.**RemainingCost** [= *value*]

Elements   The **RemainingCost** property syntax has these parts:

Part	Description
object	An object expression that evaluates to an object in the Applies To list.
value	A numeric expression of the remaining cost for the project, resource, or task.

See Also   **ActualCost** Property, **BaselineCost** Property, **Cost** Property, **CostVariance** Property, **RemainingDuration** Property, **RemainingWork** Property.

RemainingDuration Property

Applies To   **Project** Object, **Projects** Collection; **Task** Object, **Tasks** Collection.

Description   Returns or sets the remaining duration (in minutes) of a project or task. Read only for **Project** object.

Syntax   *object*.**RemainingDuration** [= *value*]

Elements   The **RemainingDuration** property syntax has these parts:

Part	Description
object	An object expression that evaluates to an object in the ...
value	A numeric expression of the remaining duration of ... minutes.

See Also   **ActualDuration** Property, **BaselineDuration** Property, **Duration** Property, **DurationVariance** Property, **RemainingCost** Property, **RemainingWork** Property.

RemainingWork Property

Applies To   **Assignment** Object, **Assignments** Collection; **Project** Object, **Projects** Collection; **Resource** Object, **Resources** Collection; **Task** Object, **Tasks** Collection.

Description   Returns or sets the remaining work (in minutes) for an assignment, project, resource, or task. Read only for **Project** or **Resource**, and **Task** objects with one or more resources.

Syntax   *object*.**RemainingWork** [= *value*]

Elements   The **RemainingWork** property syntax has these parts:

Part	Description
object	An object expression that evaluates to an object in the Applies To list.
value	A numeric expression of the remaining work for the assignment, resource, or task, in minutes.

See Also   **ActualWork** Property, **BaselineWork** Property, **RemainingCost** Property, **RemainingDuration** Property, **Work** Property, **WorkVariance** Property.

ReportList Method

Applies To   **Project** Object, **Projects** Collection.

Description   Returns a report name or all report names.

Syntax   *object*.**ReportList**[(*index*)]

Elements   The **ReportList** method syntax has the following object qualifier and named arguments:

Part	Description
object	An object expression that evaluates to an object in the Applies To list.
index	A numeric expression that specifies the index of the *object*.

See Also   List Object, **ReportPrint** Method, **ReportPrintPreview** Method, **Reports**
Method, **ResourceViewList** Method, **TaskViewList** Method, **ViewList** Method.

Example   The following example lists all the reports.

```
Sub SeeAllReports()
    Dim t As Variant
    For Each t In ActiveProject.ReportList
        MsgBox t
    Next t
End Sub
```

ReportPrint Method

Applies To   **Application** Object.

Description   Prints a report.

Syntax   [*object.*]**ReportPrint** *name*[, *fromPage*, *toPage*, *pageBreaks*, *draft*, *copies*,
fromDate, *toDate*, *preview*, *color*]

Elements   The **ReportPrint** method syntax has the following object qualifier and named
arguments:

Part	Description
object	An object expression that evaluates to an object in the Applies To list. Optional.
name	A string expression that specifies the name of the report to print. Required.
fromPage	A numeric expression that specifies the first page to print. Optional.
toPage	A numeric expression that specifies the last page to print. Optional.
pageBreaks	A Boolean expression that specifies whether to use manual page breaks. By default, the *pageBreaks* argument is **True**. Optional.
draft	A Boolean expression that specifies whether to print the report in draft mode. By default, the *draft* argument is **False**. Optional. This parameter applies to Microsoft Project for Microsoft Windows.
copies	A numeric expression that specifies the number of copies to print. By default, the *copies* argument is 1. Optional.

Part	Description
fromDate	A date expression that specifies the first date of the report to print. By default, the *fromDate* argument equals the start date of the project. Optional.
toDate	A date expression that specifies the last date of the report to print. By default, the *toDate* argument equals the finish date of the project. Optional.
preview	A Boolean expression that specifies whether to show an onscreen preview of the printed report. By default, the *preview* argument is **False**. Optional.
color	A Boolean expression that specifies whether the report is to be printed in color. Optional.

See Also   **ReportPrintPreview** Method, **Reports** Method.

Example   The following example creates a consolidated project, prints a report, and closes the consolidated project without saving it.

```
Sub ConsolidatedReport()
    ConsolidateProjects filenames:="project1.mpp,project2.mpp"
    ReportPrint name:="Project Summary"
    FileClose save:=pjDoNotSave
End Sub
```

ReportPrintPreview Method

Applies To   **Application** Object.

Description   Shows an onscreen preview of a printed report.

Syntax   [*object*.]**ReportPrintPreview** *name*

Elements   The **ReportPrintPreview** method syntax has the following object qualifier and named arguments:

Part	Description
object	An object expression that evaluates to an object in the Applies To list. Optional.
name	A string expression that specifies the name of a report for which to show an onscreen preview. Required.

See Also   **ReportPrint** Method, **Reports** Method.

Reports Method

Applies To   **Application** Object.

Description   Displays the Reports dialog box, which prompts the user to manage reports.

Syntax   [*object*.]**Reports**

Elements   The *object* placeholder is an object expression that evaluates to an object in the
                    Applies To list.

See Also   **ReportPrint** Method, **ReportPrintPreview** Method.

Reset Method

Applies To   **Application** Object.

Description   Resets a base calendar.

Syntax   [*object*.]**BaseCalendarReset** *name*

Elements   The **BaseCalendarReset** method syntax has the following object qualifier and
                    named arguments:

Part	Description
object	An object expression that evaluates to an object in the Applies To list. Optional.
name	A string expression that specifies the name of the base calendar to reset. Required.

Remarks   Base calendars have the following default characteristics:

- Monday through Friday are working days with two shifts (8 A.M. to 12 P.M. and 1 P.M. to 5 P.M.).

- Saturday and Sunday are nonworking days.

See Also   **BaseCalendarCreate** Method, **BaseCalendarDelete** Method,
                    BaseCalendarEditDays Method, **BaseCalendarRename** Method,
                    BaseCalendars Method, **ResourceCalendars** Method.

Example   The following example resets the Standard base calendar to the default settings.

```
Sub RestoreBaseCalendar()
   BaseCalendarReset name:="Standard"
End Sub
```

Reset Statement

Description Closes all disk files opened using the **Open** statement.

Syntax **Reset**

Remarks The **Reset** statement syntax closes all active files opened by the **Open** statement and writes the contents of all file buffers to disk.

See Also **Close** Statement, **End** Statement, **Open** Statement.

Example This example uses the **Reset** statement to close all open files and write the contents of all file buffers to disk.

```
For FileNumber = 1 To 5                    ' Loop 5 times.
    ' Open file for output.
    Open "TEST" & FileNumber For Output As #FileNumber
    Write #FileNumber, "Hello World"    ' Write data to file.
Next FileNumber
Reset    ' Close files and write contents to disk.
```

Resource Object, Resources Collection

Description A resource or the resources for a project or task.

Remarks In Microsoft Project, **Resource** objects are parents of **Assignments** collections and **Calendar** objects.

Properties **AccrueAt** Property, **ActualCost** Property, **ActualWork** Property, **Application** Property, **BaseCalendar** Property, **BaselineCost** Property, **BaselineWork** Property, **Calendar** Property, **Code** Property, **Cost** Property, **CostPerUse** Property, **CostVariance** Property, **Count** Property, **EMailAddress** Property, **Group** Property, **ID** Property, **Index** Property, **Initials** Property, **LinkedFields** Property, **MaxUnits** Property, **Name** Property, **Notes** Property, **Objects** Property, **Overallocated** Property, **OvertimeRate** Property, **OvertimeWork** Property, **Parent** Property, **PeakUnits** Property, **PercentWorkComplete** Property,

RemainingCost Property, RemainingWork Property, StandardRate Property, Textn Properties, UniqueID Property, Work Property, WorkVariance Property.

| Methods | Add Method, Assignments Method, Delete Method, GetField Method, Level Method, SetField Method, UniqueID Method. |

| See Also | Assignment Object, Assignments Collection; Calendar Object, Calendars Collection; Project Object, Projects Collection; Resource Property; Resources Method; Task Object, Tasks Collection. |

Resource Property

| Applies To | Cell Object. |

| Description | Returns a resource in the active cell. |

| Syntax | *object*.Resource |

| Elements | The *object* placeholder is an object expression that evaluates to an object in the Applies To list. |

| See Also | ActiveCell Property; ActiveSelection Property; Resource Object, Resources Collection; Task Property. |

ResourceAddressBook Method

| Applies To | Application Object. |

| Description | Displays the address book from mail to allow the user to select resources for the project. |

| Syntax | [*object*.]ResourceAddressBook |

| Elements | The *object* placeholder is an object expression that evaluates to an object in the Applies To list |

| Remarks | Available only in Resource views or from the Resource Assignment dialog. |

| See Also | MailProjectMailCustomize Method, MailRoutingSlip Method, MailSendProjectMail Method, MailSystem Property, MailUpdateProject Method. |

ResourceAssignment Method

Applies To   **Application** Object.

Description   Assigns, removes, or replaces the resources of the selected tasks.

Syntax   [*object.*]**ResourceAssignment** [*resources, operation, with*]

Elements   The **ResourceAssignment** method syntax has the following object qualifier and
named arguments:

Part	Description
object	An object expression that evaluates to an object in the Applies To list. Optional.
resources	A string expression that specifies the names of the resources you want to assign, remove, or replace in the selected tasks. Optional.
operation	A constant that specifies the operation you want to perform on the resources you specify with the *resources* argument. If you omit the *operation* argument, Microsoft Project assigns the resources to the selected tasks. Optional.
with	A string expression that specifies the names of the resources that replace the resources of the selected tasks. Microsoft Project ignores the *with* argument unless you specify **pjReplace** for the *operation* argument.

The *operation* argument has these settings:

pjAssign	0	The resources you specify are assigned to the selected tasks.
pjRemove	1	The resources you specify are removed from the selected tasks.
pjReplace	2	The resources you specify in the *with* argument replace the resources specified in the *resources* argument.
pjChange	3	The resource units for the resource you specify are changed. This constant can be used only for a single resource.

See Also   **Add** Method, **Delete** Method.

Example   The following example prompts the user for the name of a resource, and then
assigns that resource to the selected tasks.

```
Sub AssignResourceToSelectedTasks()
    Dim Entry    ' The name of the resource to add to selected tasks
    Dim R        ' Resource object used in For Each...Next loop
    Dim Found    ' Whether or not the resource is in the active project

    ' Prompt the user for the name of a resource.
    Entry = InputBox("Enter the name of the resource you want" & _
            " to add to the selected tasks.")

    ' Assume resource doesn't exist in the active project.
    Found = False

    ' Look for the resource.
    For Each R in ActiveProject.Resources
        If Entry = R.Name Then Found = True
    Next R

    ' If the resource is found, then assign it to selected tasks.
    If Found Then
        ResourceAssignment Resources := Entry, Operation := PjAssign

    ' Otherwise tell user that resource doesn't exist.
    Else
        MsgBox("There is no resource in the active project named " & _
            Entry & ".")
    End If
End Sub
```

ResourceCalendarEditDays Method

Applies To   **Application** Object.

Description   Edits days in a resource calendar.

Syntax   [*object*.]**ResourceCalendarEditDays** *projectName*, *resourceName*[, *startDate*, *endDate*, *weekday*, *working*, *default*, *from1*, *to1*, *from2*, *to2*, *from3*, *to3*]

Elements   The **ResourceCalendarEditDays** method syntax has the following object qualifier and named arguments:

Part	Description
object	An object expression that evaluates to an object in the Applies To list. Optional.
projectName	A string expression that specifies the name of the project containing the resource calendar to edit. Required.
resourceName	A string expression that specifies the name of the resource to edit. Required.
startDate	A date expression that specifies the first date to edit. Optional.
endDate	A date expression that specifies the last date to edit. Optional.
weekday	A constant that specifies the weekday to edit. Optional.
working	A Boolean expression that specifies whether the days you specify are working days. Optional.
default	A Boolean expression that specifies whether the resource calendar uses the values in the corresponding base calendar as defaults. By default, the *default* argument is **False**. Optional.
from1	A string expression that specifies the start time of the first shift. Optional.
to1	A string expression that specifies the finish time of the first shift. Optional.
from2	A string expression that specifies the start time of the second shift. Optional.
to2	A string expression that specifies the finish time of the second shift. Optional.
from3	A string expression that specifies the start time of the third shift. Optional.
to3	A string expression that specifies the finish time of the third shift. Optional.

The *weekday* argument has these settings:

jSunday	1	Sunday
pjMonday	2	Monday
pjTuesday	3	Tuesday
pjWednesday	4	Wednesday
pjThursday	5	Thursday
pjFriday	6	Friday
pjSaturday	7	Saturday

See Also   **ResourceCalendarReset** Method, **ResourceCalendars** Method.

ResourceCalendarReset Method

Applies To   **Application** Object.

Description   Resets a resource calendar.

Syntax   [*object*.]**ResourceCalendarReset** *projectName*, *resourceName*[, *baseCalendar*]

Elements   The **ResourceCalendarReset** method syntax has the following object qualifier named arguments:

Part	Description
object	An object expression that evaluates to an object in the Applies To list. Optional.
projectName	A string expression that specifies the name of the project containing the resource calendar to reset. Required.
resourceName	A string expression that specifies the resource for the calendar to reset. Required.
baseCalendar	A string expression that specifies the base calendar on which to base the new settings of the resource calendar. Optional.

See Also   **ResourceCalendarEditDays** Method, **ResourceCalendars** Method.

ResourceCalendars Method

Applies To   **Application** Object.

Description   Displays the Change Working Time dialog box, which prompts the user to manage calendars.

Syntax   [*object*.]**ResourceCalendars**

Elements   The *object* placeholder is an object expression that evaluates to an object in the Applies To list.

See Also   **ResourceCalendarEditDays** Method, **ResourceCalendarReset** Method.

ResourceDetails Method

Applies To	**Application** Object.
Description	Displays the details fom the address book in mail on the selected or given resource.
Syntax	*object*.**ResourceDetails** [*name*]
Elements	The **ResourceDetails** method has the following object qualifier and named arguments:

Part	Description
object	An object expression that evaluates to an object in the Applies To list. Optional.
name	A string expression used to locate a resource in the address book. If the name is found, the properties dialog is displayed. If the name is not found, mail displays the check names dialog to allow the user to choose a vaild name from the address book. If a resource name is not given, the selected resource is used. Optional.

Remarks	Available only in Resource views, from the Resource Management toolbar, or from the Resource Information dialog.
See Also	**MailProjectMailCustomize** Method, **MailRoutingSlip** Method, **MailSendProjectMail** Method, **MailSystem** Property, **MailUpdateProject** Method.

ResourceFilterList Method

Applies To	**Project** Object, **Projects** Collection.
Description	Returns a resource filter name or all resource filter names.
Syntax	*object*.**ResourceFilterList**[(*index*)]
Elements	The **ResourceFilterList** method syntax has the following object qualifier and named arguments:

Part	Description
object	An object expression that evaluates to an object in the Applies To list.
index	A numeric expression that specifies the index of the *object*.

See Also   **CurrentFilter** Property, **FilterApply** Method, **FilterEdit** Method, **Filters** Method, **List** Object, **ReportList** Method, **ResourceTableList** Method, **ResourceViewList** Method, **TaskFilterList** Method, **ViewList** Method.

Example   The following example lists all the resource filters.

```
Sub SeeAllResFilters()
    Dim t As Variant
    For Each t In ActiveProject.ResourceFilterList
        MsgBox t
    Next t
End Sub
```

ResourceGraphBarStyles Method

Applies To   **Application** Object.

Description   Sets the styles of bars on the Resource Graph.

Syntax   [*object.*]**ResourceGraphBarStyles** [*topLeftShowAs, topLeftColor, topLeftPattern, bottomLeftShowAs, bottomLeftColor, bottomLeftPattern, topRightShowAs, topRightColor, topRightPattern, bottomRightShowAs, bottomRightColor, bottomRightPattern, showValues, showAvailabilityLine, percentBarOverlap*]

Elements   The **ResourceGraphBarStyles** method syntax has the following object qualifier and named arguments:

Part	Description
object	An object expression that evaluates to an object in the Applies To list. Optional.
topLeftShowAs	A constant that specifies the bar type for the category in the upper left corner of the Bar Styles dialog box. Optional.
topLeftColor	A constant that specifies the bar color for the category in the upper left corner of the Bar Styles dialog box. Optional.
topLeftPattern	A constant that specifies the bar pattern for the category in the upper left corner of the Bar Styles dialog box. Optional.

Part	Description
bottomLeftShowAs	A constant that specifies the bar type for the category in the lower left corner of the Bar Styles dialog box. Optional.
bottomLeftColor	A constant that specifies the bar color for the category in the lower left corner of the Bar Styles dialog box. Optional.
bottomLeftPattern	A constant that specifies the bar pattern for the category in the lower left corner of the Bar Styles dialog box. Optional.
topRightShowAs	A constant that specifies the bar style for the category in the upper right corner of the Bar Styles dialog box. Optional.
topRightColor	A constant that specifies the bar color for the category in the upper right corner of the Bar Styles dialog box. Optional.
topRightPattern	A constant that specifies the bar pattern for the category in the upper right corner of the Bar Styles dialog box. Optional.
bottomRightShowAs	A constant that specifies the bar style for the category in the lower right corner of the Bar Styles dialog box. Optional.
bottomRightColor	A constant that specifies the bar color for the category in the lower right corner of the Bar Styles dialog box. Optional.
bottomRightPattern	A constant that specifies the bar pattern for the category in the lower right corner of the Bar Styles dialog box. Optional.
showValues	A Boolean expression that specifies whether to display corresponding values below the displayed bars. Optional.
showAvailabilityLine	A Boolean expression that specifies whether to display a horizontal line where a resource reaches its maximum availability. Optional.
percentBarOverlap	A numeric expression from 0 to 100 that specifies the overlap percentage of displayed bars. Optional.

The *topLeftShowAs*, *bottomLeftShowAs*, *topRightShowAs*, and *bottomRightShowAs* arguments have these settings:

pjBar	0	Bar chart
pjArea	1	Area chart
pjStep	2	Step area chart
pjLine	3	Line chart
pjStepLine	4	Step line chart
pjDoNotShow	5	Invisible

The *topLeftColor*, *bottomLeftColor*, *topRightColor*, and *bottomRightColor* arguments have these settings:

pjBlack	0	Black
pjRed	1	Red
pjYellow	2	Yellow
pjLime	3	Lime
pjAqua	4	Aqua
pjBlue	5	Blue
pjFuchsia	6	Fuchsia
pjWhite	7	White
pjMaroon	8	Maroon
pjGreen	9	Green
pjOlive	10	Olive
pjNavy	11	Navy
pjPurple	12	Purple
pjTeal	13	Teal
pjGray	14	Gray
pjSilver	15	Silver

The *topLeftPattern*, *bottomLeftPattern*, *topRightPattern*, and *bottomRightPattern* arguments have these settings for nonline shapes:

pjHollow	0	Hollow
pjSolid	1	Solid
pjLightFill	2	Light fill
pjMediumFill	3	Medium fill
pjDarkFill	4	Dark fill
pjDiagonalLeft	5	Diagonal left
pjDiagonalRight	6	Diagonal right
pjDiagonalCross	7	Diagonal cross

pjLineVertical	8	Vertical line
pjLineHorizontal	9	Horizontal line
pjLineCross	10	Crossed line

The *topLeftPattern*, *bottomLeftPattern*, *topRightPattern*, and *bottomRightPattern* arguments have these settings for line shapes:

pjNone	0	None
pjContinuous	1	Continuous
pjGraphDash	2	Dash
pjDot	3	Dot
pjDashDot	4	Dash-dot
pjDashDotDot	5	Dash-dot-dot

See Also   **ViewShowAvailability** Method, **ViewShowCost** Method, **ViewShowCumulativeCost** Method, **ViewShowCumulativeWork** Method, **ViewShowNotes** Method, **ViewShowObjects** Method, **ViewShowOverallocation** Method, **ViewShowPeakUnits** Method, **ViewShowPercentAllocation** Method, **ViewShowPredecessorsSuccessors** Method, **ViewShowResourcesPredecessors** Method, **ViewShowResourcesSuccessors** Method, **ViewShowSchedule** Method, **ViewShowSelectedTasks** Method, **ViewShowWork** Method.

ResourceGroup Property

Applies To   **Project** Object, **Projects** Collection; **Task** Object, **Tasks** Collection.

Description   The names of groups associated with the resources for a task.

Syntax   *object*.**ResourceGroup**

Elements   The *object* placeholder is an object expression that evaluates to an object in the Applies To list.

Remarks   For example, if Bob's group is "Writers" and Greg's group is "Editors", and Greg and Bob are assigned to the same task, then the **ResourceGroup** property for that task returns "Writers,Editors".

Note   This example assumes that the list separator character is the comma (,). You can set the list separator character with the **ListSeparator** property.

See Also **Group** Property, **ResourceInitials** Property, **ResourceNames** Property, **ResourcePoolName** Property.

ResourceID Property

Applies To **Assignment** Object, **Assignments** Collection.

Description Returns the identification number of a resource in an assignment.

Syntax *object*.**ResourceID**

Elements The *object* placeholder is an object expression that evaluates to an object in the Applies To list.

See Also **ProjectID** Property, **ResourceName** Property, **TaskID** Property, **TaskName** Property.

ResourceInitials Property

Applies To **Task** Object, **Tasks** Collection.

Description Returns the initials of the resources assigned to a task.

Syntax *object*.**ResourceInitials**

Elements The *object* placeholder is an object expression that evaluates to an object in the Applies To list.

Remarks The **ResourceInitials** property returns "KI,TI,KD,AT,RS,BB" if the initials of the resources assigned to the task you specify are KI, TI, KD, AT, RS, and BB respectively.

Note This example assumes that the list separator character is the comma (,). You can determine the list separator character with the **ListSeparator** property.

See Also **ResourceGroup** Property, **ResourceID** Property, **ResourceNames** Property, **TaskID** Property.

ResourceName Property

Applies To	**Assignment** Object, **Assignments** Collection.
Description	Returns the name of the resource in an assignment.
Syntax	*object*.**ResourceName**
Elements	The *object* placeholder is an object expression that evaluates to an object in the Applies To list.
See Also	**ProjectID** Property, **ResourceID** Property, **TaskID** Property, **TaskName** Property.

ResourceNames Property

Applies To	**Project** Object, **Projects** Collection; **Task** Object, **Tasks** Collection.
Description	Returns the names of the resources assigned to a task.
Syntax	*object*.**ResourceNames**
Elements	The *object* placeholder is an object expression that evaluates to an object in the Applies To list.
Remarks	For a task with more than one resource, the **ResourceNames** property returns the names of the resources, separated by the list separator character.
	For example, the **ResourceNames** property returns "Tamara,Tanya" if the list separator character is the comma (,) and the task has two resources named Tamara and Tanya.
	In Microsoft Windows, the list separator character is specified in the Regional settings of the Microsoft Windows Control Panel.
See Also	**Predecessors** Property, **Successors** Property.

ResourcePoolName Property

Applies To	**Project** Object, **Projects** Collection.

Description	Returns the filename of the resource pool used by a project. Returns the name of the project if it is not using a resource pool.
Syntax	*object*.**ResourcePoolName**
Elements	The *object* placeholder is an object expression that evaluates to an object in the Applies To list.
See Also	**ResourceSharing** Method, **ResourceSharingPoolAction** Method.

Resources Method

Applies To	**Project** Object, **Projects** Collection; **Selection** Object; **Task** Object, **Tasks** Collection.
Description	Returns a resource or the resources in a project, selection, or task.
Syntax	*object*.**Resources**[(*index*)]
Elements	The **Resources** method syntax has the following object qualifier and named arguments:

Part	Description
object	An object expression that evaluates to an object in the Applies To list.
index	A numeric expression that specifies the index of the *object*.

See Also	**ActiveSelection** Property; **Assignment** Object, **Assignments** Collection; **Resource** Object, **Resources** Collection; **ResourceAssignment** Method.
Example	The following example displays the name of each resource assigned to the selected task in a message box.

```
Sub DisplayResourceNames()
    For Each r in ActiveCell.Task.Resources
        MsgBox r.Name
    Next r
End Sub
```

ResourceSharing Method

Applies To	**Application** Object.
Description	Controls resource sharing.
Syntax	[*object*.]**ResourceSharing** [*share*, *name*, *pool*]
Elements	The **ResourceSharing** method syntax has the following object qualifier and named arguments:

Part	Description
object	An object expression that evaluates to an object in the Applies To list. Optional.
share	A Boolean expression that specifies whether to share resources. Optional.
name	A string expression that specifies the filename of the resource pool. Optional.
pool	A Boolean expression that specifies whether resources in the pool take precedence over resources in the local project. Optional.

See Also	**ResourcePoolName** Property, **Resources** Method, **ResourceSharingPoolAction** Method.

ResourceSharingPoolAction Method

Applies To	**Application** Object.
Description	Performs actions on a resource pool.
Syntax	[*object*.]**ResourceSharingPoolAction** *action*[, *fileName*, *readOnly*]
Elements	The **ResourceSharingPoolAction** method syntax has the following object qualifier and named arguments:

Part	Description
object	An object expression that evaluates to an object in the Applies To list. Optional.
action	A constant that specifies the actions to perform on the resource pool. Required.
fileName	A string expression that specifies the filename of the resource pool on which to perform the action. Optional.
readOnly	A Boolean expression that specifies whether to open files with read-only access. Optional.

The *action* argument has these settings:

pjPoolTakesPrecedence	1	Causes the resource pool to take precedence over the sharers.
pjSharersTakePrecedence	2	Causes the sharers to take precedence over the resource pool.
pjOpenSharer	3	Opens the sharer (the file specified with the *fileName* argument).
pjOpenAllSharers	4	Opens all sharers into a consolidated project.
pjUnlinkSharer	5	Unlinks the sharer from the resource pool. (The sharer is specified with the *fileName* argument.)

See Also   **ResourcePoolName** Property, **ResourceSharing** Method.

ResourceTableList Method

Applies To   **Project** Object, **Projects** Collection.

Description   Returns a resource table name or all resource table names.

Syntax   *object*.**ResourceTableList**[(*index*)]

Elements   The **ResourceTableList** method syntax has the following object qualifier and named arguments:

Part	Description
object	An object expression that evaluates to an object in the Applies To list.
index	A numeric expression that specifies the index of the *object*.

See Also   **CurrentTable** Property, **List** Object, **ReportList** Method, **ResourceFilterList** Method, **ResourceViewList** Method, **TableApply** Method, **TableEdit** Method, **Tables** Method, **TaskTableList** Method, **ViewList** Method.

Example   The following example lists all the resource tables.

```
Sub SeeAllResTables()
    Dim t As Variant
    For Each t In ActiveProject.ResourceTableList
        MsgBox t
    Next t
End Sub
```

ResourceViewList Method

Applies To   **Project** Object, **Projects** Collection.

Description   Returns a resource view name or all resource view names.

Syntax   *object*.**ResourceViewList**[(*index*)]

Elements   The **ResourceViewList** method syntax has the following object qualifier and named arguments:

Part	Description
object	An object expression that evaluates to an object in the Applies To list.
index	A numeric expression that specifies the index of the *object*.

See Also   **CurrentView** Property, **List** Object, **ReportList** Method, **ResourceFilterList** Method, **ResourceTableList** Method, **TaskViewList** Method, **ViewApply** Method, **ViewEditCombination** Method, **ViewEditSingle** Method, **ViewList** Method, **Views** Method.

Example   The following example lists all the resource views.

```
Sub SeeAllResViews()
    Dim t As Variant
    For Each t In ActiveProject.ResourceViewList
        MsgBox t
    Next t
End Sub
```

Resume Property

Applies To   **Project** Object, **Projects** Collection; **Task** Object, **Tasks** Collection.

Description   Returns the date a project or task will resume.

Syntax   *object*.**Resume**

Elements   The *object* placeholder is an object expression that evaluates to an object in the Applies To list.

See Also   **ResumeNoEarlierThan** Property, **Stop** Property.

Resume Statement

Description   Resumes execution after an error-handling routine is finished.

Syntax   **Resume [0]**

Resume Next

Resume *line*

Elements   The **Resume** statement syntax can have any of the following forms:

Statement	Description
Resume [0]	If the error occurred in the same procedure as the error handler, execution resumes with the one that caused the error. If the error occurred in another procedure, execution resumes at the statement that last called out of the procedure containing the error-handling routine.
Resume Next	If the error occurred in the same procedure as the error handler, execution resumes with the statement immediately following the statement that caused the error. If the error occurred in another procedure, execution resumes with the statement immediately following the statement that last called out of the procedure containing the error-handling routine.
Resume *line*	Execution resumes at *line*, which is a line label or line number. The argument *line* must be in the same procedure as the error handler.

Remarks

If you use a **Resume** statement anywhere except in an error-handling routine, an error occurs.

When an error-handling routine is active and the end of the procedure (an **End Sub**, **End Function**, or **End Property** statement) is encountered before a **Resume** statement is encountered, an error occurs because a logical error is presumed to have been made inadvertently. However, if an **Exit Sub**, **Exit Function**, or **Exit Property** statement is encountered while an error handler is active, no error occurs because it is considered a deliberate redirection of execution.

See Also

On Error Statement.

Example

This example uses the **Resume** statement to end error handling in a procedure and resume execution with the statement that caused the error. Error number 55 is generated to illustrate its usage.

```
Sub ResumeStatementDemo()
    On Error GoTo ErrorHandler      ' Enable error-handling routine.
    Open "TESTFILE" For Output As #1 ' Open file for output.
    Kill "TESTFILE"                  ' Attempt to delete open file.
    Exit Sub                      ' Exit Sub before error handler.
ErrorHandler:                     ' Error-handling routine.
    Select Case Err                  ' Evaluate Error Number.
        Case 55                   ' "File already open" error.
            Close #1                 ' Close open file.
        Case Else

                                  ' Handle other situations here...

    End Select
    Resume                        ' Resume execution at same line
                                  ' that caused the error.
    End Sub
```

ResumeNoEarlierThan Property

Applies To	**Project** Object, **Projects** Collection; **Task** Object, **Tasks** Collection.
Description	Returns or sets the earliest date on which a task can resume.
Syntax	*object*.**ResumeNoEarlierThan** [= *value*]
Elements	The **ResumeNoEarlierThan** property syntax has the following parts:

Part	Description
object	An object expression that evaluates to an object in the Applies To list.
value	A date expression that specifies the earliest date the task can resume.

See Also	**Resume** Property, **Stop** Property.

RevisionNumber Property

Applies To	**Project** Object, **Projects** Collection.
Description	Returns the number of times a project has been saved.
Syntax	*object*.**RevisionNumber**
Elements	The *object* placeholder is an object expression that evaluates to an object in the Applies To list.
See Also	**CreationDate** Property, **LastSaveDate** Property, **LastSavedBy** Property, **Saved** Property.
Example	The following example displays the revision number for the active project.

```
Sub GetRevisionNumber()
    MsgBox ActiveProject.RevisionNumber
End Sub
```

RGB Function

Description   Returns a whole number representing an RGB color value.

Syntax   **RGB** (*red*, *green*, *blue*)

Elements   The **RGB** function syntax has these named-argument parts:

Part	Description
red	Whole number in the range 0 to 255, inclusive, that represents the red component of the color.
green	Whole number in the range 0 to 255, inclusive, that represents the green component of the color.
blue	Whole number in the range 0 to 255, inclusive, that represents the blue component of the color.

Remarks   Application methods and properties that accept a color specification expect that specification to be a whole number representing an RGB color value. An RGB color value specifies the relative intensity of red, green, and blue, which combined cause a specific color to be displayed.

The value for any argument to **RGB** that exceeds 255 is assumed to be 255.

The following table lists some standard colors and the red, green and blue values they include:

Black	0	0	0
Blue	0	0	255
Green	0	255	0
Cyan	0	255	255
Red	255	0	0
Magenta	255	0	255
Yellow	255	255	0
White	255	255	255

Note The RGB values returned by this function are incompatible with those used by the Macintosh operating system. They may be used within the context of Microsoft applications for the Macintosh, but should not be used when communicating color changes directly to the Macintosh operating system.

Example

This example shows how the **RGB** function is used to return a whole number representing an **RGB** color value. It is used for those application methods and properties that accept a color specification. The object MyObject and its property are used here for illustration purposes only.

```
Red = RGB(255, 0, 0)                ' Return the value for Red.
I = 75                             ' Initialize offset.
RGBValue = RGB(I, 64 + I, 128 + I)  ' Same as RGB(75, 139, 203).
MyObject.Color = RGB(255, 0, 0)     ' Set the Color property of
                                   ' MyObject to Red.
```

Right Function

Description

Returns a specified number of characters from the right side of a string.

Syntax

Right(*string,length*)

Elements

The **Right** function syntax has these named-argument parts:

Part	Description
string	String expression from which the rightmost characters are returned. If *string* contains no valid data, **Null** is returned.
length	Numeric expression indicating how many characters to return. If 0, a zero-length string is returned. If greater than or equal to the number of characters in *string*, the entire string is returned.

Remarks

To determine the number of characters in *string*, use the **Len** function.

Note   Another function (RightB) is provided for use with the double-byte character sets (DBCS) used in some Asian locales. Instead of specifying the number of characters to return, *length* specifies the number of bytes. In areas where DBCS is not used, RightB behaves the same as Right.

See Also

Left Function, **Len** Function, **Mid** Function.

Example

This example uses the **Right** function to return a specified number of characters from the right side of a string.

```
        AnyString = "Hello World"   ' Define string.
    MyStr = Right(AnyString, 1) ' Returns "d".
    MyStr = Right(AnyString, 6) ' Returns " World".
    MyStr = Right(AnyString, 20)' Returns "Hello World".
```

RmDir Statement

Description	Removes an existing directory or folder.
Syntax	**RmDir** *path*
Elements	The *path* named argument is a string expression that identifies the directory or folder to be removed—may include drive. If no drive is specified, **RmDir** removes the directory or folder on the current drive.
Remarks	An error occurs if you try to use **RmDir** on a directory or folder containing files. Use the **Kill** statement to delete all files before attempting to remove a directory or folder.
See Also	**ChDir** Statement, **CurDir** Function, **Kill** Statement, **MkDir** Statement.
Example	This example uses the **RmDir** statement to remove an existing directory or folder.

```
    ' Assume that MYDIR is an empty directory or folder.
    RmDir "MYDIR"    ' Remove MYDIR.
```

Rnd Function

Description	Returns a random number.
Syntax	**Rnd**[(*number*)]
Elements	The *number* named argument can be any valid numeric expression.
Remarks	The **Rnd** function returns a value less than 1 but greater than or equal to 0.
	The value of *number* determines how **Rnd** generates a random number:

If *number* is:	Rnd generates:
Less than zero	The same number every time, using *number* as the seed.
Greater than zero	The next random number in the sequence.
Equal to zero	The most recently generated number.
Not supplied	The next random number in the sequence.

For any given initial seed, the same number sequence is generated because each successive call to the **Rnd** function uses the previous number as a seed for the next number in the sequence.

Use the **Randomize** statement without an argument to provide a random seed based on the system timer to initialize the random-number generator before **Rnd** is called.

To produce random integers in a given range, use this formula:

```
Int((upperbound - lowerbound + 1) * Rnd + lowerbound)
```

Here, *upperbound* is the highest number in the range, and *lowerbound* is the lowest number in the range.

See Also   **Randomize** Statement, **Timer** Function.

Example   This example uses the **Rnd** function to generate a random integer value from 1 to 6.

```
MyValue = Int((6 * Rnd) + 1) ' Generate random value between 1 and 6.
```

Rollup Property

Applies To   **Project** Object, **Projects** Collection; **Task** Object, **Tasks** Collection.

Description   Returns or sets whether the dates of a subtask appear on its corresponding summary task bar.

Syntax   *object*.**Rollup** [= *value*]

Elements   The **Rollup** property syntax has these parts:

Part	Description
object	An object expression that evaluates to an object in the Applies To list.
value	A Boolean expression that specifies whether the dates of the task appear on its corresponding summary task bar, as shown under Settings.

Settings

The **Rollup** property has these settings:

Setting	Description
True	The dates of the task appear on its corresponding summary task bar.
False	The dates of the task do not appear on its corresponding summary task bar.

See Also

Marked Property, **Milestone** Property.

Example

The following example sets the Rollup property to **True** for milestone tasks, and **False** for other tasks in the active project.

```
Sub DisplayMilestonesInSummaryBars()
    Dim T    ' Task object used in For Each loop

    ' Cycle through tasks in active project.
    For Each T In ActiveProject.Tasks

        ' If task is a milestone, set its Rollup property to True.
        If T.Summary Or T.Milestone Then
            T.Rollup = True

        ' If task isn't a summary task or milestone, set
        ' its Rollup property to False.
        Else
            T.Rollup = False
        End If
    Next T
End Sub
```

RowClear Method

Applies To

Application Object.

Description

Clears the active row.

Syntax	[*object*.]**RowClear**
Elements	The *object* placeholder is an object expression that evaluates to an object in the Applies To list.
See Also	**EditClear** Method, **RowDelete** Method, **RowInsert** Method.

RowDelete Method

Applies To	**Application** Object.
Description	Deletes the active row or the row that contains the active cell.
Syntax	[*object*.]**RowDelete**
Elements	The *object* placeholder is an object expression that evaluates to an object in the Applies To list.
See Also	**ColumnBestFit** Method, **ColumnDelete** Method, **ColumnInsert** Method, **RowInsert** Method.

RowInsert Method

Applies To	**Application** Object.
Description	Inserts a row above the active row.
Syntax	[*object*.]**RowInsert**
Elements	The *object* placeholder is an object expression that evaluates to an object in the Applies To list.
See Also	**ColumnBestFit** Method, **ColumnDelete** Method, **ColumnInsert** Method, **RowDelete** Method.

RSet Statement

Description	Right aligns a string within a string variable.
Syntax	**RSet** *stringvar* = *string*

Elements

The **RSet** statement syntax has these parts:

Part	Description
stringvar	Name of a string variable.
string	String expression to be right aligned within *stringvar*.

Remarks

RSet replaces any leftover characters in *stringvar* with spaces, back to its beginning.

RSet can't be used with user-defined types.

See Also

LSet Statement.

Example

This example uses the **RSet** statement to right align a string within a string variable.

```
MyString = "0123456789"      ' Initialize string.
RSet MyString = "Right->"    ' MyString contains "   Right->".
```

Saved Property

Applies To

Project Object, **Projects** Collection.

Description

Returns whether a project has changed since it was last saved.

Syntax

object.**Saved**

Elements

The *object* placeholder is an object expression that evaluates to an object in the Applies To list.

Settings

The **Saved** property has these settings:

Setting	Description
True	The project has not changed since it was last saved.
False	The project has changed since it was last saved.

See Also

CreationDate Property, **FullName** Property, **HasPassword** Property, **LastSaveDate** Property, **LastSavedBy** Property, **Name** Property, **Path** Property, **ReadOnly** Property, **ReadOnlyRecommended** Property, **RevisionNumber** Property, **WriteReserved** Property.

ScheduleFromStart Property

Applies To	**Project** Object, **Projects** Collection.
Description	Returns or sets whether Microsoft Project calculates projects forward from their start dates or backward from their finish dates.
Syntax	[*object*.]**ScheduleFromStart** [= *value*]
Elements	The **ScheduleFromStart** property syntax has these parts:

Part	Description
object	An object expression that evaluates to an object in the Applies To list.
value	A Boolean expression that specifies the direction Microsoft Project calculates projects, as shown under Settings.

Settings   The **ScheduleFromStart** property has these settings:

Setting	Description
True	Microsoft Project calculates projects forward from their start dates.
False	Microsoft Project calculates projects backward from their finish dates.

See Also	**Author** Property, **Comments** Property, **Company** Property, **CurrentDate** Property, **Keywords** Property, **Manager** Property, **Notes** Property, **Subject** Property, **Template** Property, **Title** Property.
Example	The following example returns whether Microsoft Project calculates projects forward from their start dates or backward from their finish dates.

```
Sub SeeDirectionOfSchedule()
    MsgBox ActiveProject.ScheduleFromStart
End Sub
```

SchedulePlusReminderSet Method

Applies To	**Application** Object.

Description	Sets a reminder in Microsoft Schedule+ for the start time or finish time of the active tasks.
Syntax	[*object*.]**SchedulePlusReminderSet** [*start, leadTime*]
Elements	The **SchedulePlusReminderSet** method syntax has the following object qualifier and named arguments:

Part	Description
object	An object expression that evaluates to an object in the Applies To list. Optional.
start	A Boolean expression that specifies whether to set the reminder for the start time or finish time of the active tasks. By default, the *start* argument is **True**. Optional.
leadTime	A string expression that specifies the lead time for Schedule+ reminders. By default, the *leadTime* argument is "15m", which triggers reminders 15 minutes before the start time or after the finish time of the tasks. Optional.

Remarks	This method applies to Microsoft Project for Microsoft Windows.
See Also	**MailRoutingSlip** Method, **MailSend** Method, **MailSendProjectMail** Method, **MailSendScheduleNote** Method.

Second Function

Description	Returns a whole number between 0 and 59, inclusive, representing the second of the minute.
Syntax	**Second**(*time*)
Elements	The *time* named argument is limited to a time or numbers and strings, in any combination, that can represent a time. If *time* contains no valid data, **Null** is returned.
See Also	**Day** Function, **Hour** Function, **Minute** Function, **Now** Function, **Time** Function, **Time** Statement.
Example	This example uses the **Second** function to obtain the second of the minute from a specified time.

```
' In the development environment, the time (date literal) will display
' in short format using the locale settings of your code.
MyTime = #4:35:17 PM#       ' Assign a time.
MySecond = Second(MyTime)   ' MySecond contains 17.
```

Seek Function

Description   Returns the current read/write position within a file opened using the **Open**
statement.

Syntax   **Seek(***filenumber***)**

Elements   The ***filenumber*** named argument is any valid file number.

Remarks   **Seek** returns a value between 1 and 2,147,483,647 (equivalent to 2^31-1),
inclusive. For files open in **Random** mode, **Seek** returns the number of the next
record read or written. For files opened in **Binary**, **Output**, **Append**, or **Input**
mode, **Seek** returns the byte position at which the next operation is to take place.
The first byte in a file is at position 1, the second byte is at position 2, and so on.

See Also   **Get** Statement, **Open** Statement, **Put** Statement, **Seek** Statement.

Example   This example uses the **Seek** function to return the current file position.

```
' For files opened in random-file mode, Seek returns number of next
' record.  Assume TESTFILE is a file containing records of the
' user-defined type Record.
Type Record ' Define user-defined type.
    ID As Integer
    Name As String * 20
End Type
```

```
Dim MyRecord As Record   ' Declare variable.
' Open file in random-file mode.
Open "TESTFILE" For Random As #1 Len = Len(MyRecord)
Do While Not EOF(1)      ' Loop until end of file.
    Get #1, , MyRecord   ' Read next record.
    Debug.Print Seek(1) ' Print record number to Debug
                        ' window.
Loop
Close #1                ' Close file.


' For files opened in modes other than random mode, Seek returns the
' byte position at which the next operation will take place. Assume
' TESTFILE is a file containing a few lines of text.
Open "TESTFILE" For Input As #1 ' Open file for reading.
Do While Not EOF(1)      ' Loop until end of file.
    MyChar = Input(1,#1)' Read next character of data.
    Debug.Print Seek(1) ' Print byte position to Debug
                        ' window.
Loop
Close #1                ' Close file.
```

Seek Statement

Description   Sets the position for the next read or write within a file opened using the **Open** statement.

Syntax   **Seek** [#]*filenumber,position*

Elements   The **Seek** statement syntax has these parts:

Part	Description
filenumber	Any valid file number.
position	Number in the range 1 to 2,147,483,647, inclusive, that indicates where the next read or write should occur.

Remarks   Record numbers specified in **Get** and **Put** statements override file positioning done by **Seek**.

Performing a file write after doing a **Seek** operation beyond the end of a file extends the file. If you attempt a **Seek** operation to a negative or zero position, an error occurs.

See Also   **Get** Statement, **Open** Statement, **Put** Statement, **Seek** Function.

Example   This example uses the **Seek** statement to set the position for the next read or write within a file.

```
' For files opened in random-file mode, Seek sets the next
' record. Assume TESTFILE is a file containing records of the
' user-defined type Record.
Type Record ' Define user-defined type.
    ID As Integer
    Name As String * 20
End Type

Dim MyRecord As Record   ' Declare variable.
' Open file in random-file mode.
Open "TESTFILE" For Random As #1 Len = Len(MyRecord)
MaxSize = LOF(1) \ Len(MyRecord) ' Get number of records in file.
' The loop reads all records starting from the last.
For RecordNumber = MaxSize To 1 Step - 1
    Seek #1, RecordNumber    ' Set position.
    Get #1, , MyRecord       ' Read record.
Next RecordNumber
Close #1' Close file.

' For files opened in modes other than random mode, Seek sets the
' byte position at which the next operation will take place. Assume
' TESTFILE is a file containing a few lines of text.
Open "TESTFILE" For Input As #1 ' Open file for input.
MaxSize = LOF(1)' Get size of file in bytes.
' The loop reads all characters starting from the last.
For NextChar = MaxSize To 1 Step -1
    Seek #1, NextChar    ' Set position.
    MyChar = Input(1,#1)' Read character.
Next NextChar
Close #1' Close file.
```

Select Case Statement

Description   Executes one of several groups of statements, depending on the value of an expression.

Syntax	**Select Case** *testexpression*
	[**Case** *expressionlist-n*
	    [*statements-n*]] . . .
	[**Case Else**
	    [*elsestatements*]]
	End Select

Elements

The **Select Case** statement syntax has these parts:

Part	Description
testexpression	Any numeric or string expression.
expressionlist-n	Comma-delimited list of one or more of the following forms: *expression*, *expression* **To** *expression*, **Is** *comparisonoperator expression*. The **To** keyword specifies a range of values. If you use the **To** keyword, the smaller value must appear before **To**. Use the **Is** keyword with comparison operators (except **Is** and **Like**) to specify a range of values. If not supplied, the **Is** keyword is automatically inserted.
statements-n	One or more statements executed if *testexpression* matches any part of *expressionlist-n*.
elsestatements	One or more statements executed if *testexpression* doesn't match any of the **Case** clause.

Remarks

If *testexpression* matches any *expressionlist* expression associated with a **Case** clause, the *statements* following that **Case** clause are executed up to the next **Case** clause, or, for the last clause, up to the **End Select**. Control then passes to the statement following **End Select**. If *testexpression* matches an *expressionlist* expression in more than one **Case** clause, only the statements following the first match are executed.

The **Case Else** clause is used to indicate the *statements* to be executed if no match is found between the *testexpression* and an *expressionlist* in any of the other **Case** selections. When there is no **Case Else** statement and no expression listed in the **Case** clauses matches *testexpression*, execution continues at the statement following **End Select**.

Although not required, it is a good idea to have a **Case Else** statement in your **Select Case** block to handle unforeseen *testexpression* values.

You can use multiple expressions or ranges in each **Case** clause. For example, the following line is valid:

```
Case 1 To 4, 7 To 9, 11, 13, Is > MaxNumber
```

Note The **Is** comparison operator is not the same as the **Is** keyword used in the **Select Case** statement.

You also can specify ranges and multiple expressions for character strings. In the following example, **Case** matches strings that are exactly equal to everything, strings that fall between nuts and soup in alphabetical order, and the current value of TestItem:

```
Case "everything", "nuts" To "soup", TestItem
```

Select Case statements can be nested. Each **Select Case** statement must have a matching **End Select** statement.

See Also

If...Then...Else Statement; **On...GoSub**, **On...GoTo** Statements; **Option Compare** Statement.

Example

This example uses the **Select Case** statement to evaluate the value of a variable. The second **Case** clause contains the value of the variable being evaluated and therefore only the statement associated with it is executed.

```
Number = 8              ' Initialize variable.
Select Case Number       ' Evaluate Number.
Case 1 To 5             ' Number between 1 and 5.
   MyString = "Between 1 and 5"
Case 6, 7, 8, 9, 10      ' Number between 6 and 10.
   ' This is the only Case clause that evaluates to True.
   MyString = "Between 6 and 10"
Case Else                ' Other values.
   MyString = "Not between 1 and 10"
End Select
```

SelectAll Method

Applies To

Application Object.

Description

Selects all cells on the active sheet.

Syntax

[*object.*]**SelectAll**

Elements

The *object* placeholder is an object expression that evaluates to an object in the Applies To list.

See Also

SelectCell Method, **SelectColumn** Method, **SelectRange** Method, **SelectResourceField** Method, **SelectRow** Method, **SelectTaskField** Method.

SelectBeginning Method

Applies To	**Application** Object.
Description	Selects the first cell in the active table.
Syntax	[*object*.]**SelectBeginning** [*extend*]
Elements	The **SelectBeginning** method syntax has the following object qualifier and named arguments:

Part	Description
object	An object expression that evaluates to an object in the Applies To list.
extend	A Boolean expression that specifies whether to extend the current selection. By default, the *extend* argument is **False**.

See Also	**SelectAll** Method, **SelectCell** Method, **SelectCellDown** Method, **SelectCellLeft** Method, **SelectCellRight** Method, **SelectCellUp** Method, **SelectColumn** Method, **SelectEnd** Method, **SelectionExtend** Method, **SelectRange** Method, **SelectResourceCell** Method, **SelectResourceColumn** Method, **SelectResourceField** Method, **SelectRow** Method, **SelectRowEnd** Method, **SelectRowStart** Method, **SelectSheet** Method, **SelectTaskCell** Method, **SelectTaskColumn** Method, **SelectTaskField** Method.

SelectCell Method

Applies To	**Application** Object.
Description	Selects a cell.
Syntax	[*object*.]**SelectCell** [*row, column, rowRelative*]
Elements	The **SelectCell** method syntax has the following object qualifier and named arguments:

Part	Description
object	An object expression that evaluates to an object in the Applies To list. Optional.
row	A numeric expression that specifies the row number (when the *rowRelative* argument is **False**) or the relative row position (when the *rowRelative* argument is **True**) of the cell to select. Optional.
column	A numeric expression that specifies the column number of the cell to select. Optional.
rowRelative	A Boolean expression that specifies whether the row number is absolute or relative to the active cell. By default, the *rowRelative* argument is **True**. Optional.

See Also

SelectAll Method, **SelectBeginning** Method, **SelectCellDown** Method, **SelectCellLeft** Method, **SelectCellRight** Method, **SelectCellUp** Method, **SelectColumn** Method, **SelectEnd** Method, **SelectionExtend** Method, **SelectRange** Method, **SelectResourceCell** Method, **SelectResourceColumn** Method, **SelectResourceField** Method, **SelectRow** Method, **SelectRowEnd** Method, **SelectRowStart** Method, **SelectSheet** Method, **SelectTaskCell** Method, **SelectTaskColumn** Method, **SelectTaskField** Method.

SelectCellDown Method

Applies To   **Application** Object.

Description   Selects cells downward from the current selection.

Syntax   [*object*.]**SelectCellDown** [*numCells*, *extend*]

Elements   The **SelectCellDown** method syntax has the following object qualifier and named arguments:

Part	Description
object	An object expression that evaluates to an object in the Applies To list. Optional.
numCells	A numeric expression that specifies the number of cells to select downward from the current selection. By default, the *numCells* argument is 1. Optional.
extend	A Boolean expression that specifies whether to extend the current selection. By default, the *extend* argument is **False**. Optional.

See Also**SelectAll** Method, **SelectBeginning** Method, **SelectCell** Method, **SelectCellLeft** Method, **SelectCellRight** Method, **SelectCellUp** Method, **SelectColumn** Method, **SelectEnd** Method, **SelectionExtend** Method, **SelectRange** Method, **SelectResourceCell** Method, **SelectResourceColumn** Method, **SelectResourceField** Method, **SelectRow** Method, **SelectRowEnd** Method, **SelectRowStart** Method, **SelectSheet** Method, **SelectTaskCell** Method, **SelectTaskColumn** Method, **SelectTaskField** Method.

SelectCellLeft Method

Applies To   **Application** Object.

Description   Selects cells to the left of the current selection.

Syntax   [*object.*]**SelectCellLeft** [*numCells*, *extend*]

Elements   The **SelectCellLeft** method syntax has the following object qualifier and named arguments:

Part	Description
object	An object expression that evaluates to an object in the Applies To list. Optional.
numCells	A numeric expression that specifies the number of cells to select to the left of the current selection. By default, the *numCells* argument is 1. Optional.
extend	A Boolean expression that specifies whether to extend the current selection. By default, the *extend* argument is **False**. Optional.

See Also   **SelectAll** Method, **SelectBeginning** Method, **SelectCell** Method, **SelectCellDown** Method, **SelectCellRight** Method, **SelectCellUp** Method, **SelectColumn** Method, **SelectEnd** Method, **SelectionExtend** Method, **SelectRange** Method, **SelectResourceCell** Method, **SelectResourceColumn** Method, **SelectResourceField** Method, **SelectRow** Method, **SelectRowEnd** Method, **SelectRowStart** Method, **SelectSheet** Method, **SelectTaskCell** Method, **SelectTaskColumn** Method, **SelectTaskField** Method.

SelectCellRight Method

Applies To   **Application** Object.

Description	Selects cells to the right of the current selection.
Syntax	[*object.*]**SelectCellRight** [*numCells*, *extend*]
Elements	The **SelectCellRight** method syntax has the following object qualifier and named arguments:

Part	Description
object	An object expression that evaluates to an object in the Applies To list. Optional.
numCells	A numeric expression that specifies the number of cells to select to the right of the current selection. By default, the *numCells* argument is 1. Optional.
extend	A Boolean expression that specifies whether to extend the current selection. By default, the *extend* argument is **False**. Optional.

See Also	**SelectAll** Method, **SelectBeginning** Method, **SelectCell** Method, **SelectCellDown** Method, **SelectCellLeft** Method, **SelectCellUp** Method, **SelectColumn** Method, **SelectEnd** Method, **SelectionExtend** Method, **SelectRange** Method, **SelectResourceCell** Method, **SelectResourceColumn** Method, **SelectResourceField** Method, **SelectRow** Method, **SelectRowEnd** Method, **SelectRowStart** Method, **SelectSheet** Method, **SelectTaskCell** Method, **SelectTaskColumn** Method, **SelectTaskField** Method.

SelectCellUp Method

Applies To	**Application** Object.
Description	Selects cells upward from the current selection.
Syntax	[*object.*]**SelectCellUp** [*numCells*, *extend*]
Elements	The **SelectCellUp** method syntax has the following object qualifier and named arguments:

Part	Description
object	An object expression that evaluates to an object in the Applies To list. Optional.
numCells	A numeric expression that specifies the number of cells to select upward from the current selection. By default, the ***numCells*** argument is 1. Optional.
extend	A Boolean expression that specifies whether to extend the current selection. By default, the ***extend*** argument is **False**. Optional.

See Also

SelectAll Method, **SelectBeginning** Method, **SelectCell** Method, **SelectCellDown** Method, **SelectCellLeft** Method, **SelectCellRight** Method, **SelectColumn** Method, **SelectEnd** Method, **SelectionExtend** Method, **SelectRange** Method, **SelectResourceCell** Method, **SelectResourceColumn** Method, **SelectResourceField** Method, **SelectRow** Method, **SelectRowEnd** Method, **SelectRowStart** Method, **SelectSheet** Method, **SelectTaskCell** Method, **SelectTaskColumn** Method, **SelectTaskField** Method.

SelectColumn Method

Applies To   **Application** Object.

Description   Selects one or more columns.

Syntax   [*object.*]**SelectColumn** *column*[, *additional, extend, add*]

Elements   The **SelectColumn** method syntax has the following object qualifier and named arguments:

Part	Description
object	An object expression that evaluates to an object in the Applies To list. Optional.
column	A numeric expression that specifies the name of the column to select. By default, the ***column*** argument equals the name of the active column. Required.
additional	A numeric expression that specifies a number of additional columns. Optional.
extend	A Boolean expression that specifies whether to extend the active selection into the new selection. Optional.
add	A Boolean expression that specifies whether to add the new selection to the active selection. Optional.

See Also   **SelectionExtend** Method, **SelectResourceColumn** Method, **SelectTaskColumn** Method.

SelectEnd Method

Applies To   **Application** Object.

Description   Selects the last cell in the active table that contains a resource or task.

Syntax   [*object.*]**SelectEnd** [*extend*]

Elements   The **SelectEnd** method syntax has the following object qualifier and named arguments:

Part	Description
object	An object expression that evaluates to an object in the Applies To list.
extend	A Boolean expression that specifies whether to extend the current selection. By default, the *extend* argument is **False**.

See Also   **SelectAll** Method, **SelectBeginning** Method, **SelectCell** Method, **SelectCellDown** Method, **SelectCellLeft** Method, **SelectCellRight** Method, **SelectCellUp** Method, **SelectColumn** Method, **SelectionExtend** Method, **SelectRange** Method, **SelectResourceCell** Method, **SelectResourceColumn** Method, **SelectResourceField** Method, **SelectRow** Method, **SelectRowEnd** Method, **SelectRowStart** Method, **SelectSheet** Method, **SelectTaskCell** Method, **SelectTaskColumn** Method, **SelectTaskField** Method.

Selection Object

Description   The active selection.

Properties   **Application** Property, **Parent** Property

Methods   **FieldIDList** Method, **FieldNameList** Method, **Resources** Method, **Tasks** Method

SelectionExtend Method

Applies To	**Application** Object.
Description	Turns selection extending on or off.
Syntax	[*object*.]**SelectionExtend** [*extend, add*]
Elements	The **SelectionExtend** method syntax has the following object qualifier and named arguments:

Part	Description
object	An object expression that evaluates to an object in the Applies To list.
extend	A Boolean expression that specifies whether to turn on extend mode. By default, the *extend* argument is **False**.
add	A Boolean expression that specifies whether to turn on add mode. By default, the *add* argument is **False**.

Remarks	If the *extend* argument is true, then the *add* argument is ignored.
See Also	**SelectBeginning** Method, **SelectCellDown** Method, **SelectCellLeft** Method, **SelectCellRight** Method, **SelectCellUp** Method, **SelectEnd** Method, **SelectRowEnd** Method, **SelectRowStart** Method.

SelectRange Method

Applies To	**Application** Object.
Description	Selects one or more cells.
Syntax	[*object*.]**SelectRange** *row, column*[, *rowRelative, width, height, extend, add*]
Elements	The **SelectRange** method syntax has the following object qualifier and named arguments:

Part	Description
object	An object expression that evaluates to an object in the Applies To list. Optional.
row	A numeric expression that specifies the row containing the cell you want to select. Required.
column	A numeric expression that specifies the number of the column containing the cell you want to select. Required.
rowRelative	A Boolean expression that specifies whether the location of the new selection is relative to the active selection. By default, the *rowRelative* argument is **True**. Optional. The *rowRelative* argument has these settings:

	True	The location of the new selection is relative to the active selection.
	False	The location of the new selection is absolute.

Part	Description
width	A numeric expression that specifies the width of the selection. Optional.
height	A numeric expression that specifies the height of the selection. Optional.
extend	A Boolean expression that specifies whether to extend the active selection into the new selection. Optional.
add	A Boolean expression that specifies whether to add the new selection to the active selection. Optional.

See Also   **SelectAll** Method, **SelectCell** Method, **SelectColumn** Method, **SelectionExtend** Method, **SelectRow** Method.

SelectResourceCell Method

Applies To   **Application** Object.

Description   Selects a cell containing resource information.

Syntax   [*object*.]**SelectResourceCell** [*row, column, rowRelative*]

Elements   The **SelectResourceCell** method syntax has the following object qualifier and named arguments:

Part	Description
object	An object expression that evaluates to an object in the Applies To list. Optional.
row	A numeric expression that specifies the row number (when the *rowRelative* argument is **False**) or the relative row position (when the *rowRelative* argument is **True**) of the cell to select. Optional.
column	A string expression that specifies the field name of the cell to select. Optional.
rowRelative	A Boolean expression that specifies whether the row number is absolute or relative to the active cell. Optional.

See Also

SelectAll Method, **SelectBeginning** Method, **SelectCell** Method, **SelectCellDown** Method, **SelectCellLeft** Method, **SelectCellRight** Method, **SelectCellUp** Method, **SelectColumn** Method, **SelectEnd** Method, **SelectionExtend** Method, **SelectRange** Method, **SelectResourceColumn** Method, **SelectResourceField** Method, **SelectRow** Method, **SelectRowEnd** Method, **SelectRowStart** Method, **SelectSheet** Method, **SelectTaskCell** Method, **SelectTaskColumn** Method, **SelectTaskField** Method.

SelectResourceColumn Method

Applies To   **Application** Object.

Description   Selects a column containing resource information.

Syntax   [*object*.]**SelectResourceColumn** *column*[*, additional, extend, add*]

Elements   The **SelectResourceColumn** method syntax has the following object qualifier and named arguments:

Part	Description
object	An object expression that evaluates to an object in the Applies To list. Optional.
column	A string expression that specifies the field name of the column to select. Required.
additional	A numeric expression that specifies the number of additional columns to select. By default, the *additional* argument is 0. Optional.

Part	Description
extend	A Boolean expression that specifies whether to extend the current selection. By default, the *extend* argument is **False**. Optional.
add	A Boolean expression that specifies whether to add the new selection to the current selection. By default, the *add* argument is **False**. Optional.

See Also

SelectAll Method, **SelectBeginning** Method, **SelectCell** Method, **SelectCellDown** Method, **SelectCellLeft** Method, **SelectCellRight** Method, **SelectCellUp** Method, **SelectColumn** Method, **SelectEnd** Method, **SelectionExtend** Method, **SelectRange** Method, **SelectResourceCell** Method, **SelectResourceField** Method, **SelectRow** Method, **SelectRowEnd** Method, **SelectRowStart** Method, **SelectSheet** Method, **SelectTaskCell** Method, **SelectTaskColumn** Method, **SelectTaskField** Method.

SelectResourceField Method

Applies To

Application Object.

Description

Selects a resource field.

Syntax

[*object*.]**SelectResourceField** *row*, *column*[, *rowRelative*, *width*, *height*, *extend*, *add*]

Elements

The **SelectResourceField** method syntax has the following object qualifier and named arguments:

Part	Description
object	An object expression that evaluates to an object in the Applies To list. Optional.
row	A numeric expression that specifies the row containing the field you want to select. Required.
column	A string expression that specifies the name of the column containing the field you want to select. Required.
rowRelative	A Boolean expression that specifies whether the location of the new selection is absolute or relative to the active selection. Optional.
width	A numeric expression that specifies the width of the selection. Optional.
height	A numeric expression that specifies the height of the selection. Optional.

Part	Description
extend	A Boolean expression that specifies whether to extend the active selection into the new selection. Optional.
add	A Boolean expression that specifies whether to add the new selection to the active selection. Optional.

See Also   **SelectionExtend** Method, **SelectRange** Method, **SelectResourceCell** Method, **SelectResourceColumn** Method, **SelectTaskField** Method.

SelectRow Method

Applies To   **Application** Object.

Description   Selects one or more rows.

Syntax   [*object.*]**SelectRow** *row*[*, rowRelative, height, extend, add*]

Elements   The **SelectRow** method syntax has the following object qualifier and named arguments:

Part	Description
object	An object expression that evaluates to an object in the Applies To list. Optional.
row	A numeric expression that specifies the row containing the field you want to select. Required.
rowRelative	A Boolean expression that specifies whether the location of the new selection is absolute or relative to the active selection. Optional.
height	A numeric expression that specifies the height of the selection. Optional.
extend	A Boolean expression that specifies whether to extend the active selection into the new selection. Optional.
add	A Boolean expression that specifies whether to add the new selection to the active selection. Optional.

See Also   **RowClear** Method, **RowDelete** Method, **RowInsert** Method, **SelectColumn** Method, **SelectionExtend** Method, **SelectRowEnd** Method, **SelectRowStart** Method.

SelectRowEnd Method

Applies To   **Application** Object.

Description   Selects the last cell in the row containing the active cell.

Syntax   [*object.*]**SelectRowEnd** [*extend*]

Elements   The **SelectRowEnd** method syntax has the following object qualifier and named arguments:

Part	Description
object	An object expression that evaluates to an object in the Applies To list.
extend	A Boolean expression that specifies whether to extend the current selection. By default, the *extend* argument is **False**.

See Also   **SelectAll** Method, **SelectBeginning** Method, **SelectCell** Method, **SelectCellDown** Method, **SelectCellLeft** Method, **SelectCellRight** Method, **SelectCellUp** Method, **SelectColumn** Method, **SelectEnd** Method, **SelectionExtend** Method, **SelectRange** Method, **SelectResourceCell** Method, **SelectResourceColumn** Method, **SelectResourceField** Method, **SelectRow** Method, **SelectRowStart** Method, **SelectSheet** Method, **SelectTaskCell** Method, **SelectTaskColumn** Method, **SelectTaskField** Method.

SelectRowStart Method

Applies To   **Application** Object.

Description   Selects the first cell in the row containing the active cell.

Syntax   [*object.*]**SelectRowStart** [*extend*]

Elements   The **SelectRowStart** method syntax has the following object qualifier and named arguments:

Part	Description
object	An object expression that evaluates to an object in the Applies To list.
extend	A Boolean expression that specifies whether to extend the current selection. By default, the *extend* argument is **False**.

See Also	**SelectAll** Method, **SelectBeginning** Method, **SelectCell** Method, **SelectCellDown** Method, **SelectCellLeft** Method, **SelectCellRight** Method, **SelectCellUp** Method, **SelectColumn** Method, **SelectEnd** Method, **SelectionExtend** Method, **SelectRange** Method, **SelectResourceCell** Method, **SelectResourceColumn** Method, **SelectResourceField** Method, **SelectRow** Method, **SelectRowEnd** Method, **SelectSheet** Method, **SelectTaskCell** Method, **SelectTaskColumn** Method, **SelectTaskField** Method.

SelectSheet Method

Applies To	**Application** Object.
Description	Selects all cells in the active table.
Syntax	[*object*.]**SelectSheet**
Elements	The *object* placeholder is an object expression that evaluates to an object in the Applies To list.
See Also	**SelectAll** Method, **SelectBeginning** Method, **SelectCell** Method, **SelectCellDown** Method, **SelectCellLeft** Method, **SelectCellRight** Method, **SelectCellUp** Method, **SelectColumn** Method, **SelectEnd** Method, **SelectionExtend** Method, **SelectRange** Method, **SelectResourceCell** Method, **SelectResourceColumn** Method, **SelectResourceField** Method, **SelectRow** Method, **SelectRowEnd** Method, **SelectRowStart** Method, **SelectTaskCell** Method, **SelectTaskColumn** Method, **SelectTaskField** Method.

SelectTaskCell Method

Applies To	**Application** Object.
Description	Selects a cell containing task information.
Syntax	[*object*.]**SelectTaskCell** [*row, column, rowRelative*]
Elements	The **SelectTaskCell** method syntax has the following object qualifier and named arguments:

Part	Description
object	An object expression that evaluates to an object in the Applies To list. Optional.
row	A numeric expression that specifies the row number (when the *rowRelative* argument is **False**) or the relative row position (when the *rowRelative* argument is **True**) of the task cell to select. Optional.
column	A string expression that specifies the field name of the task cell to select. Optional.
rowRelative	A Boolean expression that specifies whether the row number is absolute or relative to the active cell. Optional.

See Also
    SelectAll Method, **SelectBeginning** Method, **SelectCell** Method, **SelectCellDown** Method, **SelectCellLeft** Method, **SelectCellRight** Method, **SelectCellUp** Method, **SelectColumn** Method, **SelectEnd** Method, **SelectionExtend** Method, **SelectRange** Method, **SelectResourceCell** Method, **SelectResourceColumn** Method, **SelectResourceField** Method, **SelectRow** Method, **SelectRowEnd** Method, **SelectRowStart** Method, **SelectSheet** Method, **SelectTaskColumn** Method, **SelectTaskField** Method.

SelectTaskColumn Method

Applies To   **Application** Object.

Description   Selects a column containing task information.

Syntax   [*object*.]**SelectTaskColumn** *column*[, *additional*, *extend*, *add*]

Elements   The **SelectTaskColumn** method syntax has the following object qualifier and named arguments:

Part	Description
object	An object expression that evaluates to an object in the Applies To list. Optional.
column	A string expression that specifies the field name of the column to select. Required.
additional	A numeric expression that specifies the number of additional columns to select. By default, the *additional* argument is 0. Optional.

Part	Description
extend	A Boolean expression that specifies whether to extend the current selection. By default, the *extend* argument is **False**. Optional.
add	A Boolean expression that specifies whether to add the new selection to the current selection. By default, the *add* argument is **False**. Optional.

See Also   **SelectAll** Method, **SelectBeginning** Method, **SelectCell** Method, **SelectCellDown** Method, **SelectCellLeft** Method, **SelectCellRight** Method, **SelectCellUp** Method, **SelectColumn** Method, **SelectEnd** Method, **SelectionExtend** Method, **SelectRange** Method, **SelectResourceCell** Method, **SelectResourceColumn** Method, **SelectResourceField** Method, **SelectRow** Method, **SelectRowEnd** Method, **SelectRowStart** Method, **SelectSheet** Method, **SelectTaskCell** Method, **SelectTaskField** Method.

SelectTaskField Method

Applies To   **Application** Object.

Description   Selects a task field.

Syntax   [*object*.]**SelectTaskField** *row, column*[, *rowRelative, width, height, extend, add*]

Elements   The **SelectTaskField** method syntax has the following object qualifier and named arguments:

Part	Description
object	An object expression that evaluates to an object in the Applies To list. Optional.
row	A numeric expression that specifies the row containing the field you want to select. Required.
column	A string expression that specifies the name of the column containing the field you want to select. Required.
rowRelative	A Boolean expression that specifies whether the location of the new selection is absolute or relative to the active selection. Optional.
width	A numeric expression that specifies the width of the selection. Optional.
height	A numeric expression that specifies the height of the selection. Optional.

Part	Description
extend	A Boolean expression that specifies whether to extend the active selection into the new selection. Optional.
add	A Boolean expression that specifies whether to add the new selection to the active selection. Optional.

See Also

SelectionExtend Method, **SelectRange** Method, **SelectResourceField** Method, **SelectTaskCell** Method, **SelectTaskColumn** Method.

SendKeys Statement

Description

Sends one or more keystrokes to the active window as if typed at the keyboard; not available on the Macintosh.

Syntax

SendKeys *string*[,*wait*]

Elements

The **SendKeys** statement syntax has these named-argument parts:

Part	Description
string	String expression specifying the keystroke(s) to send.
wait	Boolean value specifying the wait mode. If **False** (default), control is returned to the procedure immediately after the keys are sent. If **True**, keystrokes must be processed before control is returned to the procedure.

Remarks

Each key is represented by one or more characters. To specify a single keyboard character, use the character itself. For example, to represent the letter A, use "A" for *string*. If you want to represent more than one character, append each additional character to the one preceding it. To represent the letters A, B, and C, use "ABC" for *string*.

The plus sign (+), caret (^), percent sign (%), tilde (~), and parentheses ( ) have special meanings to **SendKeys**. To specify one of these characters, enclose it within braces. For example, to specify the plus sign, use {+}. Brackets ([ ]) have no special meaning to **SendKeys**, but you must enclose them in braces as well, because in other applications, brackets do have a special meaning that may be significant when dynamic data exchange (DDE) occurs. To send brace characters, use {{} and {}}.

To specify characters that aren't displayed when you press a key (such as ENTER or TAB) and keys that represent actions rather than characters, use the codes shown below:

Key	Code
BACKSPACE	{BACKSPACE}, {BS}, or {BKSP}
BREAK	{BREAK}
CAPS LOCK	{CAPSLOCK}
DEL	{DELETE} or {DEL}
DOWN ARROW	{DOWN}
END	{END}
ENTER	{ENTER}
ESC	{ESC}
HELP	{HELP}
HOME	{HOME}
INS	{INSERT}
LEFT ARROW	{LEFT}
NUM LOCK	{NUMLOCK}
PAGE DOWN	{PGDN}
PAGE UP	{PGUP}
PRINT SCREEN	{PRTSC}
RIGHT ARROW	{RIGHT}
SCROLL LOCK	{SCROLLLOCK}
TAB	{TAB}
UP ARROW	{UP}
F1	{F1}
F2	{F2}
F3	{F3}
F4	{F4}
F5	{F5}
F6	{F6}
F7	{F7}
F8	{F8}
F9	{F9}
F10	{F10}
F11	{F11}
F12	{F12}
F13	{F13}
F14	{F14}

Key	Code
F15	{F15}
F16	{F16}

To specify keys combined with any combination of the SHIFT, CTRL, and ALT keys, precede the regular key code with one or more of the following codes:

Key	Code
SHIFT	+
CTRL (CONTROL)	
ALT	%

To specify that any combination of SHIFT, CTRL, and ALT should be held down while several other keys are pressed, enclose the code for those keys in parentheses. For example, to specify to hold down SHIFT while E and C are pressed, use "+(EC)". To specify to hold down SHIFT while E is pressed, followed by C without SHIFT, use "+EC".

To specify repeating keys, use the form {key number}. You must put a space between key and number. For example, {LEFT 42} means press the LEFT ARROW key 42 times; {h 10} means press h 10 times.

Note **SendKeys** can't send keystrokes to an application that is not designed to run in Microsoft Windows. **Sendkeys** also can't send the PRINT SCREEN (PRTSC) key to any application.

See Also   **AppActivate** Statement, **DoEvents** Statement.

Example   This example uses the **Shell** function to run the Calculator application included with Microsoft Windows; it then uses the **SendKeys** statement to send keystrokes to add some numbers and then quit the Calculator. The **SendKeys** statement is not available on the Macintosh.

```
ReturnValue = Shell("Calc.exe", 1)   ' Run Calculator.
AppActivate ReturnValue              ' Activate the Calculator.
For I = 1 To 100                   ' Set up counting loop.
    SendKeys I & "{+}", True          ' Send keystrokes to Calculator
Next I                             ' to add each value of I.
SendKeys "=", True                    ' Get grand total.
SendKeys "%{F4}", True                ' Send Alt+F4 to close Calculator.
```

Set Statement

Description

Declares the name, arguments, and code that form the body of a **Property** procedure, which sets a reference to an object.

Syntax

[**Public** | **Private**][**Static**] **Property Set** *name* [(*arglist*)]

    [*statements*]
    [**Exit Property**]
    [*statements*]
End Property

Elements

The **Property Set** statement syntax has these parts:

Part	Description
Public	Indicates that the **Property Set** procedure is accessible to all other procedures in all modules. If used in a private module (one that contains an **Option Private** statement), the procedure is not available outside the project.
Private	Indicates that the **Property Set** procedure is accessible only to other procedures in the module where it is declared.
Static	Indicates that the **Property Set** procedure's local variables are preserved between calls. The **Static** attribute doesn't affect variables that are declared outside the **Property Set** procedure, even if they are used in the procedure.
name	Name of the **Property Set** procedure; follows standard variable naming conventions, except that the name can be the same as a **Property Get** or **Property Let** procedure in the same module.
arglist	List of variables representing arguments that are passed to the **Property Set** procedure when it is called. Multiple variables are separated by commas. The last argument is the object reference used on the right-hand side of an object reference assignment.
statements	Any group of statements to be executed within the body of the **Property** procedure.

The *arglist* argument has the following syntax and parts:

[**ByVal** | **ByRef**] *varname*[( )][**As** *type*]

Part	Description
ByVal	Indicates that the argument is passed by value.
ByRef	Indicates that the argument is passed by reference.
varname	Name of the variable representing the argument; follows standard variable naming conventions.
type	Data type of the argument passed to the **Property Set** procedure; may be **Boolean**, **Integer**, **Long**, **Currency**, **Single**, **Double**, **Date**, **String** (variable length only), **Object**, **Variant**, a user-defined type, or an object type.

Note Every Property Set statement must define at least one argument for the procedure it defines. That argument (or the last argument if there is more than one) will contain the actual object reference for the property when the procedure defined by the Property Set statement is invoked.

Remarks

If not explicitly specified using either **Public** or **Private**, **Property** procedures are **Public** by default. If **Static** is not used, the value of local variables is not preserved between calls.

All executable code must be in procedures. You can't define a **Property Set** procedure inside another **Sub**, **Function**, or **Property** procedure.

The **Exit Property** keywords cause an immediate exit from a **Property Set** procedure. Program execution continues with the statement following the statement that called the **Property Set** procedure. Any number of **Exit Property** statements can appear anywhere in a **Property Set** procedure.

Like a **Function** and **Property Get** procedure, a **Property Set** procedure is a separate procedure that can take arguments, perform a series of statements, and change the value of its arguments. However, unlike a **Function** and **Property Get** procedure, both of which return a value, a **Property Set** procedure can only be used on the left side of an object reference assignment (**Set** statement).

See Also

Function Statement, **Property Get** Statement, **Property Let** Statement, **Sub** Statement.

Example

This example uses the **Set** statement to assign object references to variables.

```
Set MyObject = YourObject       ' Assign object reference.
' MyObject and YourObject refer to the same object.
YourObject.Text = "Hello World" ' Initialize property.
MyStr = MyObject.Text           ' Returns "Hello World".
' Discontinue association. MyObject no longer refers to YourObject.
Set MyObject = Nothing
```

SetActiveCell Method

Applies To	**Application** Object.
Description	Sets the value of the active cell.
Syntax	[*object*.]**SetActiveCell** *value*[, *create*]
Elements	The **SetActiveCell** method syntax has the following object qualifier and named arguments:

Part	Description
object	An object expression that evaluates to an object in the Applies To list. Optional.
value	A string expression that specifies a new value for the active cell. Required.
create	A Boolean expression that specifies whether to create a new task or resource when setting the value of the active cell. By default, the *create* argument is **True**. Optional.

See Also	**SelectRange** Method, **SelectResourceCell** Method, **SelectTaskCell** Method.
Example	The following example enters the specified text in the active cell.

```
Sub AddCommentToTable
    Dim M As String
    M = InputBox("Enter your comment: ")
    SetActiveCell M, False
End Sub
```

SetAttr Statement

Description	Sets attribute information for a file.
Syntax	**SetAttr** *pathname,attributes*
Elements	The **SetAttr** statement syntax has these named-argument parts:

Part	Description
pathname	String expression that specifies a file name—may include directory or folder, and drive.
attributes	Constant or numeric expression, the sum of which specifies file attributes.

Constants and values for *attributes* are:

vbNormal	0	Normal (default).
vbReadOnly	1	Read-only.
vbHidden	2	Hidden.
vbSystem	4	System—not available on the Macintosh.
vbArchive	32	File has changed since last backup—not available on the Macintosh.

Note These constants are specified by Visual Basic. As a result, the names can be used anywhere in your code in place of the actual values.

Remarks   A run-time error occurs if you try to set the attributes of an open file.

See Also   **FileAttr** Function, **GetAttr** Function.

Example   This example uses the **SetAttr** statement to set attributes for a file.

```
SetAttr "TESTFILE", vbHidden                ' Set hidden attribute.
SetAttr "TESTFILE", vbHidden + vbReadOnly   ' Set hidden and Read-only
                                            ' attributes.
```

SetField Method

Applies To   **Application** Object; **Resource** Object, **Resources** Collection; **Task** Object, **Tasks** Collection.

Description   Sets the value in a field for the selected task or resource. The **SetField** method may apply to an **Application** object (Syntax 1), or to a **Resource** or **Task** object (Syntax 2).

Syntax 1   [*object*.]**SetField** *field*, *value*[, *create*]

Syntax 2   *object*.**SetField** *fieldID*, *value*

Elements

The **SetField** Method syntax has the following object qualifier and named arguments:

Part	Description
object	An object expression that evaluates to an object in the Applies To list. Optional for Syntax 1; required for Syntax 2.
field	A string expression that specifies the name of the field set. Required.
fieldID	A constant that specifies the field to set. Required.
value	A string expression that specifies the value of the field. Required.
create	A Boolean expression that specifies whether to create a new task or resource. By default, the *create* argument is **True**. Optional.

The *fieldID* argument has these settings:

pjResourceRemainingWork	22	Remaining work
pjResourceAccrueAt	19	Accrue at
pjResourceActualCost	11	Actual cost
pjResourceActualWork	14	Actual work
pjResourceBaseCalendar	5	Base calendar
pjResourceBaselineCost	17	Baseline cost
pjResourceBaselineWork	15	Baseline work
pjResourceCode	10	Code
pjResourceCost	12	Cost
pjResourceCostPerUse	18	Cost per use
pjResourceCostVariance	24	Cost variance
pjResourceEMailAddress	35	Electronic mail address
pjResourceGroup	3	Group
pjResourceID	0	Resource
pjResourceInitials	2	Initials
pjResourceLinkedFields	34	Linked fields
pjResourceMaxUnits	4	Max units
pjResourceName	1	Name
pjResourceNotes	20	Notes
pjResourceObjects	33	Objects
pjResourceOverallocated	25	Overallocated
pjResourceOvertimeRate	7	Overtime rate
pjResourceOvertimeWork	16	Overtime work

pjResourcePeakUnits	26	Peak units
pjResourcePercentWorkComplete	29	Percent work complete
pjResourceRemainingCost	21	Remaining cost
pjResourceSheetNotes	28	Sheet notes
pjResourceStandardRate	6	Standard rate
pjResourceText1	8	Text1
pjResourceText2	9	Text2
pjResourceText3	30	Text3
pjResourceText4	31	Text4
pjResourceText5	32	Text5
pjResourceUniqueID	27	UniqueID
pjResourceWork	13	Work
pjResourceWorkVariance	23	Work variance
pjTaskActualCost	7	Actual cost
pjTaskActualDuration	28	Actual duration
pjTaskActualFinish	42	Actual finish
pjTaskActualStart	41	Actual start
pjTaskActualWork	2	Actual work
pjTaskBaselineCost	6	Baseline cost
pjTaskBaselineDuration	27	Baseline duration
pjTaskBaselineFinish	44	Baseline finish
pjTaskBaselineStart	43	Baseline start
pjTaskBaselineWork	1	Baseline work
pjTaskBCWP	11	BCWP
pjTaskBCWS	12	BCWS
pjTaskConfirmed	110	Confirmed
pjTaskConstraintDate	18	Constraint date
pjTaskConstraintType	17	Constraint type
pjTaskContact	112	Contact
pjTaskCost	5	Cost
pjTaskCost1	106	Cost1
pjTaskCost2	107	Cost2
pjTaskCost3	108	Cost3
pjTaskCostVariance	9	Cost variance
pjTaskCreated	93	Created
pjTaskCritical	19	Critical

pjTaskCV	83	CV
pjTaskDelay	20	Delay
pjTaskDuration	29	Duration
pjTaskDuration1	103	Duration1
pjTaskDuration2	104	Duration2
pjTaskDuration3	105	Duration3
pjTaskDurationVariance	30	Duration variance
pjTaskEarlyFinish	38	Early finish
pjTaskEarlyStart	37	Early start
pjTaskFinish	36	Finish
pjTaskFinish1	53	Finish1
pjTaskFinish2	56	Finish2
pjTaskFinish3	59	Finish3
pjTaskFinish4	62	Finish4
pjTaskFinish5	65	Finish5
pjTaskFinishVariance	46	Finish variance
pjTaskFixedCost	8	Fixed cost
pjTaskFixedDuration	34	Fixed duration
pjTaskFlag1	72	Flag1
pjTaskFlag10	81	Flag10
pjTaskFlag2	73	Flag2
pjTaskFlag3	74	Flag3
pjTaskFlag4	75	Flag4
pjTaskFlag5	76	Flag5
pjTaskFlag6	77	Flag6
pjTaskFlag7	78	Flag7
pjTaskFlag8	79	Flag8
pjTaskFlag9	80	Flag9
pjTaskFreeSlack	21	Free slack
pjTaskHideBar	109	Hide bar
pjTaskID	23	Task ID
pjTaskLateFinish	40	Late finish
pjTaskLateStart	39	Late start
pjTaskLinkedFields	98	Linked fields
pjTaskMarked	71	Marked
pjTaskMilestone	24	Milestone

pjTaskName	14	Name
pjTaskNotes	15	Notes
pjTaskNumber1	87	Number1
pjTaskNumber2	88	Number2
pjTaskNumber3	89	Number3
pjTaskNumber4	90	Number4
pjTaskNumber5	91	Number5
pjTaskObjects	97	Objects
pjTaskOutlineLevel	85	Outline level
pjTaskOutlineNumber	102	Outline number
pjTaskPercentComplete	32	Percent complete
pjTaskPercentWorkComplete	33	Percent work complete
pjTaskPredecessors	47	Predecessors
pjTaskPriority	25	Priority
pjTaskProject	84	Project
pjTaskRemainingCost	10	Remaining cost
pjTaskRemainingDuration	31	Remaining duration
pjTaskRemainingWork	4	Remaining work
pjTaskResourceGroup	113	Resource group
pjTaskResourceInitials	50	Resource initials
pjTaskResourceNames	49	Resource names
pjTaskResume	99	Resume
pjTaskResumeNoEarlierThan	101	Resume no earlier than
pjTaskRollup	82	Rollup
pjTaskSheetNotes	94	Sheet notes
pjTaskStart	35	Start
pjTaskStart1	52	Start1
pjTaskStart2	55	Start2
pjTaskStart3	58	Start3
pjTaskStart4	61	Start4
pjTaskStart5	64	Start5
pjTaskStartVariance	45	Start variance
pjTaskStop	100	Stop
pjTaskSubproject	26	Subproject
pjTaskSuccessors	48	Successors
pjTaskSummary	92	Summary

pjTaskSV	13	SV
pjTaskText1	51	Text1
pjTaskText10	70	Text10
pjTaskText2	54	Text2
pjTaskText3	57	Text3
pjTaskText4	60	Text4
pjTaskText5	63	Text5
pjTaskText6	66	Text6
pjTaskText7	67	Text7
pjTaskText8	68	Text8
pjTaskText9	69	Text9
pjTaskTotalSlack	22	Total slack
pjTaskUniqueID	86	UniqueID
pjTaskUniquePredecessors	95	Predecessors
pjTaskUniqueSuccessors	96	Successors
pjTaskUpdateNeeded	111	Update needed
pjTaskWBS	16	WBS
pjTaskWork	0	Work
pjTaskWorkVariance	3	Work variance

See Also **GetField** Method, **SetMatchingField** Method, **SetResourceField** Method, **SetTaskField** Method.

SetMatchingField Method

Applies To **Application** Object.

Description Sets the value in the field of selected tasks or resources that meet the criteria you specify.

Syntax [*object*.]**SetMatchingField** *field, value, checkField, checkValue*[, *checkTest, checkOperation, checkField2, checkValue2, checkTest2*]

Elements The **SetMatchingField** method syntax has the following object qualifier and named arguments:

Part	Description
object	An object expression that evaluates to an object in the Applies To list. Optional.
field	A string expression that specifies the name of the field to set. Required.
value	A string expression that specifies the value to which the field is set. Required.
checkField	A string expression that specifies the name of the field to check. Required.
checkValue	A string expression that specifies the value to compare with the value in the checked field. Required.
checkTest	A string expression that specifies how to compare the values you specify with the *checkField* and *checkValue* arguments. By default, the *checkTest* argument is "equals". Optional.
checkOperation	A string expression that specifies how to connect the first set of criteria with the second set of criteria, if the second set is specified. You can set the *checkOperation* argument to "And" or "Or". By default, the *checkOperation* argument is "And". Optional.
checkField2	A string expression that specifies the name of the second field to check. Optional.
checkValue2	A string expression that specifies the value to compare with the value in the second checked field. Optional.
checkTest2	A string expression that specifies how to compare the values you specify with the *checkField2* and *checkValue2* arguments. By default, the *checkTest2* argument is "equals". Optional.

The *checkTest* and *checkTest2* arguments have these settings:

Setting	Search the field you specify with the *field* argument for a value that
"equals"	Equals the value you specify with the *value* argument.
"not equals"	Does not equal the value you specify with the *value* argument.
"greater"	Is greater than the value you specify with the *value* argument.
"gtr or equal"	Is greater than or equal to the value you specify with the *value* argument.
"less"	Is less than the value you specify with the *value* argument.
"less or equal"	Is less than or equal to the value you specify with the *value* argument.
"within"	Is within the value you specify with the *value* argument.
"not within"	Is not within the value you specify with the *value* argument.

Setting	Search the field you specify with the *field* argument for a value that
"contains"	Contains the value you specify with the *value* argument.
"doesn't contain"	Does not contain the value you specify with the *value* argument.
"contains exactly"	Exactly contains the value you specify with the *value* argument.

See Also   **SetField** Method, **SetResourceField** Method, **SetTaskField** Method.

SetResourceField Method

Applies To   **Application** Object.

Description   Sets the value of a resource field.

Syntax   [*object*.]**SetResourceField** *field*, *value*[, *allSelectedResources*, *create*, *resourceID*]

Elements   The **SetResourceField** method syntax has the following object qualifier and named arguments:

Part	Description
object	An object expression that evaluates to an object in the Applies To list. Optional.
field	A string expression that specifies the name of the resource field to set. Required.
value	A string expression that specifies the value of the resource field. Required.
allSelectedResources	A Boolean expression that specifies whether to set the value of the field for all selected resources. By default, the *allSelectedResources* argument is **False**. Optional. **True** Sets the value of the field for the selected resources. **False** Sets the value of the field for the active resource.
create	A Boolean expression that specifies whether to create a new field. By default, the *create* argument is **True**. Optional.
resourceID	A numeric expression that specifies the identification number of the resource containing the field to set. Optional.

See Also

SetField Method, **SetMatchingField** Method, **SetTaskField** Method.

SetTaskField Method

Applies To   **Application** Object.

Description   Sets the value of a task field.

Syntax   [*object*.]**SetTaskField** *field, value*[, *allSelectedTasks, create, taskID*]

Elements   The **SetTaskField** method syntax has the following object qualifier and named arguments:

Part	Description
object	An object expression that evaluates to an object in the Applies To list. Optional.
field	A string expression that specifies the name of the task field to set. Required.
value	A string expression that specifies the value of the task field. Required.
allSelectedTasks	A Boolean expression that specifies whether to set the value of the field for all selected tasks. By default, the *allSelectedTasks* argument is **False**. Optional.
	True Sets the value of the field for the selected tasks.
	False Sets the value of the field for the active task.
create	A Boolean expression that specifies whether to create a new field. By default, the *create* argument is **True**. Optional.
taskID	A numeric expression that specifies the identification number of the task containing the field to set. Optional.

See Also   **SetField** Method, **SetMatchingField** Method, **SetResourceField** Method.

Sgn Function

Description   Returns an integer indicating the sign of a number.

Syntax   **Sgn**(*number*)

Elements	The *number* argument can be any valid numeric expression.
Return Values	

If number is	Sgn returns
Greater than zero	1
Equal to zero	0
Less than zero	-1

Remarks	The sign of the *number* argument determines the return value of the **Sgn** function.
See Also	**Abs** Function.
Example	This example uses the **Sgn** function to determine the sign of a number.

```
MyVar1 = 12: MyVar2 = -2.4: MyVar3 = 0
MySign = Sgn(MyVar1)' Returns 1.
MySign = Sgn(MyVar2)' Returns -1.
MySign = Sgn(MyVar3)' Returns 0.
```

Shell Function

Description	Runs an executable program.
Syntax	**Shell(*pathname*[,*windowstyle*])**
Elements	The **Shell** function syntax has these named-argument parts:

Part	Description
pathname	Name of the program to execute and any required arguments or command line switches; may include directory or folder and drive. May also be the name of a document that has been associated with an executable program.
	On the Macintosh, you can use the **MacID** function to specify an application's signature instead of its name. The following example uses the signature for Microsoft Word:
	`Shell MacID("MSWD")`
windowstyle	Number corresponding to the style of the window in which the program is to be run. In Microsoft Windows, if *windowstyle* is omitted, the program is started minimized with focus. On the Macintosh (System 7.0 or later), *windowstyle* only determines whether or not the application gets the focus when it is run.

The *windowstyle* named argument has these values:

Value	Window Style
1, 5, 9	Normal with focus.
2	Minimized with focus.
3	Maximized with focus.
4,8	Normal without focus.
6,7	Minimized without focus.

Remarks

If you use the **MacID** function with **Shell** in Microsoft Windows, an error occurs.

If the **Shell** function successfully executes the named file, it returns the task identification (ID) of the started program. The task ID is a unique number that identifies the running program. If the **Shell** function can't start the named program, an error occurs.

Note   The **Shell** function runs other programs asynchronously. This means you can't depend on a program started with **Shell** to be finished executing before the statements following the **Shell** function in your application are executed.

See Also

AppActivate Statement, **MacID** Function.

Example

This example uses the **Shell** function to run an application specified by the user. On the Macintosh, using the **MacID** function ensures that the application can be launched even if the file name of the application has been changed. The **Shell** function is not available on the Macintosh prior to System 7.0.

```
' In Microsoft Windows.
' Specifying 1 as the second argument runs the application normally and
' gives it the focus.
RetVal = Shell("C:\WINDOWS\CALC.EXE", 1) ' Run Calculator.

' On the Macintosh.
' Both statements launch Microsoft Excel.
RetVal = Shell("Microsoft Excel")    ' Specify file name.
RetVal = Shell(MacID("XCEL"))        ' Specify signature.
```

Shift Object

Description

A work shift for a day, month, period, weekday, or year.

Properties

Application Property, **Finish** Property, **Index** Property, **Parent** Property, **Start** Property

Methods	**Clear** Method
See Also	**Day** Object, **Days** Collection; **Month** Object, **Months** Collection; **Period** Object; **Shift**n Property; **Weekday** Object, **Weekdays** Collection; **Year** Object, **Years** Collection.

Shift*n* Property

Applies To	**Day** Object, **Days** Collection; **Month** Object, **Months** Collection; **Period** Object; **Weekday** Object, **Weekdays** Collection; **Year** Object, **Years** Collection.
Description	Returns a shift of a day, month, period, weekday, or year.
Syntax	*object*.**Shift**n
Elements	The **Shift**n property syntaxes have the following object qualifier and named arguments:

Part	Description
object	An object expression that evaluates to an object in the Applies To list.
n	A number from 1 to 3.

See Also	**Calendar** Object, **Calendars** Collection; **Shift** Object.
Example	The following example schedules a half-day of work on Fridays by creating a 8 A.M. to noon shift.

```
Sub HalfDayFridays()
    with ActiveProject.Calendar.Weekdays(pjFriday)
        .Shift1.Start = #8:00:00 AM#
        .Shift1.Finish = #12:00:00 PM#
        .Shift2.Clear
        .Shift3.Clear
    End with
End Sub
```

ShowCriticalSlack Property

Applies To	**Project** Object, **Projects** Collection.
Description	Returns or sets how much slack causes a task to be displayed as a critical task.

Syntax	[*object.*]**ShowCriticalSlack** [= *value*]
Elements	The **ShowCriticalSlack** property syntax has these parts:

Part	Description
object	An object expression that evaluates to an object in the Applies To list.
value	A numeric expression that specifies a number of days. If its slack time does not exceed this number of days, Microsoft Project displays a task as critical.

See Also   **Calculation** Property, **ListSeparator** Property, **StartOnCurrentDate** Property, **StartYearIn** Property, **UserName** Property.

ShowTipOfDay Property

Applies To	**Application** Object.
Description	Returns or sets whether the Tip of the Day appears when Microsoft Project is started.
Syntax	[*object.*]**ShowTipOfDay** [= *value*]
Elements	The **ShowTipOfDay** property syntax has the following parts:

Part	Description
object	An object expression that evaluates to an object in the Applies To list.
value	A Boolean expression that specifies whether the Tip of the Day appears when Microsoft Project is started.

See Also   **LoadLastFile** Property, **OptionsGeneral** Method, **ShowToolTips** Property, **ShowWelcome** Property.

ShowToolTips Property

Applies To	**Application** Object.
Description	Returns or sets whether ToolTips are enabled.
Syntax	[*object.*]**ShowToolTips** [= *value*]
Elements	The **ShowToolTips** property syntax has the following parts:

Part	Description
object	An object expression that evaluates to an object in the Applies To list.
value	A Boolean expression that specifies whether ToolTips are enabled.

See Also   **LoadLastFile** Property, **OptionsGeneral** Method, **ShowTipOfDay** Property, **ShowWelcome** Property.

ShowWelcome Property

Applies To   **Application** Object.

Description   Returns or sets whether the Welcome dialog box appears when Microsoft Project is started.

Syntax   [*object.*]**ShowWelcome** [= *value*]

Elements   The **ShowWelcome** property syntax has the following parts:

Part	Description
object	An object expression that evaluates to an object in the Applies To list.
value	A Boolean expression that specifies whether the Welcome dialog box appears when Microsoft Project is started.

See Also   **LoadLastFile** Property, **OptionsGeneral** Method, **ShowTipOfDay** Property, **ShowToolTips** Property.

Sin Function

Description   Returns the sine of an angle.

Syntax   **Sin(*number*)**

Elements   The ***number*** named argument can be any valid numeric expression that expresses an angle in radians.

Remarks   The **Sin** function takes an angle and returns the ratio of two sides of a right triangle. The ratio is the length of the side opposite the angle divided by the length of the hypotenuse.

The result lies in the range -1 to 1.

To convert degrees to radians, multiply degrees by pi/180. To convert radians to degrees, multiply radians by 180/pi.

See Also   **Atn** Function, **Cos** Function, Derived Math Functions, **Tan** Function.

Example   This example uses the **Sin** function to return the sine of an angle.

```
MyAngle = 1.3                    ' Define angle in radians.
MyCosecant = 1 / Sin(MyAngle)    ' Calculate cosecant.
```

Single Data Type

Description   **Single** (single-precision floating-point) variables are stored as 32-bit (4-byte) numbers, ranging in value from -3.402823E38 to -1.401298E-45 for negative values and from 1.401298E-45 to 3.402823E38 for positive values. The type-declaration character for **Single** is **!** (character code 33).

See Also   **CSng** Function, Data Type Summary, **Deftype** Statements, **Double** Data Type, **Variant** Data Type.

Sort Method

Applies To   **Application** Object.

Description   Sorts the tasks or resources in the active pane.

Syntax   [*object*.]**Sort** [*key1, ascending1, key2, ascending2, key3, ascending3, renumber, outline*]

Elements   The **Sort** method syntax has the following object qualifier and named arguments:

Part	Description
object	An object expression that evaluates to an object in the Applies To list. Optional.
key1	A string expression that specifies the name of the primary field to sort. By default, the Sort dialog box appears, which prompts the user to specify sorting information. Optional.
ascending1	A Boolean expression that specifies whether to sort the primary field in ascending or descending order. By default, the *ascending1* argument is **True**. Optional.

Part	Description
key2	A string expression that specifies the name of a secondary field to sort. Optional.
ascending2	A Boolean expression that specifies whether to sort the secondary field in ascending or descending order. By default, the *ascending2* argument is **True**. Optional.
key3	A string expression that specifies the name of a tertiary field to sort. Optional.
ascending3	A Boolean expression that specifies whether to sort the tertiary field in ascending or descending order. By default, the *ascending3* argument is **True**. Optional.
renumber	A Boolean expression that specifies whether to renumber tasks after sorting them. For task views, the *renumber* argument can be **True** only if the *outline* argument is **True**. If the *outline* argument is **True**, then the *renumber* argument defaults to the current setting in the Sort dialog. If the *outline* argument is False, the *renumber* argument is ignored. Optional.
outline	A Boolean expression that specifies whether to preserve the outline level of tasks or resources after sorting them. By default, the *outline* argument is **True**. Optional.

See Also   **EditGoto** Method, **Filters** Method, **Find** Method, **Macro** Method.

Example   The following example sorts the tasks in the active project by priority, and then renumbers the tasks.

```
Sub SortByPriority()
    Sort key1:="Priority", ascending1:=True, renumber:=True, _
        outline:=False
End Sub
```

Space Function

Description   Returns a string consisting of the specified number of spaces.

Syntax   **Space(*number*)**

Elements   The *number* named argument is the number of spaces you want in the string.

Remarks   The **Space** function is useful for formatting output and clearing data in fixed-length strings.

See Also   **Spc** Function, **String** Function.

Example

This example uses the **Space** function to return a string consisting of a specified number of spaces.

```
' Returns a string with 10 spaces.
MyString = Space(10)
' Insert 10 spaces between 2 strings.
MyString = "Hello" & Space(10) & "World"
```

Spc Function

Description

Used with the **Print #** statement or the **Print** method to position output.

Syntax

Spc(*n***)**

Elements

The *n* argument is the number of spaces to insert before displaying or printing the next expression in a list.

Remarks

If *n* is less than the output-line width, the next print position immediately follows the number of spaces printed. If *n* is greater than the output-line width, **Spc** calculates the next print position using the formula:

currentprintposition + (*n* **Mod** *width*)

For example, if the current print position is 24, the output-line width is 80 and you specify **Spc(90)**, the next print will start at position 34 (current print position + the remainder of 90/80). If the difference between the current print position and the output-line width is less than *n* (or *n* **Mod** *width*), the **Spc** function skips to the beginning of the next line and generates a number of spaces equal to *n* - (*width* - *currentprintposition*).

Note   Make sure your tabular columns are wide enough to accommodate wider letters.

When you use the **Print** method with a proportionally spaced font, the width of space characters printed using the **Spc** function is always an average of the width of all characters in the point size for the chosen font. However, there is no correlation between the number of characters printed and the number of fixed-width columns those characters occupy. For example, the uppercase letter W occupies more than one fixed-width column and the lowercase letter I occupies less.

See Also

Print # Statement, **Print** Method, **Space** Function, **Tab** Function, **Width #** Statement.

Example

This example uses the **Spc** function to position output in a file and in the Debug window.

```
' The Spc function can be used with the Print # statement.
Open "TESTFILE" For Output As #1 ' Open file for output.
Print #1, "10 spaces between here"; Spc(10); "and here."
Close #1' Close file.
' The following statement causes the text to be printed in the Debug
' window, preceded by 30 spaces.
Debug.Print Spc(30); "Thirty spaces later..."
```

SpellingCheck Method

Applies To   **Application** Object.

Description   Checks the spelling in the active project.

Syntax   [*object.*]**SpellingCheck**

Elements   The *object* placeholder is an object expression that evaluates to an object in the Applies To list.

Remarks   The **SpellingCheck** method has the same effect as the Spelling command on the Tools menu.

See Also   **OptionsSpelling** Method.

Sqr Function

Description   Returns the square root of a number.

Syntax   **Sqr(*number*)**

Elements   The ***number*** named argument can be any valid numeric expression greater than or equal to 0.

Example   This example uses the **Sqr** function to calculate the square root of a number.

```
MySqr = Sqr(4)   ' Returns 2.
MySqr = Sqr(23)  ' Returns 4.795832.
MySqr = Sqr(0)   ' Returns 0.
MySqr = Sqr(-4)  ' Generates run-time error.
```

StandardRate Property

Applies To   **Project** Object, **Projects** Collection.

Description   Returns or sets the default standard rate of pay for resources.

Syntax   [*object*.]**DefaultResourceStandardRate** [= *value*]

Elements   The **DefaultResourceStandardRate** property syntax has these parts:

Part	Description
object	An object expression that evaluates to an object in the Applies To list.
value	A string expression that specifies the default standard rate of pay for resources.

See Also   **DefaultDurationUnits** Property, **DefaultFixedDuration** Property, **DefaultResourceOvertimeRate** Property, **DefaultView** Property, **DefaultWorkUnits** Property.

Start Property

Applies To   **Project** Object, **Projects** Collection; **Task** Object, **Tasks** Collection.

Description   Returns the earliest date on which a task can start.

Syntax   *object*.**EarlyStart**

Elements   The *object* placeholder is an object expression that evaluates to an object in the Applies To list.

See Also   **EarlyFinish** Property, **LateFinish** Property, **LateStart** Property.

Start*n* Property

Applies To   **Project** Object, **Projects** Collection; **Task** Object, **Tasks** Collection.

Description   Returns or sets the value in an additional start field for a project or task.

Syntax	*object*.**Start***n* [= *value*]
Elements	The **Start***n* property syntax has the following parts:

Part	Description
object	An object expression that evaluates to an object in the Applies To list.
n	A number from 1 to 5.
value	A date expression that specifies the value for the additional start field.

See Also	**ActualStart** Property, **BaselineSave** Method, **BaselineStart** Property, **Start** Property.

StartOnCurrentDate Property

Applies To	**Project** Object, **Projects** Collection.
Description	Returns or sets whether tasks start on the current date or the project start date.
Syntax	[*object*.]**StartOnCurrentDate** [= *value*]
Elements	The **StartOnCurrentDate** property syntax has these parts:

Part	Description
object	An object expression that evaluates to an object in the Applies To list.
value	A Boolean expression that specifies when tasks start, as shown under Settings.

Settings	The **StartOnCurrentDate** property has these settings:

Setting	Description
True	Tasks start on the current date.
False	Tasks start on the project start date.

See Also	**Calculation** Property, **ListSeparator** Property, **ShowCriticalSlack** Property, **StartYearIn** Property, **UserName** Property.

StartVariance Property

Applies To	**Project** Object, **Projects** Collection; **Task** Object, **Tasks** Collection.

Description	Returns the variance, in minutes, between the baseline start date and the start date of a project or task.
Syntax	*object*.**StartVariance**
Elements	The *object* placeholder is an object expression that evaluates to an object in the Applies To list.
See Also	**ActualStart** Property, **BaselineStart** Property, **CostVariance** Property, **DurationVariance** Property, **FinishVariance** Property, **Start** Property, **WorkVariance** Property.
Example	The following example displays the number of tasks in the active project that have started late.

```
Sub CountLateTasks()
    Dim T          ' Task object used in For Each loop
    Dim LateTasks    ' The number of late tasks

    LateTasks = 0

    ' Look for late tasks in the active project.
    For Each T In ActiveProject.Tasks
        If T.BaselineStart < ActiveProject.CurrentDate And _
           T.StartVariance > 0 Then LateTasks = LateTasks + 1
    Next T

    ' Display the number of late tasks in the active project.
    MsgBox "There are " & LateTasks & " late tasks in this project."
End Sub
```

StartWeekOn Property

Applies To	**Application** Object.
Description	Returns or sets whether weeks start on Sunday.
Syntax	[*object*.]**StartWeekOn** [= *value*]
Elements	The **StartWeekOn** property syntax has the following parts:

Part	Description
object	An object expression that evaluates to an object in the Applies To list.
value	A Boolean expression that specifies whether weeks start on Sunday.

See Also **DefaultFinishTime** Property, **DefaultStartTime** Property, **HoursPerDay** Property, **HoursPerWeek** Property, **OptionsCalendar** Method, **StartYearIn** Property.

StartYearIn Property

Applies To	**Application** Object.
Description	Returns or sets the start of the fiscal year.
Syntax	[*object*.]**StartYearIn** [= *value*]
Elements	The **StartYearIn** property syntax has these parts:

Part	Description
object	An object expression that evaluates to an object in the Applies To list.
value	A constant that specifies the first month of the fiscal year, as shown under Settings.

Settings The **StartYearIn** property syntax has these settings:

Setting	Description
pjJanuary	The fiscal year starts in January.
pjFebruary	The fiscal year starts in February.
pjMarch	The fiscal year starts in March.
pjApril	The fiscal year starts in April.
pjMay	The fiscal year starts in May.
pjJune	The fiscal year starts in June.
pjJuly	The fiscal year starts in July.
pjAugust	The fiscal year starts in August.
pjSeptember	The fiscal year starts in September.
pjOctober	The fiscal year starts in October.
pjNovember	The fiscal year starts in November.
pjDecember	The fiscal year starts in December.

See Also **Calculation** Property, **ListSeparator** Property, **ShowCriticalSlack** Property, **StartOnCurrentDate** Property, **UserName** Property.

Static Statement

Description

Used at the procedure level to declare variables and allocate storage space. Variables declared with the **Static** statement retain their value as long as the code is running.

Syntax

Static *varname*[(([*subscripts*])][**As** *type*][,*varname*[(([*subscripts*])][**As** *type*]] **. . .**

Elements

The **Static** statement syntax has these parts:

Part	Description
varname	Name of the variable; follows standard variable naming conventions.
subscripts	Dimensions of an array variable; up to 60 multiple dimensions may be declared. The *subscripts* argument uses the following syntax:
	[*lower* **To**] *upper* [,[*lower* **To**] *upper*] **. . .**
type	Data type of the variable; may be **Boolean**, **Integer**, **Long**, **Currency**, **Single**, **Double**, **Date**, **String** (for variable-length strings), **String** * *length* (for fixed-length strings), **Object**, **Variant**, a user-defined type, or an object type. Use a separate **As** *type* clause for each variable being defined.

Remarks

Once the module code is running, variables declared with the **Static** statement retain their value until the module is reset or restarted. Use the **Static** statement in nonstatic procedures to explicitly declare **Static** variables.

Use a **Static** statement within a procedure to declare the data type of a **Static** variable. For example, the following statement declares a fixed-size array of integers:

```
Static EmployeeNumber(200) As Integer
```

If you do not specify a data type or object type, and there is no **Def***type* statement in the module, the variable is **Variant** by default.

Note The Static statement and the Static keyword affect the lifetime of variables differently. If you declare a procedure using the Static keyword (as in `Static Sub CountSales ()`), the storage space for all local variables within the procedure is allocated once and the value of the variables is preserved for the entire time the code is running. For nonstatic procedures, storage space for variables is allocated each time the procedure is called and released when the procedure is exited. The Static statement is used to declare variables within nonstatic procedures to preserve their value as long as the program is running.

When variables are initialized, a numeric variable is initialized to 0, a variable-length string is initialized to a zero-length string, and a fixed-length string is filled with zeros. **Variant** variables are initialized to **Empty**. Each element of a user-defined type variable is initialized as if it was a separate variable. A variable that refers to an object must be assigned an existing object using the **Set** statement before it can be used. Until it is assigned an object, the declared object variable has the special value **Nothing**, which indicates that it does not refer to any particular instance of an object.

Tip When you use the Static statement in a procedure, it is a generally accepted programming practice to put the Static statement at the beginning of the procedure with any Dim statements.

See Also

Array Function, **Dim** Statement, **Function** Statement, **Option Base** Statement, **Private** Statement, **Public** Statement, **ReDim** Statement, **Sub** Statement.

Example

This example uses the **Static** statement to retain the value of a variable as long as module code is running.

```
' Function definition.
Function KeepTotal(Number)
    ' Only the variable Accumulate preserves its value between calls.
    Static Accumulate
    Accumulate = Accumulate + Number
    KeepTotal = Accumulate
End Function

' Static function definition.
Static Function MyFunction(Arg1, Arg2, Arg3)
    ' All local variables preserve value between function calls.
    Accumulate = Arg1 + Arg2 + Arg3
    Half = Accumulate / 2
    MyFunction = Half
End Function
```

Stop Property

Applies To

Project Object, **Projects** Collection; **Task** Object, **Tasks** Collection.

Description

Returns the date on which a project or task stops.

Syntax

object.**Stop**

Elements

The *object* placeholder is an object expression that evaluates to an object in the Applies To list.

See Also   **Resume** Property, **ResumeNoEarlierThan** Property.

Stop Statement

Description   Suspends execution.

Syntax   **Stop**

Remarks   You can place **Stop** statements anywhere in procedures to suspend execution. Using the **Stop** statement is similar to setting a breakpoint in the code.

The **Stop** statement suspends execution, but unlike **End**, it doesn't close any files or clear variables.

See Also   **End** Statement.

Example   This example uses the **Stop** statement to suspend execution for each iteration through the **For...Next** loop.

```
For I = 1 To 10 ' Start For...Next loop.
   Debug.Print I   ' Print I to Debug window.
    Stop          ' Stop each time through.
Next I
```

Str Function

Description   Returns a string representation of a number.

Syntax   **Str(*number*)**

Elements   The ***number*** named argument is any valid numeric expression.

Remarks   When numbers are converted to strings, a leading space is always reserved for the sign of ***number***. If ***number*** is positive, the returned string contains a leading space and the plus sign is implied.

Use the **Format** function to convert numeric values you want formatted as dates, times, or currency or in other user-defined formats. Unlike **Str**, the **Format** function doesn't include a leading space for the sign of ***number***.

Note   The **Str** function recognizes only the period (.) as a valid decimal separator. When a possibility exists that different decimal separators may be used (for example, in international applications), you should use **CStr** to convert a number to a string.

See Also   **Format** Function.

StrComp Function

Description   Returns a value indicating the result of a string comparison.

Syntax   **StrComp**(*string1*,*string2*[,*compare*])

Elements   The **StrComp** function syntax has these parts:

Part	Description
string1	Any valid string expression.
string2	Any valid string expression.
compare	Number specifying the type of string comparison. Specify a **1** to perform a textual comparison. Specify a **0** (default) to perform a binary comparison. If *compare* is **Null**, an error occurs. If *compare* is omitted, the setting of **Option Compare** is used to determine the type of comparison.

Return Values

Value	Description
-1	*string1* is less than *string2*.
0	*string1* is equal to *string2*.
1	*string1* is greater than *string2*.
Null	*string1* or *string2* is **Null**.

Remarks

Note   When **Option Compare Text** is specified, comparisons are textual and case-insensitive. When **Option Compare Binary** is specified, comparisons are strictly binary.

See Also   **Option Compare** Statement.

Example

This example uses the **StrComp** function to return the results of a string comparison. If 1 is supplied as the third argument, a textual comparison is performed; whereas, if the third argument is 0 or omitted, a binary comparison is performed.

```
MyStr1 = "ABCD": MyStr2 = "abcd"     ' Define variables.
MyComp = StrComp(MyStr1, MyStr2, 1)  ' Returns 0.
MyComp = StrComp(MyStr1, MyStr2, 0)  ' Returns -1.
MyComp = StrComp(MyStr2, MyStr1)     ' Returns 1.
```

String Data Type

Description

There are two kinds of strings:

- Variable-length strings, which can contain up to approximately 2 billion (2^31) characters (approximately 64K (2^16) characters for Microsoft Windows version 3.1 and earlier).

- Fixed-length strings, which contain a declared number of characters (less than 64K).

The type-declaration character for **String** is **$** (character code 36). The codes for **String** characters range from 0 to 255. The first 128 characters (0-127) of the character set correspond to the letters and symbols on a standard U.S. keyboard. These first 128 characters are the same as those defined by the ASCII character set. The second 128 characters (128-255) represent special characters, such as letters in international alphabets, accents, currency symbols, and fractions.

See Also

CStr Function, Data Type Summary, **Def**_type_ Statements, **String** Function, **Variant** Data Type.

String Function

Description

Returns a repeating character string of the length specified.

Syntax

String(_number,character_**)**

Elements

The **String** function syntax has these named-argument parts:

Part	Description
number	Length of the returned string. If *number* contains no valid data, **Null** is returned.
character	Character code specifying the character or string expression whose first character is used to build the return string. If *character* contains no valid data, **Null** is returned.

Remarks

If you specify a number for *character* greater than 255, **String** converts the number to a valid character code using the formula:

character **Mod** 256

See Also

Space Function, **String** Data Type.

Example

This example uses the **String** function to return repeating character strings of the length specified.

```
MyString = String(5, "*")    ' Returns "*****".
MyString = String(5, 42)     ' Returns "*****".
MyString = String(10, "ABC") ' Returns "AAAAAAAAAA".
```

Sub Statement

Description

Declares the name, arguments, and code that form the body of a **Sub** procedure.

Syntax

[**Private** | **Public**][**Static**] **Sub** *name* [(*arglist*)]
    [*statements*]
    [**Exit Sub**]
    [*statements*]
End Sub

Elements

The **Sub** statement syntax has these parts:

Part	Description
Public	Indicates that the **Sub** procedure is accessible to all other procedures in all modules. If used in a private module (one that contains an **Option Private** statement) the procedure is not available outside the project.
Private	Indicates that the **Sub** procedure is accessible only to other procedures in the module where it is declared.
Static	Indicates that the **Sub** procedure's local variables are preserved between calls. The **Static** attribute doesn't affect variables that are declared outside the **Sub**, even if they are used in the procedure.

Part	Description
name	Name of the **Sub**; follows standard variable naming conventions.
arglist	List of variables representing arguments that are passed to the **Sub** procedure when it is called. Multiple variables are separated by commas.
statements	Any group of statements to be executed within the body of the **Sub** procedure.

The *arglist* argument has the following syntax and parts:

[[**Optional**][**ByVal** | **ByRef**][**ParamArray**] *varname*[( )] **As** *type*]

Part	Description
Optional	Indicates that an argument is not required. If used, all subsequent arguments in *arglist* must also be optional and declared using the **Optional** keyword. All **Optional** arguments must be **Variant**. **Optional** can't be used for any argument if **ParamArray** is used.
ByVal	Indicates that the argument is passed by value.
ByRef	Indicates that the argument is passed by reference.
ParamArray	Used only as the last argument in *arglist* to indicate that the final argument is an **Optional** array of **Variant** elements. The **ParamArray** keyword allows you to provide an arbitrary number of arguments. May not be used with **ByVal**, **ByRef**, or **Optional**.
varname	Name of the variable representing the argument; follows standard variable naming conventions.
type	Data type of the argument passed to the procedure; may be **Boolean**, **Integer**, **Long**, **Currency**, **Single**, **Double**, **Date**, **String** (variable length only), **Object**, **Variant**, a user-defined type, or an object type.

Remarks

If not explicitly specified using either **Public** or **Private**, **Sub** procedures are **Public** by default. If **Static** is not used, the value of local variables is not preserved between calls.

All executable code must be in procedures. You can't define a **Sub** procedure inside another **Sub**, **Function**, or **Property** procedure.

The **Exit Sub** keyword causes an immediate exit from a **Sub** procedure. Program execution continues with the statement following the statement that called the **Sub** procedure. Any number of **Exit Sub** statements can appear anywhere in a **Sub** procedure.

Like a **Function** procedure, a **Sub** procedure is a separate procedure that can take arguments, perform a series of statements, and change the value of its arguments. However, unlike a **Function** procedure, which returns a value, a **Sub** procedure can't be used in an expression.

You call a **Sub** procedure using the procedure name followed by the argument list. See the **Call** statement for specific information on how to call **Sub** procedures.

Caution Sub procedures can be recursive; that is, they can call themselves to perform a given task. However, recursion can lead to stack overflow. The Static keyword usually is not used with recursive Sub procedures.

Variables used in **Sub** procedures fall into two categories: those that are explicitly declared within the procedure and those that are not. Variables that are explicitly declared in a procedure (using **Dim** or the equivalent) are always local to the procedure. Other variables used but not explicitly declared in a procedure are also local unless they are explicitly declared at some higher level outside the procedure.

Caution A procedure can use a variable that is not explicitly declared in the procedure, but a name conflict can occur if anything you have defined at the module level has the same name. If your procedure refers to an undeclared variable that has the same name as another procedure, constant or variable, it is assumed that your procedure is referring to that module-level name. Explicitly declare variables to avoid this kind of conflict. You can use an Option Explicit statement to force explicit declaration of variables.

Note You can't use GoSub, GoTo, or Return to enter or exit a Sub procedure.

See Also

Call Statement, **Dim** Statement, **Function** Statement, **Option Explicit** Statement, **Property Get** Statement, **Property Let** Statement, **Property Set** Statement, **Static** Statement.

Example

This example uses the **Sub** statement to declare the name, arguments and code that form the body of a **Sub** procedure.

```
' Sub procedure definition.
Sub SubComputeArea(Length, Width)      ' Sub with two arguments.
    Dim Area As Double                 ' Declare local variable.
    If Length = 0 Or Width = 0 Then    ' If either argument = 0.
        Exit Sub                       ' Exit Sub immediately.
    End If
    Area = Length * Width              ' Calculate area of rectangle.
    Debug.Print Area                   ' Print Area to Debug window.
End Sub
```

Subject Property

Applies To   **Project** Object, **Projects** Collection.

Description   Returns or sets the subject of a project.

Syntax   *object*.**Subject** [= *value*]

Elements   The **Subject** property syntax has these parts:

Part	Description
object	An object expression that evaluates to an object in the Applies To list.
value	A string expression that specifies the subject of the project.

See Also   **Author** Property, **Comments** Property, **Company** Property, **Keywords** Property, **Manager** Property, **Notes** Property.

SubProject Property

Applies To   **Task** Object, **Tasks** Collection.

Description   Returns or sets the subproject for a task.

Syntax   *object*.**SubProject** [= *value*]

Elements   The **SubProject** property syntax has the following parts:

Part	Description
object	An object expression that evaluates to an object in the Applies To list.
value	A string expression that specifies the filename of a subproject for the task.

See Also   **ConstraintType** Property, **Priority** Property.

Example   The following example sets a subproject for specified tasks in open projects.

```
Sub SetSubProject()
    Dim TaskName' The task name entered by the user
    Dim SubPName' The subproject filename entered by the user
    Dim P As Project' Project object used in For Each loop
    Dim T As Task    ' Task object used in For Each loop
```

```
            ' Prompt the user for a subproject filename and task name.
            TaskName = InputBox("Enter the name of a task.")
            SubPName = InputBox("Enter the filename of a subproject" & _
                    " for the task.")

            ' Set the subproject for each instance of the task in open projects.
            For Each P In Projects
                For Each T In P.Tasks
                    If T.Name = TaskName Then T.SubProject = SubPName
                Next T
            Next P
        End Sub
```

SubscriberOptions Method

Applies To	**Application** Object.
Description	Sets options for subscribers.
Syntax	[*object.*]**SubscriberOptions** (*Name*, *Field*[, *IsTask*, *UniqueID*, *Automatically*, *Action*])
Elements	The **SubscriberOptions** method has the following object qualifier and named arguments:

Part	Description
object	An object expression that evaluates to an object in the Applies To list. Optional.
Name	The name of the edition. Required..
Field	The field name or MPX field number to subscribe to. Required.
IsTask	A Boolean expression that returns a value indicating whether an expression references a task. By default, *IsTask* = **TRUE**. Optional.
UniqueID	A list of the unique IDs of the tasks or resources to subscribe to. The list is separated by the list separator character. Optional.
Automatically	A constant that specifies whether to save automatically or manually. Optional.
Action	A constant that specifies whether to cancel or update the subscriber. Optional.

The *Automatically* argument has these settings:

pjAutomaticUpdate	4	Updates automatically.
pjManualUpdate	5	Updates manually.

The *Action* argument has these settings:

pjCancel	1	Cancels the subscriber.
pjUpdateSubscriber	2	Updates the subscriber.

Remarks   This method applies to Microsoft Project for the Macintosh.

See Also   **EditionStopAll** Method, **PublisherOptions** Method, **SubscribeTo** Method.

SubscribeTo Method

Applies To   **Application** Object.

Description   Subscribes into selected items.

Syntax   [*object*.]**SubscribeTo** (*Edition*[, *Format*])

Elements   The **CreatePublisher** method has the following object qualifier and named arguments:

Part	Description
object	An object expression that evaluates to an object in the Applies To list. Optional.
Edition	The path name to an edition. Required.
Format	A constant that specifies how to subscribe when in the Gantt Chart. Default is **pjText**. Optional.

The *Format* argument has these settings:

pjText	1	All.
pjPicture	2	Picture only.

Remarks   This method applies to Microsoft Project for the Macintosh.

See Also   **CreatePublisher** Method, **SubscriberOptions** Method.

Successors Property

Applies To   **Task** Object, **Tasks** Collection.

Description   Returns the unique identification numbers of the successors of a task.

Syntax   *object*.**UniqueIDSuccessors**

Elements   The *object* placeholder is an object expression that evaluates to an object in the Applies To list.

Remarks   For example, the **UniqueIDSuccessors** property returns "3,9,8" if the unique identification numbers of the successor tasks are 3, 9, and 8.

Note This example assumes that the list separator character is the comma (,). You can determine the list separator character with the **ListSeparator** property.

See Also   **SuccessorTasks** Method, **UniqueID** Property, **UniqueIDPredecessors** Property.

SuccessorTasks Method

Applies To   **Task** Object, **Tasks** Collection.

Description   Returns a task or the tasks that are successors of a task.

Syntax   *object*.**SuccessorTasks**[(*index*)]

Elements   The **SuccessorTasks** method syntax has the following object qualifier and named arguments:

Part	Description
object	An object expression that evaluates to an object in the Applies To list.
index	A numeric expression that specifies the index of the *object*.

See Also   **LinkSuccessors** Method, **PredecessorTasks** Method, **Successors** Property, **Tasks** Method.

Summary Property

Applies To	**Project** Object, **Projects** Collection; **Task** Object, **Tasks** Collection.
Description	Returns a value that indicates whether a task is a summary task.
Syntax	*object*.**Summary**
Elements	The *object* placeholder is an object expression that evaluates to an object in the Applies To list.
Settings	The **Summary** property has the following settings:

Setting	Description
True	The task is a summary task.
False	The task is not a summary task.

See Also	**OutlineHideSubtasks** Method, **OutlineShowAllTasks** Method, **OutlineShowSubtasks** Method.

SupportsMultipleDocuments Property

Applies To	**Application** Object.
Description	Returns whether Microsoft Project supports multiple documents (projects); always **True** for Microsoft Project.
Syntax	[*object*.]**SupportsMultipleDocuments**
Elements	The *object* placeholder is an object expression that evaluates to an object in the Applies To list.
Remarks	The **SupportsMultipleDocuments** property always returns **True** because Microsoft Project can always have more than one document (project) open at a time.
	The **SupportsMultipleDocuments** property is useful with OLE automation. For example, suppose you want to open a second document in the application referred to by a variable. If the variable refers to one of several possible applications, you may want to use the **SupportsMultipleDocuments** property to confirm that the

application currently referenced by the variable can have more than one document open at a time.

See Also	**MoveAfterReturn** Property, **Name** Property, **OperatingSystem** Property, **SupportsMultipleWindows** Property, **Version** Property.

SupportsMultipleWindows Property

Applies To	**Application** Object.
Description	Returns whether Microsoft Project can have more than one window open at a time; always **True** for Microsoft Project.
Syntax	[*object*.]**SupportsMultipleWindows**
Elements	The *object* placeholder is an object expression that evaluates to an object in the Applies To list.
Remarks	The **SupportsMultipleWindows** property always returns **True** because Microsoft Project can always have more than one window open at a time.
	The **SupportsMultipleWindows** property is useful with OLE automation. For example, suppose you want to open a second window in the application referred to by a variable. If the variable refers to one of several possible applications, you may want to use the **SupportsMultipleWindows** property to confirm that the application currently referenced by the variable can have more than one window open at a time.
See Also	**MoveAfterReturn** Property, **Name** Property, **OperatingSystem** Property, **SupportsMultipleDocuments** Property, **Version** Property.

SV Property

Applies To	**Project** Object, **Projects** Collection; **Task** Object, **Tasks** Collection.
Description	Returns the SV of a project or task.
Syntax	*object*.**SV**
Elements	The *object* placeholder is an object expression that evaluates to an object in the Applies To list.
See Also	**BCWP** Property, **CV** Property.

Tab Function

Description   Used with the **Print #** statement or the **Print** method to position output.

Syntax   **Tab**[(*n*)]

Elements   The *n* argument is the column number to tab to before displaying or printing the next expression in a list. If omitted, **Tab** moves the cursor to the beginning of the next print zone. This allows **Tab** to be used instead of a comma in locales where the comma is used as a decimal separator.

Remarks   If the current print position on the current line is greater than *n*, **Tab** skips to the *n*th column on the next output line. If *n* is less than 1, **Tab** moves the print position to column 1. If *n* is greater than the output-line width, **Tab** calculates the next print position using the formula:

n **Mod** *width*

For example, if width is 80 and you specify **Tab**(90), the next print will start at column 10 (the remainder of 90/80). If *n* is less than the current print position, printing begins on the next line at the calculated print position. If the calculated print position is greater than the current print position, printing begins at the calculated print position on the same line.

The leftmost print position on an output line is always 1. When you use the **Print #** statement to print to files, the rightmost print position is the current width of the output file, which you can set using the **Width #** statement.

Note Make sure your tabular columns are wide enough to accommodate wider letters.

When you use the **Tab** function with the **Print** method, the print surface is divided into uniform, fixed-width columns. The width of each column is an average of the width of all characters in the point size for the chosen font. However, there is no correlation between the number of characters printed and the number of fixed-width columns those characters occupy. For example, the uppercase letter W occupies more than one fixed-width column and the lowercase letter I occupies less.

See Also   **Print #** Statement, **Print** Method, **Space** Function, **Spc** Function, **Width #** Statement.

Example   This example uses the **Tab** function to position output in a file or in the Debug window.

```
' The Tab function can be used with the Print # statement.
Open "TESTFILE" For Output As #1 ' Open file for output.
' The second word prints at column 20.
Print #1, "Hello"; Tab(20); "World."
' If the argument is omitted, cursor is moved to the next print zone.
Print #1, "Hello"; Tab ; "World"
Close #1' Close file.

' The Tab function can also be used with the Print method.
' The following statement prints text starting at column 10.
Debug.Print Tab(10); "10 columns from start."
```

TableApply Method

Applies To	**Application** Object.
Description	Applies a table to the active view.
Syntax	[*object*.]**TableApply** *name*
Elements	The **TableApply** method syntax has the following object qualifier and named arguments:

Part	Description
object	An object expression that evaluates to an object in the Applies To list. Optional.
name	A string expression that specifies the name of the table to apply. Required.

See Also	**OrganizerDeleteItem** Method, **TableEdit** Method, **Tables** Method.
Example	The following example applies the Variance table to the active view.

```
Sub ApplyVarianceTable()
    TableApply "Variance"
End Sub
```

TableEdit Method

Applies To	**Application** Object.

Description   Creates or edits a table.

Syntax   [*object.*]**TableEdit** *name, taskTable*[*, create, overwriteExisting, newName,*
fieldName, newFieldName, title, width, align, showInMenu, lockFirstColumn,
dateFormat, rowHeight, columnPosition]

Elements   The **TableEdit** method syntax has the following object qualifier and named
arguments:

Part	Description
object	An object expression that evaluates to an object in the Applies To list. Optional.
name	A string expression that specifies the name of a table to edit, create, or copy. Required.
taskTable	A Boolean expression that specifies whether the active table contains information on tasks or resources. Required.
create	A Boolean expression that specifies whether to create a new table. By default, the *create* argument is **False**. Optional. The *create* argument has these settings:

	True	A new table is created. If the *newName* argument is **Empty**, the new table is given the name you specify with the *name* argument. Otherwise, the new table is a copy of the table you specify with the *name* argument, and the new table is given the name you specify with the *newName* argument.
	False	A new table is not created.

Part	Description
overwriteExisting	A Boolean expression that specifies whether to replace the existing table with a new table. By default, the *overwriteExisting* argument is **False**. Optional.
newName	A string expression that specifies a new name for the existing (*create* argument is **False**) or new (*create* argument is **True**) table. By default, the *newName* argument is **Empty**. If the *newName* argument is **Empty** and the *create* argument is **False**, the table you specify with the *name* argument retains its current name. Optional.
fieldName	A string expression that specifies the name of a field to change. Optional.
newFieldName	A string expression that specifies the name of a new field. The field you specify with the *newFieldName* argument replaces the field you specify with the *fieldName* argument. Optional.
title	A string expression that specifies a title for the field you specify with the *fieldName* argument. Optional.

Part	Description
width	A numeric expression that specifies the width of the active columns, in points. By default, the *width* argument is 10 for new fields. Optional.
align	A constant that specifies how to align the text in the field you specify with the *fieldName* argument. By default, the *align* argument is **pjRight**. Optional.
showInMenu	A Boolean expression that specifies whether to show the name of the table in the Tables menu. (The Tables menu appears when you choose Table from the View menu.) By default, the *showInMenu* argument is **False**. Optional.
lockFirstColumn	A Boolean expression that specifies whether to lock — or prevent changes to — the first column of the table. By default, the *lockFirstColumn* argument is **False**. Optional.
dateFormat	A constant that specifies the format for the date fields in the table. By default, the *dateFormat* argument is **pjDateDefault**. Optional.
rowHeight	A numeric expression that specifies the height of the rows in the table. By default, the *rowHeight* argument is 1. Optional.
columnPosition	A numeric expression that specifies which column to edit. (Columns are numbered from the left to right, starting with 0.) If you specify a value for the *newFieldName* argument, a new column is inserted in the table. If you set the *columnPosition* argument to 0, the new field is inserted in the first column (*lockFirstColumn* is **False**) or the second column (*lockFirstColumn* is **True**) of the table. Set the *columnPosition* argument to -1 to specify the last column of the table. By default, the *columnPosition* argument is -1. Optional.

The *align* argument has these settings:

Constant	Description
pjLeft	The text is flushed left.
pjCenter	The text is centered.
pjRight	The text is flushed right.

The *dateFormat* argument has these settings:

pjDateDefault	-1	The default format, as specified on the View tab of the Options dialog box. (To display the Options dialog box, choose Options from the Tools menu.)
pjDate_mm_dd_yy_hh_mmAM	0	1/31/94 12:33 PM
pjDate_mm_dd_yy	1	1/31/94
pjDate_mmmm_dd_yyyy_hh_mmAM	2	January 31, 1994 12:33 PM
pjDate_mmmm_dd_yyyy	3	January 31, 1994
pjDate_mmm_dd_hh_mmAM	4	Jan 31 12:33 PM
pjDate_mmm_dd_yyy	5	Jan 31 '94
pjDate_mmmm_dd	6	January 31
pjDate_mmm_dd	7	Jan 31
pjDate_ddd_mm_dd_yy_hh_mmAM	8	Mon 1/31/94 12:33 PM
pjDate_ddd_mm_dd_yy	9	Mon 1/31/94
pjDate_ddd_mmm_dd_yyy	10	Mon Jan 31, '94
pjDate_ddd_hh_mmAM	11	Mon 12:33 PM
pjDate_mm_dd	12	1/31
pjDate_dd	13	31
pjDate_hh_mmAM	14	12:33 PM
pjDate_ddd_mmm_dd	15	Mon Jan 31
pjDate_ddd_mm_dd	16	Mon 1/31
pjDate_ddd_dd	17	Mon 31
pjDate_Www_dd	18	W05/1
pjDate_Www_dd_yy_hh_mmAM	19	W05/1/94 12:33 PM

Remarks   In Microsoft Windows, to specify the order of the items in a date format, such as years, months, and days, use the Regional settings in the Windows Control Panel.

See Also   **TableApply** Method, **Tables** Method.

Example   The following example creates a new table named Flags, but doesn't show the new table in the Table menu.

```
Sub CreateNewFlagTable()
    TableEdit name := "Flags", taskTable := True, create := True, _
        fieldName := "Priority", showInMenu := False
End Sub
```

Tables Method

Applies To	**Application** Object.
Description	Displays the More Tables dialog box, which prompts the user to manage tables.
Syntax	[*object*.]**Tables**
Elements	The *object* placeholder is an object expression that evaluates to an object in the Applies To list.
Remarks	The **Tables** method has the same effect as the More Tables command on the View menu.
See Also	**TableApply** Method, **TableEdit** Method.

Tan Function

Description	Returns the tangent of an angle.
Syntax	**Tan(*number*)**
Elements	The ***number*** named argument can be any valid numeric expression that expresses an angle in radians.
Remarks	**Tan** takes an angle and returns the ratio of two sides of a right triangle. The ratio is the length of the side opposite an angle divided by the length of the side adjacent to the angle.
	To convert degrees to radians, multiply degrees by pi/180. To convert radians to degrees, multiply radians by 180/pi.
See Also	**Atn** Function, **Cos** Function, Derived Math Functions, **Sin** Function.
Example	This example uses the **Tan** function to return the tangent of an angle.

```
MyAngle = 1.3                  ' Define angle in radians.
MyCotangent = 1 / Tan(MyAngle)   ' Calculate cotangent.
```

Task Object, Tasks Collection

Description   A task or tasks.

Remarks   In Microsoft Project, **Task** objects are parents of **Assignments** collections.

Properties   **ActualCost** Property, **ActualDuration** Property, **ActualFinish** Property, **ActualStart** Property, **ActualWork** Property, **Application** Property, **BaselineCost** Property, **BaselineDuration** Property, **BaselineFinish** Property, **BaselineStart** Property, **BaselineWork** Property, **BCWP** Property, **Confirmed** Property, **ConstraintDate** Property, **ConstraintType** Property, **Contact** Property, **Cost** Property, **Costn** Property, **CostVariance** Property, **Count** Property, **Created** Property, **Critical** Property, **CV** Property, **Delay** Property, **Duration** Property, **Durationn** Property, **DurationVariance** Property, **EarlyFinish** Property, **EarlyStart** Property, **Finish** Property, **Finishn** Property, **FinishVariance** Property, **FixedCost** Property, **FixedDuration** Property, **Flagn** Properties, **FreeSlack** Property, **HideBar** Property, **ID** Property, **Index** Property, **LateFinish** Property, **LateStart** Property, **LinkedFields** Property, **Marked** Property, **Milestone** Property, **Name** Property, **Notes** Property, **Numbern** Properties, **Objects** Property, **OutlineLevel** Property, **OutlineNumber** Property, **OutlineParent** Property, **Parent** Property, **PercentComplete** Property, **PercentWorkComplete** Property, **Predecessors** Property, **Priority** Property, **Project** Property, **RemainingCost** Property, **RemainingDuration** Property, **RemainingWork** Property, **ResourceGroup** Property, **ResourceInitials** Property, **ResourceNames** Property, **Resume** Property, **ResumeNoEarlierThan** Property, **Rollup** Property, **Start** Property, **Startn** Property, **StartVariance** Property, **Stop** Property, **SubProject** Property, **Successors** Property, **Summary** Property, **SV** Property, **Textn** Properties, **TotalSlack** Property, **UniqueID** Property, **UniqueIDPredecessors** Property, **UniqueIDSuccessors** Property, **UpdateNeeded** Property, **Work** Property, **WorkVariance** Property

Methods   **Add** Method, **Assignments** Method, **Delete** Method, **GetField** Method, **LinkPredecessors** Method, **LinkSuccessors** Method, **OutlineChildren** Method, **OutlineHideSubtasks** Method, **OutlineIndent** Method, **OutlineOutdent** Method, **OutlineShowAllTasks** Method, **OutlineShowSubtasks** Method, **PredecessorTasks** Method, **Resources** Method, **SetField** Method, **SuccessorTasks** Method, **UniqueID** Method, **UnlinkPredecessors** Method, **UnlinkSuccessors** Method

See Also   **Assignment** Object, **Assignments** Collection; **Task** Property; **Tasks** Method.

Task Property

Applies To	**Project** Object, **Projects** Collection.
Description	Returns or sets whether the summary task for a project is visible.
Syntax	*object*.**DisplayProjectSummaryTask** [= *value*]
Elements	The **DisplayProjectSummaryTask** property syntax has the following parts:

Part	Description
object	An object expression that evaluates to an object in the Applies To list.
value	A Boolean expression that specifies whether the project summary task is visible.

See Also	**OptionsView** Method.
Example	The following example creates a new project and displays its summary task.

```
Sub NewProject()
    FileNew
    ActiveProject.DisplayProjectSummaryTask = True
End Sub
```

TaskFilterList Method

Applies To	**Project** Object, **Projects** Collection.
Description	Returns a task filter name or all task filter names.
Syntax	*object*.**TaskFilterList**[(***index***)]
Elements	The **TaskFilterList** method syntax has the following object qualifier and named arguments:

Part	Description
object	An object expression that evaluates to an object in the Applies To list.
index	A numeric expression that specifies the index of the *object*.

See Also	**CurrentFilter** Property, **FilterApply** Method, **FilterEdit** Method, **Filters** Method, **List** Object, **ReportList** Method, **ResourceFilterList** Method, **TaskTableList** Method, **TaskViewList** Method, **ViewList** Method.
Example	The following example lists all the task filters.

```
Sub SeeAllFilters()
    Dim t As Variant
    For Each t in ActiveProject.TaskFilterList
        MsgBox t
    Next t
End Sub
```

TaskID Property

Applies To	**Assignment** Object, **Assignments** Collection.
Description	Returns the identification number of a task in an assignment.
Syntax	*object*.**TaskID**
Elements	The *object* placeholder is an object expression that evaluates to an object in the Applies To list.
See Also	**ProjectID** Property, **ResourceID** Property, **ResourceName** Property, **TaskName** Property.

TaskName Property

Applies To	**Assignment** Object, **Assignments** Collection.
Description	Returns the name of the task in an assignment.
Syntax	*object*.**TaskName**
Elements	The *object* placeholder is an object expression that evaluates to an object in the Applies To list.
See Also	**ProjectID** Property, **ResourceID** Property, **ResourceName** Property, **TaskID** Property.

TaskTableList Method

Applies To	**Project** Object, **Projects** Collection.
Description	Returns a task table name or all task table names.
Syntax	*object*.**TaskTableList**[(*index*)]
Elements	The **TaskTableList** method syntax has the following object qualifier and named arguments:

Part	Description
object	An object expression that evaluates to an object in the Applies To list.
index	A numeric expression that specifies the index of the *object*.

See Also	**CurrentTable** Property, **List** Object, **ReportList** Method, **ResourceTableList** Method, **TableApply** Method, **TableEdit** Method, **Tables** Method, **TaskFilterList** Method, **TaskViewList** Method, **ViewList** Method.
Example	The following example lists all the task tables.

```
Sub SeeAllTables()
    Dim t As Variant
    For Each t In ActiveProject.TaskTableList
        MsgBox t
    Next t
End Sub
```

TaskViewList Method

Applies To	**Project** Object, **Projects** Collection.
Description	Returns a task view name or all task view names.
Syntax	*object*.**TaskViewList**[(*index*)]
Elements	The **TaskViewList** method syntax has the following object qualifier and named arguments:

Part	Description
object	An object expression that evaluates to an object in the Applies To list.
index	A numeric expression that specifies the index of the *object*.

See Also

CurrentView Property, **List** Object, **ReportList** Method, **ResourceViewList** Method, **TaskFilterList** Method, **TaskTableList** Method, **ViewApply** Method, **ViewEditCombination** Method, **ViewEditSingle** Method, **ViewList** Method, **Views** Method.

Example

The following example lists all the task views.

```
Sub SeeAllTaskViews()
    Dim t As Variant
    For Each t In ActiveProject.TaskViewList
        MsgBox t
    Next t
End Sub
```

Template Property

Applies To

Project Object, **Projects** Collection.

Description

Returns the name of the template associated with a project.

Syntax

object.**Template**

Elements

The *object* placeholder is an object expression that evaluates to an object in the Applies To list.

See Also

Author Property, **Comments** Property, **Company** Property, **Keywords** Property, **Manager** Property, **Notes** Property, **Subject** Property, **Title** Property.

Example

The following example creates a new project based on the template of the active project.

```
Sub CreateNewProject()
    FileOpen ActiveProject.Template
End Sub
```

Text*n* Properties

Applies To	**Project** Object, **Projects** Collection; **Resource** Object, **Resources** Collection; **Task** Object, **Tasks** Collection.
Description	Returns or sets text associated with a resource or task.
Syntax	*object*.**Text***n* [= *value*]
Elements	The **Text***n* property syntaxes have the following parts:

Part	Description
object	An object expression that evaluates to an object in the Applies To list.
n	A number from 1 to 5 (**Resource** object) or from 1 to 10 (**Task** or **Project** object).
value	A string expression that specifies the text associated with the resource or task.

See Also	**Flag***n* Properties, **Notes** Property, **Number***n* Properties, **Summary** Property.

TextStyles Method

Applies To	**Application** Object.
Description	Sets the text styles for tasks and resources in the active view.
Syntax	[*object*.]**TextStyles** *item*[, *font*, *size*, *bold*, *italic*, *underline*, *color*]
Elements	The **TextStyles** method syntax has the following object qualifier and named arguments:

Part	Description
object	An object expression that evaluates to an object in the Applies To list. Optional.
item	A constant that specifies the type of text to change. Required.
font	A string expression that specifies the name of the font. The *font* argument is ignored if the active view is the PERT Chart and the *item* argument is not **pjAll**. Optional.

Part	Description
size	A string expression that specifies the size of the font. The *size* argument is ignored if the active view is the PERT Chart and the *item* argument is not **pjAll**. Optional.
bold	A Boolean expression that specifies whether the font is bold. Optional.
italic	A Boolean expression that specifies whether the font is italic. Optional.
underline	A Boolean expression that specifies whether the font is underlined. Optional.
color	A constant that specifies the color of the font. Optional.

If the active view is the Gantt Chart, the *item* argument has these settings:

pjAll	0	All
pjNoncritical	1	Noncritical tasks
pjCritical	2	Critical tasks
pjMilestone	3	Milestone tasks
pjSummary	4	Summary tasks
pjProjectSummary	5	Project summary tasks
pjMarked	6	Marked tasks
pjTaskFilterHighlight	7	Filter-highlighted tasks
pjTaskRowColumnTitles	8	Row and column titles
pjGanttMajorTimescale	9	Major timescale
pjGanttMinorTimescale	10	Minor timescale
pjBarTextLeft	11	Text to the left of Gantt bars
pjBarTextRight	12	Text to the right of Gantt bars
pjBarTextTop	13	Text above Gantt bars
pjBarTextBottom	14	Text below Gantt bars
pjBarTextInside	15	Text inside Gantt bars

If the active view is the Calendar, the *item* argument has these settings:

pjAll	0	All
pjNoncritical	1	Noncritical tasks
pjCritical	2	Critical tasks
pjMilestone	3	Milestone tasks
pjSummary	4	Summary tasks

pjProjectSummary	5	Project summary tasks
pjMarked	6	Marked tasks
pjTaskFilterHighlight	7	Filter-highlighted tasks
pjMonthlyTitles	8	Monthly titles
pjDailyTitles	9	Daily titles
pjWeeklyTitles	10	Weekly titles
pjMonthPreviews	11	Month previews
pjDateBoxTopRight	12	Text in the upper-right corner of date boxes
pjDateBoxTopLeft	13	Text in the upper-left corner of date boxes
pjDateBoxBottomRight	14	Text in the lower-right corner of date boxes
pjDateBoxBottomLeft	15	Text in the lower-left corner of date boxes

If the active view is the Task Sheet, the *item* argument has these settings:

pjAll	0	All
pjNoncritical	1	Noncritical tasks
pjCritical	2	Critical tasks
pjMilestone	3	Milestone tasks
pjSummary	4	Summary tasks
pjProjectSummary	5	Project summary tasks
pjMarked	6	Marked tasks
pjTaskFilterHighlight	7	Filter-highlighted tasks
pjTaskRowColumnTitles	8	Titles for rows and columns

If the active view is the PERT Chart, the *item* argument has these settings:

pjAll	0	All
pjPERTCritical	1	Critical tasks
pjPERTNonCritical	2	Noncritical tasks
pjCriticalMilestone	3	Critical milestone tasks
pjNoncriticalMilestone	4	Noncritical milestone tasks
pjCriticalSummary	5	Critical summary tasks
pjNoncriticalSummary	6	Noncritical summary tasks
pjCriticalSubproject	7	Critical subproject tasks

pjNoncriticalSubproject	8	Noncritical subproject tasks
pjCriticalMarked	9	Critical marked tasks
pjNoncriticalMarked	10	Noncritical marked tasks

If the active view is the Resource Graph, the *item* argument has these settings:

pjAll	0	All
pjAllocated	1	Allocated resources
pjOverallocated	2	Overallocated resources
pjGraphMajorTimescale	3	Major timescale
pjGraphMinorTimescale	4	Minor timescale
pjTickLabels	5	Tick labels
pjLegendLabels	6	Legend labels

If the active view is the Resource Usage Graph, the *item* argument has these settings:

pjAll	0	All
pjAllocated	1	Allocated resources
pjOverallocated	2	Overallocated resources
pjResourceFilterHighlight	3	Filter-highlighted resources
pjResourceRowColumnTitles	4	Row and column titles
pjUsageMajorTimescale	5	Major timescale
pjUsageMinorTimescale	6	Minor timescale

If the active view is the Resource Sheet, the *item* argument has these settings:

pjAll	0	All
pjAllocated	1	Allocated resources
pjOverallocated	2	Overallocated resources
pjResourceFilterHighlight	3	Filter-highlighted resources
pjResourceRowColumnTitles	4	Row and column titles

The *color* argument has these settings:

pjBlack	0	Black
pjRed	1	Red
pjYellow	2	Yellow

pjLime	3	Lime
pjAqua	4	Aqua
pjBlue	5	Blue
pjFuchsia	6	Fuchsia
pjWhite	7	White
pjMaroon	8	Maroon
pjGreen	9	Green
pjOlive	10	Olive
pjNavy	11	Navy
pjPurple	12	Purple
pjTeal	13	Teal
pjGray	14	Gray
pjSilver	15	Silver

See Also   **BarBoxStyles** Method, **Font** Method, **FontBold** Method, **FontItalic** Method, **FontUnderline** Method, **GanttBarStyleEdit** Method.

ThousandsSeparator Property

Applies To   **Application** Object.

Description   Returns the thousands separator character.

Syntax   [*object*.]**ThousandsSeparator**

Elements   The *object* placeholder is an object expression that evaluates to an object in the Applies To list.

Remarks   Microsoft Project for Microsoft Windows sets the **ThousandsSeparator** property equal to the corresponding value in the Regional settings of the Microsoft Windows Control Panel.

On the Macintosh, using System 7.1 and later, you can use the Numbers control panel to change this value.

See Also   **DecimalSeparator** Property.

Time Function

Description   Returns the current system time.

Syntax   **Time**

Remarks   To set the system time, use the **Time** statement.

See Also   **Date** Function, **Date** Statement, **Time** Statement, **Timer** Function.

Example   This example uses the **Time** function to return the current system time.

```
MyTime = Time    ' Return current system time.
```

Time Statement

Description   Sets the system time.

Syntax   **Time** = *time*

Elements   The *time* argument is limited to expressions that can represent a time. If *time* contains no valid data, **Null** is returned.

Remarks   If *time* is a string, **Time** attempts to convert it to a time using the time separators you specified for your system. If it can't be converted to a valid time, an error occurs.

Note If you use the **Time** statement to set the time on computers using versions of MS-DOS earlier than version 3.3, the change remains in effect only until you change it again or turn off your computer. Many computers have a battery-powered CMOS RAM that retains date and time information when the computer is turned off. However, to permanently change the time on computers running earlier versions of MS-DOS, you may have to use your Setup disk or perform some equivalent action. Refer to the documentation for your particular system.

See Also   **Date** Function, **Date** Statement, **Time** Function.

Example	This example uses the **Time** statement to set the computer system time to a user-defined time.

```
MyTime = #4:35:17 PM#    ' Assign a time.
Time = MyTime           ' Set system time to MyTime.
```

TimeLeadingZero Property

Applies To	**Application** Object.
Description	Returns **True** if Microsoft Project displays zeroes before times with single-digit hours; returns **False** otherwise.
Syntax	[*object*.]**TimeLeadingZero**
Elements	The *object* placeholder is an object expression that evaluates to an object in the Applies To list.
Remarks	Microsoft Project for Microsoft Windows sets the **TimeLeadingZero** property equal to the corresponding value in the Regional settings of the Microsoft Windows Control Panel.
	On the Macintosh, using System 7.1 and later, you can use the Date & Time control panel to change this value.
See Also	**AMText** Property, **PMText** Property, **TimeSeparator** Property, **TwelveHourTimeFormat** Property.

Timer Function

Description	Returns the number of seconds elapsed since midnight.
Syntax	**Timer**
Remarks	The return value of the **Timer** function is automatically used with the **Randomize** statement to generate a seed for the **Rnd** (random-number) function.
See Also	**Randomize** Statement, **Rnd** Function, **Time** Function.

Example

This example uses the **Timer** function to record the number of seconds taken to print output to the Debug window.

```
Start = Timer    ' Set start time.
For I = 1 to 50  ' Loop 50 times.
    Debug.Print I    ' Print to Debug window.
Next I
Finish = Timer   ' Set end time.
TotalTime = Finish - Start   ' Calculate total time.
```

Timescale Method

Applies To

Application Object.

Description

Zooms in on or out from the Gantt Chart, Resource Graph, and Resource Usage view to show information about tasks or resources in a certain duration.

Syntax

[*object*.]**ZoomTimescale** [*duration*, *entire*, *selection*, *reset*]

Elements

The **ZoomTimescale** method syntax has the following object qualifier and named arguments:

Part	Description
object	An object expression that evaluates to an object in the Applies To list. Optional.
duration	A string expression that specifies the duration to display in the view. Optional.
entire	A Boolean expression that specifies whether to display the entire project in the view. By default, the *entire* argument is **False**. Optional.
selection	A Boolean expression that specifies whether to display the selected tasks in the view. By default, the *selection* argument is **False**. Optional.
reset	A Boolean expression that specifies whether to reset the view to its default size. By default, the *reset* argument is **False**. Optional.

See Also

ZoomIn Method, **ZoomOut** Method, **ZoomPERT** Method.

Example

The following example fits the entire project in the current view.

```
Sub Display()
    ZoomTimescale entire := True
End Sub
```

TimescaledData Method

Applies To   **Application** Object.

Description   Returns a list of work or cost information for a task and resource over intervals in a time period.

Syntax   [*object*.]**TimescaledData**(*taskID*, *resourceID*, *startDate*, *endDate*[, *type*, *timescaleUnit*, *count*])

Elements   The **TimescaledData** statement syntax has the following object qualifier and named arguments:

Part	Description
object	An object expression that evaluates to an object in the Applies To list. Optional.
taskID	A numeric expression that specifies the identification number of the task. Required.
resourceID	A numeric expression that specifies the identification number of the resource. Required.
startDate	A date expression that specifies the start date. The start date is rounded to the beginning of the interval in which it falls. Required.
endDate	A date expression that specifies the finish date. The finish date is rounded to the end of the interval in which it falls. Required.
type	A constant that specifies the type of information. By default, the *type* argument is **pjWork**. Optional.
timescaleUnit	A constant that specifies the timescale unit. By default, the *timescaleUnit* argument is **pjTimescaleWeek**. Optional.
count	A numeric expression that specifies the number of timescale units. By default, the *count* argument is 1. Optional.

The *type* argument has these settings:

pjWork	0	Work
pjCost	1	Cost
pjCumulativeWork	2	Cumulative work
pjCumulativeCost	3	Cumulative cost

The *timescaleUnit* argument has these settings:

pjTimescaleYears	0	Years
pjTimescaleQuarters	1	Quarters
pjTimescaleMonths	2	Months
pjTimescaleWeeks	3	Weeks
pjTimescaleDays	4	Days
pjTimescaleHours	5	Hours
pjTimescaleMinutes	6	Minutes

Remarks

The *startDate* and *endDate* arguments are rounded to the start and end of the intervals in which they fall.

See Also

Assignments Method, **Resources** Method, **Tasks** Method, **TimescaleEdit** Method.

Example

The following example displays the number of hours per week that a resource will work on a task for the next month.

```
Sub AssignmentsOverTime()
    Dim t, r, temp

    Open "usage.csv" For Output As #1

    For Each t In ActiveProject.Tasks
        If Not (t is Nothing) Then
            Print #1, t.Name
            For Each r In t.Resources
                temp = TimescaledData(t.ID, r.ID, _
                    ActiveProject.ProjectStart, _
                    ActiveProject.ProjectFinish, pjWork, _
                    pjTimescaleWeeks)
                Print #1, r.name & ListSeparator & temp
            Next r
        End If
    Next t

    Close #1
End Sub
```

TimescaleEdit Method

Applies To	**Application** Object.
Description	Formats timescales for the following: Gantt Chart, Resource Graph, and Resource Usage view.
Syntax	[*object.*]**TimescaleEdit** [*majorUnits, minorUnits, majorLabel, minorLabel, majorAlign, minorAlign, majorCount, minorCount, majorTicks, minorTicks, enlarge, separator*]
Elements	The **TimescaleEdit** method syntax has the following object qualifier and named arguments:

Part	Description
object	An object expression that evaluates to an object in the Applies To list. Optional.
majorUnits	A constant that specifies the major units for the timescale. Optional.
minorUnits	A constant that specifies the minor units for the timescale. Optional.
majorLabel	A constant that specifies the major label for the timescale. Optional.
minorLabel	A constant that specifies the minor label for the timescale. Optional.
majorAlign	A constant that specifies the alignment of major units on the timescale. Optional.
minorAlign	A constant that specifies the alignment of minor units on the timescale. Optional.
majorCount	A numeric expression that specifies the number of major timescale units to display together. Optional.
minorCount	A numeric expression that specifies the number of minor timescale units to display together. Optional.
majorTicks	A Boolean expression that specifies whether to display ticks between the major timescale units. Optional.
minorTicks	A Boolean expression that specifies whether to display ticks between the minor timescale units. Optional.

Part	Description
enlarge	A numeric expression from 25 to 1000 that specifies the scaling factor for the timescale. Optional.
separator	A Boolean expression that specifies whether to draw a line between the major and minor timescales. Optional.

The *majorUnits* and *minorUnits* arguments have these settings:

pjTimescaleYears	0	Years
pjTimescaleQuarters	1	Quarters
pjTimescaleMonths	2	Months
pjTimescaleWeeks	3	Weeks
pjTimescaleDays	4	Days
pjTimescaleHours	5	Hours
pjTimescaleMinutes	6	Minutes

If the *majorUnits* and *minorUnits* arguments equal **pjTimescaleYears**, the *majorLabel* and *minorLabel* arguments have these settings:

Constant	Examples of the date format
pjYear_yyyy	1994, 1995
pjYear_yyy	'94, '95
pjYear_yy	94, 95
pjYearFromEnd_yy	3, 2, 1 (year from the finish date of the project)
pjYearFromEnd_Yyy	Y3, Y2, Y1 (year from the finish date of the project)
pjYearFromEnd_Year_yy	Year 2, Year 1 (year from the finish date of the project)
pjYearFromStart_yy	1, 2, 3 (year from the start date of the project)
pjYearFromStart_Yyy	Y1, Y2, Y3 (year from the start date of the project)
pjYearFromStart_Year_yy	Year 1, Year 2 (year from the start date of the project)

If the *majorUnits* and *minorUnits* arguments equal **pjTimescaleQuarters**, the *majorLabel* and *minorLabel* arguments have these settings:

Constant	Examples of the date format
pjQuarter_q	1, 2
pjQuarter_qQyy	1Q94, 2Q94
pjQuarter_qqq_Quarter	1st Quarter, 2nd Quarter
pjQuarter_Qq	Q1, Q2
pjQuarter_Qq_yyy	Q1 '94, Q2 '94
pjQuarter_Qtr_q	Qtr 1, Qtr 2
pjQuarter_Qtr_q_yyyy	Qtr 1, 1994; Qtr 2, 1994
pjQuarterFromEnd_q	3, 2, 1 (quarter from the finish date of the project)
pjQuarterFromEnd_Qq	Q3, Q2, Q1 (quarter from the finish date of the project)
pjQuarterFromEnd_Quarter_q	Quarter 2, Quarter 1 (quarter from the finish date of the project)
pjQuarterFromStart_q	3, 2, 1 (quarter from the start date of the project)
pjQuarterFromStart_Qq	Q3, Q2, Q1 (quarter from the start date of the project)
pjQuarterFromStart_Quarter_q	Quarter 2, Quarter 1 (quarter from the start date of the project)

If the *majorUnits* and *minorUnits* arguments equal **pjTimescaleMonths**, the *majorLabel* and *minorLabel* arguments have these settings:

Constant	Examples of the date format
pjMonth_mm	1, 2
pjMonth_mm_yy	1/94, 2/94
pjMonth_mm_yyy	1 '94, 2 '94
pjMonth_m	J, F
pjMonth_mmm	Jan, Feb
pjMonth_mmm_yyy	Jan '94, Feb '94
pjMonth_mmmm	January, February
pjMonth_mmmm_yyyy	January 1994, February 1994
pjMonthFromEnd_mm	5, 4 (month from the finish date of project)
pjMonthFromEnd_Mmm	M5, M4 (month from the finish date of project)
pjMonthFromEnd_Month_mm	Month5, Month4 (month from the finish date of project)

Constant	Examples of the date format
pjMonthFromStart_mm	1, 2 (month from the start date of project)
pjMonthFromStart_Mmm	M1, M2 (month from the start date of project)
pjMonthFromStart_Month_mm	Month1, Month2 (month from the start date of project)

If the *majorUnits* and *minorUnits* arguments equal **pjTimescaleWeeks**, the *majorLabel* and *minorLabel* arguments have these settings:

Constant	Examples of the date format
pjWeek_mm_dd	1/31, 2/7
pjWeek_mm_dd_yy	1/31/94, 2/7/94
pjWeek_m_dd	J 31, F 7
pjWeek_mmm_dd	Jan 31, Feb 7
pjWeek_mmm_dd_yyy	Jan 31, '94
pjWeek_mmmm_dd	January 31, February 7
pjWeek_mmmm_dd_yyyy	January 31, 1994; February 7, 1994
pjWeek_di_mm_dd	M 1/31, M 2/7
pjWeek_di_m_dd	M J 31, M F 7
pjWeek_di_mmm_dd	M Jan 31, M Feb 7
pjWeek_ddi_mm_dd	Mo 1/31, Mo 2/7
pjWeek_ddi_m_dd	Mo J 31, Mo F 7
pjWeek_ddi_mmm_dd	Mo Jan 31, Mo Feb 7
pjWeek_ddd_mm_dd	Mon 1/31, Mon 2/7
pjWeek_ddd_mm_dd_yy	Mon 1/31/94, Mon 2/7/94
pjWeek_ddd_dd	Mon 31, Mon 7
pjWeek_ddd_ww	Mon 5, Mon 6 (number of the week in the year)
pjWeek_ddd_m_dd	Mon J 31, Mon F 7
pjWeek_ddd_mmm_dd	Mon Jan 31, Mon Feb 7
pjWeek_ddd_mmm_dd_yyy	Mon Jan 31, '94; Mon Feb 7, '94
pjWeek_ddd_mmmm_dd	Mon January 31, Mon February 7
pjWeek_ddd_mmmm_dd_yyy	Mon January 31, '94; Mon February 7, '94

If the *majorUnits* and *minorUnits* arguments equal **pjTimescaleDays**, the *majorLabel* and *minorLabel* arguments have these settings:

Constant	Examples of date format
pjDay_mm_dd	1/31, 2/1
pjDay_mm_dd_yy	1/31/94, 2/1/94
pjDay_m_dd	J 31, F1
pjDay_mmm_dd	Jan 31, Feb 1
pjDay_mmm_dd_yyy	Jan 31, '94; Feb 1, '94
pjDay_di	M, T
pjDay_di_mm_dd	M 1/31, T 2/1
pjDay_di_dd	M 31, T 1
pjDay_di_m_dd	M J 31, T F 1
pjDay_didd	M31, T1
pjDay_ddi	Mo, Tu
pjDay_ddi_mm_dd	Mo 1/31, Tu 2/1
pjDay_ddi_dd	Mo 31, Tu 1
pjDay_ddi_m_dd	Mo J 31, Tu F 1
pjDay_ddd	Mon, Tue
pjDay_ddd_mm_dd	Mon 1/31, Tue 2/1
pjDay_ddd_mm_dd_yy	Mon 1/31/94; Tue 2/1/94
pjDay_ddd_dd	Mon 31, Tue 1
pjDay_ddd_m_dd	Mon J 31, Tue F 1
pjDay_ddd_mmm_dd	Mon Jan 31, Tue Feb 1
pjDay_ddd_mmm_dd_yyy	Mon Jan 31, '94; Tue Feb 1, '94
pjDay_ddd_mmmm_dd	Mon January 31, Tue February 1
pjDay_dddd	Monday, Tuesday
pjDayFromEnd_dd	4, 3 (day from the end date of the project)
pjDayFromEnd_Ddd	D4, D3 (day from the end date of the project)
pjDayFromEnd_Day_dd	Day 4, Day 3 day from the end date of the project)
pjDayFromStart_dd	1, 2 (day from the start date of the project)
pjDayFromStart_Ddd	D1, D2 (day from the start date of the project)
pjDayFromStart_Day_dd	Day 1, Day 2 (day from the start date of the project)
pjDayOfMonth_dd	1, 2 (day of the month)
pjDayOfYear_dd	1, 2 (day of the year)
pjDayOfYear_dd_yyyy	1 1994, 2 1994 (day of the year and the year)
pjDayOfYear_dd_yyy	1 '94, 2 '94 (day of the year and the year)

If the *majorUnits* and *minorUnits* arguments equal **pjTimescaleHours**, the *majorLabel* and *minorLabel* arguments have these settings:

Constant	Examples of the date format
pjHour_mm_dd_hhAM	1/31, 11 AM; 1/31, 12 PM
pjHour_hh	11, 12
pjHour_hh_mmAM	11:00 AM, 12:00 PM
pjHour_hhAM	11 AM, 12 PM
pjHour_mmm_dd_hhAM	Jan 31, 11 AM; Jan 31, 12 PM
pjHour_ddd_mmm_dd_hhAM	Mon Jan 31, 11 AM; Mon Jan 31, 12 PM
pjHourFromEnd_hh	3, 2, 1 (hour from the finish date of the project)
pjHourFromEnd_Hhh	H3, H2, H1 (hour the finish date of the project)
pjHourFromEnd_Hour_hh	Hour 2, Hour 1 (hour from the finish date of the project)
pjHourFromStart_hh	1, 2, 3 (hour from the start date of the project)
pjHourFromStart_Hhh	H1, H2, H3 (hour from the start date of the project)
pjHourFromStart_Hour_hh	Hour 1, Hour 2 (hour from the start date of the project)

If the *majorUnits* and *minorUnits* arguments equal **pjTimescaleMinutes**, the *majorLabel* and *minorLabel* arguments have these settings:

Constant	Examples of the date format
pjMinute_hh_mmAM	11:45 AM, 11:46 AM
pjMinute_mm	45, 46
pjMinuteFromEnd_mm	3, 2, 1 (minute from the finish date of the project)
pjMinuteFromEnd_Mmm	M3, M2, M1 (minute from the finish date of the project)
pjMinuteFromEnd_Minute_mm	Minute 2, Minute 1 (minute from the finish date of the project)
pjMinuteFromStart_mm	1, 2, 3 (minute from the start date of the project)
pjMinuteFromStart_Mmm	M1, M2, M3 (minute from the start date of the project)
pjMinuteFromStart_Minute_mm	Minute 1, Minute 2 (minute from the start date of the project)

The *majorAlign* and *minorAlign* arguments have these settings:

pjLeft	0	Flush left
pjCenter	1	Center
pjRight	2	Flush right

See Also   **Timescale** Method, **TimescaleNonWorking** Method.

TimescaleNonWorking Method

Applies To   **Application** Object.

Description   Sets the format of nonworking times.

Syntax   [*object*.]**TimescaleNonWorking** [*draw*, *calendar*, *color*, *pattern*]

Elements   The **TimescaleNonWorking** method syntax has the following object qualifier and named arguments:

Part	Description
object	An object expression that evaluates to an object in the Applies To list. Optional.
draw	A constant that specifies how to denote nonworking times. Optional.
calendar	A string expression that specifies the name of the calendar to format. Optional.
color	A constant that specifies the color of nonworking times. Optional.
pattern	A constant that specifies the pattern for nonworking times. Optional.

The *draw* argument has these settings:

pjBehind	0	Draws nonworking times behind Gantt bars.
pjInFront	1	Draws nonworking times in front of Gantt bars.
pjDoNotDraw	2	Does not draw nonworking times.

The *color* argument has these settings:

pjBlack	0	Black
pjRed	1	Red
pjYellow	2	Yellow
pjLime	3	Lime
pjAqua	4	Aqua
pjBlue	5	Blue
pjFuchsia	6	Fuchsia
pjWhite	7	White
pjMaroon	8	Maroon
pjGreen	9	Green
pjOlive	10	Olive
pjNavy	11	Navy
pjPurple	12	Purple
pjTeal	13	Teal
pjGray	14	Gray
pjSilver	15	Silver

The *pattern* argument has these settings:

pjHollow	0	Hollow
pjSolid	1	Solid
pjLightFill	2	Light fill
pjMediumFill	3	Medium fill
pjDarkFill	4	Dark fill
pjDiagonalLeft	5	Diagonal left
pjDiagonalRight	6	Diagonal right
pjDiagonalCross	7	Diagonal cross
pjLineVertical	8	Vertical line
pjLineHorizontal	9	Horizontal line
pjLineCross	10	Crossed line

See Also   **Timescale** Method, **TimescaleEdit** Method.

TimeSeparator Property

Applies To   **Application** Object.

Description   Returns the time separator character.

Syntax   [*object.*]**TimeSeparator**

Elements   The *object* placeholder is an object expression that evaluates to an object in the Applies To list.

Remarks   Microsoft Project for Microsoft Windows sets the **TimeSeparator** property equal to the corresponding value in the Regional settings of the Microsoft Windows Control Panel.

On the Macintosh, using System 7.1 and later, you can use the Date & Time control panel to change this value.

See Also   **AMText** Property, **PMText** Property, **TimeLeadingZero** Property, **TwelveHourTimeFormat** Property.

TimeSerial Function

Description   Returns a date containing the time for a specific hour, minute, and second.

Syntax   **TimeSerial(***hour,minute,second***)**

Elements   The **TimeSerial** function syntax has these named-argument parts:

Part	Description
hour	Number between 0 (12:00 A.M.) and 23 (11:00 P.M.), inclusive, or a numeric expression.
minute	Number between 0 and 59, inclusive, or a numeric expression.
second	Number between 0 and 59, inclusive, or a numeric expression.

Remarks   To specify a time, such as 11:59:59, the range of numbers for each **TimeSerial** argument should be in the normally accepted range for the unit; that is, 0-23 for hours and 0-59 for minutes and seconds. However, you can also specify relative times for each argument using any numeric expression that represents some number of hours, minutes, or seconds before or after a certain time. The following example uses expressions instead of absolute time numbers. The **TimeSerial** function returns a time for 15 minutes before (0 - 15) six hours before noon (12 - 6), or 5:45:00 A.M.

```
TimeSerial(12 - 6, 0 - 15, 0)
```

If the time specified by the three arguments, either directly or by expression, falls outside the acceptable range of times, an error occurs.

See Also   **DateSerial** Function, **DateValue** Function, **Hour** Function, **Minute** Function, **Now** Function, **Second** Function, **TimeValue** Function.

Example   This example uses the **TimeSerial** function to return a time for the specified hour, minute and second.

```
' MyTime contains the time for 4:35:17 PM
MyTime = TimeSerial(16, 35, 17) ' Return time.
```

TimeValue Function

Description   Returns a time.

Syntax   **TimeValue(*time*)**

Elements   The *time* named argument is normally a string expression representing a time from 0:00:00 (12:00:00 A.M.) to 23:59:59 (11:59:59 P.M.), inclusive. However, *time* can also be any expression that represents a time in that range. If *time* contains no valid data, **Null** is returned.

Remarks   You can enter valid times using a 12- or 24-hour clock. For example, `"2:24PM"` and `"14:24"` are both valid time arguments.

If the *time* argument contains date information, **TimeValue** doesn't this information. However, if *time* includes invalid date information, an error occurs.

See Also   **DateSerial** Function, **DateValue** Function, **Hour** Function, **Minute** Function, **Now** Function, **Second** Function, **TimeSerial** Function.

Example   This example uses the **TimeValue** function to convert a string to a time. In general, it is bad programming practice to hard code dates/ times as strings as shown in this example. Use date literals instead.

```
MyTime = TimeValue("4:35:17 PM") ' Return time.
```

TipOfTheDay Method

Applies To	**Application** Object.
Description	Displays the Tip of the Day.
Syntax	[*object*.]**TipOfTheDay**
Elements	The *object* placeholder is an object expression that evaluates to an object in the Applies To list.
See Also	**ShowTipOfDay** Property.

Title Property

Applies To	**Project** Object, **Projects** Collection.
Description	Returns or sets the title of a project.
Syntax	*object*.**Title** [= *value*]
Elements	The **Title** property syntax has these parts:

Part	Description
object	An object expression that evaluates to an object in the Applies To list.
value	A string expression that specifies the title of the project.

See Also	**Author** Property, **Comments** Property, **Company** Property, **Keywords** Property, **Manager** Property, **Notes** Property, **Subject** Property.
Example	The following example prompts the user to set the title of the active project.

```
Sub SetTitleForActiveProject()
    ActiveProject.Title = InputBox("Enter a title for this project.")
End Sub
```

ToolbarCopyToolFace Method

Applies To   **Application** Object.

Description   Copies the face of a toolbar button to the Clipboard.

Syntax   [*object*.]**ToolbarCopyToolFace** *toolbarName*, *buttonIndex*

Elements   The **ToolbarCopyToolFace** method syntax has the following object qualifier and named arguments:

Part	Description
object	An object expression that evaluates to an object in the Applies To list. Optional.
toolbarName	A string expression that specifies the name of the toolbar containing the button face to copy. Required.
buttonIndex	A numeric expression that specifies the toolbar index of the button face to copy. Required.

Remarks   The **ToolbarCopyToolFace** method has no effect unless the specified toolbar is visible and the specified button face is not a combo box.

See Also   **ToolbarCustomizeTool** Method, **ToolbarDeleteTool** Method, **ToolbarInsertTool** Method, **ToolbarPasteToolFace** Method, **Toolbars** Method, **ToolbarsCustomize** Method.

ToolbarCustomizeTool Method

Applies To   **Application** Object.

Description   Displays the Customize Tool dialog box, which allows the user to customize a toolbar button face, command, description, and ToolTip.

Syntax   [*object*.]**ToolbarCustomizeTool** *toolbarName*, *buttonIndex*[, *command*, *faceIndex*, *description*, *toolTip*]

Elements   The **ToolbarCustomizeTool** method syntax has the following object qualifier and named arguments:

Part	Description
object	An object expression that evaluates to an object in the Applies To list. Optional.
toolbarName	A string expression that specifies the name of the toolbar to customize. Required.
buttonIndex	A numeric expression that specifies the toolbar index of the button to customize. Required.
command	A string expression that specifies the macro or command that corresponds to the inserted button. Optional.
faceIndex	A numeric expression that specifies the button library index of the button face to insert. Optional.
description	A string expression that specifies the description for the toolbar button. Optional.
toolTip	A string expression that specifies the ToolTip for the toolbar button. Optional.

Remarks

The **ToolbarCustomizeTool** method has no effect unless the specified toolbar is visible and the specified button face is not a combo box.

See Also

ToolbarCopyToolFace Method, **ToolbarDeleteTool** Method, **ToolbarInsertTool** Method, **ToolbarPasteToolFace** Method, **Toolbars** Method, **ToolbarsCustomize** Method.

ToolbarDeleteTool Method

Applies To

Application Object.

Description

Deletes a toolbar button from a toolbar.

Syntax

[*object*.]**ToolbarDeleteTool** *toolbarName, buttonIndex*

Elements

The **ToolbarDeleteTool** method syntax has the following object qualifier and named arguments:

Part	Description
object	An object expression that evaluates to an object in the Applies To list. Optional.
toolbarName	A string expression that specifies the name of the toolbar containing the button to delete. Required.
buttonIndex	A numeric expression that specifies the toolbar index of the button to delete. Required.

Remarks　　The **ToolbarDeleteTool** method has no effect unless the specified toolbar is visible.

See Also　　**ToolbarCopyToolFace** Method, **ToolbarCustomizeTool** Method, **ToolbarInsertTool** Method, **ToolbarPasteToolFace** Method, **Toolbars** Method, **ToolbarsCustomize** Method.

ToolbarInsertTool Method

Applies To　　**Application** Object.

Description　　Inserts a toolbar button on a toolbar.

Syntax　　[*object*.]**ToolbarInsertTool** *toolbarName, buttonIndex*[, *command, faceIndex, description, toolTip*]

Elements　　The **ToolbarInsertTool** method syntax has the following object qualifier and named arguments:

Part	Description
object	An object expression that evaluates to an object in the Applies To list. Optional.
toolbarName	A string expression that specifies the name of the toolbar on which to insert a button. Required.
buttonIndex	A numeric expression that specifies the toolbar index of the button to insert. Required.
command	A string expression that specifies the macro or command that corresponds to the inserted button. Optional.
faceIndex	A numeric expression that specifies the button library index of the button face to insert. Optional.
description	A string expression that specifies the description for the toolbar button. Optional.
toolTip	A string expression that specifies the ToolTip for the toolbar button. Optional.

Remarks　　The **ToolbarInsertTool** method has no effect unless the specified toolbar is visible.

See Also　　**ToolbarCopyToolFace** Method, **ToolbarCustomizeTool** Method, **ToolbarDeleteTool** Method, **ToolbarPasteToolFace** Method, **Toolbars** Method, **ToolbarsCustomize** Method.

ToolbarPasteToolFace Method

Applies To	**Application** Object.
Description	Pastes a bitmap from the Clipboard onto a toolbar button face.
Syntax	[*object*.]**ToolbarPasteToolFace** *toolbarName, buttonIndex*
Elements	The **ToolbarPasteToolFace** method syntax has the following object qualifier and named arguments:

Part	Description
object	An object expression that evaluates to an object in the Applies To list. Optional.
toolbarName	A string expression that specifies the name of the toolbar on which to paste the button face. Required.
buttonIndex	A numeric expression that specifies the toolbar index of the button on which to paste the button face. Required.

Remarks	The **ToolbarPasteToolFace** method has no effect unless the specified toolbar is visible.
See Also	**ToolbarCopyToolFace** Method, **ToolbarCustomizeTool** Method, **ToolbarDeleteTool** Method, **ToolbarInsertTool** Method, **Toolbars** Method, **ToolbarsCustomize** Method.

Toolbars Method

Applies To	**Application** Object.
Description	Manages toolbars.
Syntax	[*object*.]**Toolbars** [*action, toolbarName, newToolbarName*]
Elements	The **Toolbars** method syntax has the following object qualifier and named arguments:

Part	Description
object	An object expression that evaluates to an object in the Applies To list. Optional.
action	A constant that specifies the action to perform. Optional.
toolbarName	A string expression that specifies the name of the toolbar to edit. Optional.
newToolbarName	A string expression that specifies the new name for an existing toolbar, or the name for a new toolbar. Optional.

The *action* argument has these settings:

pjToggle	1	Shows the toolbar, if it is hidden; hides the toolbar, if it is visible.
pjDelete	2	Deletes the toolbar, if it is a custom toolbar.
pjReset	2	Resets the toolbar, if it is a built-in toolbar.
pjCreate	3	Creates a new toolbar.
pjRename	5	Renames the toolbar.
pjCopy	4	Copies the toolbar.
pjShow	6	Shows the toolbar.
pjHide	7	Hides the toolbar.

See Also

ToolbarCopyToolFace Method, **ToolbarCustomizeTool** Method, **ToolbarDeleteTool** Method, **ToolbarInsertTool** Method, **ToolbarPasteToolFace** Method, **ToolbarsCustomize** Method.

ToolbarsCustomize Method

Applies To **Application** Object.

Description Displays the Customize Toolbars dialog box, which prompts the user to customize toolbars.

Syntax [*object*.]**ToolbarsCustomize**

Elements The *object* placeholder is an object expression that evaluates to an object in the Applies To list.

See Also **ToolbarCopyToolFace** Method, **ToolbarCustomizeTool** Method, **ToolbarDeleteTool** Method, **ToolbarInsertTool** Method, **ToolbarPasteToolFace** Method, **Toolbars** Method.

Top Property

Applies To   **Application** Object; **Window** Object, **Windows** Collection.

Description   Returns or sets the distance of the main window from the top edge of the screen (**Application** object) or the distance of a project window from the top edge of the main window (**Window** object).

Syntax   *object.***Top** [= *value*]

Elements   The **Top** property syntax has these parts:

Part	Description
object	An object expression that evaluates to an object in the Applies To list.
value	A numeric expression that specifies the distance, in points, of the main window from the top edge of the screen, or the distance, in points, of a document window from the top edge of the main window.

Remarks   The position of the window is measured from the top of the main screen, not from the bottom of the menu bar. For Microsoft Project for the Macintosh, this property is supported read-only for the **Application** object.

See Also   **Caption** Property, **Height** Property, **Left** Property, **UsableHeight** Property, **UsableWidth** Property, **Visible** Property, **Width** Property, **WindowState** Property.

TopPane Property

Applies To   **Window** Object, **Windows** Collection.

Description   Returns the top pane of a window.

Syntax   [*object.*]**TopPane**

Elements   The *object* placeholder is an object expression that evaluates to an object in the Applies To list.

See Also   **ActivePane** Property, **BottomPane** Property, **Pane** Object.

TotalSlack Property

Applies To	**Project** Object, **Projects** Collection; **Task** Object, **Tasks** Collection.
Description	Returns the total slack for a task, in minutes.
Syntax	*object*.**TotalSlack**
Elements	The *object* placeholder is an object expression that evaluates to an object in the Applies To list.
See Also	**Critical** Property, **Delay** Property, **FreeSlack** Property.

Trappable Errors

Description   Trappable errors can occur while an application is running. Some of these can also occur during development or compile time. You can test and respond to trappable errors using the **On Error** statement and the **Err** function.

Code	Message
3	Return without GoSub
5	Invalid procedure call
6	Overflow
7	Out of memory
9	Subscript out of range
10	Duplicate definition
11	Division by zero
13	Type mismatch
14	Out of string space
16	String formula too complex
17	Can't perform requested operation
18	User interrupt occurred
20	Resume without error
28	Out of stack space
35	Sub or Function not defined

Code	Message
48	Error in loading DLL
49	Bad DLL calling convention
51	Internal error
52	Bad file name or number
53	File not found
54	Bad file mode
55	File already open
57	Device I/O error
58	File already exists
59	Bad record length
61	Disk full
62	Input past end of file
63	Bad record number
67	Too many files
68	Device unavailable
70	Permission denied
71	Disk not ready
74	Can't rename with different drive
75	Path/File access error
76	Path not found
91	Object variable not set
92	For loop not initialized
93	Invalid pattern string
94	Invalid use of Null
95	User-defined error
323	Can't load module; invalid format
423	Property or method not found
424	Object required
430	Class does not support OLE Automation
438	Object doesn't support this property or method
440	OLE Automation error
445	Object doesn't support this action
446	Object doesn't support named arguments
447	Object doesn't support current locale setting
448	Named argument not found

Code	Message
449	Argument not optional
450	Wrong number of arguments
451	Object not a collection
452	Invalid ordinal
453	Specified DLL function not found
454	Code resource not found
455	Code resource lock error

See Also

CVErr Function; **Err** Statement; **Err, Erl** Functions; **Error** Function; **Error** Statement; **Resume** Statement.

TwelveHourTimeFormat Property

Applies To

Application Object.

Description

Returns whether times appear in 12-hour or 24-hour format.

Syntax

[*object.*]**TwelveHourTimeFormat**

Elements

The *object* placeholder represents an object expression that evaluates to an object in the Applies To list.

Settings

The **TwelveHourTimeFormat** property has these settings:

Setting	Description
True	Times appear in 12-hour format.
False	Times appear in 24-hour format.

Remarks

Microsoft Project for Microsoft Windows sets the **TwelveHourTimeFormat** property equal to the corresponding value in the Regional settings of the Microsoft Windows Control Panel.

On the Macintosh, Microsoft Project sets the **TwelveHourTimeFormat** property equal to the corresponding value in the System settings.

See Also

AMText Property, **PMText** Property, **TimeLeadingZero** Property, **TimeSeparator** Property.

TypeName Function

Description   Returns a string that provides information about a variable.

Syntax   **TypeName(*varname*)**

Elements   The ***varname*** named argument can be any variable except a variable of a user-defined type.

Remarks   The string returned by **TypeName** can be any one of the following:

String Returned	Variable contains
objecttype	An OLE Automation object whose type is *objecttype*.
Integer	An integer.
Long	A long integer.
Single	A single-precision floating point number.
Double	A double-precision floating point number.
Currency	A currency value.
Date	A date.
String	A string.
Boolean	A Boolean value.
Error	An error value.
Empty	Uninitialized.
Null	No valid data.
Object	An object that doesn't support OLE Automation.
Unknown	An OLE Automation object whose type is unknown.
Nothing	An object variable that doesn't refer to an object.

If ***varname*** is an array, the returned string can be any one of the possible returned strings (or **Variant**) with empty parentheses appended. For example, if ***varname*** is an array of integers, **TypeName** returns `"Integer()"`.

See Also   Data Type Summary, **IsArray** Function, **IsDate** Function, **IsEmpty** Function, **IsError** Function, **IsMissing** Function, **IsNull** Function, **IsNumeric** Function, **IsObject** Function, **Variant** Data Type, **VarType** Function.

Example

This example uses the **TypeName** function to return information about a variable.

```
' Declare variables.
Dim StrVar As String, IntVar As Integer, CurVar As Currency
Dim ArrayVar (1 To 5) As Integer
NullVar = Null              ' Assign Null value.
MyType = TypeName(StrVar)   ' Returns "String".
MyType = TypeName(IntVar)   ' Returns "Integer".
MyType = TypeName(CurVar)   ' Returns "Currency".
MyType = TypeName(NullVar)  ' Returns "Null".
MyType = TypeName(ArrayVar) ' Returns "Integer()".
```

Type Statement

Description

Used at module level to define a user-defined data type containing one or more elements.

Syntax

[Private | Public] **Type** *varname*
    elementname [([*subscripts*])] As ***type***
    [*elementname* [([*subscripts*])] As ***type***]
    . . .
End Type

Elements

The **Type** statement syntax has these parts:

Part	Description
Public	Used to declare user-defined types that are available to all procedures in all modules in all projects.
Private	Used to declare user-defined types that are available only within the module where the declaration is made.
varname	Name of the user-defined type; follows standard variable naming conventions.
elementname	Name of an element of the user-defined type. Element names also follow standard variable naming conventions, except that reserved words can be used.
subscripts	Dimensions of an array element. Use only parentheses when declaring an array whose size can change.
type	Data type of the element; may be **Boolean**, **Integer**, **Long**, **Currency**, **Single**, **Double**, **Date**, **String**, **String** * *length* (for fixed-length strings), **Object**, **Variant**, another user-defined type, or an object type.

Remarks

The **Type** statement can be used only at module level. Once you have declared a user-defined type using the **Type** statement, you can declare a variable of that type anywhere within the scope of the declaration. Use **Dim**, **Private**, **Public**, **ReDim**, or **Static** to declare a variable of a user-defined type.

Line numbers and line labels aren't allowed in **Type...End Type** blocks.

User-defined types are often used with data records, which frequently consist of a number of related elements of different data types.

The following example shows the use of fixed-size arrays in a user-defined type:

```
Type StateData
    CityCode (1 To 100) As Integer ' Declare a static array.
    County As String * 30
End Type
Dim Washington(1 To 100) As StateData
```

In the preceding example, StateData includes the CityCode static array, and the record Washington has the same structure as StateData.

When you declare a fixed-size array within a user-defined type, its dimensions must be declared with numeric literals or constants rather than variables.

The setting of the **Option Base** statement determines the lower bound for arrays within user-defined types.

Example

This example uses the **Type** statement to define a user-defined data type. The **Type** statement is used at the module level only.

```
Type EmployeeRecord               ' Create user-defined type.
    ID As Integer                 ' Define elements of type.
    Name As String * 20
    Address As String * 30
    Phone As Long
    HireDate As Date
End Type
Dim MyRecord As EmployeeRecord    ' Declare variable.
MyRecord.ID = 12003               ' Assign a value to an element.
```

UBound Function

Description   Returns the largest available subscript for the indicated dimension of an array.

Syntax   **UBound**(*arrayname*[,*dimension*])

Elements   The **UBound** function syntax has these parts:

Part	Description
arrayname	Name of the array variable; follows standard variable naming conventions.
dimension	Whole number indicating which dimension's upper bound is returned. Use 1 for the first dimension, 2 for the second, and so on. If *dimension* is omitted, 1 is assumed.

Remarks   The **UBound** function is used with the **LBound** function to determine the size of an array. Use the **LBound** function to find the lower limit of an array dimension.

UBound returns the values listed in the table below for an array with these dimensions:

```
Dim A(1 To 100, 0 To 3, -3 To 4)
```

Statement	Return Value
UBound(A, 1)	100
UBound(A, 2)	3
UBound(A, 3)	4

See Also   **Dim** Statement, **LBound** Function, **Option Base** Statement, **Public** Statement, **ReDim** Statement, **Static** Statement.

Example   This example uses the **UBound** function to determine the largest available subscript for the indicated dimension of an array.

```
Dim MyArray(1 To 10, 5 To 15, 10 To 20)  ' Declare array variables.
Dim AnyArray(10)
Upper = UBound(MyArray, 1)                    ' Returns 10.
Upper = UBound(MyArray, 3)                    ' Returns 20.
Upper = UBound(AnyArray)                       ' Returns 10.
```

UCase Function

Description   Returns a string that has been converted to uppercase.

Syntax   **UCase(*string*)**

Elements   The ***string*** named argument is any valid string expression. If ***string*** contains no valid data, **Null** is returned.

Remarks   Only lowercase letters are converted to uppercase; all uppercase letters and nonletter characters remain unchanged.

See Also   **LCase** Function.

Example   This example uses the **UCase** function to return an uppercase version of a string.

```
LowerCase = "Hello World 1234"    ' String to convert.
UpperCase = UCase(LowerCase)      ' Returns "HELLO WORLD 1234".
```

UniqueID Method

Applies To   **Assignment** Object, **Assignments** Collection; **Resource** Object, **Resources** Collection; **Task** Object, **Tasks** Collection.

Description   Returns the task, resource, or assignment with the given unique identification number from its containing collection.

Syntax   *object*.**UniqueID(*index*)**

Elements   The **UniqueID** method syntax has the following object qualifier and named arguments:

Part	Description
object	An object expression that evaluates to an object in the Applies To list.
index	A numeric expression that specifies the index of the *object*.

See Also   **Assignment** Object, **Assignments** Collection; **Assignments** Method; **Resource** Object, **Resources** Collection; **Resources** Method; **Task** Object, **Tasks** Collection; **Tasks** Method; **UniqueID** Property.

UniqueID Property

Applies To	**Assignment** Object, **Assignments** Collection; **Project** Object, **Projects** Collection; **Resource** Object, **Resources** Collection; **Task** Object, **Tasks** Collection.
Description	Returns the unique identification number of a task, resource or resource assignment.
Syntax	*object*.**UniqueID**
Elements	The *object* placeholder is an object expression that evaluates to an object in the Applies To list.
See Also	**ID** Property.

UniqueIDPredecessors Property

Applies To	**Task** Object, **Tasks** Collection.
Description	Returns the unique identification numbers of the predecessors of a task.
Syntax	*object*.**UniqueIDPredecessors**
Elements	The *object* placeholder is an object expression that evaluates to an object in the Applies To list.
Remarks	For example, the **UniqueIDPredecessors** property returns "5,4,1" if the unique identification numbers of the predecessor tasks are 5, 4, and 1.

Note This example assumes that the list separator character is the comma (,). You can determine the list separator character with the **ListSeparator** property.

See Also	**PredecessorTasks** Method, **UniqueID** Property, **UniqueIDSuccessors** Property.

UniqueIDSuccessors Property

Applies To   **Task** Object, **Tasks** Collection.

Description   Returns the unique identification numbers of the successors of a task.

Syntax   *object*.**UniqueIDSuccessors**

Elements   The *object* placeholder is an object expression that evaluates to an object in the Applies To list.

Remarks   For example, the **UniqueIDSuccessors** property returns "3,9,8" if the unique identification numbers of the successor tasks are 3, 9, and 8.

Note This example assumes that the list separator character is the comma (,). You can determine the list separator character with the **ListSeparator** property.

See Also   **SuccessorTasks** Method, **UniqueID** Property, **UniqueIDPredecessors** Property.

Units Property

Applies To   **Project** Object, **Projects** Collection.

Description   Returns or sets the default duration units.

Syntax   [*object*.]**DefaultDurationUnits** [= *value*]

Elements   The **DefaultDurationUnits** property syntax has these parts:

Part	Description
object	An object expression that evaluates to an object in the Applies To list.
value	A constant that specifies the default duration units, as shown under Settings.

Elements   The **DefaultDurationUnits** property has these settings:

Setting	Description
pjMinutes	The default duration units are minutes.
pjHours	The default duration units are hours.
pjDays	The default duration units are days.
pjWeeks	The default duration units are weeks.

See Also　　**DefaultFixedDuration** Property, **DefaultResourceOvertimeRate** Property, **DefaultResourceStandardRate** Property, **DefaultView** Property, **DefaultWorkUnits** Property.

UnlinkPredecessors Method

Applies To　　**Task** Object, **Tasks** Collection.

Description　　Removes predecessors from one or more tasks.

Syntax　　*object*.**UnlinkPredecessors** *tasks*

Elements　　The **UnlinkPredecessors** method syntax has the following object qualifier and named arguments:

Part	Description
object	An object expression that evaluates to an object in the Applies To list. Required.
tasks	A **Task** object. The predecessor tasks you specify with the *tasks* argument are removed from the tasks you specify with the object expression. Required.

See Also　　**LinkPredecessors** Method, **LinkSuccessors** Method, **Predecessors** Property, **Successors** Property, **UnlinkSuccessors** Method.

UnlinkSuccessors Method

Applies To　　**Task** Object, **Tasks** Collection.

Description　　Removes successors from one or more tasks.

Syntax　　*object*.**UnlinkSuccessors** *tasks*

Elements

The **UnlinkSuccessors** method syntax has the following object qualifier and named arguments:

Part	Description
object	An object expression that evaluates to an object in the Applies To list. Required.
tasks	A **Task** object. The successor tasks you specify with the *tasks* argument are removed from the tasks you specify with the object expression. Required.

See Also

LinkPredecessors Method, **LinkSuccessors** Method, **Predecessors** Property, **Successors** Property, **UnlinkPredecessors** Method.

Example

The following example removes a successor from every task in the active project.

```
Sub RemoveSuccessor()
    Dim Entry    ' Successor specified by user
    Dim SuccTask ' Successor task object
    Dim T        ' Task object used in For Each loop
    Dim S        ' Successor (task object) used in loop

    ' Prompt the user for the name of a successor to unlink.
    Entry = InputBox("Enter the name of a successor to unlink" & _
            " from every task in this project.")

    Set SuccTask = Nothing
    ' Look for the name of the successor in tasks of the active project.
    For Each T In ActiveProject.Tasks
        If T.Name = Entry Then
            Set SuccTask = T
            Exit For
        End If
    Next T
    ' Remove the successor from every task in the active project.
    If Not (SuccTask Is Nothing) Then
        For Each T In ActiveProject.Tasks
            For Each S In T.SuccessorTasks
                If S.Name = Entry Then
                    T.UnlinkSuccessors SuccTask
                    Exit For
                End If
            Next S
        Next T
    End If
End Sub
```

UnlinkTasks Method

Applies To	**Application** Object.
Description	Unlinks the active tasks.
Syntax	[*object*.]**UnlinkTasks**
Elements	The *object* placeholder is an object expression that evaluates to an object in the Applies To list.
See Also	**LinkTasks** Method, **LinkTasksEdit** Method, **UniqueID** Property.

UpdateNeeded Property

Applies To	**Project** Object, **Projects** Collection; **Task** Object, **Tasks** Collection.
Description	Returns whether the resources assigned to a task need to be updated as to the status of the task.
Syntax	*object*.**UpdateNeeded**
Elements	The *object* placeholder is an object expression that evaluates to an object in the Applies To list.
Remarks	This method applies to Microsoft Project for Microsoft Windows.
See Also	**Confirmed** Property, **EMailAddress** Property, **MailSendProjectMail** Method.

UpdateProject Method

Applies To	**Application** Object.
Description	Uses feedback from Microsoft Project mail to update a project.
Syntax	*object*.**MailUpdateProject** [*dataFile*]
Elements	The **MailUpdateProject** property syntax has the following parts:

Part	Description
object	An object expression that evaluates to an object in the Applies To list. Required.
dataFile	A string expression that specifies the name of the file on which to base the update. Optional.

Remarks This method applies to Microsoft Project for Microsoft Windows.

See Also **MailLogOff** Method, **MailLogOn** Method, **MailRoutingSlip** Method, **MailSend** Method, **MailSendProjectMail** Method, **MailSendScheduleNote** Method, **MailSession** Property, **MailSystem** Property.

UpdateTasks Method

Applies To **Application** Object.

Description Updates the active tasks.

Syntax [*object.*]**UpdateTasks** [*percentComplete, actualDuration, remainingDuration, actualStart, actualFinish, notes*]

Elements The **UpdateTasks** method syntax has the following object qualifier and named arguments:

Part	Description
object	An object expression that evaluates to an object in the Applies To list. Optional.
percentComplete	A string expression that specifies the percent complete of the active tasks. Optional.
actualDuration	A string expression that specifies the actual duration of the active tasks. Optional.
remainingDuration	A string expression that specifies the remaining duration of the active tasks. Optional.
actualStart	A string expression that specifies the actual start date of the active tasks. Optional.
actualFinish	A string expression that specifies the actual finish date of the active tasks. Optional.
notes	A string expression for comments. Optional.

See Also **BaselineSave** Method, **UpdateProject** Method.

UsableHeight Property

Applies To   **Application** Object.

Description   Returns the maximum height, in points, of a project window.

Syntax   [*object*.]**UsableHeight**

Elements   The *object* placeholder is an object expression that evaluates to an object in the Applies To list.

Remarks   The **UsableHeight** property equals the total amount of vertical space inside the main window minus the space taken up by toolbars, menu bars, status bars, scroll bars, and the title bar.

See Also   **Caption** Property, **Height** Property, **Left** Property, **Top** Property, **UsableWidth** Property, **Visible** Property, **Width** Property, **WindowState** Property.

Example   The following example moves the windows of every open project inside the main window.

```
Sub FitWindows()

    Dim W    ' The Window object used in For Each loop
    For Each W in Application.Windows

        ' Adjust the height of each window, if necessary.
        If W.Height > UsableHeight Then
            W.Height = UsableHeight
            W.Top = 0

        ' Adjust the vertical position of each window, if necessary.
        ElseIf W.Top + W.Height > UsableHeight Then
            W.Top = W.Top - (W.Top + W.Height - UsableHeight)
        End If

        ' Adjust the width of each window, if necessary.
        If W.Width > UsableWidth Then
            W.Width = UsableWidth
            W.Left = 0

        ' Adjust the horizontal position of each window, if necessary.
        ElseIf W.Left + W.Width > UsableWidth Then
            W.Left = W.Left - (W.Left + W.Width - UsableWidth)
        End If
    Next
End Sub
```

UsableWidth Property

Applies To   **Application** Object.

Description   Returns the maximum width, in points, of a project window.

Syntax   [*object*.]**UsableWidth**

Elements   The *object* placeholder is an object expression that evaluates to an object in the Applies To list.

Remarks   The **UsableWidth** property equals the total amount of horizontal space inside the main window minus the space taken up by toolbars and scroll bars.

See Also   **Caption** Property, **Height** Property, **Left** Property, **Top** Property, **UsableHeight** Property, **Visible** Property, **Width** Property, **WindowState** Property.

User-Defined Data Type

Description   Any data type you define using the **Type** statement. User-defined data types can contain one or more elements of any data type, array, or a previously defined user-defined type. For example:

```
Type MyType
    MyName As String     ' String variable stores a name.
    MyBirthDate As Date  ' Date variable stores a birthdate.
    MySex as Integer     ' Integer variable stores sex (0 for
End Type                 ' female, 1 for male.
```

See Also   Data Type Summary, **Type** Statement.

UserName Property

Applies To   **Application** Object.

Description   Returns or sets the name of the user.

Syntax   [*object*.]**UserName** [= *value*]

Elements	The **UserName** property syntax has these parts:

Part	Description
object	An object expression that evaluates to an object in the Applies To list.
value	A string expression that specifies the name of the current user.

Remarks

Use the **UserName** property to customize Microsoft Project options or macros for a particular user.

Suppose you have written a macro called PrintReport that prints the report MINE.MPP when you press Ctrl+R, but another user wants to use the same shortcut keys to print the report YOURS.MPP. You can edit the PrintReport macro so it checks the Username property, prints MINE.MPP if you are the current user, and prints YOURS.MPP otherwise.

See Also

Calculation Property, **ListSeparator** Property, **ShowCriticalSlack** Property, **StartOnCurrentDate** Property, **StartYearIn** Property.

Example

The following example sets preferences in Microsoft Project according to the name of the current user.

```
Sub GetUserName()

    ' Prompt user for his or her name.
    UserName = InputBox("What's your name?", , UserName)

    ' If user is Tamara, then set certain preferences.
    If UserName = "Tamara" Then
        DisplayScheduleMessages = False
        BarRounding On:=False
        Calculation = True

    ' If user is not Tamara, then set default preferences.
    Else
        DisplayScheduleMessages = True
        BarRounding On:=True
        Calculation = False
    End If
End Sub
```

Val Function

Description

Returns the numbers contained in a string.

Syntax

Val(*string*)

Elements

The *string* named argument is any valid string expression.

Remarks

The **Val** function stops reading the string at the first character it can't recognize as part of a number. Symbols and characters that are often considered parts of numeric values, such as dollar signs and commas, are not recognized. However, the function recognizes radix prefixes &O (for octal) and &H (for hexadecimal). Blanks, tabs, and linefeeds are stripped from the argument.

The following returns the value 1615198:

```
Val("   1615 198th Street N.E.")
```

In the code below, **Val** returns the decimal value -1 for the hexadecimal value shown:

```
Val("&HFFFF")
```

Note   The **Val** function recognizes only the period (.) as a valid decimal separator. When a possibility exists that different decimal separators may be used (for example, in international applications), you should use **CDbl** instead to convert a string to a number.

See Also

CDbl Function, **Str** Function.

Example

This example uses the **Val** function to return the numbers contained in a string.

```
MyValue = Val("2457")       ' Returns 2457.
MyValue = Val(" 2 45 7")    ' Returns 2457.
MyValue = Val("24 and 57")  ' Returns 24.
```

Variant Data Type

Description

The **Variant** data type is the data type that all variables become if not explicitly declared as some other type (using statements such as **Dim**, **Private**, **Public**, or **Static**). The **Variant** data type has no type-declaration character.

The **Variant** is a special data type that can contain any kind of data as well as the special values **Empty**, **Error**, and **Null**. You can determine how the data in a **Variant** is treated using the **VarType** or **TypeName** function.

Numeric data can be any integer or real number value ranging from -1.797693134862315E308 to -4.94066E-324 for negative values and from 4.94066E-324 to 1.797693134862315E308 for positive values. Generally, numeric **Variant** data is maintained in its original data type within the **Variant**. For example, if you assign an **Integer** to a **Variant**, subsequent operations treat the **Variant** as if it were an **Integer**. However, if an arithmetic operation is performed on a **Variant** containing an **Integer**, a **Long**, or a **Single**, and the result exceeds the normal range for the original data type, the result is promoted within the **Variant** to the next larger data type. An **Integer** is promoted to a **Long**, and a **Long** and a **Single** are promoted to a **Double**. An error occurs when **Variant** variables containing **Currency** and **Double** values exceed their respective ranges.

You can use the **Variant** data type in place of any data type to work with data in a more flexible way. If the contents of a **Variant** variable are digits, they may be either the string representation of the digits or their actual value, depending on the context. For example:

```
Dim MyVar As Variant
MyVar = 98052
```

In the example shown above, MyVar contains a numeric representation—the actual value 98052. Arithmetic operators work as expected on **Variant** variables that contain numeric values or string data that can be interpreted as numbers. If you use the + operator to add MyVar to another **Variant** containing a number or to a variable of a numeric data type, the result is an arithmetic sum. See the information about addition and concatenation operators for complete information on how to use them with **Variant** data.

The value **Empty** denotes a **Variant** variable that hasn't been initialized (assigned an initial value). A **Variant** containing **Empty** is 0 if it is used in a numeric context and a zero-length string ("") if it is used in a string context.

Don't confuse **Empty** with **Null**. **Null** indicates that the **Variant** variable intentionally contains no valid data.

In a **Variant**, **Error** is a special value used to indicate that an error condition has occurred in a procedure. However, unlike for other kinds of errors, normal application-level error handling does not occur. This allows the programmer, or the application itself, to take some alternative based on the error value. **Error** values are created by converting real numbers to error values using the **CVErr** function.

See Also   **CVar** Function, **CVErr** Function, Data Type Summary, **Def**_type_ Statements, **Dim** Statement, **Private** Statement, **Public** Statement, **Static** Statement, **TypeName** Function, **VarType** Function.

VarType Function

Description   Returns a value indicating the subtype of a variable.

Syntax	**VarType**(*varname*)
Elements	The ***varname*** named argument can be any variable except a variable of a user-defined type.

Return Values

0	vbEmpty	Empty (uninitialized).
1	vbNull	Null (no valid data).
2	vbInteger	Integer.
3	vbLong	Long integer.
4	vbSingle	Single-precision floating point number.
5	vbDouble	Double-precision floating point number.
6	vbCurrency	Currency.
7	vbDate	Date.
8	vbString	String.
9	vbObject	OLE Automation object.
10	vbError	Error.
11	vbBoolean	Boolean.
12	vbVariant	Variant (used only with arrays of Variants).
13	vbDataobject	Non-OLE Automation object.
8192	vbArray	Array.

Note These constants are specified by Visual Basic. As a result, the names can be used anywhere in your code in place of the actual values.

Remarks	The **VarType** function never returns the value for vbArray by itself. It is always added to some other value to indicate an array of a particular type. The constant vbVariant is only returned in conjunction with vbArray to indicate that the argument to the **VarType** function is an array of type **Variant**. For example, the value returned for an array of integers is calculated as vbInteger + vbArray, or 8194.
See Also	Data Type Summary, **IsArray** Function, **IsDate** Function, **IsEmpty** Function, **IsError** Function, **IsMissing** Function, **IsNull** Function, **IsNumeric** Function, **IsObject** Function, **TypeName** Function, **Variant** Data Type.
Example	This example uses **VarType** to determine the subtype of a variable.

```
' Initialize variables.
IntVar = 459: StrVar = "Hello World": DateVar = #2/12/69#
MyCheck = VarType(IntVar)    ' Returns 2.
MyCheck = VarType(DateVar)   ' Returns 7.
MyCheck = VarType(StrVar)    ' Returns 8.
```

Version Property

Applies To   **Application** Object.

Description   Returns the version number of Microsoft Project.

Syntax   [*object.*]**Version**

Elements   The *object* placeholder is an object expression that evaluates to an object in the Applies To list.

Remarks   The **Version** property returns "4.1" for Microsoft Project version 4.1.

See Also   **MoveAfterReturn** Property, **Name** Property, **OperatingSystem** Property, **SupportsMultipleDocuments** Property, **SupportsMultipleWindows** Property.

ViewApply Method

Applies To   **Application** Object.

Description   Sets the view in the active window.

Syntax   [*object.*]**ViewApply** *name*[, *singlePane, toggle*]

Elements   The **ViewApply** method syntax has the following object qualifier and named arguments:

Part	Description
object	An object expression that evaluates to an object in the Applies To list. Optional.
name	A string expression that specifies the name of the view to display in the active window. Required.
singlePane	A Boolean expression that specifies whether the view consists of one (**True**) or two (**False**) panes. By default, the *singlePane* argument is **False**. Optional.
toggle	A Boolean expression that specifies whether to change the number of panes in the active window. If you specify **True** for the *toggle* argument, the active window changes from one pane to two panes or from two panes to one pane. The *toggle* argument is ignored if you specify **True** for the *singlePane* argument. By default, the *toggle* argument is **False**. Optional.

See Also	**FormViewShow** Method, **ViewEditCombination** Method, **ViewEditSingle** Method, **Views** Method, **WindowSplit** Method.
Example	The following example sets the active window to a single-pane view of the Module Editor.

```
Sub ChangeWindowToModuleEditor()
    ViewApply name:="Module Editor", singlePane:=True
End Sub
```

ViewEditCombination Method

Applies To	**Application** Object.
Description	Creates or edits a combination view.
Syntax	[*object*.]**ViewEditCombination** [*name, create, newName, topView, bottomView, showInMenu*]
Elements	The **ViewEditCombination** method syntax has the following object qualifier and named arguments:

Part	Description
object	An object expression that evaluates to an object in the Applies To list. Optional.
name	A string expression that specifies the name of a two-pane view to edit, create, or copy. By default, the *name* argument is the name of the active view.
create	A Boolean expression that specifies whether to create a new two-pane view. By default, the *create* argument is **False**. Optional. The *create* argument has these settings:

	True	A new view is created. If the *newName* argument is **Empty**, the new view is given the name you specify with the *name* argument. Otherwise, the new view is a copy of the view you specify with the *name* argument, and the new view is given the name you specify with the *newName* argument.
	False	A new view is not created.

Part	Description
newName	A string expression that specifies a new name for the view you specify with the *name* argument (*create* argument is **False**) or a name for the new view you create (*create* argument is **True**). By default, the *newName* argument is **Empty**. If the *newName* argument is **Empty** and the *create* argument is **False**, the view you specify with the *name* argument retains its current name. Optional.
topView	A string expression that specifies the name of the view to display in the upper pane. If you're creating a view, this will be in the upper pane. If you're editing a view, the view will be edited with this in the upper pane. Optional.
bottomView	A string expression that specifies the name of the view to display in the lower pane. If you're creating a view, this will be in the lower pane. If you're editing a view, the view will be edited with this in the lower pane. Optional.
showInMenu	A Boolean expression that specifies whether to show the name of the view in the View menu. By default, the *showInMenu* argument is **False**. Optional.

See Also

OrganizerDeleteItem Method, **ViewApply** Method, **ViewEditSingle** Method, **Views** Method.

Example

The following example creates a new combination view with the Resource Sheet view and the Resource Graph in the upper and lower panes respectively.

```
Sub DisplayKrisView()
    ViewEditCombination name:= "Kris' View", create:= True, _
        topView:= "Resource Sheet", bottomView:= "Resource Graph"
End Sub
```

ViewEditSingle Method

Applies To   **Application** Object.

Description   Creates or edits a single-pane view.

Syntax   [*object*.]**ViewEditSingle** [*name, create, newName, screen, showInMenu, highlightFilter, table, filter*]

Elements   The **ViewEditSingle** method syntax has the following object qualifier and named arguments:

Part	Description
object	An object expression that evaluates to an object in the Applies To list. Optional.
name	A string expression that specifies the name of a one-pane view to edit, create, or copy. By default, the *name* argument is the name of the active view. Optional.
create	A Boolean expression that specifies whether to create a new one-pane view. By default, the *create* argument is **False**. Optional. The *create* argument has these settings:

	True	A new view is created. If the *newName* argument is **Empty**, the new view is given the name you specify with the *name* argument. Otherwise, the new view is a copy of the view you specify with the *name* argument, and the new view is given the name you specify with the *newName* argument.
	False	A new view is not created.

Part	Description
newName	A string expression that specifies a new name for the view you specify with the *name* argument (*create* argument is **False**) or a name for the new view you create (*create* argument is **True**). By default, the *newName* argument is **Empty**. If the *newName* argument is **Empty** and the *create* argument is **False**, the view you specify with the *name* argument retains its current name. Optional.
screen	A constant that specifies the view to display. Optional.
showInMenu	A Boolean expression that specifies whether to show the name of the view in the View menu. By default, the *showInMenu* argument is **False**. Optional.
highlightFilter	A Boolean expression that specifies whether to highlight filtered items. By default, the *highlightFilter* argument is **False**. Optional.
table	A string expression that specifies the name of a table to display in the view. Required for a new view.
filter	A string expression that specifies a filter to apply to the view. Required for a new view.

The *screen* argument has these settings:

pjGantt	1	Gantt Chart
pjPERT	2	PERT Chart
pjTaskPERT	3	Task PERT view
pjTaskForm	4	Task Form
pjTaskSheet	5	Task Sheet

pjResourceForm	6	Resource Form
pjResourceSheet	7	Resource Sheet
pjResourceUsage	8	Resource Usage view
pjResourceGraph	9	Resource Graph
pjTaskDetailsForm	10	Task Details Form
pjTaskNameForm	11	Task Name Form
pjResourceNameForm	12	Resource Name Form
pjCalendar	13	Calendar view
pjModuleEditor	14	Module Editor view

See Also

OrganizerDeleteItem Method, **ViewApply** Method, **ViewEditCombination** Method, **Views** Method.

Example

The following example creates a new view for tasks currently in progress.

```
Sub Display()
    ViewEditSingle name := "Kris' Task Schedule", create := True, _
        filter:="In Progress Tasks", table := "Schedule"
End Sub
```

ViewList Method

Applies To

Project Object, **Projects** Collection.

Description

Returns a resource view name or all resource view names.

Syntax

object.**ResourceViewList**[(*index*)]

Elements

The **ResourceViewList** method syntax has the following object qualifier and named arguments:

Part	Description
object	An object expression that evaluates to an object in the Applies To list.
index	A numeric expression that specifies the index of the *object*.

See Also

CurrentView Property, **List** Object, **ReportList** Method, **ResourceFilterList** Method, **ResourceTableList** Method, **TaskViewList** Method, **ViewApply** Method, **ViewEditCombination** Method, **ViewEditSingle** Method, **ViewList** Method, **Views** Method.

Example

The following example lists all the resource views.

```
Sub SeeAllResViews()
    Dim t As Variant
    For Each t In ActiveProject.ResourceViewList
        MsgBox t
    Next t
End Sub
```

Views Method

Applies To   **Application** Object.

Description   Displays the More Views dialog box, which prompts the user to manage views.

Syntax   [*object*.]**Views**

Elements   The *object* placeholder is an object expression that evaluates to an object in the Applies To list.

Remarks   The **Views** method has the same effect as the More Views command on the View menu.

See Also   **OrganizerDeleteItem** Method, **ViewApply** Method, **ViewEditCombination** Method, **ViewEditSingle** Method.

ViewShowAvailability Method

Applies To   **Application** Object.

Description   Displays availability information in the active Resource Usage view.

Syntax   [*object*.]**ViewShowAvailability**

Elements   The *object* placeholder is an object expression that evaluates to an object in the Applies To list.

Remarks   The **ViewShowAvailability** method has no effect unless the active window contains the Resource Usage view.

See Also   **ViewShowCost** Method, **ViewShowCumulativeCost** Method, **ViewShowCumulativeWork** Method, **ViewShowNotes** Method, **ViewShowObjects** Method, **ViewShowOverallocation** Method, **ViewShowPeakUnits** Method, **ViewShowPercentAllocation** Method,

ViewShowPredecessorsSuccessors Method, **ViewShowResourcesPredecessors**
Method, **ViewShowResourcesSuccessors** Method, **ViewShowSchedule** Method,
ViewShowSelectedTasks Method, **ViewShowWork** Method.

ViewShowCost Method

Applies To	**Application** Object.
Description	Displays cost information in the active view.
Syntax	[*object*.]**ViewShowCost**
Elements	The *object* placeholder is an object expression that evaluates to an object in the Applies To list.
Remarks	The **ViewShowCost** method has no effect unless the active window contains one of the following views: Resource Usage, Task Form, Task Details Form, Task Name Form, Resource Form, or Resource Name Form.
See Also	**ViewShowAvailability** Method, **ViewShowCumulativeCost** Method, **ViewShowCumulativeWork** Method, **ViewShowNotes** Method, **ViewShowObjects** Method, **ViewShowOverallocation** Method, **ViewShowPeakUnits** Method, **ViewShowPercentAllocation** Method, **ViewShowPredecessorsSuccessors** Method, **ViewShowResourcesPredecessors** Method, **ViewShowResourcesSuccessors** Method, **ViewShowSchedule** Method, **ViewShowSelectedTasks** Method, **ViewShowWork** Method.

ViewShowCumulativeCost Method

Applies To	**Application** Object.
Description	Displays cumulative cost information in the active Resource Usage view.
Syntax	[*object*.]**ViewShowCumulativeCost**
Elements	The *object* placeholder is an object expression that evaluates to an object in the Applies To list.
Remarks	The **ViewShowCumulativeCost** method has no effect unless the active window contains the Resource Usage view.

See Also   **ViewShowAvailability** Method, **ViewShowCost** Method,
ViewShowCumulativeWork Method, **ViewShowNotes** Method,
ViewShowObjects Method, **ViewShowOverallocation** Method,
ViewShowPeakUnits Method, **ViewShowPercentAllocation** Method,
ViewShowPredecessorsSuccessors Method, **ViewShowResourcesPredecessors**
Method, **ViewShowResourcesSuccessors** Method, **ViewShowSchedule** Method,
ViewShowSelectedTasks Method, **ViewShowWork** Method.

ViewShowCumulativeWork Method

Applies To   **Application** Object.

Description   Displays cumulative work information in the active Resource Usage view.

Syntax   [*object*.]**ViewShowCumulativeWork**

Elements   The *object* placeholder is an object expression that evaluates to an object in the
Applies To list.

Remarks   The **ViewShowCumulativeWork** method has no effect unless the active window
contains the Resource Usage view.

See Also   **ViewShowAvailability** Method, **ViewShowCost** Method,
ViewShowCumulativeCost Method, **ViewShowNotes** Method,
ViewShowObjects Method, **ViewShowOverallocation** Method,
ViewShowPeakUnits Method, **ViewShowPercentAllocation** Method,
ViewShowPredecessorsSuccessors Method, **ViewShowResourcesPredecessors**
Method, **ViewShowResourcesSuccessors** Method, **ViewShowSchedule** Method,
ViewShowSelectedTasks Method, **ViewShowWork** Method.

ViewShowNotes Method

Applies To   **Application** Object.

Description   Displays note information in the active view.

Syntax   [*object*.]**ViewShowNotes**

Elements   The *object* placeholder is an object expression that evaluates to an object in the
Applies To list.

Remarks	The **ViewShowNotes** method has no effect unless the active window contains the Task Form, Task Details Form, Task Name Form, Resource Form, or Resource Name Form.
See Also	**ViewShowAvailability** Method, **ViewShowCost** Method, **ViewShowCumulativeCost** Method, **ViewShowCumulativeWork** Method, **ViewShowObjects** Method, **ViewShowOverallocation** Method, **ViewShowPeakUnits** Method, **ViewShowPercentAllocation** Method, **ViewShowPredecessorsSuccessors** Method, **ViewShowResourcesPredecessors** Method, **ViewShowResourcesSuccessors** Method, **ViewShowSchedule** Method, **ViewShowSelectedTasks** Method, **ViewShowWork** Method.

ViewShowObjects Method

Applies To	**Application Object**.
Description	Displays object information in the active view.
Syntax	[*object*.]**ViewShowObjects**
Elements	The *object* placeholder is an object expression that evaluates to an object in the Applies To list.
Remarks	The **ViewShowObjects** method has no effect unless the active window contains the Task Form, Task Details Form, Task Name Form, Resource Form, or Resource Name Form.
See Also	**ViewShowAvailability** Method, **ViewShowCost** Method, **ViewShowCumulativeCost** Method, **ViewShowCumulativeWork** Method, **ViewShowNotes** Method, **ViewShowOverallocation** Method, **ViewShowPeakUnits** Method, **ViewShowPercentAllocation** Method, **ViewShowPredecessorsSuccessors** Method, **ViewShowResourcesPredecessors** Method, **ViewShowResourcesSuccessors** Method, **ViewShowSchedule** Method, **ViewShowSelectedTasks** Method, **ViewShowWork** Method.

ViewShowOverallocation Method

Applies To	**Application** Object.
Description	Displays overallocation information in the active Resource Usage view.
Syntax	[*object*.]**ViewShowOverallocation**

Elements	The *object* placeholder is an object expression that evaluates to an object in the Applies To list.
Remarks	The **ViewShowOverallocation** method has no effect unless the active window contains the Resource Usage view.
See Also	**ViewShowAvailability** Method, **ViewShowCost** Method, **ViewShowCumulativeCost** Method, **ViewShowCumulativeWork** Method, **ViewShowNotes** Method, **ViewShowObjects** Method, **ViewShowPeakUnits** Method, **ViewShowPercentAllocation** Method, **ViewShowPredecessorsSuccessors** Method, **ViewShowResourcesPredecessors** Method, **ViewShowResourcesSuccessors** Method, **ViewShowSchedule** Method, **ViewShowSelectedTasks** Method, **ViewShowWork** Method.

ViewShowPeakUnits Method

Applies To	**Application** Object.
Description	Displays peak units information in the active Resource Usage view.
Syntax	[*object*.]**ViewShowPeakUnits**
Elements	The *object* placeholder is an object expression that evaluates to an object in the Applies To list.
Remarks	The **ViewShowPeakUnits** method has no effect unless the active window contains the Resource Usage view.
See Also	**ViewShowAvailability** Method, **ViewShowCost** Method, **ViewShowCumulativeCost** Method, **ViewShowCumulativeWork** Method, **ViewShowNotes** Method, **ViewShowObjects** Method, **ViewShowOverallocation** Method, **ViewShowPercentAllocation** Method, **ViewShowPredecessorsSuccessors** Method, **ViewShowResourcesPredecessors** Method, **ViewShowResourcesSuccessors** Method, **ViewShowSchedule** Method, **ViewShowSelectedTasks** Method, **ViewShowWork** Method.

ViewShowPercentAllocation Method

Applies To	**Application** Object.
Description	Displays percent allocation information in the active Resource Usage view.
Syntax	[*object*.]**ViewShowPercentAllocation**

Elements	The *object* placeholder is an object expression that evaluates to an object in the Applies To list.
Remarks	The **ViewShowPercentAllocation** method has no effect unless the active window contains the Resource Usage view.
See Also	**ViewShowAvailability** Method, **ViewShowCost** Method, **ViewShowCumulativeCost** Method, **ViewShowCumulativeWork** Method, **ViewShowNotes** Method, **ViewShowObjects** Method, **ViewShowOverallocation** Method, **ViewShowPeakUnits** Method, **ViewShowPredecessorsSuccessors** Method, **ViewShowResourcesPredecessors** Method, **ViewShowResourcesSuccessors** Method, **ViewShowSchedule** Method, **ViewShowSelectedTasks** Method, **ViewShowWork** Method.

ViewShowPredecessorsSuccessors Method

Applies To	**Application** Object.
Description	Displays predecessors and successors information in the active view.
Syntax	[*object*.]**ViewShowPredecessorsSuccessors**
Elements	The *object* placeholder is an object expression that evaluates to an object in the Applies To list.
Remarks	The **ViewShowPredecessorsSuccessors** method has no effect unless the active window contains the Task Form, Task Details Form, or Task Name Form.
See Also	**ViewShowAvailability** Method, **ViewShowCost** Method, **ViewShowCumulativeCost** Method, **ViewShowCumulativeWork** Method, **ViewShowNotes** Method, **ViewShowObjects** Method, **ViewShowOverallocation** Method, **ViewShowPeakUnits** Method, **ViewShowPercentAllocation** Method, **ViewShowResourcesPredecessors** Method, **ViewShowResourcesSuccessors** Method, **ViewShowSchedule** Method, **ViewShowSelectedTasks** Method, **ViewShowWork** Method.

ViewShowResourcesPredecessors Method

Applies To	**Application** Object.
Description	Displays resources and predecessors information in the active Task Form view.
Syntax	[*object*.]**ViewShowResourcesPredecessors**

Elements	The *object* placeholder is an object expression that evaluates to an object in the Applies To list.
Remarks	The **ViewShowResourcesPredecessors** method has no effect unless the active window contains one of the following views: Task Form, Task Details Form, and Task Name Form.
See Also	**ViewShowAvailability** Method, **ViewShowCost** Method, **ViewShowCumulativeCost** Method, **ViewShowCumulativeWork** Method, **ViewShowNotes** Method, **ViewShowObjects** Method, **ViewShowOverallocation** Method, **ViewShowPeakUnits** Method, **ViewShowPercentAllocation** Method, **ViewShowPredecessorsSuccessors** Method, **ViewShowResourcesSuccessors** Method, **ViewShowSchedule** Method, **ViewShowSelectedTasks** Method, **ViewShowWork** Method.

ViewShowResourcesSuccessors Method

Applies To	**Application** Object.
Description	Displays resources and successors information in the active view.
Syntax	[*object*.]**ViewShowResourcesSuccessors**
Elements	The *object* placeholder is an object expression that evaluates to an object in the Applies To list.
Remarks	The **ViewShowResourcesSuccessors** method has no effect unless the active window contains one of the following views: Task Form, Task Details Form, and Task Name Form.
See Also	**ViewShowAvailability** Method, **ViewShowCost** Method, **ViewShowCumulativeCost** Method, **ViewShowCumulativeWork** Method, **ViewShowNotes** Method, **ViewShowObjects** Method, **ViewShowOverallocation** Method, **ViewShowPeakUnits** Method, **ViewShowPercentAllocation** Method, **ViewShowPredecessorsSuccessors** Method, **ViewShowResourcesPredecessors** Method, **ViewShowSchedule** Method, **ViewShowSelectedTasks** Method, **ViewShowWork** Method.

ViewShowSchedule Method

Applies To	**Application** Object.

Description	Displays the schedule fields in a resource or task form.
Syntax	[*object.*]**ViewShowSchedule**
Elements	The *object* placeholder is an object expression that evaluates to an object in the Applies To list.
Remarks	The **ViewShowSchedule** method has no effect unless the active view contains a resource or task form.
See Also	**ViewShowAvailability** Method, **ViewShowCost** Method, **ViewShowCumulativeCost** Method, **ViewShowCumulativeWork** Method, **ViewShowNotes** Method, **ViewShowObjects** Method, **ViewShowOverallocation** Method, **ViewShowPeakUnits** Method, **ViewShowPercentAllocation** Method, **ViewShowPredecessorsSuccessors** Method, **ViewShowResourcesPredecessors** Method, **ViewShowResourcesSuccessors** Method, **ViewShowSelectedTasks** Method, **ViewShowWork** Method.

ViewShowSelectedTasks Method

Applies To	**Application** Object.
Description	Determines which tasks appear in the active Resource Usage view.
Syntax	[*object.*]**ViewShowSelectedTasks** [*show*]
Elements	The **ViewShowSelectedTasks** method syntax has the following object qualifier and named arguments:

Part	Description
object	An object expression that evaluates to an object in the Applies To list.
show	A Boolean expression that specifies whether to show selected tasks in the Resource Usage view. If you set the *show* argument to **False**, the Resource Usage view displays information from all tasks in the project. By default, the *show* argument is **True** if the active Resource Usage view shows selected tasks only; otherwise the *show* argument is **False**.

Remarks	The **ViewShowSelectedTasks** method has no effect unless the Resource Usage form is in the lower pane of the active window.
See Also	**ViewShowAvailability** Method, **ViewShowCost** Method, **ViewShowCumulativeCost** Method, **ViewShowCumulativeWork** Method, **ViewShowNotes** Method, **ViewShowObjects** Method, **ViewShowOverallocation** Method, **ViewShowPeakUnits** Method, **ViewShowPercentAllocation** Method,

ViewShowPredecessorsSuccessors Method, ViewShowResourcesPredecessors
Method, ViewShowResourcesSuccessors Method, ViewShowSchedule Method,
ViewShowWork Method.

ViewShowWork Method

Applies To   **Application** Object.

Description   Displays work information in the active pane.

Syntax   [*object*.]**ViewShowWork**

Elements   The *object* placeholder is an object expression that evaluates to an object in the
Applies To list.

Remarks   The **ViewShowWork** method has no effect unless the active window contains one
of the following views: Resource Allocation, Resource Graph, Resource Usage,
Resource Form, Resource Name Form, Task Details Form, or Task Name Form.

See Also   **ViewShowAvailability** Method, **ViewShowCost** Method,
ViewShowCumulativeCost Method, **ViewShowCumulativeWork** Method,
ViewShowNotes Method, **ViewShowObjects** Method, **ViewShowOverallocation**
Method, **ViewShowPeakUnits** Method, **ViewShowPercentAllocation** Method,
ViewShowPredecessorsSuccessors Method, **ViewShowResourcesPredecessors**
Method, **ViewShowResourcesSuccessors** Method, **ViewShowSchedule** Method,
ViewShowSelectedTasks Method.

Visible Property

Applies To   **Application** Object; **Window** Object, **Windows** Collection.

Description   Returns or sets whether the main application window or a project window is visible.

Syntax   *object*.**Visible** [= *value*]

Elements   The **Visible** property has the following parts:

Part	Description
object	An object expression that evaluates to an object in the Applies To list.
value	A Boolean expression that specifies whether the main application or project window is visible.

Remarks   For the **Application** object, the **Visible** property affects the state of the window. Setting **Visible** to **False** hides the application window. Setting **Visible** to **True** restores the application window. For Microsoft Project for the Macintosh, this property is supported read-only.

See Also   **WindowHide** Method, **WindowUnhide** Method.

WBS Property

Applies To   **Project** Object, **Projects** Collection; **Task** Object, **Tasks** Collection.

Description   Returns or sets the WBS code of a task.

Syntax   *object*.**WBS** [= *value*]

Elements   The **WBS** property syntax has these parts:

Part	Description
object	An object expression that evaluates to an object in the Applies To list.
value	A string expression that specifies the WBS code of the task.

See Also   **ConstraintDate** Property, **ConstraintType** Property, **Flagn** Properties, **Name** Property, **Notes** Property, **Numbern** Properties, **Priority** Property, **SubProject** Property, **Summary** Property, **Textn** Properties.

Weekday Function

Description   Returns a whole number representing the day of the week.

Syntax   **Weekday(*date*)**

Elements   The *date* named argument is limited to numbers or strings, in any combination, that can represent a date. If *date* contains no valid data, **Null** is returned.

Value	Description
	Return Values
1	Sunday
2	Monday
3	Tuesday
4	Wednesday
5	Thursday
6	Friday
7	Saturday

See Also **Date** Function, **Date** Statement, **Day** Function, **Month** Function, **Now** Function, **Year** Function.

Example This example uses the **Weekday** function to obtain the day of the week from a specified date.

```
MyDate = #February 12, 1969#      ' Assign a date.
MyWeekDay = Weekday(MyDate)       ' MyWeekDay contains 4 since it
                             ' was a Wednesday.
```

Weekday Object, Weekdays Collection

Description A weekday or the weekdays in a calendar.

Remarks In Microsoft Project, **Weekday** objects are parents of **Shift** object.

Properties **Application** Property, **Calendar** Property, **Count** Property, **Index** Property, **Name** Property, **Parent** Property, **Shiftn** Property, **Working** Property

See Also **Calendar** Object, **Calendars** Collection; **Shift** Object; **Weekdays** Method.

Weekdays Method

Applies To **Calendar** Object, **Calendars** Collection.

Description Returns a weekday or the weekdays in a calendar.

Syntax *object*.**Weekdays**[(*index*)]

Elements The **Weekdays** method syntax has the following object qualifier and named arguments:

Part	Description
object	An object expression that evaluates to an object in the Applies To list.
index	A numeric expression from 1 (Sunday) to 7 (Saturday) that specifies the index of the *object* or a string expression that specifies a three-letter abbreviation for or the full name of a weekday.

See Also　　**Calendar** Object, **Calendars** Collection; **Weekday** Object, **Weekdays** Collection.

Example　　The following example makes Friday a nonworking day in the calendar for the active project.

```
Sub MakeFridaysNonworking()
    ActiveProject.Calendar.Weekdays(6).Working = False
End Sub
```

While...Wend Statement

Description　　Executes a series of statements as long as a given condition is **True**.

Syntax　　**While** *condition*
　　　　[*statements*]
　　Wend

Elements　　The **While...Wend** statement syntax has these parts:

Part	Description
condition	Numeric or string expression that evaluates to **True** or **False**.
statements	One or more statements executed while condition is **True**.

Remarks　　If *condition* is **True**, all statements in *statements* are executed until the **Wend** statement is encountered. Control then returns to the **While** statement and *condition* is again checked. If *condition* is still **True**, the process is repeated. If it is not **True**, execution resumes with the statement following the **Wend** statement.

While...Wend loops can be nested to any level. Each **Wend** matches the most recent **While**.

Caution　Do not branch into the body of a **While...Wend** loop without executing the **While** statement. Doing so may cause run-time errors or other problems that are difficult to locate.

Tip The **Do...Loop** statement provides a more structured and flexible way to perform looping.

See Also	**Do...Loop** Statement, **With** Statement.

Example

This example uses the **While...Wend** statement to increment a counter variable. The statements in the loop are executed as long as the condition evaluates to **True**.

```
Counter = 0                    ' Initialize variable.
While Counter < 20              ' Test value of Counter.
    Counter = Counter + 1     ' Increment Counter.
Wend
Debug.Print Counter            ' Prints 20 in Debug window.
```

Width # Statement

Description

Assigns an output-line width to a file opened using the **Open** statement.

Syntax

Width #*filenumber*,*width*

Elements

The **Width** statement syntax has these parts:

Part	Description
filenumber	Any valid file number.
width	Numeric expression in the range 0 to 255, inclusive, that indicates how many characters appear on a line before a new line is started. If *width* equals 0, there is no limit to the length of a line. The default value for *width* is 0.

See Also

Open Statement, **Print #** Statement

Example

This example uses the **Width** statement to set the output-line width for a file.

```
Open "TESTFILE" For Output As #1 ' Open file for output.
Width #1, 5                     ' Set output-line width to 5.
For I = 0 To 9                  ' Loop 10 times.
    Print #1, Chr(48 + I);       ' This prints 5 characters per line.
Next I
Close #1                        ' Close file.
```

Width Property

Applies To   **Application** Object.

Description   Returns the maximum width, in points, of a project window.

Syntax   [*object*.]**UsableWidth**

Elements   The *object* placeholder is an object expression that evaluates to an object in the Applies To list.

Remarks   The **UsableWidth** property equals the total amount of horizontal space inside the main window minus the space taken up by toolbars and scroll bars.

See Also   **Caption** Property, **Height** Property, **Left** Property, **Top** Property, **UsableHeight** Property, **Visible** Property, **Width** Property, **WindowState** Property.

Window Object, Windows Collection

Description   A window or the windows open in an application or project.

Remarks   In Microsoft Project, **Window** objects are parents of **Pane** objects.

Properties   **ActivePane** Property, **ActiveWindow** Property, **Application** Property, **BottomPane** Property, **Caption** Property, **Count** Property, **Height** Property, **Index** Property, **Left** Property, **Parent** Property, **Top** Property, **TopPane** Property, **Visible** Property, **Width** Property, **WindowState** Property

Methods   **Activate** Method, **Close** Method

See Also   **Application** Object; **Pane** Object; **Project** Object, **Projects** Collection; **Windows** Method.

WindowActivate Method

Applies To   **Application** Object.

Description   Activates a window.

Syntax   [*object*.]**WindowActivate** [*windowName*, *topPane*, *dialogID*]

Elements	The **WindowActivate** method syntax has the following object qualifier and named arguments:

Part	Description
object	An object expression that evaluates to an object in the Applies To list. Optional.
windowName	A string expression that specifies the name of the window to activate. The name of a window is the exact text that appears in the caption of the window. By default, the *windowName* argument equals the name of the active window. Optional.
topPane	A Boolean expression that specifies whether to activate the upper or lower pane. By default, the *topPane* argument is **True**. Optional.
dialogID	A constant that specifies the name of a dialog box to display. Optional.

The *dialogID* argument has these settings:

pjResourceAssignment	4087	Displays the Resource Assignment dialog box, which prompts the user to assign resources to the active tasks.
pjCustomizeToolbars	4124	Displays the Customize Toolbars dialog box, which prompts the user to customize toolbars.

See Also	**Activate** Method, **WindowArrangeAll** Method, **WindowHide** Method, **WindowMoreWindows** Method, **WindowNewWindow** Method, **WindowNext** Method, **WindowPrev** Method, **WindowUnhide** Method.
Example	The following examples allow the user to specify and activate a "hot" window. If you assign the ActivateHotWindow **Sub** procedure to a shortcut key, you can press that key to quickly activate the hot window.

```
Global HotWindowName      ' The name of the current hot window.

Sub ActivateHotWindow()
    Dim IsOpen   ' Whether or not the current hot window is open.
    Dim I        ' Index for For...Next loop.
    IsOpen = False   ' Assume the hot window is not open.
    For I = 1 to Windows.Count   ' Look for the current hot window.
        If LCase(Windows(I).Caption) = LCase(HotWindowName) Then
            IsOpen = True
            Exit For
        End If
    Next I
```

```
                         ' If the current hot window is not open or defined, then run
                         ' the ChangeHotWindow Sub procedure.
                         If Len(HotWindowName) = 0 Or Not IsOpen Then
                             MsgBox ("The current hot window is not open or has" & _
                                 " not been defined.")
                             ChangeHotWindowName

                         ' Otherwise, if the hot window is open, then activate it.
                         Else
                             WindowActivate (HotWindowName)
                         End If
                 End Sub

                 Sub ChangeHotWindowName()
                     Dim Entry    ' The text entered by the user.
                     Entry = InputBox("Enter the name of the hot window.")

                     ' If the user chooses Cancel, then exit the Sub procedure.
                     If Entry = Empty Then Exit Sub

                     ' Otherwise, set the name of the hot window and then activate it.
                     HotWindowName = Entry
                     ActivateHotWindow
                 End Sub
```

WindowArrangeAll Method

Applies To   **Application** Object.

Description   Arranges all the open windows in Microsoft Project.

Syntax   [*object.*]**WindowArrangeAll**

Elements   The *object* placeholder is an object expression that evaluates to an object in the Applies To list.

See Also   **WindowActivate** Method, **WindowHide** Method, **WindowMoreWindows** Method, **WindowNewWindow** Method, **WindowNext** Method, **WindowPrev** Method, **WindowUnhide** Method.

WindowHide Method

Applies To   **Application** Object.

Description   Hides a window.

Syntax   [*object.*]**WindowHide** [*name*]

Elements   The **WindowHide** method syntax has the following object qualifier and named arguments:

Part	Description
object	An object expression that evaluates to an object in the Applies To list.
name	A string expression that specifies the name of a window to hide. The name of a window is the exact text that appears in the caption of the window. By default, the active window is hidden.

See Also   **Visible** Property, **WindowActivate** Method, **WindowArrangeAll** Method, **WindowMoreWindows** Method, **WindowNewWindow** Method, **WindowNext** Method, **WindowPrev** Method, **WindowUnhide** Method.

Example   The following example hides all windows except the active window.

```
Sub HideAllWindowsExceptActive()
    Dim I

    For I = 1 To Windows.Count
        If Windows(I) <> ActiveWindow And Windows(I).Visible Then
            WindowHide Windows(I).Caption
        End If
    Next I
End Sub
```

WindowMoreWindows Method

Applies To   **Application** Object.

Description   Displays the Window Activate dialog box, which prompts the user to activate a window.

Syntax	[*object*.]**WindowMoreWindows**
Elements	The *object* placeholder is an object expression that evaluates to an object in the Applies To list.
See Also	**WindowActivate** Method, **WindowArrangeAll** Method, **WindowHide** Method, **WindowNewWindow** Method, **WindowNext** Method, **WindowPrev** Method, **WindowUnhide** Method.

WindowNewWindow Method

Applies To	**Application** Object.
Description	Creates a new window.
Syntax	[*object*.]**WindowNewWindow** [*projects*, *view*, *allProjects*, *ShowDialog*]
Elements	The **WindowNewWindow** method syntax has the following object qualifier and named arguments:

Part	Description
object	An object expression that evaluates to an object in the Applies To list. Optional.
projects	A string expression that specifies the names of one or more projects, separated by the list separator character. The new window contains data from the projects you specify. By default, Microsoft Project creates a copy of the active window. Optional.
view	A string expression that specifies the name of an initial view for the new window. By default, the *view* argument equals the **DefaultView** property. Optional.
allProjects	A Boolean expression that specifies whether the new window contains data from all open projects. When **True**, the *allProjects* argument overrides the *projects* argument. By default, the *allProjects* argument is **False**. Optional.
showDialog	A Boolean expression that specifies whether the New Window dialog will be displayed so a view or project can be selected. By default, the *showDialog* argument is **False**. Optional.

See Also	**ConsolidateProjects** Method, **WindowActivate** Method, **WindowArrangeAll** Method, **WindowHide** Method, **WindowMoreWindows** Method, **WindowNext** Method, **WindowPrev** Method, **WindowUnhide** Method.

Example

The following example creates a new window that combines the data from all open projects.

```
Sub NewCombineProjectsInNewWindow()
    WindowNewWindow allProjects := True
End Sub
```

WindowNext Method

Applies To   **Application** Object.

Description   Activates the next window.

Syntax   [*object.*]**WindowNext** [*noWrap*]

Elements   The **WindowNext** method syntax has the following object qualifier and named arguments:

Part	Description
object	An object expression that evaluates to an object in the Applies To list.
noWrap	A Boolean expression that specifies whether to activate the first window when the last window is active. By default, the *noWrap* argument is **False**.

See Also   **WindowActivate** Method, **WindowArrangeAll** Method, **WindowHide** Method, **WindowMoreWindows** Method, **WindowNewWindow** Method, **WindowPrev** Method, **WindowUnhide** Method.

WindowPrev Method

Applies To   **Application** Object.

Description   Activates the previous window.

Syntax   [*object.*]**WindowPrev** [*noWrap*]

Elements   The **WindowNext** method syntax has the following object qualifier and named arguments:

Part	Description
object	An object expression that evaluates to an object in the Applies To list.
noWrap	A Boolean expression that specifies whether to activate the last window when the first window is active. By default, the *noWrap* argument is **False**.

See Also   **WindowActivate** Method, **WindowArrangeAll** Method, **WindowHide** Method, **WindowMoreWindows** Method, **WindowNewWindow** Method, **WindowNext** Method, **WindowUnhide** Method.

Windows Method

Applies To   **Application** Object.

Description   Displays the Window Activate dialog box, which prompts the user to activate a window.

Syntax   [*object*.]**WindowMoreWindows**

Elements   The *object* placeholder is an object expression that evaluates to an object in the Applies To list.

See Also   **WindowActivate** Method, **WindowArrangeAll** Method, **WindowHide** Method, **WindowNewWindow** Method, **WindowNext** Method, **WindowPrev** Method, **WindowUnhide** Method.

WindowSplit Method

Applies To   **Application** Object.

Description   Creates a lower pane for the active window. Closes the lower pane, if it already exists.

Syntax   [*object*.]**WindowSplit**

Elements   The *object* placeholder is an object expression that evaluates to an object in the Applies To list.

See Also   **FormViewShow** Method, **ViewApply** Method.

WindowState Property

Applies To   **Application** Object; **Window** Object, **Windows** Collection.

Description   Returns or sets the state of the main window (**Application** object) or all project windows (**Window** object).

Syntax   *object*.**WindowState** [= *value*]

Elements   The **WindowState** property syntax has these parts:

Part	Description
object	An object expression that evaluates to an object in the Applies To list.
value	**pjMaximized**, **pjMinimized**, or **pjNormal**. Optional.

Settings   The **WindowState** property syntax has these settings:

pjNormal	1	Restores the window to its last nonmaximized and nonminimized state.
pjMinimized	2	Minimizes the window. Applies to Microsoft Windows.
pjMaximized	3	Maximizes the window. On the Macintosh, this parameter toggles the window between its maximized and restored states.

Remarks   For Microsoft Project for the Macintosh, this property is supported read-only for the **Application** object.

See Also   **Caption** Property, **Height** Property, **Left** Property, **Top** Property, **UsableHeight** Property, **UsableWidth** Property, **Visible** Property, **Width** Property.

Example   The following example maximizes all project windows.

```
Sub MaximizeProjectWindows()
    ActiveWindow.WindowState = pjMaximized
End Sub
```

WindowUnhide Method

Applies To   **Application** Object.

Description   Shows a hidden window.

Syntax   [*object*.]**WindowUnhide** [*name*]

Elements   The **WindowUnhide** method syntax has the following object qualifier and named arguments:

Part	Description
object	An object expression that evaluates to an object in the Applies To list.
name	A string expression that specifies the name of a hidden window to show. The name of a window is the exact text that appears in the caption of the window. By default, the Unhide dialog box appears, which prompts the user to show a hidden window in the active project.

See Also   **Visible** Property, **WindowActivate** Method, **WindowArrangeAll** Method, **WindowHide** Method, **WindowMoreWindows** Method, **WindowNewWindow** Method, **WindowNext** Method, **WindowPrev** Method.

Example   The following example unhides all open windows.

```
Sub UnhideAllWindows()
    Dim I

    For I = 1 To Windows.Count
        If Not Windows(I).Visible Then
            WindowUnhide Windows(I).Caption
        End If
    Next I
End Sub
```

With Statement

Description   Executes a series of statements on a single object or a user-defined type.

Syntax

With *object*
    [*statements*]
End With

Elements

The **With** statement syntax has these parts:

Part	Description
object	Name of an object or a user-defined type.
statements	One or more statements to be executed on *object*.

Remarks

The **With** statement allows you to perform a series of statements on a specified object without requalifying the name of the object. For example, if you have a number of different properties to change on a single object, it is more convenient to place the property assignment statements within the **With** control structure, referring to the object once instead of referring to it with each property assignment. The following example illustrates use of the **With** statement to assign values to several properties of the same object.

```
With MyLabel
    .Height = 2000
    .Width = 2000
    .Caption = "This is MyLabel"
End With
```

You can nest **With** statements by placing one **With** loop within another. Each *object* must be unique.

See Also

Do...Loop Statement, **While...Wend** Statement.

Example

This example uses the **With** statement to execute a series of statements on a single object. The object MyObject and its properties are generic names used for illustration purposes only.

```
With MyObject
    ' Same as MyObject.Height = 100
    .Height = 100
    .Caption = "Hello World"
    With .Font
        ' Same as MyObject.Font.Color = Red.
        .Color = Red
        .Bold = True
    End With
End With
```

Work Property

Applies To	**Assignment** Object, **Assignments** Collection; **Resource** Object, **Resources** Collection.
Description	Returns or sets the overtime work for an assignment. Returns the overtime work for a resource.
Syntax	*object*.**OvertimeWork** [= *value*]
Elements	The **OvertimeWork** property syntax has the following parts:

Part	Description
object	An object expression that evaluates to an object in the Applies To list.
value	A numeric expression that specifies the duration of overtime work for the resource.

See Also	**ActualWork** Property, **BaselineWork** Property, **OvertimeRate** Property, **Work** Property.

Working Property

Applies To	**Day** Object, **Days** Collection; **Month** Object, **Months** Collection; **Period** Object; **Weekday** Object, **Weekdays** Collection; **Year** Object, **Years** Collection.
Description	Returns or sets whether every day in a calendar period is a working day.
Syntax	*object*.**Working** [= *value*]
Elements	The **Working** property syntax has the following parts:

Part	Description
object	An object expression that evaluates to an object in the Applies To list.
value	A Boolean expression that specifies whether every day in the calendar period is a working day, as shown under Settings.

Settings	The **Working** property has the following settings:

Setting	Description
True	Every day in the calendar period is a working day.
False	Every day in the calendar period is not a working day.

See Also   **Clear** Method, **Default** Method, **Reset** Method.

Example   The following example makes June, July, and August nonworking months for resources in the "Student" group of the active project.

```
Sub GiveStudentsSummerOff()
    Dim R   ' Resource object used in For Each loop
    Dim Y   ' Year object used in For Each loop

    ' Look for resources in the "Student" group of the active project.
    For Each R In ActiveProject.Resources

        ' Give the summer off to resources in the "Student" group.
        If R.Group = "Student" Then
            For Each Y In R.Calendar.Years
                Y.Months("June").Working = False
                Y.Months("July").Working = False
                Y.Months("August").Working = False
            Next Y
        End If
    Next R
End Sub
```

WorkVariance Property

Applies To   **Project** Object, **Projects** Collection; **Resource** Object, **Resources** Collection; **Task** Object, **Tasks** Collection.

Description   Returns the variance between the baseline work and the work for a project or task.

Syntax   *object*.**WorkVariance**

Elements   The *object* placeholder is an object expression that evaluates to an object in the Applies To list.

See Also   **ActualWork** Property, **BaselineWork** Property, **CostVariance** Property, **DurationVariance** Property, **FinishVariance** Property, **RemainingWork** Property, **StartVariance** Property, **Work** Property.

Write # Statement

Description	Writes raw data to a sequential file.
Syntax	**Write** #*filenumber*[,*outputlist*]
Elements	The **Write** statement syntax has these parts:

Part	Description
filenumber	Any valid file number.
outputlist	One or more comma-delimited numeric or string expressions to write to a file.

Remarks

If you omit *outputlist* and include a comma after *filenumber*, a blank line prints to the file. Multiple expressions can be separated with a space, a semicolon, or a comma. A space has the same effect as a semicolon.

When **Write #** is used to output data to a file, several universal assumptions are followed so the data can always be read and correctly interpreted using **Input #**, regardless of locale:

- Numeric data is always output using the period (.) as the decimal separator.
- For Boolean data, either #TRUE# or #FALSE# is printed. The **True** and **False** keywords are not translated, regardless of locale.
- Date data is written to the file using the universal date format. When either the date or the time component is missing or zero, only the provided part gets written to the file.
- Nothing is written to the file if *outputlist* data is **Empty**. However, for **Null** data, #NULL# is output.
- For error data, the output appears as #ERROR errorcode#. The **Error** keyword is not translated, regardless of locale.

Unlike the **Print #** statement, the **Write #** statement inserts commas between items and quotation marks around strings as they are written to the file. You don't have to put explicit delimiters in the list. **Write #** inserts a newline character (carriage return or carriage return-linefeed) after it has written the final character in *outputlist* to the file.

See Also   **Input #** Statement, **Open** Statement, **Print #** Statement.

Example

This example uses the **Write #** statement to write raw data to a sequential file.

```
Open "TESTFILE" For Output As 1 ' Open file for output.
Write #1, "Hello World", 234    ' Written data is comma delimited.
Write #1,                       ' Write blank line.

' Assign Boolean, Date, Null and Error values.
MyBool = False : MyDate = #February 12, 1969# : MyNull = Null
MyError = CVErr(32767)
' Boolean data is written as #TRUE# or #FALSE#. Date literals are
' written in universal date format. Null data is written as #NULL#.
' Error data is written as #ERROR errorcode#.
Write #1, MyBool ; " is a Boolean value"
Write #1, MyDate ; " is a date"
Write #1, MyNull ; " is a null value"
Write #1, MyError ; " is an error value"
Close #1' Close file.
```

WriteReserved Property

Applies To   **Project** Object, **Projects** Collection.

Description   Returns whether a password is required to open a project for read-write access.

Syntax   *object*.**WriteReserved**

Elements   The *object* placeholder is an object expression that evaluates to an object in the Applies To list.

See Also   **HasPassword** Property, **ReadOnly** Property.

Xor Operator

Description   Used to perform a logical exclusion on two expressions.

Syntax   *result = expression1* **Xor** *expression2*

Elements   The **Xor** operator syntax has these parts:

Part	Description
result	Any numeric variable.
expression1	Any expression.
expression2	Any expression.

Remarks

If one, and only one, of the expressions evaluates **True**, *result* is **True**. However, if either expression is a **Null**, *result* is also a **Null**. When neither expression is a **Null**, *result* is determined according to the following table:

True	**True**	**False**
True	**False**	**True**
False	**True**	**True**
False	**False**	**False**

The **Xor** operator also performs a bit-wise comparison of identically positioned bits in two numeric expressions and sets the corresponding bit in *result* according to the following truth table:

0	0	0
0	1	1
1	0	1
1	1	0

See Also

Operator Precedence.

Example

This example uses the **Xor** operator to perform logical exclusion on two expressions.

```
A = 10: B = 8: C = 6 : D = Null  ' Initialize variables.
MyCheck = A > B Xor B > C         ' Returns False.
MyCheck = B > A Xor B > C         ' Returns True.
MyCheck = B > A Xor C > B         ' Returns False.
MyCheck = B > D Xor A > B         ' Returns Null.
MyCheck = A Xor B                 ' Returns 2 (bit-wise comparison).
```

Year Function

Description   Returns a whole number representing the year.

Syntax   **Year(***date***)**

Elements   The *date* named argument is limited to a date or numbers and strings, in any combination, that can represent a date. If *date* contains no valid data, **Null** is returned.

See Also   **Date** Function, **Date** Statement, **Day** Function, **Month** Function, **Now** Function, **Weekday** Function.

Example   This example uses the **Year** function to obtain the year from a specified date.

```
' In the development environment, the date literal will display in short
' format using the locale settings of your code.
MyDate = #February 12, 1969#    ' Assign a date.
MyYear = Year(MyDate)           ' MyYear contains 1969.
```

Year Object, Years Collection

Description   A year or the years in a calendar.

Remarks   In Microsoft Project, **Year** objects are parents of **Months** collections and **Shift** object.

Properties   **Application** Property, **Calendar** Property, **Count** Property, **Index** Property, **Name** Property, **Parent** Property, **Shiftn** Property, **Working** Property

Methods   **Default** Method, **Months** Method

See Also   **Calendar** Object, **Calendars** Collection; **Month** Object, **Months** Collection; **Shift** Object; **Years** Method.

Years Method

Applies To   **Calendar** Object, **Calendars** Collection.

Description   Returns a year or the years in a calendar.

Syntax   *object*.**Years**[(*index*)]

Elements   The **Years** method syntax has the following object qualifier and named arguments:

Part	Description
object	An object expression that evaluates to an object in the Applies To list.
index	A numeric expression that specifies the index of the *object*.

See Also	**Calendar** Object, **Calendars** Collection; **Days** Method; **Months** Method; **Period** Method; **Year** Object, **Years** Collection.
Example	The following example makes January 1 of every year a nonworking day.

```
Sub NewYearsDayOff()
    For each y in ActiveProject.Calendar.Years
        y.Months(1).Days(1).Working = False
    Next y
End Sub
```

Zoom Method

Applies To	**Application** Object.
Description	Displays a Zoom dialog box, which prompts the user to zoom in on or out from the active view.
Syntax	[*object*.]**Zoom**
Elements	The *object* placeholder is an object expression that evaluates to an object in the Applies To list.
Remarks	The Zoom method has no effect unless the active window contains one of the following views: Gantt Chart, PERT Chart, Calendar, Resource Graph, or Resource Usage.
See Also	**ZoomIn** Method, **ZoomOut** Method, **ZoomPERT** Method, **ZoomTimescale** Method.

ZoomCalendar Method

Applies To	**Application** Object.
Description	Zooms in on or out from the Calendar.
Syntax	[*object*.]**ZoomCalendar** [*numWeeks, startDate, endDate*]
Elements	The **ZoomCalendar** method syntax has the following object qualifier and named arguments:

Part	Description
object	An object expression that evaluates to an object in the Applies To list. Optional.
numWeeks	A numeric expression that specifies the number of weeks to display. If you specify values for the *startDate* and *endDate* arguments, the *numWeeks* argument is ignored. Optional.
startDate	A string expression that specifies the first date to display. Optional.
endDate	A string expression that specifies the last date to display. Optional.

Remarks The **ZoomCalendar** method has no effect unless the Calendar is the active view.

See Also **Zoom** Method, **ZoomPERT** Method, **ZoomTimescale** Method.

Example The following example displays four weeks at a time in Calendar view.

```
Sub FourWeekCalendar()
    ZoomCalendar numWeeks:=4
End Sub
```

ZoomIn Method

Applies To **Application** Object.

Description Zooms in on the active view.

Syntax [*object*.]**ZoomIn**

Elements The *object* placeholder is an object expression that evaluates to an object in the Applies To list.

See Also **Zoom** Method, **ZoomOut** Method, **ZoomPERT** Method, **ZoomTimescale** Method.

ZoomOut Method

Applies To **Application** Object.

Description Zooms out from the active view.

Syntax	[*object*.]**ZoomOut**
Elements	The *object* placeholder is an object expression that evaluates to an object in the Applies To list.
See Also	**Zoom** Method, **ZoomIn** Method, **ZoomPERT** Method, **ZoomTimescale** Method.

ZoomPERT Method

Applies To	**Application** Object.
Description	Zooms in on or out from the PERT Chart.
Syntax	[*object*.]**ZoomPERT** [*percent, entire*]
Elements	The **ZoomPERT** method syntax has the following object qualifier and named arguments:

Part	Description
object	An object expression that evaluates to an object in the Applies To list. Optional.
percent	A numeric expression that specifies the percentage—between 25 and 400—to reduce or enlarge the PERT Chart. Optional.
entire	A Boolean expression that specifies whether to display all tasks on the screen. By default, the *entire* argument is **False**. Optional.

See Also	**ZoomIn** Method, **ZoomOut** Method, **ZoomTimescale** Method.
Example	The following example fits all tasks in the current view.

```
Sub Display()
    ZoomPERT entire := True
End Sub
```

ZoomTimescale Method

Applies To	**Application** Object.
Description	Zooms in on or out from the Gantt Chart, Resource Graph, and Resource Usage view to show information about tasks or resources in a certain duration.
Syntax	[*object*.]**ZoomTimescale** [*duration, entire, selection, reset*]

Elements

The **ZoomTimescale** method syntax has the following object qualifier and named arguments:

Part	Description
object	An object expression that evaluates to an object in the Applies To list. Optional.
duration	A string expression that specifies the duration to display in the view. Optional.
entire	A Boolean expression that specifies whether to display the entire project in the view. By default, the *entire* argument is **False**. Optional.
selection	A Boolean expression that specifies whether to display the selected tasks in the view. By default, the *selection* argument is **False**. Optional.
reset	A Boolean expression that specifies whether to reset the view to its default size. By default, the *reset* argument is **False**. Optional.

See Also

ZoomIn Method, **ZoomOut** Method, **ZoomPERT** Method.

Example

The following example fits the entire project in the current view.

```
Sub Display()
    ZoomTimescale entire := True
End Sub
```

Learn to integrate **objects** from **Microsoft Office**
for Windows 95

with custom **Visual Basic** objects.

U.S.A. $39.95
U.K. £37.49 [V.A.T. included]
Canada $53.95
ISBN 1-55615-899-8

Learn how to coordinate applications for optimal performance. A custom program that uses multiple applications to provide a unified solution must act as a unit. Correct coordination among applications can make or break your solution. This book teaches you how to design your application for maximum effectiveness when it uses Microsoft Office 95 and Visual Basic applications simultaneously. You'll learn how to code for optimal performance. No Visual Basic programmer should be without this valuable information.

Get Matt Curland's powerful programming tool. Use the Object Navigator, included on the companion CD, to:

- Locate elusive functionality in any object library with full sub-string search
- Graphically build complete hierarchical code expressions that can be pasted directly into your code

If your goal is building object-oriented applications with Visual Basic and Microsoft Office for Windows 95 applications, this is the guide that will get you on track and keep you there.

Microsoft Press

Unleash the power of
Microsoft® Visual Basic® with
HARDCORE VISUAL BASIC!

Visual Basic wizard Bruce McKinney shows how to blast through the so-called limits of Visual Basic and reach the powerful object-oriented development tool that lurks within. The result: applications with better performance and more functionality.

Valuable Information Included on CD!

■ Thousands of lines of code that illustrate advanced programming techniques with the Windows API and the new object-oriented features of Visual Basic 4

■ The Windows API type library and other useful tools, such as Property Shop, Bug Wizard, Time It, and the VBUTIL dynamic-link library

HARDCORE VISUAL BASIC provides developers and programmers with detailed coverage of such topics as:

■ Exploring the Spirit of Basic—Language purification, the Basic Hungarian naming convention, efficient code versus correct code, and Basic wrappers for un-Basic hacks

■ Taking Control of Windows®—Calling the Windows API, understanding C in Basic, and mastering messages and processes

■ Programming Objects, Basic Style—Classes and objects, the form class, collecting objects, and creating new controls by delegating to classes

■ Painting Pictures—The Basic way of drawing, painting, and animating

■ Reusing Code—Modular packages for sorting, shuffling, searching, and parsing; reusable Search, Replace, About, and Color Select forms; and classes for editing, animating, managing the keyboard, handling menus, and sharing memory between programs

■ Programming in Different Environments—Code for MS-DOS®, Windows 3.1, Windows 95, Windows NT®, and OLE

If you want to push Visual Basic to the max, HARDCORE VISUAL BASIC is your guide—it's essential for any serious Visual Basic programmer's library.

"HARDCORE VISUAL BASIC is a book for people who like Basic but don't like limits. It's for people who won't take no for an answer. If you're willing to go the extra mile for better performance and more functionality, you'll have fun with this book."

—Bruce McKinney

Microsoft Press® books are available wherever quality books are sold and through CompuServe's Electronic Mall—
GO MSP—or our Web page, http://www.microsoft.com/mspress/. Call **1-800-MSPRESS** for more information or to place a credit card order.* Please refer to BBK when placing your order. Prices subject to change.

*In Canada, contact Macmillan Canada, Attn: Microsoft Press Dept., 164 Commander Blvd., Agincourt, Ontario, Canada MIS 3C7, or call 1-800-667-1115. Outside the U.S. and Canada, write to International Coordinator, Microsoft Press, One Microsoft Way, Redmond, WA 98052-6399, or fax +1-206-936-7329.

ISBN 1-55615-667-7
664 pages, one CD-ROM
$39.95 ($53.95 Canada)

Microsoft *Press*

For Virginia.

Contents

12 Working with macros and forms 361

13 Working with other Office programs 393

14 Collaborating with colleagues 411

Introduction

Part of the Microsoft Office 2013 suite of programs, Microsoft Excel 2013 is a full-featured spreadsheet program that helps you quickly and efficiently develop dynamic, professional workbooks to summarize and present your data. *Microsoft Excel 2013 Step by Step* offers a comprehensive look at the features of Excel that most people will use most frequently.

Who this book is for

Microsoft Excel 2013 Step by Step and other books in the *Step by Step* series are designed for beginning-level to intermediate-level computer users. Examples shown in the book generally pertain to small and medium businesses but teach skills that can be used in organizations of any size. Whether you are already comfortable working in Excel and want to learn about new features in Excel 2013 or are new to Excel, this book provides invaluable hands-on experience so that you can create, modify, and share workbooks with ease.

How this book is organized

This book is divided into 14 chapters. Chapters 1–4 address basic skills such as identifying the different Excel programs, customizing the program window, setting up workbooks, managing data within workbooks, creating formulas to summarize your data, and formatting your workbooks. Chapters 5–10 show you how to analyze your data in more depth through sorting and filtering, creating alternative data sets for scenario analysis, summarizing data by using charts, and creating PivotTables and PivotCharts. Chapters 11–14 cover printing, working with macros and forms, working with other Microsoft Office programs, and collaborating with colleagues.

The first part of Chapter 1 contains introductory information that will primarily be of interest to readers who are new to Excel or are upgrading from Excel 2010 or an earlier version. If you have worked with a more recent version of Excel, you might want to skip that material.

This book has been designed to lead you step by step through all the tasks you're most likely to want to perform with Excel 2013. If you start at the beginning and work your way through all the exercises, you will gain enough proficiency to be able to create and work with most types of Excel workbooks. However, each topic is self-contained, so you can jump in anywhere to acquire exactly the skills you need.

Download the practice files

Before you can complete the exercises in this book, you need to download the book's practice files to your computer. These practice files can be downloaded from the following page:

http://go.microsoft.com/FWLink/?Linkid=275457

> **IMPORTANT** The Excel 2013 program is not available from this website. You should purchase and install that program before using this book.

The following table lists the practice files for this book.

Chapter	File
Chapter 1: Getting started with Excel 2013	DataLabels.xlsx
	ExceptionSummary.xlsx
	ExceptionTracking.xlsx
	MisroutedPackages.xlsx
	PackageCounts.xlsx
	RouteVolume.xlsx
Chapter 2: Working with data and Excel tables	2013Q1ShipmentsByCategory.xlsx
	AverageDeliveries.xlsx
	DriverSortTimes.xlsx
	MailingNames.xlsx
	Series.xlsx
	ServiceLevels.xlsx
Chapter 3: Performing calculations on data	ConveyerBid.xlsx
	FuelSurcharges.xlsx
	ITExpenses.xlsx
	PackagingCosts.xlsx
	SavingsIncentive.xlsx
	VehicleMiles.xlsx

Chapter	File
Chapter 4: Changing workbook appearance	CallCenter.xlsx
	Dashboard.xlsx
	ExecutiveSearch.xlsx
	HourlyExceptions.xlsx
	HourlyTracking.xlsx
	VehicleMileSummary.xlsx
Chapter 5: Focusing on specific data by using filters	Credit.xlsx
	ForFollowUp.xlsx
	PackageExceptions.xlsx
	Slicers.xlsx
Chapter 6: Reordering and summarizing data	GroupByQuarter.xlsx
	ShipmentLog.xlsx
	ShippingCustom.xlsx
	ShippingSummary.xlsx
Chapter 7: Combining data from multiple sources	Consolidate.xlsx
	DailyCallSummary.xlsx
	FebruaryCalls.xlsx
	FleetOperatingCosts.xlsx
	JanuaryCalls.xlsx
	OperatingExpenseDashboard.xlsx
Chapter 8: Analyzing data and alternative data sets	2DayScenario.xlsx
	AdBuy.xlsx
	DriverSortTimes.xlsx
	MultipleScenarios.xlsx
	PackageAnalysis.xlsx
	RateProjections.xlsx
	TargetValues.xlsx
Chapter 9: Creating charts and graphics	FutureVolumes_start.xlsx
	MonthAndCategory_start.xlsx
	OrgChart_start.xlsx
	RevenueAnalysis_start.xlsx
	RevenueSummary_start.xlsx
	Shapes_start.xlsx
	VolumeByCenter_start.xlsx
	YearlyPackageVolume_start.xlsx

Chapter	File
Chapter 10: Using PivotTables and PivotCharts	Creating.txt
	Creating.xlsx
	Editing.xlsx
	Focusing.xlsx
	Formatting.xlsx
	RevenueAnalysis.xlsx
Chapter 11: Printing worksheets and charts	ConsolidatedMessenger.png
	CorporateRevenue.xlsx
	HourlyPickups.xlsx
	PickupsByHour.xlsx
	RevenueByCustomer.xlsx
	SummaryByCustomer.xlsx
Chapter 12: Working with macros and forms	PackageWeight.xlsm
	PerformanceDashboard.xlsm
	RunOnOpen.xlsm
	VolumeHighlights.xlsm
	YearlySalesSummary.xlsm
Chapter 13: Working with other Office programs	2013YearlyRevenueSummary.pptx
	Hyperlink.xlsx
	LevelDescriptions.xlsx
	RevenueByServiceLevel.xlsx
	RevenueChart.xlsx
	RevenueSummary.pptx
	SummaryPresentation.xlsx
Chapter 14: Collaborating with colleagues	CategoryXML.xlsx
	CostProjections.xlsx
	ExceptionTracking.xml
	ProjectionChangeTracking.xlsx
	ProjectionsDistro.xlsx
	ProjectionsForComment.xlsx
	ProjectionsSigned.xlsx
	SecureInfo.xlsx
	ShipmentSummary.xlsx
	SkyDriveFile.xlsx

Your companion ebook

With the ebook edition of this book, you can do the following:

- Search the full text
- Print
- Copy and paste

To download your ebook, please see the instruction page at the back of the book.

Getting support and giving feedback

The following sections provide information about getting help with Excel 2013 or the contents of this book and contacting us to provide feedback or report errors.

Errata

We've made every effort to ensure the accuracy of this book and its companion content. Any errors that have been reported since this book was published are listed on our Microsoft Press site at oreilly.com:

http://go.microsoft.com/FWLink/?Linkid=275456

If you find an error that is not already listed, you can report it to us through the same page.

If you need additional support, email Microsoft Press Book Support at *mspinput@microsoft.com*.

Please note that product support for Microsoft software is not offered through the addresses above.

We want to hear from you

At Microsoft Press, your satisfaction is our top priority, and your feedback our most valuable asset. Please tell us what you think of this book at:

http://www.microsoft.com/learning/booksurvey

The survey is short, and we read every one of your comments and ideas. Thanks in advance for your input!

Stay in touch

Let's keep the conversation going! We're on Twitter at: *http://twitter.com/MicrosoftPress*.

Chapter at a glance

Customize

Customize the Excel 2013 program window,
page 13

Create

Create workbooks,
page 25

Modify

Modify workbooks,
page 30

Merge

Merge and unmerge cells,
page 39

Getting started with Excel 2013

1

IN THIS CHAPTER, YOU WILL LEARN HOW TO

- Identify the different Excel 2013 programs.

- Identify new features of Excel 2013.

- Customize the Excel 2013 program window.

- Create workbooks.

- Modify workbooks.

- Modify worksheets.

- Merge and unmerge cells.

When you create a Microsoft Excel 2013 workbook, the program presents a blank workbook that contains one worksheet. You can add or delete worksheets, hide worksheets within the workbook without deleting them, and change the order of your worksheets within the workbook. You can also copy a worksheet to another workbook or move the worksheet without leaving a copy of the worksheet in the first workbook. If you and your colleagues work with a large number of documents, you can define property values to make your workbooks easier to find when you and your colleagues attempt to locate them by searching in File Explorer or by using Windows 8 Search.

TIP In Windows 8, File Explorer has replaced Windows Explorer. Throughout this book, this browsing utility is referred to by its Windows 8 name. If your computer is running Windows 7, use Windows Explorer instead.

You can also make Excel easier to use by customizing the Excel program window to fit your work style. If you have several workbooks open at the same time, you can move between the workbook windows quickly. However, if you switch between workbooks frequently, you might find it easier to resize the workbooks so they don't take up the entire Excel window. If you do this, you can switch to the workbook that you want to modify by clicking the title bar of the workbook you want.

The Microsoft Office User Experience team has enhanced your ability to customize the Excel user interface. If you find that you use a command frequently, you can add it to the Quick Access Toolbar so it's never more than one click away. If you use a set of commands frequently, you can create a custom ribbon tab so they appear in one place. You can also hide, display, or change the order of the tabs on the ribbon.

In this chapter, you'll get an overview of the different Excel programs that are available and discover features that are available in Excel 2013. You'll also create and modify workbooks and worksheets, make workbooks easier to find, and customize the Excel 2013 program window.

PRACTICE FILES To complete the exercises in this chapter, you need the practice files contained in the Chapter01 practice file folder. For more information, see "Download the practice files" in this book's Introduction.

Identifying the different Excel 2013 programs

The Microsoft Office 2013 suite includes programs that give you the ability to create and manage every type of file you need to work effectively at home, business, or school. The programs include Microsoft Word 2013, Excel 2013, Outlook 2013, PowerPoint 2013, Access 2013, InfoPath 2013, Lync 2013, OneNote 2013, and Publisher 2013. You can purchase the programs as part of a package that includes multiple programs or purchase most of the programs individually.

With the Office 2013 programs, you can find the tools you need quickly and, because they were designed as an integrated package, you'll find that most of the skills you learn in one program transfer readily to the others. That flexibility extends well beyond your personal computer. In addition to the traditional desktop Excel program, you can also use Excel 2013 on devices with ARM chips and over the web. The following describes the different Excel 2013 programs that are available to you:

- **Microsoft Excel 2013 desktop edition** This program is installed directly on your computer. It includes all of the capabilities built into Excel 2013. You can purchase the desktop edition as part of an Office program suite, as a separate program, or as part of the Office 365 subscription package that lets you install the desktop versions of Office programs over the Internet.

TIP Office 365 is a cloud-based subscription licensing solution. Some of the Office 365 subscription levels provide access to the full Excel 2013 program, Excel Web App, or both.

- **Microsoft Excel 2013 RT** Microsoft developed an edition of Windows 8 for devices powered by an ARM processor. Devices running this edition of Windows 8, called Windows RT, come with an edition of Office 2013 named Microsoft Office 2013 RT. The Office 2013 RT program suite includes Excel, OneNote, PowerPoint, and Word.

Excel 2013 RT takes advantage of ARM devices' touch screen capabilities by including Touch Mode. When you enable Touch Mode, the Excel 2013 RT interface changes slightly to make it easier to work with the program by tapping the screen with your finger or a stylus and by providing an on-screen keyboard through which you can enter data. You can also work with Excel 2013 RT by using a physical keyboard, a mouse, and your device's track pad.

TIP Excel 2013 RT includes almost all of the functionality found in the Excel 2013 full desktop program; the main difference is that Excel 2013 RT does not support macros. If you open a macro-enabled workbook in Excel 2013 RT, the macros will be disabled.

- **Microsoft Excel 2013 Web App** Information workers require their data to be available to them at all times, not just when they're using their personal computers. To provide mobile workers with access to their data, Microsoft developed Office Web Apps, which include online versions of Excel, Word, PowerPoint, and OneNote. Office Web Apps are available as part of an Office 365 subscription or for free as part of the Microsoft SkyDrive cloud service.

You can use Excel Web App to edit files stored in your SkyDrive account or on a Microsoft SharePoint site. Excel Web App displays your Excel 2010 and Excel 2013 files as they appear in the desktop program and includes all of the functions you use to summarize your data. You can also view and manipulate (but not create) PivotTables, add charts, and format your data to communicate its meaning clearly.

Excel Web App also includes the capabilities to share your workbooks online, to embed them as part of another webpage, and to create web-accessible surveys that save user responses directly to an Excel workbook in your SkyDrive account.

After you open a file by using Excel Web App, you can choose to continue editing the file in your browser (such as Windows Internet Explorer 10) or open the file in the desktop program. When you open the file in your desktop program, any changes you save are written to the version of the file on your SkyDrive account. This practice means that you will always have access to the most recent version of your file, regardless of where and how you access it.

- **Microsoft Excel Mobile** If you have a Windows Phone 8 device, you can use Excel Mobile to view and manipulate your workbooks. You can create formulas, change the formatting of worksheet cells, sort and filter your data, and summarize your data by using charts. You can also connect your phone to your SkyDrive account, so all of those files will be available even if you don't have a notebook or other computer to work with at the moment.

Identifying new features of Excel 2013

Excel 2013 includes all of the most useful capabilities included in previous versions of the program. If you've used an earlier version of Excel, you probably want to know about the new features introduced in Excel 2013. The following sections summarize the most important changes from Excel 2010, Excel 2007, and Excel 2003.

If you are upgrading from Excel 2010

For users of Excel 2010, you'll find that Excel 2013 extends the program's existing capabilities and adds some very useful new ones. The features introduced in Excel 2013 include:

- **Windows 8 functionality** Excel 2013, like all Office 2013 programs, takes full advantage of the capabilities of the Windows 8 operating system. When it is running on a computer running Windows 8, Excel embodies the new presentation elements and enables you to use a touch interface to interact with your data.

- **A window for each workbook** Every workbook now has its own program window.

- **New functions** More than 50 new functions are available, which you can use to summarize your data, handle errors in your formulas, and bring in data from online resources.

- **Flash Fill** If your data is in list form, you can combine, extract, or format the data in a cell. When you continue the operation, Excel detects your pattern and offers to extend it for every row in the list.

- **Quick Analysis Lens** Clicking the Quick Analysis action button, which appears next to a selected cell range, displays different ways to visually represent your data. Clicking an icon creates the analysis instantly.

- **Recommended PivotTable** PivotTables create interactive and flexible data summaries. You can have Excel recommend a series of PivotTables to create from your data, click the one you want, and keep working.

- **Recommended Charts** As with Recommended PivotTables, Excel recommends the most suitable charts based on patterns in your data. You can display the suggested charts, click the one you want, and modify it so it's perfect.

- **Chart formatting control** You can fine-tune your charts quickly and easily. Change the title, layout, or other elements of your charts from a new and interactive interface.

- **Chart animations** When you change the underlying data in a chart, Excel updates your chart and highlights the change by using an animation.

- **Cloud capability** You can now share workbooks stored online or post part of a workbook to your social network by posting a link to the file.

- **Online presentation capability** You can share your workbook and collaborate in real time with others as part of a Microsoft Lync conversation or meeting. You can also allow others to take control of your workbook during the conversation or meeting.

If you are upgrading from Excel 2007

In addition to the features added in Excel 2013, the Excel programming team introduced the following features in Excel 2010:

- **Manage Excel files and settings in the Backstage view** When the User Experience and Excel teams focused on the Excel 2007 user interface, they discovered that several workbook management tasks that contained content-related tasks were sprinkled among the ribbon tabs. The Excel team moved all of the workbook management tasks to the Backstage view, which users can access by clicking the File tab.

- **Preview data by using Paste Preview** With this feature, you can preview how your data will appear in the worksheet before you commit to the paste.

- **Customize the Excel 2010 user interface** The ability to make simple modifications to the Quick Access Toolbar has been broadened to include many more options for changing the ribbon interface. You can hide or display built-in ribbon tabs, change the order of built-in ribbon tabs, add custom groups to a ribbon tab, and create custom ribbon tabs, which can also contain custom groups.

- **Summarize data by using more accurate functions** In earlier versions of Excel, the program contained statistical, scientific, engineering, and financial functions that would return inaccurate results in some relatively rare circumstances. The Excel programming team identified the functions that returned inaccurate results and collaborated with academic and industry analysts to improve the functions' accuracy.

- **Summarize data by using sparklines** In his book *Beautiful Evidence* (Graphics Press), Edward Tufte describes sparklines as "intense, simple, wordlike graphics." Sparklines take the form of small charts that summarize data in a single cell. These small but powerful additions to Excel 2010 and Excel 2013 enhance the program's reporting and summary capabilities.

- **Filter PivotTable data by using slicers** Slicers visually indicate which values appear in a PivotTable and which are hidden. They are particularly useful when you are presenting data to an audience that contains visual thinkers who might not be skilled at working with numerical values.

- **Filter PivotTable data by using search filters** Excel 2007 introduced several new ways to filter PivotTables. These filtering capabilities have been extended with the introduction of search filters. With a search filter, you begin entering a sequence of characters that occur in the term (or terms) by which you want to filter. As you enter these characters, the filter list of the PivotTable field displays only those terms that reflect the values entered into the search filter box.

- **Visualize data by using improved conditional formats** The Excel programming team greatly extended the capabilities of the data bar and icon set conditional formats introduced in Excel 2007. The team also enabled you to create conditional formats that refer to cells on worksheets other than the one on which you're defining the format.

- **Create and display math equations** With the updated equation designer, you can create any equation you require. The editor has several common equations built in, such as the quadratic formula and the Pythagorean theorem, but it also contains numerous templates that you can use to create custom equations quickly.

- **Edit pictures within Excel 2010** One very helpful capability is the ability to remove the background elements of an image. Removing an image's background enables you to create a composite image in which the foreground elements are placed in front of another background. For example, you can focus on a flower's bloom and remove most of the leaves and stem from the photo. After you isolate the foreground image, you can place the bloom in front of another background.

If you are upgrading from Excel 2003

In addition to the changes in Excel 2010 and Excel 2013, users upgrading from Excel 2003 will notice several more significant changes:

- **The ribbon** Unlike in previous versions of Excel, in which you hunted through a complex toolbar and menu system to find the commands you wanted, you can use the ribbon user interface to find everything you need at the top of the program window.

- **Larger data collection capability** The larger worksheet includes more than 1 million rows and 16,000 columns.

- **New file format** The Excel file format (.xlsx) uses XML and file compression techniques to reduce the size of a typical file by 50 percent.

- **Expanded cell and worksheet formatting** Vast improvements have been made to the color management and formatting options found in previous versions of the program. You can have as many different colors in a workbook as you like, for example, and you can assign a design theme to a workbook.

- **Excel tables** These enable you to enter and summarize your data efficiently. If you want to enter data in a new table row, all you have to do is enter the data in the row below the table. When you press Tab or Enter after entering the last cell's values, Excel expands the table to include your new data. You can also have Excel display a Totals row, which summarizes your table's data by using a function that you specify.

- **Improved charting** With the charting engine, you can create more attractive charts.

- **Formula AutoComplete** When you enter formulas into an Excel worksheet cell, the program displays a list of options from which you can choose for each formula element, greatly accelerating formula entry.

- **Additional formulas** With the added formulas, such as AVERAGEIFS, users can summarize data conditionally.

- **Conditional formatting** With conditional formats, users can create data bars and color scales, assign icon sets to values, assign multiple conditional formats to a cell, and assign more than three conditional formatting rules to a cell.

Working with the ribbon

As with all Office 2013 programs, the Excel ribbon is dynamic, meaning that as its width changes, its buttons adapt to the available space. As a result, a button might be large or small, it might or might not have a label, or it might even be an entry in a list.

For example, when sufficient horizontal space is available, the buttons on the Home tab are spread out, and the available commands in each group are visible.

If you decrease the horizontal space available to the ribbon, small button labels disappear and entire groups of buttons might hide under one button that represents the entire group. Clicking the group button displays a list of the commands available in that group.

When the ribbon becomes too narrow to display all the groups, a scroll arrow appears at its right end. Clicking the scroll arrow displays the hidden groups.

The width of the ribbon depends on three factors:

- **Program window width** Maximizing the program window provides the most space for the ribbon. To maximize the window, click the **Maximize** button, drag the borders of a nonmaximized window, or drag the window to the top of the screen.

- **Screen resolution** Screen resolution is the size of your screen display expressed as pixels wide × pixels high. Your screen resolution options are dependent on the display adapter installed in your computer, and on your monitor. Common screen resolutions range from 800 × 600 to 2560 × 1600. The greater the number of pixels wide (the first number), the greater the number of buttons that can be shown on the ribbon.

To change your screen resolution:

1 Display the **Screen Resolution** control panel item in one of the following ways:

- Right-click the Windows desktop, and then click **Screen Resolution**.

- Enter screen resolution in Windows 8 Search, and then click **Adjust screen resolution** in the **Settings** results.

- Open the **Display** control panel item, and then click **Adjust resolution**.

2 On the **Screen Resolution** page, click the **Resolution** arrow, click or drag to select the screen resolution you want, and then click **Apply** or **OK**.

- **The magnification of your screen display** If you change the screen magnification setting in Windows, text and user interface elements are larger and therefore more legible, but fewer elements fit on the screen. You can set the magnification from 100 to 500 percent.

You can change the screen magnification from the Display page of the Appearance And Personalization control panel item. You can display the Display page directly from Control Panel or by using one of the following methods:

- Right-click the Windows desktop, click **Personalize**, and then in the lower-left corner of the **Personalization** window, click **Display**.

- Enter display in Windows 8 Search, and then click **Display** in the **Settings** results.

To change the screen magnification to 125 percent or 150 percent, click that option on the Display page. To select another magnification, click the Custom Sizing Options link and then, in the Custom Sizing Options dialog box, click the magnification you want in the drop-down list or drag the ruler to change the magnification even more.

After you click OK in the Custom Sizing Options dialog box, the custom magnification is shown on the Display page along with any warnings about possible problems with selecting that magnification. Click Apply on the Display page to apply the selected magnification.

Customizing the Excel 2013 program window

How you use Excel 2013 depends on your personal working style and the type of data collections you manage. The Excel product team interviews customers, observes how differing organizations use the program, and sets up the user interface so that many users won't need to change it to work effectively. If you do want to change the program window, including the user interface, you can. You can change how Excel displays your worksheets; zoom in on worksheet data; add frequently used commands to the Quick Access Toolbar; hide, display, and reorder ribbon tabs; and create custom tabs to make groups of commands readily accessible.

Zooming in on a worksheet

One way to make Excel easier to work with is to change the program's zoom level. Just as you can "zoom in" with a camera to increase the size of an object in the camera's viewer, you can use the zoom setting to change the size of objects within the Excel program window. For example, if Peter Villadsen, the Consolidated Messenger European Distribution Center Manager, displayed a worksheet that summarized his distribution center's package volume by month, he could click the View tab and then, in the Zoom group, click the Zoom button to open the Zoom dialog box. The Zoom dialog box contains controls that he can use to select a preset magnification level or to enter a custom magnification level. He could also use the Zoom control in the lower-right corner of the Excel window.

Clicking the Zoom In control increases the size of items in the program window by 10 percent, whereas clicking the Zoom Out control decreases the size of items in the program window by 10 percent. If you want more fine-grained control of your zoom level, you can use the slider control to select a specific zoom level or click the magnification level indicator, which indicates the zoom percentage, and use the Zoom dialog box to set a custom magnification level.

The Zoom group on the View tab contains the Zoom To Selection button, which fills the program window with the contents of any selected cells, up to the program's maximum zoom level of 400 percent.

TIP The minimum zoom level in Excel is 10 percent.

Arranging multiple workbook windows

As you work with Excel, you will probably need to have more than one workbook open at a time. For example, you could open a workbook that contains customer contact information and copy it into another workbook to be used as the source data for a mass mailing you create in Word. When you have multiple workbooks open simultaneously, you can switch between them by clicking the View tab and then, in the Window group, clicking the Switch Windows button and clicking the name of the workbook you want to view.

You can arrange your workbooks on the desktop so that most of the active workbook is shown but the others are easily accessible. To do so, click the View tab and then, in the Window group, click the Arrange All button. Then, in the Arrange Windows dialog box, click Cascade.

Many Excel workbooks contain formulas on one worksheet that derive their value from data on another worksheet, which means you need to change between two worksheets every time you want to test how modifying your data changes the formula's result. However, an easier way to approach this is to display two copies of the same workbook simultaneously,

displaying the worksheet that contains the data in the original window and displaying the worksheet with the formula in the new window. When you change the data in either copy of the workbook, Excel updates the other copy. To display two copies of the same workbook, open the workbook and then, on the View tab, in the Window group, click New Window to opens a second copy of the workbook. To display the workbooks side by side, on the View tab, click Arrange All. Then, in the Arrange Windows dialog box, click Vertical and then click OK.

If the original workbook's name is MisroutedPackages, Excel displays the name MisroutedPackages:1 on the original workbook's title bar and MisroutedPackages:2 on the second workbook's title bar.

TROUBLESHOOTING If the controls in the Window group on the View tab don't affect your workbooks as you expect, you might have a program, such as SkyDrive for PC, open in the background that prevents those capabilities from functioning.

Adapting exercise steps

The screen shots shown in this book were captured at a screen resolution of 1024 × 768, at 100-percent magnification. If your settings are different, the ribbon on your screen might not look the same as the one shown in this book. As a result, exercise instructions that involve the ribbon might require a little adaptation. This book's instructions use this format:

- On the **Insert** tab, in the **Illustrations** group, click the **Chart** button.

If the command is in a list, the instructions use this format:

- On the **Home** tab, in the **Editing** group, click the **Find** arrow and then, in the **Find** list, click **Go To**.

If your display settings cause a button to appear differently on your screen than it does in this book, you can easily adapt the steps to locate the command. First click the specified tab, and then locate the specified group. If a group has been collapsed into a group list or under a group button, click the list or button to display the group's commands. If you can't immediately identify the button you want, point to likely candidates to display their names in ScreenTips.

This book provides instructions based on traditional keyboard and mouse input methods. If you're using Excel on a touch-enabled device, you might be giving commands by tapping with your finger or with a stylus. If so, substitute a tapping action any time the instructions ask you to click a user interface element. Also note that when the instructions ask you to enter information in Excel, you can do so by typing on a keyboard, tapping in the entry field under discussion to display and use the on-screen keyboard, or even speaking aloud, depending on your computer setup and your personal preferences.

In this exercise, you'll change a worksheet's zoom level, zoom to maximize the display of a selected cell range, switch between workbooks, and arrange all open workbooks on your screen.

 SET UP You need the PackageCounts and MisroutedPackages workbooks located in the Chapter01 practice file folder to complete this exercise. Open both workbooks, and then follow the steps.

1   In the **MisroutedPackages** workbook, in the lower-right corner of the Excel window, click the **Zoom In** control five times to change the worksheet's zoom level to **150%**.

2   Select cells **B2:C11**.

3   On the **View** tab, in the **Zoom** group, click the **Zoom to Selection** button to display the selected cells so that they fill the program window.

	A	B	C
2		**Region**	**2012 Exception Rate**
3		Northeast	0.0021%
4		Atlantic	0.0025%
5		Southeast	0.0026%
6		North Central	0.0026%
7		Midwest	0.0020%
8		Southwest	0.0018%
9		Mountain West	0.0002%
10		Northwest	0.0004%
11		Central	0.0011%

Sheet1

4   On the **View** tab, in the **Zoom** group, click the **Zoom** button to open the **Zoom** dialog box.

5   Click **100%**, and then click **OK** to return the worksheet to its default zoom level.

6   On the **View** tab, in the **Window** group, click the **Switch Windows** button, and then click **PackageCounts** to display the **PackageCounts** workbook.

7   On the **View** tab, in the **Window** group, click the **Arrange All** button to open the **Arrange Windows** dialog box.

8   Click **Cascade**, and then click **OK** to cascade the open workbook windows.

 CLEAN UP Close the PackageCounts and MisroutedPackages workbooks, saving your changes if you want to.

Adding buttons to the Quick Access Toolbar

As you continue to work with Excel 2013, you might discover that you use certain commands much more frequently than others. If your workbooks draw data from external sources, for example, you might find yourself displaying the Data tab and then, in the Connections group, clicking the Refresh All button much more often than the program's designers might have expected. You can make any button accessible with one click by adding the button to the Quick Access Toolbar, located just above the ribbon in the upper-left corner of the Excel program window.

To add a button to the Quick Access Toolbar, click the File tab to display the Backstage view, and then click Options in the left pane. In the Excel Options dialog box, display the Customize The Quick Access Toolbar page. This page contains two panes. The pane on the left lists all of the controls that are available within a specified category, and the pane on the right lists the controls currently displayed on the Quick Access Toolbar. To add a command to the Quick Access Toolbar, in the Choose Commands From list, click the category that contains the control you want to add. Excel displays the available commands in the

pane below the Choose Commands From field. Click the control you want, and then click the Add button.

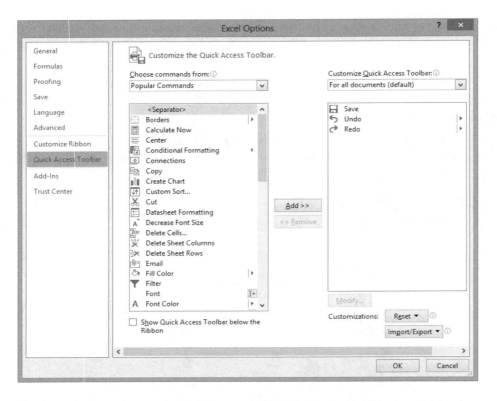

You can change a button's position on the Quick Access Toolbar by clicking its name in the right pane and then clicking either the Move Up or Move Down button at the right edge of the dialog box. To remove a button from the Quick Access Toolbar, click the button's name in the right pane, and then click the Remove button. When you're done making your changes, click the OK button. If you prefer not to save your changes, click the Cancel button. If you saved your changes but want to return the Quick Access Toolbar to its original state, click the Reset button and then click either Reset Only Quick Access Toolbar, which removes any changes you made to the Quick Access Toolbar, or Reset All Customizations, which returns the entire ribbon interface to its original state.

You can also choose whether your Quick Access Toolbar changes affect all your workbooks or just the active workbook. To control how Excel applies your change, in the Customize Quick Access Toolbar list, click either For All Documents to apply the change to all of your workbooks or For Workbook to apply the change to the active workbook only.

If you'd like to export your Quick Access Toolbar customizations to a file that can be used to apply those changes to another Excel 2013 installation, click the Import/Export button and then click Export All Customizations. Use the controls in the dialog box that opens to save your file. When you're ready to apply saved customizations to Excel, click the Import/Export button, click Import Customization File, select the file in the File Open dialog box, and click Open.

Customizing the ribbon

Excel enhances your ability to customize the entire ribbon by enabling you to hide and display ribbon tabs, reorder tabs displayed on the ribbon, customize existing tabs (including tool tabs, which appear when specific items are selected), and create custom tabs.

To begin customizing the ribbon, display the Backstage view and then click Options. In the Excel Options dialog box, click Customize Ribbon to display the Customize The Ribbon page.

To select which tabs appear in the tabs pane on the right side of the screen, click the Customize The Ribbon field's arrow and then click either Main Tabs, which displays the tabs that can appear on the standard ribbon; Tool Tabs, which displays the tabs that appear when you click an item such as a drawing object or PivotTable; or All Tabs.

TIP The procedures taught in this section apply to both the main tabs and the tool tabs.

Each tab's name has a check box next to it. If a tab's check box is selected, then that tab appears on the ribbon. You can hide a tab by clearing the check box and bring the tab back by selecting the check box. You can also change the order in which the tabs are displayed on the ribbon. To do so, click the name of the tab you want to move and then click the Move Up or Move Down arrow to reposition the selected tab.

Just as you can change the order of the tabs on the ribbon, you can change the order in which groups of commands appear on a tab. For example, the Page Layout tab contains five groups: Themes, Page Setup, Scale To Fit, Sheet Options, and Arrange. If you use the Themes group less frequently than the other groups, you could move the group to the right end of the tab by clicking the group's name and then clicking the Move Down button until the group appears in the position you want.

To remove a group from a built-in tab, click the name of the group in the right pane and click the Remove button. If you remove a group from a built-in tab and later decide you want to put it back on the tab, display the tab in the right pane. Then, click the Choose Commands From field's arrow and click Main Tabs. With the tab displayed, in the left pane, click the expand control (which looks like a plus sign) next to the name of the tab that contains the group you want to add back. You can now click the name of the group in the left pane and click the Add button to put the group back on the selected tab.

The built-in tabs are designed efficiently, so adding new command groups might crowd the other items on the tab and make those controls harder to find. Rather than adding controls to an existing tab, you can create a custom tab and then add groups and commands to it. To create a custom tab, click the New Tab button on the Customize The Ribbon page of the Excel Options dialog box. When you do, a new tab named New Tab (Custom), which contains a group named New Group (Custom), appears in the tab list.

You can add an existing group to your new tab by clicking the Choose Commands From field's arrow, selecting a collection of commands, clicking the group you want to add, and then clicking the Add button. You can also add individual commands to your tab by clicking a command in the command list and clicking the Add button. To add a command to your tab's custom group, click the new group in the right tab list, click the command in the left list, and then click the Add button. If you want to add another custom group to your new tab, click the new tab, or any of the groups within that tab, and then click New Group.

TIP You can change the order of the groups and commands on your custom ribbon tabs by using the techniques described earlier in this section.

The New Tab (Custom) name doesn't tell you anything about the commands on your new tab, so you can rename it to reflect its contents. To rename any tab on the ribbon, display the Customize The Ribbon page of the Excel Options dialog box, click the tab you want to modify, and then click the Rename button. Enter the tab's new name in the Rename dialog box, and click OK. To rename any group on the ribbon, click the name of the group, and then click Rename. When you do, the Rename dialog box appears. Enter a new name for the group in the Display Name box and click OK.

If you'd like to export your ribbon customizations to a file that can be used to apply those changes to another Excel 2013 installation, click the Import/Export button and then click Export All Customizations. Use the controls in the dialog box that opens to save your file. When you're ready to apply saved customizations to Excel, click the Import/Export button, click Import Customization File, select the file in the File Open dialog box, and click Open.

When you're done customizing the ribbon, click the OK button to save your changes or click Cancel to keep the user interface as it was before you started this round of changes. You can also change a tab, or the entire ribbon, back to the state it was in when you installed Excel. To restore a single tab, click the tab you want to restore, click the Reset button, and then click Reset Only Selected Ribbon Tab. To restore the entire ribbon, including the Quick Access Toolbar, click the Reset button and then click Reset All Customizations.

Maximizing usable space in the program window

You can increase the amount of space available inside the program window by hiding the ribbon, the formula bar, or the row and column labels.

To hide the ribbon, double-click the active tab label. The tab labels remain visible at the top of the program window, but the tab content is hidden. To temporarily redisplay the ribbon, click the tab label you want. Then click any button on the tab, or click away from the tab, to rehide it. To permanently redisplay the ribbon, double-click any tab label.

KEYBOARD SHORTCUT Press Ctrl+F1 to hide and unhide the ribbon. For a complete list of keyboard shortcuts, see "Keyboard shortcuts" at the end of this book.

To hide the formula bar, clear the Formula Bar check box in the Show/Hide group on the View tab. To hide the row and column labels, clear the Headings check box in the Show/Hide group on the View tab.

In this exercise, you'll add a button to the Quick Access Toolbar and customize the ribbon.

➡ SET UP You need the PackageCounts workbook located in the Chapter01 practice file folder to complete this exercise. Open the workbook, and then follow the steps.

1 Click the **File** tab to display the **Backstage** view, and then click **Options** to open the **Excel Options** dialog box.

2 Click **Quick Access Toolbar** to display the **Customize The Quick Access Toolbar** page.

3   Click the **Choose commands from** arrow, and then in the list, click **Review Tab** to display the commands in the **Review Tab** category in the command list.

4   Click the **Spelling** command, and then click **Add** to add the **Spelling** command to the **Quick Access Toolbar**.

5   Click **Customize Ribbon** to display the **Customize The Ribbon** page of the **Excel Options** dialog box.

6   If necessary, click the **Customize the Ribbon** box's arrow and click **Main Tabs**. In the right tab list, click the **Review** tab and then click the **Move Up** button three times to move the **Review** tab between the **Insert** and **Page Layout** tabs.

7   Click the **New Tab** button to create a tab named **New Tab (Custom)**, which appears below the most recently active tab in the **Main Tabs** list.

8   Click the **New Tab (Custom)** tab name, click the **Rename** button, enter My Commands in the **Display Name** box, and click **OK** to change the new tab's name to **My Commands**.

9   Click the **New Group (Custom)** group's name and then click the **Rename** button. In the **Rename** dialog box, click the icon that looks like a paint palette (second row, fourth from the right). Then, in the **Display name** box, enter Formatting, and click **OK** to change the new group's name to **Formatting**.

10   In the right tab list, click the **My Commands** tab name. Then, on the left side of the dialog box, click the **Choose Commands From** box's arrow and click **Main Tabs** to display that group of tabs in the left tab list.

11   In the left tab list, click the **Home** tab's expand control, click the **Styles** group's name, and then click the **Add** button to add the **Styles** group to the **My Commands** tab.

12   In the left tab list, below the **Home** tab, click the **Number** group's expand control to display the commands in the **Number** group.

13   In the right tab list, click the **Formatting** group you created earlier. Then, in the left tab list, click the **Number Format** item and click the **Add** button to add the **Number Format** item to the **Formatting** custom group.

14   Click **OK** to save your ribbon customizations, and then click the **My Commands** tab on the ribbon to display the contents of the new tab.

IMPORTANT The remaining exercises in this book assume that you are using Excel 2013 as it was installed on your computer. After you complete this exercise, you should reset the ribbon to its original configuration so that the instructions in the remaining exercises in the book are consistent with your copy of Excel.

✖ CLEAN UP Close all open workbooks, saving your changes if you want to.

Creating workbooks

Every time you want to gather and store data that isn't closely related to any of your other existing data, you should create a new workbook. The default workbook in Excel has one worksheet, although you can add more worksheets or delete existing worksheets if you want. Creating a workbook is a straightforward process—you just display the Backstage view, click New, and click the tile that represents the type of workbook you want.

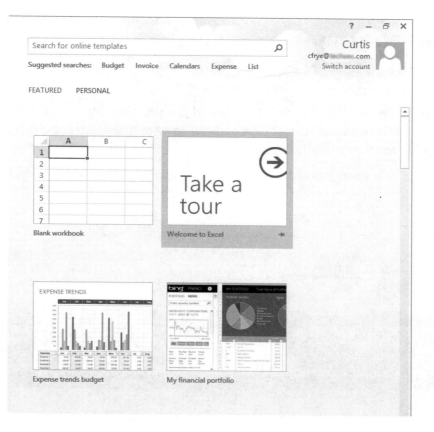

KEYBOARD SHORTCUT Press Ctrl+N to create a blank workbook.

When you start Excel, the program displays the Start experience. With the Start experience, you can select which type of workbook to create. You can create a blank workbook by clicking the Blank Workbook tile or click one of the built-in templates available in Excel. You can then begin to enter data into the worksheet's cells. You could also open an existing workbook and work with its contents. In this book's exercises, you'll work with workbooks created for Consolidated Messenger, a fictional global shipping company. After you make changes to a workbook, you can save it to preserve your work.

KEYBOARD SHORTCUT Press Ctrl+S to save a workbook.

TIP Readers frequently ask, "How often should I save my files?" It is good practice to save your changes every half hour or even every five minutes, but the best time to save a file is whenever you make a change that you would hate to have to make again.

When you save a file, you overwrite the previous copy of the file. If you have made changes that you want to save, but you also want to keep a copy of the file as it was when you saved it previously, you can use the Save As command to specify a name for the new file. To open the Save As dialog box, in the Backstage view, click Save As.

KEYBOARD SHORTCUT Press F12 to open the Save As dialog box.

You can also use the controls in the Save As dialog box to specify a different format for the new file and a different location in which to save the new version of the file. For example, Lori Penor, the chief operating officer of Consolidated Messenger, might want to save an Excel file that tracks consulting expenses as an Excel 2003 file if she needs to share the file with a consulting firm that uses Excel 2003.

After you create a file, you can add information to make the file easier to find when you search by using File Explorer or Windows 8 Search to search for it. Each category of information, or property, stores specific information about your file. In Windows, you can search for files based on the file's author or title, or by keywords associated with the file. A file that tracks the postal code destinations of all packages sent from a vendor might have the keywords *postal*, *destination*, and *origin* associated with it.

To set values for your workbook's built-in properties, you can display the Backstage view, click Info, click Properties, and then click Show Document Panel to display the Document Properties panel below the ribbon. The standard version of the Document Properties panel has fields for the file's author, title, subject, keywords, category, and status, and any comments about the file.

You can also create custom properties by clicking the arrow located to the right of the Document Properties label, and clicking Advanced Properties to open the Properties dialog box. On the Custom page of the Properties dialog box, you can click one of the existing custom categories or create your own by entering a new property name in the Name field, clicking the Type arrow and selecting a data type (for example, Text, Date, Number, or Yes/No), selecting or entering a value in the Value field, and then clicking Add. If you want to delete an existing custom property, point to the Properties list, click the property you want to get rid of, and click Delete. After you finish making your changes, click the OK button. To hide the Document Properties panel, click the Close button in the upper-right corner of the panel.

When you're done modifying a workbook, you should save your changes and then, to close the file, display the Backstage view and then click Close. You can also click the Close button in the upper-right corner of the workbook window.

KEYBOARD SHORTCUT Press Ctrl+W to close a workbook.

In this exercise, you'll close an open workbook, create a new workbook, save the workbook with a new name, assign values to the workbook's standard properties, and create a custom property.

➡ SET UP You need the ExceptionSummary workbook located in the Chapter01 practice file folder to complete this exercise. Open the workbook, and then follow the steps.

1   Click the **File** tab to display the **Backstage** view, and then click **Close** to close the **ExceptionSummary** workbook.

2   Display the **Backstage** view, and then click **New** to display the **New** page.

3   Click **Blank workbook**, and then click **Create** to open a new, blank workbook.

4   Display the **Backstage** view, click **Save As**, click **Computer**, and then click **Browse** to open the **Save As** dialog box.

5   Use the navigation controls to display the **Chapter01** folder. In the **File name** field, enter Exceptions2013.

6   Click the **Save** button to save your work and close the **Save As** dialog box.

7   Display the **Backstage** view, click **Info**, click **Properties**, and then click **Show Document Panel** to display the **Document Properties** panel.

8   In the **Keywords** field, enter exceptions, regional, percentage.

9   In the **Category** field, enter performance.

10   Click the arrow at the right end of the **Document Properties** button, and then click **Advanced Properties** to open the **Exceptions2013 Properties** dialog box.

11   Click the **Custom** tab to display the **Custom** page.

12   In the **Name** field, enter Performance.

13   In the **Value** field, enter Exceptions.

14   Click the **Add** button, and then click **OK** to save the properties and close the
       Exceptions2013 Properties dialog box.

❌ CLEAN UP Close the Exceptions2013 workbook, saving your changes if you want to.

Modifying workbooks

Most of the time, you create a workbook to record information about a particular activity,
such as the number of packages that a regional distribution center handles or the average
time a driver takes to complete all deliveries on a route. Each worksheet within that workbook should represent a subdivision of that activity. To display a particular worksheet, click
the worksheet's tab on the tab bar (just below the grid of cells).

In the case of Consolidated Messenger, the workbook used to track daily package volumes
could have a separate worksheet for each regional distribution center. As mentioned earlier,

new Excel workbooks contain one worksheet; because Consolidated Messenger uses nine regional distribution centers, you would need to create eight new worksheets. To create a new worksheet, click the New Sheet button (which looks like a plus sign in a circle) at the right edge of the tab bar.

When you create a worksheet, Excel assigns it a generic name such as *Sheet2*, *Sheet3*, or *Sheet4*. After you decide what type of data you want to store on a worksheet, you should change the default worksheet name to something more descriptive. For example, you could change the name of Sheet1 in the regional distribution center tracking workbook to *Northeast*. When you want to change a worksheet's name, double-click the worksheet's tab on the tab bar to highlight the worksheet name, enter the new name, and press Enter.

Another way to work with more than one worksheet is to copy a worksheet from another workbook to the current workbook. One circumstance in which you might consider copying worksheets to the current workbook is if you have a list of your current employees in another workbook. You can copy worksheets from another workbook by right-clicking the tab of the sheet you want to copy and, on the shortcut menu, clicking Move Or Copy to open the Move Or Copy dialog box.

TIP When you select the Create A Copy check box, Excel leaves the copied worksheet in its original workbook, whereas clearing the check box causes Excel to delete the worksheet from its original workbook.

After the worksheet is in the target workbook, you can change the worksheets' order to make the data easier to locate within the workbook. To change a worksheet's location in the workbook, you drag its sheet tab to the location you want on the tab bar. If you want to remove a worksheet from the tab bar without deleting the worksheet, you can do so by right-clicking the worksheet's tab on the tab bar and clicking Hide on the shortcut menu. When you want Excel to redisplay the worksheet, right-click any visible sheet tab and then click Unhide. In the Unhide dialog box, click the name of the sheet you want to display, and click OK.

To differentiate a worksheet from others, or to visually indicate groups or categories of worksheets in a multiple-worksheet workbook, you can change the color of a worksheet tab. To do so, right-click the tab, point to Tab Color, and then click the color you want.

TIP If you copy a worksheet to another workbook, and the destination workbook has the same Office Theme applied as the active workbook, the worksheet retains its tab color. If the destination workbook has another theme applied, the worksheet's tab color changes to reflect that theme. For more information about Office themes, see Chapter 4, "Changing workbook appearance."

If you determine that you no longer need a particular worksheet, such as one you created to store some figures temporarily, you can delete the worksheet quickly. To do so, right-click its sheet tab, and then click Delete.

In this exercise, you'll insert and rename a worksheet, change a worksheet's position in a workbook, hide and unhide a worksheet, copy a worksheet to another workbook, change a worksheet's tab color, and delete a worksheet.

➡ SET UP You need the ExceptionTracking workbook located in the Chapter01 practice file folder to complete this exercise. Open the workbook, and then follow the steps.

1   On the tab bar, click the **New Sheet** button to create a new worksheet.

2   Right-click the new worksheet's sheet tab, and then click **Rename** to highlight the new worksheet's name.

3   Enter 2013, and then press **Enter**.

4   On the tab bar, double-click the **Sheet1** sheet tab to highlight the worksheet's name.

5   Enter 2012, and then press **Enter**.

6   Right-click the **2013** sheet tab, point to **Tab Color**, and then, in the **Standard Colors** palette, click the green swatch to change the **2013** sheet tab to green.

7   On the tab bar, drag the **2012** sheet tab to the right of the **Scratch Pad** sheet tab.

8   Right-click the **2013** sheet tab, and then click **Hide** to remove the **2013** sheet tab from the tab bar.

9   Right-click the **2012** sheet tab, and then click **Move or Copy** to open the **Move or Copy** dialog box.

Move or Copy dialog box showing:
Move selected sheets
To book:
ExceptionTracking.xlsx
Before sheet:
Scratch Pad
2012
(move to end)
☐ Create a copy
OK   Cancel

10   Click the **To book** arrow, and then in the list, click **(new book)**.

11   Select the **Create a copy** check box.

12   Click **OK** to create a new workbook and copy the selected worksheet into it.

13   On the **Quick Access Toolbar**, click **Save** to open the **Save As** dialog box.

14   In the **File name** field, enter 2012 Archive, and then press **Enter** to save the workbook.

15   On the **View** tab, click the **Switch Windows** button, and then click **ExceptionTracking** to display the **ExceptionTracking** workbook.

16   On the tab bar, right-click the **Scratch Pad** sheet tab, and then click **Delete**. In the dialog box that opens, click **Delete** to confirm the operation.

17   Right-click the **2012** sheet tab, and then click **Unhide** to open the **Unhide** dialog box.

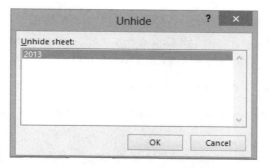

18   Click **2013**, and then click **OK** to close the **Unhide** dialog box and display the **2013** worksheet in the workbook.

✕ CLEAN UP Close the ExceptionTracking workbook and the 2012 Archive workbook, saving your changes if you want to.

Modifying worksheets

After you put up the signposts that make your data easy to find, you can take other steps to make the data in your workbooks easier to work with. For example, you can change the width of a column or the height of a row in a worksheet by dragging the column's right border or the row's bottom border to the position you want. Increasing a column's width or a row's height increases the space between cell contents, making your data easier to read and work with.

TIP You can apply the same change to more than one row or column by selecting the rows or columns you want to change and then dragging the border of one of the selected rows or columns to the location you want. When you release the mouse button, all the selected rows or columns change to the new height or width.

Inserting rows, columns, and cells

Modifying column width and row height can make a workbook's contents easier to work with, but you can also insert a row or column between cells that contain data to make your data easier to read. Adding space between the edge of a worksheet and cells that contain data, or perhaps between a label and the data to which it refers, makes the workbook's contents less crowded. You insert rows by clicking a cell and clicking the Home tab on the ribbon. Then, in the Cells group, in the Insert list, click Insert Sheet Rows. Excel inserts a row above the row that contains the active cell. You insert a column in much the same way, by choosing Insert Sheet Columns from the Insert list. When you do this, Excel inserts a column to the left of the active cell.

When you insert a row, column, or cell in a worksheet that has had formatting applied, the Insert Options button appears. When you click the Insert Options button, Excel displays a list of choices you can make about how the inserted row or column should be formatted, as described in the following table.

Option	Action
Format Same As Above	Applies the formatting of the row above the inserted row to the new row
Format Same As Below	Applies the formatting of the row below the inserted row to the new row
Format Same As Left	Applies the formatting of the column to the left of the inserted column to the new column
Format Same As Right	Applies the formatting of the column to the right of the inserted column to the new column
Clear Formatting	Applies the default format to the new row or column

If you want to delete a row or column, right-click the row or column head and then, on the shortcut menu that appears, click Delete. You can temporarily hide rows or columns by selecting those rows or columns and then, on the Home tab, in the Cells group, clicking the Format button, pointing to Hide & Unhide, and then clicking either Hide Rows or Hide Columns. The rows or columns you selected disappear, but they aren't gone for good as they would be if you'd used Delete. Instead, they have just been removed from the display until you call them back. To return the hidden rows to the display, select the row or column headers on either side of the hidden rows or columns. Then, on the Home tab, in the Cells group, click the Format button, point to Hide & Unhide, and then click either Unhide Rows or Unhide Columns.

IMPORTANT If you hide the first row or column in a worksheet, you must click the Select All button in the upper-left corner of the worksheet (above the first row header and to the left of the first column header) or press Ctrl+A to select the entire worksheet. Then, on the Home tab, in the Cells group, click Format, point to Hide & Unhide, and then click either Unhide Rows or Unhide Columns to make the hidden data visible again.

Just as you can insert rows or columns, you can insert individual cells into a worksheet. To insert a cell, click the cell that is currently in the position where you want the new cell to appear. On the Home tab, in the Cells group, in the Insert list, click Insert Cells to open the Insert dialog box. In the Insert dialog box, you can choose whether to shift the cells surrounding the inserted cell down (if your data is arranged as a column) or to the right (if your data is arranged as a row). When you click OK, the new cell appears, and the contents of affected cells shift down or to the right, as appropriate. Similarly, if you want to delete a block of cells, select the cells, and on the Home tab, in the Cells group, in the Delete list, click Delete Cells to open the Delete dialog box—complete with options that you can use to choose how to shift the position of the cells around the deleted cells.

TIP The Insert dialog box also includes options you can click to insert a new row or column; the Delete dialog box has similar options for deleting an entire row or column.

If you want to move the data in a group of cells to another location in your worksheet, select the cells you want to move and point to the selection's border. When the pointer changes to a four-pointed arrow, you can drag the selected cells to the desired location on the worksheet. If the destination cells contain data, Excel displays a dialog box asking whether you want to overwrite the destination cells' contents. If you want to replace the existing values, click OK. If you don't want to overwrite the existing values, click Cancel and insert the required number of cells to accommodate the data you want to move.

In this exercise, you'll insert a column and row into a worksheet, specify insert options, hide a column, insert a cell into a worksheet, delete a cell from a worksheet, and move a group of cells within the worksheet.

SET UP You need the RouteVolume workbook located in the Chapter01 practice file folder to complete this exercise. Open the workbook, and then follow the steps.

1   On the **May 12** worksheet, select cell **A1**.

2   On the **Home** tab, in the **Cells** group, click the **Insert** arrow, and then in the list, click **Insert Sheet Columns** to create a new column **A**.

3   In the **Insert** list, click **Insert Sheet Rows** to create a new row **1**.

4   Click the **Insert Options** button that appears below the lower-right corner of the selected cell, and then click **Clear Formatting** to remove the formatting from the new row **1**.

5   Right-click the column header of column **E**, and then click **Hide** to remove column **E** from the display.

	A	B	C	D	F
1					
2		Route	Volume		
3		1	6413		
4		2	2208		
5		3	7052		
6		4	9229		
7		5	1425		
8		6	4329		
9		7	8410		
10		8	8785		
11		9	5812		
12		10	1112		
13					

6   On the tab bar, click the **May 13** sheet tab to display the worksheet of the same name.

7   Click cell **B6**.

8   On the **Home** tab, in the **Cells** group, click the **Delete** arrow, and then in the list, click **Delete Cells** to open the **Delete** dialog box.

Delete

Delete
- ○ Shift cells left
- ● Shift cells up
- ○ Entire row
- ○ Entire column

[OK]   [Cancel]

9   If necessary, click **Shift cells up**, and then click **OK**. Excel deletes cell **B6**, moving the cells below it up to fill in the gap.

10   Click cell **C6**.

11   In the **Cells** group, in the **Insert** list, click **Insert Cells** to open the **Insert** dialog box.

12   If necessary, click **Shift cells down**, and then click **OK** to close the **Insert** dialog box, create a new cell **C6**, and move cells **C6:C11** down to accommodate the inserted cell.

13   In cell **C6**, enter **4499**, and then press **Enter**.

14   Select cells **E13:F13**.

15   Point to the border of the selected cells. When the pointer changes to a four-pointed arrow, drag the selected cells to cells **B13:C13**. The dragged cells replace cells **B13:C13**.

	A	B	C	D
1				
2		Route	Volume	
3		1	6413	
4		2	2208	
5		3	7052	
6		4	4499	
7		5	9229	
8		6	1425	
9		7	4329	
10		8	8410	
11		9	8785	
12		10	5812	
13		11	5509	
14				
15				

 CLEAN UP Close the RouteVolume workbook, saving your changes if you want to.

Merging and unmerging cells

Most Excel worksheets contain data about a specific subject, such as packages shipped, revenue, or operating costs. One of the best ways to communicate the contents of a worksheet is to use a label. For example, you might create a list of Consolidated Messenger's delivery regions with the city where the region's distribution hub is located.

◢	A	B	C
1			
2		**Distribution Center Hubs**	
3		Listed by region name and city	
4			
5		Northeast	Boston
6		Atlantic	Baltimore
7		Southeast	Atlanta
8		North Central	Cleveland
9		Midwest	St. Louis
10		Southwest	Albuquerque
11		Mountain West	Denver
12		Northwest	Portland
13		Central	Omaha
14			

The text *Distribution Center Hubs* appears to span two cells, B2 and C2, but is in fact contained within cell B2. If you select cell B2, Excel highlights the cell's border, which obscures the text. If you want to combine cells B2 and C2 into a single cell, you can do so by merging the cells into a single cell.

To merge two or more cells, you select the cells, click the Home tab, click Merge & Center, and then click Merge Cells. Now when you click cell B2, the selection border extends along the entire merged cell without blocking the text.

	A	B	C
1			
2		**Distribution Center Hubs**	
3		Listed by region name and city	
4			
5		Northeast	Boston
6		Atlantic	Baltimore
7		Southeast	Atlanta
8		North Central	Cleveland
9		Midwest	St. Louis
10		Southwest	Albuquerque
11		Mountain West	Denver
12		Northwest	Portland
13		Central	Omaha
14			

IMPORTANT When you merge two or more cells, Excel retains just the text in the range's top left cell. All other text is deleted.

When you click the Merge & Center button, a list of options appears. In addition to merging cells, you can click Merge & Center to combine the selected cells into a single cell and center the text within the merged cell. You should strongly consider using the Merge & Center option for label text, such as above a list of data where the title spans more than one column.

You can also merge the cells in multiple rows at the same time. For example, suppose your list has a main heading and a subheading. You can merge the cells in the two rows that contain headings by clicking the Home tab, clicking Merge & Center, and then clicking Merge Across.

◢	A	B	C
1			
2		**Distribution Center Hubs**	
3		Listed by region name and city	
4			
5		Northeast	Boston
6		Atlantic	Baltimore
7		Southeast	Atlanta
8		North Central	Cleveland
9		Midwest	St. Louis
10		Southwest	Albuquerque
11		Mountain West	Denver
12		Northwest	Portland
13		Central	Omaha
14			

IMPORTANT When you select the header cells, click the Home tab, click Merge & Center, and then click either Merge & Center or Merge Cells, Excel deletes any text that's not in the top-left cell of the selected range.

If you want to split merged cells into their individual cells, click the Home tab, click Merge & Center, and then click Unmerge Cells.

In this exercise, you will merge cells, unmerge cells, merge and center cells, and use Merge Across to combine cells in several rows into one merged cell per row.

SET UP You need the DataLabels workbook located in the Chapter01 practice file folder to complete this exercise. Open the workbook, and then follow the steps.

1   Select cells **B2:D2**.

2   Click the **Home** tab, click the **Merge & Center** arrow, and then click **Merge Cells** to merge the cells into a single cell.

3   Select cells **B3:F3**.

4   Click the **Home** tab, click the **Merge & Center** arrow, and then click **Merge & Center** to merge the cells into a single cell and center its contents.

5   Select cells **B5:E8**.

6   Click the **Home** tab, click the **Merge & Center** arrow, and then click **Merge Across** to merge the cells in each row into a single cell. The operation creates four merged cells.

	A	B	C	D	E	F
1						
2		**Delivery Category**				
3		**Brief descriptions of each category**				
4						
5		Overnight: next day delivery by 3PM				
6		2Day: second-day delivery by 6PM				
7		3Day: third-day delivery by 6PM				
8		Ground: delivery in 3-5 days by 6PM				
9						

7   Select cell **B2**.

8   Click the **Home** tab, click the **Merge & Center** arrow, and then click **Unmerge Cells** to split the merged cell into its original cells.

9   Select cells **B2:D2**.

10   Click the **Home** tab, click the **Merge & Center** arrow, and then click **Merge & Center** to merge the cells into a single cell and center its contents.

CLEAN UP Close the DataLabels workbook, saving your changes if you want to.

Key points

- Save your work whenever you do something you'd hate to have to do again.

- Assigning values to a workbook's properties makes it easier to find your workbook by searching in File Explorer or by using Windows 8 Search.

- Be sure to give your worksheets descriptive names.

- If you want to use a worksheet's data in another workbook, you can send a copy of the worksheet to that other workbook without deleting the original worksheet.

- You can delete a worksheet you no longer need, but you can also hide a worksheet in a workbook. When you need the data on the worksheet, you can unhide it.

- You can save yourself a lot of cutting and pasting by inserting and deleting worksheet cells, columns, and rows.

- By merging cells, you can add data labels that span multiple columns.

- Customize your Excel 2013 program window by changing how it displays your workbooks, zooming in on data, adding frequently used buttons to the Quick Access Toolbar, and rearranging or customizing the ribbon to meet your needs.

Chapter at a glance

Manage

Manage data by using Flash Fill,
page 50

	A	B	C	D
1	**LastName**	**FirstName**	**Initial**	**FullName**
2	Ray	Mike		Mike Ray
3	Basalik	Evan	B	Evan Basalik
4	Roth	Daniel	C	Daniel Roth
5	Kahn	Wendy		Wendy Kahn
6				

Rearrange

Move data within a workbook,
page 54

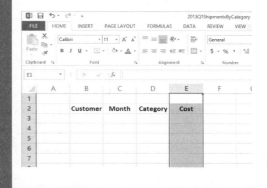

Find

Find and replace data,
page 58

Define

Define Excel tables,
page 67

	A	B	C	D
1				
2		**Customer**	**Month**	**Program Savings**
3		Contoso	January	$ 182,423
4		Contoso	February	$ 173,486
5		Contoso	March	$ 88,027
6		Fabrikam	January	$ 139,434
7		Fabrikam	February	$ 29,461
8		Fabrikam	March	$ 91,295
9		Lucerne Publishing	January	$ 136,922
10		Lucerne Publishing	February	$ 161,370
11		Lucerne Publishing	March	$ 160,250
12		Wide World Importers	January	$ 109,903
13		Wide World Importers	February	$ 102,243
14		Wide World Importers	March	$ 105,077
15		Total		$ 1,479,891
16				

Working with data and Excel tables

2

IN THIS CHAPTER, YOU WILL LEARN HOW TO

- Enter and revise data.

- Manage data by using Flash Fill.

- Move data within a workbook.

- Find and replace data.

- Correct and expand upon worksheet data.

- Define Excel tables.

With Microsoft Excel 2013, you can visualize and present information effectively by using charts, graphics, and formatting, but the data is the most important part of any workbook. By learning to enter data efficiently, you will make fewer data entry errors and give yourself more time to analyze your data so you can make decisions about your organization's performance and direction.

Excel provides a wide variety of tools you can use to enter and manage worksheet data effectively. For example, you can organize your data into Excel tables, which enables you to store and analyze your data quickly and efficiently. Also, you can enter a data series quickly, repeat one or more values, and control how Excel formats cells, columns, and rows moved from one part of a worksheet to another with a minimum of effort. With Excel, you can check the spelling of worksheet text, look up alternative words by using the Thesaurus, and translate words to foreign languages.

In this chapter, you'll enter and revise Excel data, manage data by using Flash Fill, move data within a workbook, find and replace existing data, use proofing and reference tools to enhance your data, and organize your data by defining Excel tables.

PRACTICE FILES To complete the exercises in this chapter, you need the practice files contained in the Chapter02 practice file folder. For more information, see "Download the practice files" in this book's Introduction.

Entering and revising data

After you create a workbook, you can begin entering data. The simplest way to enter data is to click a cell and enter a value. This method works very well when you're entering a few pieces of data, but it is less than ideal when you're entering long sequences or series of values. For example, Craig Dewar, the VP of Marketing for Consolidated Messenger, might want to create a worksheet that lists the monthly program savings that large customers can realize if they sign exclusive delivery contracts with Consolidated Messenger. To record those numbers, he would need to create a worksheet tracking each customer's monthly program savings.

	A	B	C	D	E
1					
2		**Customer**	**Month**	**Program Savings**	
3		Contoso	January	$ 182,423	
4		Contoso	February	$ 173,486	
5		Contoso	March	$ 88,027	
6		Fabrikam	January	$ 139,434	
7		Fabrikam	February	$ 29,461	
8		Fabrikam	March	$ 91,295	
9		Lucerne Publishing	January	$ 136,922	
10		Lucerne Publishing	February	$ 161,370	
11		Lucerne Publishing	March	$ 160,250	
12		Wide World Importers	January	$ 109,903	
13		Wide World Importers	February	$ 102,243	
14		Wide World Importers	March	$ 105,077	
15					

Repeatedly entering the sequence January, February, March, and so on can be handled by copying and pasting the first occurrence of the sequence, but there's an easier way to do it: use AutoFill. With AutoFill, you enter the first element in a recognized series, click the fill handle at the lower-right corner of the cell, and drag the fill handle until the series extends far enough to accommodate your data. By using a similar tool, FillSeries, you can enter two values in a series and use the fill handle to extend the series in your worksheet. For example, if you want to create a series starting at 2 and increasing by 2, you can enter 2 in the first cell and 4 in the second cell, select both cells, and then use the fill handle to extend the series to the end value you want.

You do have some control over how Excel extends the values in a series when you drag the fill handle. For example, if you drag the fill handle up (or to the left), Excel extends the series to include previous values. If you enter January in a cell and then drag that cell's fill handle up (or to the left), Excel places December in the first cell, November in the second cell, and so on.

Another way to control how Excel extends a data series is by pressing the Ctrl key while you drag the fill handle. For example, if you press the Ctrl key while you drag the fill handle, Excel repeats the value January in each cell you add to the series.

TIP Be sure to experiment with how the fill handle extends your series and how pressing the Ctrl key changes that behavior. Using the fill handle can save you a lot of time entering data.

Other data entry techniques you'll use in this section are AutoComplete, which detects when a value you're entering is similar to previously entered values; Pick From Drop-Down List, from which you can choose a value from among the existing values in the active cell's worksheet column; and Ctrl+Enter, which you can use to enter a value in multiple cells simultaneously.

TROUBLESHOOTING If an AutoComplete suggestion doesn't appear as you begin entering a cell value, the option might be turned off. To turn on AutoComplete, click the File tab, and then click Options. In the Excel Options dialog box, display the Advanced page. In the Editing Options area of the page, select the Enable AutoComplete For Cell Values check box, and then click OK.

The following table summarizes these data entry techniques.

Method	Action
AutoFill	Enter the first value in a recognized series and use the fill handle to extend the series.
FillSeries	Enter the first two values in a series and use the fill handle to extend the series.
AutoComplete	Enter the first few letters in a cell, and if a similar value exists in the same column, Excel suggests the existing value.
Pick From Drop-Down List	Right-click a cell, and then click Pick From Drop-Down List. A list of existing values in the cell's column is displayed. Click the value you want to enter into the cell.
Ctrl+Enter	Select a range of cells, each of which you want to contain the same data, enter the data in the active cell, and press Ctrl+Enter.

Another handy feature in Excel is the AutoFill Options button that appears next to data you add to a worksheet by using the fill handle.

Clicking the AutoFill Options button displays a list of actions Excel can take regarding the cells affected by your fill operation. The options in the list are summarized in the following table.

Option	Action
Copy Cells	This copies the contents of the selected cells to the cells indicated by the fill operation.
Fill Series	This action fills the cells indicated by the fill operation with the next items in the series.
Fill Formatting Only	This copies the format of the selected cell to the cells indicated by the fill operation, but does not place any values in the target cells.
Fill Without Formatting	This action fills the cells indicated by the fill operation with the next items in the series, but ignores any formatting applied to the source cells.
Fill Days (or Fill Weekdays, Fill Months, and so on)	The appearance of this option changes according to the series you extend. For example, if you extend the values Wed, Thu, and Fri, Excel presents two options, Fill Days and Fill Weekdays, and you can select which one you intended. If you do not use a recognized sequence, this option does not appear.
Flash Fill	This action fills the cells by using the Flash Fill capability, which fills the values by identifying a pattern in the worksheet's data.

In this exercise, you'll enter data by using multiple methods and control how Excel formats an extended data series.

→ SET UP You need the Series workbook located in the Chapter02 practice file folder to complete this exercise. Start Excel, and open the workbook. Then follow the steps.

1   On the **Monthly** worksheet, select cell **B3**, and then drag the fill handle down through **B7** to repeat the value **Fabrikam** in cells **B4:B7**.

2   Select cell **C3**, and while pressing the **Ctrl** key, drag the fill handle down through **C7** to repeat the value **January** in cells **C4:C7**.

3   Select cell **B8**, and then enter the letter **F**, which causes Excel to display the characters **abrikam** highlighted in gray.

	A	B	C	D	E	F
1						
2		Customer	Month	Category	Amount	
3		Fabrikam	January	Ground	$ 14,501.98	
4		Fabrikam	January	3Day	$ 3,501.75	
5		Fabrikam	January	2Day	$ 5,599.10	
6		Fabrikam	January	Overnight	$ 35,907.82	
7		Fabrikam	January	Priority Overnight	$ 17,333.25	
8		Fabrikam				
9						

4   Press **Tab** to accept the value **Fabrikam** for the cell.

5   In cell **C8**, enter **February**.

6   Right-click cell **D8**, and then click **Pick From Drop-down List** to display a list of values in column **D**.

	A	B	C	D	E	F
1						
2		Customer	Month	Category	Amount	
3		Fabrikam	January	Ground	$ 14,501.98	
4		Fabrikam	January	3Day	$ 3,501.75	
5		Fabrikam	January	2Day	$ 5,599.10	
6		Fabrikam	January	Overnight	$ 35,907.82	
7		Fabrikam	January	Priority Overnight	$ 17,333.25	
8		Fabrikam	February			
9				2Day		
10				3Day		
11				Ground		
12				Overnight		
				Priority Overnight		

7   From the list, click **2Day**, which then appears in cell **D8**.

8   In cell **E8**, enter 11802.14, and then press **Tab** or **Enter** to enter the value into the cell.

9   Select cell **B2**, and then drag the fill handle through cells **C2:E2** to fill the cells with the value **Customer**.

10   Click the **AutoFill Options** button, and then click **Fill Formatting Only** to restore the original values in cells **C2:E2** and apply the formatting of cell **B2** to those cells.

✕ CLEAN UP Close the Series workbook, saving your changes if you want to.

Managing data by using Flash Fill

When you manage data in Excel, you will often find that you want to combine values from several cells into a single value. For example, Consolidated Messenger might have a list of individuals to contact about arranging bulk shipping contracts for their companies.

	A	B	C	D
1	**LastName**	**FirstName**	**Initial**	**FullName**
2	Ray	Mike		
3	Basalik	Evan	B	
4	Roth	Daniel	C	
5	Kahn	Wendy		

The contacts' names appear in three columns: LastName, FirstName, and Initial. Note that not every contact has a middle initial. If you want to combine each row's LastName, FirstName, and Initial value into a single name, you click in the blank cell to the right of the first row's Initial column and enter the combination as you want it to appear. When you're done, press Enter to move down a row and enter the second row's value. After you start typing, Flash Fill, which is new in Excel 2013, displays suggestions based on how it predicts you want to fill in the rest of the values.

	A	B	C	D
1	**LastName**	**FirstName**	**Initial**	**FullName**
2	Ray	Mike		Mike Ray
3	Basalik	Evan	B	Evan Basalik
4	Roth	Daniel	C	Daniel Roth
5	Kahn	Wendy		Wendy Kahn
6				

Note that the Flash Fill suggestions did not include Initial values for rows that have a value in that cell. You can correct that omission by clicking in the FullName cell next to a row that does contain an Initial value and then entering the name as you would like it to appear. When you do, Flash Fill recognizes the new pattern for this subset of the data and offers to fill in the values.

	A	B	C	D
1	**LastName**	**FirstName**	**Initial**	**FullName**
2	Ray	Mike		Mike Ray
3	Basalik	Evan	B	Evan B Basalik
4	Roth	Daniel	C	Daniel C Roth
5	Kahn	Wendy		Wendy Kahn
6				

IMPORTANT For Flash Fill to function, you must enter the desired value in a cell next to the data you based your list on and make two consecutive edits. "Two consecutive edits" means that you must enter the desired value in one cell and then immediately start entering a value in a cell in the range you want Flash Fill to populate.

With Flash Fill, you can also pull data segments out of a larger, compound value. For example, suppose you received a customer database where the city, state, and postal code of each mailing address was combined in a single cell.

	A	B	C
1	**CityStateZip**	**State**	
2	Vienna, VA 22180		
3	Portland, OR 97220		
4	Mt. Crawford, VA 22841		
5	Syracuse, NY 13214		
6			

This data follows a consistent pattern, with the city followed by a comma before the two-letter state abbreviation. Because Flash Fill can detect this pattern, you can perform two consecutive edits to have the program suggest values for the remaining cells to the right of the existing data.

	A	B	C
1	**CityStateZip**	**State**	
2	Vienna, VA 22180	VA	
3	Portland, OR 97220	OR	
4	Mt. Crawford, VA 22841	VA	
5	Syracuse, NY 13214	NY	
6			

TIP If for some reason Flash Fill doesn't offer to complete the values in a data range, click a cell in the range you want Flash Fill to populate and then, on the Data tab of the ribbon, click Flash Fill.

In this exercise, you'll combine and correct data by using Flash Fill.

➡ SET UP You need the MailingNames workbook located in the Chapter02 practice file folder to complete this exercise. Open the workbook, and then follow the steps.

1   On the **Names** worksheet, enter **Mark Hassall** in cell **D2** and press **Enter**.

2   In cell **D3**, start entering the first name **Justin**. As you do, the Flash Fill logic suggests a series of values to fill in cells **D3:D5**.

3   Press **Enter** to accept the suggestions, even though some of them don't include the individual's middle initial.

4   Edit the value in cell **D3** so it reads Justin K. Harrison, and press **Enter** to have Flash Fill update the name in cell **D3** and the name in **D4**.

	A	B	C	D	
1	**LastName**	**FirstName**	**Initial**	**FullName**	
2	Hassall	Mark		Mark Hassall	
3	Harrison	Justin	K	Justin K. Harrison	
4	Pionsky	Idan	L	Idan L. Pionsky	
5	Preston	Chris		Chris Preston	

5   On the tab bar, click the **Addresses** sheet tab to display the **Addresses** worksheet.

6   Select cells **E2:F5** and then, on the **Home** tab, click the **Number Format** arrow. Then click **Text**.

7   In cell **F2**, enter 03214, and then press **Enter**.

8   In cell **F3**, start entering 07921 to have Flash Fill suggest values for the corrected series.

9   Press **Enter** to accept the suggested values.

10   Edit the value in cell **F4** so it reads 98012.

❌ CLEAN UP Close the MailingNames workbook, saving your changes if you want to.

Moving data within a workbook

You can move to a specific cell in lots of ways, but the most direct method is to click the desired cell. The cell you click will be outlined in black, and its contents, if any, will appear in the formula bar. When a cell is outlined, it is the active cell, meaning that you can modify its contents. You use a similar method to select multiple cells (referred to as a *cell range*)—just click the first cell in the range, and drag the mouse pointer over the remaining cells you want to select. After you select the cell or cells you want to work with, you can cut, copy, delete, or change the format of the contents of the cell or cells. For instance, Gregory Weber, the Northwest Distribution Center Manager for Consolidated Messenger, might want to copy the cells that contain a set of column labels to a new page that summarizes similar data.

IMPORTANT If you select a group of cells, the first cell you click is designated as the active cell.

You're not limited to selecting cells individually or as part of a range. For example, you might need to move a column of price data one column to the right to make room for a column of headings that indicate to which service category (ground, three-day express, two-day express, overnight, or priority overnight) a set of numbers belongs. To move an entire column (or entire columns) of data at a time, you click the column's header, located at the top of the worksheet. Clicking a column header highlights every cell in that column and enables you to copy or cut the column and paste it elsewhere in the workbook. Similarly, clicking a row's header highlights every cell in that row, enabling you to copy or cut the row and paste it elsewhere in the workbook.

When you copy a cell, cell range, row, or column, Excel copies the cells' contents and formatting. In versions prior to Excel 2010, you would paste the cut or copied items and then click the Paste Options button to select which aspects of the cut or copied cells to paste into the target cells. The problem with using the Paste Options button was that there was no way to tell what your pasted data would look like until you completed the paste operation. If you didn't like the way the pasted data looked, you had to click the Paste Options button again and try another option.

With the Paste Live Preview capability in Excel, you can view what your pasted data will look like before committing to the paste operation. To preview your data by using Paste Live Preview, cut or copy worksheet data and then, on the Home tab of the ribbon, in the Clipboard group, click the Paste button's arrow to display a menu containing the Paste gal-

lery, and point to one of the icons. When you do, Excel displays a preview of how your data will appear if you click that paste option.

If you position the pointer over one icon in the Paste gallery and then move it over another icon without clicking, Excel will update the preview to reflect the new option. Depending on the cells' contents, two or more of the paste options might lead to the same result.

TROUBLESHOOTING If pointing to an icon in the Paste gallery doesn't result in a live preview, that option might be turned off. To turn Paste Live Preview on, click the File tab, and then click Options to open the Excel Options dialog box. Click General, select the Enable Live Preview check box, and click OK.

After you click an icon to complete the paste operation, Excel displays the Paste Options button next to the pasted cells. Clicking the Paste Options button displays the Paste Options gallery as well, but pointing to one of those icons doesn't generate a preview. If you want to display Paste Live Preview again, you will need to press Ctrl+Z to undo the paste operation and, if necessary, cut or copy the data again to use the icons in the Home tab's Clipboard group.

TROUBLESHOOTING If the Paste Options button doesn't appear, you can turn the feature on by clicking the File tab and then clicking Options to open the Excel Options dialog box. In the Excel Options dialog box, display the Advanced page and then, in the Cut, Copy, And Paste area, select the Show Paste Options Buttons When Content Is Pasted check box. Click OK to close the dialog box and save your setting.

After cutting or copying data to the Microsoft Office Clipboard, you can access additional paste options from the Paste gallery and from the Paste Special dialog box, which you display by clicking Paste Special at the bottom of the Paste menu.

In the Paste Special dialog box, you can specify the aspect of the Clipboard contents you want to paste, restricting the pasted data to values, formats, comments, or one of several other options. You can perform mathematical operations involving the cut or copied data and the existing data in the cells you paste the content into. You can transpose data—change rows to columns and columns to rows—when you paste it, by clicking the Transpose thumbnail in the Paste gallery or by selecting the Transpose check box in the Paste Special dialog box.

In this exercise, you'll copy a set of data headers to another worksheet, move a column of data within a worksheet, and use Paste Live Preview to control the appearance of copied data.

SET UP You need the 2013Q1ShipmentsByCategory workbook located in the Chapter02 practice file folder to complete this exercise. Open the workbook, and then follow the steps.

1   On the **Count** worksheet, select cells **B2:D2**.

2   On the **Home** tab, in the **Clipboard** group, click the **Copy** button to copy the contents of cells **B2:D2** to the Clipboard.

     KEYBOARD SHORTCUT Press Ctrl+C to copy worksheet contents to the Clipboard. For a complete list of keyboard shortcuts, see "Keyboard shortcuts" at the end of this book.

3   On the tab bar, click the **Sales** tab to display that worksheet.

4   Select cell **B2**.

5   On the **Home** tab, in the **Clipboard** group, click the **Paste** button's arrow, point to the first icon in the **Paste** group, and then click the **Keep Source Formatting** icon (the final icon in the first row of the **Paste** gallery). Notice that Excel displays how the data would look if you pasted the copied values without formatting, and then pastes the header values into cells **B2:D2**, retaining the original cells' formatting.

6   Right-click the column header of column **I**, and then click **Cut**, which causes Excel to outline column **I** with a marquee.

7   Right-click the header of column **E**, and then, in the **Paste Options** area, click **Paste** to paste the contents of column **I** into column **E**.

     KEYBOARD SHORTCUT Press Ctrl+V to paste worksheet contents exactly as they appear in the original cell.

CLEAN UP Close the 2013Q1ShipmentsByCategory workbook, saving your changes if you want to.

Finding and replacing data

Excel worksheets can hold more than one million rows of data, so in large data collections, it's unlikely that you would have the time to move through a worksheet one row at a time to locate the data you want to find. You can locate specific data in an Excel worksheet by using the Find And Replace dialog box, which has two pages (one named Find, the other named Replace) that you can use to search for cells that contain particular values. Using the controls on the Find page identifies cells that contain the data you specify; by using the controls on the Replace page, you can substitute one value for another. For example, if one of Consolidated Messenger's customers changes its company name, you can change every instance of the old name to the new name by using the Replace functionality.

When you need more control over the data that you find and replace—for instance, if you want to find cells in which the entire cell value matches the value you're searching for—you can click the Options button to expand the Find And Replace dialog box.

One way you can use the extra options in the Find And Replace dialog box is to use a specific format to identify data that requires review. As an example, Consolidated Messenger VP of Marketing Craig Dewar could make corporate sales plans based on a projected budget for the next year and mark his trial figures by using a specific format. After the executive board finalizes the numbers, he could use the Find Format capability in the Find And Replace dialog box to locate the old values and change them by hand.

The following table summarizes the Find And Replace dialog box controls' functions.

Control	Function
Find What field	Contains the value you want to find or replace
Find All button	Identifies every cell that contains the value in the Find What field
Find Next button	Selects the next cell that contains the value in the Find What field
Replace With field	Contains the value to overwrite the value in the Find What field
Replace All button	Replaces every instance of the value in the Find What field with the value in the Replace With field
Replace button	Replaces the highlighted occurrence of the value in the Find What field and highlights the next cell that contains that value
Options button	Expands the Find And Replace dialog box to display additional capabilities
Format button	Opens the Find Format dialog box, which you can use to specify the format of values to be found or values to be replaced
Within box	Enables you to select whether to search the active worksheet or the entire workbook
Search box	Enables you to select whether to search by rows or by columns
Look In box	Enables you to select whether to search cell formulas or values

Control	Function
Match Case check box	When selected, requires that all matches have the same capital-ization as the text in the Find What field (for example, cat doesn't match Cat)
Match Entire Cell Contents check box	Requires that the cell contain exactly the same value as in the Find What field (for example, Cat doesn't match Catherine)
Close button	Closes the Find And Replace dialog box

To change a value by hand, select the cell, and then either enter a new value in the cell or, in the formula bar, select the value you want to replace and enter the new value. You can also double-click a cell and edit its contents within the cell.

In this exercise, you'll find a specific value in a worksheet, replace every occurrence of a company name in a worksheet, and find a cell that has a specific formatting.

SET UP You need the AverageDeliveries workbook located in the Chapter02 practice file folder to complete this exercise. Open the workbook, and then follow the steps.

1 If necessary, click the **Time Summary** sheet tab to display the **Time Summary** worksheet.

2 On the **Home** tab, in the **Editing** group, click **Find & Select**, and then click **Find** to display the **Find** page of the **Find and Replace** dialog box.

KEYBOARD SHORTCUT Press Ctrl+F to display the Find page of the Find And Replace dialog box.

3 In the **Find what** field, enter 103.

4 Click **Find Next** to have Excel select cell **B5**, which contains the value **103**.

	A	B	C	D	E	F	G	H	I	J
1										
2		Route	Deliveries	End Time						
3		101	552	5:03 PM						
4		102	480	4:15 PM						
5		103	324	4:18 PM		Find and Replace			?	×
6		104	492	3:56 PM		Find	Replace			
7		105	486	4:02 PM		Find what:	103			
8		106	277	5:30 PM						
9		107	560	6:45 PM					Options >>	
10		108	413	4:31 PM						
11		109	254	4:18 PM		Find All	Find Next		Close	
12		110	595	5:49 PM						
13		111	459	3:30 PM						
14		112	338	4:14 PM						

5   Delete the value in the **Find what** field, and then click the **Options** button to display additional search options.

6   Click **Format** to open the **Find Format** dialog box.

7   Click the **Font** tab to display the **Font** page of the dialog box.

8   In the **Font style** list, click **Italic**, and then click **OK** to close the **Find Format** dialog box.

9   Click **Find Next**, which causes Excel to select cell **D25**.

10   Click **Close** to close the **Find and Replace** dialog box.

11   On the tab bar, click the **Customer Summary** sheet tab to display the **Customer Summary** worksheet.

12   On the **Home** tab, in the **Editing** group, click **Find & Select**, and then click **Replace** to open the **Find and Replace** dialog box with the **Replace** page displayed.

KEYBOARD SHORTCUT Press Ctrl+H to display the Replace page of the Find And Replace dialog box.

13   Click the **Format** arrow to the right of the **Find what** field, and then in the list, click **Clear Find Format** to remove the format from the **Find What** field.

14   In the **Find what** field, enter Contoso.

15   In the **Replace with** field, enter Northwind Traders.

16   Click **Replace All**, which causes Excel to display a message box indicating that Excel made three replacements.

17   Click **OK** to close the message box.

18   Click **Close** to close the **Find and Replace** dialog box.

✖ CLEAN UP Close the AverageDeliveries workbook, saving your changes if you want to.

Correcting and expanding upon worksheet data

After you enter your data, you should take the time to check and correct it. You do need to verify visually that each piece of numeric data is correct, but you can make sure that your worksheet's text is spelled correctly by using the Excel spelling checker. When the spelling checker encounters a word it doesn't recognize, it highlights the word and offers suggestions representing its best guess of the correct word. You can then edit the word directly, pick the proper word from the list of suggestions, or have the spelling checker ignore the misspelling. You can also use the spelling checker to add new words to a custom dictionary

so that Excel will recognize them later, saving you time by not requiring you to identify the words as correct every time they occur in your worksheets.

TIP After you make a change in a workbook, you can usually remove the change as long as you haven't closed the workbook. To undo a change, click the Undo button on the Quick Access Toolbar. If you decide you want to keep a change, you can use the Redo command to restore it.

If you're not sure of your word choice, or if you use a word that is almost but not quite right for your intended meaning, you can check for alternative words by using the Thesaurus. Several other research tools are also available, such as the Bing search engine and the Microsoft Encarta dictionary, to which you can refer as you create your workbooks. To display those tools, on the Review tab, in the Proofing group, click Research to display the Research pane.

Research ▾ ✕

Search for:

timely ➡

All Reference Books ▾

← Back ▾ → ▾

▲ Encarta Dictionary:
English (North America)
▲ time·ly (adjective)

time·ly [ˈtaimli]

occurring at good time

happening or done at
the right time or an
appropriate time

• a timely intervention

▲ time·li·ness (noun)

time·li·ness See time·ly

▲ time·ly (adverb)

time·ly See time·ly

▷ Thesaurus: English
(United States)
▷ Translation
▷ Can't find it?

🌐 Get services on Office
Marketplace

🔍 Research options...

Finally, if you want to translate a word from one language to another, you can do so by selecting the cell that contains the value you want to translate, displaying the Review tab, and then, in the Language group, clicking Translate. The Research pane opens (or changes if it's already open) and displays controls you can use to select the original and destination languages.

Research ▾ ✕

Search for:

timely ➡

Translation ▾

← Back ▾ → ▾

▲ **Translation**

Translate a word or sentence.

From

English (United States) ▾

To

French (France) ▾

Translation options...

▲ **Bilingual Dictionary**

▲ **timely**

['taɪmlɪ] *adjective*
opportun

▲ **Can't find it?**

Try one of these alternatives or see Help for hints on refining your search.

Other places to search

Search for 'timely' in:

🌐 Get services on Office Marketplace

🔍 Research options...

IMPORTANT Excel translates a sentence by using word substitutions, which means that the translation routine doesn't always pick the best word for a given context. The translated sentence might not capture your exact meaning.

In this exercise, you'll check a worksheet's spelling, add two new terms to a dictionary, search for an alternative word by using the Thesaurus, and translate a word from English into French.

➡ SET UP You need the ServiceLevels workbook located in the Chapter02 practice file folder to complete this exercise. Open the workbook, and then follow the steps.

1   On the **Review** tab, in the **Proofing** group, click **Spelling** to open the **Spelling** dialog box with the first misspelled word in the worksheet displayed in the **Not in Dictionary** field.

Spelling: English (United States)	?	×

Not in Dictionary:

shiped	Ignore Once
	Ignore All
	Add to Dictionary

Suggestions:

shipped	Change
shaped	
shied	Change All
sniped	
shined	AutoCorrect
swiped	

Dictionary language: English (United States)

Options...	Undo Last	Cancel

2   Verify that the word **shipped** is highlighted in the **Suggestions** pane, and then click **Change** to correct the word and display the next questioned word: **withn**.

3   Click **Change** to correct the word and display the next questioned word: **TwoDay**.

4   Click **Add to Dictionary** to add the word to the dictionary and display the next questioned word: **ThreeDay**.

5   Click **Add to Dictionary** to add the word to the dictionary.

6   If necessary, click **Close** to close the **Spelling** dialog box. When you do, the **Spelling** dialog box closes and a message box appears, indicating that the spelling check is complete for the worksheet.

7   Click **OK** to close the message box.

8   Click cell **B6** and then, on the **Review** tab, in the **Proofing** group, click **Thesaurus** to display a list of synonyms for the word **Overnight**.

9   On the **Review** tab, in the **Language** group, click **Translate** to display the translation tools in the **Research** pane.

10 If necessary, in the **From** list, click **English (U.S.)**.

11 In the **To** list, click **French (France)**. The **Research** pane displays French words that mean *overnight*.

Research

Search for:

Overnight

Translation

← Back | → |

▲ **Translation**

Translate a word or sentence.

From

English (United States)

To

French (France)

Translation options...

▲ **Bilingual Dictionary**

▲ **overnight**

adverb stay, travel
la nuit; FIGURATIVE:
change, learn etc du
jour au lendemain

▲ **Can't find it?**

Try one of these
alternatives or see Help for
hints on refining your
search.

Other places to search

Get services on Office
Marketplace

Research options...

CLEAN UP Close the ServiceLevels workbook, saving your changes if you want to.

Defining Excel tables

With Excel, you've always been able to manage lists of data effectively, enabling you to sort your worksheet data based on the values in one or more columns, limit the data displayed by using criteria (for example, show only those routes with fewer than 100 stops), and create formulas that summarize the values in visible (that is, unfiltered) cells. In Excel 2007, the Excel product team extended your ability to manage your data by introducing Excel tables. Excel 2013 offers you the same capability.

	A	B	C	D
1				
2		Customer ▼	Month ▼	Program Savings ▼
3		Contoso	January	$ 182,423
4		Contoso	February	$ 173,486
5		Contoso	March	$ 88,027
6		Fabrikam	January	$ 139,434
7		Fabrikam	February	$ 29,461
8		Fabrikam	March	$ 91,295
9		Lucerne Publishing	January	$ 136,922
10		Lucerne Publishing	February	$ 161,370
11		Lucerne Publishing	March	$ 160,250
12		Wide World Importers	January	$ 109,903
13		Wide World Importers	February	$ 102,243
14		Wide World Importers	March	$ 105,077

To create an Excel table, enter a series of column headers in adjacent cells, and then enter a row of data below the headers. Click any header or data cell into which you just entered, and then, on the Home tab, in the Styles group, click Format As Table. Then, from the gallery that appears, click the style you want to apply to the table. When the Format As Table dialog box opens, verify that the cells in the Where Is The Data For Your Table? field reflect your current selection and that the My Table Has Headers check box is selected, and then click OK.

Excel can also create an Excel table from an existing cell range as long as the range has no blank rows or columns within the data and there is no extraneous data in cells immediately below or next to the list. To create the Excel table, click any cell in the range and then, on the Home tab, in the Styles group, click the Format As Table button and select a table style. If your existing data has formatting applied to it, that formatting remains applied to those cells when you create the Excel table. If you want Excel to replace the existing formatting with the Excel table's formatting, right-click the table style you want to apply and then click Apply And Clear Formatting.

When you want to add data to an Excel table, click the rightmost cell in the bottom row of the Excel table and press the Tab key to create a new row. You can also select a cell in the row immediately below the last row in the table or a cell in the column immediately to the right of the table and enter a value into the cell. After you enter the value and move out of the cell, the AutoCorrect Options action button appears. If you didn't mean to include the data in the Excel table, you can click Undo Table AutoExpansion to exclude the cells from

the Excel table. If you never want Excel to include adjacent data in an Excel table again, click Stop Automatically Expanding Tables.

TIP To stop Table AutoExpansion before it starts, click the File tab, and then click Options. In the Excel Options dialog box, click Proofing, and then click the AutoCorrect Options button to open the AutoCorrect dialog box. Click the AutoFormat As You Type tab, clear the Include New Rows And Columns In Table check box, and then click OK twice.

You can add rows and columns to an Excel table, or remove them from an Excel table without deleting the cells' contents, by dragging the resize handle at the Excel table's lower-right corner. If your Excel table's headers contain a recognizable series of values (such as Region1, Region2, and Region3), and you drag the resize handle to create a fourth column, Excel creates the column with the label *Region4*—the next value in the series.

Excel tables often contain data that you can summarize by calculating a sum or average, or by finding the maximum or minimum value in a column. To summarize one or more columns of data, you can add a Total row to your Excel table.

	A	B	C	D
1				
2		Customer ▾	Month ▾	Program Savings ▾
3		Contoso	January	$ 182,423
4		Contoso	February	$ 173,486
5		Contoso	March	$ 88,027
6		Fabrikam	January	$ 139,434
7		Fabrikam	February	$ 29,461
8		Fabrikam	March	$ 91,295
9		Lucerne Publishing	January	$ 136,922
10		Lucerne Publishing	February	$ 161,370
11		Lucerne Publishing	March	$ 160,250
12		Wide World Importers	January	$ 109,903
13		Wide World Importers	February	$ 102,243
14		Wide World Importers	March	$ 105,077
15		Total		$ 1,479,891 ▾
16				

When you add the Total row, Excel creates a formula that summarizes the values in the rightmost Excel table column. To change that summary operation, or to add a summary operation to any other cell in the Total row, click the cell, click the arrow that appears, and then click the summary operation you want to apply. Clicking the More Functions menu

item opens the Insert Function dialog box, from which you can select any of the functions available in Excel.

Much as it does when you create a new worksheet, Excel gives your Excel tables generic names such as Table1 and Table2. You can change an Excel table's name to something easier to recognize by clicking any cell in the table, clicking the Design tool tab, and then, in the Properties group, editing the value in the Table Name box. Changing an Excel table name might not seem important, but it helps make formulas that summarize Excel table data much easier to understand. You should make a habit of renaming your Excel tables so you can recognize the data they contain.

SEE ALSO For more information about using the Insert Function dialog box and about referring to tables in formulas, see "Creating formulas to calculate values" in Chapter 3, "Performing calculations on data."

If for any reason you want to convert your Excel table back to a normal range of cells, click any cell in the Excel table and then, on the Design tool tab, in the Tools group, click Convert To Range. When Excel displays a message box asking if you're sure you want to convert the table to a range, click OK.

In this exercise, you'll create an Excel table from existing data, add data to an Excel table, add a Total row, change that row's summary operation, and rename the Excel table.

➡ SET UP You need the DriverSortTimes workbook located in the Chapter02 practice file folder to complete this exercise. Open the workbook, and then follow the steps.

1   Select cell **B2**.

2   On the **Home** tab, in the **Styles** group, click **Format as Table**, and then select a table style to open the **Format As Table** dialog box.

3   Verify that the range =$B$2:$C$17 is displayed in the **Where is the data for your table?** field and that the **My table has headers** check box is selected, and then click **OK** to create an Excel table from your data and display the **Design** tool tab.

4   In cell **B18**, enter D116, press **Tab**, enter 100 in cell **C18**, and then press **Enter** to have Excel include the data in your Excel table.

5   Select a cell in the table. Then on the **Design** tool tab, in the **Table Style Options** group, select the **Total Row** check box to add a **Total** row to the bottom of your Excel table.

6   Select cell **C19**, click the arrow that appears at the right edge of the cell, and then click **Average** to change the summary operation to **Average**.

Driver ▼	Sorting Minutes ▼
D101	102
D102	162
D103	165
D104	91
D105	103
D106	127
D107	112
D108	137
D109	102
D110	147
D111	163
D112	109
D113	91
D114	107
D115	93
D116	100
Total	**119.4375** ▼

7   On the **Design** tool tab, in the **Properties** group, enter the value SortTimes in the **Table Name** field, and then press **Enter** to rename your Excel table.

✖ CLEAN UP Close the DriverSortTimes workbook, saving your changes if you want to.

Key points

- You can enter a series of data quickly by entering one or more values in adjacent cells, selecting the cells, and then dragging the fill handle. To change how dragging the fill handle extends a data series, hold down the Ctrl key.

- Dragging a fill handle displays the Auto Fill Options button, which you can use to specify whether to copy the selected cells' values, extend a recognized series, or apply the selected cells' formatting to the new cells.

- Managing data by using Flash Fill enables you to separate cell entries into their components, apply formatting, and fix values such as postal codes that have had their leading zeros removed.

- With Excel, you can enter data by selecting items from a list, using AutoComplete, or pressing Ctrl+Enter. You should experiment with these techniques and use the one that best fits your circumstances.

- When you copy (or cut) and paste cells, columns, or rows, you can use the Paste Live Preview capability to preview how your data will appear before you commit to the paste operation.

- After you paste cells, rows, or columns into your worksheet, Excel displays the Paste Options action button. You can use its controls to change which aspects of the cut or copied elements Excel applies to the pasted elements.

- By using the options in the Paste Special dialog box, you can paste only specific aspects of cut or copied data, perform mathematical operations, transpose data, or delete blank cells when pasting.

- You can find and replace data within a worksheet by searching for specific values or by searching for cells that have a particular format applied.

- Excel provides a variety of powerful proofing and research tools, enabling you to check your workbook's spelling, find alternative words by using the Thesaurus, and translate words between languages.

- With Excel tables, you can organize and summarize your data effectively.

2

Chapter at a glance

Name

Name groups of data,
page 76

Summarize

Summarize data that meets specific
conditions, page 90

Calculate

Use array formulas,
page 96

Correct

Find and correct errors in calculations,
page 99

Performing calculations on data

3

IN THIS CHAPTER, YOU WILL LEARN HOW TO

- Name groups of data.
- Create formulas to calculate values.
- Summarize data that meets specific conditions.
- Work with iterative calculation options and automatic workbook calculation.
- Use array formulas.
- Find and correct errors in calculations.

Microsoft Excel 2013 workbooks give you a handy place to store and organize your data, but you can also do a lot more with your data in Excel. One important task you can perform is to calculate totals for the values in a series of related cells. You can also use Excel to discover other information about the data you select, such as the maximum or minimum value in a group of cells. By finding the maximum or minimum value in a group, you can identify your best salesperson, product categories you might need to pay more attention to, or suppliers that consistently give you the best deal. Regardless of your bookkeeping needs, Excel gives you the ability to find the information you want. And if you make an error, you can find the cause and correct it quickly.

Many times, you can't access the information you want without referencing more than one cell, and it's also often true that you'll use the data in the same group of cells for more than one calculation. Excel makes it easy to reference a number of cells at once, enabling you to define your calculations quickly.

In this chapter, you'll streamline references to groups of data on your worksheets and create and correct formulas that summarize an organization's business operations.

Naming groups of data

When you work with large amounts of data, it's often useful to identify groups of cells that contain related data. For example, you can create a worksheet in which cells C3:I3 hold the number of packages Consolidated Messenger's Northeast processing facility handled from 5:00 P.M. to 12:00 A.M. on the previous day.

	A	B	C	D	E	F	G	H	I	J
1										
2			5:00 PM	6:00 PM	7:00 PM	8:00 PM	9:00 PM	10:00 PM	11:00 PM	
3		Northeast	14,776	21,061	22,111	13,412	11,459	11,038	5,732	
4		Atlantic	7,755	5,579	13,778	13,774	5,352	17,209	15,822	
5		Southeast	11,578	11,867	5,627	5,625	7,148	24,487	20,262	
6		North Central	6,807	11,223	12,136	24,653	23,876	9,817	7,410	
7		Midwest	7,926	15,404	7,702	10,338	10,734	14,021	20,557	
8		Southwest	22,320	15,431	24,276	8,968	10,066	23,602	11,216	
9		Mountain West	23,398	19,838	21,591	24,305	21,431	8,338	6,941	
10		Northwest	9,482	5,672	14,689	18,795	9,388	8,069	19,776	
11		Central	16,424	13,289	18,546	19,762	20,770	11,202	6,403	
12										

Instead of specifying the cells individually every time you want to use the data they contain, you can define those cells as a range (also called a *named range*). For example, you can group the items from the cells described in the preceding paragraph into a range named *NortheastPreviousDay*. Whenever you want to use the contents of that range in a calculation, you can simply use the name of the range instead of specifying each cell individually.

TIP Yes, you could just name the range *Northeast*, but if you use the range's values in a formula in another worksheet, the more descriptive range name tells you and your colleagues exactly what data is used in the calculation.

To create a named range, select the cells you want to include in your range, click the Formulas tab, and then, in the Defined Names group, click Define Name to display the New Name dialog box. In the New Name dialog box, enter a name in the Name field, verify that the cells you selected appear in the Refers To field, and then click OK. You can also add a comment about the range in the Comment field and select whether you want to make the name available for formulas in the entire workbook or just on an individual worksheet.

If the cells you want to define as a named range have labels in a row or column that's part of the cell group, you can use those labels as the names of the named ranges. For example, if your data appears in worksheet cells B4:I12 and the values in column B are the row labels, you can make each row its own named range. To create a series of named ranges from a group of cells, select all of the data cells, including the labels, click the Formulas tab and then, in the Defined Names group, click Create From Selection to open the Create Names From Selection dialog box. In the Create Names From Selection dialog box, select the check box that represents the labels' position in the selected range, and then click OK.

A final way to create a named range is to select the cells you want in the range, click in the Name box next to the formula box, and then enter the name for the range. You can display the ranges available in a workbook by clicking the Name arrow.

To manage the named ranges in a workbook, click the Formulas tab, and then, in the Defined Names group, click Name Manager to open the Name Manager dialog box.

When you click a named range, Excel displays the cells it encompasses in the Refers To field. Clicking the Edit button opens the Edit Name dialog box, which is a version of the New Name dialog box, enabling you to change a named range's definition; for example, by adding a column. You can also use the controls in the Name Manager dialog box to delete a named range (the range, not the data) by clicking it, clicking the Delete button, and then clicking OK in the confirmation dialog box that opens.

TIP If your workbook contains a lot of named ranges, you can click the Filter button in the Name Manager dialog box and select a criterion to limit the names displayed in the Name Manager dialog box.

In this exercise, you'll create a named range to streamline references to a group of cells. You'll also edit a named range and use a named range in a formula.

SET UP You need the VehicleMiles workbook located in the Chapter03 practice file folder to complete this exercise. Open the workbook, and then follow the steps.

1. Select cells **C4:G4**, intentionally leaving cell H4 out of this selection. You will edit the named range later in this exercise.

2. In the **Name** box at the left end of the formula bar, enter **V101LastWeek**, and then press **Enter** to create a named range named *V101LastWeek*.

3. On the **Formulas** tab, in the **Defined Names** group, click **Name Manager** to open the **Name Manager** dialog box.

4. Click the **V101LastWeek** name. The cell range to which the **V101LastWeek** name refers appears in the **Refers to** box at the bottom of the **Name Manager** dialog box.

5. Edit the cell range in the **Refers to** box to =MilesLastWeek!$C$4:$H$4 (change the **G** to an **H**), and then click the check mark button to the left of the box to finalize the update.

6. Click **Close** to close the **Name Manager** dialog box.

7   Select the cell range **C5:H5**.

8   On the **Formulas** tab, in the **Defined Names** group, click **Define Name** to open the **New Name** dialog box.

9   In the **Name** field, enter V102LastWeek.

10   Verify that the definition in the **Refers to** field is =**MilesLastWeek!$C$5:$H$5**.

11   Click **OK** to create the name and close the **New Name** dialog box.

12   In cell **A1**, enter the formula =**SUM(V102LastWeek)** and press **Enter**. When you do, the total of all miles for vehicle V102 appears in the cell.

❌ CLEAN UP Close the VehicleMiles workbook, saving your changes if you want to.

Operators and precedence

When you create an Excel formula, you use the built-in functions and arithmetic operators that define operations such as addition and multiplication. In Excel, mathematical operators are evaluated in the order shown in the following table.

Operator	Description
−	Negation (e.g., −1)
%	Percentage
^	Exponentiation
* and /	Multiplication and Division
+ and −	Addition and Subtraction
&	Concatenation (adding two strings together)
=, >, <, >=, <=, and <>	Equals, Greater Than, Less Than, Greater Than or Equal To, Less Than or Equal To, and Not Equal To

If two operators at the same level, such as + and −, occur in the same equation, Excel evaluates them in left-to-right order. For example, the operations in the formula = *4 + 8 * 3 − 6* would be evaluated in this order:

1   *8 * 3*, with a result of 24

2   *4 + 24*, with a result of 28

3   *28 − 6*, with a final result of 22

You can control the order in which operations are evaluated by using parentheses. Operations in parentheses are always evaluated first. For example, if the previous equation were rewritten as = *(4 + 8) * 3 – 6*, the operations would be evaluated in this order:

1. *(4 + 8)*, with a result of 12
2. *12 * 3*, with a result of 36
3. *36 – 6*, with a final result of 30

If you have multiple levels of parentheses, Excel evaluates the expressions within the innermost set of parentheses first and works its way out. As with operations on the same level, such as + and –, expressions in the same parenthetical level are evaluated in left-to-right order.

For example, the formula = *4 + (3 + 8 * (2 + 5)) – 7* would be evaluated in this order:

1. *(2 + 5)*, with a result of 7
2. *7 * 8*, with a result of 56
3. *56 + 3*, with a result of 59
4. *4 + 59*, with a result of 63
5. *63 – 7*, with a final result of 56

Creating formulas to calculate values

After you add your data to a worksheet and define ranges to simplify data references, you can create a formula, which is an expression that performs calculations on your data. For example, you can calculate the total cost of a customer's shipments, figure the average number of packages for all Wednesdays in the month of January, or find the highest and lowest daily package volumes for a week, month, or year.

To write an Excel formula, you begin the cell's contents with an equal (=) sign; when Excel identifies it, it knows that the expression following it should be interpreted as a calculation, not text. After the equal sign, enter the formula. For example, you can find the sum of the numbers in cells C2 and C3 by using the formula *=C2+C3*. After you have entered a formula

into a cell, you can revise it by clicking the cell and then editing the formula in the formula box. For example, you can change the preceding formula to =C3-C2, which calculates the difference between the contents of cells C2 and C3.

TROUBLESHOOTING If Excel treats your formula as text, make sure the equal sign is the first character. If Excel still displays your formula as text, check whether the cell has the Text format applied to it. If it does, change the cell's format to a format that suits the value you want to calculate.

Entering the cell references for 15 or 20 cells in a calculation would be tedious, but Excel makes it easy to enter complex calculations. To create a new calculation, click the Formulas tab, and then in the Function Library group, click Insert Function. The Insert Function dialog box opens, with a list of functions, or predefined formulas, from which you can choose.

The following table describes some of the most useful functions in the list.

Function	Description
SUM	Finds the sum of the numbers in the specified cells
AVERAGE	Finds the average of the numbers in the specified cells
COUNT	Finds the number of cells in the specified range that contain numbers
MAX	Finds the largest value in the specified cells
MIN	Finds the smallest value in the specified cells

Two other functions you might use are the *NOW* and *PMT* functions. The *NOW* function displays the time Excel updated the workbook's formulas, so the value will change every time the workbook recalculates. The proper form for this function is =*NOW()*. To update the value to the current date and time, press the F9 key or display the Formulas tab and then, in the Calculation group, click the Calculate Now button.

The *PMT* function is a bit more complex. It calculates payments due on a loan, assuming a constant interest rate and constant payments. To perform its calculations, the *PMT* function requires an interest rate, the number of payments, and the starting balance. The elements to be entered into the function are called *arguments* and must be entered in a certain order. That order is written as *PMT(rate, nper, pv, fv, type)*. The following table summarizes the arguments in the *PMT* function.

Argument	Description
rate	The interest rate, to be divided by 12 for a loan with monthly payments, by 4 for quarterly payments, and so on
nper	The total number of payments for the loan
pv	The amount loaned (pv is short for present value, or principal)
fv	The amount to be left over at the end of the payment cycle (usually left blank, which indicates 0)
type	0 or 1, indicating whether payments are made at the beginning or at the end of the month (usually left blank, which indicates 0, or the end of the month)

If Consolidated Messenger wanted to borrow $2,000,000 at a 6 percent interest rate and pay the loan back over 24 months, you could use the *PMT* function to figure out the monthly payments. In this case, the function would be written =*PMT(6%/12, 24, 2000000)*, which calculates a monthly payment of $88,641.22.

TIP Because the payment calculated by the *PMT* function represents money that flows out of your bank account, the result is a negative number. If you want the result to be expressed as a positive number, multiply the formula's result by -1.

You can also use the names of any ranges you defined to supply values for a formula. For example, if the named range NortheastLastDay refers to cells C4:I4, you can calculate the average of cells C4:I4 with the formula =*AVERAGE(NortheastLastDay)*. With Excel, you can add functions, named ranges, and table references to your formulas more efficiently by using the Formula AutoComplete capability. Just as AutoComplete offers to fill in a cell's text value when Excel recognizes that the value you're entering matches a previous entry, Formula AutoComplete offers to help you fill in a function, named range, or table reference while you create a formula.

As an example, consider a worksheet that contains a two-column Excel table named *Exceptions*. The first column is labeled *Route*; the second is labeled *Count*.

	A	B
1	**Route**	**Count**
2	101	8
3	102	5
4	103	8
5	104	12
6	105	5
7	106	2
8	107	4
9	108	4
10	109	2
11	110	7
12		

You refer to a table by entering the table name, followed by the column or row name in square brackets. For example, the table reference *Exceptions[Count]* would refer to the Count column in the Exceptions table.

To create a formula that finds the total number of exceptions by using the *SUM* function, you begin by entering =*SU*. When you enter the letter *S*, Formula AutoComplete lists functions that begin with the letter *S*; when you enter the letter *U*, Excel narrows the list down to the functions that start with the letters *SU*.

	A	B	C	D	E	F	G	H
1	**Route**	**Count**		=SU				
2	101	8		SUBSTITUTE	Replaces existing text with new text in a text string			
3	102	5		SUBTOTAL				
4	103	8		SUM				
5	104	12		SUMIF				
6	105	5		SUMIFS				
7	106	2		SUMPRODUCT				
8	107	4		SUMSQ				
9	108	4		SUMX2MY2				
10	109	2		SUMX2PY2				
11	110	7		SUMXMY2				
12								

To add the *SUM* function (followed by an opening parenthesis) to the formula, click *SUM* and then press Tab. To begin adding the table reference, enter the letter *E*. Excel displays a list of available functions, tables, and named ranges that start with the letter *E*. Click Exceptions, and press Tab to add the table reference to the formula. Then, because you want to summarize the values in the table's Count column, enter a left square bracket and then, in the list of available table items, click Count. To finish creating the formula, enter a right square bracket followed by a closing parenthesis to create the formula *=SUM(Exceptions[Count])*.

If you want to include a series of contiguous cells in a formula, but you haven't defined the cells as a named range, you can click the first cell in the range and drag to the last cell. If the cells aren't contiguous, hold down the Ctrl key and select all of the cells to be included. In both cases, when you release the mouse button, the references of the cells you selected appear in the formula.

TIP Excel highlights each cell range used in a formula in one of several colors.

	A	B	C	D	E	F	G	H	I	J	K
1											
2		Conveyer									
3		350' track	$14,012.00								
4		Catch bin	$ 895.00								
5		Motor	$ 1,249.00								
6		Chain drive	$ 1,495.00			=sum(C3,C6,C14,C17					
7		Sorting table	$ 675.00			SUM(number1, [number2], [number3], **[number4]**, [number5], ...)					
8		Subtotal		$ 18,326.00							
9											
10		**Loading Dock**									
11		Concrete	$ 2,169.00								
12		Labor	$ 4,500.00								
13		Posts	$ 300.00								
14		Excavation	$ 2,500.00								
15		Drain	$ 1,800.00								
16		Rails	$ 495.00								
17		Stairs	$ 1,295.00								
18		Subtotal		$ 13,059.00							
19											
20		**Build Total**		$ 31,385.00							
21		**Labor Percentage**									

In addition to using the Ctrl key to add cells to a selection, you can expand a selection by using a wide range of keyboard shortcuts.

The following table summarizes many of those shortcuts.

Key sequence	Description
Shift+Right Arrow	Extend the selection one cell to the right.
Shift+Left Arrow	Extend the selection one cell to the left.
Shift+Up Arrow	Extend the selection up one cell.
Shift+Down Arrow	Extend the selection down one cell.
Ctrl+Shift+Right Arrow	Extend the selection to the last non-blank cell in the row.
Ctrl+Shift+Left Arrow	Extend the selection to the first non-blank cell in the row.
Ctrl+Shift+Up Arrow	Extend the selection to the first non-blank cell in the column.
Ctrl+Shift+Down Arrow	Extend the selection to the last non-blank cell in the column.
Ctrl+*	Select the entire active region.
Shift+Home	Extend the selection to the beginning of the row.
Ctrl+Shift+Home	Extend the selection to the beginning of the worksheet.
Ctrl+Shift+End	Extend the selection to the end of the worksheet.
Shift+Page Down	Extend the selection down one screen.
Shift+Page Up	Extend the selection up one screen.

SEE ALSO For a complete list of keyboard shortcuts, see "Keyboard shortcuts" at the end of this book.

After you create a formula, you can copy it and paste it into another cell. When you do, Excel tries to change the formula so that it works in the new cells. For instance, suppose you have a worksheet in which cell D8 contains the formula =SUM(C2:C6). Clicking cell D8, copying the cell's contents, and then pasting the result into cell D16 writes =SUM(C10:C14) into cell D16. Excel has reinterpreted the formula so that it fits the surrounding cells! Excel knows it can reinterpret the cells used in the formula because the formula uses a relative reference, or a reference that can change if the formula is copied to another cell. Relative references are written with just the cell row and column (for example, *C14*).

Relative references are useful when you summarize rows of data and want to use the same formula for each row. As an example, suppose you have a worksheet with two columns of data, labeled *SalePrice* and *Rate*, and you want to calculate your sales representative's commission by multiplying the two values in a row. To calculate the commission for the first sale, you would enter the formula =*A2*B2* in cell C2.

FILE | **HOME** | **INSERT** | **PAGE LAYOUT** | **FORMULAS** | **DATA**

C2 f_x =A2*B2

	A	B	C	D	E
1	**Sale Price**	**Rate**	**Commission**		
2	$ 7,364	6%	$ 441.84		
3	$ 8,135	6%			
4	$ 4,128	6%			
5	$ 17,103	6%			
6	$ 5,865	6%			
7	$ 18,188	6%			
8					

Selecting cell C2 and dragging the fill handle through cell C7 copies the formula from cell C2 into each of the other cells. Because you created the formula by using relative references, Excel updates each cell's formula to reflect its position relative to the starting cell (in this case, cell C2.) The formula in cell C7, for example, is *=A7*B7*.

C7 f_x =A7*B7

	A	B	C
1	**Sale Price**	**Rate**	**Commission**
2	$ 7,364	6%	$ 441.84
3	$ 8,135	6%	$ 488.10
4	$ 4,128	6%	$ 247.68
5	$ 17,103	6%	$ 1,026.18
6	$ 5,865	6%	$ 351.90
7	$ 18,188	6%	$ 1,091.28

You can use a similar technique when you add a formula to an Excel table column. If the sale price and rate data were in an Excel table and you created the formula *=A2*B2* in cell C2, Excel would apply the formula to every other cell in the column. Because you used relative references in the formula, the formulas would change to reflect each cell's distance from the original cell.

	A	B	C
1	**Sale Price** ▾	**Rate** ▾	**Commission** ▾
2	$ 7,364	6%	$ 441.84
3	$ 8,135	6%	$ 488.10
4	$ 4,128	6%	$ 247.68
5	$ 17,103	6%	$ 1,026.18
6	$ 5,865	6%	$ 351.90
7	$ 18,188	6%	$ 1,091.28

If you want a cell reference to remain constant when the formula using it is copied to another cell, you can use an absolute reference. To write a cell reference as an absolute reference, enter $ before the row letter and the column number. For example, if you want the formula in cell D16 to show the sum of values in cells C10 through C14 regardless of the cell into which it is pasted, you can write the formula as =SUM($C$10:$C$14).

TIP Another way to ensure that your cell references don't change when you copy the formula to another cell is to click the cell that contains the formula, copy the formula's text in the formula bar, press the Esc key to exit cut-and-copy mode, click the cell in which you want to paste the formula, and press Ctrl+V. Excel doesn't change the cell references when you copy your formula to another cell in this manner.

One quick way to change a cell reference from relative to absolute is to select the cell reference in the formula box and then press F4. Pressing F4 cycles a cell reference through the four possible types of references:

- Relative columns and rows (for example, C4)

- Absolute columns and rows (for example, $C$4)

- Relative columns and absolute rows (for example, C$4)

- Absolute columns and relative rows (for example, $C4)

In this exercise, you'll create a formula manually, revise it to include additional cells, create a formula that contains an Excel table reference, create a formula with relative references, and change the formula so it contains absolute references.

SET UP You need the ITExpenses workbook located in the Chapter03 practice file folder to complete this exercise. Open the workbook, and then follow the steps.

1   If necessary, display the **Summary** worksheet. Then, in cell **F9**, enter =C4, and press **Enter** to create the formula and display the value **$385,671.00** in cell **F9**.

2   Select cell **F9** and enter =SU to erase the existing formula and display the **Formula AutoComplete** list, which contains possible functions to use in the formula.

3   In the **Formula AutoComplete** list, click **SUM**, and then press **Tab** to change the contents of the formula bar to =SUM(.

4   Click cell **C3**, press **Ctrl+Shift+Down Arrow** to extend the selection to cell **C8**, enter) (a closing parenthesis) to make the formula bar's contents =SUM(C3:C8), and then press **Enter** to display the value **$2,562,966.00** in cell **F9**.

5   In cell **F10**, enter =SUM(C4:C5), and then press **Enter**.

6   In cell **D4**, enter =SUM($C$3:C4) and press **Enter** to add the formula to the cell.

7   Click cell **D4** and then drag the cell's fill handle until the selection covers cell **D8**. The formulas keep the cell reference **$C$3** absolute, but change the second cell reference to reflect the new cells' positions relative to the original formula.

8   On the tab bar, click the **JuneLabor** sheet tab to display the **JuneLabor** worksheet.

9   In cell **F13**, enter =SUM(J to display **JuneSummary**, the name of the table in the **JuneLabor** worksheet, in the **Formula AutoComplete** list.

10 Press **Tab** to extend the formula to read =SUM(JuneSummary.

11 Enter [, and then in the **Formula AutoComplete** list, click **Labor Expense**, and press **Tab** to extend the formula to read =SUM(JuneSummary[Labor Expense.

	A	B	C	D	E	F	G	H
1								
2		Region	Labor Expense					
3		Northeast	$ 64,685.00					
4		Atlantic	$ 99,001.00					
5		Southeast	$ 91,039.00					
6		North Central	$ 40,036.00					
7		Midwest	$ 77,238.00					
8		Southwest	$ 43,303.00					
9		Mountain West	$ 45,994.00					
10		Northwest	$ 95,633.00					
11		Central	$ 80,122.00					
12								
13					Total	=SUM(JuneSummary[Labor Expense		
14						SUM(number1, [number2], ...)		
15								
16								

12   Enter]) to complete the formula, and then press **Enter** to display the value **$637,051.00** in cell **F13**.

❌ CLEAN UP **Close the ITExpenses workbook, saving your changes if you want to.**

Summarizing data that meets specific conditions

Another use for formulas is to display messages when certain conditions are met. For instance, Consolidated Messenger's VP of Marketing, Craig Dewar, might have agreed to examine the rates charged to corporate customers who were billed for more than $100,000 during a calendar year. This kind of formula is called a *conditional formula*; one way to create a conditional formula in Excel is to use the *IF* function. To create a conditional formula, you click the cell to hold the formula and open the Insert Function dialog box. From within the dialog box, click *IF* in the list of available functions, and then click OK. When you do, the Function Arguments dialog box opens.

Function Arguments	?	×
IF		
Logical_test		= logical
Value_if_true		= any
Value_if_false		= any
		=
Checks whether a condition is met, and returns one value if TRUE, and another value if FALSE.		
Logical_test is any value or expression that can be evaluated to TRUE or FALSE.		
Formula result =		
Help on this function	OK	Cancel

When you work with an *IF* function, the Function Arguments dialog box has three boxes: Logical_test, Value_if_true, and Value_if_false. The Logical_test box holds the condition you want to check. If the customer's year-to-date shipping bill appears in cell G8, the expression would be *G8>100000*.

Now you need to have Excel display messages that indicate whether Craig Dewar should evaluate the account for a possible rate adjustment. To have Excel print a message from an *IF* function, you enclose the message in quotes in the Value_if_true or Value_if_false box. In this case, you would enter *"High-volume shipper—evaluate for rate decrease"* (including the quotation marks) in the Value_if_true box and *"Does not qualify at this time."* in the Value_if_false box.

Excel also includes several other conditional functions you can use to summarize your data, as shown in the following table.

Function	Description
AVERAGEIF	Finds the average of values within a cell range that meet a specified criterion
AVERAGEIFS	Finds the average of values within a cell range that meet multiple criteria
COUNT	Counts the number of cells in a range that contain a numerical value
COUNTA	Counts the number of cells in a range that are not empty
COUNTBLANK	Counts the number of cells in a range that are empty
COUNTIF	Counts the number of cells in a range that meet a specified criterion
COUNTIFS	Counts the number of cells in a range that meet multiple criteria
IFERROR	Displays one value if a formula results in an error and another if it doesn't
SUMIF	Finds the sum of values in a range that meet a single criterion
SUMIFS	Finds the sum of values in a range that meet multiple criteria

You can use the *IFERROR* function to display a custom error message, instead of relying on the default Excel error messages to explain what happened. For example, you could use an *IFERROR* formula when looking up the CustomerID value from cell G8 in the Customers table by using the *VLOOKUP* function. One way to create such a formula is by using *=IFERROR(VLOOKUP(G8,Customers,2,false),"Customer not found")*. If the function finds a match for the CustomerID in cell G8, it displays the customer's name; if it doesn't find a match, it displays the text *Customer not found*.

SEE ALSO For more information about the VLOOKUP function, see "Looking up information in a worksheet" in Chapter 6, "Reordering and summarizing data."

Just as the *COUNTIF* function counts the number of cells that meet a criterion and the *SUMIF* function finds the total of values in cells that meet a criterion, the *AVERAGEIF* function finds the average of values in cells that meet a criterion. To create a formula by using the *AVERAGEIF* function, you define the range to be examined for the criterion, the criterion, and, if required, the range from which to draw the values. As an example, consider a worksheet that lists each customer's ID number, name, state, and total monthly shipping bill.

	A	B	C	D
1	CustomerID	CustomerName	State	Total
2	OD100	Contoso	WA	$118,476.00
3	OD101	Fabrikam	WA	$125,511.00
4	OD102	Northwind Traders	OR	$103,228.00
5	OD103	Adventure Works	WA	$ 86,552.00
6				

If you want to find the average order value for customers from the state of Washington (abbreviated in the worksheet as WA), you can create the formula =AVERAGEIF(C2:C5, "=WA", D2:D5).

The *SUMIFS*, *AVERAGEIFS*, and *COUNTIFS* functions extend the capabilities of the *SUMIF*, *AVERAGEIF*, and *COUNTIF* functions to allow for multiple criteria. If you want to find the sum of all orders of at least $100,000 placed by companies in Washington, you can create the formula =SUMIFS(D2:D5, C2:C5, "=WA", D2:D5, ">=100000").

The *AVERAGEIFS* and *SUMIFS* functions start with a data range that contains values that the formula summarizes; you then list the data ranges and the criteria to apply to that range. In generic terms, the syntax runs =AVERAGEIFS(data_range, criteria_range1, criteria1[,criteria_range2, criteria2...]). The part of the syntax in square brackets (which aren't used when you create the formula) is optional, so an *AVERAGEIFS* or *SUMIFS* formula that contains a single criterion will work. The *COUNTIFS* function, which doesn't perform any calculations, doesn't need a data range—you just provide the criteria ranges and criteria. For example, you could find the number of customers from Washington who were billed at least $100,000 by using the formula =COUNTIFS(C2:C5, "=WA", D2:D5, ">=100000").

In this exercise, you'll create a conditional formula that displays a message if a condition is true, find the average of worksheet values that meet one criterion, and find the sum of worksheet values that meet two criteria.

 SET UP You need the PackagingCosts workbook located in the Chapter03 practice file folder to complete this exercise. Open the workbook, and then follow the steps.

1   In cell **G3**, enter the formula =IF(F3>=35000, "Request discount", "No discount available"), and press **Enter** to create the formula, which displays *Request discount* if the value in cell F3 is at least 35,000 and displays *No discount available* if not. The value **Request discount** appears in cell **G3**.

2   Click cell **G3**, and drag the fill handle down until it covers cell **G14**. Excel copies the formula in cell **G3** to cells **G4:G14**, adjusting the formula to reflect the cells' addresses. The results of the copied formulas appear in cells **G4:G14**.

3   In cell **I3**, enter the formula =AVERAGEIF(C3:C14, "=Box", F3:F14) and press **Enter** to display the average cost per category of boxes, **$46,102.50**, in cell **I3**.

4   In cell **I6**, enter =SUMIFS(F3:F14, C3:C14, "=Envelope", E3:E14, "=International"), and press **Enter** to display the value **$45,753.00**, which represents the total cost of all envelopes used for international shipments, in cell **I6**.

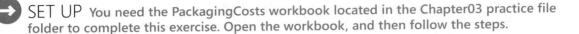

 CLEAN UP Close the PackagingCosts workbook, saving your changes if you want to.

Working with iterative calculation options and automatic workbook calculation

Excel formulas use values in other cells to calculate their results. If you create a formula that refers to the cell that contains the formula, you have created a circular reference. Under most circumstances, Excel treats circular references as a mistake for two reasons. First, the vast majority of Excel formulas don't refer to their own cell, so a circular reference is unusual enough to be identified as an error. The second, more serious consideration is that a formula with a circular reference can slow down your workbook. Because Excel repeats, or iterates, the calculation, you need to set limits on how many times the program repeats the operation.

You can control your workbook's calculation options by clicking the File tab on the ribbon, clicking Options to open the Excel Options dialog box, clicking Formulas to display that page of the Excel Options dialog box, and selecting the calculation option you want.

The Calculation Options section of the Formulas page in the dialog box has three available settings:

- **Automatic** The default setting, which recalculates a worksheet whenever a value affecting a formula changes

- **Automatic except for data tables** Recalculates a worksheet whenever a value changes but doesn't recalculate data tables

- **Manual** Requires you to press **F9** or click the **Formulas** tab and click the **Calculate Now** button to recalculate your worksheet

In the Calculation Options section, you can also choose to allow or disallow iterative calculations. Selecting the Enable Iterative Calculation check box lets Excel repeat calculations for cells that contain formulas with circular references. The default Maximum Iterations value of 100 and Maximum Change of 0.001 are appropriate for all but the most unusual circumstances. Click OK to accept your changes.

TIP You can also have Excel recalculate its formulas by clicking the Formulas tab on the ribbon, clicking the Calculation Options button, and selecting the behavior you want.

In this exercise, you'll create a formula that has a circular reference and then change the program's iterative calculation options to find the result.

→ SET UP You need the SavingsIncentive workbook located in the Chapter03 practice file folder to complete this exercise. Open the workbook, and then follow the steps.

1   Click the **Formulas** tab, click the **Calculation Options** button, and then click **Manual**.

2   In cell **B6**, enter the formula **=B7*B9** and press **Enter** to display the initial result of the formula, which is **$1,600.00**. Note that this result is incorrect because the Gross Savings minus the Savings Incentive should equal the Net Savings value, which it does not.

3   Press **F9** to recalculate the worksheet. When you do, Excel displays a message box indicating that you have created a circular reference.

	A	B	C	D	E	F	G
1	**Savings Incentive Program**						
2							
3	**Previous Expense**	$ 145,000.00					
4	**New Expense**	$ 125,000.00					
5	**Gross Savings**	$ 20,000.00					
6	**Savings Incentive**	$ 1,481.48					
7	**Net Savings**	$ 18,518.52					
8							
9	**Incentive Rate**	8%					
10		Microsoft Excel				✕	
11							
12	⚠	Careful, we found one or more circular references in your workbook that might cause your formulas to calculate incorrectly.					
13		FYI: A circular reference can be a formula that refers to its own cell value, or refers to a cell dependent on its own cell value.					
14							
15		OK	Help				
16							

4   Click **OK** to close the message box.

5   Click the **File** tab and then click **Options** to open the **Excel Options** dialog box.

6   Click the **Formulas** category label.

7   Select the **Enable iterative calculation** check box, and then click **OK** to close the **Excel Options** dialog box.

8   Press **F9** to recalculate the worksheet. The correct values of **$1,481.48** and **$18,518.52** appear in cells **B6** and **B7**, respectively.

9   Click the **Formulas** tab, click the **Calculation Options** button, and then click **Automatic**.

❌ CLEAN UP Close the PackagingCosts workbook, saving your changes if you want to.

Using array formulas

Most Excel formulas calculate values to be displayed in a single cell. For example, you could add the formulas *=B1*B4*, *=B1*B5*, and *=B1*B6* to consecutive worksheet cells to calculate shipping insurance costs based on the value of a package's contents.

	A	B	C
1	**Insurance Rate**	2.5%	
2			
3	**PackageID**	**Value**	**Premium**
4	PK000352	$ 591.00	
5	PK000353	$1,713.00	
6	PK000354	$3,039.00	
7			

Rather than add the same formula to multiple cells one cell at a time, you can add a formula to every cell in the target range at once by creating an array formula. To create an array formula, you enter the formula's arguments and press Ctrl+Shift+Enter to identify the formula as an array formula. To calculate package insurance rates for values in the cell range B4:B6 and the rate in cell B1, you would select a range of cells with the same shape as the value range and enter the formula =B1*B4:B6. In this case, the values are in a three-cell column, so you must select a range of the same shape, such as C4:C6.

	A	B	C
1	**Insurance Rate**	2.5%	
2			
3	**PackageID**	**Value**	**Premium**
4	PK000352	$ 591.00	=B1*B4:B6
5	PK000353	$ 1,713.00	
6	PK000354	$ 3,039.00	
7			

IMPORTANT If you enter the array formula into a range of the wrong shape, Excel displays duplicate results, incomplete results, or error messages depending on how the target range differs from the value range.

When you press Ctrl+Shift+Enter, Excel creates an array formula in the selected cells. The formula appears within a pair of curly braces to indicate it is an array formula. In this case, the formula in cells C4:C6 is {=B1*B4:B6}.

IMPORTANT You can't add curly braces to a formula to make it an array formula—you must press Ctrl+Shift+Enter to create it.

In addition to creating an array formula that combines a single cell's value with an array, you can create array formulas that use two separate arrays. For example, Consolidated Messenger might establish a goal to reduce sorting time in each of four distribution centers.

▲	A	B	C	D
1	Center	Previous Time	Target Percentage	Target Time
2	North	145	85%	
3	South	180	90%	
4	East	195	75%	
5	West	205	70%	
6				

This worksheet stores the previous sorting times in minutes and percentage target in cells B2:B5 and C2:C5, respectively. The array formula to calculate the targets for each of the four centers is =B2:B5*C2:C5, which, when entered into cells D2:D5 by pressing Ctrl+Shift+Enter, would appear as {= B2:B5*C2:C5}.

To edit an array formula, you must select every cell that contains the array formula, click the formula bar to activate it, edit the formula on the formula bar, and then press Ctrl+Shift+Enter to re-enter the formula as an array formula.

TIP Many operations that used to require an array formula can now be calculated by using functions such as *SUMIFS* and *COUNTIFS*.

In this exercise, you'll create and edit array formulas.

→ SET UP You need the FuelSurcharges workbook located in the Chapter03 practice file folder to complete this exercise. Open the workbook, and then follow the steps.

1 If necessary, click the **Fuel** sheet tab to display the **Fuel** worksheet.

2 Select cells **C11:F11**.

3 Enter the formula =C3*C9:F9 and then press **Ctrl+Shift+Enter** to add the formula {=C3*C9:F9} to cells **C11:F11**.

4 With cells **C11:F11** still selected, click the formula bar, edit the formula so it reads =C3*C10:F10, and then press **Ctrl+Shift+Enter** to change the array formula to {=C3*C10:F10}.

5 Click the **Volume** sheet tab to display the **Volume** worksheet.

6 Select cells **D4:D7**.

7 Enter the formula =B4:B7*C4:C7 and then press **Ctrl+Shift+Enter** to add the formula {=B4:B7*C4:C7} to cells **D4:D7**.

✖ CLEAN UP Close the FuelSurcharges workbook, saving your changes if you want to.

Finding and correcting errors in calculations

Including calculations in a worksheet gives you valuable answers to questions about your data. As is always true, however, it is possible for errors to creep into your formulas. With Excel, you can find the source of errors in your formulas by identifying the cells used in a particular calculation and describing any errors that have occurred. The process of examining a worksheet for errors is referred to as *auditing*.

Excel identifies errors in several ways. The first way is to display an error code in the cell holding the formula that is generating the error.

◢	A	B	C	D	E	F
1						
2		Category	Expenses			
3		Hardware	$1,469,002.00			
4		Desktop Software	$ 385,671.00			
5		Server Software	$ 599,101.00			
6		Maintenance	$ 64,703.00			
7		Cable	$ 11,240.00			
8		Backup Power Supply	$ 33,249.00			
9					Total ◈	#NAME?
10					Software Total	
11						

When a cell with an erroneous formula is the active cell, an Error button is displayed next to it. Pointing to the Error button causes it to display an arrow on the button's right edge. Clicking the arrow displays a menu with options that provide information about the error and offer to help you fix it.

The following table lists the most common error codes and what they mean.

Error code	Description
#####	The column isn't wide enough to display the value.
#VALUE!	The formula has the wrong type of argument (such as text in a cell where a numerical value is required).
#NAME?	The formula contains text that Excel doesn't recognize (such as an unknown named range).
#REF!	The formula refers to a cell that doesn't exist (which can happen whenever cells are deleted).
#DIV/0!	The formula attempts to divide by zero.
#N/A!	The formula attempts to use a value that is not available in the target range. This error often occurs when a user enters an invalid lookup value in a VLOOKUP formula.

Another technique you can use to find the source of formula errors is to ensure that the appropriate cells are providing values for the formula. For example, you might want to calculate the total number of deliveries for a service level, but you could accidentally create a formula referring to the service levels' names instead of their package quantities. You can identify the source of an error by having Excel trace a cell's *precedents*, which are the cells that have values used in the active cell's formula. To do so, click the Formulas tab, and then in the Formula Auditing group, click Trace Precedents. When you do, Excel identifies those cells by drawing a blue tracer arrow from the precedents to the active cell.

You can also audit your worksheet by identifying cells that contain formulas that use a value from a given cell. For example, you might use one region's daily package total in a formula that calculates the average number of packages delivered for all regions on a given day. Cells that use another cell's value in their calculations are known as *dependents*, meaning that they depend on the value in the other cell to derive their own value. As with tracing precedents, you can click the Formulas tab, and then in the Formula Auditing group, click Trace Dependents to have Excel draw blue arrows from the active cell to those cells that have calculations based on that value.

	A	B	C	D	E	F
1						
2		Category	Expenses			
3		Hardware	$1,469,002.00			
4		Desktop Software	$ ●385,671.00			
5		Server Software	$ 599,101.00			
6		Maintenance	$ 64,703.00			
7		Cable	$ 11,240.00			
8		Backup Power Supply	$ 33,249.00			
9					Total	$ 2,562,966.00
10					Software Total	$ 984,772.00
11						

If the cells identified by the tracer arrows aren't the correct cells, you can hide the arrows and correct the formula. To hide the tracer arrows on a worksheet, display the Formulas tab, and then in the Formula Auditing group, click Remove Arrows.

If you prefer to have the elements of a formula error presented as text in a dialog box, you can use the Error Checking dialog box to view the error and the formula in the cell in which the error occurs. To open the Error Checking dialog box, display the Formulas tab, and then in the Formula Auditing group, click the Error Checking button. You can use the controls in the Error Checking dialog box to move through the formula one step at a time, to choose to ignore the error, or to move to the next or the previous error. If you click the Options button in the dialog box, you can also use the controls in the Excel Options dialog box to change how Excel determines what is an error and what isn't.

TIP You can have the Error Checking tool ignore formulas that don't use every cell in a region (such as a row or column). If you clear the Formulas Which Omit Cells In A Region check box, you can create formulas that don't add up every value in a row or column (or rectangle) without Excel marking them as an error.

For times when you just want to display the results of each step of a formula and don't need the full power of the Error Checking tool, you can use the Evaluate Formula dialog box to move through each element of the formula. To open the Evaluate Formula dialog box, you display the Formulas tab and then, in the Formula Auditing group, click the Evaluate Formula button. The Evaluate Formula dialog box is useful for examining formulas that don't produce an error but aren't generating the result you expect.

Finally, you can monitor the value in a cell regardless of where in your workbook you are by opening a Watch Window that displays the value in the cell. For example, if one of your formulas uses values from cells in other worksheets or even other workbooks, you can set a watch on the cell that contains the formula and then change the values in the other cells.

To set a watch, click the cell you want to monitor, and then on the Formulas tab, in the Formula Auditing group, click Watch Window. Click Add Watch to have Excel monitor the selected cell.

As soon as you enter the new value, the Watch Window displays the new result of the formula. When you're done watching the formula, select the watch, click Delete Watch, and close the Watch Window.

In this exercise, you'll use the formula-auditing capabilities in Excel to identify and correct errors in a formula.

 SET UP You need the ConveyerBid workbook located in the Chapter03 practice file folder to complete this exercise. Open the workbook, and then follow the steps.

1 Click cell **D21**.

2 On the **Formulas** tab, in the **Formula Auditing** group, click **Watch Window** to open the **Watch Window**.

3 Click **Add Watch**, and then in the **Add Watch** dialog box, click **Add** to add cell **D21** to the watch list.

4 Click cell **D8**, which activates the cell and displays **=SUM(C3:C7)** in the formula bar.

5 On the **Formulas** tab, in the **Formula Auditing** group, click the **Trace Precedents** button to display a blue arrow that begins at the cell range **C3:C7** and points to cell **D8**, indicating that the cells in the range **C3:C7** provide the values for the formula in cell **D8**.

⊿	A	B	C	D
1				
2		**Conveyer**		
3		350' track	$ 14,012.00	
4		Catch bin	$ 395.00	
5		Motor	$ 1,249.00	
6		Chain drive	$ 1,495.00	
7		Sorting table	$ 675.00	
8		*Subtotal*		$ 18,326.00
9				

6   On the **Formulas** tab, in the **Formula Auditing** group, click the **Remove Arrows** button to remove the tracer arrow.

7   Click cell **A1**.

8   On the **Formulas** tab, in the **Formula Auditing** group, click the **Error Checking** button to open the **Error Checking** dialog box, which displays the error found in cell D21.

Error Checking dialog box:

Error in cell D21
= C12/D19

Divide by Zero Error
The formula or function used is dividing by zero or empty cells.

Help on this error
Show Calculation Steps...
Ignore Error
Edit in Formula Bar
Options...
Previous   Next

9   Click **Next** to move to the next error. Excel displays a message box indicating that there are no more errors in the worksheet.

10   Click **OK** to close both the message box and the **Error Checking** dialog box.

11   On the **Formulas** tab, in the **Formula Auditing** group, click the **Error Checking** arrow, and then in the list, click **Trace Error**. Blue arrows appear, pointing to cell **D21** from cells **C12** and **D19**. These arrows indicate that using the values (or lack of values, in this case) in the indicated cells generates the error in cell D21.

12   On the **Formulas** tab, in the **Formula Auditing** group, click **Remove Arrows** to hide the arrows.

13   In the formula box, delete the existing formula, enter **=C12/D20**, and then press **Enter**. The value **14%** appears in cell **D21** and the change is reflected in the Watch Window.

14   Click cell **D21**.

15   On the **Formulas** tab, in the **Formula Auditing** group, click the **Evaluate Formula** button to open the **Evaluate Formula** dialog box, which displays the formula from cell **D21**.

16   Click **Evaluate** three times to step through the formula's elements, and then click **Close** to close the **Evaluate Formula** dialog box.

17   In the **Watch Window**, click the watch in the list.

18   Click **Delete Watch** to erase the watch.

19   On the **Formulas** tab, in the **Formula Auditing** group, click **Watch Window** to close the **Watch Window**.

✖ CLEAN UP Close the ConveyerBid workbook, saving your changes if you want to.

Key points

- You can add a group of cells to a formula by entering the formula, and then at the spot in the formula in which you want to name the cells, selecting the cells.

- By creating named ranges, you can refer to entire blocks of cells by using a single term, saving you lots of time and effort. You can use a similar technique with Excel table data, referring to an entire Excel table or one or more table columns.

- When you write a formula, be sure you use absolute referencing ($A$1) if you want the formula to remain the same when it's copied from one cell to another, or use relative referencing (A1) if you want the formula to change to reflect its new position in the worksheet.

- Instead of entering a formula from scratch, you can use the Insert Function dialog box to help you.

- With iterative calculations, you can manage formulas that have circular references.

- You can use array formulas to summarize ranges of values by creating a single formula.

- You can monitor how the value in a cell changes by adding a watch to the Watch Window.

- To find out which formulas refer to the values in the selected cell, use Trace Dependents; if you want to find out which cells provide values for the formula in the active cell, use Trace Precedents.

- You can step through the calculations of a formula in the Evaluate Formula dialog box or go through a more rigorous error-checking procedure by using the Error Checking tool.

3

Chapter at a glance

Define

Define styles,
page 113

Apply

Apply workbook themes and Excel table
styles, page 119

Change

Change the appearance of data based on its
value, page 131

Distribution Capacity		
Northeast		47%
Atlantic		75%
Southeast		39%
North Central		54%
Midwest		40%
Southwest		73%
Mountain West		51%
Northwest		69%
Central		41%

Add

Add images to worksheets,
page 138

	A	B	C	D
1				
2		Call Volume		
3		Northeast	13,769	
4		Atlantic	19,511	
5		Southeast	11,111	
6		North Central	24,972	
7		Midwest	11,809	
8		Southwest	20,339	
9		Mountain West	20,127	
10		Northwest	12,137	
11		Central	20,047	
12				

Changing workbook appearance

4

IN THIS CHAPTER, YOU WILL LEARN HOW TO

- Format cells.

- Define styles.

- Apply workbook themes and Excel table styles.

- Make numbers easier to read.

- Change the appearance of data based on its value.

- Add images to worksheets.

Entering data into a workbook efficiently saves you time, but you must also ensure that your data is easy to read. Microsoft Excel 2013 gives you a wide variety of ways to make your data easier to understand; for example, you can change the font, character size, or color used to present a cell's contents. Changing how data appears on a worksheet helps set the contents of a cell apart from the contents of surrounding cells. The simplest example of that concept is a data label. If a column on your worksheet contains a list of days, you can easily set apart a label (for example, *Day*) by presenting it in bold type that's noticeably larger than the type used to present the data to which it refers. To save time, you can define several custom formats and then apply them quickly to the desired cells.

You might also want to specially format a cell's contents to reflect the value in that cell. For example, Lori Penor, the chief operating officer of Consolidated Messenger, might want to create a worksheet that displays the percentage of improperly delivered packages from each regional distribution center. If that percentage exceeds a threshold, she could have Excel display a red traffic light icon, indicating that the center's performance is out of tolerance and requires attention.

In this chapter, you'll change the appearance of data, apply existing formats to data, make numbers easier to read, change data's appearance based on its value, and add images to worksheets.

Formatting cells

Excel spreadsheets can hold and process lots of data, but when you manage numerous spreadsheets it can be hard to remember from a worksheet's title exactly what data is kept in that worksheet. Data labels give you and your colleagues information about data in a worksheet, but it's important to format the labels so that they stand out visually. To make your data labels or any other data stand out, you can change the format of the cells that hold your data.

	A	B	C	D
1				
2		**Call Volume**		
3		Northeast	13,769	
4		Atlantic	19,511	
5		Southeast	11,111	
6		North Central	24,972	
7		Midwest	11,809	
8		Southwest	20,339	
9		Mountain West	20,127	
10		Northwest	12,137	
11		Central	20,047	
12				

Most of the tools you need to change a cell's format can be found on the Home tab. You can apply the formatting represented on a button by selecting the cells you want to apply the style to and then clicking that button. If you want to set your data labels apart by making them appear bold, click the Bold button. If you have already made a cell's contents bold, selecting the cell and clicking the Bold button will remove the formatting.

TIP Deleting a cell's contents doesn't delete the cell's formatting. To delete a selected cell's formatting, on the Home tab, in the Editing group, click the Clear button (which looks like an eraser), and then click Clear Formats. Clicking Clear All from the same list will remove the cell's contents and formatting.

Buttons in the Home tab's Font group that give you choices, such as Font Color, have an arrow at the right edge of the button. Clicking the arrow displays a list of options accessible for that button, such as the fonts available on your system or the colors you can assign to a cell.

Another way you can make a cell stand apart from its neighbors is to add a border around the cell. To place a border around one or more cells, select the cells, and then choose the border type you want by selecting from the Border list in the Font group. Excel does provide more options: to display the full range of border types and styles, in the Border list, click More Borders. The Border page of the Format Cells dialog box contains the full range of tools you can use to define your cells' borders.

You can also make a group of cells stand apart from its neighbors by changing its shading, which is the color that fills the cells. On a worksheet that tracks total package volume for the past month, Lori Penor could change the fill color of the cells holding her data labels to make the labels stand out even more than by changing the labels' text formatting.

TIP You can display the most commonly used formatting controls by right-clicking a selected range. When you do, a Mini Toolbar containing a subset of the Home tab formatting tools appears above the shortcut menu.

If you want to change the attributes of every cell in a row or column, you can click the header of the row or column you want to modify and then select the format you want.

One task you can't perform by using the tools on the Home tab is to change the standard font for a workbook, which is used in the Name box and on the formula bar. The standard font when you install Excel is Calibri, a simple font that is easy to read on a computer screen and on the printed page. If you want to choose another font, click the File tab, and then click Options. On the General page of the Excel Options dialog box, set the values in the Use This Font and Font Size list boxes to pick your new display font.

In this exercise, you'll emphasize a worksheet's title by changing the format of cell data, and you'll add a border to a cell range and then change a cell range's fill color. After those tasks are complete, you'll change the default font for the workbook.

→ SET UP You need the VehicleMileSummary workbook located in the Chapter04 practice file folder to complete this exercise. Open the workbook, and then follow the steps.

1 Click cell **D2**.

2 On the **Home** tab, in the **Font** group, click the **Bold** button to display the cell's contents in bold type.

3 In the **Font** group, click the **Font Size** arrow, and then in the list, click **18** to increase the size of the text in cell **D2**.

	A	B	C	D	E	F	G	H	I
1									
2				Vehicle Mile Summary					
3									
4			Day						
5		VehicleID	Monday	Tuesday	Wednesday	Thursday	Friday	Saturday	
6		V101	159	144	124	108	125	165	
7		V102	113	106	111	116	119	97	
8		V103	87	154	124	128	111	100	
9		V104	137	100	158	96	127	158	
10		V105	86	132	154	97	154	165	
11		V106	159	163	155	101	89	160	
12		V107	111	165	155	92	91	94	
13		V108	101	162	123	87	93	140	
14		V109	164	159	116	97	149	120	
15		V110	100	107	143	144	152	132	

4 Click cell **B5**, hold down the **Ctrl** key, and click cell **C4** to select the noncontiguous cells.

5 On the **Home** tab, in the **Font** group, click the **Bold** button to display the cells' contents in bold type.

6 Select the cell ranges **B6:B15** and **C5:H5**.

7   In the **Font** group, click the **Italic** button to display the cell's contents in italic type.

◢	A	B	C	D	E	F	G	H
1								
2			**Vehicle Mile Summary**					
3								
4			Day					
5		VehicleID	*Monday*	*Tuesday*	*Wednesday*	*Thursday*	*Friday*	*Saturday*
6		*V101*	159	144	124	108	125	165
7		*V102*	113	106	111	116	119	97
8		*V103*	87	154	124	128	111	100
9		*V104*	137	100	158	96	127	158
10		*V105*	86	132	154	97	154	165
11		*V106*	159	163	155	101	89	160
12		*V107*	111	165	155	92	91	94
13		*V108*	101	162	123	87	93	140
14		*V109*	164	159	116	97	149	120
15		*V110*	100	107	143	144	152	132
16								

8   Select the cell range **C6:H15**.

9   In the **Font** group, click the **Border** arrow, and then in the list, click **Outside Borders** to place a border around the outside edge of the selected cells.

10   Select the cell range **B4:H15**.

11   In the **Border** list, click **Thick Box Border** to place a thick border around the outside edge of the selected cells.

12   Select the cell ranges **B4:B15** and **C4:H5**.

13   In the **Font** group, click the **Fill Color** arrow, and then in the **Standard Colors** palette, click the yellow swatch to change the selected cells' background color to yellow.

◢	A	B	C	D	E	F	G	H
1								
2				**Vehicle Mile Summary**				
3								
4			Day					
5		VehicleID	Monday	Tuesday	Wednesday	Thursday	Friday	Saturday
6		V101	159	144	124	108	125	165
7		V102	113	106	111	116	119	97
8		V103	87	154	124	128	111	100
9		V104	137	100	158	96	127	158
10		V105	86	132	154	97	154	165
11		V106	159	163	155	101	89	160
12		V107	111	165	155	92	91	94
13		V108	101	162	123	87	93	140
14		V109	164	159	116	97	149	120
15		V110	100	107	143	144	152	132

14   Click the **File** tab, and then click **Options** to open the **Excel Options** dialog box.

15   If necessary, click **General** to display the **General** page.

16   In the **When creating new workbooks** area, in the **Use this as the default font** list, click **Verdana**. **Verdana** appears in the **Use This Font** field.

17   Click **Cancel** to close the **Excel Options** dialog box without saving your change.

❌ CLEAN UP Close the VehicleMileSummary workbook, saving your changes if you want to.

Defining styles

As you work with Excel, you will probably develop preferred formats for data labels, titles, and other worksheet elements. Instead of adding a format's characteristics one element at a time to the target cells, you can have Excel store the format and recall it as needed. You can find the predefined formats by displaying the Home tab, and then in the Styles group, clicking Cell Styles.

Clicking a style from the Cell Styles gallery applies the style to the selected cells, but Excel also displays a live preview of a format when you point to it. If none of the existing styles is what you want, you can create your own style by clicking New Cell Style below the gallery to display the Style dialog box. In the Style dialog box, enter the name of your new style in the Style Name field, and then click Format. The Format Cells dialog box opens.

After you set the characteristics of your new style, click OK to make your style available in the Cell Styles gallery. If you ever want to delete a custom style, display the Cell Styles gallery, right-click the style, and then click Delete.

The Style dialog box is quite versatile, but it's overkill if all you want to do is apply formatting changes you made to a cell to the contents of another cell. To do so, use the Format Painter button, found in the Home tab's Clipboard group. Just click the cell that has the format you want to copy, click the Format Painter button, and select the target cells to have Excel apply the copied format to the target range.

TIP If you want to apply the same formatting to multiple cells by using the Format Painter button, double-click the Format Painter button and then click the cells to which you want to apply the formatting. When you're done applying the formatting, press the Esc key.

In this exercise, you'll create a style and apply the new style to a data label.

→ SET UP You need the HourlyExceptions workbook located in the Chapter04 practice file folder to complete this exercise. Open the workbook, and then follow the steps.

1   On the **Home** tab, in the **Styles** group, click **Cell Styles**, and then click **New Cell Style** to open the **Style** dialog box.

2   In the **Style name** field, enter Crosstab Column Heading.

3   Click the **Format** button to open the **Format Cells** dialog box.

4   Click the **Alignment** tab.

5   In the **Horizontal** list, click **Center**. **Center** appears in the **Horizontal** field.

6   Click the **Font** tab.

7   In the **Font style** list, click **Italic** to display the text in the **Preview** pane in italicized text.

8 Click the **Number** tab to display the **Number** page of the **Format Cells** dialog box.

9 In the **Category** list, click **Time** to display the available time formats.

10 In the **Type** pane, click **1:30 PM**.

11 Click **OK** to save your changes. The **Format Cells** dialog box closes, and your new style's definition appears in the **Style** dialog box.

12 Click **OK** to close the **Style** dialog box.

13 Select cells **C4:N4**.

14 On the **Home** tab, in the **Styles** group, click **Cell Styles**. Your new style appears at the top of the gallery, in the **Custom** area.

Custom

Crosstab Col...

Good, Bad and Neutral

Normal	Bad	Good	Neutral

Data and Model

Calculation	Check Cell	*Explanatory ...*	Input	Linked Cell	Note
Output	Warning Text				

Titles and Headings

Heading 1	Heading 2	Heading 3	Heading 4	Title	Total

Themed Cell Styles

20% - Accent1	20% - Accent2	20% - Accent3	20% - Accent4	20% - Accent5	20% - Accent6
40% - Accent1	40% - Accent2	40% - Accent3	40% - Accent4	40% - Accent5	40% - Accent6
60% - Accent1	60% - Accent2	60% - Accent3	60% - Accent4	60% - Accent5	60% - Accent6
Accent1	Accent2	Accent3	Accent4	Accent5	Accent6

Number Format

Comma	Comma [0]	Currency	Currency [0]	Percent

New Cell Style...

Merge Styles...

15   Click the **Crosstab Column Heading** style to apply your new style to the selected cells.

✕ CLEAN UP Close the HourlyExceptions workbook, saving your changes if you want to.

Applying workbook themes and Excel table styles

Microsoft Office 2013 includes powerful design tools that you can use to create attractive, professional documents quickly. The Excel product team implemented the new design capabilities by defining workbook themes and Excel table styles. A theme is a way to specify the fonts, colors, and graphic effects that appear in a workbook. Excel comes with many themes installed.

To apply an existing workbook theme, display the Page Layout tab. Then, in the Themes group, click Themes, and click the theme you want to apply to your workbook. By default, Excel applies the Office theme to your workbooks.

When you apply formatting to a workbook element, Excel displays colors that are available within the active theme. For example, selecting a worksheet cell and then clicking the Font Color button's arrow displays a menu containing two palettes of colors you can use. The theme colors appear in the Theme Colors palette, the standard colors appear in the Standard Colors palette, and the More Colors link, which displays the Colors dialog box, appears at the bottom of the menu. If you format workbook elements by using colors from the Theme Colors palette, applying a different theme changes that object's colors.

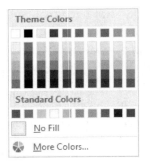

You can change a theme's colors, fonts, and graphic effects by displaying the Page Layout tab and then, in the Themes group, selecting new values from the Colors, Fonts, and Effects lists. To save your changes as a new theme, display the Page Layout tab, and in the Themes group, click Themes, and then click Save Current Theme. Use the controls in the Save Current Theme dialog box that opens to record your theme for later use. Later, when you click the Themes button, your custom theme will appear at the top of the gallery.

TIP When you save a theme, you save it as an Office Theme file. You can apply the theme to other Office 2013 documents as well.

Just as you can define and apply themes to entire workbooks, you can apply and define Excel table styles. You select an Excel table's initial style when you create it; to create a new style, display the Home tab, and in the Styles group, click Format As Table. In the Format As Table gallery, click New Table Style to open the New Table Style dialog box.

Enter a name for the new style, select the first table element you want to format, and then click Format to display the Format Cells dialog box. Define the element's formatting, and then click OK. When the New Table Style dialog box reopens, its Preview pane displays the overall table style and the Element Formatting area describes the selected element's appearance. Also, in the Table Element list, Excel displays the element's name in bold to indicate it has been changed. To make the new style the default for new Excel tables created in the current workbook, select the Set As Default Table Style For This Document check box. When you click OK, Excel saves the new table style.

TIP To remove formatting from a table element, click the name of the table element and then click the Clear button.

In this exercise, you'll create a new workbook theme, change a workbook's theme, create a new table style, and apply the new style to an Excel table.

SET UP You need the HourlyTracking workbook located in the Chapter04 practice file folder to complete this exercise. Open the workbook, and then follow the steps.

1   If necessary, click any cell in the Excel table to make the table active.

2   On the **Home** tab, in the **Styles** group, click **Format as Table**, and then click the style at the upper-left corner of the **Table Styles** gallery. Doing so applies the style to the table.

3   On the **Home** tab, in the **Styles** group, click **Format as Table**, and then click **New Table Style** to open the **New Table Style** dialog box.

4   In the **Name** field, enter Exception Default.

5   In the **Table Element** list, click **Header Row**.

6   Click **Format** to open the **Format Cells** dialog box.

7   Click the **Fill** tab to display the **Fill** page.

8   In the first row of color swatches, just below the **No Color** button, click the third swatch from the left to display that new background color in the **Sample** pane of the dialog box.

9   Click **OK** to close the **Format Cells** dialog box. When the **New Table Style** dialog box reopens, the **Header Row** table element appears in bold, and the **Preview** pane's header row is shaded.

10   In the **Table Element** list, click **Second Row Stripe**, and then click **Format** to open the **Format Cells** dialog box.

11   Just below the **No Color** button, click the third swatch from the left again to have the new background color appear in the **Sample** pane of the dialog box.

12   Click **OK** to close the **Format Cells** dialog box. When the **New Table Style** dialog box reopens, the **Second Row Stripe** table element appears in bold, and every second row is shaded in the **Preview** pane.

New Table Style

Name: Exception Default

Table Element:

- Whole Table
- First Column Stripe
- Second Column Stripe
- First Row Stripe
- **Second Row Stripe**
- Last Column
- First Column
- **Header Row**
- Total Row

[Format] [Clear]

Preview

Stripe Size

1

Element Formatting:

Shaded

☐ Set as default table style for this document

[OK] [Cancel]

13 Click **OK** to close the **New Table Style** dialog box.

14 On the **Home** tab, in the **Styles** group, click **Format as Table**. In the gallery, in the **Custom** area, click the new format to apply it to your table.

15 On the **Page Layout** tab, in the **Themes** group, click the **Fonts** arrow, and then in the list, click **Consolas-Verdana** to change the theme's font.

	A	B	C	D	E
1					
2		Day ▾	Region ▾	Hour ▾	Exceptions ▾
3		7/29/2013	Northeast	5:00 PM	104
4		7/29/2013	Atlantic	5:00 PM	37
5		7/29/2013	Southeast	5:00 PM	22
6		7/29/2013	North Central	5:00 PM	19
7		7/29/2013	Midwest	5:00 PM	37
8		7/29/2013	Southwest	5:00 PM	72
9		7/29/2013	Mountain West	5:00 PM	8
10		7/29/2013	Northwest	5:00 PM	35
11		7/29/2013	Central	5:00 PM	14
12		7/29/2013	Northeast	6:00 PM	119
13		7/29/2013	Atlantic	6:00 PM	44
14		7/29/2013	Southeast	6:00 PM	37
15		7/29/2013	North Central	6:00 PM	28
16		7/29/2013	Midwest	6:00 PM	45
17		7/29/2013	Southwest	6:00 PM	75
18		7/29/2013	Mountain West	6:00 PM	10
19		7/29/2013	Northwest	6:00 PM	44
20		7/29/2013	Central	6:00 PM	17

16   In the **Themes** group, click the **Themes** button, and then click **Save Current Theme** to open the **Save Current Theme** dialog box.

17   In the **File name** field, enter Verdana Office, and then click **Save** to save your theme.

18   In the **Themes** group, click the **Themes** button, and then click **Organic** to apply the new theme to your workbook.

❌ CLEAN UP Close the HourlyTracking workbook, saving your changes if you want to.

Making numbers easier to read

Changing the format of the cells in your worksheet can make your data much easier to read, both by setting data labels apart from the actual data and by adding borders to define the boundaries between labels and data even more clearly. Of course, using formatting options to change the font and appearance of a cell's contents doesn't help with idiosyncratic data types such as dates, phone numbers, or currency values.

As an example, consider US phone numbers. These numbers are 10 digits long and have a 3-digit area code, a 3-digit exchange, and a 4-digit line number written in the form (###) ###-####. Although it's certainly possible to enter a phone number with the expected formatting in a cell, it's much simpler to enter a sequence of 10 digits and have Excel change the data's appearance.

You can tell Excel to expect a phone number in a cell by displaying the Number page of the Format Cells dialog box and displaying the formats available for the Special category.

Clicking Phone Number in the Type list tells Excel to format 10-digit numbers in the standard phone number format. You can view this in operation if you compare the contents of the active cell and the contents of the formula box for a cell with the Phone Number formatting.

C3	▼	:	×	✓	f_x	5035550109			

	A	B	C	D	E
1					
2			**Phone Number**		
3			(503) 555-0109		
4					
5					

TROUBLESHOOTING If you enter a 9-digit number in a field that expects a phone number, no error message will appear; instead, a 2-digit area code appears. For example, the number 425550012 would be displayed as (42) 555-0012. An 11-digit number would be displayed with a 4-digit area code. If the phone number doesn't look right, you probably left out a digit or included an extra one, so you should make sure your entry is correct.

Just as you can instruct Excel to expect a phone number in a cell, you can also have it expect a date or a currency amount. You can make those changes from the Format Cells dialog box by choosing either the Date category or the Currency category. Using the Date category, you can pick the format for the date (and determine whether the date's appearance changes due to the Locale setting of the operating system on the computer viewing the workbook). In a similar vein, selecting the Currency category displays controls to set the number of places after the decimal point, the currency symbol to use, and the way in which Excel should display negative numbers.

TIP With the Excel user interface, you can make the most common format changes by displaying the Home tab of the ribbon and then, in the Number group, either clicking a button representing a built-in format or selecting a format from the Number Format list.

You can also create a custom numeric format to add a word or phrase to a number in a cell. For example, you can add the phrase *per month* to a cell that has a formula that calculates average monthly sales for a year to ensure that you and your colleagues will recognize the figure as a monthly average. To create a custom number format, click the Home tab, and then click the Number dialog box launcher (found at the lower-right corner of the Number group on the ribbon) to display the Format Cells dialog box. Then, if necessary, click the Number tab.

In the Category list, click Custom to display the available custom number formats in the Type list. You can then click the base format you want and modify it in the Type box. For example, clicking the 0.00 format causes Excel to format any number in a cell with two digits to the right of the decimal point.

TIP The zeros in the format indicate that the position in the format can accept any number as a valid value.

To customize the format, click in the Type box and add any symbols or text you want to the format. For example, entering a dollar ($) sign to the left of the existing format and then entering *"per month"* (including quote marks) to the right of the existing format causes the number 1,500 to be displayed as *$1500.00 per month*.

IMPORTANT You need to enclose any text to be displayed as part of the format in quotes so that Excel recognizes the text as a string to be displayed in the cell.

In this exercise, you'll assign date, phone number, and currency formats to ranges of cells.

 SET UP You need the ExecutiveSearch workbook located in the Chapter04 practice file folder to complete this exercise. Open the workbook, and then follow the steps.

1   Click cell **A3**.

2   On the **Home** tab, click the **Font** dialog box launcher to open the **Format Cells** dialog box.

3   If necessary, click the **Number** tab.

4   In the **Category** list, click **Date** to display the available date formats in the **Type** list.

```
Format Cells                                    ?   ×

Number  Alignment  Font  Border  Fill  Protection

Category:
  General        ⌃   Sample
  Number               8/25/2013
  Currency
  Accounting         Type:
  Date               *3/14/2012                         ⌃
  Time               *Wednesday, March 14, 2012
  Percentage         3/14
  Fraction           3/14/12
  Scientific         03/14/12
  Text               14-Mar
  Special            14-Mar-12                           ⌄
  Custom
                     Locale (location):
                     English (United States)             ⌄
                ⌄

  Date formats display date and time serial numbers as date values.  Date formats that begin with
  an asterisk (*) respond to changes in regional date and time settings that are specified for the
  operating system. Formats without an asterisk are not affected by operating system settings.


                                            OK          Cancel
```

5   In the **Type** list, click **3/14/12**.

6   Click **OK** to display the contents of cell **A3** using the new format.

7   Click cell **G3**.

8   On the **Home** tab, in the **Number** group, click the **Number Format** arrow, and then click **More Number Formats**.

9   If necessary, click the **Number** tab in the **Format Cells** dialog box.

10   In the **Category** list, click **Special** to display the available special formats in the **Type** list.

11   In the **Type** list, click **Phone Number**, and then click **OK** to display the contents of the cell as **(425) 555-0102**, matching the format you selected, and to close the **Format Cells** dialog box.

12   Click cell **H3**.

13   Click the **Font** dialog box launcher.

14   If necessary, click the **Number** tab in the **Format Cells** dialog box.

15   In the **Category** list, click **Custom** to display the available custom formats in the **Type** list.

16   In the **Type** list, click the **#,##0** item to display #,##0 in the **Type** box.

17   In the **Type** box, click to the left of the existing format, and enter $. Then click to the right of the format, and type " before bonuses" (note the space after the opening quote).

18   Click **OK** to close the dialog box.

D	E	F	G	H	I
City	**State**	**ZIP**	**Phone**	**CurrentSalary**	
Redmond	WA	22841	(425) 555-0102	$255,000 before bonuses	

✖ CLEAN UP Close the ExecutiveSearch workbook, saving your changes if you want to.

Changing the appearance of data based on its value

By recording package volumes, vehicle miles, and other business data in a worksheet, you can make important decisions about your operations. As explained earlier in this chapter, you can change the appearance of data labels and the worksheet itself to make interpreting your data easier.

Another way you can make your data easier to interpret is to have Excel change the appearance of your data based on its value. These formats are called *conditional formats* because the data must meet certain conditions, defined in conditional formatting rules, to have a format applied to it. For example, if chief operating officer Lori Penor wanted to highlight any Thursdays with higher-than-average weekday package volumes, she could define a conditional format that tests the value in the cell recording total sales and changes the format of the cell's contents when the condition is met.

To create a conditional format, you select the cells to which you want to apply the format, display the Home tab, and then in the Styles group, click Conditional Formatting to display a menu of possible conditional formats. In Excel, you can define conditional formats that change how the program displays data in cells that contain values above or below the average values of the related cells, that contain values near the top or bottom of the value range, or that contain values duplicated elsewhere in the selected range.

When you select which kind of condition to create, Excel opens a dialog box that contains fields and controls that you can use to define your rule. To display all of the rules for the selected cells, display the Home tab, and then in the Styles group, click Conditional Formatting. On the menu, click Manage Rules to display the Conditional Formatting Rules Manager dialog box.

With the Conditional Formatting Rules Manager, you can control your conditional formats in the following ways:

- Create a new rule by clicking the **New Rule** button.
- Change a rule by clicking the rule and then clicking the **Edit Rule** button.
- Remove a rule by clicking the rule and then clicking the **Delete Rule** button.
- Move a rule up or down in the order by clicking the rule and then clicking the **Move Up** button or **Move Down** button.
- Control whether Excel continues evaluating conditional formats after it finds a rule to apply by selecting or clearing a rule's **Stop If True** check box.
- Save any new rules and close the **Conditional Formatting Rules Manager** by clicking **OK**.
- Save any new rules without closing the **Conditional Formatting Rules Manager** by clicking **Apply**.
- Discard any unsaved changes by clicking **Cancel**.

TIP Clicking the New Rule button in the Conditional Formatting Rules Manager opens the New Formatting Rule dialog box. The commands in the New Formatting Rule dialog box duplicate the options displayed when you click the Conditional Formatting button in the Styles group on the Home tab.

After you create a rule, you can change the format applied if the rule is true by clicking the rule and then clicking the Edit Rule button to display the Edit Formatting Rule dialog box.

In that dialog box, click the Format button to display the Format Cells dialog box. After you define your format, click OK to display the rule.

Edit Formatting Rule	?	×

Select a Rule Type:

- Format all cells based on their values
- Format only cells that contain
- Format only top or bottom ranked values
- Format only values that are above or below average
- Format only unique or duplicate values
- Use a formula to determine which cells to format

Edit the Rule Description:

Format only cells with:

Cell Value ∨	greater than ∨	=0.00023	📑

Preview: AaBbCcYyZz   Format...

OK   Cancel

IMPORTANT Excel doesn't check to make sure that your conditions are logically consistent, so you need to be sure that you plan and enter your conditions correctly.

Using Excel, you can also create three other types of conditional formats: data bars, color scales, and icon sets. Data bars summarize the relative magnitude of values in a cell range by extending a band of color across the cell.

Distribution Capacity	
Northeast	47%
Atlantic	75%
Southeast	39%
North Central	54%
Midwest	40%
Southwest	73%
Mountain West	51%
Northwest	69%
Central	41%

You can create two types of data bars in Excel 2013: solid fill and gradient fill. When data bars were introduced in Excel 2007, they filled cells with a color band that decreased in intensity as it moved across the cell. This gradient fill pattern made it a bit difficult to determine the relative length of two data bars because the end points weren't as distinct as they would have been if the bars were a solid color. In Excel 2013, you can choose between a solid fill pattern, which makes the right edge of the bars easier to discern, and a gradient fill, which you can use if you share your workbook with colleagues who use Excel 2007.

Excel also draws data bars differently than was done in Excel 2007. Excel 2007 drew a very short data bar for the lowest value in a range and a very long data bar for the highest value. The problem was that similar values could be represented by data bars of very different lengths if there wasn't much variance among the values in the conditionally formatted range. In Excel 2013, data bars compare values based on their distance from zero, so similar values are summarized by using data bars of similar lengths.

TIP Excel 2013 data bars summarize negative values by using bars that extend to the left of a baseline that the program draws in a cell. You can control how your data bars summarize negative values by clicking the Negative Value And Axis button, which can be accessed from either the New Formatting Rule dialog box or the Edit Formatting Rule dialog box.

Color scales compare the relative magnitude of values in a cell range by applying colors from a two-color or three-color set to your cells. The intensity of a cell's color reflects the value's tendency toward the top or bottom of the values in the range.

Distribution Capacity	
Northeast	47%
Atlantic	75%
Southeast	39%
North Central	54%
Midwest	40%
Southwest	73%
Mountain West	51%
Northwest	69%
Central	41%

Icon sets are collections of three, four, or five images that Excel displays when certain rules are met.

Distribution Capacity		
Northeast	◙	47%
Atlantic	◙	75%
Southeast	◙	39%
North Central	◙	54%
Midwest	◙	40%
Southwest	◙	73%
Mountain West	◙	51%
Northwest	◙	69%
Central	◙	41%

When icon sets were introduced in Excel 2007, you could apply an icon set as a whole, but you couldn't create custom icon sets or choose to have Excel 2007 display no icon if the value in a cell met a criterion. In Excel 2013, you can display any icon from any set for any criterion or display no icon.

When you click a color scale or icon set in the Conditional Formatting Rules Manager and then click the Edit Rule button, you can control when Excel applies a color or icon to your data.

IMPORTANT Be sure that you do not include cells that contain summary formulas in your conditionally formatted ranges. The values, which could be much higher or lower than your regular cell data, could throw off your comparisons.

In this exercise, you'll create a series of conditional formats to change the appearance of data in worksheet cells that display the package volume and delivery exception rates of a regional distribution center.

SET UP You need the Dashboard workbook located in the Chapter04 practice file folder to complete this exercise. Open the workbook, and then follow the steps.

1   Select cells **C4:C12**.

2   On the **Home** tab, in the **Styles** group, click **Conditional Formatting**. On the menu, point to **Color Scales**, and then in the top row of the palette, click the second pattern from the left to apply the format to the selected range.

Package Exception Rate	
Northeast	0.003%
Atlantic	0.008%
Southeast	0.013%
North Central	0.004%
Midwest	0.018%
Southwest	0.001%
Mountain West	0.045%
Northwest	0.002%
Central	0.038%

3   Select cells **F4:F12**.

4   On the **Home** tab, in the **Styles** group, click **Conditional Formatting**. On the menu, point to **Data Bars**, and then, in the **Solid Fill** group, click the orange data bar format to apply the format to the selected range.

5   Select cells **I4:I12**.

6   On the **Home** tab, in the **Styles** group, click **Conditional Formatting**. On the menu, point to **Icon Sets**, and then in the left column of the list of formats, click the three traffic lights that have black borders to apply that format to the selected cells.

Distribution Capacity		
Northeast	⬤	47%
Atlantic	⬤	75%
Southeast	⬤	39%
North Central	⬤	54%
Midwest	⬤	40%
Southwest	⬤	73%
Mountain West	⬤	51%
Northwest	⬤	69%
Central	⬤	41%

7   With the range **I4:I12** still selected, on the **Home** tab, in the **Styles** group, click **Conditional Formatting**, and then click **Manage Rules** to open the **Conditional Formatting Rules Manager**.

8   Click the **Icon Set** rule, and then click **Edit Rule** to open the **Edit Formatting Rule** dialog box.

Edit Formatting Rule

Select a Rule Type:
- Format all cells based on their values
- Format only cells that contain
- Format only top or bottom ranked values
- Format only values that are above or below average
- Format only unique or duplicate values
- Use a formula to determine which cells to format

Edit the Rule Description:

Format all cells based on their values:

Format Style: Icon Sets   Reverse Icon Order

Icon Style: [icons]   ☐ Show Icon Only

Display each icon according to these rules:

Icon				Value		Type	
●	when value is	>=		67		Percent	
●	when < 67 and	>=		33		Percent	
●	when < 33						

OK   Cancel

9   Click the **Reverse Icon Order** button to reconfigure the rules so the red light icon is at the top and the green light icon is at the bottom.

10   In the red light icon's row, in the **Type** list, click **Number**.

11   In the red light icon's **Value** field, enter 0.7.

12   In the yellow light icon's row, in the **Type** list, click **Number**.

13   In the yellow light icon **Value** field, enter 0.5.

14   Click **OK** twice to close the **Edit Formatting Rule** dialog box and the **Conditional Formatting Rules Manager** to apply the format to the selected cell range.

15   Click cell **C15**.

16   On the **Home** tab, in the **Styles** group, click **Conditional Formatting**. On the menu, point to **Highlight Cells Rules**, and then click **Less Than** to open the **Less Than** dialog box.

17   In the left field, enter 96%.

18   In the **With** list, click **Red text**.

19 Click **OK** to close the **Less Than** dialog box. Excel displays the text in cell **C15** in red.

	A	B	C	D	E	F	G	H	I	J
1										
2										
3		**Package Exception Rate**			**Package Volume**			**Distribution Capacity**		
4		Northeast	0.003%		Northeast	1,912,447		Northeast		47%
5		Atlantic	0.008%		Atlantic	1,933,574		Atlantic		75%
6		Southeast	0.013%		Southeast	1,333,292		Southeast		39%
7		North Central	0.004%		North Central	1,811,459		North Central		54%
8		Midwest	0.018%		Midwest	1,140,803		Midwest		40%
9		Southwest	0.001%		Southwest	1,911,884		Southwest		73%
10		Mountain West	0.045%		Mountain West	1,787,293		Mountain West		51%
11		Northwest	0.002%		Northwest	1,631,350		Northwest		69%
12		Central	0.038%		Central	1,660,040		Central		41%
13										
14										
15		**Customer Satisfaction**	88%							
16										

✖ CLEAN UP **Close the Dashboard workbook, saving your changes if you want to.**

Adding images to worksheets

Establishing a strong corporate identity helps customers remember your organization in addition to the products and services you offer. Setting aside the obvious need for sound management, two important physical attributes of a strong retail business are a well-conceived shop space and an eye-catching, easy-to-remember logo. After you or your graphic artist has created a logo, you should add the logo to all your documents, especially any that might be viewed by your customers. Not only does the logo mark the documents as coming from your company, it also serves as an advertisement, encouraging anyone who views your worksheets to call or visit your company.

One way to add a picture to a worksheet is to display the Insert tab, and then in the Illustrations group, click Picture. Clicking Picture displays the Insert Picture dialog box, from which you can locate the picture you want to add from your hard disk. When you insert a picture, the Format tool tab appears on the ribbon. You can use the tools on the Format tool tab to change the picture's contrast, brightness, and other attributes. With the controls in the Picture Styles group, you can place a border around the picture, change the picture's shape, or change a picture's effects (such as shadow, reflection, or three-dimensional effects). Other tools, found in the Arrange and Size groups, enable you to rotate, reposition, and resize the picture.

▲	A	B	C	D	E	F	G	H	I
1									
2		**Call Volume**							
3		Northeast	13,769						
4		Atlantic	19,511						
5		Southeast	11,111						
6		North Central	24,972						
7		Midwest	11,809						
8		Southwest	20,339						
9		Mountain West	20,127						
10		Northwest	12,137						
11		Central	20,047						
12									
13									

You can also resize a picture by clicking it and then dragging one of the handles that appears on the graphic. If you accidentally resize a graphic by dragging a handle, just click the Undo button to remove your change.

Excel 2013 includes a built-in capability that you can use to remove the background of an image you insert into a workbook. To do so, click the image and then, on the Format tool tab, in the Adjust group, click Remove Background. When you do, Excel attempts to identify the foreground and background of the image.

You can drag the handles on the inner square of the background removal tool to change how the tool analyzes the image. When you have adjusted the outline to identify the elements of the image you want to keep, click the Keep Changes button on the Background Removal tool tab to complete the operation.

If you want to generate a repeating image in the background of a worksheet to form a tiled pattern behind your worksheet's data, you can display the Page Layout tab, and then in the Page Setup group, click Background. In the Insert Pictures dialog box, click Browse to open the Sheet Background dialog box, navigate to the folder that contains the image you want to serve as the background for your worksheet, click the image, and click OK.

TIP To remove a background image from a worksheet, display the Page Layout tab, and then in the Page Setup group, click Delete Background.

To achieve a watermark-type effect that has words displayed behind the worksheet data, save the watermark information as an image, and then use the image as the sheet background; you could also insert the image in the header or footer, and then resize or scale it to position the watermark information where you want it.

In this exercise, you'll add an image to an existing worksheet, change its location on the worksheet, reduce the size of the image, and then set another image as a repeating background for the worksheet.

 SET UP You need the CallCenter workbook and the phone and texture images located in the Chapter04 practice file folder to complete this exercise. Open the workbook, and then follow the steps.

1   On the **Insert** tab, in the **Illustrations** group, click **Pictures** to open the **Insert Picture** dialog box.

2   Navigate to the **Chapter04** practice file folder, and then double-click the **phone** image file to add the image to your worksheet.

3   On the **Format** tool tab, in the **Adjust** group, click **Remove Background** to have Excel attempt to separate the image's foreground from its background.

4   Drag the handles at the upper-left and lower-right corners of the outline until the entire phone, including the cord, is within the frame.

5   On the **Background Removal** tab, click **Keep Changes** to remove the highlighted
     image elements.

6   Move the image to the upper-left corner of the worksheet, click and hold the handle
     at the lower-right corner of the image, and drag it up and to the left until the image
     no longer obscures the **Call Volume** label.

	A	B	C	D
1				
2		Call Volume		
3		Northeast	13,769	
4		Atlantic	19,511	
5		Southeast	11,111	
6		North Central	24,972	
7		Midwest	11,809	
8		Southwest	20,339	
9		Mountain West	20,127	
10		Northwest	12,137	
11		Central	20,047	
12				

7   On the **Page Layout** tab, in the **Page Setup** group, click **Background** to open the **Insert Pictures** dialog box.

8   Next to **From a File**, click **Browse** to open the **Sheet Background** dialog box.

9   Navigate to the **Chapter04** practice file folder, and then double-click the **texture** image file to repeat the image as a background pattern.

◢	A	B	C	D
1				
2		**Call Volume**		
3		Northeast	13,769	
4		Atlantic	19,511	
5		Southeast	11,111	
6		North Central	24,972	
7		Midwest	11,809	
8		Southwest	20,339	
9		Mountain West	20,127	
10		Northwest	12,137	
11		Central	20,047	
12				

10 On the **Page Layout** tab, in the **Page Setup** group, click **Delete Background** to remove the background image.

❌ CLEAN UP Close the CallCenter workbook, saving your changes if you want to.

Key points

- If you don't like the default font in which Excel displays your data, you can change it.

- You can use cell formatting, including borders, alignment, and fill colors, to emphasize certain cells in your worksheets. This emphasis is particularly useful for making column and row labels stand out from the data.

- Excel comes with several existing styles that you can use to change the appearance of individual cells. You can also create new styles to make formatting your workbooks easier.

- If you want to apply the formatting from one cell to another cell, use the Format Painter to copy the format quickly.

- You can choose from quite a few built-in document themes and Excel table formats to apply to groups of cells. If you find one you like, use it and save yourself lots of formatting time.

- Using conditional formats, you can set rules so that Excel changes the appearance of a cell's contents based on its value.

- Adding images can make your worksheets more visually appealing and make your data easier to understand. Excel 2013 greatly enhances your ability to manage your images without leaving Excel.

4

Chapter at a glance

Restrict

Limit data that appears on your screen,
page 146

◢	A	B	C	D
1				
2		Date	Exceptions	
10		3/8/2013	53	
11		3/9/2013	73	
12		3/10/2013	64	
13		3/11/2013	53	
14		3/12/2013	47	
15		3/13/2013	91	
16		3/14/2013	91	
34				

Filter

Filter Excel table data by using slicers,
page 153

◢	A	B	C		D	E	F		G	H	I	J
1	Month	Region	Packages		Month				Region			
2	January	North Central	132,897		January				North Central			
3	February	North Central	320,203		February				Northeast			
4	March	North Central	309,410		March				Northwest			
5	April	North Central	433,735		April							
6	May	North Central	326,941		May							
7	June	North Central	147,505		June							
8	July	North Central	460,907		July							
9	August	North Central	404,524		August							
10	September	North Central	237,127		September							
11	October	North Central	358,402		October							
12	November	North Central	435,538		November							
13	December	North Central	208,264		December							
14	January	Northeast	497,347									
15	February	Northeast	149,755									
16	March	Northeast	122,280									
17	April	Northeast	178,259									
18	May	Northeast	231,714									
19	June	Northeast	473,094									
20	July	Northeast	139,887									

Manipulate

Manipulate worksheet data,
page 158

D	E	F	G	H	I	J
						Summary
Date	Center	Route	Cost	Investigate		$ 15.76
3/30/2013	Northeast	RT310	$ 12.08	No		
3/30/2013	Midwest	RT892	$ 14.88	Yes		
3/30/2013	Northwest	RT424	$ 13.61	No		
3/30/2013	Northeast	RT995	$ 10.64	No		
3/30/2013	Midwest	RT827	$ 15.26	No		
3/30/2013	Central	RT341	$ 18.86	No		
3/30/2013	Central	RT864	$ 15.71	Yes		
3/30/2013	Central	RT277	$ 18.50	No		
3/31/2013	South	RT983	$ 19.87	No		
3/31/2013	Southwest	RT827	$ 18.01	No		
3/31/2013	South	RT942	$ 19.85	No		
3/31/2013	South	RT940	$ 15.61	No		
3/31/2013	Southwest	RT751	$ 12.84	No		
4/1/2013	Midwest	RT436	$ 13.94	No		
4/1/2013	Midwest	RT758	$ 17.55	No		

Define

Define valid sets of values for ranges of cells,
page 166

Data Validation dialog box — Settings tab:
- Validation criteria
- Allow: Whole number
- ☑ Ignore blank
- Data: between
- Minimum: 1000
- Maximum: 2000
- ☐ Apply these changes to all other cells with the same settings
- Clear All — OK — Cancel

Focusing on specific data by using filters

IN THIS CHAPTER, YOU WILL LEARN HOW TO

- Limit data that appears on your screen.

- Filter Excel table data by using slicers.

- Manipulate worksheet data.

- Define valid sets of values for ranges of cells.

With Microsoft Excel 2013, you can manage huge data collections, but storing more than 1 million rows of data doesn't help you make business decisions unless you have the ability to focus on the most important data in a worksheet. Focusing on the most relevant data in a worksheet facilitates decision making, whether that data represents the 10 busiest days in a month or revenue streams that you might need to reevaluate. Excel offers a number of powerful and flexible tools with which you can limit the data displayed in your worksheet. When your worksheet displays the subset of data you need to make a decision, you can perform calculations on that data. You can discover what percentage of monthly revenue was earned in the 10 best days in the month, find your total revenue for particular days of the week, or locate the slowest business day of the month.

Just as you can limit the data displayed by your worksheets, you can create validation rules that limit the data entered into them as well. By setting rules for data entered into cells, you can catch many of the most common data entry errors, such as entering values that are too small or too large, or attempting to enter a word in a cell that requires a number. If you add a validation rule to worksheet cells after data has been entered into them, you can circle any invalid data so that you know what to correct.

In this chapter, you'll limit the data that appears on your screen, manipulate worksheet data, and create validation rules that limit data entry to appropriate values.

Limiting data that appears on your screen

Excel spreadsheets can hold as much data as you need them to, but you might not want to work with all the data in a worksheet at the same time. For example, you might want to review the revenue figures for your company during the first third, second third, and final third of a month. You can limit the data shown on a worksheet by creating a filter, which is a rule that selects rows to be shown in a worksheet.

To create a filter, you click a cell in the data you want to filter and then, on the Home tab, in the Editing group, click Sort & Filter and then click Filter. When you do, Excel displays a filter arrow at the right edge of the top cell in each column of the data. The arrow indicates that the Excel AutoFilter capability is active.

> **IMPORTANT** When you turn on filtering, Excel treats the cells in the active cell's column as a range. To ensure that the filtering works properly, you should always have a label at the top of the column you want to filter. If you don't, Excel treats the first value in the list as the label and doesn't include it in the list of values by which you can filter the data.

Clicking the filter arrow displays a menu of filtering options and a list of the unique values in the column. The first few commands in the list are sorting commands, followed by the Clear Filter command and then the Filter By Color command. The next command that appears in the list depends on the type of data in the column. For example, if the column contains a set of dates, the command will be Date Filters. Clicking the command displays a list of commands specific to that data type.

	A	B	C	D	E	F
2		**ExceptionID** ▾	**PackageID** ▾	**Date** ▾	Equals...	
3		EX10	⬆ Sort Oldest to Newest		Before...	
4		EX10	⬇ Sort Newest to Oldest		After...	
5		EX10	Sort by Color ▸		Between...	
6		EX10				
7		EX10	⧖ Clear Filter From "Date"		Tomorrow	
8		EX10	Filter by Color ▸		Today	
9		EX10	Date Filters ▸		Yesterday	
10		EX10				
11		EX10	Search (All) 🔍 ▾		Next Week	
12		EX10	☑ (Select All)		This Week	
13		EX10	⊟ ☑ 2013		Last Week	
14		EX10	⊞ ☑ March		Next Month	
15		EX10	⊞ ☑ April		This Month	
16		EX10			Last Month	
17		EX10			Next Quarter	
18		EX10			This Quarter	
19		EX10			Last Quarter	
20		EX10			Next Year	
21		EX10	OK Cancel		This Year	
22		EX10			Last Year	
23		EX1000021	PI34920139	4/2/2013	Year to Date	
24		EX1000022	PI34920140	4/2/2013	All Dates in the Period ▸	
25		EX1000023	PI34920141	4/2/2013	Custom Filter...	
26		EX1000024	PI34920142	4/2/2013		

| ◂ ▸ | **ByRoute** | MarchDailyCount | ⊕ |

READY

TIP When a column contains several types of data, the filter command becomes Number Filters.

When you click a filtering option, Excel displays a dialog box in which you can define the filter's criteria. As an example, you could create a filter that displays only dates after 3/31/2013.

	A	B	C	D	E	F
2		ExceptionID ▾	PackageID ▾	Date ▾	Center ▾	Route ▾
16		EX1000014	PI34920132	4/1/2013	Midwest	RT436
17		EX1000015	PI34920133	4/1/2013	Midwest	RT758
18		EX1000016	PI34920134	4/1/2013	Midwest	RT529
19		EX1000017	PI34920135	4/1/2013	Northeast	RT243
20		EX1000018	PI34920136	4/1/2013	Northeast	RT189
21		EX1000019	PI34920137	4/1/2013	Northwest	RT714
22		EX1000020	PI34920138	4/2/2013	Central	RT151
23		EX1000021	PI34920139	4/2/2013	Midwest	RT543
24		EX1000022	PI34920140	4/2/2013	Southwest	RT208
25		EX1000023	PI34920141	4/2/2013	South	RT145
26		EX1000024	PI34920142	4/2/2013	Central	RT250
27		EX1000025	PI34920143	4/2/2013	Midwest	RT852
28						

If you want to display the highest or lowest values in a data column, you can create a Top 10 filter. Choosing the Top 10 command from the menu doesn't just limit the display to the top 10 values. Instead, it opens the Top 10 AutoFilter dialog box. From within this dialog box, you can choose whether to show values from the top or bottom of the list, define the number of items you want to display, and choose whether the number in the middle box indicates the number of items or the percentage of items to be shown when the filter is applied. By using the Top 10 AutoFilter dialog box, you can find your top 10 salespeople or identify the top 5 percent of your customers.

Excel 2013 includes a capability called the *search filter*, which you can use to type a search string that Excel uses to identify which items to display in an Excel table or a data list. To use a search filter, click a column's filter arrow and start entering a character string in the Search box. As you enter the character string, Excel limits the items displayed at the bottom of the filter panel to those that contain the character or characters you've entered. When the filter list's items represent the values you want to display, click OK.

When you point to Text Filters (or Date Filters for date values or Number Filters for number values) and then click Custom Filter, you can define a rule that Excel uses to decide which rows to show after the filter is applied. For instance, you can create a rule that determines that only days with package volumes of less than 100,000 should be shown in your worksheet. With those results in front of you, you might be able to determine whether the weather or another factor resulted in slower business on those days.

Excel indicates that a column has a filter applied by changing the appearance of the column's filter arrow to include an icon that looks like a funnel. After you finish examining your data by using a filter, you can remove the filter by clicking the column's filter arrow and then clicking Clear Filter. To turn off filtering entirely and remove the filter arrows, display the Home tab and then, in the Editing group, click Sort & Filter and then click Filter.

In this exercise, you'll filter worksheet data by using a series of AutoFilter commands, create a filter showing the five days with the highest delivery exception counts in a month, create a search filter, and create a custom filter.

SET UP You need the PackageExceptions workbook located in the Chapter05 practice file folder to complete this exercise. Open the workbook, and then follow the steps.

1   On the **ByRoute** worksheet, click any cell in the cell range **B2:F27**.

2   On the **Home** tab, in the **Editing** group, click **Sort & Filter**, and then click **Filter** to display a filter arrow in each column's header cell.

3   Click the **Date** column filter arrow and then, from the menu that appears, clear the **March** check box. When you do, Excel removes the check from the **March** check box and changes the state of the **Select All** and **2013** check boxes to indicate that some items within those categories have been filtered.

	A	B	C	D	E	F
2		ExceptionID ▾	PackageID ▾	Date ▾	Center ▾	Route ▾
3		EX10 ᴬ↓ Sort Oldest to Newest			Northeast	RT310
4		EX10 ᶻ↓ Sort Newest to Oldest			Midwest	RT892
5		EX10 Sort by Color ▸			Northwest	RT424
6		EX10			Northeast	RT995
7		EX10 ▾ₓ Clear Filter From "Date"			Midwest	RT827
8		EX10 Filter by Color ▸			Central	RT341
9		EX10 Date Filters ▸			Central	RT864
10		EX10			Central	RT277
11		EX10 Search (All) 🔍 ⌄			South	RT983
12		EX10 ▣ (Select All)			Southwest	RT827
13		EX10 ⊟ ▣ 2013			South	RT942
14		EX10 ⊞ ☐ March			South	RT940
15		EX10 ⊞ ☑ April			Southwest	RT751
16		EX10			Midwest	RT436
17		EX10			Midwest	RT758
18		EX10			Midwest	RT529
19		EX10			Northeast	RT243
20		EX10			Northeast	RT189
21		EX10 OK Cancel			Northwest	RT714
22		EX10			Central	RT151
23		EX1000021	PI34920139	4/2/2013	Midwest	RT543

4   Click **OK** to hide all rows that contain a date from the month of March.

5   Click the **Center** column filter arrow and then, from the menu that appears, clear the **Select All** check box to clear all the check boxes in the list.

6   Select the **Midwest** check box, and then click **OK** to display only those exceptions that occurred in the Midwest distribution center during the month of April.

A	B	C	D	E	F
	ExceptionID ▼	PackageID ▼	Date ⊤	Center ⊤	Route ▼
	EX1000014	PI34920132	4/1/2013	Midwest	RT436
	EX1000015	PI34920133	4/1/2013	Midwest	RT758
	EX1000016	PI34920134	4/1/2013	Midwest	RT529
	EX1000021	PI34920139	4/2/2013	Midwest	RT543
	EX1000025	PI34920143	4/2/2013	Midwest	RT852

7   On the **Home** tab, in the **Editing** group, click **Sort & Filter**, and then click **Clear** to clear all active filters but leave the filter arrows in place.

8   Click the **Route** column header's filter arrow, and then enter **RT9** in the **Search** box to narrow the filter list so it displays only those routes with an identifier that includes the characters *RT9*.

9   Click **OK** to apply the filter and display exceptions that occurred on routes with identifiers that contain the string *RT9*.

10   Click the **MarchDailyCount** sheet tab to display its worksheet.

11   Click any cell in the Excel table.

12   Click the **Exceptions** column filter arrow, point to **Number Filters**, and then click **Top 10** to open the **Top 10 AutoFilter** dialog box.

13   In the middle field, enter **5** and then click **OK** to display the table rows that contain the five highest values in the **Exceptions** column.

	A	B	C	D
1				
2		Date ▾	Exceptions ▾	
18		3/16/2013	144	
21		3/19/2013	128	
22		3/20/2013	144	
23		3/21/2013	138	
24		3/22/2013	137	
34				

14   Click the **Exceptions** column filter arrow, and then click **Clear Filter from "Exceptions"** to remove the filter.

15   Click the **Date** column filter arrow, point to **Date Filters**, and then click **Custom Filter** to open the **Custom AutoFilter** dialog box.

16   In the upper-left list, click **is after or equal to**.

17   In the upper-right list, click **3/8/2013**.

18   In the lower-left list, click **is before or equal to**.

19   In the lower-right list, click **3/14/2013**.

20   Click **OK**. Because you left the **And** option selected, Excel displays all table rows that contain a date from 3/8/2013 to 3/14/2013, inclusive.

	A	B	C	D
1				
2		Date ▾	Exceptions ▾	
10		3/8/2013	53	
11		3/9/2013	73	
12		3/10/2013	64	
13		3/11/2013	53	
14		3/12/2013	47	
15		3/13/2013	91	
16		3/14/2013	91	
34				
35				

21   On the **Quick Access Toolbar**, click the **Undo** button to remove your filter and restore the table to its unfiltered state.

 CLEAN UP Close the PackageExceptions workbook, saving your changes if you want to.

Filtering Excel table data by using slicers

In versions of Excel prior to Excel 2013, the only visual indication that you have applied a filter to an Excel table column is the indicator added to a column's filter arrow. The indicator lets users know that there is an active filter applied to that column but provides no information about which values are displayed and which are hidden. Beginning with Excel 2010, you could use slicers to provide a visual indication of which items are currently displayed or hidden in a PivotTable. Excel 2013 extends that ability to filtering an Excel table.

To create a slicer, click any cell in an Excel table and then, on the Insert tab, in the Filters group, click Slicer to display the Insert Slicers dialog box.

Select the check box next to the columns for which you want to create a slicer, and click OK. When you do, Excel displays a slicer for each column you identified.

	A	B	C	D	E	F	G
1	Month	Region	Packages				
2	January	North Central	132,897	Region			
3	February	North Central	320,203				
4	March	North Central	309,410	North Central			
5	April	North Central	433,735	Northeast			
6	May	North Central	326,941	Northwest			
7	June	North Central	147,505				
8	July	North Central	460,907				
9	August	North Central	404,524				
10	September	North Central	237,127				
11	October	North Central	358,402				
12	November	North Central	435,538				
13	December	North Central	208,264				
14	January	Northeast	497,347				
15	February	Northeast	149,755				
16	March	Northeast	122,280				

TIP If you have already applied a filter to the column for which you display a slicer, the slicer reflects the filter's result.

A slicer displays the values within the Excel table column you identified. Any value displayed in color (or gray if you select a gray-and-white color scheme) appears within the table. Values displayed in light gray or white do not appear in the table.

Clicking an item in a slicer changes that item's state—if a value is currently displayed in a table, clicking the value hides it. If it's hidden, clicking its value in the slicer displays it in the table. As with other objects in an Excel workbook, you can use the Shift and Ctrl keys to help define your selections. For example, suppose you create a slicer for the Month column while every month is displayed.

Month	
January	
February	
March	
April	
May	
June	
July	
August	
September	
October	
November	
December	

If you want to hide every month except January, February, and March, you click the January item to hide every month except January. Then hold down the Shift key and click March to have Excel display just the data for the months of January, February, and March. You can then add another month, such as July, to the filter by holding down the Ctrl key and clicking July in the slicer.

	A	B	C	D	E	F	G
1	Month	Region	Packages	Month			
2	January	North Central	132,897	January			
3	February	North Central	320,203				
4	March	North Central	309,410	February			
8	July	North Central	460,907	March			
14	January	Northeast	497,347				
15	February	Northeast	149,755	April			
16	March	Northeast	122,280	May			
20	July	Northeast	139,887	June			
26	January	Northwest	344,484				
27	February	Northwest	466,331	July			
28	March	Northwest	448,363	August			
32	July	Northwest	155,604				
38				September			
39				October			
40				November			
41				December			
42							
43							

To use a slicer to remove a filter, click the Clear Filter button in the upper-right corner of the slicer. If you want to resize a slicer, you can do so by dragging the resize handle in the lower-right corner of the slicer. To delete the slicer, right-click its title bar and then click the menu command that starts with the word *Remove*. For example, the Month column's menu command would be Remove Month.

TIP You can change a slicer's formatting by clicking the slicer and then, on the Slicer Tools Options tool tab, clicking a style in the Slicer Styles gallery.

In this exercise, you'll filter the contents of an Excel table by using a slicer.

SET UP You need the Slicers workbook located in the Chapter05 practice file folder to complete this exercise. Open the workbook, and then follow the steps.

1   Click any cell in the Excel table.

2   On the **Insert** tab of the ribbon, click the **Slicer** button to display the **Insert Slicers** dialog box.

3   Select the **Month** and **Region** check boxes, and then click **OK** to add slicers for the **Month** and **Region** columns.

A	B	C	D	E	F	G	H	I	J

Month	Region	Packages
January	North Central	132,897
February	North Central	320,203
March	North Central	309,410
April	North Central	433,735
May	North Central	326,941
June	North Central	147,505
July	North Central	460,907
August	North Central	404,524
September	North Central	237,127
October	North Central	358,402
November	North Central	435,538
December	North Central	208,264
January	Northeast	497,347
February	Northeast	149,755
March	Northeast	122,280
April	Northeast	178,259
May	Northeast	231,714
June	Northeast	473,094
July	Northeast	139,887

Month: January, February, March, April, May, June, July, August, September, October, November, December

Region: North Central, Northeast, Northwest

4   In the **Month** slicer, click the **January** item and then, holding down the **Shift** key, click the **April** item. Excel updates your table to display values for the months of January, February, March, and April.

5   In the **Region** slicer, click the **North Central** item and then, holding down the **Ctrl** key, click the **Northwest** item. Excel updates your table to display values for the North Central and Northwest regions.

6   Right-click the **Region** slicer and then click **Remove "Region"** to delete it. Excel deletes the slicer and removes its filter from the table.

7   In the **Month** slicer, click the **June** item to display results for the month of June.

8   In the **Month** slicer, click the **Clear Filter** button to remove the filter and display the entire table.

9   Right-click the **Month** slicer and then click **Remove "Month"** to delete it.

✖ CLEAN UP Close the Slicers workbook, saving your changes if you want to.

5

Manipulating worksheet data

Excel offers a wide range of tools you can use to summarize worksheet data. This section shows you how to select rows at random by using the *RAND* and *RANDBETWEEN* functions, how to summarize worksheet data by using the *SUBTOTAL* and *AGGREGATE* functions, and how to display a list of unique values within a data set.

Selecting list rows at random

In addition to filtering the data that is stored in your Excel worksheets, you can choose rows at random from a list. Selecting rows randomly is useful for choosing which customers will receive a special offer, deciding which days of the month to audit, or picking prize winners at an employee party.

To choose rows randomly, you can use the *RAND* function, which generates a random value between 0 and 1, and compare the value it returns with a test value included in the formula. As an example, suppose Consolidated Messenger wanted to offer approximately 30 percent of its customers a discount on their next shipment. A formula that returns a *TRUE* value 30 percent of the time would be *RAND<=0.3*; that is, whenever the random value was between 0 and 0.3, the result would be *TRUE*. You could use this formula to select each row in a list with a probability of 30 percent. A formula that displays *TRUE* when the value is equal to or less than 30 percent, and *FALSE* otherwise, would be *=IF(RAND()<=0.3,"True","False")*.

If you recalculate this formula 10 times, it's very unlikely that exactly three *TRUE* results and seven *FALSE* results would occur. Just as flipping a coin can result in the same result 10 times in a row by chance, so can the *RAND* function's results appear to be off if you only recalculate it a few times. However, if you were to recalculate the function 10,000 times, it is extremely likely that the number of *TRUE* results would be very close to 30 percent.

TIP Because the *RAND* function is a volatile function (it recalculates its results every time you update the worksheet), you should copy the cells that contain the *RAND* function in a formula and paste the formulas' values back into their original cells. To do so, select the cells that contain the *RAND* formulas and press Ctrl+C to copy the cell's contents. Then, on the Home tab, in the Clipboard group, in the Paste list, click Paste Values to replace the formula with its current result. If you don't replace the formulas with their results, you will never have a permanent record of which rows were selected.

The *RANDBETWEEN* function generates a random whole number within a defined range. For example, the formula *=RANDBETWEEN(1,100)* would generate a random integer value from 1 to 100, inclusive. The *RANDBETWEEN* function is very useful for creating sample data collections for presentations. Before the *RANDBETWEEN* function was introduced, you had to create formulas that added, subtracted, multiplied, and divided the results of the *RAND* function, which are always decimal values between 0 and 1, to create your data.

Summarizing worksheets by using hidden and filtered rows

The ability to analyze the data that's most vital to your current needs is important, but there are some limitations to how you can summarize your filtered data by using functions such as *SUM* and *AVERAGE*. One limitation is that any formulas you create that include the *SUM* and *AVERAGE* functions don't change their calculations if some of the rows used in the formula are hidden by the filter.

Excel provides two ways to summarize just the visible cells in a filtered data list. The first method is to use AutoCalculate. To use AutoCalculate, you select the cells you want to summarize. When you do, Excel displays the average of the values in the cells, the sum of the values in the cells, and the number of visible cells (the count) in the selection. You'll find the display on the status bar at the lower edge of the Excel window.

AVERAGE: $15.76   COUNT: 25   SUM: $394.06   ⊞ ▣ ▥ — | + 100%

When you use AutoCalculate, you aren't limited to finding the sum, average, and count of the selected cells. To display the other functions you can use, right-click the status bar and select the function you want from the shortcut menu. If a check mark appears next to a function's name, that function's result appears on the status bar. Clicking a selected function name removes that function from the status bar.

AutoCalculate is great for finding a quick total or average for filtered cells, but it doesn't make the result available in the worksheet. Formulas such as *=SUM(C3:C26)* always consider every cell in the range, regardless of whether you hide a cell's row by right-clicking the row's header and then clicking Hide, so you need to create a formula by using either the *SUBTOTAL* function or the *AGGREGATE* function to summarize just those values that are visible in your worksheet. With the *SUBTOTAL* function, you can summarize every value in a range or summarize only those values in rows you haven't manually hidden. The *SUBTOTAL* function has this syntax: *SUBTOTAL(function_num, ref1, ref2, ...)*. The *function_num* argument holds the number of the operation you want to use to summarize your data. (The operation

5

numbers are summarized in a table later in this section.) The *ref1*, *ref2*, and further arguments represent up to 29 ranges to include in the calculation.

As an example, assume you have a worksheet where you hid rows 20 through 26 manually. In this case, the formula *=SUBTOTAL(9, C3:C26, E3:E26, G3:G26)* would find the sum of all values in the ranges C3:C26, E3:E26, and G3:G26, regardless of whether that range contained any hidden rows. The formula *=SUBTOTAL(109, C3:C26, E3:E26, G3:G26)* would find the sum of all values in cells C3:C19, E3:E19, and G3:G19, ignoring the values in the manually hidden rows.

> **IMPORTANT** Be sure to place your *SUBTOTAL* formula in a row that is even with or above the headers in the range you're filtering. If you don't, your filter might hide the formula's result!

The following table lists the summary operations available for the *SUBTOTAL* formula. Excel displays the available summary operations as part of the Formula AutoComplete functionality, so you don't need to remember the operation numbers or look them up in the Help system.

Operation number (includes hidden values)	Operation number (ignores values in manually hidden rows)	Function	Description
1	101	AVERAGE	Returns the average of the values in the range
2	102	COUNT	Counts the cells in the range that contain a number
3	103	COUNTA	Counts the nonblank cells in the range
4	104	MAX	Returns the largest (maximum) value in the range
5	105	MIN	Returns the smallest (minimum) value in the range
6	106	PRODUCT	Returns the result of multiplying all numbers in the range

Operation number (includes hidden values)	Operation number (ignores values in manually hidden rows)	Function	Description
7	107	STDEV.S	Calculates the standard deviation of the values in the range by examining a sample of the values
8	108	STDEV.P	Calculates the standard deviation of the values in the range by using all the values
9	109	SUM	Returns the result of adding all numbers in the range together
10	110	VAR.S	Calculates the variance of the values in the range by examining a sample of the values
11	111	VAR.P	Calculates the variance of the values in the range by using all of the values

As the previous table shows, the *SUBTOTAL* function has two sets of operations. The first set (operations 1 through 11) represents operations that include hidden values in their summary, and the second set (operations 101 through 111) represents operations that summarize only values visible in the worksheet. Operations 1 through 11 summarize all cells in a range, regardless of whether the range contains any manually hidden rows. By contrast, operations 101 through 111 ignore any values in manually hidden rows. What the *SUBTOTAL* function doesn't do, however, is change its result to reflect rows hidden by using a filter.

The *AGGREGATE* function extends the capabilities of the *SUBTOTAL* function. With it, you can select from a broader range of functions and use another argument to determine which, if any, values to ignore in the calculation. *AGGREGATE* has two possible syntaxes, depending on the summary operation you select. The first syntax is *=AGGREGATE(function_num, options, ref1...)*, which is similar to the syntax of the *SUBTOTAL* function. The other possible syntax, *=AGGREGATE(function_num, options, array, [k])*, is used to create *AGGREGATE* functions that use the *LARGE, SMALL, PERCENTILE.INC, QUARTILE.INC, PERCENTILE.EXC,* and *QUARTILE.EXC* operations.

The following table summarizes the summary operations available for use in the *AGGREGATE* function.

Number	Function	Description
1	AVERAGE	Returns the average of the values in the range.
2	COUNT	Counts the cells in the range that contain a number.
3	COUNTA	Counts the nonblank cells in the range.
4	MAX	Returns the largest (maximum) value in the range.
5	MIN	Returns the smallest (minimum) value in the range.
6	PRODUCT	Returns the result of multiplying all numbers in the range.
7	STDEV.S	Calculates the standard deviation of the values in the range by examining a sample of the values.
8	STDEV.P	Calculates the standard deviation of the values in the range by using all the values.
9	SUM	Returns the result of adding all numbers in the range together.
10	VAR.S	Calculates the variance of the values in the range by examining a sample of the values.
11	VAR.P	Calculates the variance of the values in the range by using all of the values.
12	MEDIAN	Returns the value in the middle of a group of values.
13	MODE.SNGL	Returns the most frequently occurring number from a group of numbers.
14	LARGE	Returns the k-th largest value in a data set; k is specified by using the last function argument. If k is left blank, Excel returns the largest value.
15	SMALL	Returns the k-th smallest value in a data set; k is specified by using the last function argument. If k is left blank, Excel returns the smallest value.
16	PERCENTILE.INC	Returns the k-th percentile of values in a range, where k is a value from 0 to 1, inclusive.

Number	Function	Description
17	QUARTILE.INC	Returns the quartile value of a data set, based on a percentage from 0 to 1, inclusive.
18	PERCENTILE.EXC	Returns the k-th percentile of values in a range, where k is a value from 0 to 1, exclusive.
19	QUARTILE.EXC	Returns the quartile value of a data set, based on a percentage from 0 to 1, exclusive.

With the second argument, *options*, you can select which items the *AGGREGATE* function should ignore. These items can include hidden rows, errors, and *SUBTOTAL* and *AGGREGATE* functions. The following table summarizes the values available for the *options* argument and the effect they have on the function's results.

Number	Description
0	Ignore nested *SUBTOTAL* and *AGGREGATE* functions
1	Ignore hidden rows and nested *SUBTOTAL* and *AGGREGATE* functions
2	Ignore error values and nested *SUBTOTAL* and *AGGREGATE* functions
3	Ignore hidden rows, error values, and nested *SUBTOTAL* and *AGGREGATE* functions
4	Ignore nothing
5	Ignore hidden rows
6	Ignore error values
7	Ignore hidden rows and error values

5

Finding unique values within a data set

Summarizing numerical values can provide valuable information that helps you run your business. It can also be helpful to know how many different values appear within a column. For example, you might want to display all of the countries in which Consolidated Messenger has customers. If you want to display a list of the unique values in a column, click any cell in the data set, display the Data tab and then, in the Sort & Filter group, click Advanced to display the Advanced Filter dialog box.

In the List Range field, enter the reference of the cell range you want to examine for unique values, select the Unique Records Only check box, and then click OK to have Excel display the row that contains the first occurrence of each value in the column.

> **IMPORTANT** Excel treats the first cell in the data range as a header cell, so it doesn't consider the cell as it builds the list of unique values. Be sure to include the header cell in your data range!

In this exercise, you'll select random rows from a list of exceptions to identify package delivery misadventures to investigate, create an *AGGREGATE* formula to summarize the visible cells in a filtered worksheet, and find the unique values in one column of data.

➡ SET UP You need the ForFollowUp workbook located in the Chapter05 practice file folder to complete this exercise. Open the workbook, and then follow the steps.

1   Select cells **G3:G27**. When you do, the average of the values in the selected cells, the number of cells selected, and the total of the values in the selected cells appear in the **AutoCalculate** area of the status bar.

2   In cell **J2**, enter the formula =AGGREGATE(1,1,G3:G27). The value *$15.76* appears in cell **J2**.

3　On the **Data** tab, in the **Sort & Filter** group, click **Advanced** to open the **Advanced Filter** dialog box.

4　In the **List range** field, enter **E2:E27**.

5　Select the **Unique records only** check box, and then click **OK** to display the rows that contain the first occurrence of each different value in the selected range.

> **TIP** Remember that you must include cell E2, the header cell, in the List Range field so that the filter doesn't display two occurrences of Northeast in the unique values list. To test what happens when you don't include the header cell, try changing the range in the List Range field to E3:E27, selecting the Unique Records Only check box, and clicking OK.

	B	C	D	E	F	G	H	I	J	K
2	ExceptionID	PackageID	Date	Center	Route	Cost	Investigate		$ 15.76	
3	EX1000001	PI34920119	3/30/2013	Northeast	RT310	$ 12.08				
4	EX1000002	PI34920120	3/30/2013	Midwest	RT892	$ 14.88				
5	EX1000003	PI34920121	3/30/2013	Northwest	RT424	$ 13.61				
8	EX1000006	PI34920124	3/30/2013	Central	RT341	$ 18.86				
11	EX1000009	PI34920127	3/31/2013	South	RT983	$ 19.87				
12	EX1000010	PI34920128	3/31/2013	Southwest	RT827	$ 18.01				
28										

6　On the **Data** tab, in the **Sort & Filter** group, click **Clear** to remove the filter.

7　In cell **H3**, enter the formula **=IF(RAND()<0.15,"Yes","No")**, and press **Enter**. A value of *Yes* or *No* appears in cell **H3**, depending on the *RAND* function result.

8　Select cell **H3**, and then drag the fill handle down until it covers cell **H27** to copy the formula into every cell in the range **H3:H27**.

9　With the range **H3:H27** still selected, on the **Home** tab, in the **Clipboard** group, click the **Copy** button. Excel copies the cell range's contents to the Microsoft Office Clipboard.

10　Click the **Paste** arrow, and then in the **Paste** gallery that appears, click the first icon in the **Paste Values** group to replace the cells' formulas with the formulas' current results.

5

	D	E	F	G	H	I	J
							Summary
	Date	**Center**	**Route**	**Cost**	**Investigate**		$ 15.76
	3/30/2013	Northeast	RT310	$ 12.08	No		
	3/30/2013	Midwest	RT892	$ 14.88	Yes		
	3/30/2013	Northwest	RT424	$ 13.61	No		
	3/30/2013	Northeast	RT995	$ 10.64	No		
	3/30/2013	Midwest	RT827	$ 15.26	No		
	3/30/2013	Central	RT341	$ 18.86	No		
	3/30/2013	Central	RT864	$ 15.71	Yes		
	3/30/2013	Central	RT277	$ 18.50	No		
	3/31/2013	South	RT983	$ 19.87	No		
	3/31/2013	Southwest	RT827	$ 18.01	No		
	3/31/2013	South	RT942	$ 19.85	No		
	3/31/2013	South	RT940	$ 15.61	No		
	3/31/2013	Southwest	RT751	$ 12.84	No		
	4/1/2013	Midwest	RT436	$ 13.94	No		
	4/1/2013	Midwest	RT758	$ 17.55	No		

✖ CLEAN UP Close the ForFollowUp workbook, saving your changes if you want to.

Defining valid sets of values for ranges of cells

Part of creating efficient and easy-to-use worksheets is to do what you can to ensure the data entered into your worksheets is as accurate as possible. Although it isn't possible to catch every typographical or transcription error, you can set up a validation rule to make sure that the data entered into a cell meets certain standards.

To create a validation rule, display the Data tab on the ribbon and then, in the Data Tools group, click the Data Validation button to open the Data Validation dialog box. You can use the controls in the Data Validation dialog box to define the type of data that Excel should allow in the cell and then, depending on the data type you choose, to set the conditions data must meet to be accepted in the cell. For example, you can set the conditions so that Excel knows to look for a whole number value between 1,000 and 2,000.

Setting accurate validation rules can help you and your colleagues avoid entering a customer's name in the cell designated to hold the phone number or setting a credit limit above a certain level. To require a user to enter a numeric value in a cell, display the Settings page of the Data Validation dialog box, and, depending on your needs, choose either Whole Number or Decimal from the Allow list.

If you want to set the same validation rule for a group of cells, you can do so by selecting the cells to which you want to apply the rule (such as a column in which you enter the credit limit of customers of Consolidated Messenger) and setting the rule by using the Data Validation dialog box. One important fact you should keep in mind is that, with Excel, you can create validation rules for cells in which you have already entered data. Excel doesn't tell you whether any of those cells contain data that violates your rule at the moment you create the rule, but you can find out by having Excel circle any worksheet cells containing data that violates the cell's validation rule. To do so, display the Data tab and then, in the Data Tools group, click the Data Validation arrow. On the menu, click the Circle Invalid Data button to circle cells with invalid data.

	A	B	C	D
1				
2		Date	Exceptions	
3		3/1/2013	73	
4		3/2/2013	89	
5		3/3/2013	47	
6		3/4/2013	109	
7		3/5/2013	115	
8		3/6/2013	109	
9		3/7/2013	118	
10		3/8/2013	53	
11		3/9/2013	73	
12		3/10/2013	64	

When you're ready to hide the circles, in the Data Validation list, click Clear Validation Circles.

Of course, it's frustrating if you want to enter data into a cell and, when a message box appears that tells you the data you tried to enter isn't acceptable, you aren't given the rules you need to follow. With Excel, you can create a message that tells the user which values are expected before the data is entered and then, if the conditions aren't met, reiterate the conditions in a custom error message.

You can turn off data validation in a cell by displaying the Settings page of the Data Validation dialog box and clicking the Clear All button in the lower-left corner of the dialog box.

In this exercise, you'll create a data validation rule that limits the credit line of Consolidated Messenger customers to $25,000, add an input message mentioning the limitation, and then create an error message if someone enters a value greater than $25,000. After you create your rule and messages, you'll test them.

➔ SET UP You need the Credit workbook located in the Chapter05 practice file folder to complete this exercise. Open the workbook, and then follow the steps.

1   Select the cell range **J4:J7**. Note that cell **J7** is currently blank; you will add a value to it later in this exercise.

2   On the **Data** tab, in the **Data Tools** group, click **Data Validation** to open the **Data Validation** dialog box, which displays the **Settings** page.

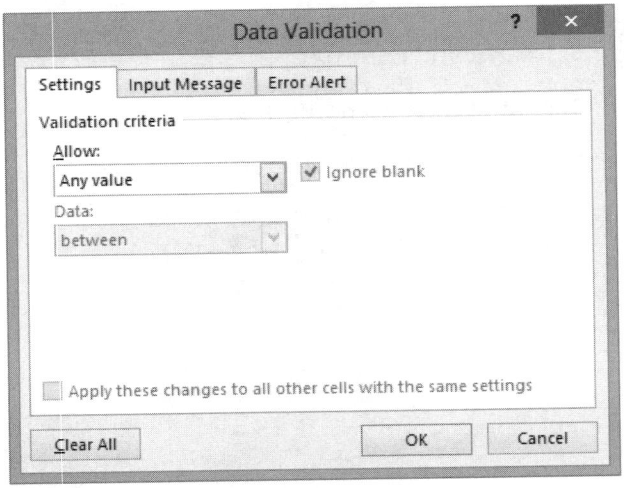

3   In the **Allow** list, click **Whole Number**. Boxes labeled **Minimum** and **Maximum** appear below the **Data** box.

4   In the **Data** list, click **less than or equal to** remove the **Minimum** box.

5   In the **Maximum** box, enter **25000**.

6   Clear the **Ignore blank** check box.

7   Click the **Input Message** tab to display the **Input Message** page.

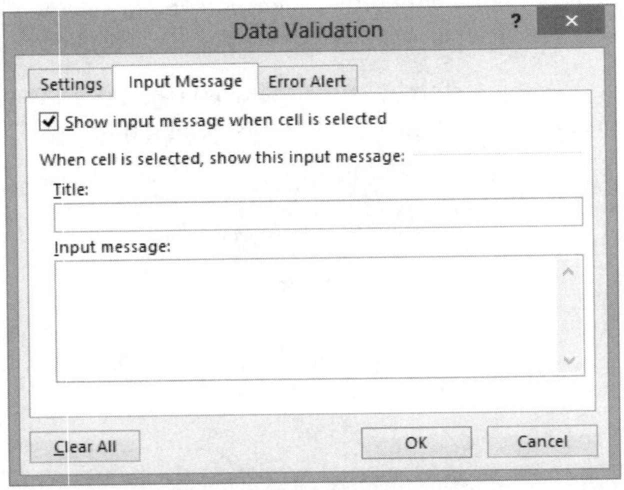

8   In the **Title** box, enter **Enter Limit**.

9   In the **Input Message** box, enter Please enter the customer's credit limit, omitting the dollar sign and any commas.

10   Click the **Error Alert** tab to display the **Error Alert** page.

11   In the **Style** list, click **Stop** to change the icon that appears on your message box.

12   In the **Title** box, enter Error, and then click **OK**.

13   Click cell **J7**. When you do, a ScreenTip with the title *Enter Limit* and the text *Please enter the customer's credit limit, omitting the dollar sign and any commas* appears near cell **J7**.

14   Enter 25001, and press **Enter**. A stop box with the title **Error** opens. Leaving the **Error message** box blank in step 12 causes Excel to use its default message.

15   Click **Cancel** to close the error box.

IMPORTANT By clicking Retry, you can edit the bad value, whereas clicking Cancel deletes the entry.

16   Click cell **J7** to make it the active cell and display the ScreenTip.

17   Enter **25000**, and press **Enter**.

18   On the **Data** tab, in the **Data Tools** group, click the **Data Validation** arrow and then, in the list, click **Circle Invalid Data**. A red circle appears around the value in cell **J4**.

	E	F	G	H	I	J	
	Address	**City**	**State**	**ZIP**	**Phone**	**Limit**	
	11020 Microsoft Way	Redmond	WA	98073	(425) 555-1001	$ 26,000.00	
	1480 Microsoft Way	Redmond	WA	98073	(425) 555-1098	$ 7,500.00	
	891A Microsoft Way	Redmond	WA	98073	(425) 555-1287	$ 15,000.00	
						$ 25,000.00	

19   In the **Data Validation** list, click **Clear Validation Circles** to remove the red circle from around the value in cell **J4**.

✖ CLEAN UP   **Close the Credit workbook, saving your changes if you want to.**

Key points

- A number of filters are defined in Excel. (You might find that the one you want is already available.)

- Filtering an Excel worksheet based on values in a single column is easy to do, but you can create a custom filter to limit your data based on the values in more than one column as well.

- With the search filter capability, you can limit the data in your worksheets based on characters the terms contain.

- Don't forget that you can get a running total (or an average, or any one of several other summary operations) for the values in a group of cells. Just select the cells and look on the status bar: the result will be there.

- Use data validation techniques to improve the accuracy of data entered into your worksheets and to identify data that doesn't meet the guidelines you set.

Chapter at a glance

Sort

Sort worksheet data,
page 174

Customize

Sort data by using custom lists,
page 179

Organize

Organize data into levels,
page 183

Find

Look up information in a worksheet,
page 189

Reordering and summarizing data

6

IN THIS CHAPTER, YOU WILL LEARN HOW TO

- Sort worksheet data.

- Sort data by using custom lists.

- Organize data into levels.

- Look up information in a worksheet.

Most of the time, when you enter data in a Microsoft Excel worksheet, you will enter it in chronological order. For example, you could enter hourly shipment data in a worksheet, starting with the first hour of the day and ending with the last hour. The data would naturally be displayed in the order you entered it, but that might not always be the best arrangement to answer your questions. For instance, you might want to sort your data so that the top row in your worksheet shows the day of the month with the highest package volume, with subsequent rows displaying the remaining days in decreasing order of package volumes handled. You can also sort data based on the contents of more than one column. A good example is sorting package handling data by week, day, and then hour of the day.

After you have sorted your data into the order you want, you can find partial totals, or subtotals, for groups of cells within a given range. Yes, you can create formulas to find the sum, average, or standard deviation of data in a cell range, but you can do the same thing much more quickly by having Excel calculate the total for rows that have the same value in one of their columns. For example, if your worksheet holds sales data for a list of services, you can calculate subtotals for each product category.

When you calculate subtotals in a worksheet, Excel creates an outline that marks the cell ranges used in each subtotal. For example, if the first 10 rows of a worksheet contain overnight shipping data, and the second 10 rows contain second-day shipping data, Excel divides the rows into two units. You can use the markers on the worksheet to hide or display the rows used to calculate a subtotal; in this case, you can hide all the rows that contain overnight shipping data, hide all the rows that contain second-day shipping data, hide both, or show both.

Excel also has a capability you might expect to find only in a database program—you can enter a value in a cell and have Excel look in a named range to find a corresponding value. For instance, you can have a two-column named range with one column displaying customer identification numbers and the second column displaying the name of the company assigned each number. When you use a VLOOKUP formula that references the named range, colleagues using your workbook can enter a customer identification number in a cell and have the name of the corresponding company appear in the cell that has the formula.

In this chapter, you'll sort your data by using one or more criteria, calculate subtotals, organize your data into levels, and look up information in a worksheet.

PRACTICE FILES To complete the exercises in this chapter, you need the practice files contained in the Chapter06 practice file folder. For more information, see "Download the practice files" in this book's Introduction.

Sorting worksheet data

Although Excel makes it easy to enter your business data and to manage it after you've saved it in a worksheet, unsorted data will rarely answer every question you want to ask it. For example, you might want to discover which of your services generates the most profits or which service costs the most for you to provide. You can discover that information by sorting your data.

When you sort data in a worksheet, you rearrange the worksheet rows based on the contents of cells in a particular column or set of columns. For instance, you can sort a worksheet to find your highest-revenue services.

You can sort a group of rows in a worksheet in a number of ways, but the first step is to identify the column that will provide the values by which the rows should be sorted. In the revenue example, you could find the highest revenue totals by sorting on the cells in the Revenue column. First you would select the cells in the Revenue column and display the

Home tab. Then, in the Editing group, in the Sort & Filter list, click Sort Largest To Smallest. Clicking Sort Largest To Smallest makes Excel put the row with the highest value in the Revenue column at the top of the worksheet and continue down to the lowest value.

	A	B	C	D
1				
2		Service	Revenue	
3		Overnight	$ 1,598,643	
4		3Day	$ 1,000,142	
5		Ground	$ 994,775	
6		2Day	$ 745,600	
7		Priority Overnigh	$ 502,991	
8				
9				

If you want to sort the rows in the opposite order, from the lowest revenue to the highest, select the cells in the Revenue column and then, in the Sort & Filter list, click Sort Smallest To Largest.

TIP The exact set of values that appears in the Sort & Filter list changes to reflect the data in your column. If your column contains numerical values, you'll find the options Sort Largest To Smallest, Sort Smallest To Largest, and Custom List. If your column contains text values, the options are Sort A To Z (ascending order), Sort Z To A (descending order), and Custom List. And if your column contains dates, the options are Sort Newest To Oldest, Sort Oldest To Newest, and Custom List.

By using the Sort Smallest To Largest and Sort Largest To Smallest options, you can sort rows in a worksheet quickly, but you can use these options only to sort the worksheet based on the contents of one column, even though you might want to sort by two columns. For example, you might want to order the worksheet rows by service category and then by total so that you can display the customers that use each service category most frequently. You can sort rows in a worksheet by the contents of more than one column by using the Sort dialog box, in which you can pick any number of columns to use as sort criteria and choose whether to sort the rows in ascending or descending order.

6

To open the Sort dialog box, click Custom Sort in the Sort & Filter list.

If your data has a header row, select the My Data Has Headers check box so the column headers will appear in the Sort By list. After you identify the column by which you want to sort, you can use the options in the Sort On list to select whether you want to sort by a cell's value (the default), a cell's fill color, a cell's font color, or an icon displayed in the cell.

SEE ALSO For more information about creating conditional formats that change a cell's formatting or display an icon to reflect the cell's value, see "Changing the appearance of data based on its value" in Chapter 4, "Changing workbook appearance."

Finally, from the Order list, you can select how you want Excel to sort the column values. As with the Sort & Filter button's list, the exact values that appear in the Order list change to reflect the data to be sorted.

Adding, moving, copying, and deleting sorting levels are a matter of clicking the appropriate button in the Sort dialog box. To add a second level to your sort, click the Add Level button.

TIP In Excel 2003 and earlier versions of the program, you could define a maximum of three sorting levels. Beginning with Excel 2007, you can create up to 64 sorting levels.

To delete a level, click the level in the list, and then click Delete Level. By clicking the Copy Level button, you can put all the settings from one rule into another, saving yourself some work if you need to change only one item. By clicking the Move Up and Move Down buttons, which display an upward-pointing arrow and a downward-pointing arrow, respectively, you can change a sorting level's position in the order. Finally, clicking the Options button opens the Sort Options dialog box, which you can use to make a sorting level case sensitive and to change the orientation of the sort.

In this exercise, you'll sort worksheet data, sort by multiple criteria, change the order in which sorting criteria are applied, and sort data by color.

➡ SET UP You need the ShippingSummary workbook located in the Chapter06 practice file folder to complete this exercise. Open the workbook, and then follow the steps.

1 Click cell **C3**. On the **Home** tab, in the **Editing** group, click the **Sort & Filter** button and then, in the list, click **Sort A to Z**. Excel sorts the data by season, with the seasons listed in alphabetical order.

2 In the **Sort & Filter** list, click **Custom Sort** to open the **Sort** dialog box and display the parameters of the sort you just applied.

3 If it's not already selected, select the **My data has headers** check box.

4 In the **Column** list, click **Customer**. If necessary, in the **Sort On** list, click **Values**; then in the **Order** list, click **A to Z**.

5 Click **Add Level** to create a new sorting level.

6   In the new **Column** list, click **Revenue**.

7   In the new **Order** list, click **Largest to Smallest**.

8   Click **OK** to close the **Sort** dialog box and sort the data list.

⬜	A	B	C	D	E
1					
2		Customer	Season	Revenue	
3		Contoso	Spring	$201,438.00	
4		Contoso	Winter	$183,651.00	
5		Contoso	Fall	$118,299.00	
6		Contoso	Summer	$114,452.00	
7		Fabrikam	Fall	$255,599.00	
8		Fabrikam	Summer	$183,632.00	
9		Fabrikam	Spring	$139,170.00	
10		Fabrikam	Winter	$100,508.00	
11		Northwind Traders	Fall	$188,851.00	
12		Northwind Traders	Winter	$174,336.00	
13		Northwind Traders	Summer	$129,732.00	
14		Northwind Traders	Spring	$120,666.00	
15					

9   In the **Sort & Filter** list, click **Custom Sort** to open the **Sort** dialog box.

10   Click **Then by**, which selects the **Revenue** sorting rule.

11   Click the **Move Up** button to move the **Revenue** sorting rule above the **Customer** sorting rule.

12   Click **OK** to close the **Sort** dialog box and sort the data list.

13   Click cell **C3**. Then on the **Home** tab, in the **Editing** group, click **Sort & Filter**, and click **Custom Sort** to open the **Sort** dialog box.

14   In the **Sort by** row, in the **Column** list, click **Revenue**.

15   In the **Sort on** list, click **Cell Color**.

16   In the new list control that appears in the **Sort by** row, click **On Bottom** to have Excel put the **Revenue** cells that have no cell color on the bottom.

17   Click **OK** to have Excel sort the data list.

❌ CLEAN UP Close the ShippingSummary workbook, saving your changes if you want to.

Sorting data by using custom lists

The default setting for Excel is to sort numbers according to their values and to sort words in alphabetical order, but that pattern doesn't work for some sets of values. One example in which sorting a list of values in alphabetical order would yield incorrect results is the months of the year. In an alphabetical calendar, April is the first month and September is the last! Fortunately, Excel recognizes a number of special lists, such as days of the week and months of the year. You can have Excel sort the contents of a worksheet based on values in a known list; if needed, you can create your own list of values. For example, the default lists of weekdays in Excel start with Sunday. If you keep your business records based on a Monday-through-Sunday week, you can create a new list that has Monday as the first day and Sunday as the last.

To create a new list, enter the list of values you want to use as your list into a contiguous cell range, select the cells, click the File tab, and then click Options. On the Advanced page of the Excel Options dialog box, in the General group near the bottom of the page, click the Edit Custom Lists button to open the Custom Lists dialog box.

The selected cell range's reference appears in the Import List From Cells field. To record your list, click the Import button.

If you prefer, you can enter the list in the List Entries box, to the right of the Custom Lists box.

TIP Another benefit of creating a custom list is that dragging the fill handle of a list cell that contains a value causes Excel to extend the series for you. For example, if you create the list *Spring, Summer, Fall, Winter*, then enter *Summer* in a cell and drag the cell's fill handle, Excel extends the series as *Fall, Winter, Spring, Summer, Fall*, and so on.

To use a custom list as a sorting criterion, open the Sort dialog box, click the rule's Order arrow, click Custom List, and select your list from the dialog box that opens.

TIP The Data tab of the ribbon also contains a Sort & Filter group with controls you can use to sort and filter your data.

In this exercise, you'll sort data by using a custom list.

SET UP You need the ShippingCustom workbook located in the Chapter06 practice file folder to complete this exercise. Open the workbook, and then follow the steps.

1   Select cells **G4:G7**, click the **File** tab, and then click **Options** to open the **Excel Options** dialog box.

2   On the **Advanced** page, in the **General** group toward the bottom of the page, click **Edit Custom Lists** to open the **Custom Lists** dialog box.

3   Verify that the cell range **$G$4:$G$7** appears in the **Import list from cells** field, and then click **Import** to add the new list to the **Custom Lists** box.

4   Click **OK** twice to close the **Custom Lists** dialog box and the **Excel Options** dialog box.

5   Click cell **C3**.

6   On the **Home** tab, in the **Editing** group, click **Sort & Filter**, and then click **Custom Sort** to open the **Sort** dialog box.

7   Click the rule in the **Sort by** row, and then click **Delete Level** to remove the sorting rule.

8   If necessary, in the new **Sort by** row, in the **Column** list, click **Season**.

9   In the same row, in the **Order** list, click **Custom List** to open the **Custom Lists** dialog box.

10   In the **Custom lists** box, click **Spring, Summer, Fall, Winter**.

11   Click **OK** twice to close the **Custom Lists** dialog box and the **Sort** dialog box so that Excel sorts the data list.

	A	B	C	D	E
1					
2		Customer	Season	Revenue	
3		Contoso	Spring	$201,438.00	
4		Fabrikam	Spring	$139,170.00	
5		Northwind Traders	Spring	$120,666.00	
6		Contoso	Summer	$114,452.00	
7		Fabrikam	Summer	$183,632.00	
8		Northwind Traders	Summer	$129,732.00	
9		Contoso	Fall	$118,299.00	
10		Fabrikam	Fall	$255,599.00	
11		Northwind Traders	Fall	$188,851.00	
12		Contoso	Winter	$183,651.00	
13		Fabrikam	Winter	$100,508.00	
14		Northwind Traders	Winter	$174,336.00	
15					

✖ CLEAN UP Close the ShippingCustom workbook, saving your changes if you want to.

Organizing data into levels

After you have sorted the rows in an Excel worksheet or entered the data so that it doesn't need to be sorted, you can have Excel calculate subtotals or totals for a portion of the data. In a worksheet with sales data for three different product categories, for example, you can sort the products by category, select all the cells that contain data, and then open the Subtotal dialog box. To open the Subtotal dialog box, display the Data tab and then, in the Outline group, click Subtotal.

In the Subtotal dialog box, you can choose the column on which to base your subtotals (such as every change of value in the Year column), the summary calculation you want to perform, and the column or columns that have values to be summarized. After you define your subtotals, they appear in your worksheet.

1 2 3		A	B	C	D
	1	Year	Quarter	Month	Package Volume
	2	2012	1	January	5,213,292
	3	2012	1	February	2,038,516
	4	2012	1	March	2,489,601
	5	2012	2	April	9,051,231
	6	2012	2	May	5,225,156
	7	2012	2	June	3,266,644
	8	2012	3	July	2,078,794
	9	2012	3	August	1,591,434
	10	2012	3	September	8,518,985
	11	2012	4	October	1,973,050
	12	2012	4	November	7,599,195
	13	2012	4	December	9,757,876
	14	2012 Total			58,803,774
	15	2013	1	January	5,304,039
	16	2013	1	February	5,465,096
	17	2013	1	March	1,007,799

When you add subtotals to a worksheet, Excel also defines groups based on the rows used to calculate a subtotal. The groupings form an outline of your worksheet based on the criteria you used to create the subtotals. For example, all the rows representing months in the year 2012 could be in one group, rows representing months in 2013 in another, and so on. The outline area at the left of your worksheet holds controls you can use to hide or display groups of rows in your worksheet.

Three types of controls can appear in the outline area: Hide Detail buttons, Show Detail buttons, and level buttons. The Hide Detail button beside a group can be clicked to hide the rows in that group. In a worksheet that has a subtotal group consisting of rows 2 through 13, clicking the Hide Detail button next to row 14 would hide rows 2 through 13 but leave the row holding the subtotal for that group, row 14, visible.

1 2 3		A	B	C	D	E
	1	Year	Quarter	Month	Package Volume	
+	14	2012 Total			58,803,774	
	15	2013	1	January	5,304,039	
	16	2013	1	February	5,465,096	
	17	2013	1	March	1,007,799	
	18	2013	2	April	4,010,287	
	19	2013	2	May	4,817,070	
	20	2013	2	June	8,155,717	
	21	2013	3	July	6,552,370	
	22	2013	3	August	2,295,635	
	23	2013	3	September	7,115,883	
	24	2013	4	October	1,362,767	
	25	2013	4	November	8,935,488	
	26	2013	4	December	9,537,077	
−	27	2013 Total			64,559,228	
−	28	Grand Total			123,363,002	
	29					

When you hide a group of rows, the button displayed next to the group changes to a Show Detail button. Clicking a group's Show Detail button restores the rows in the group to the worksheet.

The level buttons are the other buttons in the outline area of a worksheet that has subtotals. Each button represents a level of organization in a worksheet; clicking a level button hides all levels of detail below that of the button you clicked. The following table describes the data contained at each level of a worksheet that has three levels of organization.

Level	Description
1	Grand total
2	Subtotals for each group
3	Individual rows in the worksheet

Clicking the Level 2 button in the worksheet would hide the rows with data on, for example, each month's revenue, but would leave the row that contains the grand total (Level 1) and all rows that contain the subtotal for each year (Level 2) visible in the worksheet.

			A	B	C	D	E
		1	Year	Quarter	Month	Package Volume	
+		14	2012 Total			58,803,774	
+		27	2013 Total			64,559,228	
−		28	Grand Total			123,363,002	
		29					

If you want to, you can add levels of detail to the outline that Excel creates. For example, you might want to be able to hide revenues from April to June, which you know are traditionally strong months. To create a new outline group within an existing group, select the rows you want to group; on the Data tab, in the Outline group, point to Group, and then click Group.

You can remove a group by selecting the rows in the group and then, in the Outline group, clicking Ungroup.

TIP If you want to remove all subtotals from a worksheet, open the Subtotal dialog box, and click the Remove All button.

In this exercise, you'll add subtotals to a worksheet and then show and hide different groups of data in your worksheet by using the outline that appears.

→ SET UP You need the GroupByQuarter workbook located in the Chapter06 practice file folder to complete this exercise. Open the workbook, and then follow the steps.

1   Click any cell in the data list. Then, on the **Data** tab, in the **Outline** group, click **Subtotal** to open the **Subtotal** dialog box. The **Subtotal** dialog box displays the default options to add a subtotal at every change in the **Year** column, to return the sum of the values in the subtotaled rows, and to add a row with the subtotal of values in the **Package Volume** column below the final selected row.

2   Click **OK** to close the **Subtotal** dialog box. New rows appear with subtotals for package volume during each year represented in the worksheet. The new rows are numbered **14** and **27**. A row that contains the grand total of all rows also appears; that row is row **28**. A new area with outline bars and group-level indicators appears to the left of column **A**.

	A	B	C	D	E
1	Year	Quarter	Month	Package Volume	
2	2012	1	January	5,213,292	
3	2012	1	February	2,038,516	
4	2012	1	March	2,489,601	
5	2012	2	April	9,051,231	
6	2012	2	May	5,225,156	
7	2012	2	June	3,266,644	
8	2012	3	July	2,078,794	
9	2012	3	August	1,591,434	
10	2012	3	September	8,518,985	
11	2012	4	October	1,973,050	
12	2012	4	November	7,599,195	
13	2012	4	December	9,757,876	
14	2012 Total			58,803,774	
15	2013	1	January	5,304,039	
16	2013	1	February	5,465,096	
17	2013	1	March	1,007,799	
18	2013	2	April	4,010,287	
19	2013	2	May	4,817,070	
20	2013	2	June	8,155,717	
21	2013	3	July	6,552,370	
22	2013	3	August	2,295,635	
23	2013	3	September	7,115,883	
24	2013	4	October	1,362,767	
25	2013	4	November	8,935,488	
26	2013	4	December	9,537,077	
27	2013 Total			64,559,228	
28	Grand Total			123,363,002	

Sheet1   ⊕

6

3   Click the row heading of row **5**, and drag to the row heading of row **7** to select rows **5** through **7**.

4   On the **Data** tab, in the **Outline** group, click **Group** to make rows **5** through **7** into a new group. An outline bar appears on a new level in the outline area, and a corresponding **Level 4** button appears at the top of the outline area.

5   In the outline area, click the **Hide Detail** button next to row **8** to hide rows **5** through **7**. The **Hide Detail** button you clicked changes to a **Show Detail** button.

	A	B	C	D	E
2	2012	1	January	5,213,292	
3	2012	1	February	2,038,516	
4	2012	1	March	2,489,601	
8	2012	3	July	2,078,794	
9	2012	3	August	1,591,434	
10	2012	3	September	8,518,985	
11	2012	4	October	1,973,050	
12	2012	4	November	7,599,195	
13	2012	4	December	9,757,876	
14	**2012 Total**			58,803,774	
15	2013	1	January	5,304,039	
16	2013	1	February	5,465,096	
17	2013	1	March	1,007,799	

6   In the outline area, click the **Show Detail** button next to row **8** to display rows **5** through **7**. In the outline area, click the **Level 1** button to hide all rows except row **1** with the column headings and row **28** with the grand total.

7   In the outline area, click the **Level 2** button to display the rows that have the subtotals for each year.

8   In the outline area, click the **Level 3** button to display all rows except rows **5** through **7**.

9   In the outline area, click the **Level 4** button to display rows **5** through **7**.

❌ CLEAN UP Close the GroupByQuarter workbook, saving your changes if you want to.

Looking up information in a worksheet

Whenever you create a worksheet that holds information about a list of distinct items, such as products offered for sale by a company, you should ensure that at least one column in the list contains a unique value that distinguishes that row (and the item the row represents) from every other row in the list. Assigning each row a column that contains a unique value means that you can associate data in one list with data in another list. For example, if you assign every customer a unique identification number, you can store a customer's contact information in one worksheet and all orders for that customer in another worksheet. You can then associate the customer's orders and contact information without writing the contact information in a worksheet every time the customer places an order.

In the case of shipments handled by Consolidated Messenger, the column that contains those unique values, also known as the *primary key column*, is the ShipmentID column.

	A	B	C	D	E	F
1						
2		ShipmentID	Destination			
3						
4						
5						
6		ShipmentID	CustomerID	Date	OriginationPostalCode	DestinationPostalCode
7		SI3049210	CI384471	5/20/2007	59686	77408
8		SI3049211	CI495231	5/20/2007	24348	91936
9		SI3049212	CI429120	5/20/2007	70216	83501
10		SI3049213	CI418125	5/20/2007	84196	21660
11		SI3049214	CI782990	5/20/2007	13193	92518
12		SI3049215	CI102300	5/20/2007	27910	76842
13		SI3049216	CI560742	5/20/2007	73820	21393
14		SI3049217	CI483289	5/20/2007	34245	33975

6

If you know a shipment's ShipmentID, it's no trouble to look through a list of 20 or 30 items to find a particular shipment. If, however, you have a list of many thousands of shipments, looking through the list to find one would take quite a bit of time. Instead, you can use the *VLOOKUP* function so that your colleagues can enter a ShipmentID in a cell and have the corresponding details appear in another cell.

The *VLOOKUP* function finds a value in the leftmost column of a named range, such as a table, and then returns the value from the specified cell to the right of the cell that has the found value. A properly formed *VLOOKUP* function has four arguments (data that is passed to the function), as shown in the following definition: =VLOOKUP(lookup_value, table_array, col_index_num, range_lookup).

The following table summarizes the values Excel expects for each of these arguments.

Argument	Expected value
lookup_value	The value to be found in the first column of the named range specified by the *table_array* argument. The *lookup_value* argument can be a value, a cell reference, or a text string.
table_array	The multicolumn range or name of the range or Excel table to be searched.
col_index_num	The number of the column in the named range that has the value to be returned.
range_lookup	A *TRUE* or *FALSE* value, indicating whether the function should find an approximate match (*TRUE*) or an exact match (*FALSE*) for the *lookup_value*. If left blank, the default value for this argument is *TRUE*.

IMPORTANT When *range_lookup* is left blank or set to *TRUE*, for *VLOOKUP* to work properly the rows in the named range specified in the *table_array* argument must be sorted in ascending order based on the values in the leftmost column of the named range.

The *VLOOKUP* function works a bit differently depending on whether the *range_lookup* argument is set to *TRUE* or *FALSE*. The following list summarizes how the function works based on the value of *range_lookup*:

- If the *range_lookup* argument is left blank or set to *TRUE*, and *VLOOKUP* doesn't find an exact match for *lookup_value*, the function returns the largest value that is less than *lookup_value*.

- If the *range_lookup* argument is left blank or set to *TRUE*, and *lookup_value* is smaller than the smallest value in the named range, an *#N/A* error is returned.

- If the *range_lookup* argument is left blank or set to *TRUE*, and *lookup_value* is larger than all values in the named range, the largest value in the named range is returned.

- If the *range_lookup* argument is set to *FALSE*, and *VLOOKUP* doesn't find an exact match for *lookup_value*, the function returns an *#N/A* error.

As an example of a *VLOOKUP* function, consider an Excel table that has its headers in row 1 and the first column in column A of the worksheet. If the *=VLOOKUP (D2, Table1, 2, TRUE)* formula is used, when you enter *CI02* in cell D2 and press Enter, the *VLOOKUP* function searches the first column of the table, finds an exact match, and returns the value *Northwind Traders* to cell E2.

	A	B	C	D	E	F
E2		fx	=VLOOKUP(D2,Table1,2,TRUE)			
1	**CustomerID** ▼	**Customer** ▼		**CustomerID**	**Company Name**	
2	CI101	Fabrikam		CI102	Northwind Traders	
3	CI102	Northwind Traders				
4	CI103	Tailspin Toys				
5	CI104	Contoso				
6						

TIP The related *HLOOKUP* function matches a value in a column of the first row of a table and returns the value in the specified row number of the same column. The letter "H" in the *HLOOKUP* function name refers to the horizontal layout of the data, just as the "V" in the *VLOOKUP* function name refers to the data's vertical layout. For more information on using the *HLOOKUP* function, click the Excel Help button, enter *HLOOKUP* in the search terms box, and then click Search.

IMPORTANT Be sure to format the cell in which you enter the *VLOOKUP* formula with the same format as the data you want the formula to display. For example, if you create a *VLOOKUP* formula in cell G14 that finds a date, you must apply a date cell format to cell G14 for the result of the formula to display properly.

In this exercise, you'll create a *VLOOKUP* function to return the destination postal code of deliveries that have ShipmentIDs entered in a specific cell.

 SET UP You need the ShipmentLog workbook located in the Chapter06 practice file folder to complete this exercise. Open the workbook, and then follow the steps.

1   In cell **C3**, enter the formula =VLOOKUP(B3, Shipments, 5, FALSE). Cell **B3**, which the formula uses to look up values in the **Shipments** table, is blank, so the **#N/A** error code appears in cell **C3**.

2   In cell **B3**, enter SI3049224, and press **Enter**. The value **51102** appears in cell **C3**.

3   In cell **C3**, edit the formula so that it reads =VLOOKUP(B3, Shipments, 2, FALSE). The formula now finds its target value in table column 2 (the **CustomerID** column), so the value **CI512191** appears in cell **C3**.

4   In cell **C3**, edit the formula so that it reads =VLOOKUP(B3, Shipments, 4, TRUE). Changing the last argument to *TRUE* enables the *VLOOKUP* formula to find an approximate match for the **ShipmentID** in cell **B3**, whereas changing the column to **4** means the formula gets its result from the **OriginationPostalCode** column. The value **14020** appears in cell **C3**.

C3		▼	⋮	×	✓	fx	=VLOOKUP(B3,Shipments,4,TRUE)		

⊿	A	B	C	D	E	F
1						
2		ShipmentID	Postal Code			
3		SI3049224	14020			
4						
5						
6		ShipmentID ⌄	CustomerID ⌄	Date ⌄	OriginationPostalCode ⌄	DestinationPostalCode ⌄
7		SI3049210	CI384471	5/20/2007	59686	77408
8		SI3049211	CI495231	5/20/2007	24348	91936
9		SI3049212	CI429120	5/20/2007	70216	83501
10		SI3049213	CI418125	5/20/2007	84196	21660
11		SI3049214	CI782990	5/20/2007	13193	92518
12		SI3049215	CI102300	5/20/2007	27910	76842
13		SI3049216	CI560742	5/20/2007	73820	21393
14		SI3049217	CI483289	5/20/2007	34245	33975
15		SI3049218	CI762179	5/20/2007	87569	11471
16		SI3049219	CI278943	5/20/2007	28371	72853
17		SI3049220	CI213987	5/20/2007	18024	31069
18		SI3049221	CI907745	5/20/2007	70812	53604
19		SI3049222	CI299868	5/20/2007	33242	23892
20		SI3049223	CI503324	5/20/2007	58997	37121
21		SI3049224	CI512191	5/20/2007	14020	51102
22		SI3049225	CI932656	5/20/2007	56345	28404
23		SI3049226	CI514577	5/20/2007	34262	99198
24		SI3049227	CI803799	5/20/2007	92043	65330

5   In cell **B3**, enter SI3049209. The value in cell **B3** is smaller than the smallest value in the **Shipments** table's first column, so the *VLOOKUP* formula displays the #N/A error code in cell **C3**.

6   In cell **B3**, enter SI3049245. The **ShipmentID** entered into cell **B3** is greater than the last value in the table's first column, so the *VLOOKUP* formula displays the last value in the target column (in this case, the fourth column). Therefore, the incorrect value **44493** appears in cell **C3**. The error occurs because the *range_lookup* argument is set to *TRUE*.

✖ CLEAN UP Close the ShipmentLog workbook, saving your changes if you want to.

Key points

- You can rearrange the data in a worksheet quickly by clicking either the Sort Ascending or Sort Descending button in the Sort & Filter group on the Data tab.

- Don't forget that you can sort the rows in a worksheet by using orders other than alphabetical or numerical. For example, you can sort a series of days based on their order in the week or by cell color.

- If none of the existing sort orders (days, weekdays, and so on) meets your needs, you can create your own custom sort order.

- You can divide the data in your worksheet into levels and find a subtotal for each level.

- By creating subtotals, you can show or hide groups of data in your worksheets.

- You can use the *VLOOKUP* function to look up a value in one column of data and return a value from another column in the same row.

6

Chapter at a glance

Templates

Use workbooks as templates for other workbooks, page 196

Link

Link to data in other worksheets and workbooks, page 204

	E	F	G	H	I
1					
2	**Facilities**			**Transportation**	
3					
4	Power	$ 1,800,000.00		Truck Fuel	$ 24,808,206
5	Water	$ 900,000.00		Truck Maintenance	
6	Rent	$ 2,350,000.00		Airplane Fuel	
7	Mortgage	$ 4,590,210.00		Airplane Maintenance	

Consolidate

Consolidate multiple sets of data into a single workbook, page 209

	A	B	C	D	E	F	G	H
1								
2								
3			Hour					
4		Call Center	9:00 AM	10:00 AM	11:00 AM	12:00 PM	1:00 PM	2:00 PM
5		Northeast	15931	15958	13140	25367	19558	20624
6		Atlantic	28432	22326	15436	20884	30000	19770
7		Southeast	13132	12568	19732	14762	18885	20882
8		North Central	17588	26324	24121	24453	20048	21994
9		Midwest	24875	19965	19386	11374	26007	29378
10		Southwest	15353	27755	19718	17889	22116	28816
11		Mountain West	21516	28321	9754	26384	15926	23572
12		Northwest	19806	24154	12389	10151	24078	11642
13		Central	21018	24884	18655	31525	13407	19683
14								

Combining data from multiple sources

IN THIS CHAPTER, YOU WILL LEARN HOW TO

- Use workbooks as templates for other workbooks.

- Link to data in other worksheets and workbooks.

- Consolidate multiple sets of data into a single workbook.

Microsoft Excel 2013 gives you a wide range of tools with which to format, summarize, and present your data. After you have created a workbook to hold data about a particular subject, you can create as many worksheets as you need to make that data easier to find within your workbook. For example, you can create a workbook to store sales data for a year, with each worksheet representing a month in that year. To ensure that every year's workbook has a similar appearance, you can create a workbook with the characteristics you want (such as more than the standard number of worksheets, custom worksheet formatting, or a particular color for the workbook's sheet tabs) and save it as a pattern, or *template*, for similar workbooks you will create in the future. The benefit of ensuring that all your sales data worksheets have the same layout is that you and your colleagues immediately know where to look for specific totals. You can use that knowledge to summarize, or consolidate, that data into a single worksheet.

A consequence of organizing your data into different workbooks and worksheets is that you need ways to manage, combine, and summarize data from more than one Excel file. You can always copy data from one worksheet to another, but if the original value were to change, that change would not be reflected in the cell range to which you copied the data. Rather than remembering which cells you need to update when a value changes, you can create a link to the original cell. That way, Excel will update the value for you whenever you open the workbook. If multiple worksheets hold related values, you can use links to summarize those values in a single worksheet.

In this chapter, you'll use a workbook as a template for other workbooks, work with more than one set of data, link to data in other workbooks, and summarize multiple sets of data.

PRACTICE FILES To complete the exercises in this chapter, you need the practice files contained in the Chapter07 practice file folder. For more information, see "Download the practice files" in this book's Introduction.

Using workbooks as templates for other workbooks

After you decide on the type of data you want to store in a workbook and what that workbook should look like, you probably want to be able to create similar workbooks without adding all of the formatting and formulas again. For example, you might have established a design for your monthly sales-tracking workbook.

When you have settled on a design for your workbooks, you can save one of the workbooks as a template for similar workbooks you will create in the future. You can leave the workbook's labels to aid data entry, but you should remove any existing data from a workbook that you save as a template, both to avoid data entry errors and to remove any confusion as to whether the workbook is a template. You can also remove any worksheets you and your colleagues won't need by right-clicking the tab of an unneeded worksheet and, on the shortcut menu that appears, clicking Delete.

If you want your template workbook to have more than the standard number of worksheets (such as 12 worksheets to track shipments for a year, by month), you can add worksheets by clicking the Insert Worksheet button that appears to the right of the existing worksheet tabs.

Before you create your first template, you should identify the path to the default template folder on your computer. The path for users whose Windows local settings are English (US) is typically Program Files (x86)\Microsoft Office\Templates\1033. The language identifier for English (US) is 1033, which is why the path includes that identifier. You can enter that path as your default template path on the Save page of the Excel Options dialog box. To open the Excel Options dialog box, click the File tab and then click Options. In the dialog box, click Save and then, in the Default Personal Templates Location box, enter the template folder's path.

TIP You can discover your template folder's path by opening File Explorer and navigating to the template folder, starting with the Program Files or Program Files (x86) folder, depending on your installation. To copy the path of the folder, click the folder icon at the left end of the File Explorer address box at the top of the File Explorer window and then press Ctrl+C.

To create a template from an existing workbook, save the model workbook as an Excel template file (a file with an .xltx extension), which is a file format you can choose from the Save As Type dialog box. If you ever want to change the template, you can open it like a standard workbook and make your changes. When you have completed your work, save the file by clicking the Save button on the Quick Access Toolbar—it will still be a template.

TIP You can also save your Excel 2013 workbook either as an Excel 97–2003 template (.xlt) or as a macro-enabled Excel 2013 workbook template (.xltm). For information about using macros in Excel 2013 workbooks, see Chapter 12, "Working with macros and forms."

After you save a workbook as a template, you can use it as a model for new workbooks. To create a workbook from a template in Excel, click the File tab to display the Backstage view, and then click New.

7

The New page of the Backstage view displays the blank workbook template, sample templates, a search box you can use to locate helpful templates on Office.com, and a set of sample search terms.

From the list of available templates, you can click the template you want to use as the model for your workbook. Excel creates a new workbook (an .xlsx workbook file, not an .xltx template file) with the template's formatting and contents in place.

In addition to creating a workbook template, you can add a worksheet based on a template to your workbook by right-clicking a sheet tab and then clicking Insert to open the Insert dialog box.

The Insert dialog box splits its contents into two pages. The General page contains icons you can click to insert a blank worksheet, a chart sheet, and any worksheet templates available to you.

TIP The MS Excel 4.0 Macro and MS Excel 5.0 Dialog icons on the General page are there to help users integrate older Excel spreadsheet solutions into Excel 2013.

The Spreadsheet Solutions page contains a set of useful templates for a variety of financial and personal tasks.

To add a spreadsheet from the Insert dialog box to your workbook, click the template you want, and then click OK. When you click a template, a preview of that template's contents appears in the preview pane, so you can verify you've selected the template you want.

In this exercise, you'll create a workbook from an existing template, save a template to track hourly call volumes to each regional center, and insert a worksheet based on a worksheet template into a new workbook.

→ SET UP You need the DailyCallSummary workbook located in the Chapter07 practice file folder to complete this exercise. Open the workbook, and then follow the steps.

1   Click the **File** tab, and then in the **Backstage** view, click **Save As**.

2   On the **Save As** page, click **Computer**.

3   Click **Browse** to open the **Save As** dialog box.

4   In the **Save as type** list, click **Excel Template**.

5   Click **Save** to save the workbook as a template and close the **Save As** dialog box.

   TIP You must remember where you saved your template file to use it later. If you updated the Default Personal Templates Location setting in the Excel Options dialog box and saved the file in that folder, the template you just created will appear on the New page of the Backstage view.

6   In the **Backstage** view, click **Close** to close the **DailyCallSummary** workbook.

7   Display the **Backstage** view again, and then click **New**.

8   In the templates gallery, click **Expense Trends Budget** to display information about the template.

9   Click **Create** to create a workbook based on the selected template.

10   On the **Quick Access Toolbar**, click the **Save** button to display the **Backstage** view.

11   On the **Save As** page of the **Backstage** view, click **Computer** and then click **Browse** to open the **Save As** dialog box.

12   In the **File name** box, enter ExpenseReport. Use the dialog box controls to browse to the **Chapter07** folder, and then click **Save** to save your workbook.

13   In the **Backstage** view, click **Open** to display that page, and then click **Recent Workbooks**. In the **Recent Workbooks** list, click the **DailyCallSummary** workbook file (not the template) to display the **DailyCallSummary** workbook.

	A	B	C	D	E	F	G
1							
2							
3			**Hour**				
4		**Call Center**	*9:00 AM*	*10:00 AM*	*11:00 AM*	*12:00 PM*	*1:00 PM*
5		*Northeast*					
6		*Atlantic*					
7		*Southeast*					
8		*North Central*					
9		*Midwest*					
10		*Southwest*					
11		*Mountain West*					
12		*Northwest*					
13		*Central*					
14							

14　　Right-click the **Daily** sheet tab, and then click **Insert** to open the **Insert** dialog box.

15　　On the **Spreadsheet Solutions** page, click **TimeCard**, and then click **OK** to create a new worksheet based on the template.

✖ CLEAN UP Close the DailyCallSummary and ExpenseReport workbooks, saving your changes if you want to.

Linking to data in other worksheets and workbooks

Copying and pasting data from one workbook to another is a quick and easy way to gather related data in one place, but there is a substantial limitation: if the data from the original cell changes, the change is not reflected in the cell to which the data was copied. In other words, copying and pasting a cell's contents doesn't create a relationship between the original cell and the target cell.

You can ensure that the data in the target cell reflects any changes in the original cell by creating a link between the two cells. Instead of entering a value into the target cell by typing or pasting, you create a formula that identifies the source from which Excel will derive the target cell's value and updates the value when it changes in the source cell.

To create a link between cells, open both the workbook that contains the cell from which you want to pull the value and the workbook that has the target cell. Then click the target cell and enter an equal sign, signifying that you want to create a formula. After you enter the equal sign, activate the workbook that has the cell from which you want to derive the value, click that cell, and then press the Enter key.

When you switch back to the workbook with the target cell, you will find that Excel has filled in the formula with a reference to the cell you clicked.

| I4 | ▾ | ⋮ | ✕ ✓ | f_x | ='[FleetOperatingCosts.xlsx]Truck Fuel'!$C$15 |

	E	F	G	H	I
1					
2	**Facilities**			**Transportation**	
3					
4	Power	$ 1,800,000.00		Truck Fuel	$ 24,808,206
5	Water	$ 900,000.00		Truck Maintenance	
6	Rent	$ 2,350,000.00		Airplane Fuel	
7	Mortgage	$ 4,590,210.00		Airplane Maintenance	

For example, the reference *='[FleetOperatingCosts.xlsx]Truck Fuel'!$C$15* gives three pieces of information: the workbook, the worksheet, and the cell you clicked in the worksheet. The first element of the reference (the name of the workbook) is enclosed in square brackets; the end of the second element (the worksheet) is marked with an exclamation point; and the third element (the cell reference) has a dollar sign before both the row and the column identifier. The single quotes around the workbook name and worksheet name are there to account for the space in the Truck Fuel worksheet's name. This type of reference is known as a *3-D* reference, reflecting the three dimensions (workbook, worksheet, and cell range) that you need in order to point to a group of cells in another workbook.

TIP For references to cells in the same workbook, the workbook information is omitted. Likewise, references to cells in the same worksheet don't use a worksheet identifier.

You can also link to cells in an Excel table. Such links include the workbook name, worksheet name, name of the Excel table, and row and column references of the cell to which you've linked. Creating a link to the Cost column's cell in a table's Totals row, for example, results in a reference such as *='FleetOperatingCosts.xlsx'!Truck Maintenance[[#Totals],[Cost]]*.

IMPORTANT Hiding or displaying a table's Totals row affects any links to a cell in that row. Hiding the Totals row causes references to that row to display a *#REF!* error message.

Whenever you open a workbook that contains a link to another document, Excel tries to update the information in linked cells. If the program can't find the source, as would happen if a workbook or worksheet is deleted or renamed, an alert box appears, telling you that there is a broken link. At that point, you can click the Update button and then the Edit Links button to open the Edit Links dialog box and find which link is broken. After you identify the broken link, you can close the Edit Links dialog box, click the cell containing the broken link, and create a new link to the data you want.

If you enter a link and you make an error, a *#REF!* error message appears in the cell that contains the link. To fix the link, click the cell, delete its contents, and then either reenter the link or create it by using the method described earlier in this section.

TIP Excel tracks workbook changes, such as when you change a workbook's name, very well. Unless you delete a worksheet or workbook, or move a workbook to a new folder, odds are good that Excel can update your link references automatically to reflect the change.

In this exercise, you'll create a link to another workbook, make the link's reference invalid, use the Edit Links dialog box to break the link, and then re-create the link correctly.

➜ SET UP You need the OperatingExpenseDashboard and FleetOperatingCosts workbooks located in the Chapter07 practice file folder to complete this exercise. Open the workbooks, and then follow the steps.

1   In the **OperatingExpenseDashboard** workbook, in cell I6, enter =, but do not press Enter.

2   On the **View** tab, in the **Window** group, click **Switch Windows** and then, in the list, click **FleetOperatingCosts** to display the **FleetOperatingCosts** workbook.

3   If necessary, click the **Plane Repair** sheet tab to display the **Plane Repair** worksheet, and then click cell **C15**. Excel updates the formula to ='**[FleetOperatingCosts.xlsx]Plane Repair'!$C$15**.

4   Press **Enter**. Excel displays the **OperatingExpenseDashboard** workbook; the value **$2,410,871** appears in cell I6.

TIP Yes, cell C15 on the Plane Repair worksheet contains the wrong total for the Airplane Fuel category; that's why you replace it later in this exercise.

5   In the **Switch Windows** list, click **FleetOperatingCosts** to display the **FleetOperatingCosts** workbook.

6   Right-click the **Plane Repair** sheet tab, and then click **Delete**. In the message box that appears, click **Delete** to confirm that you want to delete the worksheet.

7   In the **Switch Windows** list, click **OperatingExpenseDashboard** to display the **OperatingExpenseDashboard** workbook. Note that cell **I6** shows a **#REF!** error because the worksheet containing the linked cell has been deleted.

	E	F	G	H	I
1					
2	**Facilities**			**Transportation**	
3					
4	Power	$ 1,800,000.00		Truck Fuel	
5	Water	$ 900,000.00		Truck Maintenance	
6	Rent	$ 2,350,000.00		Airplane Fuel	#REF!
7	Mortgage	$ 4,590,210.00		Airplane Maintenance	
8					

8   On the **Data** tab, in the **Connections** group, click **Edit Links** to open the **Edit Links** dialog box.

Edit Links

Source	Type	Update	Status
FleetOperatingCosts.xlsx	Worksheet	A	Unknown

Update Values
Change Source...
Open Source
Break Link
Check Status

Location: C:\Users\Curt\Documents\Writing\Excel 2013 SBS...\Chapter07
Item:
Update: ⦿ Automatic ○ Manual

Startup Prompt...   Close

9   Click **Break Link**. Excel displays a warning box asking if you're sure you want to break the link.

10 Click **Break Links** to close the warning box and remove the link from the workbook.

11 Click **Close** to close the **Edit Links** dialog box.

12 In cell **I6**, enter =, but do not press Enter.

13 In the **Switch Windows** list, click **FleetOperatingCosts** to display the **FleetOperatingCosts** workbook.

14 Click the **Plane Fuel** sheet tab to display the **Plane Fuel** worksheet.

15 Click cell **C15**, and then press **Enter** to complete the formula. Excel displays the **OperatingExpenseDashboard** workbook with the value **$52,466,303** in cell **I6**.

I6			×	✓	fx	='[FleetOperatingCosts.xlsx]Plane Fuel'!$C$15	
	E	F	G	H		I	
1							
2	**Facilities**			**Transportation**			
3							
4	Power	$ 1,800,000.00		Truck Fuel			
5	Water	$ 900,000.00		Truck Maintenance			
6	Rent	$ 2,350,000.00		Airplane Fuel		$ 52,466,303	
7	Mortgage	$ 4,590,210.00		Airplane Maintenance			
8							

 CLEAN UP Close the OperatingExpenseDashboard and FleetOperatingCosts workbooks, saving your changes if you want to.

Consolidating multiple sets of data into a single workbook

When you create a series of worksheets that contain similar data, perhaps by using a template, you build a consistent set of workbooks in which data is stored in a predictable place. For example, consider a workbook template that uses cell C5 to record the number of calls received from 9:00 A.M. to 10:00 A.M. by the Northeast distribution center.

	A	B	C	D	E	F	G
1							
2							
3			**Hour**				
4		**Call Center**	*9:00 AM*	*10:00 AM*	*11:00 AM*	*12:00 PM*	*1:00 PM*
5		*Northeast*					
6		*Atlantic*					
7		*Southeast*					
8		*North Central*					
9		*Midwest*					
10		*Southwest*					
11		*Mountain West*					
12		*Northwest*					
13		*Central*					
14							

Using links to bring data from one worksheet to another gives you a great deal of power to combine data from several sources into a single resource. For example, you can create a worksheet that lists the total revenue just for certain months of a year, use links to draw the values from the worksheets in which the sales were recorded, and then create a formula to perform calculations on the data. However, for large worksheets with hundreds of cells filled with data, creating links from every cell is a time-consuming process. Also, to calculate a sum or an average for the data, you would need to include links to cells in every workbook.

Fortunately, there is an easier way to combine data from multiple worksheets into a single worksheet. By using this process, called *data consolidation*, you can define ranges of cells from multiple worksheets and have Excel summarize the data. You define these ranges in the Consolidate dialog box.

7

Consolidate   ?   ✕

Function:
Sum

Reference:
                                              Browse...

All references:

                                              Add

                                              Delete

Use labels in
☐ Top row
☐ Left column   ☐ Create links to source data

                    OK   Close

IMPORTANT The ranges must all have the same shape.

After you open the dialog box, you move to the worksheet that contains the first cell range you want to include in your summary. When you select the cells, the 3-D reference for the range appears in the Consolidate dialog box. Clicking Add stores the reference. You can then choose the other cell ranges that contain data you want to include in the summary, or you can remove a range from the calculation by clicking the range and then clicking Delete.

Cells that are in the same relative position in the ranges have their contents summarized together. When you consolidate the ranges, the cell in the upper-left corner of one range is added to the cell in the upper-left corner of every other range, even if those ranges are in different areas of the worksheet. After you choose the ranges to be used in your summary, you can choose the calculation to perform on the data (sum, average, and so on). When you're done selecting ranges to use in the calculation, click OK to have Excel summarize the data on your target worksheet.

IMPORTANT You can define only one data consolidation summary per workbook.

In this exercise, you'll define a data consolidation range consisting of ranges from two other workbooks. You'll then add the contents of the ranges and show the results in a worksheet.

SET UP You need the Consolidate, JanuaryCalls, and FebruaryCalls workbooks located in the Chapter07 practice file folder to complete this exercise. Open the workbooks, and then follow the steps.

1   In the **Consolidate** workbook, on the **Data** tab, in the **Data Tools** group, click **Consolidate** to open the **Consolidate** dialog box.

2   Click the **Collapse Dialog** button at the right edge of the **Reference** field to contract the **Consolidate** dialog box.

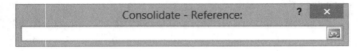

3   On the **View** tab, in the **Window** group, click **Switch Windows** and then, in the list, click **JanuaryCalls** to display the **JanuaryCalls** workbook.

4   Select the cell range **C5:O13**, and then click the **Expand Dialog** button to restore the **Consolidate** dialog box to its full size.

5   Click **Add** to add the selected range to the **All references** box.

7

6   Click the **Collapse Dialog** button again to contract the **Consolidate** dialog box.

7   In the **Switch Windows** list, click **FebruaryCalls** to display the **FebruaryCalls** workbook.

8   Select the cell range **C5:O13**, and then click the **Expand Dialog** button to restore the **Consolidate** dialog box to its full size.

9   Click **Add** to add the range '[FebruaryCalls.xlsx]February'!$C$5:$O$13 to the **All references** box.

10   Click **OK** to consolidate the **JanuaryCalls** and **FebruaryCalls** workbook data into the range C5:O13 in the **Consolidate** workbook. You didn't change the **SUM** operation in the **Function** box, so the values in the **Consolidate** workbook are the sum of the other workbooks' values.

	A	B	C	D	E	F	G	H
1								
2								
3			Hour					
4		Call Center	9:00 AM	10:00 AM	11:00 AM	12:00 PM	1:00 PM	2:00 PM
5		Northeast	15931	15958	13140	25367	19558	20624
6		Atlantic	28432	22326	15436	20884	30000	19770
7		Southeast	13132	12568	19732	14762	18885	20882
8		North Central	17588	26324	24121	24453	20048	21994
9		Midwest	24875	19965	19386	11374	26007	29378
10		Southwest	15353	27755	19718	17889	22116	28816
11		Mountain West	21516	28321	9754	26384	15926	23572
12		Northwest	19806	24154	12389	10151	24078	11642
13		Central	21018	24884	18655	31525	13407	19683
14								

✖ CLEAN UP Close the Consolidate, JanuaryCalls, and FebruaryCalls workbooks, saving your changes if you want to.

Key points

- If you create a lot of workbooks that have the same layout and design, saving a workbook with the common elements (and no data) will save you time when you create similar workbooks in the future.

- You can use data in other worksheets or workbooks in your formulas. You create a link by clicking the cell, which creates a 3-D reference to that cell.

- When you create a link to a cell in a table's Totals row, hiding the Totals row causes Excel to display a #REF! error in the cell in which you created the link.

7

Chapter at a glance

Examine

Examine data by using the Quick Analysis Lens, page 216

FORMATTING	CHARTS	**TOTALS**	TABLES	SPARKLINES
Sum	Average	Count	% Total	Running Total	Sum

Formulas automatically calculate totals for you.

Define

Define an alternative data set, page 219

Scenario Manager

Scenarios:
2DayIncrease

Add...
Delete
Edit...
Merge...
Summary...

Changing cells: $C$5
Comment: Created by Curtis Frye on 11/28/2012

Show   Close

Optimize

Find optimal solutions by using Solver, page 233

Solver Results

Solver found a solution. All Constraints and optimality conditions are satisfied.

Reports
Answer

○ Keep Solver Solution
○ Restore Original Values

☐ Return to Solver Parameters Dialog   ☐ Outline Reports

OK   Cancel   Save Scenario...

Solver found a solution. All Constraints and optimality conditions are satisfied.

When the GRG engine is used, Solver has found at least a local optimal solution. When Simplex LP is used, this means Solver has found a global optimal solution.

Analyze

Analyze data by using descriptive statistics, page 240

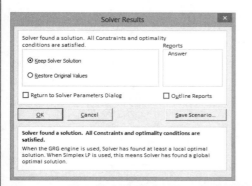

	A	B	C
1	Column1		
2			
3	Mean	120.7333	
4	Standard Error	7.036955	
5	Median	109	
6	Mode	102	
7	Standard Deviation	27.25401	
8	Sample Variance	742.781	
9	Kurtosis	-1.17215	
10	Skewness	0.642027	
11	Range	74	
12	Minimum	91	

Analyzing data and alternative data sets

8

IN THIS CHAPTER, YOU WILL LEARN HOW TO

- Examine data by using the Quick Analysis Lens.

- Define an alternative data set.

- Define multiple alternative data sets.

- Analyze data by using data tables.

- Vary your data to get a specific result by using Goal Seek.

- Find optimal solutions by using Solver.

- Analyze data by using descriptive statistics.

When you store data in a Microsoft Excel 2013 workbook, you can use that data, either by itself or as part of a calculation, to discover important information about your organization. You can summarize your data quickly by creating charts, calculating totals, or applying conditional formatting. When you track total sales on a time basis, you can find your best and worst sales periods and correlate them with outside events. For businesses such as Consolidated Messenger, package volume increases dramatically during the holidays as customers ship gifts to friends and family members.

The data in your worksheets is great for answering the question, "What happened?" The data is less useful for answering "what-if" questions, such as, "How much money would we save if we reduced our labor to 20 percent of our total costs?" You can always save an alternative version of a workbook and create formulas that calculate the effects of your changes, but you can do the same thing in your existing workbooks by defining one or more alternative data sets and switching between the original data and the new sets you create. Within a single workbook, you can create a data table that calculates the effects of changing one or two variables in a formula.

Excel also provides the tools to determine the input values that would be required for a formula to produce a specified result. For example, the chief operating officer of Consolidated Messenger, Lori Penor, could find out to what level the revenues from three-day shipping would need to rise for that category to account for 25 percent of total revenue.

In this chapter, you'll examine data by using the Quick Analysis Lens, define alternative data sets, and use different methods to determine the necessary inputs to make a calculation produce a specific result.

PRACTICE FILES To complete the exercises in this chapter, you need the practice files contained in the Chapter08 practice file folder. For more information, see "Download the practice files" in this book's Introduction.

Examining data by using the Quick Analysis Lens

One of the refinements in Excel 2013 is the addition of the Quick Analysis Lens, which brings the most commonly used formatting, charting, and summary tools into one convenient location. To examine data by using the Quick Analysis Lens tools, select the data you want to summarize. When you select a range, Excel displays the Quick Analysis button in the lower-right corner of the range. Clicking the Quick Analysis button displays the tools you can use to analyze your data.

KEYBOARD SHORTCUT Press Ctrl+Q to display the Quick Analysis Lens tools. For a complete list of keyboard shortcuts, see "Keyboard shortcuts" at the end of this book.

	A	B	C
1	Region	Packages	
2	Northeast	440,971	
3	Atlantic	304,246	
4	Southeast	444,006	
5	North Central	466,687	
6	Midwest	400,713	
7	Southwest	402,456	
8	Mountain Wes	370,176	
9	Northwest	209,013	
10	Central	234,993	
11			
12			

The Quick Analysis Lens provides a wide range of tools that you can use, including the ability to create an Excel table or PivotTable, insert a chart, or add conditional formatting. You can also add total columns and rows to your data range. For example, you can click the Totals tab of the Quick Analysis Lens, and then click Running Total for columns, identified by the icon labeled Running Total and the blue row at the bottom of the button, to add a row that calculates the running total for each column.

Formulas automatically calculate totals for you.

You can add one summary column and one summary row to each data range. If you select a new summary column or row when one exists, Excel displays a confirmation dialog box to verify that you want to replace the existing summary. When you click Yes, Excel makes the change.

In this exercise, you'll use the Quick Analysis Lens to analyze data.

SET UP You need the PackageAnalysis workbook located in the Chapter08 practice file folder to complete this exercise. Open the workbook, and then follow the steps.

1   Click any cell in the data range.

2   Press **Ctrl+*** to select the entire data range.

3   Click the **Quick Analysis** button to display the tools available in the **Quick Analysis** gallery.

4   Click the **Totals** tab to display the tools on that tab, point to (but don't click) the **Sum** button that has the blue row at the bottom to display a live preview of the effect of clicking the button, and then click the **Sum** button to add a sum total to the bottom of the data range.

	A	B	C
1	Region	Packages	
2	Northeast	440,971	
3	Atlantic	304,246	
4	Southeast	444,006	
5	North Central	466,687	
6	Midwest	400,713	
7	Southwest	402,456	
8	Mountain Wes	370,176	
9	Northwest	209,013	
10	Central	234,993	
11	Sum	3,273,261	
12			

TIP When your data range is an Excel table, as it is in this exercise, you can show or hide the summary by displaying or hiding the table's Total row.

5   In the **Quick Analysis** gallery, click the **Totals** tab again. Then click the arrow on the far right of the gallery to scroll to the right.

6   Click the **% Total** button that has the yellow column at the right edge to add that summary column to the worksheet.

	A	B	C
1	Region	Packages	% Total
2	Northeast	440,971	13.47%
3	Atlantic	304,246	9.29%
4	Southeast	444,006	13.56%
5	North Central	466,687	14.26%
6	Midwest	400,713	12.24%
7	Southwest	402,456	12.30%
8	Mountain Wes	370,176	11.31%
9	Northwest	209,013	6.39%
10	Central	234,993	7.18%
11	Sum	3,273,261	
12			

❌ CLEAN UP Close the PackageAnalysis workbook, saving your changes if you want to.

Defining an alternative data set

When you save data in an Excel worksheet, you create a record that reflects the character-istics of an event or object. That data could represent the number of deliveries in an hour on a particular day, the price of a new delivery option, or the percentage of total revenue accounted for by a delivery option. After the data is in place, you can create formulas to generate totals, find averages, and sort the rows in a worksheet based on the contents of one or more columns. However, if you want to perform a what-if analysis or explore the impact that changes in your data would have on any of the calculations in your workbooks, you need to change your data.

The problem with manipulating data that reflects an event or item is that when you change any data to affect a calculation, you run the risk of destroying the original data if you acci-dentally save your changes. You can avoid ruining your original data by creating a duplicate workbook and making your changes to it, but you can also create alternative data sets, or *scenarios*, within an existing workbook.

When you create a scenario, you give Excel alternative values for a list of cells in a work-sheet. You can use the Scenario Manager to add, delete, and edit scenarios.

8

Clicking the Add button displays the Add Scenario dialog box.

From within this dialog box, you can name the scenario and identify the cells for which you want to define alternative values. After you click OK, the Scenario Values dialog box opens with fields for you to enter the new values.

Clicking OK returns you to the Scenario Manager dialog box. From there, clicking the Show button replaces the values in the original worksheet with the alternative values you just defined in the scenario. Any formulas referencing cells that have changed values will recalculate their results. You can then remove the scenario by clicking the Undo button on the Quick Access Toolbar.

IMPORTANT If you save and close a workbook while a scenario is in effect, those values become the default values for the cells changed by the scenario! You should seriously consider creating a scenario that contains the original values of the cells you change or creating a scenario summary worksheet (described in the next section, "Defining multiple alternative data sets").

In this exercise, you'll create a scenario to measure the projected impact on total revenue of a rate increase on two-day shipping.

 SET UP You need the 2DayScenario workbook located in the Chapter08 practice file folder to complete this exercise. Open the workbook, and then follow the steps.

1   On the **Data** tab, in the **Data Tools** group, click **What-If Analysis** and then, in the list, click **Scenario Manager** to open the **Scenario Manager** dialog box.

2   Click **Add** to open the **Add Scenario** dialog box.

3   In the **Scenario name** field, enter **2DayIncrease**.

4   At the right edge of the **Changing cells** field, click the **Collapse Dialog** button so the worksheet contents are visible.

5   In the worksheet, click cell **C5** and then, in the **Add Scenario** dialog box, click the **Expand Dialog** button. $C$5 appears in the **Changing Cells** field, and the dialog box title changes to **Edit Scenario**.

	8

Edit Scenario dialog box:

Scenario name:
2DayIncrease

Changing cells:
$C$5

Ctrl+click cells to select non-adjacent changing cells.

Comment:
Created by Curtis Frye on 11/28/2012

Protection
☑ Prevent changes
☐ Hide

[OK]   [Cancel]

6　Click **OK** to open the **Scenario Values** dialog box.

7　In the value field, enter **13.2**, and then click **OK**. The **Scenario Values** dialog box closes, and the **Scenario Manager** dialog box opens again.

8　If necessary, drag the **Scenario Manager** dialog box to another location on the screen so that you can view the entire table.

9　In the **Scenario Manager** dialog box, click **Show**. Excel applies the scenario, changing the value in cell **C5** to **$13.20**, which in turn increases the value in cell **E8** to **$747,450,000.00**.

	A	B	C	D	E	F
1						
2		Service	Base Rate	Packages	Revenue	
3		Ground	$ 8.15	14,000,000	$ 114,100,000.00	
4		3Day	$ 10.25	9,000,000	$ 92,250,000.00	
5		2Day	$ 13.20	9,000,000	$ 118,800,000.00	
6		Overnight	$ 17.50	23,000,000	$ 402,500,000.00	
7		Priority Overnight	$ 24.75	800,000	$ 19,800,000.00	
8		Total			$ 747,450,000.00	

Scenario Manager ? ×

Scenarios:

2DayIncrease

Add...
Delete
Edit...
Merge...
Summary...

Changing cells: $C$5
Comment: Created by Curtis Frye on 11/28/2012

Show　Close

10　In the **Scenario Manager** dialog box, click **Close**.

11 On the **Quick Access Toolbar**, click the **Undo** button to remove the effect of the scenario and prevent Excel from overwriting the original values with the scenario's values if you decide to save the workbook.

❌ CLEAN UP Close the 2DayScenario workbook, saving your changes if you want to.

Defining multiple alternative data sets

One great feature of Excel scenarios is that you're not limited to creating one alternative data set—you can create as many scenarios as you like and apply them by using the Scenario Manager. To apply more than one scenario by using the Scenario Manager, click the name of the first scenario you want to display, click the Show button, and then do the same for any subsequent scenarios. The values you defined as part of those scenarios will appear in your worksheet, and Excel will update any calculations involving the changed cells.

TIP If you apply a scenario to a worksheet and then apply another scenario to the same worksheet, both sets of changes appear. If multiple scenarios change the same cell, the cell will contain the value in the most recently applied scenario.

Applying multiple scenarios alters the values in your worksheets. You can understand how those changes affect your formulas, but Excel also gives you a way to view the results of all your scenarios in a single, separate worksheet. To create a worksheet in your current workbook that summarizes the changes caused by your scenarios, open the Scenario Manager, and then click the Summary button. When you do, the Scenario Summary dialog box opens.

8

From within the dialog box, you can choose the type of summary worksheet you want to create and the cells you want to display in the summary worksheet. To choose the cells to display in the summary, click the Collapse Dialog button at the right of the Result Cells field, select the cells you want to display, and then expand the dialog box. After you verify that the range in the box represents the cells you want to have included on the summary sheet, click OK to create the new worksheet.

It's a good idea to create an "undo" scenario named *Normal* that holds the original values of the cells you're going to change before they're changed in other scenarios. For example, if you create a scenario named *High Fuel Costs* that changes the sales figures in three cells, your Normal scenario restores those cells to their original values. That way, even if you accidentally modify your worksheet, you can apply the Normal scenario and not have to reconstruct the worksheet from scratch.

TIP Each scenario can change a maximum of 32 cells, so you might need to create more than one scenario to ensure that you can restore a worksheet.

In this exercise, you'll create scenarios to represent projected revenue increases from two rate changes, view the scenarios, and then summarize the scenario results in a new worksheet.

➡ SET UP **You need the MultipleScenarios workbook located in the Chapter08 practice file folder to complete this exercise. Open the workbook, and then follow the steps.**

1   On the **Data** tab, in the **Data Tools** group, click **What-If Analysis** and then, in the list, click **Scenario Manager** to open the **Scenario Manager** dialog box.

2   Click **Add** to open the **Add Scenario** dialog box.

3   In the **Scenario name** field, enter 3DayIncrease.

4   At the right edge of the **Changing cells** field, click the **Collapse Dialog** button to collapse the **Add Scenario** dialog box.

5   In the worksheet, click cell **C4** and then, in the dialog box, click the **Expand Dialog** button. $C$4 appears in the **Changing Cells** field, and the dialog box title changes to **Edit Scenario**.

6   Click **OK** to open the **Scenario Values** dialog box.

7   In the value field, enter **11.50**.

8   Click **OK** to close the **Scenario Values** dialog box and open the **Scenario Manager**.

9   Click **Add** to open the **Add Scenario** dialog box.

10   In the **Scenario name** field, enter Ground and Overnight Increase.

11   At the right edge of the **Changing cells** field, click the **Collapse Dialog** button to collapse the **Add Scenario** dialog box.

12   Click cell **C3**, hold down the **Ctrl** key, and click cell **C6**. Then click the **Expand Dialog** button. **$C$3,$C$6** appears in the **Changing Cells** field, and the dialog box title changes to **Edit Scenario**.

Edit Scenario	?	✕

Scenario name:

Ground and Overnight Increase

Changing cells:

$C$3,$C$6

Ctrl+click cells to select non-adjacent changing cells.

Comment:

Created by Curtis Frye on 11/28/2012

Protection

☑ Prevent changes

☐ Hide

OK	Cancel

13   Click **OK** to open the **Scenario Values** dialog box.

14   In the **$C$3** field, enter **10.15**.

15   In the **$C$6** field, enter **18.5**.

16   Click **OK** to close the **Scenario Values** dialog box and open the **Scenario Manager** dialog box.

8

17 Click **Summary** to open the **Scenario Summary** dialog box.

18 Verify that **Scenario summary** is selected and that cell **E8** appears in the **Result cells** field.

19 Click **OK** to create a **Scenario Summary** worksheet.

		Current Values:	3DayIncrease	Ground and Overnight Increase
Scenario Summary				
Changing Cells:				
	$C$4	$ 10.25	$ 11.50	$ 10.25
	$C$3	$ 8.15	$ 8.15	$ 10.15
	$C$6	$ 17.50	$ 17.50	$ 18.50
Result Cells:				
	$E$8	$ 739,800,000.00	$ 751,050,000.00	$ 790,800,000.00

Notes: Current Values column represents values of changing cells at time Scenario Summary Report was created. Changing cells for each scenario are highlighted in gray.

✖ CLEAN UP Close the MultipleScenarios workbook, saving your changes if you want to.

Analyzing data by using data tables

When you examine business data in Excel, you will often want to discover the result of formulas if you provide different inputs. For example, the executive team of Consolidated Messenger might want to calculate the change in revenue from raising shipping rates, increasing package volume, or both. In Excel 2013, you can calculate the results of those changes by using a data table.

To create a data table that has one variable, you create a worksheet that contains the data required to calculate the variations in the table.

	A	B	C	D
1	**Revenue Increases**			**Revenue**
2	Year	2012		$ 2,102,600.70
3	Increase	0%	2%	
4	Package Count	237,582	5%	
5	Rate	$ 8.85	8%	
6				

> **IMPORTANT** The data and formulas must be laid out in a rectangle so the data table you create will appear in the lower-right corner of the cell range you select.

The formula used to summarize the base data appears in cell D2, the cells with the changing values are the range C3:C5, and the cells to contain the calculations based on those values are D3:D5. To create the single-variable data table, select the cell range C2:D5, which encompasses the changing rates, summary formula, and target cells. Then, on the Data tab, click What-If Analysis, and then click Data Table to display the Data Table dialog box.

8

Now you need to identify the cell that contains the summary formula's value that will change in the data table's cells. In this case, that cell is B3. Because the target cells D3:D5 are laid out as a column, you enter the cell address B3 in the Column Input Cell box and click OK.

TIP If your target cells were laid out as a row, you would enter the address of the cell that contains the value to be changed in the Row Input Cell box.

When you click OK, Excel fills in the results of the data table, using the replacement values in cells C3:C5 to provide the values for cells D3:D5.

	A	B	C	D
1	**Revenue Increases**			Revenue
2	Year	2012		$ 2,102,600.70
3	Increase	0%	2%	$ 2,107,352.34
4	Package Count	237,582	5%	$ 2,114,479.80
5	Rate	$ 8.85	8%	$ 2,121,607.26
6				

To create a two-variable data table, you lay your data out with one set of replacement values as row headers and the other set as column headers. For example, you could build a worksheet to calculate total revenue as a function of both rate increases and package count increases.

	A	B	C	D	E
1	**Revenue Increases**	Revenue			
2	Year	2012	$ 2,102,600.70	260,000	300,000
3	Increase	0%	2%		
4	Package Count	237,582	5%		
5	Rate	$ 8.85	8%		
6					

In this case, you select the cell range C2:E5 and then, on the Data tab, click What-If Analysis and then click Data Table to display the Data Table dialog box. Because you're creating a two-variable data table, you need to enter cell addresses for both the Column Input Cell and Row Input Cell. In this case, the column input cell is B3, which represents the rate increase, and the row input cell is B4, which contains the package count. When you click OK, Excel creates your data table.

	A	B	C	D	E
1	**Revenue Increases**	Revenue			
2	Year	2012	$ 2,102,600.70	260,000	300,000
3	Increase	0%	2%	$ 2,306,200.00	$ 2,661,000.00
4	Package Count	237,582	5%	$ 2,314,000.00	$ 2,670,000.00
5	Rate	$ 8.85	8%	$ 2,321,800.00	$ 2,679,000.00
6					

TIP You can't edit the formulas Excel creates when you define a data table. You can only change them successfully by creating another data table that includes the same cells.

In this exercise, you'll create one-variable and two-variable data tables.

→ SET UP You need the RateProjections workbook located in the Chapter08 practice file folder to complete this exercise. Open the workbook, and then follow the steps.

1   If necessary, click the **RateIncreases** sheet tab to display that worksheet.

2   Select cells **C2:D5**.

3   On the **Data** tab, in the **Data Tools** group, click the **What-If Analysis** button and then, in the list, click **Data Table**.

4   In the **Column input cell** box, enter **B3**.

5   Click **OK** to close the **Data Table** dialog box and fill the what-if values into cells **D3:D5**.

6   Click the **RateAndVolume** sheet tab to display that worksheet.

7   Select cells **C2:E5**.

8   On the **Data** tab, in the **Data Tools** group, click the **What-If Analysis** button and then, in the list, click **Data Table**.

9   In the **Row input cell** box, enter **B4**.

10   In the **Column input cell** box, enter **B3**.

11   Click **OK** to close the **Data Table** dialog box and update your worksheet.

▲	A	B	C	D	E
1	**Revenue Increases**		Revenue		
2	Year	2012	$ 2,102,600.70	260,000	300,000
3	Increase	0%	2.00%	$ 2,306,200.00	$ 2,661,000.00
4	Package Count	237,582	4.75%	$ 2,313,350.00	$ 2,669,250.00
5	Rate	$ 8.85	9.25%	$ 2,325,050.00	$ 2,682,750.00
6					

 CLEAN UP Close the RateProjections workbook, saving your changes if you want to.

Varying your data to get a specific result by using Goal Seek

When you run an organization, you must track how every element performs, both in absolute terms and in relation to other parts of the organization. Just as you might want to reward your employees for maintaining a perfect safety record and keeping down your insurance rates, you might also want to stop carrying products you cannot sell.

When you plan how you want to grow your business, you should have specific goals in mind for each department or product category. For example, Lori Penor of Consolidated Messenger might have the goal of reducing the firm's labor costs by 20 percent as compared to the previous year. Finding the labor amount that represents a 20-percent decrease is simple, but expressing goals in other ways can make finding the solution more challenging. Instead of decreasing labor costs 20 percent over the previous year, Lori might want to decrease labor costs so they represent no more than 20 percent of the company's total outlay.

As an example, consider a worksheet that holds cost figures for Consolidated Messenger's operations and uses those figures to calculate both total costs and the share each category has of that total.

	A	B	C	D	E	F	G	H
1								
2			Labor	Transportation	Taxes	Facilities	Total	
3		Cost	$ 18,000,382.00	$35,000,000.00	$ 7,000,000.00	$ 19,000,000.00	$ 79,000,382.00	
4		Share	22.79%	44.30%	8.86%	24.05%		
5								

IMPORTANT In the worksheet, the values in the Share row are displayed as percentages, but the underlying values are decimals. For example, Excel represents *0.3064* as *30.64%*.

Although it would certainly be possible to figure the target number that would make labor costs represent 20 percent of the total, there is an easier way to do it in Excel: by using Goal Seek. To use Goal Seek, you display the Data tab and then, in the Data Tools group, click What-If Analysis. On the menu that is displayed, click Goal Seek to open the Goal Seek dialog box.

IMPORTANT If you save a workbook with the results of a Goal Seek calculation in place, you will overwrite the values in your workbook.

In the dialog box, you identify the cell that has the target value; in this example, it is cell C4, which has the percentage of costs accounted for by the Labor category. The To Value field has the target value (.2, which is equivalent to 20 percent), and the By Changing Cell field identifies the cell that has the value Excel should change to generate the target value of 20 percent in cell C4. In this example, the cell to be changed is C3.

Clicking OK tells Excel to find a solution for the goal you set. When Excel finishes its work, the new values appear in the designated cells, and the Goal Seek Status dialog box opens.

TIP Goal Seek finds the closest solution it can without exceeding the target value. In this case, the closest percentage it could find was 19.97 percent.

In this exercise, you'll use Goal Seek to determine how much you need to decrease transportation costs so that those costs make up no more than 40 percent of Consolidated Messenger's operating costs.

 SET UP You need the TargetValues workbook located in the Chapter08 practice file folder to complete this exercise. Open the workbook, and then follow the steps.

1   On the **Data** tab, in the **Data Tools** group, click the **What-If Analysis** button, and then, in the list, click **Goal Seek** to open the **Goal Seek** dialog box.

2   In the **Set cell** field, enter **D4**.

3   In the **To value** field, enter **40%**.

4   In the **By changing cell** field, enter **D3**.

5   Click **OK** to display the solution in both the worksheet and the **Goal Seek Status** dialog box. The target value of 0.4 is equivalent to the 40 percent value you entered earlier.

	A	B	C	D	E	F	G	H
1								
2			**Labor**	**Transportation**	**Taxes**	**Facilities**	**Total**	
3		Cost	$ 18,000,382.00	$29,336,849.65	$ 7,000,000.00	$ 19,000,000.00	$ 73,337,231.65	
4		Share	24.54%	40.00%	9.54%	25.91%		
5								
6								
7								
8								
9								
10								
11								
12								
13								
14								

Goal Seek Status

Goal Seeking with Cell D4 found a solution.

Target value: 0.4
Current value: 40.00%

6   Click **Cancel** to close the **Goal Seek Status** dialog box without saving the new worksheet values.

CLEAN UP Close the TargetValues workbook, saving your changes if you want to.

Finding optimal solutions by using Solver

Goal Seek is a great tool for finding out how much you need to change a single input value to generate a desired result from a formula, but it's of no help if you want to find the best mix of several input values. For example, marketing vice president Craig Dewar might want to advertise in four national magazines to drive customers to Consolidated Messenger's website, but he might not know the best mix of ads to reach the greatest number of readers. He asked the publishers for ad pricing and readership numbers, which he recorded in a spreadsheet, along with the minimum number of ads per publication (three) and the minimum number of times he wants the ad to be seen (10,000,000). Because one of the magazines has a high percentage of corporate executive readers, Craig does want to take out at least four ads in that publication, despite its relatively low readership. The goal of the ad campaign is for the ads to be seen as many times as possible without costing the company more than the $3,000,000 budget.

	Magazine	Cost per Ad	Readers	Number of Ads	Total Cost	Audience
5	Mag1	$ 30,000.00	100,000	8	$ 240,000.00	800,000
6	Mag2	$ 40,000.00	400,000	8	$ 320,000.00	3,200,000
7	Mag3	$ 27,000.00	350,000	8	$ 216,000.00	2,800,000
8	Mag4	$ 80,000.00	200,000	10	$ 800,000.00	2,000,000
9	Totals				$ 1,576,000.00	8,800,000

	Constraints		
11		Total Budget	$ 3,000,000.00
12		Minimum Audience	10,000,000
13		Minimum Ads for Magazines 1 through 3	8
14		Minimum Ads for Magazine 4	10
15		Maximum Ads in Any Magazine	20

TIP It helps to spell out every aspect of your problem so that you can identify the cells you want Solver to use in its calculations.

If you performed a complete installation when you installed Excel on your computer, the Solver button is available on the Data tab in the Analysis group. If not, you need to install the Solver Add-In. To do so, click the File tab, and then click Options. In the Excel Options dialog box, click Add-Ins to display the Add-Ins page. At the bottom of the dialog box, in the Manage list, click Excel Add-Ins, and then click Go to display the Add-Ins dialog box. Select the Solver Add-In check box and click OK to install Solver.

TIP You might be prompted for the Microsoft Office system installation CD. If so, put the CD in your CD drive, and click OK.

After the installation is complete, Solver appears on the Data tab, in the Analysis group. Clicking Solver displays the Solver Parameters dialog box.

The first step of setting up your Solver problem is to identify the cell that contains the summary formula you want to establish as your objective. To identify that cell, click in the Set Objective box, click the target cell in the worksheet, and then select the option that represents whether you want to minimize the cell's value, maximize the cell's value, or make the cell take on a specific value. Next, you click in the By Changing Variable Cells box and select the cells Solver should vary to change the value in the objective cell.

If you want to require Solver to find solutions that use only integer values (that is, values that are whole numbers and have no decimal component), you can do so by clicking the Options button in the Solver Parameters dialog box to open the Options dialog box.

If necessary, clear the Ignore Integer Constraints check box and click OK to save your setting and return to the Solver Parameters dialog box.

Finally, you can create constraints that will set the limits for the values Solver can use. To do so, click Add to open the Add Constraint dialog box. You add constraints to the Solver problem by selecting the cells to which you want to apply the constraint, selecting the comparison operation (such as less than or equal to, greater than or equal to, or must be an integer), and clicking in the Constraint box to select the cell with the value of the constraint. You could also enter a value in the Constraint box, but referring to a cell makes it possible for you to change the constraint later without opening Solver.

TIP After you run Solver, you can use the commands in the Solver Results dialog box to save the results as changes to your worksheet or create a scenario based on the changed data.

In this exercise, you'll use Solver to determine the best mix of ads given the following constraints:

- You want to maximize the number of people who view the ads.
- You must buy at least 8 ads in three magazines and at least 10 in the fourth.
- You can't buy part of an ad (that is, all numbers must be integers).
- You can buy no more than 20 ads in any one magazine.
- You must reach at least 10,000,000 people.
- Your ad budget is $3,000,000.

→ SET UP **You need the AdBuy workbook located in the Chapter08 practice file folder to complete this exercise. Open the workbook, and then follow the steps.**

1   If the **Solver** button doesn't appear in the **Analysis** group on the **Data** tab, follow the instructions described earlier to install it.

2   In the **Analysis** group on the **Data** tab, click **Solver** to open the **Solver Parameters** dialog box.

3   In the **Solver Parameters** dialog box, click **Options** to open the **Options** dialog box.

4   On the **All Methods** page of the dialog box, clear the **Ignore Integer Constraints** check box, and then click **OK**.

5   Click in the **Set Objective** box, and then click cell **G9**. **$G$9** appears in the **Set Objective** field.

6   Click **Max**.

7   Click in the **By Changing Variable Cells** field, and select cells **E5:E8**. **$E$5:$E$8** appears in the **By Changing Variable Cells** field.

8   Click **Add** to open the **Add Constraint** dialog box.

9   Select cells **E5:E8**. **$E$5:$E$8** appears in the **Cell Reference** field.

10 In the operator list, click **int**. Then click **Add**. Excel adds the constraint to the Solver problem, and the **Add Constraint** dialog box clears to accept the next constraint.

11 Click cell **F9**. **$F$9** appears in the **Cell Reference** field. Verify that the operator **<=** appears in the operator field.

12 Click in the **Constraint** field, and then click cell **G11**. **=$G$11** appears in the **Constraint** field.

13 Click **Add**. Excel adds the constraint to the Solver problem, and the **Add Constraint** dialog box clears to accept the next constraint.

14 Click cell **G9**. **$G$9** appears in the **Cell Reference** field.

15 In the operator list, click **>=**.

16 Click in the **Constraint** field, and then click cell **G12**. **=$G$12** appears in the **Constraint** field.

17 Click **Add**. Excel adds the constraint to the Solver problem, and the **Add Constraint** dialog box clears to accept the next constraint.

18 Select cells **E5:E7**. **$E$5:$E$7** appears in the **Cell Reference** field.

19 In the operator list, click **>=**.

20 Click in the **Constraint** field, and then click cell **G13**. **=$G$13** appears in the
Constraint field.

21 Click **Add**. Excel adds the constraint to the Solver problem, and the **Add Constraint**
dialog box clears to accept the next constraint.

22 Click cell **E8**. **$E$8** appears in the **Cell Reference** field.

23 In the operator list, click **>=**.

24 Click in the **Constraint** field, and then click cell **G14**. **=$G$14** appears in the
Constraint field.

25 Click **Add**. Excel adds the constraint to the Solver problem, and the **Add Constraint**
dialog box clears to accept the next constraint.

26 Select cells **E5:E8**. **$E$5:$E$8** appears in the **Cell Reference** field.

27 Verify that the **<=** operator appears in the operator field, click in the **Constraint** field,
and then click cell **G15**. **=$G$15** appears in the **Constraint** field.

28 Click **OK**. Excel adds the constraint to the Solver problem and closes the **Add
Constraint** dialog box, and the **Solver Parameters** dialog box opens again.

Solver Parameters

Se_t Objective: $G$9

To: ⦿ _M_ax   ◯ Mi_n_   ◯ _V_alue Of: 0

_B_y Changing Variable Cells:

$E$5:$E$8

S_u_bject to the Constraints:

```
$E$5:$E$7 > = $G$13
$E$5:$E$8 < = $G$15
$E$5:$E$8 = integer
$E$8 > = $G$14
$F$9 < = $G$11
$G$9 > = $G$12
```

- Add
- _C_hange
- _D_elete
- _R_eset All
- Load/Save

☐ Ma_k_e Unconstrained Variables Non-Negative

Se_l_ect a Solving Method: GRG Nonlinear ▾   O_p_tions

Solving Method

Select the GRG Nonlinear engine for Solver Problems that are smooth nonlinear. Select the LP Simplex engine for linear Solver Problems, and select the Evolutionary engine for Solver problems that are non-smooth.

_H_elp   _S_olve   Cl_o_se

8

29   Click **Solve**. The **Solver Results** dialog box opens, indicating that Solver found a solution. The result is displayed in the body of the worksheet.

The table shown in the spreadsheet:

Magazine	Cost per Ad	Readers	Number of Ads	Total Cost	Audience
Mag1	$ 30,000.00	100,000	20	$ 600,000.00	2,000,000
Mag2	$ 40,000.00	400,000	20	$ 800,000.00	8,000,000
Mag3	$ 27,000.00	350,000	20	$ 540,000.00	7,000,000
Mag4	$ 80,000.00	200,000	13	$ 1,040,000.00	2,600,000
Totals				$ 2,980,000.00	19,600,000

Solver Results dialog:

Solver found a solution. All Constraints and optimality conditions are satisfied.

Reports: Answer

○ Keep Solver Solution
○ Restore Original Values

☐ Return to Solver Parameters Dialog   ☐ Outline Reports

OK   Cancel   Save Scenario...

Solver found a solution. All Constraints and optimality conditions are satisfied.

When the GRG engine is used, Solver has found at least a local optimal solution. When Simplex LP is used, this means Solver has found a global optimal solution.

Ad Buy Constraints

30   Click **OK** to close the **Solver Results** dialog box.

❌ CLEAN UP Close the AdBuy workbook, saving your changes if you want to.

Analyzing data by using descriptive statistics

Experienced business people can tell a lot about numbers just by looking at them, such as whether the numbers "feel right." That is, the sales figures are about where they're supposed to be for a particular hour, day, or month; the average seems about right; and sales have increased from year to year. When you need more than an informal assessment, however, you can use the tools in the Analysis ToolPak.

If the Data Analysis item isn't visible in the Analysis group on the Data tab, you can install it. To do so, click the File tab, and then click Options. In the Excel Options dialog box, click Add-Ins to display the Add-Ins page. At the bottom of the dialog box, in the Manage list, click Excel Add-Ins, and then click Go to display the Add-Ins dialog box. Select the Analysis ToolPak check box and click OK.

TIP You might be prompted for the Microsoft Office system installation CD. If so, put the CD in your CD drive, and click OK.

After the installation is complete, the Data Analysis option appears in the Analysis group on the Data tab.

In the list that appears when you click the Data Analysis button, click the item representing the type of data analysis you want to perform, click OK, and use the commands in the resulting dialog box to analyze your data.

In this exercise, you'll use the Analysis ToolPak to generate descriptive statistics of driver sorting time data.

SET UP You need the DriverSortTimes workbook located in the Chapter08 practice file folder to complete this exercise. Open the workbook, and then follow the steps.

1   On the **Data** tab, in the **Analysis** group, click **Data Analysis** to open the **Data Analysis** dialog box.

2   Click **Descriptive Statistics**, and then click **OK** to open the **Descriptive Statistics** dialog box.

8

3   Click in the **Input Range** field, and then select cells **C3:C17**. **$C$3:$C$17** appears in the **Input Range** field.

4   Select the **Summary statistics** check box.

5   Click **OK**. A new worksheet that contains summary statistics about the selected data appears.

	A	B	C
1	Column1		
2			
3	Mean	120.7333	
4	Standard Error	7.036955	
5	Median	109	
6	Mode	102	
7	Standard Deviation	27.25401	
8	Sample Variance	742.781	
9	Kurtosis	-1.17215	
10	Skewness	0.642027	
11	Range	74	
12	Minimum	91	
13	Maximum	165	
14	Sum	1811	
15	Count	15	
16			

 CLEAN UP Close the DriverSortTimes workbook, saving your changes if you want to.

Key points

- The Quick Analysis Lens puts the most popular summary analysis tools at your fingertips.

- By using scenarios, you can describe many potential business cases within a single workbook.

- It's usually a good idea to create a "normal" scenario that you can use to reset your worksheet.

- Remember that you can change up to 32 cells in a scenario, but no more.

- You can summarize your scenarios on a new worksheet to compare how each scenario approaches the data.

- You can use data tables to create useful what-if scenarios by changing one or two variables that provide input to a summary formula.

- You can use Goal Seek to determine what value you need in a single cell to generate the result you want from a formula.

- If you want to vary the values in more than one cell to find the optimal mix of inputs for a calculation, use the Solver Add-In.

- Advanced statistical tools are available in the Analysis ToolPak. You can use them to examine your data thoroughly.

8

Chapter at a glance

Charts

Customize the appearance of charts,
page 254

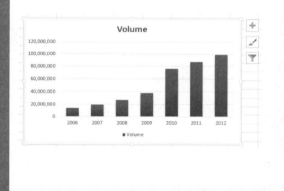

Trendlines

Find trends in your data,
page 262

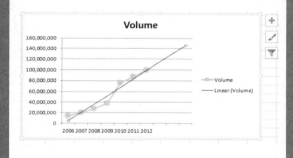

Diagrams

Create diagrams by using SmartArt,
page 273

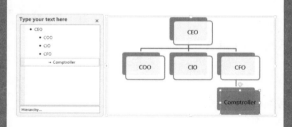

Shapes

Create shapes and mathematical equations,
page 278

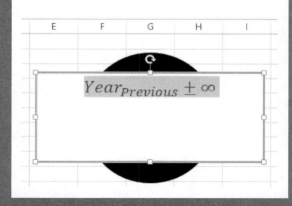

Creating charts and graphics

9

IN THIS CHAPTER, YOU WILL LEARN HOW TO

- Create charts.

- Customize the appearance of charts.

- Find trends in your data.

- Create dual-axis charts.

- Summarize your data by using sparklines.

- Create diagrams by using SmartArt.

- Create shapes and mathematical equations.

When you enter data into a Microsoft Excel 2013 worksheet, you create a record of important events, whether they are individual sales, sales for an hour of a day, or the price of a product. However, a list of values in cells can't communicate easily the overall trends in the data. The best way to communicate trends in a large collection of data is by creating a chart, which summarizes data visually. In addition to the standard charts, with Excel 2013, you can create compact charts called sparklines, which summarize a data series by using a graph contained within a single cell.

You have a great deal of control over your charts' appearance—you can change the color of any chart element, choose a different chart type to better summarize the underlying data, and change the display properties of text and numbers in a chart. If the data in the worksheet used to create a chart represents a progression through time, such as sales over several months, you can have Excel extrapolate future sales and add a trendline to the graph that represents that prediction.

In this chapter, you'll create a chart and customize its elements, find trends in your data, create a dual-axis chart, summarize data by using sparklines, create diagrams by using SmartArt, and create shapes that contain mathematical equations.

Creating charts

With Excel 2013, you can create charts quickly by using the Quick Analysis Lens, which displays recommended charts to summarize your data. To display recommended charts, select the entire data range you want to chart, click the Quick Analysis button, and then click Charts to display the types of charts that Excel recommends.

You can display a live preview of each recommended chart by pointing to the icon that represents that chart. Clicking the icon adds the chart to your worksheet.

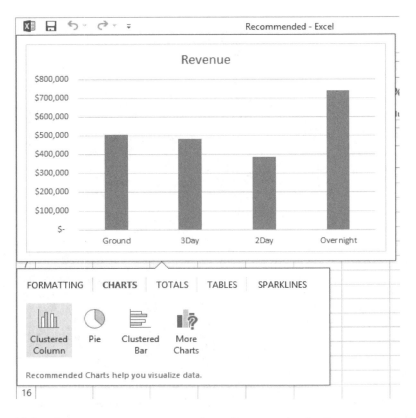

If the chart you want to create doesn't appear in the Recommended Charts gallery, select the data that you want to summarize visually and then, on the Insert tab, in the Charts group, click the type of chart that you want to create to have Excel display the available chart subtypes. When you point to a subtype, Excel displays a live preview of what the chart will look like if you click that subtype.

When you click a chart subtype, Excel creates the chart by using the default layout and color scheme defined in your workbook's theme.

KEYBOARD SHORTCUT Press Alt+F11 to create a chart of the default type on the current worksheet or press F11 to create a new chart sheet. Unless you or another user changed the default, Excel creates a column chart. For a complete list of keyboard shortcuts, see "Keyboard shortcuts" at the end of this book.

If Excel doesn't plot your data the way that you want it to appear, you can change the axis on which Excel plots a data column. The most common reason for incorrect data plotting is that the column to be plotted on the horizontal axis contains numerical data instead of textual data. For example, if your data includes a Year column and a Maintenance column, instead of plotting maintenance data for each consecutive year along the horizontal axis, Excel plots both of those columns in the body of the chart and creates a sequential series to provide values for the horizontal axis.

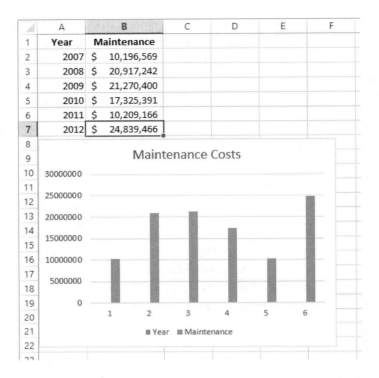

You can change which data Excel applies to the vertical axis (also known as the *y-axis*) and the horizontal axis (also known as the *x-axis*). To make that change, select the chart and then, on the Design tab, in the Data group, click Select Data to open the Select Data Source dialog box.

As shown in the preceding graphic, the Year column doesn't belong in the Legend Entries (Series) pane, which corresponds to a column chart's vertical axis. To remove a column from an axis, select the column's name, and then click Remove. To add the column to the Horizontal (Category) Axis Labels pane, click that pane's Edit button to display the Axis Labels dialog box, which you can use to select a range of cells on a worksheet to provide values for an axis.

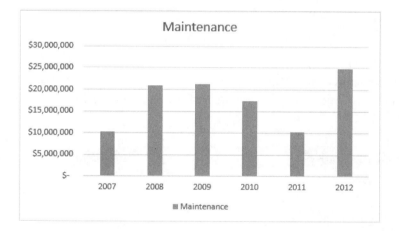

In the Axis Labels dialog box, click the Collapse Dialog button at the right edge of the Axis Label Range field, select the cells to provide the values for the horizontal axis (not including the column header, if any), click the Expand Dialog button, and then click OK. Click OK again to close the Select Data Source dialog box and revise your chart.

After you create your chart, you can change its size to reflect whether the chart should dominate its worksheet or take on a role as another informative element on the worksheet. For example, Gary Schare, the chief executive officer of Consolidated Messenger, could create a

workbook that summarizes the performance of each of his company's business units. In that case, he would display the chart and data for each business unit on the same worksheet, so he would want to make his charts small.

To resize a chart, select the chart, and then drag one of the handles on the chart's edges. By using the handles in the middle of the edges, you can resize the chart in one direction. When you drag a handle on the left or right edge, the chart gets narrower or wider, whereas when you drag the handles on the chart's top and bottom edges, the chart gets shorter or taller. You can drag a corner handle to change the chart's height and width at the same time; and you can hold down the Shift key as you drag the corner handle to change the chart's size without changing its proportions.

Just as you can control a chart's size, you can also control its location. To move a chart within a worksheet, drag the chart to the desired location. If you want to move the chart to a new worksheet, click the chart and then, on the Design tool tab, in the Location group, click Move Chart to open the Move Chart dialog box.

To move the chart to a new chart sheet, click New Sheet and enter the new sheet's name in the accompanying field. Clicking New Sheet creates a chart sheet that contains only your chart. You can still resize the chart on that sheet, but when Excel creates the new chart sheet, the chart takes up the full sheet.

To move the chart to an existing worksheet, click Object In and then, in the Object In list, click the worksheet to which you want to move the chart.

In this exercise, you'll create a chart, change how the chart plots your data, move your chart within a worksheet, and move your chart to its own chart sheet.

 SET UP You need the YearlyPackageVolume workbook located in the Chapter09 practice file folder to complete this exercise. Open the workbook, and then follow the steps.

1 On the **Data** worksheet, click any cell in the Excel table, and then press **Ctrl+*** to select the entire table.

2 In the lower-right corner of the Excel table, click the **Quick Analysis** button to display tools available in the **Quick Analysis** gallery.

3 Click the **Charts** tab to display the available chart types.

4 Click **Line** to create the recommended line chart.

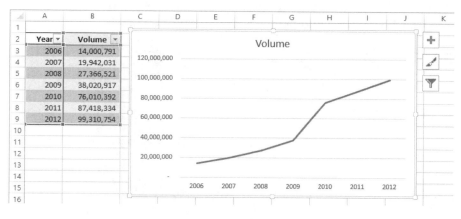

5 Press **Ctrl+Z** to undo the last action and remove the chart from your worksheet.

6 On the **Insert** tab, in the **Charts** group, click **Bar** and then, in the **2D Bar** group, click the first chart subtype, **Clustered Bar**. Excel creates the chart, with both the **Year** and **Volume** data series plotted in the body of the chart.

7 On the **Design** tab, in the **Data** group, click **Select Data** to open the **Select Data Source** dialog box.

8 In the **Legend Entries (Series)** area, click **Year**.

9 Click **Remove** to delete the **Year** series.

10 In the **Horizontal (Category) Axis Labels** area, click **Edit** to open the **Axis Labels** dialog box.

11 Select cells **A3:A9**, and then click **OK**. The **Axis Labels** dialog box closes, and the **Select Data Source** dialog box reappears with the years in the **Horizontal (Category) Axis Labels** area.

12   Click **OK**. Excel redraws your chart, using the years as the values for the horizontal axis.

13   Point to (don't click) the body of the chart, and when the pointer changes to a four-headed arrow drag the chart up and to the left so that it covers the Excel table.

14   On the **Design** tab, in the **Location** group, click **Move Chart** to open the **Move Chart** dialog box.

15   Click **New sheet**, enter Volume Chart in the sheet name box, and then click **OK**. Your chart appears on a chart sheet named *Volume Chart*.

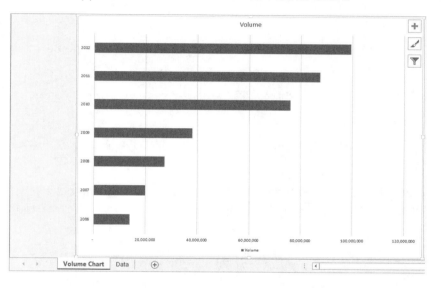

✖ CLEAN UP Close the YearlyPackageVolume workbook, saving your changes if you want to.

Customizing the appearance of charts

If you want to change a chart's appearance, select the chart and then click the Chart Styles button, which appears in a group of three buttons. These buttons, which are new in Excel 2013, put chart formatting and data controls within easy reach of your chart.

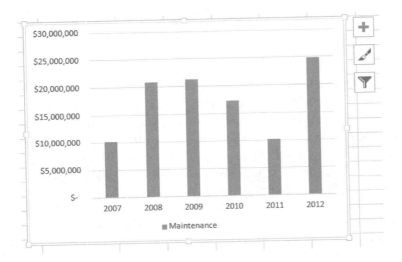

The Chart Styles gallery has two tabs: Style and Color. You can select a new look for you chart by choosing from the many styles on the Style.

TIP If you prefer to work with the ribbon, these same styles appear in the Chart Styles gallery on the Design tab.

Clicking the Color tab in the Chart Styles gallery displays a series of color schemes that you can select to change your chart's appearance.

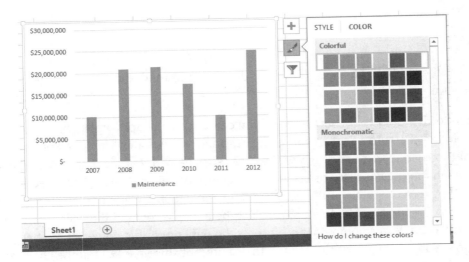

TIP The styles in the Chart Styles gallery are tied to your workbook's theme. If you change your workbook's theme, Excel changes your chart's appearance to reflect the new theme's colors.

When you create a chart by using the tools in the Charts group on the Insert tab, Excel creates an attractive chart that focuses on the data. In most cases, the chart has a title, legend (list of data series displayed in the chart), horizontal lines in the body of the chart to make it easier to discern individual values, and axis labels. If you want to create a chart that has more or different elements, such as additional data labels for each data point plotted on your chart, you can do so by selecting the chart and then, on the Design tab, in the Chart Layouts group, clicking Quick Layouts and then clicking the layout you want.

If you don't find the exact chart layout you want, you can select the chart and then click the Chart Elements action button, which appears to the right of the chart, to control each element's appearance and options.

By selecting the Gridlines check box, you can determine whether the chart displays horizontal and vertical gridlines.

In addition to changing your chart's layout, you can control the appearance of each element within the chart. To select a chart element to format, click that element. For example, if you want to change the formatting of the data series named Volume in the column chart you created in the previous exercise, you can click any column in the series to select the entire series. Any formatting changes you make then apply to every point in the entire series. If you want to change a single data point, select the entire series, and then click the chart element (for example, a column) that represents the data point that you want to change. For example, you can highlight the column that represents the year 2011 in the chart you created in the previous exercise.

You can display a list of the selectable chart elements by selecting the chart and then, on the Format tab, in the Current Selection group, clicking the Chart Elements arrow. Then click the desired chart element to select it.

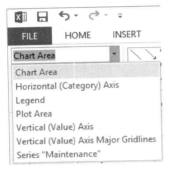

After you select the chart element, you can drag one of the element's handles to resize the element or drag the element to another location within the chart. To change the chart element's format, use the tools and dialog box launchers in the Shape Styles, Word Art Styles, Arrange, and Size groups on the Format tab to change the element's appearance. You can also select the chart element and then, on the Format tab, in the Current Selection group, click Format Selection to display a Format pane that you can use to change the chart element's appearance.

You can also display a similar set of formatting controls for a chart element by clicking the Chart Elements action button, pointing to the name of the element you want to change, clicking the right-pointing triangle that appears, and then clicking More Options. Doing so displays the pane related to that element.

With the third action button, Chart Filters, you can focus on specific data in your chart. Clicking the Chart Filters action button displays a filter interface that is very similar to that used to limit the data displayed in an Excel table.

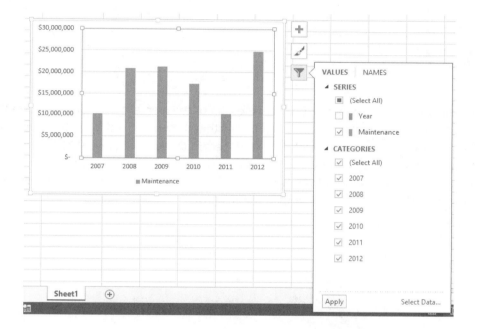

Selecting or clearing a check box displays or hides data related to a specific value within a series, which you can select as well.

If you think you want to apply the same set of changes to charts you'll create in the future, you can save your chart as a chart template. When you select the data that you want to summarize visually and apply the chart template, you'll create consistently formatted charts in a minimum of steps. To save a chart as a chart template, right-click the chart and then click Save As Template. Use the controls in the dialog box that opens to name and save your template. Then, to create a chart based on that template, select the data that you want to summarize and on the Insert tab, in the Charts group, click the dialog box launcher in the lower-right corner of the group to open the Insert Chart dialog box. On the All Charts tab, click Templates, click the template you want to use, and then click OK.

TIP You can apply a template to an existing chart by selecting the chart and then, on the Design tab, in the Type group, clicking Change Chart Type to open the Change Chart Type dialog box. Click Templates, click the template you want to use, and then click OK.

In this exercise, you'll change a chart's layout, apply a new Chart Style, change the number format of the values on the vertical axis, save the chart as a chart template, and apply the template to another chart.

SET UP You need the VolumeByCenter workbook located in the Chapter09 practice file folder to complete this exercise. Open the workbook, and then follow the steps.

1   On the **Presentation** worksheet, select the chart.

2   On the **Design** tab, in the **Chart Layouts** group, click **Quick Layouts**, and then click the first chart layout **Layout 1**.

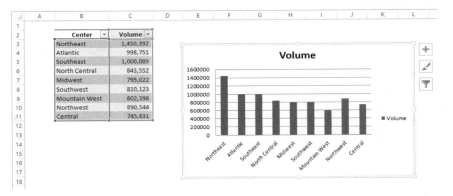

3   To the right of the chart, click the **Chart Styles** action button to display the **Chart Styles** gallery.

4   Click **Style 7** to change the chart's style.

5   Click the **Chart Styles** action button to hide the **Chart Styles** gallery.

6   Click the **Chart Elements** action button, point to the **Axes** entry, click the right-pointing triangle that appears, and then click **More Options** to display the **Format Axis** pane.

7   In the pane, click **Axis Options**, and then click **Vertical (Value) Axis**.

8   Click **Number** to display the **Number** options in the **Format Axis** pane.

9   In the **Category** list, click **Number** to display the **Number** category's style options.

10   In the **Decimal places** field, enter 0.

11   If necessary, select the **Use 1000 Separator (,)** check box.

12   Click the pane's **Close button**. Excel closes the pane and updates the chart's appearance.

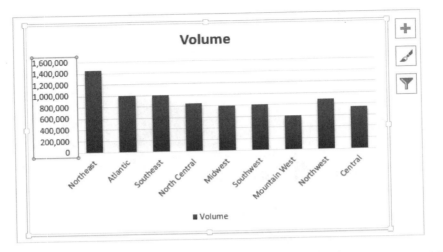

13   Right-click the chart and then click **Save As Template** to open the **Save Chart Template** dialog box.

14   In the **File name** field, enter Cool Blue.

15   Click **Save** to save your template.

16   On the tab bar, click the **Yearly Summary** sheet tab to display the **Yearly Summary** worksheet.

17   Select the chart and then, on the **Design** tab, in the **Type** group, click **Change Chart Type** to open the **Change Chart Type** dialog box.

18   Click **Templates** to display the **My Templates** list.

19   Click the **Cool Blue** custom template, and then click **OK** to apply the template to your chart.

9

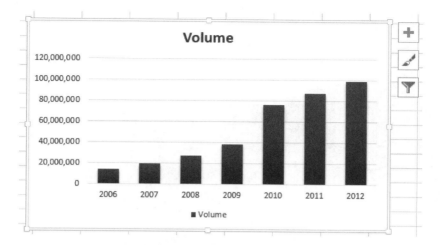

CLEAN UP Close the VolumeByCenter workbook, saving your changes if you want to.

Finding trends in your data

You can use the data in Excel workbooks to discover how your business has performed in the past, but you can also have Excel make its best guess—for example, as to future shipping revenues if the current trend continues. Consider a graph that shows the fleet maintenance costs for the years 2006 through 2012 for Consolidated Messenger.

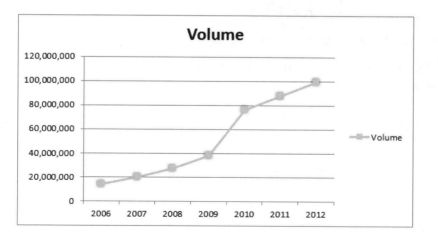

The total has increased from 2006 to 2012, but the growth hasn't been uniform, so guessing how much maintenance costs would increase if the overall trend continued would require difficult mathematical computations. Fortunately, Excel can perform that

math. To have Excel project future values in the maintenance costs data series, click the chart, click the Chart Elements action button, point to Trendline, click the right-pointing triangle that appears, and then click More Options to display the Format Trendline pane.

On the Trendline Options page of the Format Trendline pane, you can choose the data distribution that Excel should expect when it makes its projection.

TIP If you don't know which distribution to choose, use Linear, which applies to most business data. The other distributions are used for scientific and engineering applications and you will most likely know, or be told by a colleague, when to use them.

After you choose the distribution type, you can tell Excel how far ahead to project the data trend. The horizontal axis of the chart used in this example shows revenues by year from 2006 to 2012. To tell Excel how far in the future to look, enter a number in the Forecast area's Forward box. In this case, to look ahead one year, enter *1* in the Forward box, and then click OK to add the trendline to the chart.

TIP When you click the Trendline button in the Analysis group, one of the options Excel displays is Linear Forecast Trendline, which adds a trendline with a two-period forecast.

As with other chart elements, you can double-click the trendline to open a formatting dialog box and change the line's appearance.

In this exercise, you'll add a trendline to a chart.

SET UP You need the FutureVolumes workbook located in the Chapter09 practice file folder to complete this exercise. Open the workbook, and then follow the steps.

1   Select the chart.

2   Click the **Chart Elements** action button, point to **Trendline**, click the right-pointing triangle that appears, and then click **More Options**. The **Format Trendline** pane appears.

3   If necessary, in the **Trend/Regression Type** area, click **Linear**.

4   In the **Forecast** area, in the **Forward** field, enter **3**.

5   Click the pane's **Close button** to add the trendline to the chart.

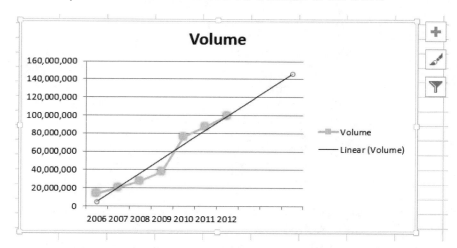

CLEAN UP Close the FutureVolumes workbook, saving your changes if you want to.

Creating dual-axis charts

The Excel 2013 charting engine provides you with the flexibility to plot more than one data series, even if the series use two different scales. For example, Consolidated Messenger might track seasonal package volumes for each regional distribution center by category and, as part of the same data collection, track the number of improperly routed packages.

	A	B	C
1	Month	Volume	Exceptions
2	January	191,442	45
3	February	155,371	31
4	March	207,614	41
5	April	111,977	31
6	May	283,284	29
7	June	109,175	39
8	July	298,858	37
9	August	170,936	47
10	Septembe	195,520	39
11	October	134,432	34
12	Novembe	150,993	23
13	Decembe	195,378	21
14			

When you have two differing but related data series in a table, you can summarize the data by using a dual-axis chart. To create a dual-axis chart, click any cell in the data you want to chart and then, on the Insert tab, click the type of chart you want to create. When you do, Excel plots both data series by using that chart type.

9

You can plot these two data series using separate axes by creating a combo chart. To do that, click the chart and then, on the Design tool tab, click Change Chart Type to display the dialog box of the same name. In the Change Chart Type dialog box, click the All Charts tab, and then click Combo to display the Combo charts page.

You can now use the controls in the Choose The Chart Type And Axis For Your Data Series area of the dialog box to select how to plot each series. To choose how to format a series, click the Chart Type arrow for that series and select its chart type. If you want the series to be plotted in relation to the values on the left vertical axis, leave the Secondary Axis check box cleared. To have the series plotted in relation to the values on the right vertical axis, select the Secondary Axis check box.

When you click OK, Excel creates your chart.

In this exercise, you'll create a dual-axis chart.

→ SET UP You need the DualAnalysis workbook located in the Chapter09 practice file folder to complete this exercise. Open the workbook, and then follow the steps.

1 Click any cell in the Excel table.

2 Click the **Insert** tab and then, in the **Charts** group, click the **Insert Column Chart** button and click the first **2D Column** chart subtype, **Clustered Column**. When you do, Excel creates a chart with the two data series.

3 Right-click the **Chart Title** text box and click **Edit Text**. Enter Comparison for the chart title.

4 On the **Design** tool tab, click the **Change Chart Type** button to open the **Change Chart Type** dialog box.

5 If necessary, click the **All Charts** tab to display that page of the dialog box. Then, in the list of chart types, click **Combo** to display the **Combo Chart** interface.

6 Verify that the **Volume** series will be plotted by using a **Clustered Column** chart and that the **Exceptions** series will be plotted by using a **Line** chart.

7 Select the **Secondary Axis** check box next to the **Exceptions** series. Doing so adds a second vertical axis to the right edge of the chart. The values on this axis reflect the values in the **Exceptions** series.

9

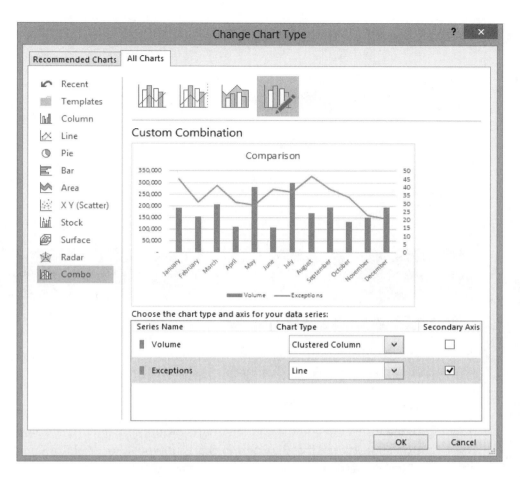

8   Click **OK** to create the chart.

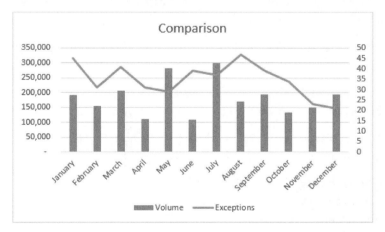

CLEAN UP Close the DualAnalysis workbook, saving your changes if you want to.

Summarizing your data by using sparklines

You can create charts in Excel workbooks to summarize your data visually by using legends, labels, and colors to highlight aspects of your data. It is possible to create very small charts to summarize your data in an overview worksheet, but you can also use *sparklines* to create compact, informative charts that provide valuable context for your data.

Edward Tufte introduced sparklines in his book *Beautiful Evidence* (Graphics Press, 2006), with the goal of creating charts that imparted their information in approximately the same space as a word of printed text. In Excel, a sparkline occupies a single cell, which makes it ideal for use in summary worksheets. As an example, suppose Lori Penor wanted to summarize the monthly revenue data for one of Consolidated Messenger's local branches.

	A	B	C	D	E	F
1						
2		Month	Revenue	Target	Difference	
3		January	$1,538,468	$1,600,000	$ (61,532)	
4		February	$1,474,289	$1,600,000	$ (125,711)	
5		March	$1,416,242	$1,600,000	$ (183,758)	
6		April	$1,685,377	$1,600,000	$ 85,377	
7		May	$1,573,046	$1,600,000	$ (26,954)	
8		June	$1,979,077	$1,600,000	$ 379,077	
9		July	$1,600,000	$1,600,000	$ -	
10		August	$2,417,226	$1,600,000	$ 817,226	
11		September	$1,872,026	$1,600,000	$ 272,026	
12		October	$2,097,478	$1,600,000	$ 497,478	
13		November	$2,876,025	$2,750,000	$ 126,025	
14		December	$3,825,430	$4,000,000	$ (174,570)	
15						

Lori can create three types of sparklines: line, column, and win/loss. The line and column sparklines are compact versions of the standard line and column charts. The win/loss sparkline indicates whether a cell value is positive (a win), negative (a loss), or zero (a tie). To create a line sparkline, you select the data you want to summarize and then, on the Insert tab, in the Sparklines group, click the Line button. When you do, Excel displays the Create Sparklines dialog box.

Create Sparklines ? ✕

Choose the data that you want

Data Range: C3:C14 🔲

Choose where you want the sparklines to be placed

Location Range: _____ 🔲

OK   Cancel

The data range you selected appears in the Data Range box. If the data range is not correct, you can click the Collapse Dialog button to the right of the Data Range box, select the correct cells, and then click the Expand Dialog button. Then, in the Location Range box, enter the address of the cell into which you want to place your sparkline. When you click OK, Excel creates a line sparkline in the cell you specified.

B	C	D	E	F	G	H
Month	**Revenue**	**Target**	**Difference**		**Trend**	**By Month**
January	$1,538,468	$1,600,000	$ (61,532)			
February	$1,474,289	$1,600,000	$ (125,711)			
March	$1,416,242	$1,600,000	$ (183,758)			
April	$1,685,377	$1,600,000	$ 85,377			
May	$1,573,046	$1,600,000	$ (26,954)			
June	$1,979,077	$1,600,000	$ 379,077			
July	$1,600,000	$1,600,000	$ -			
August	$2,417,226	$1,600,000	$ 817,226			
September	$1,872,026	$1,600,000	$ 272,026			
October	$2,097,478	$1,600,000	$ 497,478			
November	$2,876,025	$2,750,000	$ 126,025			
December	$3,825,430	$4,000,000	$ (174,570)			

You follow the same basic procedure to create a column sparkline, except that instead of clicking the Line button in the Sparklines group on the Insert tab, you click the Column button. To create a win/loss sparkline, you need to ensure that your data contains, or could contain, both positive and negative values. If you measured monthly revenue for

Consolidated Messenger, every value would be positive and the win/loss sparkline would impart no meaningful information. Comparing revenue to revenue targets, however, could result in positive, negative, or tie values, which can be meaningfully summarized by using a win/loss sparkline.

To create a win/loss sparkline, follow the same data selection process and click the Win/Loss button.

Months in which Consolidated Messenger's branch exceeded its revenue target appear in the top half of the cell in blue, months in which the branch fell short of its target appear in the bottom half of the cell in red, and the month in which the revenue was exactly the same as the target is blank.

After you create a sparkline, you can change its appearance. Because a sparkline takes up the entire interior of a single cell, resizing that cell's row or column resizes the sparkline. You can also change a sparkline's formatting. When you click a sparkline, Excel displays the Design tool tab.

You can use the tools on the Design tool tab to select a new style; show or hide value markers; change the color of your sparkline or the markers; edit the data used to create the sparkline; modify the labels on the sparkline's axes; or group, ungroup, or clear sparklines. You can't delete a sparkline by clicking its cell and then pressing the Delete or Backspace key—you must click the cell and then, on the Design tool tab, click the Clear button.

TIP Remember that sparklines work best when displayed in compact form. If you find yourself adding markers and labels to a sparkline, you might consider using a regular chart to take advantage of its wider range of formatting and customization options.

In this exercise, you'll create a line, column, and win/loss sparkline, change the sparkline's formatting, and clear a sparkline from a cell.

➡ SET UP You need the RevenueSummary workbook located in the Chapter09 practice file folder to complete this exercise. Open the workbook, and then follow the steps.

1   Select the cell range **C3:C14**.

2   On the **Insert** tab, in the **Sparklines** group, click **Line** to open the **Create Sparklines** dialog box.

3   Verify that **C3:C14** appears in the **Data Range** box. Then, in the **Location Range** box, enter **G3** and click **OK**. Excel creates a line sparkline in cell **G3**.

4   Select the cell range **C3:C14**.

5   On the **Insert** tab, in the **Sparklines** group, click **Column**. The **Create Sparklines** dialog box opens again.

6   Verify that **C3:C14** appears in the **Data Range** box. Then, in the **Location Range** box, enter **H3** and click **OK**. Excel creates a column sparkline in cell **H3**.

7   Drag the right edge of the column **H** header to the right until the cell's width is approximately doubled. Excel displays more details in the sparkline.

8   Select the cell range **E3:E14**.

9   On the **Insert** tab, in the **Sparklines** group, click **Win/Loss**. The **Create Sparklines** dialog box opens again.

10   Verify that **E3:E14** appears in the **Data Range** box. Then, in the **Location Range** box, enter **I3** and click **OK**. Excel creates a win/loss sparkline in cell **I3**.

11   With cell **I3** still selected, on the **Design** tool tab, in the **Style** gallery, click the right-most sparkline style. Excel changes the win/loss sparkline's appearance.

12   Click cell **G3** and then, on the **Design** tool tab, in the **Group** group, click the **Clear** button and then click **Clear Selected Sparkline**. The sparkline disappears.

✖ CLEAN UP Close the RevenueSummary workbook, saving your changes if you want to.

Creating diagrams by using SmartArt

As an international delivery company, Consolidated Messenger's business processes are quite complex. Many times, chief operating officer Lori Penor summarizes the company's processes for the board of directors by creating diagrams. Excel has just the tool she needs to create those diagrams: SmartArt. To create a SmartArt graphic, on the Insert tab, in the Illustrations group, click SmartArt to display the Choose A SmartArt Graphic dialog box.

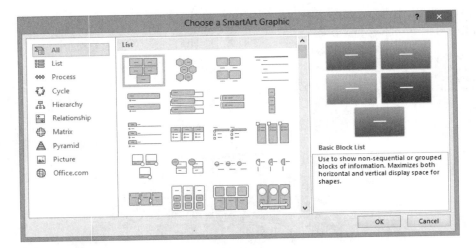

When you click one of the thumbnails in the center pane of the Choose A SmartArt Graphic dialog box, Excel displays a description of the diagram type you selected in the rightmost pane of the dialog box. Clicking All displays every available SmartArt graphic type. The following table lists the types of diagrams you can create by using the Choose A SmartArt Graphic dialog box.

TIP The Office.com category contains SmartArt diagrams available online through Office.com.

Diagram	Description
List	Shows a series of items that typically require a large amount of text to explain
Process	Shows a progression of sequential steps through a task, process, or workflow
Cycle	Shows a process with a continuous cycle or relationships of core elements
Hierarchy	Shows hierarchical relationships, such as those within a company
Relationship	Shows the relationships between two or more items
Matrix	Shows the relationship of components to a whole by using quadrants
Pyramid	Shows proportional, foundation-based, or hierarchical relationships such as a series of skills
Picture	Shows one or more images with captions

TIP Some of the diagram types can be used to illustrate several types of relationships. Be sure to examine all your options before you decide on the type of diagram to use to illustrate your point.

After you click the button that represents the type of diagram you want to create, click OK to add the diagram to your worksheet.

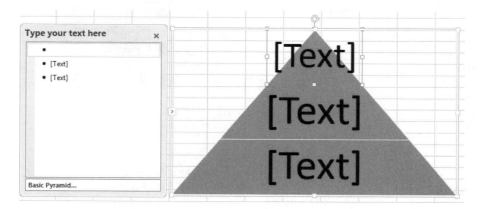

While the diagram is selected, Excel displays the Design and Format tool tabs. You can use the tools on the Design tool tab to change the graphic's layout, style, or color scheme. The Design tool tab also contains the Create Graphic group, which is home to tools you can use to add a shape to the SmartArt graphic, add text to the graphic, and promote or demote shapes within the graphic.

As an example, consider a process diagram that describes how Consolidated Messenger handles a package within one of the company's regional distribution centers.

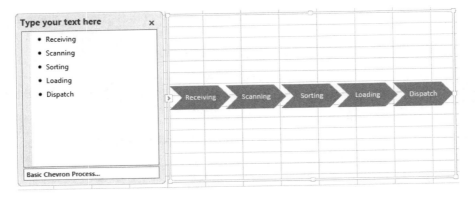

In the text pane, located to the left of the SmartArt graphic, you can add text to a shape without having to click and type within the shape. If you enter the process steps in the wrong order, you can move a shape by right-clicking the shape you want to move and then clicking Cut on the shortcut menu that appears. To paste the shape back into the graphic, right-click the shape to the left of where you want the pasted shape to appear, and then click Paste. For example, if you have a five-step process and accidentally switch the second and third steps, you can move the third step to the second position by right-clicking the third step, clicking Cut, right-clicking the first shape, and then clicking Paste.

If you want to add a shape to a SmartArt graphic, to add a step to a process, for instance, click a shape next to the position you want the new shape to occupy and then, on the Design tool tab, in the Create Graphic group, click Add Shape, and then click the option that represents where you want the new shape to appear in relation to the selected shape.

TIP The options that appear when you click Add Shape depend on the type of SmartArt graphic you created and which graphic element is selected. For instance, the options for an organizational chart are Add Shape After, Add Shape Before, Add Shape Above, Add Shape Below, and Add Assistant.

You can edit the graphic's elements by using the buttons on the Format tool tab or by right-clicking the shape and then clicking Format Shape to display the Format Shape pane. If you have selected the text in a shape, you can use the tools in the Font group on the Home tab to change the text's appearance.

TIP You can use the controls in the Format Shape dialog box to change the shape's fill color, borders, shadow, three-dimensional appearance, and text box properties.

In this exercise, you'll create an organization chart, fill in the shapes, delete a shape, add a shape, change the layout of the diagram without changing the information it embodies, and change the formatting of one of the diagram elements.

→ SET UP You need the OrgChart workbook located in the Chapter09 practice file folder to complete this exercise. Open the workbook, and then follow the steps.

1 On the **Insert** tab, in the **Illustrations** group, click **SmartArt** to open the **Choose a SmartArt Graphic** dialog box.

2 Click **Hierarchy** to display the **Hierarchy** graphic subtypes.

3 Click the first subtype (**Organization Chart**), and then click **OK**. Excel creates the organization chart graphic.

4 In the **Type your text here** pane, in the first text box, enter CEO, and then press the **Down Arrow** key. The value *CEO* appears in the shape at the top level of the organization chart.

5 In the SmartArt diagram, right-click the assistant box, located below and to the left of the **CEO** shape, and then click **Cut**. Excel removes the shape and moves the shapes on the third level of the organization chart to the second level.

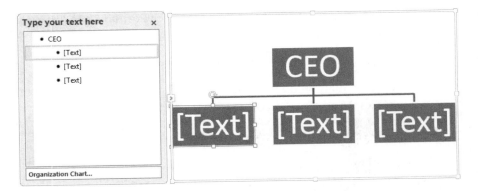

6   Click the leftmost shape on the second level of the organization chart, and then enter **COO**.

7   Click the middle shape on the second level of the organization chart, and then enter **CIO**.

8   Click the rightmost shape on the second level of the organization chart, and then enter **CFO**.

9   Click the **CFO** shape. On the **Design** tool tab, in the **Create Graphic** group, in the **Add Shape** list, click **Add Shape Below**. A new shape appears below the **CFO** shape.

10   In the new shape, type **Comptroller**.

11   On the **Design** tool tab, in the **Layouts** group, click the second layout from the left on the second line of layouts. Excel applies the new layout to your organization chart.

9

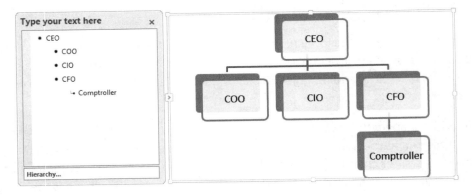

12 Right-click the **Comptroller** shape, and then click **Format Shape** to display the **Format Shape** pane.

13 If necessary, click the **Fill** category to display the fill options.

14 Verify that the **Solid fill** option is selected, click the **Color** button and then, in the **Standard Colors** area of the color picker, click the red swatch.

15 Click **Close**. Excel changes the shape's fill to red.

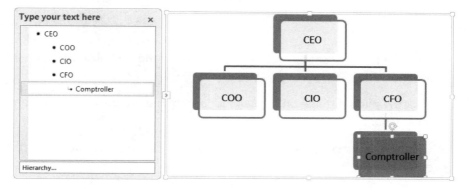

✖ CLEAN UP Close the OrgChart workbook, saving your changes if you want to.

Creating shapes and mathematical equations

With Excel, you can analyze your worksheet data in many ways, including summarizing your data and business processes visually by using charts and SmartArt. You can also augment your worksheets by adding objects such as geometric shapes, lines, flowchart symbols, and banners.

To add a shape to your worksheet, click the Insert tab and then, in the Illustrations group, click the Shapes button to display the shapes available. When you click a shape in the gallery, the pointer changes from a white arrow to a thin black crosshair. To draw your shape, click anywhere in the worksheet and drag the pointer until your shape is the size you want. When you release the mouse button, your shape appears and Excel displays the Format tool tab on the ribbon.

TIP Holding down the Shift key while you draw a shape keeps the shape's proportions constant. For example, clicking the Rectangle tool and then holding down the Shift key while you draw the shape causes you to draw a square.

You can resize a shape by clicking the shape and then dragging one of the resizing handles around the edge of the shape. You can drag a handle on a side of the shape to drag that side to a new position; when you drag a handle on the corner of the shape, you affect height and width simultaneously. If you hold down the Shift key while you drag a shape's corner, Excel keeps the shape's height and width in proportion. To rotate a shape, select the shape and then drag the white rotation handle at the top of the selection outline in a circle until the shape is in the orientation you want.

TIP You can assign your shape a specific height and width by clicking the shape and then, on the Format tool tab, in the Size group, entering the values you want in the height and width boxes.

After you create a shape, you can use the controls on the Format tool tab to change its formatting. To apply a predefined style, click the More button in the lower-right corner of the Shape Styles group's gallery and then click the style you want to apply. If none of the predefined styles are exactly what you want, you can use the Shape Fill, Shape Outline, and Shape Effects options to change those aspects of the shape's appearance.

TIP When you point to a formatting option, such as a style or option displayed in the Shape Fill, Shape Outline, or Shape Effects lists, Excel displays a live preview of how your shape would appear if you applied that formatting option. You can preview as many options as you like before committing to a change. If a live preview doesn't appear, click the File tab to display the Backstage view and then click Options to open the Excel Options dialog box. On the General page, select the Enable Live Preview check box and click OK.

9

If you want to use a shape as a label or header in a worksheet, you can add text to the shape's interior. To do so, select the shape and begin typing; when you're done adding text, click outside the shape to deselect it. You can edit a shape's text by moving the pointer over the text. When the pointer is in position for you to edit the text, it will change from a white pointer with a four-pointed arrow to a black I-bar. You can then click the text to start editing it. If you want to change the text's appearance, you can use the commands on the Home tab or on the Mini Toolbar that appears when you select the text.

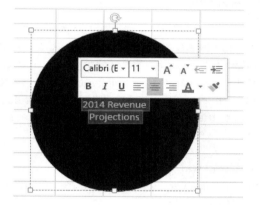

You can move a shape within your worksheet by dragging it to a new position. If your worksheet contains multiple shapes, you can align and distribute them within the worksheet. Horizontal shape alignment means that the shapes are lined up by their top edge, bottom edge, or center. Vertical shape alignment means that they have the same right edge, left edge, or center. To align a series of shapes, hold down the Ctrl key and click the shapes you want to align. Then, on the Format tool tab, in the Arrange group, click Align, and then click the alignment option you want.

Distributing shapes moves the shapes so they have a consistent horizontal or vertical distance between them. To do so, select three or more shapes on a worksheet, click the Format tool tab and then, in the Arrange group, click Align and then click either Distribute Horizontally or Distribute Vertically.

If you have multiple shapes on a worksheet, you will find that Excel arranges them from front to back, placing newer shapes in front of older shapes.

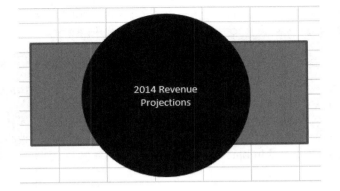

To change the order of the shapes, select the shape in the back, click the Format tool tab, and then, in the Arrange group, click Bring Forward. When you do, Excel moves the back shape in front of the front shape. Clicking Send Backward has the opposite effect, moving the selected shape one layer back in the order. If you click the Bring Forward arrow, you can choose to bring a shape all the way to the front of the order; similarly, when you click the Send Backward arrow, you can choose to send a shape to the back of the order.

One other way to work with shapes in Excel is to add mathematical equations to their interior. As an example, a business analyst might evaluate Consolidated Messenger's financial performance by using a ratio that can be expressed with an equation. To add an equation to a shape, click the shape and then, on the Insert tab, in the Symbols group, click Equation, and then click the Design tool tab to display the interface for editing equations.

TIP Clicking the Equation arrow displays a list of common equations, such as the Pythagorean Theorem, that you can add with a single click.

Click any of the controls in the Structures group to begin creating an equation of that type. You can fill in the details of a structure by adding text normally or by adding symbols from the gallery in the Symbols group.

9

In this exercise, you'll create a circle and a rectangle, change the shapes' formatting, reorder the shapes, align the shapes, add text to the circle, and then add an equation to the rectangle.

 SET UP You need the Shapes workbook located in the Chapter09 practice file folder to complete this exercise. Open the workbook, and then follow the steps.

1   On the **Insert** tab, in the **Illustrations** group, click the **Shapes** button, and then click the oval. The pointer changes to a thin black crosshair.

2   Starting near cell **C3**, hold down the **Shift** key and drag the pointer to approximately cell **E9**. Excel draws a circle.

3   On the **Format** tool tab, in the **Shapes Styles** group's gallery, click the second style. Excel formats the shape with white text and a black background.

4   On the **Insert** tab, in the **Illustrations** group, click the **Shapes** button, and then click the rectangle shape. The pointer changes to a thin black crosshair.

5   Starting near cell **G3**, drag the pointer to cell **K9**. Excel draws a rectangle.

6   On the **Format** tool tab, in the **Shapes Styles** group's gallery, click the first style. Excel formats the shape with black text, an orange border, and a white background.

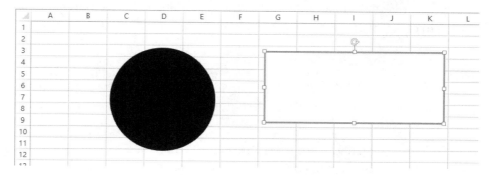

7   Click the circle and enter 2014 Revenue Projections. Then, on the **Home** tab, in the **Alignment** group, click the **Middle Align** button. Excel centers the text vertically within the circle.

8   On the **Home** tab, in the **Alignment** group, click the **Center** button. Excel centers the text horizontally within the circle.

9　Hold down **Ctrl** and click the circle and the rectangle. Then, on the **Format** tool tab, in the **Arrange** group, click the **Align Objects** button, and then click **Align Center**. Excel centers the shapes horizontally.

10　Without releasing the selection, on the **Format** tool tab, in the **Arrange** group, click the **Align Objects** button, and then click **Align Middle**. Excel centers the shapes vertically.

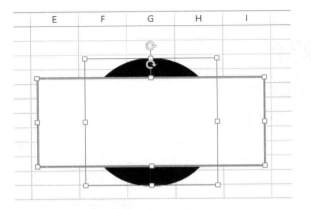

11　Click any spot on the worksheet outside of the circle and rectangle to release the selection, and then click the rectangle.

12　On the **Format** tool tab, in the **Arrange** group, click **Send Backward**. Excel moves the rectangle behind the circle.

13　Press **Ctrl+Z** to undo the last action. Excel moves the rectangle in front of the circle.

14　Click anywhere on the worksheet except on the circle or the rectangle. Click the rectangle and then, on the **Insert** tab, in the **Symbols** group, click **Equation**. The text **Type Equation Here** appears in the rectangle.

15　On the **Design** tool tab, in the **Structures** group, click the **Script** button, and then click the **Subscript** structure (the second from the left in the top row). The **Subscript** structure's outline appears in the rectangle.

9

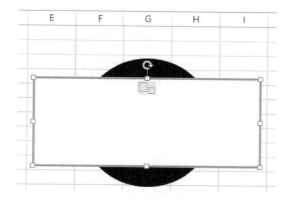

16   Click the left box of the structure and enter Year.

17   Click the right box of the structure and enter Previous.

18   Press the **Right Arrow** key once to move the cursor to the right of the word **Previous** and then, in the **Symbols** group's gallery, click the **Plus Minus** symbol (the first symbol in the top row).

19   In the **Symbols** group's gallery, click the **Infinity** symbol (the second symbol in the top row).

20   Select all of the text in the rectangle and then, on the **Home** tab, in the **Font** group, click the **Increase Font Size** button four times. Excel increases the equation text's font size.

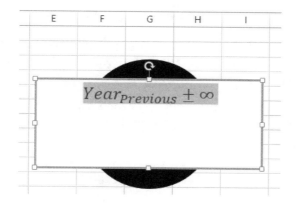

✖ CLEAN UP Close the Shapes workbook, saving your changes if you want to.

Key points

- You can use charts to summarize large sets of data in an easy-to-follow visual format.

- You're not stuck with the chart you create; if you want to change it, you can.

- If you format many of your charts the same way, creating a chart template can save you a lot of work in the future.

- Adding chart labels and a legend makes your chart much easier to follow.

- When you format your data properly, you can create dual-axis charts, which are compact and easy to read.

- If your chart data represents a series of events over time (such as monthly or yearly sales), you can use trendline analysis to extrapolate future events based on the past data.

- With sparklines, you can summarize your data in a compact space, providing valuable context for values in your worksheets.

- With Excel, you can quickly create and modify common business and organizational diagrams, such as organization charts and process diagrams.

- You can create and modify shapes to enhance your workbook's visual impact.

- The improved equation editing capabilities help Excel 2013 users communicate their thinking to their colleagues.

9

Chapter at a glance

Analyze

Analyze data dynamically by using PivotTables, page 288

	A	B	C	D	E
1					
2					
3	Sum of Volume	Column Labels			
4	Row Labels	Atlantic	Central	Midwest	Mountain West
5	January	6,042,842	6,006,191	5,720,977	5,872,046
6	February	3,098,663	2,932,222	3,456,904	2,935,951
7	March	3,210,406	3,167,785	3,046,753	3,265,252
8	April	3,002,529	2,989,245	3,125,231	3,071,049
9	May	3,368,888	3,576,763	3,280,768	3,159,233
10	June	3,208,696	2,973,980	3,035,619	3,063,572
11	July	3,115,294	3,364,482	2,945,492	3,456,576
12	August	3,237,645	3,191,591	3,441,757	3,371,850
13	September	3,072,723	2,807,222	3,166,599	2,942,925
14	October	3,261,585	3,362,250	3,333,751	3,182,437
15	November	6,137,174	6,083,306	6,236,356	6,121,929
16	December	6,279,737	6,546,678	6,099,560	5,880,670
17	Grand Total	47,036,182	47,001,715	46,889,767	46,323,490

Filter

Filter, show, and hide PivotTable data, page 298

	A	B	C	D
1	Weekday	(All)		
2				
3	Sum of Volume	Column Labels		
4	Row Labels	2012	2013	Grand Total
5	Atlantic	23276049	23760133	47036182
6	Central	23727556	23274159	47001715
7	Midwest	23643436	23246331	46889767
8	Mountain West	23075908	23247582	46323490
9	North Central	24118888	22561702	46680590
10	Northeast	24103492	24586713	48690205
11	Northwest	25028389	23604961	48633350
12	Southeast	23785488	26736115	50521603
13	Southwest	24817582	23300579	48118161
14	Grand Total	215576788	214318275	429895063

Format

Format PivotTables, page 313

	A	B	C	D	E
1					
2					
3	Sum of Volume	Column Labels			
4	Row Labels	Atlantic	Central	Midwest	Mountain West
5	⊟ 2012	23,276,049	23,727,556	23,643,436	23,075,908
6	January	2,966,264	3,143,004	2,774,877	2,942,544
7	February	1,541,726	1,407,340	2,046,448	1,552,098
8	March	1,688,027	1,594,434	1,600,920	1,641,026
9	April	1,445,436	1,548,205	1,395,802	1,653,829
10	May	1,530,319	1,813,746	1,529,086	1,516,453
11	June	1,725,770	1,431,518	1,458,009	1,551,719

Create

Create dynamic charts by using PivotCharts, page 326

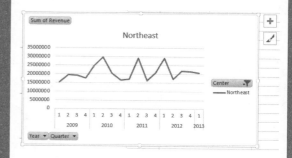

Using PivotTables and PivotCharts

IN THIS CHAPTER, YOU WILL LEARN HOW TO

- Analyze data dynamically by using PivotTables.

- Filter, show, and hide PivotTable data.

- Edit PivotTables.

- Format PivotTables.

- Create PivotTables from external data.

- Create dynamic charts by using PivotCharts.

When you create Microsoft Excel 2013 worksheets, you should consider how you want the data to appear when you show it to your colleagues. You can change the formatting of your data to emphasize the contents of specific cells, sort and filter your worksheets based on the contents of specific columns, or hide rows containing data that isn't relevant to the point you're trying to make.

One limitation of the standard Excel worksheet is that you can't easily change how the data is organized on the page. For example, in a worksheet in which each column represents an hour in the day, each row represents a day in a month, and the body of the worksheet contains the total sales for every hourly period of the month, you can't change the worksheet quickly so that it displays only sales on Tuesdays during the afternoon.

However, Excel has a tool that you can use to create worksheets that can be sorted, filtered, and rearranged dynamically to emphasize different aspects of your data. That tool is the PivotTable.

In this chapter, you'll create and edit PivotTables from an existing worksheet, focus your PivotTable data by using filters, format PivotTables, create a PivotTable that has data imported from a text file, and summarize your data visually by using a PivotChart.

Analyzing data dynamically by using PivotTables

With Excel worksheets, you can gather and present important data, but the standard worksheet can't be changed from its original configuration easily. As an example, consider a worksheet that records monthly package volumes for each of nine distribution centers in the United States.

	A	B	C	D	E
1					
2		January	February	March	April
3	Atlantic	6,042,842	3,098,663	3,210,406	3,002,529
4	Central	6,006,191	2,932,222	3,167,785	2,989,245
5	Midwest	5,720,977	3,456,904	3,046,753	3,125,231
6	Mountain West	5,872,046	2,935,951	3,265,252	3,071,049
7	North Central	6,236,863	3,785,068	2,929,397	2,677,853
8	Northeast	6,370,982	3,281,469	3,725,669	3,148,289
9	Northwest	6,108,382	4,216,668	3,640,750	2,997,048
10	Southeast	6,396,724	4,877,758	4,387,252	3,583,479
11	Southwest	5,949,454	4,413,610	3,226,583	3,006,170
12		54,704,461	32,998,313	30,599,847	27,600,893

The data in the worksheet is organized so that each row represents a distribution center and each column represents a month of the year. When presented in this arrangement, the monthly totals for all centers and the yearly total for each distribution center are given equal billing: neither set of totals stands out.

Such a neutral presentation of your data is versatile, but it has limitations. First, although you can use sorting and filtering to restrict the rows or columns shown, it's difficult to change the worksheet's organization. For example, in this worksheet, you can't easily reorganize the contents of your worksheet so that the months are assigned to the rows and the distribution centers are assigned to the columns.

To reorganize and redisplay your data dynamically, you can use the PivotTable tool. In Excel 2013, you can create Recommended PivotTables. To open the Recommended PivotTables dialog box for a data set, click any cell in the data range that you want to summarize and then, on the Insert tab of the ribbon, click Recommended PivotTables. When you do, Excel displays a set of PivotTables that you can create quickly.

Pointing to a recommended PivotTable shows a preview image of what that PivotTable would look like. To create it, just click the image of the arrangement you want to create and click OK.

TIP If Excel 2013 has no Recommended PivotTables for your data, it displays the option to create a blank PivotTable.

If none of the Recommended PivotTables meet your needs, you can create a PivotTable by adding individual fields. For instance, you can create a PivotTable with the same layout as the worksheet described previously, which emphasizes totals by month, and then change the PivotTable layout to have the rows represent the months of the year and the columns represent the distribution centers. The new layout emphasizes the totals by regional distribution center.

	A	B	C	D	E
1					
2					
3	Sum of Volume	Column Labels			
4	Row Labels	Atlantic	Central	Midwest	Mountain West
5	January	6,042,842	6,006,191	5,720,977	5,872,046
6	February	3,098,663	2,932,222	3,456,904	2,935,951
7	March	3,210,406	3,167,785	3,046,753	3,265,252
8	April	3,002,529	2,989,245	3,125,231	3,071,049
9	May	3,368,888	3,576,763	3,280,768	3,159,233
10	June	3,208,696	2,973,980	3,035,619	3,063,572
11	July	3,115,294	3,364,482	2,945,492	3,456,576
12	August	3,237,645	3,191,591	3,441,757	3,371,850
13	September	3,072,723	2,807,222	3,166,599	2,942,925
14	October	3,261,585	3,362,250	3,333,751	3,182,437
15	November	6,137,174	6,083,306	6,236,356	6,121,929
16	December	6,279,737	6,546,678	6,099,560	5,880,670
17	Grand Total	47,036,182	47,001,715	46,889,767	46,323,490

To create a PivotTable, your data must be collected in a list. Excel tables mesh perfectly with PivotTable dynamic views; not only do Excel tables have a well-defined column and row structure, but the ability to refer to an Excel table by its name also greatly simplifies PivotTable creation and management.

In the Excel table used to create the distribution PivotTable, each row of the table contains a value that represents the distribution center, date, month, week, weekday, day, and volume for every day of the years 2012 and 2013.

	B	C	D	E	F	G	H	I
1								
2	Center	Date	Year	Month	Week	Day	Weekday	Volume
3	Atlantic	1/1/2013	2013	January	1	1	Tuesday	120933
4	Atlantic	1/2/2013	2013	January	1	2	Wednesday	52979
5	Atlantic	1/3/2013	2013	January	1	3	Thursday	45683
6	Atlantic	1/4/2013	2013	January	1	4	Friday	53152
7	Atlantic	1/5/2013	2013	January	1	5	Saturday	149776
8	Atlantic	1/6/2013	2013	January	1	6	Sunday	108772
9	Atlantic	1/7/2013	2013	January	1	7	Monday	99919
10	Atlantic	1/8/2013	2013	January	2	8	Tuesday	138271
11	Atlantic	1/9/2013	2013	January	2	9	Wednesday	77451
12	Atlantic	1/10/2013	2013	January	2	10	Thursday	130536
13	Atlantic	1/11/2013	2013	January	2	11	Friday	119809

Excel needs that data when it creates the PivotTable so that it can maintain relationships among the data. If you want to filter your PivotTable so that it shows all package volumes on Thursdays in January, for example, Excel must be able to identify January 10, 2013 as a Thursday.

After you create an Excel table, you can click any cell in the table, display the Insert tab and then, in the Tables group, click PivotTable to open the Create PivotTable dialog box.

In this dialog box, you verify the data source for your PivotTable and whether you want to create a PivotTable on a new worksheet or an existing worksheet. After you click OK, Excel displays a new or existing worksheet and displays the PivotTable Fields pane.

TIP You should always place your PivotTable on its own worksheet to avoid cluttering the display.

If the PivotTable Fields pane isn't visible, you can display it by clicking any cell in the PivotTable, which displays the PivotTable Tools tabs. On the Options tool tab, in the Show/Hide group, click Field List.

To assign a field, or column of data, to an area of the PivotTable, drag the field header from the Choose Fields To Add To Report area at the top of the PivotTable Fields pane to the Drag Fields Between Areas Below area at the bottom of the pane. For example, if you drag the Volume field header to the Values area, the PivotTable displays the total of all entries in the Volume column.

It's important to note that the order in which you enter the fields in the Rows and Columns areas affects how Excel organizes the data in your PivotTable. As an example, consider a PivotTable that groups the PivotTable rows by distribution center and then by month.

3	Row Labels	Sum of Volume
4	⊟Atlantic	47036182
5	January	6042842
6	February	3098663
7	March	3210406
8	April	3002529
9	May	3368888
10	June	3208696
11	July	3115294
12	August	3237645
13	September	3072723
14	October	3261585
15	November	6137174
16	December	6279737
17	⊟Central	47001715
18	January	6006191
19	February	2932222
20	March	3167785
21	April	2989245
22	May	3576763
23	June	2973980

The same PivotTable data could also be organized by month and then by distribution center.

3	Row Labels	Sum of Volume
4	⊟January	54704461
5	Atlantic	6042842
6	Central	6006191
7	Midwest	5720977
8	Mountain West	5872046
9	North Central	6236863
10	Northeast	6370982
11	Northwest	6108382
12	Southeast	6396724
13	Southwest	5949454
14	⊟February	32998313
15	Atlantic	3098663
16	Central	2932222
17	Midwest	3456904
18	Mountain West	2935951
19	North Central	3785068
20	Northeast	3281469
21	Northwest	4216668
22	Southeast	4877758
23	Southwest	4413610

In the preceding examples, all the field headers are in the Rows area. If you drag the Center header from the Rows area to the Columns area, the PivotTable reorganizes (pivots) its data to form a different configuration.

	A	B	C	D	E
1					
2					
3	Sum of Volume	Column Labels ▼			
4	Row Labels ▼	Atlantic	Central	Midwest	Mountain West
5	January	6042842	6006191	5720977	5872046
6	February	3098663	2932222	3456904	2935951
7	March	3210406	3167785	3046753	3265252
8	April	3002529	2989245	3125231	3071049
9	May	3368888	3576763	3280768	3159233
10	June	3208696	2973980	3035619	3063572
11	July	3115294	3364482	2945492	3456576
12	August	3237645	3191591	3441757	3371850
13	September	3072723	2807222	3166599	2942925
14	October	3261585	3362250	3333751	3182437
15	November	6137174	6083306	6236356	6121929
16	December	6279737	6546678	6099560	5880670
17	Grand Total	47036182	47001715	46889767	46323490

To pivot a PivotTable, you drag a field header to a new position in the PivotTable Fields pane. As you drag a field within the pane, Excel displays a blue line in the interior of the target area so you know where the field will appear when you release the mouse button. If your data set is large or if you based your PivotTable on a data collection on another computer, it might take some time for Excel to reorganize the PivotTable after a pivot. You can have Excel delay redrawing the PivotTable by selecting the Defer Layout Update check box in the lower-left corner of the PivotTable Fields pane. When you're ready for Excel to display the reorganized PivotTable, click Update.

If you expect your PivotTable source data to change, such as when you link to an external database that records shipments or labor hours, you should ensure that your PivotTable summarizes all the available data. To do that, you can refresh the PivotTable connection to its data source. If Excel detects new data in the source table, it updates the PivotTable contents accordingly. To refresh your PivotTable, click any cell in the PivotTable and then, on the Options tool tab, in the Data group, click Refresh.

10

In this exercise, you'll create a PivotTable by using data from a table, add fields to the PivotTable, and then pivot the PivotTable.

SET UP You need the Creating workbook located in the Chapter10 practice file folder to complete this exercise. Open the workbook, and then follow the steps.

1 Click any cell in the Excel table.

2 On the **Insert** tab, in the **Tables** group, click **Recommended PivotTables** to open the **Recommended PivotTables** dialog box.

3 Click the second icon, labeled **Sum of Volume by Weekday**.

4 Click **OK** to create the PivotTable.

	A	B
1		
2		
3	**Row Labels** ▼	**Sum of Volume**
4	Sunday	61253579
5	Monday	62042322
6	Tuesday	62278691
7	Wednesday	60664392
8	Thursday	61694953
9	Friday	61441352
10	Saturday	60519774
11	**Grand Total**	**429895063**
12		

5 Click the **Sheet1** worksheet's sheet tab to display that worksheet.

6 If necessary, click any cell in the Excel table.

7 On the **Insert** tab, in the **Tables** group, click the **PivotTable** button to open the **PivotTable** dialog box.

8   Verify that the **DailyVolumes** table name appears in the **Table/Range** field and that the **New Worksheet** option is selected.

9   Click **OK** to create a PivotTable on a new worksheet.

10   In the **PivotTable Fields** pane, drag the **Center** field header to the **Rows** area. Excel adds the **Center** field values to the PivotTable row area.

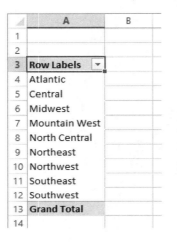

11   In the **PivotTable Fields** pane, drag the **Year** field header to the **Columns** area. Excel adds the **Year** field values to the PivotTable column area.

12   In the **PivotTable Fields** pane, drag the **Volume** field header to the **Values** area. Excel fills in the body of the PivotTable with the **Volume** field values.

13   In the **PivotTable Fields** pane, in the **Columns** area, drag the **Year** field header to the **Rows** area, and drop it beneath the **Center** field header. Excel changes the PivotTable to reflect the new organization.

10

▲	A	B
1		
2		
3	**Row Labels** ▾	**Sum of Volume**
4	⊟ **Atlantic**	**47036182**
5	2012	23276049
6	2013	23760133
7	⊟ **Central**	**47001715**
8	2012	23727556
9	2013	23274159
10	⊟ **Midwest**	**46889767**
11	2012	23643436
12	2013	23246331
13	⊟ **Mountain West**	**46323490**
14	2012	23075908
15	2013	23247582
16	⊟ **North Central**	**46680590**
17	2012	24118888
18	2013	22561702
19	⊟ **Northeast**	**48690205**
20	2012	24103492
21	2013	24586713
22	⊟ **Northwest**	**48633350**
23	2012	25028389
24	2013	23604961

 CLEAN UP Close the Creating workbook, saving your changes if you want to.

Filtering, showing, and hiding PivotTable data

PivotTables often summarize huge data sets in a relatively small worksheet. The more details you can capture and write to a table, the more flexibility you have in analyzing the data. As an example, consider all the details captured in a table in which each row contains a value that represents the distribution center, date, month, week, weekday, day, and volume for every day of the year.

	B	C	D	E	F	G	H	I
1								
2	Center ▾	Date ▾	Year ▾	Month ▾	Week ▾	Day ▾	Weekda ▾	Volume ▾
3	Atlantic	1/2/2012	2012	January	1	1	Monday	46144
4	Atlantic	1/3/2012	2012	January	1	2	Tuesday	105578
5	Atlantic	1/4/2012	2012	January	1	3	Wednesday	83669
6	Atlantic	1/5/2012	2012	January	1	4	Thursday	100240
7	Atlantic	1/6/2012	2012	January	1	5	Friday	130597
8	Atlantic	1/7/2012	2012	January	1	6	Saturday	123563
9	Atlantic	1/8/2012	2012	January	1	7	Sunday	50054
10	Atlantic	1/9/2012	2012	January	2	8	Monday	78540

Each column, in turn, contains numerous values: there are nine distribution centers, data from two years, 12 months in a year, seven weekdays, and as many as five weeks and 31 days in a month. Just as you can filter the data that appears in an Excel table or other data collection, you can filter the data displayed in a PivotTable by selecting which values you want the PivotTable to include.

SEE ALSO For more information on filtering an Excel table, see "Limiting data that appears on your screen" in Chapter 5, "Focusing on specific data by using filters."

To filter a PivotTable based on a field's contents, click the field's header in the Choose Fields To Add To Report area of the PivotTable Fields pane. When you do, Excel displays a menu of sorting and filtering options.

10

TIP You can also create selection filters for PivotTables by using slicers, which are introduced in Chapter 5, "Focusing on specific data by using filters." To display the Insert Slicers dialog box for a PivotTable, click any cell in the PivotTable, click the Analyze tool tab, and then click Insert Slicer.

The PivotTable displays several sorting options, commands for different categories of filters, and a list of items that appear in the field you want to filter. Every list item has a check box next to it. Items with a check mark in the box are currently displayed in the PivotTable, and items without a check mark are hidden.

The first entry at the top of the item list is the Select All check box. This check box can have one of three states: displaying a check mark, displaying a black square, or empty. If the Select All check box contains a check mark, then the PivotTable displays every item in the list. If the Select All check box is empty, then no filter items are selected. Finally, if the Select

All check box contains a black square, it means that some, but not all, of the items in the list are displayed. Selecting only the Northwest check box, for example, leads to a PivotTable configuration in which only the data for the Northwest center is displayed.

Sum of Volume	Column Labels	
Row Labels	Northwest	Grand Total
2012	25028389	25028389
January	3085352	3085352
February	2554130	2554130
March	1932304	1932304
April	1348145	1348145
May	1628489	1628489
June	1475038	1475038
July	1832445	1832445
August	1633582	1633582
September	1638024	1638024
October	2045639	2045639
November	3020217	3020217
December	2835024	2835024
2013	23604961	23604961
January	3023030	3023030
February	1662538	1662538
March	1708446	1708446
April	1648903	1648903
May	1607655	1607655

If you'd rather display as much PivotTable data as possible, you can hide the PivotTable Fields pane and filter the PivotTable by using the filter arrows on the Rows and Columns headers within the body of the PivotTable. When you click either of those headers, you can select a field by which you can filter; you can then define the filter by using the same controls that are available when you click a field header in the PivotTable Fields pane.

Excel indicates that a PivotTable has filters applied by placing a filter indicator next to the Columns or Rows header, as appropriate, and the filtered field name in the PivotTable Fields pane.

So far in this example, all the fields by which the PivotTable has been filtered has changed the organization of the data in the PivotTable. Adding some fields to a PivotTable, however, might create unwanted complexity. For example, you might want to filter a PivotTable by weekday, but adding the Weekday field to the body of the PivotTable expands the table unnecessarily.

10

▲	A	B	C	D	E	F
1						
2						
3	Sum of Volume	Column Labels ▾				
4		⊟2012				
5	Row Labels ▾	Sunday	Monday	Tuesday	Wednesday	Thursday
6	Atlantic	3453319	3349646	3366196	2917606	3567714
7	Central	3320819	3366199	3527584	3365866	3263079
8	Midwest	3667386	3475968	3091127	3463291	3245714
9	Mountain West	3357763	3268404	3068409	3200078	3298019
10	North Central	3457202	3741370	3215869	3428683	3686605
11	Northeast	3496199	3601318	3470147	3593310	3511717
12	Northwest	3791023	3767825	3374432	3812518	3519655
13	Southeast	3268002	3473394	3348605	3575267	3257557
14	Southwest	3178975	3570147	3396272	3632371	3872515
15	Grand Total	30990688	31614271	29858641	30988990	31222575

Instead of adding the Weekday field to the Rows or Columns area, you can drag the field to the Filters area near the bottom of the PivotTable Fields pane. Doing so leaves the body of the PivotTable unchanged, but adds a new area above the PivotTable in its worksheet.

▲	A	B	C	D
1	Weekday	(All) ▾		
2				
3	Sum of Volume	Column Labels ▾		
4	Row Labels ▾	2012	2013	Grand Total
5	Atlantic	23276049	23760133	47036182
6	Central	23727556	23274159	47001715
7	Midwest	23643436	23246331	46889767
8	Mountain West	23075908	23247582	46323490
9	North Central	24118888	22561702	46680590
10	Northeast	24103492	24586713	48690205
11	Northwest	25028389	23604961	48633350
12	Southeast	23785488	26736115	50521603
13	Southwest	24817582	23300579	48118161
14	Grand Total	215576788	214318275	429895063

TIP In Excel 2003 and earlier versions, this area was called the Page Field area.

When you click the filter arrow of a field in the Filters area, Excel displays a list of the values in the field. When you click the filter arrow, you can choose to filter by one value at a time. If you'd like to filter your PivotTable by more than one value, you can do so by selecting the Select Multiple Items check box.

If your PivotTable has more than one field in the Rows area, you can filter values in a PivotTable by hiding and collapsing levels of detail within the report. To do that, you click the Hide Detail control (which looks like a box with a minus sign in it) or the Show Detail control (which looks like a box with a plus sign in it) next to a header.

For example, you might have your data divided by year; clicking the Show Detail control next to the 2012 year header would display that year's details. Conversely, clicking the 2013 year header's Hide Detail control would hide the individual months' values and display only the year's total.

	A	B
1		
2		
3	**Row Labels** ▼	**Sum of Volume**
4	⊟ 2012	215576788
5	Atlantic	23276049
6	Central	23727556
7	Midwest	23643436
8	Mountain West	23075908
9	North Central	24118888
10	Northeast	24103492
11	Northwest	25028389
12	Southeast	23785488
13	Southwest	24817582
14	⊞ 2013	214318275
15	**Grand Total**	429895063

Excel 2013 also lets you filter PivotTables using search filters. With a search filter, you can enter in a series of characters for Excel to filter that field's values. To create a search filter, click a field's filter arrow and enter the character string that you want to search for in the filter menu's Search box.

10

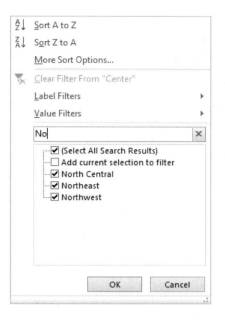

For example, if the PivotTable's Center field contains the values Atlantic, Central, Midwest, Mountain West, North Central, Northeast, Northwest, Southeast, and Southwest, entering the character string *No* limits the values to *North Central*, *Northeast*, and *Northwest*.

TIP Search filters look for the character string you specify anywhere within a field's value, not just at the start of the value. In the previous example, the search filter string *cen* would return both *Central* and *North Central*.

In this exercise, you'll focus the data displayed in a PivotTable by creating a filter, by filtering a PivotTable based on the contents of a field in the Filters area, by showing and hiding levels of detail within the body of the PivotTable, and by using the Search box.

SET UP You need the Focusing workbook located in the Chapter10 practice file folder to complete this exercise. Open the workbook, and then follow the steps.

1   On the **Sheet2** worksheet, click any cell in the PivotTable.

2   In the **Choose fields to add to report** area of the **PivotTable Fields** pane, click the **Center** field header, click the **Center** field filter arrow, and then clear the **(Select All)** check box. Excel clears all the check boxes in the filter menu.

3   Select the **Northwest** check box, and then click **OK**. Excel filters the PivotTable.

	A	B	C
1			
2			
3	Sum of Volume	Column Labels ⊤	
4	Row Labels ▼	Northwest	Grand Total
5	⊟2012	25028389	25028389
6	January	3085352	3085352
7	February	2554130	2554130
8	March	1932304	1932304
9	April	1348145	1348145
10	May	1628489	1628489
11	June	1475038	1475038
12	July	1832445	1832445
13	August	1633582	1633582
14	September	1638024	1638024
15	October	2045639	2045639
16	November	3020217	3020217
17	December	2835024	2835024
18	⊟2013	23604961	23604961
19	January	3023030	3023030
20	February	1662538	1662538
21	March	1708446	1708446

4   On the **Quick Access Toolbar**, click the **Undo** button to remove the filter.

5   In the **PivotTable Fields** pane, drag the **Weekday** field header from the **Choose fields to add to report area** to the **Filters** area in the **Drag fields between areas below** area.

6   In the **PivotTable Fields** pane, click the **Close** button to close it.

7   In the body of the worksheet, click the **Weekday** filter arrow, and then, if necessary, select the **Select Multiple Items** check box. Excel adds check boxes beside the items in the **Weekday** field filter list.

8   Clear the **All** check box to clear every check box in the list.

9   Select the **Tuesday** and **Thursday** check boxes, and then click **OK**. Excel filters the PivotTable, summarizing only those values from Tuesdays and Thursdays.

10

10   In cell **A5**, click the **Hide Detail** button. Excel collapses rows that contain data from the year 2012, leaving only the subtotal row that summarizes that year's data.

	A	B	C	D
1	Weekday	(Multiple Items) ⊤		
2				
3	Sum of Volume	Column Labels ▾		
4	Row Labels ▾	Atlantic	Central	Midwest
5	⊞ 2012	6933910	6790663	6336841
6	⊟ 2013	6783726	6541290	6650799
7	January	1017628	1087262	992605
8	February	453202	418419	515009
9	March	467334	359716	367785
10	April	458566	437695	452702
11	May	481096	516957	460397
12	June	302371	416959	450633
13	July	433346	452848	339017
14	August	564377	450209	452780
15	September	353976	278120	381304
16	October	458948	449253	570835
17	November	808929	819627	861745
18	December	983953	854225	805987
19	Grand Total	13717636	13331953	12987640

11   In cell **A5**, click the **Show Detail** button to redisplay the collapsed rows.

12   If the **PivotTable Fields** pane isn't displayed, click the **Analyze** tool tab, click **Show**, and then click **Field List**.

13   In the **PivotTable Fields** pane, click the **Month** field header arrow to open the filter menu.

14   In the **Search** box, enter Ju. Excel displays the months **June** and **July** in the filter list.

15   Click **OK** to apply the filter.

16   On the **Analyze** tool tab, click the **Actions** button, click **Clear**, and then click **Clear Filters** to remove all filters from the PivotTable.

❌ CLEAN UP Close the Focusing workbook, saving your changes if you want to.

Editing PivotTables

After you create a PivotTable, you can rename it, edit it to control how it summarizes your data, and use PivotTable cell data in a formula. As an example, consider a PivotTable named *PivotTable2* that summarizes package volumes for every Consolidated Messengers regional distribution hub.

10

	A	B	C	D	E
1					
2					
3	Sum of Volume	Column Labels ▼			
4	Row Labels ▼	Atlantic	Central	Midwest	Mountain West
5	⊟2012	23276049	23727556	23643436	23075908
6	January	2966264	3143004	2774877	2942544
7	February	1541726	1407340	2046448	1552098
8	March	1688027	1594434	1600920	1641026
9	April	1445436	1548205	1395802	1653829
10	May	1530319	1813746	1529086	1516453
11	June	1725770	1431518	1458009	1551719
12	July	1581340	1706190	1472534	1672400
13	August	1519538	1577651	1797139	1745152
14	September	1494735	1420065	1672046	1483296
15	October	1743541	1711810	1599927	1655866
16	November	3049369	2921522	3153696	2847752
17	December	2989984	3452071	3142952	2813773
18	⊟2013	23760133	23274159	23246331	23247582
19	January	3076578	2863187	2946100	2929502
20	February	1556937	1524882	1410456	1383853

Excel displays the PivotTable name when you click the PivotTable button on the Analyze tool tab. The name *PivotTable2* doesn't help you or your colleagues understand the data the PivotTable contains, particularly if you use the PivotTable data in a formula on another worksheet. To give your PivotTable a more descriptive name, click any cell in the PivotTable and then, on the Options tool tab, in the PivotTable Options group, enter the new name in the PivotTable Name field.

When you create a PivotTable with at least one field in the Rows area and one field in the Columns area of the PivotTable Fields pane, Excel adds a grand total row and column to summarize your data. You can control how and where these summary rows and columns appear by clicking any PivotTable cell and then, on the Design tool tab, in the Layout group, clicking either the Subtotals or Grand Totals button and selecting the desired layout.

After you create a PivotTable, Excel determines the best way to summarize the data in the column you assign to the Values area. For numeric data, for example, Excel uses the *SUM* function. If you want to change a PivotTable summary function, right-click any data cell in the PivotTable values area, point to Summarize Values By, and then click the desired operation. If you want to use a function other than those listed, click More Options to display the Value Field Settings dialog box. On the Summarize Values By page of the dialog box, you can choose the summary operation you want to use.

You can also change how the PivotTable displays the data in the Values area. On the Show Values As page of the Value Field Settings dialog box, you can select whether to display each cell's percentage contribution to its column's total, its row's total, or its contribution to the total of all values displayed in the PivotTable.

If you want, you can create a formula that incorporates a value from a PivotTable cell. To do so, you click the cell in which you want to create the formula, enter an equal sign, and then click the cell in the PivotTable that contains the data you want to appear in the other cell. A *GETPIVOTDATA* formula appears in the formula box of the worksheet that contains the PivotTable. When you press Enter, Excel creates the *GETPIVOTDATA* formula and displays the contents of the PivotTable cell in the target cell.

In this exercise, you'll rename a PivotTable, specify whether subtotal and grand total rows will appear, change the PivotTable summary function, display each cell's contribution to its row's total, and create a formula that incorporates a value in a PivotTable cell.

→ SET UP You need the Editing workbook located in the Chapter10 practice file folder to complete this exercise. Open the workbook, and then follow the steps.

1   On the **PivotTable** worksheet, click any cell in the PivotTable.

2   On the **Analyze** tool tab, click the **PivotTable** button and then, in the **PivotTable Name** field, enter VolumeSummary and press **Enter** to rename the PivotTable.

3   On the **Design** tool tab, in the **Layout** group, click **Subtotals**, and then click **Do Not Show Subtotals**. Excel removes the subtotal rows from the PivotTable.

4   On the **Design** tool tab, in the **Layout** group, click **Grand Totals**, and then click **On for columns only**. Excel removes the cells that calculate each row's grand total.

H	I	J	K	L	
Northwest	Southeast	Southwest			
3085352	3470295	3029490			
2554130	1988929	2692383			
1932304	1441894	1646946			
1348145	1631240	1525005			
1628489	1749378	1452226			
1475038	1422265	1428581			
1832445	1511712	1503100			
1633582	1671246	1414763			
1638024	1510884	1407402			
2045639	1427066	2888565			
3020217	2848642	2728934			
2835024	3111937	3100187			

5   On the **Quick Access Toolbar**, click the **Undo** button to reverse the last change.

6   Right-click any data cell in the PivotTable, point to **Summarize Values By**, and then click **Average** to change the **Value** field summary operation.

	A	B	C	D	E
1					
2					
3	Average of Volume	Column Labels ▼			
4	Row Labels ▼	Atlantic	Central	Midwest	Mountain West
5	⊟ 2012				
6	January	95685.93548	101387.2258	89512.16129	94920.77419
7	February	55061.64286	50262.14286	73087.42857	55432.07143
8	March	54452.48387	51433.35484	51642.58065	52936.32258
9	April	48181.2	51606.83333	46526.73333	55127.63333
10	May	49365.12903	58507.93548	49325.35484	48917.83871
11	June	57525.66667	47717.26667	48600.3	51723.96667
12	July	51010.96774	55038.3871	47501.09677	53948.3871
13	August	49017.35484	50891.96774	57972.22581	56295.22581
14	September	49824.5	47335.5	55734.86667	49443.2
15	October	56243.25806	55219.67742	51610.54839	53415.03226
16	November	101645.6333	97384.06667	105123.2	94925.06667
17	December	96451.09677	111357.129	101385.5484	90766.87097
18	⊟ 2013				
19	January	99244.45161	92360.87097	95035.48387	94500.06452
20	February	55604.89286	54460.07143	50373.42857	49423.32143

7   On the **Quick Access Toolbar**, click the **Undo** button to reverse the last change.

8   Right-click any data cell in the PivotTable, and then click **Value Field Settings** to open the **Value Field Settings** dialog box.

9   Click the **Show Values As** tab to display the **Show Values As** page.

10   In the **Show Values As** list, click **% of Row Total**.

11   Click **OK** to change how Excel calculates the values in the PivotTable.

10

	A	B	C	D	E
1					
2					
3	**Sum of Volume**	**Column Labels** ▼			
4	**Row Labels** ▼	**Atlantic**	**Central**	**Midwest**	**Mountain West**
5	⊟ **2012**				
6	January	10.75%	11.39%	10.06%	10.66%
7	February	8.63%	7.88%	11.46%	8.69%
8	March	11.40%	10.77%	10.81%	11.08%
9	April	10.68%	11.43%	10.31%	12.22%
10	May	10.76%	12.75%	10.75%	10.66%
11	June	12.70%	10.54%	10.73%	11.42%
12	July	10.94%	11.81%	10.19%	11.58%
13	August	10.43%	10.83%	12.34%	11.98%
14	September	10.95%	10.40%	12.25%	10.87%
15	October	10.57%	10.37%	9.70%	10.03%
16	November	11.38%	10.90%	11.77%	10.63%
17	December	10.68%	12.33%	11.22%	10.05%
18	⊟ **2013**				
19	January	11.35%	10.56%	10.87%	10.81%
20	February	10.28%	10.07%	9.31%	9.14%
21	March	9.64%	9.96%	9.15%	10.28%

12   On the **Quick Access Toolbar**, click the **Undo** button to reverse the last change.

13   On the **Design** tab, in the **Layout** group, click **Subtotals**, and then click **Show All Subtotals at Bottom of Group** to display subtotals in the workbook.

14   Click the **Package Summary** sheet tab to display the **Package Summary** worksheet.

15   In cell **C4**, enter =, but do not press Enter.

16   Click the **PivotTable** sheet tab to display that worksheet.

17   Click cell **K32**, and then press **Enter**. When you do, Excel creates the formula **=GETPIVOTDATA("Volume",Sheet2!$A$3,"Year",2013)** in cell **C4**.

The formula bar shows: `=GETPIVOTDATA("Volume",Sheet2!$A$3,"Year",2013)` with cell reference C4.

	A	B	C	D	E	F
1						
2		**Total Packages Handled**				
3		Calendar Year 2012	215576788			
4		Calendar Year 2013	214318275			
5						

✖ CLEAN UP Close the Focusing workbook, saving your changes if you want to.

Formatting PivotTables

PivotTables are the ideal tools for summarizing and examining large data collections, even those containing more than 10,000 or even 100,000 rows. Even though PivotTables often end up as compact summaries, you should do everything you can to make your data more comprehensible. One way to improve your data's readability is to apply a number format to the PivotTable Values field. To apply a number format to a field, right-click any cell in the field, and then click Number Format to open the Format Cells dialog box. Select or define the format you want to apply, and then click OK to enact the change.

SEE ALSO For more information on selecting and defining cell formats by using the Format Cells dialog box, see "Formatting cells" in Chapter 4, "Changing workbook appearance."

Analysts often use PivotTables to summarize and examine organizational data with an eye to making important decisions about the company. For example, chief operating officer Lori Penor might examine monthly package volumes handled by Consolidated Messenger and notice that there's a surge in package volume during the winter months in the United States.

	Northwest	Southeast	Southwest	Grand Total
	25,028,389	23,785,488	24,817,582	215,576,788
	3,085,352	3,470,295	3,029,490	27,595,133
	2,554,130	1,988,929	2,692,383	17,854,654
	1,932,304	1,441,894	1,646,946	14,804,110
	1,348,145	1,631,240	1,525,005	13,539,264
	1,628,489	1,749,378	1,452,226	14,225,789
	1,475,038	1,422,265	1,428,581	13,587,254
	1,832,445	1,511,712	1,503,100	14,448,166
	1,633,582	1,671,246	1,414,763	14,568,966
	1,638,024	1,510,884	1,407,402	13,650,679
	2,045,639	1,427,066	2,888,565	16,501,082
	3,020,217	2,848,642	2,728,934	26,798,138
	2,835,024	3,111,937	3,100,187	28,003,553

Excel extends the capabilities of your PivotTables by enabling you to apply a conditional format to the PivotTable cells. What's more, you can select whether to apply the conditional format to every cell in the Values area, to every cell at the same level as the selected cell (that is, a regular data cell, a subtotal cell, or a grand total cell) or to every cell that contains or draws its values from the selected cell's field (such as the Volume field in the previous example).

To apply a conditional format to a PivotTable field, click a cell in the Values area. On the Home tab, in the Styles group, click Conditional Formatting, and then create the desired conditional format. After you do, Excel displays a Formatting Options action button, which offers three options for applying the conditional format:

- **Selected Cells** Applies the conditional format to the selected cells only

- **All Cells Showing Sum of field_name Values** Applies the conditional format to every cell in the data area, regardless of whether the cell is in the data area, a subtotal row or column, or a grand total row or column

- **All Cells Showing Sum of field_name Values for Fields** Applies the conditional format to every cell at the same level (for example, data cell, subtotal, or grand total) as the selected cells

SEE ALSO For more information on creating conditional formats, see "Changing the appearance of data based on its value" in Chapter 4, "Changing workbook appearance."

In Excel, you can take full advantage of the Microsoft Office system enhanced formatting capabilities to apply existing formats to your PivotTables. Just as you can create Excel table formats, you can also create your own PivotTable formats to match your organization's desired color scheme.

To apply a PivotTable style, click any cell in the PivotTable and then, on the Design tool tab, in the PivotTable Styles group, click the style that you want to apply. If you want to create your own PivotTable style, click the More button to display a menu containing a gallery, and then click New PivotTable Style below the gallery to open the New PivotTable Style dialog box.

Enter a name for the style in the Name field, click the first table element you want to customize, and then click Format. Use the controls in the Format Cells dialog box to change the element's appearance. After you click OK to close the Format Cells dialog box, the New PivotTable Quick Style dialog box Preview pane displays the style's appearance. If you want Excel to use the style by default, select the Set As Default PivotTable Style For This Document check box. After you finish creating your formats, click OK to close the New PivotTable Quick Style dialog box and save your style.

The Design tool tab contains many other tools that you can use to format your PivotTable, but one of the most useful is the Banded Columns check box, which you can find in the PivotTable Style Options group. If you select a PivotTable style that offers banded rows as an option, selecting the Banded Rows check box turns banding on. If you prefer not to have Excel band the rows in your PivotTable, clearing the check box turns banding off.

In this exercise, you'll apply a number format to a PivotTable values field, apply a PivotTable style, create your own PivotTable style, apply banded rows to your PivotTable, and apply a conditional format to a PivotTable.

➡ SET UP You need the Formatting workbook located in the Chapter10 practice file folder to complete this exercise. Open the workbook, and then follow the steps.

1 On the **Sheet2** worksheet, right-click any data cell, and then click **Number Format** to open the **Format Cells** dialog box.

2 In the **Category** list, click **Number** to display the **Number** page of the dialog box.

3   In the **Decimal places** field, enter 0.

4   Select the **Use 1000 Separator (,)** check box.

5   Click **OK** to reformat your PivotTable data.

⧨	A	B	C	D
1				
2				
3	Sum of Volume	Column Labels ▾		
4	Row Labels ▾	Atlantic	Central	Midwest
5	⊟2012	23,276,049	23,727,556	23,643,436
6	January	2,966,264	3,143,004	2,774,877
7	February	1,541,726	1,407,340	2,046,448
8	March	1,688,027	1,594,434	1,600,920
9	April	1,445,436	1,548,205	1,395,802
10	May	1,530,319	1,813,746	1,529,086
11	June	1,725,770	1,431,518	1,458,009
12	July	1,581,340	1,706,190	1,472,534
13	August	1,519,538	1,577,651	1,797,139
14	September	1,494,735	1,420,065	1,672,046
15	October	1,743,541	1,711,810	1,599,927
16	November	3,049,369	2,921,522	3,153,696
17	December	2,989,984	3,452,071	3,142,952
18	⊟2013	23,760,133	23,274,159	23,246,331
19	January	3,076,578	2,863,187	2,946,100
20	February	1,556,937	1,524,882	1,410,456
21	March	1,522,379	1,573,351	1,445,833

6   If necessary, on the **Design** tool tab, in the **PivotTable Style Options** group, select the **Banded Rows** check box.

7   On the **Design** tool tab, in the **PivotTable Styles** group, click the **More** button. Then, in the top row of the gallery, click the third style from the left (**Pivot Style Light 2.**). Clicking the style causes Excel to apply it to your PivotTable.

10

▲	A	B	C	D
1				
2				
3	Sum of Volume	Column Labels ▼		
4	Row Labels ▼	Atlantic	Central	Midwest
5	⊟2012	23,276,049	23,727,556	23,643,436
6	January	2,966,264	3,143,004	2,774,877
7	February	1,541,726	1,407,340	2,046,448
8	March	1,688,027	1,594,434	1,600,920
9	April	1,445,436	1,548,205	1,395,802
10	May	1,530,319	1,813,746	1,529,086
11	June	1,725,770	1,431,518	1,458,009
12	July	1,581,340	1,706,190	1,472,534
13	August	1,519,538	1,577,651	1,797,139
14	September	1,494,735	1,420,065	1,672,046
15	October	1,743,541	1,711,810	1,599,927
16	November	3,049,369	2,921,522	3,153,696
17	December	2,989,984	3,452,071	3,142,952
18	⊟2013	23,760,133	23,274,159	23,246,331
19	January	3,076,578	2,863,187	2,946,100
20	February	1,556,937	1,524,882	1,410,456

8   In the lower-right corner of the **PivotTable Styles** menu, click the **More** button to display the gallery.

9   Click **New PivotTable Style** to open the **New PivotTable Style** dialog box.

10   In the **Name** field, enter Custom Style 1.

11   In the **Table Element** list, click **Header Row**, and then click **Format** to open the **Format Cells** dialog box.

12   On the **Font** page, in the **Color** list, click the white swatch.

13   On the **Border** page, in the **Presets** area, click **Outline**.

14   On the **Fill** page, in the **Background Color** area, click the purple swatch in the lower-right corner of the color palette.

15   Click **OK** to close the **Format Cells** dialog box. The style change appears in the **Preview** pane of the **New PivotTable Quick Style** dialog box.

16   In the **Table Element** list, click **Second Row Stripe**, and then click **Format** to open the **Format Cells** dialog box.

17   On the **Fill** page, in the middle part of the **Background Color** area, click the eighth swatch in the second row (it's a light, dusty purple).

18   Click **OK** twice to close the **Format Cells** dialog box. Your format appears in the **PivotTable Styles** group.

19   Click the **More** button in the lower-right corner of the **PivotTable Styles** group, and then click your new style to reformat the PivotTable.

20   On the **Design** tool tab, in the **PivotTable Style Options** group, clear the **Banded Rows** check box. Excel removes the banding from your PivotTable and from the preview of the custom style.

	A	B	C	D	E
1					
2					
3	Sum of Volume	Column Labels ▼			
4	Row Labels ▼	Atlantic	Central	Midwest	Mountain West
5	⊟2012	23,276,049	23,727,556	23,643,436	23,075,908
6	January	2,966,264	3,143,004	2,774,877	2,942,544
7	February	1,541,726	1,407,340	2,046,448	1,552,098
8	March	1,688,027	1,594,434	1,600,920	1,641,026
9	April	1,445,436	1,548,205	1,395,802	1,653,829
10	May	1,530,319	1,813,746	1,529,086	1,516,453
11	June	1,725,770	1,431,518	1,458,009	1,551,719

21 Select the cell ranges **K6:K17** and **K19:K30**.

22 On the **Home** tab, in the **Styles** group, click **Conditional Formatting**, point to **Color Scales**, and in the top row, click the second three-color scale from the left to apply the conditional format to the selected cells.

	I	J	K	L
	Southeast	Southwest	Grand Total	
	23,785,488	24,817,582	215,576,788	
	3,470,295	3,029,490	27,595,133	
	1,988,929	2,692,383	17,854,654	
	1,441,894	1,646,946	14,804,110	
	1,631,240	1,525,005	13,539,264	
	1,749,378	1,452,226	14,225,789	
	1,422,265	1,428,581	13,587,254	
	1,511,712	1,503,100	14,448,166	
	1,671,246	1,414,763	14,568,966	
	1,510,884	1,407,402	13,650,679	
	1,427,066	2,888,565	16,501,082	
	2,848,642	2,728,934	26,798,138	
	3,111,937	3,100,187	28,003,553	
	26,736,115	23,300,579	214,318,275	
	2,926,429	2,919,964	27,109,328	
	2,888,829	1,721,227	15,143,659	
	2,945,358	1,579,637	15,795,737	

 CLEAN UP Close the Formatting workbook, saving your changes if you want to.

Creating PivotTables from external data

Although most of the time you will create PivotTables from data stored in Excel worksheets, you can also bring data from outside sources into Excel. For example, you might need to work with data created in another spreadsheet program by using a file format that Excel can't read directly. Fortunately, you can export the data from the original program into a text file, which Excel then translates into a worksheet.

TIP The data import technique shown here isn't exclusive to PivotTables. You can use this procedure to bring data into your worksheets for any purpose.

Spreadsheet programs store data in cells, so the goal of representing spreadsheet data in a text file is to indicate where the contents of one cell end and those of the next cell begin. The character that marks the end of a cell is a *delimiter*, in that it marks the end (or "limit") of a cell. The most common cell delimiter is the comma, so the delimited sequence *15, 18, 24, 28* represents data in four cells. The problem with using commas to delimit financial data is that larger values—such as *52,802*—can be written by using commas as thousands markers. To avoid confusion when importing a text file, the most commonly used delimiter for financial data is the Tab character.

To import data from a text file, on the Data tab, click Get External Data group, and then click From Text to display the Import Text File dialog box.

From within the Import Text File dialog box, browse to the directory that contains the text file you want to import. When you double-click the file, Excel launches the Text Import wizard.

On the first page of the Text Import wizard, you can indicate whether the data file you are importing is Delimited or Fixed Width; Fixed Width means that each cell value will fall within a specific position in the file. Clicking Next to accept the default choice, Delimited (which Excel assigns after examining the data source you selected), advances you to the next wizard page.

Text Import Wizard - Step 2 of 3

This screen lets you set the delimiters your data contains. You can see how your text is affected in the preview below.

Delimiters
☑ Tab
☐ Semicolon   ☐ Treat consecutive delimiters as one
☐ Comma
☐ Space   Text qualifier: `"` ▾
☐ Other: ____

Data preview

Center	Date	Year	Month	Week	Day	Weekday	Volume
Atlantic	1/1/2013	2013	January	1	1	Tuesday	120933
Atlantic	1/2/2013	2013	January	1	2	Wednesday	52979
Atlantic	1/3/2013	2013	January	1	3	Thursday	45683
Atlantic	1/4/2013	2013	January	1	4	Friday	53152

Cancel   < Back   Next >   Finish

On this page, you can choose the delimiter for the file (in this case, Excel detected tabs in the file and selected the Tab check box for you) and you can preview what the text file will look like when imported. Clicking Next advances you to the final wizard page.

Text Import Wizard - Step 3 of 3

This screen lets you select each column and set the Data Format.

Column data format
⦿ General
○ Text   'General' converts numeric values to numbers, date values to dates, and
○ Date: MDY ▾   all remaining values to text.
○ Do not import column (skip)   Advanced...

Data preview

General	General	Gener	General	Gener	Gener	General	General
Center	Date	Year	Month	Week	Day	Weekday	Volume
Atlantic	1/1/2013	2013	January	1	1	Tuesday	120933
Atlantic	1/2/2013	2013	January	1	2	Wednesday	52979
Atlantic	1/3/2013	2013	January	1	3	Thursday	45683
Atlantic	1/4/2013	2013	January	1	4	Friday	53152

Cancel   < Back   Next >   Finish

10

On this page, you can change the data type and formatting of the columns in your data. Because you'll assign number styles and PivotTable Quick Styles after you create the PivotTable, you can click Finish to import the data into your worksheet. After the data is in Excel, you can work with it normally.

In this exercise, you'll import data into Excel from a text file and then create a PivotTable based on that data.

SET UP You need the Creating text file located in the Chapter10 practice file folder to complete this exercise. Don't open the file yet; just follow the steps.

1. Create a new Excel workbook. On the **Data** tab, click the **Get External Data** button, and then click **From Text** to open the **Import Text File** dialog box.

2. Navigate to the **Chapter10** practice file folder, and then double-click the **Creating** text file to start the **Text Import** wizard.

3. Verify that the **Delimited** option is selected, and then click **Next** to display the next page of the wizard.

4. In the **Delimiters** area, verify that the **Tab** check box is selected and also verify that the data displayed in the **Data preview** area reflects the structure you expect.

5. Click **Finish** to skip the third page of the wizard, which has commands you can use to assign specific data types to each column. Excel assigns data types for you, so you don't need to do so. After you click **Finish**, the **Import Data** dialog box opens.

6   Verify that **Existing worksheet** is selected, and then click **OK** to import the data into your workbook.

7   On the **Home** tab, in the **Styles** group, click **Format as Table**, and then click the first table style to display the **Format As Table** dialog box.

8   Verify that the **My table has headers** check box is selected and that the range =$A$1:$H$6571 appears in the **Where is the data for your table?** box, and then click **OK**.

9   In the confirmation dialog box, click **Yes** to confirm that you want to create the Excel table and break its link to the external data source. Excel creates an Excel table from your imported data.

10   On the **Insert** tab, click **PivotTable** to open the **Create PivotTable** dialog box.

11   Verify that **Select a table or range** is selected, that **Table1** appears in the **Table/Range** field, and that the **New Worksheet** option is selected.

12   Click **OK** to create the PivotTable on a new worksheet.

13   In the **PivotTable Fields** pane, drag the **Volume** field header to the **Values** area.

14   Drag the **Weekday** field header to the **Columns** area.

15   Drag the **Center** field header to the **Rows** data area.

	A	B	C	D	E	F	G	H	I
1									
2									
3	Sum of Volume	Column Labels ▼							
4	Row Labels ▼	Sunday	Monday	Tuesday	Wednesday	Thursday	Friday	Saturday	Grand Total
5	Atlantic	7113064	6785522	6701941	6513606	6349037	6828903	6744109	47036182
6	Central	6647901	6885403	6626576	6692635	6646779	6494618	7007803	47001715
7	Midwest	6675694	7115293	6742964	6333636	6847094	6563336	6611750	46889767
8	Mountain West	6491280	6762698	6861705	6566685	6465276	6570660	6605186	46323490
9	North Central	6406503	6652892	6821348	6554389	6835394	6751992	6658072	46680590
10	Northeast	6798887	7061096	7072813	6945302	6889922	7137390	6784795	48690205
11	Northwest	6661552	6997784	7144120	6775035	7380197	7077630	6597032	48633350
12	Southeast	7419464	7024506	7397212	7373977	7510823	6835314	6960307	50521603
13	Southwest	7039234	6757128	6910012	6909127	6770431	7181509	6550720	48118161
14	Grand Total	61253579	62042322	62278691	60664392	61694953	61441352	60519774	429895063
15									

❌ CLEAN UP   Close the Imported Data workbook, saving your changes if you want to.

10

Creating dynamic charts by using PivotCharts

Just as you can create PivotTables that you can reorganize on the fly to emphasize different aspects of the data in a list, you can also create dynamic charts, or PivotCharts, to reflect the contents and organization of a PivotTable.

Creating a PivotChart is fairly straightforward. Just click any cell in a list or Excel table that you would use to create a PivotTable, and then click the Insert tab. In the Charts group, click the PivotChart button to create the chart. When you do, Excel 2013 opens the Create PivotChart dialog box.

To create a PivotChart from an existing PivotTable, click a cell in the PivotTable, display the Insert tab and then, in the Charts group, click the type of chart you want to create. After you complete either of these procedures, Excel displays a new PivotChart in your workbook.

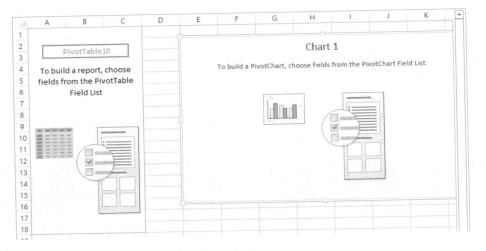

Any changes to the PivotTable on which the PivotChart is based are reflected in the PivotChart. For example, if the data in an underlying data set changes, clicking the Refresh button in the Data group on the Analyze tool tab will change the PivotChart to reflect the new data. Also, if you filter the contents of a PivotTable, the filter will be reflected in the PivotChart. For instance, if you click 2009 in the Year list of a revenue analysis PivotTable and then click OK, both the PivotTable and the PivotChart will show only revenues from 2009.

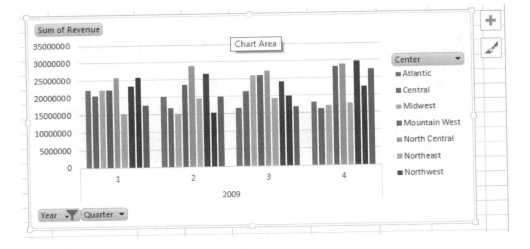

SEE ALSO For more information on manipulating PivotTables, see "Filtering, showing, and hiding PivotTable data" earlier in this chapter.

A PivotChart has tools with which you can filter the data in the PivotChart and PivotTable. Clicking the Year arrow, clicking (All) in the list that appears, and then clicking OK will restore the PivotChart to its original configuration.

If you ever want to change the chart type of an existing chart, you can do so by selecting the chart and then, on the Design tab, in the Type group, clicking Change Chart Type to display the Change Chart Type dialog box. When you select the type you want and click OK, Excel re-creates your chart.

> **IMPORTANT** If your data is the wrong type to be represented by the chart type you select, Excel displays an error message.

In this exercise, you'll create a PivotTable and associated PivotChart, change the underlying data and update the PivotChart to reflect that change, change the PivotChart's type, and then filter a PivotTable and PivotChart.

➡ SET UP You need the RevenueAnalysis workbook located in the Chapter10 practice file folder to complete this exercise. Open the workbook, and then follow the steps.

1 On the **Through 2012** worksheet, click any cell in the Excel table.

2 On the **Insert** tab, in the **Charts** group, click the **PivotChart** button to open the **Create PivotChart** dialog box.

3 Verify that the **QuarterlyRevenue** table appears in the **Table/Range** field and that **New Worksheet** is selected.

4   Click **OK** to create the PivotChart and associated PivotTable.

5   In the **PivotChart Fields** pane, drag the **Center** field header from the **Choose fields to add to report** area to the **Legend (Series)** area.

6   Drag the **Year** field header from the **Choose fields to add to report** area to the **Axis (Category)** area.

7   Drag the **Quarter** field header from the **Choose fields to add to report** area to the **Axis (Category)** area, positioning it below the **Year** field header.

8   Drag the **Revenue** field header from the **Choose fields to add to report** area to the **Values** area. Excel updates the PivotChart to reflect the field placements.

9   Click the **2013** sheet tab to display that worksheet.

10 Select the data in cells **B2:E10**, and then press **Ctrl+C**. Excel copies the data to the Microsoft Office Clipboard.

11 On the tab bar, click the **Through 2012** sheet tab to display that worksheet.

12 Select cell **B147**, and then press **Ctrl+V** to paste the data into the worksheet and include it in the Excel table.

13 Click the tab of the worksheet that contains the PivotTable and the PivotChart. The PivotChart appears.

14 Select the PivotChart and then, on the **Analyze** tool tab, in the **Data** group, click **Refresh** to add the data to your PivotChart.

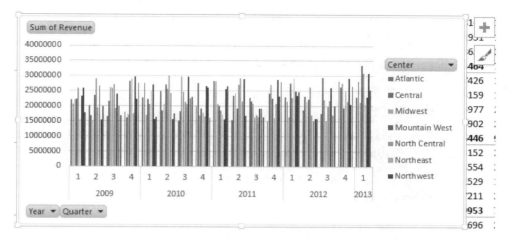

15   On the **Design** tool tab, in the **Type** group, click **Change Chart Type** to open the
      Change Chart Type dialog box.

16   Click **Line**, click the first **Line** chart subtype, and then click **OK** to change your
      PivotChart to a line chart.

17   In the **PivotTable Fields** pane, in the **Choose fields to add to report** area, point
      to the **Center** field header. Click the filter arrow that appears and then, in the filter
      menu, clear the **Select All** check box to remove the check boxes from the filter list
      items.

18   Select the **Northeast** check box, and then click **OK** to filter the PivotChart.

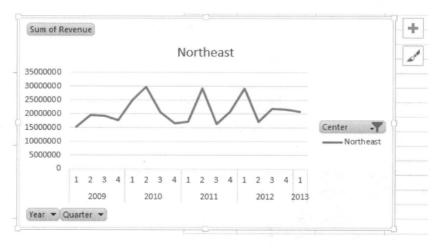

❌ CLEAN UP Close the RevenueAnalysis workbook, saving your changes if you want to.

Key points

- A PivotTable is a versatile tool that you can use to rearrange your data dynamically, enabling you to emphasize different aspects of your data without creating new worksheets.

- PivotTable data must be formatted as a list. By using a data table as the PivotTable data source, you can streamline the creation process by referring to the table name instead of being required to select the entire range that contains the data you want to summarize.

- You can choose from a variety of styles when you create PivotTables.

- With the PivotTable Fields pane, you can create your PivotTable by using a straightforward, compact tool.

- Just as you can limit the data shown in a static worksheet, you can use filters to limit the data shown in a PivotTable.

- If you have data in a compatible format, such as a text file, you can import that data into Excel and create a PivotTable from it.

- You can summarize your data visually by using a PivotChart, which you can pivot just like a PivotTable.

10

Chapter at a glance

Headers

Add headers and footers to printed pages,
page 334

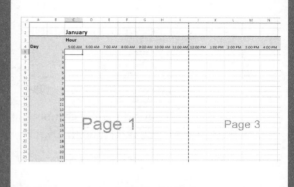

Prepare

Prepare worksheets for printing,
page 340

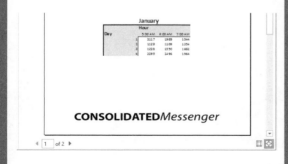

Print

Print parts of worksheets,
page 352

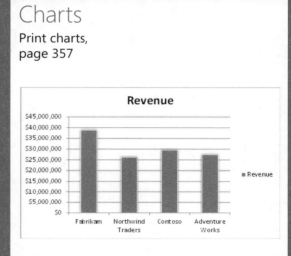

Charts

Print charts,
page 357

Printing worksheets and charts

11

IN THIS CHAPTER, YOU WILL LEARN HOW TO

- Add headers and footers to printed pages.

- Prepare worksheets for printing.

- Print worksheets.

- Print parts of worksheets.

- Print charts.

Microsoft Excel 2013 provides you with a wide range of tools that you can use to create and manipulate your data. By using filters, by sorting, and by creating PivotTables and charts, you can change your worksheets so that they convey the greatest possible amount of information. After you configure your worksheet so that it shows your data to best advantage, you can print your Excel documents to use in a presentation or include in a report. You can choose to print all or part of any of your worksheets, change how your data and charts appear on the printed page, and even suppress any error messages that might appear in your worksheets.

In this chapter, you'll add headers and footers to your worksheets, prepare your worksheets for printing, print all of and part of a worksheet, and print a chart.

PRACTICE FILES To complete the exercises in this chapter, you need the practice files contained in the Chapter11 practice file folder. For more information, see "Download the practice files" in this book's Introduction.

Adding headers and footers to printed pages

If you want to ensure that the same information appears at the top or bottom of every printed page, you can do so by adding headers or footers. A *header* is a section that appears at the top of every printed page; a *footer* is a section that appears at the bottom of every printed page. To create a header or footer in Excel, you display the Insert tab and then, in the Text group, click Header & Footer to display the Design tool tab.

When you display your workbook's headers and footers, Excel displays the workbook in Page Layout view. Page Layout view shows you exactly how your workbook will look when printed, while still enabling you to edit your file, a capability not provided by Print Preview. You can also switch to Page Layout view by displaying the View tab and then, in the Workbook Views group, clicking Page Layout.

SEE ALSO For information about editing your workbook in Print Preview mode, see "Previewing worksheets before printing" later in this chapter.

Excel divides its headers and footers into left, middle, and right sections. When you point to an editable header or footer section, Excel highlights the section to indicate that clicking the mouse button will open that header or footer section for editing.

TIP If you have a chart selected when you click the Header & Footer button on the Insert tab, Excel displays the Header/Footer page of the Page Setup dialog box instead of opening a header or footer section for editing.

When you click a header or footer section, Excel displays the Design tool tab on the ribbon. The Design tool tab contains several standard headers and footers, such as page numbers by themselves or followed by the name of the workbook. To add an Auto Header to your workbook, display the Design tool tab and then, in the Header & Footer group, click Header. Then click the header you want to apply. The list of headers that appears will vary depending on the properties and contents of your worksheet and workbook.

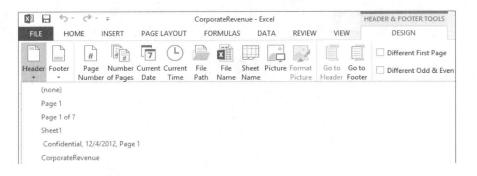

You can also create custom headers by entering your own text or by using the commands in the Header & Footer Elements group to insert a date, time, worksheet name, or page number. You can also add a graphic, such as a company logo, to a header or footer. For example, if you include a worksheet in a printed report that is distributed outside your company, adding your company's logo to the worksheet can identify the worksheet with your company. After you insert a graphic into a header or footer, the Format Picture button in the Header & Footer Elements group will become available. When you click that button, a dialog box opens with tools for editing your graphic.

When you print or display a worksheet, you might want to have different headers for odd and even pages. For example, Consolidated Messenger's document standards might require the current date on odd-numbered pages and the page number on even-numbered pages. To establish different headers and footers for odd-numbered and even-numbered pages,

11

click the View tab and then click the Page Layout button to display your workbook in Page Layout view. Click within a header or footer and then, on the Design tool tab, select the Different Odd & Even Pages check box. Now when you change a header or footer, Excel indicates whether it applies to an odd or even page.

Your worksheet's header and footer will always be the same width as the printed worksheet. If you want to adjust the vertical size of a header or footer, click the Page Layout tab, click the Margins button, and then click the Custom Margins command at the bottom of the menu to display the Margins page of the Page Setup dialog box.

The Margins page of the Page Setup dialog box has boxes for you to enter your desired header and footer sizes. Enter the values you want and then click OK to apply your changes.

In this exercise, you'll create a custom header for a workbook. You'll then add a graphic to the footer and edit the graphic by using the Format Picture dialog box.

SET UP You need the RevenueByCustomer workbook and the ConsolidatedMessenger image located in your Chapter11 practice file folder to complete this exercise. Open the workbook, and then follow the steps.

1   On the **Insert** tab, click the **Text** button, and then click **Header & Footer** to display your workbook in **Page Layout** view.

2   In the middle header section, enter **Q1 2013**, and then press **Enter**.

3   On the **Design** tool tab, in the **Header & Footer Elements** group, click **File Name** to add the **&[File]** code to the header.

4   To the right of the **&[File]** code, enter a comma, and then press the **Spacebar**.

5   On the **Design** tool tab, in the **Header & Footer Elements** group, click **Current Date**. Excel changes the contents of the middle header section to **&[File], &[Date]**.

6   Press **Tab**. Excel highlights the right header section. The workbook name and current date appear in the middle header section.

7   On the **Design** tool tab, in the **Options** group, select the **Different Odd & Even Pages** check box to print the header you defined on odd-numbered pages only and to leave the header on even-numbered pages blank. Excel changes the header label from **Header** to **Odd Page Header**.

8   On the **Design** tool tab, in the **Navigation** group, click **Go to Footer** to highlight the right footer section.

9   Click the middle footer section.

10 On the **Design** tool tab, in the **Header & Footer Elements** group, click **Picture** to open the **Insert Pictures** dialog box.

11 Click **From a File** to display the **Insert Picture** dialog box.

12 Navigate to the **Chapter11** folder, and then double-click the **ConsolidatedMessenger** image file. The code **&[Picture]** appears in the middle footer section.

13 Click any worksheet cell above the footer to display the worksheet as it will be printed.

14   Click the image in the footer and then, on the **Design** tool tab, click **Format Picture** to open the **Format Picture** dialog box.

Format Picture dialog box

15   Click the **Size** tab if the **Size** page is not already displayed.

16   In the **Scale** area of the dialog box, in the **Height** field, enter **80%**, and then press **Enter** to close the **Format Picture** dialog box.

17   Click any worksheet cell above the footer to display the reformatted picture.

18   On the **Page Layout** tab, click **Margins**, and then click the **Custom Margins** command at the bottom of the menu to display the **Margins** page of the **Page Setup** dialog box.

19   In the **Header** box, enter **.5**.

20   In the **Footer** box, enter **.5** and click **OK** to reformat your worksheet.

✖ CLEAN UP Close the RevenueByCustomer workbook, saving your changes if you want to.

Preparing worksheets for printing

When you are ready to print your workbook, you can change the workbook's properties to ensure that your worksheets display all your information and that printing is centered on the page. In Excel, all of these printing functions are gathered together in one place: the Backstage view. To preview your workbook in the Backstage view, click the File tab and then click Print.

KEYBOARD SHORTCUT Press Ctrl+P to preview your worksheet in the Backstage view. For a complete list of keyboard shortcuts, see "Keyboard shortcuts" at the end of this book.

Excel comes with three margin settings: Normal, Wide, and Narrow. Excel applies the Normal setting by default, but you can select any of the three options by displaying the workbook in the Backstage view and then, in the Settings area, clicking the Margins button and clicking the setting you want. If you want finer control over your margins, click the Margins button and then click Custom Margins to display the Margins page of the Page Setup dialog box.

If you want to display a worksheet's margins while you have its workbook open in the Backstage view, click the Show Margins button near the lower-right corner of the Backstage view.

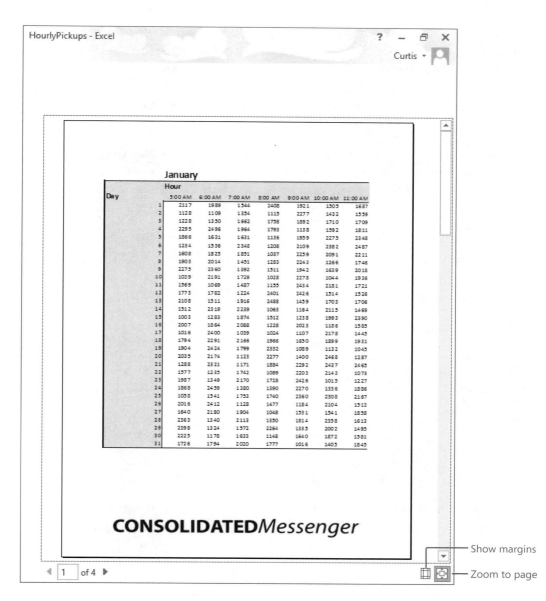

CONSOLIDATED*Messenger*

Show margins

Zoom to page

◀ | 1 | of 4 ▶

You can drag each margin line to change the corresponding margin's position, increasing or decreasing the amount of space allocated to each worksheet section. Do bear in mind that increasing the size of the header or footer reduces the size of the worksheet body, meaning that fewer rows can be printed on a page.

Another issue with printing worksheets is that the data in worksheets tends to be wider horizontally than a standard sheet of paper. You can use the commands in the Backstage

view to change the alignment of the rows and columns on the page. When the columns parallel the long edge of a piece of paper, the page is laid out in portrait mode; when the columns parallel the short edge of a piece of paper, it is in landscape mode.

Changing between portrait and landscape mode can result in a better fit, but you might find that not all of your data will fit on a single printed page. This is where the options available on the Scaling button in the Backstage view come to the rescue. By using the options on the Scaling button, you can perform three tasks: reduce the size of the worksheet's contents until the worksheet can be printed on a single page, reduce the size of the worksheet's contents until all of the worksheet's columns fit on a single page, or reduce the size of the worksheet's contents until all of the worksheet's rows fit on a single page. You can make the same changes (and more) by using the controls in the Page Setup dialog box. To display the Page Setup dialog box, click the Page Layout tab, and then click the Page Setup dialog box launcher.

Previewing worksheets before printing

You can view your worksheet as it will be printed by displaying the Backstage view and then clicking Print in the left pane. When Excel displays your worksheet in the Backstage view, it shows the active worksheet as it will be printed with its current settings. At the bottom of the Backstage view, Excel indicates how many pages the worksheet will require when printed and the number of the page you are viewing.

TIP When you display a workbook in the Backstage view, you can view the next printed page by clicking the preview image and pressing the Page Down key; to move to the previous page, press the Page Up key. You can also use the Previous and Next arrows at the bottom of the Backstage view, enter a page number in the Current Page box, or scroll through the pages by using the vertical scroll bar at the right edge of the Backstage view.

11

Changing page breaks in a worksheet

Another way to affect how your worksheet will appear on the printed page is to change where Excel assigns its page breaks. A page break is the point at which Excel prints all subsequent data on a new sheet of paper. You can make these changes indirectly by modifying a worksheet's margins, but you can do so directly by displaying your document in Page Break Preview mode. To display your worksheet in this mode, on the View tab, in the Workbook Views group, click Page Break Preview.

	A	B	C	D	E	F	G	H	I	J	K	L	M	N
1														
2			January											
3			Hour											
4	Day		5:00 AM	6:00 AM	7:00 AM	8:00 AM	9:00 AM	10:00 AM	11:00 AM	12:00 PM	1:00 PM	2:00 PM	3:00 PM	4:00 PM
5		1	2117	1989	1544	2408	1921	1505	1687	2391	1486	2075	1626	1326
6		2	1128	1109	1354	1115	2277	1432	1559	2103	2493	1317	1519	1836
7		3	1228	1350	1662	1758	1892	1710	1709	1889	1495	1405	1513	1493
8		4	2295	2496	1964	1793	1138	1592	1811	1479	2339	1839	2416	1838
9		5	1866	1631	1631	1136	1959	2275	2348	1355	1346	1947	2098	1163
10		6	1234	1536	2348	1208	2109	2382	2487	2464	1755	2086	1261	1989
11		7	1608	1825	1851	1037	2259	2091	2211	1195	1395	1727	1171	1753
12		8	1903	2014	1451	1283	2243	1266	1746	2243	1385	1414	1675	2274
13		9	2275	2360	1392	1511	1942	1639	2018	2468	2247	2493	1827	2261
14		10	1039	2191	1729	1028	2278	1044	1936	1233	1677	1988	1690	1649
15		11	1569	1069	1487	1155	2434	2181	1721	2235	1534	1407	1187	1581
16		12	1773	1782	1224	2401	2426	1514	1526	1086	1478	1943	1028	1988
17		13	2108	1511	1916	2488	1459	1703	1706	2083	2305	2348	1662	2218
18		14	1512	2319	2239	1068	1164	2115	1469	1629	2398	1970	1665	1343
19		15	1003	1288	1874	1512	1238	1993	2390	2040	1366	1422	2344	1144
20		16	2007	1864	2088	1228	2023	1186	1585	1422	1486	2232	1907	2001
21		17	1016	2400	1039	1024	1107	2178	1445	1452	1506	1605	1925	2223
22		18	1794	2291	2166	1966	1650	1899	1931	2124	1166	1630	2178	1185
23		19	1904	2424	1799	2332	1089	1132	1045	1203	1364	2346	1654	1483

The blue lines in the window represent the page breaks. If you want to set a page break manually, you can do so by displaying your worksheet in Page Break Preview mode, right-clicking the row header of the row below where you want the new page to start, and clicking Insert Page Break. In other words, if you right-click the row header of row 15 and then click Insert Page Break, row 14 will be the last row on the first printed page, and row 15 will be the first row on the second printed page. The same technique applies to columns: if you right-click the column H column header and click Insert Page Break, column G will be the last column on the first printed page, and column H will be the first column on the second printed page.

You can also add page breaks without displaying your workbook in Page Break Preview mode. To add a page break while your workbook is open in Normal view, click a row or column header and then, on the Page Layout tab, in the Page Setup area, click Breaks, and click Insert Page Break. You can use the commands in the Breaks list to delete a page break or to reset all of the page breaks in your worksheets.

IMPORTANT Be sure to click a row header or column header when you want to insert a single page break. If you view a workbook in Page Break Preview mode, right-click a cell within the body of a worksheet, and then click Insert Page Break, Excel creates both a vertical page break to the left of the selected cell and a horizontal page break above the selected cell.

To move a page break, drag the line that represents the break to its new position. Excel will change the worksheet's properties so that the area you defined will be printed on a single page.

Changing the page printing order for worksheets

When you view a document in Page Break Preview mode, Excel indicates the order in which the pages will be printed with light gray words on the worksheet pages. (These indicators appear only in Page Break Preview mode; they don't show up when the document is printed.) You can change the order in which the pages are printed by displaying the Page Layout tab, clicking the Page Setup dialog box launcher, and displaying the Sheet page of the Page Setup dialog box.

In the Page Order area of the dialog box, you can select the Over, Then Down option to change the order in which the worksheets will be printed from the default Down, Then Over. You might want to change the printing order to keep certain information together on consecutive printed pages. For example, suppose you have a worksheet that is designed to hold hourly package pickup information; the columns represent hours of the day, and the rows represent days of the month. If you want to print out consecutive days for each hour, you use Down, Then Over. In a typical configuration, pages 1 and 2 display the 5:00 A.M. to 11:00 A.M. pickups for the months of January and February, pages 3 and 4 display the 12:00 P.M. to 5:00 P.M. pickups for those months, and so on.

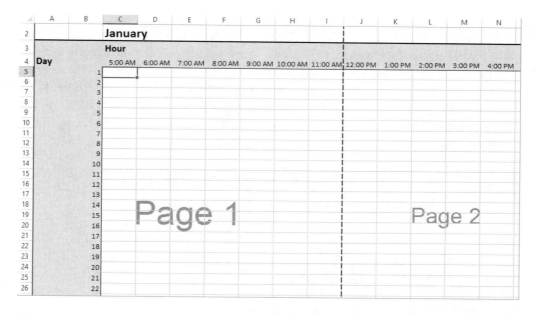

Changing the print order to Over, Then Down for the previous example would print consecutive hours for each day. Pages 1 and 2 would display the 5:00 A.M. to 5:00 P.M. pickups for January, and pages 3 and 4 would display the same pickups for February.

In this exercise, you'll preview a worksheet before printing it, change the worksheet's margins, change its orientation, reduce its size, add a page break, and change the page printing order.

➡️ SET UP You need the PickupsByHour workbook located in the Chapter11 practice file folder to complete this exercise. Open the workbook, and then follow the steps.

1. While displaying the **JanFeb** worksheet, click the **File** tab to display the **Backstage** view, and then click **Print**.

2. On the **Print** page of the **Backstage** view, click the **Orientation** button, and then click **Landscape Orientation** to reorient the worksheet.

3. In left pane of the **Backstage** view, click the **Go Back** button to return to the workbook.

11

4   On the **Page Layout** tab, in the **Scale to Fit** group, enter **80%** in the **Scale** box, and then press **Enter** to resize your worksheet.

5   Click the row header for row **38** to highlight that row.

6   On the **Page Layout** tab, in the **Page Setup** group, click **Breaks**, and then click **Insert Page Break** to set a horizontal page break above row **38**.

	A	B	C	D	E
37					
38		**February**			
39					
40				**Hour**	
41		**Day**		5:00 AM	6:00 AM
42			1	2117	1989
43			2	1128	1109
44			3	1228	1350
45			4	2295	2496

7   On the tab bar, click the **MarJun** sheet tab to display the **MarJun** worksheet.

8   On the **Page Layout** tab, in the **Page Setup** group, click **Margins**, and then click **Wide** to apply wide margins to the worksheet.

9   On the **Page Layout** tab, click the **Page Setup** dialog box launcher to open the **Page Setup** dialog box.

10 If necessary, click the **Sheet** tab to display the **Sheet** page of the dialog box.

11 In the **Page order** area, click **Over, then down**.

12 Click **OK**.

13 If you want, display the **Backstage** view, click **Print** to display the **Print** page, and then click the **Print** button to print your worksheet.

❌ CLEAN UP   Close the PickupsByHour workbook, saving your changes if you want to.

Printing worksheets

When you're ready to print a worksheet, all you have to do is display the Backstage view, click Print, and then click the Print button. If you want a little more say in how Excel prints your worksheet, you can use the commands on the Print page of the Backstage view to

determine how Excel prints your worksheet. For example, you can choose the printer to which you want to send this print job, print multiple copies of the worksheet, and select whether the copies are collated (all pages of a document are printed together) or not (multiple copies of the same page are printed together).

Info

New

Open

Save

Save As

Print

Share

Export

Close

Account

Options

Print

Copies: 1

Print

Printer

Send To OneNote 2013
Ready

Printer Properties

Settings

Print Active Sheets
Only print the active sheets

Pages: [ ] to [ ]

Collated
1,2,3   1,2,3   1,2,3

Landscape Orientation

Letter
8.5" x 11"

Normal Margins
Left: 0.7"   Right: 0.7"

Custom Scaling

Page Setup

11

If you want to print more than one worksheet from the active workbook, but not every worksheet in the workbook, you can select the worksheets to print from the tab bar. To select specific worksheets to print, hold down the Ctrl key while you click the sheet tabs of the worksheets you want. Then display the Backstage view, click Print, and click the Print button.

TIP The worksheets you select for printing do not need to be next to one another in the workbook.

One helpful option on the Sheet page of the Page Setup dialog box is the Cell Errors As box, which you can use to select how Excel will print any errors in your worksheet. You can print an error as it normally appears in the worksheet, print a blank cell in place of the error, or choose one of two other indicators that are not standard error messages.

After you prepare your workbook for printing, you can specify which elements to print by displaying the Print page of the Backstage view and then clicking the Print What button, which displays Print Active Sheets by default. To print the entire worksheet, verify that the Print What button displays Print Active Sheets, and then click the Print button. To print every worksheet in the active workbook, click the Print What button, click Print Entire Workbook, and then click the Print button.

In this exercise, you'll print nonadjacent worksheets in your workbook and suppress errors in the printed worksheet.

SET UP You need the SummaryByCustomer workbook located in the Chapter11 practice file folder to complete this exercise. Open the workbook, and then follow the steps.

1   If necessary, display the **Summary** worksheet.

2   On the **Page Layout** tab, click the **Page Setup** dialog box launcher to open the **Page Setup** dialog box.

3   Click the **Sheet** tab to display the **Sheet** page of the dialog box.

Page Setup

Page	Margins	Header/Footer	Sheet

Print area:

Print titles

Rows to repeat at top:

Columns to repeat at left:

Print

☐ Gridlines

☐ Black and white

☐ Draft quality

☐ Row and column headings

Comments: (None)

Cell errors as: displayed

Page order

◉ Down, then over

○ Over, then down

Print...   Print Preview   Options...

OK   Cancel

4   In the **Cell errors as** list, click **<blank>**.

5   Click **OK**.

6   Hold down the **Ctrl** key and then, on the tab bar, click the **Northwind** sheet tab to select the **Summary** and **Northwind** worksheets.

7   Display the **Backstage** view, and then click **Print**.

8   In the **Settings** area of the **Print** page, verify that **Print Active Sheets** is selected.

9   Click the **Go Back** button at the top of the left pane to cancel printing, or click the **Print** button if you want to print the worksheets.

11

✖ CLEAN UP Close the SummaryByCustomer workbook, saving your changes if you want to.

Printing parts of worksheets

Excel gives you a great deal of control over what your worksheets look like when you print them, but you also have a lot of control over which parts of your worksheets will be printed. For example, you can use the commands available on the Print page of the Backstage view to choose which pages of a multipage worksheet you want to print.

In the Settings area of the Print page, you can fill in the page numbers you want to print in the Pages From and To boxes.

TIP You can also use the Page Break Preview window to determine which pages to print, and if the pages aren't in an order you like, you can use the commands on the Sheet page of the Page Setup dialog box to change the order in which they will be printed.

Another way you can modify how a worksheet will be printed is to have Excel fit the entire worksheet on a specified number of pages. For example, you can have Excel resize a worksheet so that it will fit on a single printed page. Fitting a worksheet onto a single page is a handy tool when you need to add a sales or other summary to a report and don't want to spread important information across more than one page.

To have Excel fit a worksheet on a set number of pages, display the Page Layout tab and use the controls in the Scale To Fit group. In the Width and Height lists, you can select how many pages wide or tall you want your printout to be.

If you want to print a portion of a worksheet instead of the entire worksheet, you can define the area or areas that you want to have printed. To identify the area of the worksheet you want to print, select the cells with the data you want to print and, on the Page Layout tab, in the Page Setup group, click Print Area and then click Set Print Area. Excel marks the area with a dotted line around the border of the selected cells and prints only the cells you selected. To remove the selection, click Print Area, and then click Clear Print Area.

TIP You can include noncontiguous groups of cells in the area to be printed by holding down the Ctrl key as you select the cells. Noncontiguous print areas will be printed on separate pages.

After you define a print area, you can use the options in the Page Setup dialog box to position the print area on the page. Specifically, you can have Excel center the print area on the page by selecting the Horizontally and Vertically check boxes in the Center On Page area of the Margins page.

If the contents of a worksheet will take up more than one printed page, you can have Excel repeat one or more rows at the top of the page or columns at the left of the page. For example, if you want to print a lengthy worksheet that contains the mailing addresses of customers signed up to receive your company's monthly newsletter, you could repeat the column headings Name, Address, City, and so forth at the top of the page. To repeat rows at the top of each printed page, on the Page Layout tab, in the Page Setup group, click Print Titles. Excel will display the Sheet page of the Page Setup dialog box.

On the Sheet page of the Page Setup dialog box, you can use the commands in the Print Titles area to select the rows or columns to repeat. To choose rows to repeat at the top of the page, click the Collapse Dialog button next to the Rows To Repeat At Top box, select the rows, and then click the Expand Dialog button. The rows you selected appear in the Rows To Repeat At Top box.

Similarly, to have a set of columns appear at the left of every printed page, click the Collapse Dialog button next to the Columns To Repeat At Left box, select the columns, and then click the Expand Dialog button. When you're done, click OK to accept the settings.

In this exercise, you'll select certain pages of a worksheet to print, have Excel fit your printed worksheet on a set number of pages, define a multi-region print area, center the printed material on the page, and repeat columns at the left edge of each printed page.

SET UP You need the HourlyPickups workbook located in the Chapter11 practice file folder to complete this exercise. Open the workbook, and then follow the steps.

1   On the **Page Layout** tab, in the **Page Setup** group, click **Print Titles** to open the **Page Setup** dialog box with the **Sheet** page displayed.

2   At the right edge of the **Columns to repeat at left** field, click the **Collapse Dialog** button to collapse the dialog box.

3   Select the column **A** header, and drag to select the column **B** header. The reference **$A:$B** appears in the **Columns To Repeat At Left** field.

4   At the right edge of the **Columns to repeat at left** field, click the **Expand Dialog** button to expand the dialog box.

5   Click **Print Preview** to display your worksheet in the **Backstage** view.

   TIP Even though nothing in the preview indicates that columns A and B will appear on every printed page, scrolling through the preview shows those columns on each page.

January							
Hour							
Day	5:00 AM	6:00 AM	7:00 AM	8:00 AM	9:00 AM	10:00 AM	11:00 AM
1	2117	1989	1544	2408	1921	1505	1687
2	1128	1109	1354	1115	2277	1432	1559
3	1228	1350	1662	1738	1892	1710	1709
4	2295	2496	1964	1793	1138	1592	1811
5	1866	1631	1631	1136	1959	2275	2348
6	1234	1536	2348	1208	2109	2382	2487
7	1608	1875	1851	1037	2259	2091	2211
8	1903	2014	1451	1283	2243	1266	1746
9	2275	2360	1392	1511	1942	1639	2018
10	1039	2191	1729	1028	2278	1044	1936
11	1369	1069	1487	1155	2434	2181	1721
12	1773	1782	1224	2401	2426	1514	1528
13	2108	1511	1916	2488	1459	1703	1706
14	1512	2319	2239	1063	1164	2115	1469
15	1003	1283	1874	1512	1238	1993	2390
16	2007	1864	2088	1228	2023	1186	1585
17	1016	2400	1039	1024	1107	2178	1445
18	1794	2291	2166	1966	1650	1899	1931
19	1904	2424	1799	2332	1089	1132	1045
20	2035	2174	1123	2277	1400	2468	1287
21	1288	2321	1171	1884	2292	2437	2465
22	1577	1235	1742	1089	2203	2143	1073
23	1987	1349	2170	1728	2426	1015	1227
24	1868	2459	1380	1390	2270	1336	1886
25	1058	1541	1753	1740	2360	2308	2167
26	2016	2412	1128	1477	1184	2104	1513
27	1640	2180	1904	1048	1531	1541	1838
28	2363	1340	2113	1350	1814	2358	1613
29	2398	1324	1572	2264	1335	2002	1495
30	2225	1178	1633	1148	1640	1872	1581
31	1726	1794	2020	1777	1016	1405	1845

CONSOLIDATED_Messenger_

◄ 1 of 4 ►

6   Below **Pages** in the **Settings** area, in the **From** field, enter **1**; in the **To** field, enter **2**.

7   Click the **Go Back** button at the top of the left pane and then, on the ribbon, click the **Page Layout** tab; in the **Scale to Fit** group, click the **Width** arrow and then, in the list that appears, click **1 page**.

8   Click the **Height** arrow and then, in the list that appears, click **2 pages**. Excel resizes your worksheet so that it will fit on two printed pages. The new scaling and size values appear in the **Scale to Fit** group on the **Page Layout** tab.

9   Select the cell range **A1:E8**, hold down the **Ctrl** key, and then select the cell range **A38:E45**.

10 On the **Page Layout** tab, in the **Page Setup** group, click the **Print Area** button, and then click **Set Print Area**.

11 Click the **Page Setup** dialog box launcher to open the **Page Setup** dialog box.

12 On the **Margins** page of the dialog box, in the **Center on page** area, select the **Horizontally** and **Vertically** check boxes.

13 Click **Print Preview** to display your worksheet in the **Backstage** view.

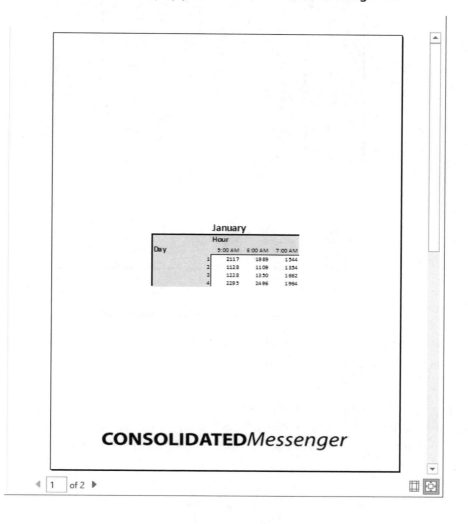

14   Click the **Go Back** button to exit the **Backstage** view and then, on the ribbon, click the **Page Layout** tab to display your worksheet in **Normal** view.

15   In the **Page Setup** group, click **Print Area**, and then click **Clear Print Area** to remove the print areas defined for the **JanFeb** worksheet.

✖ CLEAN UP Close the HourlyPickups workbook, saving your changes if you want to.

Printing charts

With charts, which are graphic representations of your Excel data, you can communicate lots of information by using a single picture. Depending on your data and the type of chart you make, you can show trends across time, indicate the revenue share for various departments in a company for a month, or project future sales by using trendline analysis. After you create a chart, you can print it to include in a report or use in a presentation.

If you embed a chart in a worksheet, however, the chart might obscure some of your data unless you move the chart elsewhere on the worksheet. That's one way to handle printing a chart or the underlying worksheet, but there are other ways that don't involve changing the layout of your worksheets.

To print a chart without printing any other part of the underlying worksheet, click the chart, display the Backstage view, and then click Print. In the Settings area of the Print page, Print Selected Chart will be the only option available. If you click anywhere on the worksheet outside the chart, the Print What area opens with Print Active Sheets selected, meaning that the chart and underlying worksheet are printed as they appear on the screen. When you're ready to print the chart, click the Print button.

TIP Even if the selected chart is smaller than the worksheet on which it resides, it will be scaled to print at the full size of the printer's page.

11

In this exercise, you'll print a chart.

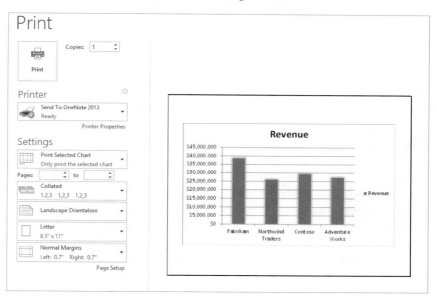

SET UP You need the CorporateRevenue workbook located in the Chapter11 practice file folder to complete this exercise. Open the workbook, and then follow the steps.

1   Select the chart.

2   Click the **File** tab to display the **Backstage** view, and then click **Print**.

3   Verify that **Print Selected Chart** is selected, and then click **Print** (or click the **Go Back** button to exit the **Backstage** view if you don't want to print the chart).

CLEAN UP Close the CorporateRevenue workbook.

Key points

- In the Backstage view, you have complete control over how your worksheets appear on the printed page. Don't be afraid to experiment until you find a look you like.

- When you display a worksheet in the Backstage view, you can preview what your worksheet will look like on paper before you print.

- You can preview where the page breaks will fall when you print a worksheet, and you can change them if you want.

- Don't forget that you can have Excel avoid printing error codes!

- You can repeat rows or columns in a printed worksheet.

- If you want to print a chart without printing the rest of the accompanying worksheet, be sure to select the chart before you start the printing procedure.

11

Chapter at a glance

Modify

Create and modify macros,
page 369

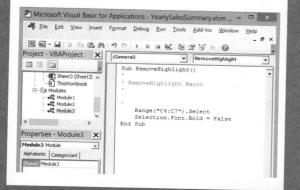

On-click

Run macros when a button is clicked,
page 372

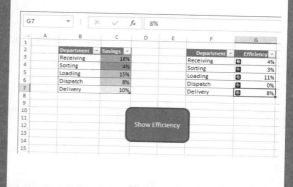

On-open

Run macros when a workbook is opened,
page 376

	A	B	C	D
1				
2		Center	Volume	
3		Northeast	1,450,392	
4		Atlantic	998,751	
5		Southeast	1,000,089	
6		North Central	843,552	
7		Midwest	795,022	
8		Southwest	810,123	
9		Mountain West	602,398	
10		Northwest	890,544	
11		Central	745,631	
12				

Controls

Insert form controls and set form properties,
page 379

UserForm1

Pounds   Ounces

Ground
3Day
2Day

○ Signature Required

○ Signature Waived

Working with macros and forms

12

IN THIS CHAPTER, YOU WILL LEARN HOW TO

- Enable and examine macros.

- Create and modify macros.

- Run macros when a button is clicked.

- Run macros when a workbook is opened.

- Insert form controls and set form properties.

Many tasks you perform in Microsoft Excel 2013 are done once (for example, entering sales data for a particular day or adding formulas to a worksheet) or can be repeated quickly by using tools in Excel (for example, changing the format of a cell range). However, you probably have one or two tasks you perform frequently that require a lot of steps to accomplish. For example, you might have several cells in a worksheet that contain important data you use quite often in presentations to your colleagues. Instead of going through a lengthy series of steps to highlight the cells that have the important information, you can create a macro, which is a recorded series of actions, to perform the steps for you. After you have created a macro, you can run, edit, or delete it as needed.

In Excel, you run and edit macros by using the items available in the Macros group on the View tab. You can make your macros easier to access by creating new buttons on the Quick Access Toolbar, to which you can assign your macros. If you run a macro to highlight specific cells in a worksheet every time you show that worksheet to a colleague, you can save time by adding a Quick Access Toolbar button that runs the macro to highlight the cells for you.

Another handy feature of Excel macros is that you can create macros that run when a workbook is opened. For example, you might want to ensure that no cells in a worksheet are highlighted when the worksheet opens. You can create a macro that removes any special formatting from your worksheet cells when its workbook opens, which enables you to emphasize the data you want as you present the information to your colleagues.

You can also use form controls and macros to create custom solutions for your business. By adding controls such as text boxes, spin controls, and list boxes, you can design a user-friendly interface for you and your colleagues to enter data quickly while minimizing errors.

In this chapter, you'll open, run, create, and modify macros; create Quick Access Toolbar buttons and shapes that you can use to run macros with a single mouse click; run a macro when a workbook is opened; and add controls and set form properties for a UserForm.

PRACTICE FILES To complete the exercises in this chapter, you need the practice files contained in the Chapter12 practice file folder. For more information, see "Download the practice files" in this book's Introduction.

Enabling and examining macros

It's possible for unscrupulous programmers to write viruses and other harmful programs by using the Microsoft Visual Basic for Applications (VBA) programming language, so you need to be sure that you don't run macros from unknown sources. In addition to running protective software such as Windows Defender, you can also change your Excel macro security settings to control when macros can be run. After you're sure a macro is safe, you can open it in the Visual Basic Editor to examine its code.

Changing macro security settings

In versions of Excel prior to Excel 2007, you could define macro security levels to determine which macros, if any, your workbooks would be allowed to run, but there was no workbook type in which all macros were disallowed. Excel 2013 has several file types that you can use to control whether a workbook will allow macros to be run. The following table summarizes the macro-related file types.

Extension	Description
.xlsx	Regular Excel workbook; macros are *disabled*
.xlsm	Regular Excel workbook; macros are *enabled*
.xltx	Excel template workbook; macros are *disabled*
.xltm	Excel template workbook; macros are *enabled*

When you open a macro-enabled workbook, the Excel program-level security settings might prevent the workbook from running the macro code. When that happens, Excel displays a security warning on the Message Bar.

To allow a workbook's macros to run, click the Enable Content button on the Message Bar. Always take the time to verify the workbook's source and consider whether you expected the workbook to contain macros before you enable the content. If you decide not to enable the macros in a workbook, click the Close button at the right edge of the Message Bar.

You can change your program-level security settings to make them more or less restrictive; to do so, click the File tab to display the Backstage view, click Options in the left pane, and then, in the Excel Options dialog box that opens, click the Trust Center category. On the page that appears, click the Trust Center Settings button to display the Trust Center dialog box.

12

The Excel default macro security level is Disable All Macros With Notification, which means that Excel displays a warning on the Message Bar but allows you to enable the macros manually. Selecting the Disable All Macros Without Notification option does exactly what the label says. If Consolidated Messenger's company policy is to disallow all macros in all Excel workbooks, its employees would select the Disable All Macros Without Notification option.

> **IMPORTANT** Because it is possible to write macros that act as viruses, potentially causing harm to your computer and spreading copies of themselves to other computers, you should never choose the Enable All Macros security setting, even if you have virus-checking software installed on your computer.

Examining macros

The best way to get an idea of how macros work is to examine an existing macro. To do that, display the View tab. In the Macros group, click the Macros button, and then click View Macros.

TIP In the Macro dialog box, you can display the macros available in other workbooks by clicking the Macros In box and selecting a workbook by name or selecting All Open Workbooks to display every macro in any open workbook. If you select either of those choices, the macro names that are displayed include the name of the workbook in which the macro is stored. Clicking This Workbook displays the macros in the active workbook.

The Macro dialog box displays a list of macros in your workbook. To view the code behind a macro, you click the macro's name and then click Edit to open the Visual Basic Editor.

```
Sub HighlightSouthern()
'
' HighlightSouthern Macro
'

'
    Range("B4:C4").Select
    With Selection.Font
        .Color = -16776961
        .TintAndShade = 0
    End With
    Range("B5:C5").Select
    With Selection.Font
        .Color = -16776961
        .TintAndShade = 0
    End With
    Range("B8:C8").Select
    With Selection.Font
        .Color = -16776961
        .TintAndShade = 0
    End With
End Sub
```

KEYBOARD SHORTCUT Press Alt+F11 to open and close the Visual Basic Editor. For a complete list of keyboard shortcuts, see "Keyboard shortcuts" at the end of this book.

Excel macros are recorded by using VBA. Consider, for example, the code for a macro that selects the cell range B4:C4 and changes the cells' formatting to bold. The first line of the macro identifies the cell range to be selected (in this case, cells C4:C9). After the macro selects the cells, the next line of the macro changes the formatting of the selected cells to bold, which has the same result as when you click a cell and then click the Bold button in the Font group on the Home tab.

To test how the macro works, you can open the Macro dialog box, click the name of the macro you want to examine, and then click Step Into. The Visual Basic Editor opens, with a highlight around the instruction that will be executed next.

To execute an instruction, press F8. The highlight moves to the next instruction, and your worksheet then changes to reflect the action that resulted from the execution of the preceding instruction.

You can run a macro without stopping after each instruction by opening the Macro dialog box, clicking the macro to run, and then clicking Run. You'll usually run the macro this way; after all, the point of using macros is to save time.

In this exercise, you'll examine a macro in the Visual Basic Editor, move through the first part of the macro one step at a time, and then run the entire macro without stopping.

→ SET UP You need the VolumeHighlights workbook located in the Chapter12 practice file folder to complete this exercise. Open the workbook, click the Enable Content button on the Message Bar (if necessary), and then follow the steps.

1　On the **View** tab, in the **Macros** group, click the **Macros** arrow and then, in the list that appears, click **View Macros** to open the **Macro** dialog box.

2　If necessary, click the **HighlightSouthern** macro, and then, to display the macro code, click **Edit**. The Visual Basic Editor opens, with the code for the **HighlightSouthern** macro displayed in the **Module1 (Code)** window.

3　In the Visual Basic Editor window, click the **Close** button to close the window and redisplay the workbook.

4　In the **Macros** list, click **View Macros** to open the **Macro** dialog box.

5　Click the **HighlightSouthern** macro, and then click **Step Into**. The macro appears in the Visual Basic Editor, with the first macro instruction highlighted.

6　Press the **F8** key to highlight the next instruction.

7　Press **F8** again to execute the step that selects the **Atlantic** row in the table.

8　Press **F8** twice to execute the steps that change the **Atlantic** row's text color to red.

9　Click the **Close** button in the Visual Basic Editor.

10　When a warning dialog box opens, indicating that closing the Visual Basic Editor will stop the debugger, click **OK**.

11　In the **Macros** list, click **View Macros** to open the **Macro** dialog box.

12　Click the **HighlightSouthern** macro.

13　Click **Run** to close the **Macro** dialog box and run the entire macro.

	A	B	C	D
1				
2		Center	Volume	
3		Northeast	1,450,392	
4		Atlantic	998,751	
5		Southeast	1,000,089	
6		North Central	843,552	
7		Midwest	795,022	
8		Southwest	810,123	
9		Mountain West	602,398	
10		Northwest	890,544	
11		Central	745,631	
12				

✖ CLEAN UP Close the VolumeHighlights workbook, saving your changes if you want to.

Creating and modifying macros

The first step of creating a macro is to plan the process you want to automate. Computers today are quite fast, so adding an extra step that doesn't affect the outcome of a process doesn't slow you down noticeably, but leaving out a step means you will need to re-record your macro. After you plan your process, you can create a macro by clicking the View tab and then, in the Macros group, clicking the Macros arrow. In the list that appears, click Record Macro. When you do, the Record Macro dialog box opens.

Record Macro ? ✕

Macro name:

Macro1

Shortcut key:

Ctrl+

Store macro in:

This Workbook

Description:

OK   Cancel

12

After you enter the name of your macro in the Macro Name box, click OK. You can now perform the actions that you want Excel to repeat later; when you're done recording your macro, in the Macros list, click Stop Recording to add your macro to the list of macros available in your workbook.

TIP The Record and Stop Recording icons also appear on the status bar.

To modify an existing macro, you can simply delete the macro and re-record it. Or if you just need to make a quick change, you can open it in the Visual Basic Editor and add to or change the macro's instructions. To delete a macro, open the Macro dialog box, click the macro you want to delete, and then click Delete.

SEE ALSO For more information about using the Visual Basic Editor, press Alt+F11 to display the Visual Basic Editor, and then press F1 to display the Visual Basic Help dialog box.

In this exercise, you'll record, edit, save, and run a macro that removes the bold formatting from selected cells.

 SET UP You need the YearlySalesSummary workbook located in the Chapter12 practice file folder to complete this exercise. Open the workbook, click the Enable Content button on the Message Bar (if necessary), and then follow the steps.

1 On the **View** tab, in the **Macros** group, click the **Macros** arrow and then, in the list that appears, click **Record Macro** to open the **Record Macro** dialog box.

2 In the **Macro name** box, replace the existing name with RemoveHighlight.

3 Click **OK** to close the **Record Macro** dialog box.

4 Select the cell range **C4:C7**. (The text in these cells is currently bold.)

5 On the **Home** tab, in the **Font** group, click the **Bold** button to remove the bold formatting.

6 On the **View** tab, in the **Macros** list, click **Stop Recording** to stop recording the macro.

7 In the **Macros** list, click **View Macros** to open the **Macro** dialog box.

8 In the **Macro name** area, click **RemoveHighlight**, and then click **Edit** to display the macro in the Visual Basic Editor.

9   Edit the line of code that currently reads **Range("C4:C7").Select** so that it reads **Range("C3:C9").Select**. This macro statement selects the cell range **C3:C9**, not the incorrect range **C4:C7**.

10 On the **Standard** toolbar of the Visual Basic Editor, click the **Save** button to save your change.

11 On the title bar of the Visual Basic Editor window, click the **Close** button.

12 Select cells **C3:C9** and format them as bold.

13 In the **Macros** list, click **View Macros** to open the **Macro** dialog box.

14 Click **RemoveHighlight**, and then click **Run**. The macro removes the bold formatting from cells **C3:C9**.

✖ CLEAN UP Close the YearlySalesSummary workbook, saving your changes if you want to.

Running macros when a button is clicked

You can quickly discover the commands built into Excel by looking though the commands on the ribbon. However, it can take a few seconds to display the View tab, open the Macro dialog box, select the macro you want to run, and click the Run button. When you're in the middle of a presentation, taking even those few seconds can reduce your momentum and force you to regain your audience's attention. Excel offers several ways for you to make your macros more accessible.

If you want to display the Macro dialog box quickly, you can add the View Macros button to the Quick Access Toolbar. To do so, click the Customize Quick Access Toolbar button at the right edge of the Quick Access Toolbar, and then click More Commands to display the Quick Access Toolbar page of the Excel Options dialog box.

SEE ALSO For more information about customizing the Quick Access Toolbar, see "Customizing the Excel 2013 program window" in Chapter 1, "Setting up a workbook."

In the Popular Commands command group, the last item in the command pane is View Macros. When you click the View Macros command, click the Add button, and then click OK, Excel adds the command to the Quick Access Toolbar and closes the Excel Options dialog box. Clicking the View Macros button on the Quick Access Toolbar opens the Macro

dialog box, which saves a significant amount of time compared to when you display the View tab and move the pointer to the far right edge of the ribbon.

If you prefer to run a macro without having to display the Macro dialog box, you can do so by adding a button representing the macro to the Quick Access Toolbar. Clicking that button runs the macro immediately, which is very handy when you create a macro for a task you perform frequently. To add a button that represents a macro to the Quick Access Toolbar, click the Customize Quick Access Toolbar button at the right edge of the Quick Access Toolbar, and then click More Commands to display the Quick Access Toolbar page of the Excel Options dialog box. From there, in the Choose Commands From list, click Macros. Click the macro that you want represented on the Quick Access Toolbar, click Add, and then click OK.

If you add more than one macro button to the Quick Access Toolbar or if you want to change the button that represents your macro on the Quick Access Toolbar, you can select a new button from more than 160 options. To assign a new button to your macro, click the macro command in the Customize Quick Access Toolbar pane and click the Modify button to display your choices. Click the symbol you want, enter a new text value to appear when a user points to the button, and then click OK twice (the first time to close the Modify Button dialog box and the second to close the Excel Options dialog box).

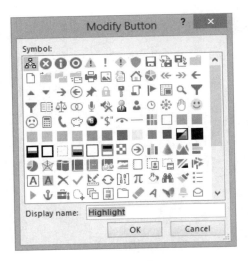

Finally, you can have Excel run a macro when you click a shape in your workbook. By assigning macros to shapes, you can create "buttons" that are graphically richer than those available on the Quick Access Toolbar. If you're so inclined, you can even create custom button layouts that represent other objects, such as a remote control. To run a macro when you

12

click a shape, right-click the shape, and then click Assign Macro on the shortcut menu that opens. In the Assign Macro dialog box, click the macro that you want to run when you click the shape, and then click OK.

> **IMPORTANT** When you assign a macro to run when you click a shape, don't change the name of the macro that appears in the Assign Macro dialog box. The name that appears refers to the object and what the object should do when it is clicked; changing the macro name breaks that connection and prevents Excel from running the macro.

In this exercise, you'll add the View Macros button to the Quick Access Toolbar, add a macro button to the Quick Access Toolbar, assign a macro to a workbook shape, and then run the macros.

➜ SET UP You need the PerformanceDashboard workbook located in the Chapter12 practice file folder to complete this exercise. Open the workbook, click the Enable Content button on the Message Bar (if necessary), and then follow the steps.

1   On the **Quick Access Toolbar**, click the **Customize Quick Access Toolbar** button, and then click **More Commands**. The **Quick Access Toolbar** page of the **Excel Options** dialog box opens, displaying the **Popular Commands** category in the **Choose Commands From** pane.

2   In the list of available commands, click **View Macros**.

3   Click **Add** to add the **View Macros** command to the **Customize Quick Access Toolbar** pane.

4   In the **Choose commands from** list, click **Macros** to display the available macros in the pane below the list.

5   In the **Choose commands from** pane, click **SavingsHighlight**.

TROUBLESHOOTING If macros in the workbook are not enabled, the SavingsHighlight macro will not appear in the list.

6   Click **Add** to add the **SavingsHighlight** macro to the **Customize Quick Access Toolbar** pane.

7   In the **Customize Quick Access Toolbar** pane, click the **SavingsHighlight** command.

8   Click **Modify** to open the **Modify Button** dialog box.

9   Click the gray button with the white circle inside it (the fourth button from the left on the top row).

10 Click **OK** twice to close the **Modify Button** dialog box and the **Excel Options** dialog box. The **View Macros** and **SavingsHighlight** buttons appear on the **Quick Access Toolbar**.

11 On the worksheet, right-click the **Show Efficiency** shape, and then click **Assign Macro** to open the **Assign Macro** dialog box.

12 Click **EfficiencyHighlight**, and then click **OK** to assign the macro to the button and close the **Assign Macro** dialog box.

13 On the **Quick Access Toolbar**, click the **SavingsHighlight** button. Excel runs the macro, which applies a conditional format to the values in the **Savings** column of the table on the left.

14   Click the **Show Efficiency** shape. Excel runs the macro, which applies a conditional format to the values in the **Efficiency** column of the table on the right.

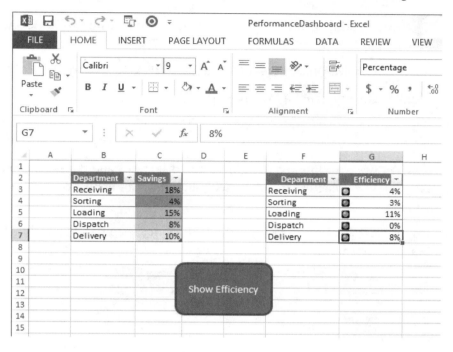

❌ CLEAN UP Close the PerformanceDashboard workbook, saving your changes if you want to.

Running macros when a workbook is opened

One advantage of writing Excel macros in VBA is that you can have Excel run a macro whenever a workbook is opened. For example, if you use a worksheet for presentations, you can create macros that render the contents of selected cells in bold type, italic, or different typefaces to set the data apart from data in neighboring cells. If you close a workbook without removing that formatting, however, the contents of your workbook will still have that formatting applied when you open it. Although this is not a catastrophe, returning the workbook to its original formatting might take a few seconds to accomplish.

Instead of running a macro manually, or even from a toolbar button or a menu, you can have Excel run a macro whenever a workbook is opened. The trick of making that happen is in the name you give the macro. Whenever Excel finds a macro with the name Auto_Open, it runs the macro when the workbook to which it is attached is opened.

TIP If you have your macro security set to the Disable With Notification level, clicking the Options button that appears on the Message Bar, selecting the Enable This Content option, and then clicking OK allows the Auto_Open macro to run.

In this exercise, you'll create and test a macro that runs whenever someone opens the workbook to which it is attached.

➔ SET UP You need the RunOnOpen workbook located in the Chapter12 practice file folder to complete this exercise. Open the workbook, click the Enable Content button on the Message Bar (if necessary), and then follow the steps.

1 On the **View** tab, in the **Macros** group, click the **Macros** arrow and then, in the list that appears, click **Record Macro** to open the **Record Macro** dialog box.

2 In the **Macro name** box, delete the existing name, and then enter Auto_Open.

3 Click **OK** to close the **Record Macro** dialog box.

4 Select the cell range **B3:C11**.

5 On the **Home** tab, in the **Font** group, click the **Bold** button twice. The first click of the **Bold** button formats all the selected cells in bold; the second click removes the bold formatting from all the selected cells.

12

6 Click cell **C11** and then, in the **Macros** list, click **Stop Recording** to stop recording your macro.

7 In the **Macros** list, click **View Macros** to open the **Macro** dialog box.

8 Click **Highlight**, and then click **Run**. The macro formats the contents of cells **C4**, **C6**, and **C10** in bold type.

	A	B	C	D
1				
2		Center	Volume	
3		Northeast	1,450,392	
4		Atlantic	998,751	
5		Southeast	1,000,089	
6		North Central	843,552	
7		Midwest	795,022	
8		Southwest	810,123	
9		Mountain West	602,398	
10		Northwest	890,544	
11		Central	745,631	
12				

9 On the **Quick Access Toolbar**, click the **Save** button.

10 Click the **Close** button to close the **RunOnOpen** workbook.

11 Display the **Backstage** view, click **Recent Workbooks**, and then click **RunOnOpen. xlsm**. If a warning appears, click **Enable Content**, and then click **OK** to enable macros. **RunOnOpen** opens, and the contents of cells **C4**, **C6**, and **C10** change immediately to regular type.

	A	B	C	D
1				
2		Center	Volume	
3		Northeast	1,450,392	
4		Atlantic	998,751	
5		Southeast	1,000,089	
6		North Central	843,552	
7		Midwest	795,022	
8		Southwest	810,123	
9		Mountain West	602,398	
10		Northwest	890,544	
11		Central	745,631	
12				

 CLEAN UP Close the RunOnOpen workbook, saving your changes if you want to.

Inserting form controls and setting form properties

UserForms are Excel objects that you create to provide a user-friendly interface for data entry. You can allow open-ended text entry by adding a text box, define specific items in a list box, or combine the two approaches in a combo box.

To create a UserForm, press Alt+F11 to open the Visual Basic Editor, and then on the Insert menu, click UserForm. You can then change the form's name by clicking in the Properties pane and entering a new value in the Name field.

You can change the size of a UserForm by dragging any of the handles on its sides or corners. By dragging a handle in the middle of a side, you can change the UserForm's height or width; dragging a handle at a UserForm's corner changes both height and width.

TIP The Name property is the internal representation of the UserForm (that is, how you will refer to it in your code), so you should consider putting the letters *frm* at the start of the name to indicate that it represents a form.

The Caption property contains the word or words that appear on a UserForm's title bar. To change the UserForm's caption, click the UserForm and then, in the Properties panel, click the box next to the Caption property and edit its value.

Adding text boxes to UserForms

You can create a text box in a UserForm so that users can enter textual information. If the Toolbox isn't displayed in the Visual Basic Editor, on the Insert menu, click Toolbox. Then click the TextBox button in the Toolbox and drag in the body of the UserForm to define the text box. When you do, the text box's properties appear in the Properties panel.

As with the UserForm object, you can change the name of a text box. To do that, click the text box control and then, in the Properties pane, enter a new value in the *Name* property's box.

12

You can also add a label to identify the control and indicate the data to be entered. To add a label, display the Toolbox, click the Label button, and drag to define the label in the body of the form. Position the label so that it's in line with the text box and then change the label's *Caption* property so that it contains the text required to identify its related control.

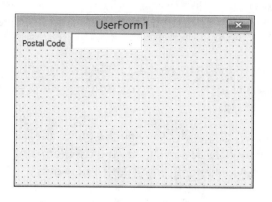

TROUBLESHOOTING A control's name may not be a reserved word, such as *Number* or *Date*.

Adding list boxes to UserForms

In a text box, users can enter any text they want into the control. If you prefer to have users select from a list of values, you can create a list box. List boxes increase data entry accuracy at the expense of user flexibility.

To create a list box, display a UserForm in the Visual Basic Editor and then, in the Toolbox, click the ListBox button, and drag on the UserForm to create the list box. When you do, the list box appears on the UserForm and its properties appear in the Properties panel on the left side of the Visual Basic Editor window.

A list box control draws its values from a range of worksheet cells. To assign a cell range to a list box, you enter the range's definition into the list box's *RowSource* property. In Excel 2013, the easiest way to define the row source for a list box is to create a one-column Excel table.

SEE ALSO For more information about creating an Excel table, see Chapter 2, "Working with data and Excel tables."

With your data source defined, enter an equal sign (=) followed by the name of the table in the *RowSource* property for your list box. When you run the UserForm, you can use the list

box's arrows to scroll through the list of available values. When you find the value you want, click it to highlight it.

> **IMPORTANT** When you enter data in a UserForm's list box, you must click the item in the list box so that it is highlighted. The item displayed isn't necessarily the selected item.

Adding combo boxes to UserForms

In a list box, users can select a value from a predetermined list of values; in a text box, they can enter any text value they want. A combo box provides either mode of entry, which is more flexible than a list box but introduces the possibility that misspellings might lead to inconsistent data entry.

To add a combo box to a UserForm, display the UserForm in the Visual Basic Editor and then, in the Toolbox, click the Combobox button. Draw the outline of the combo box on the body of the UserForm to create it.

As with the list box, you can provide its values by assigning an Excel table to the *RowSource* property, using a statement such as *=ServiceLevels*.

Adding option buttons to UserForms

With option buttons, users can indicate whether an option, such as whether a delivery requires signature confirmation, is turned on or turned off. You can also create groups of option buttons that lets users select at most one option from the group at a time.

12

To add an option button to a UserForm, display the UserForm and then, in the Toolbox, click the Option Button control. Draw the option button on the UserForm. Its properties will be displayed in the Properties panel. The most common properties you'll change are the button's *Name* and *Caption* properties.

The *Name* property controls how you refer to the option button in your VBA code. To change the control's label text, you need to change the value of the *Caption* property. For example, you could change the caption property to read *Signature*.

TIP If you want an option button to be selected by default, change its Value property from False to True.

You can also create groups of option buttons where only one of the buttons can be selected at a time. For example, you might want a user to select a shipping method from among the options of ground, two day, three day, overnight, and priority overnight. To allow only one option button of those five to be selected at a time, you assign the same *GroupName* property value to each button. You could create the Methods group to allow one selection from the alternatives.

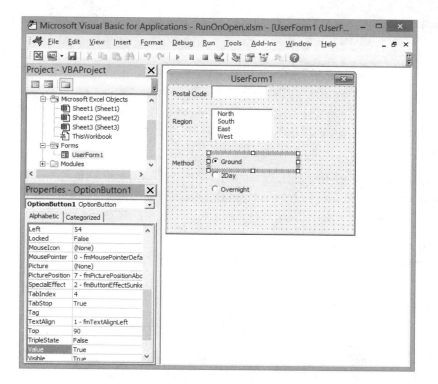

Adding graphics to UserForms

One way to add some visual interest or useful information to a VBA UserForm is by adding graphics. To add an image to a UserForm, display the UserForm in the Visual Basic Editor and then, in the Toolbox, click the Image button. Drag on the UserForm to define the frame within which the image should appear.

To select the graphic you want to display on the UserForm, click the image control on the UserForm and then, in the Properties panel, click in the box next to the Picture property name. Click the Browse button that appears, navigate to the folder that contains the image you want to add to the UserForm, click the image, and then click Open to display it.

Unless the image you selected fits exactly in the frame, just a portion of it is displayed on the UserForm. You can control the way the image fits within the frame by assigning the value you want to the *PictureSizeMode* property. That property has three possible values:

- **0 – fmPictureSizeModeClip** Displays as much of the image as possible within the frame

- **1 – fmPictureSizeModeStretch** Displays the entire image within the frame but stretches the image so that it fills the entire frame

- **3 – fmPictureSizeModeZoom** Displays the entire image within the frame but keeps the vertical and horizontal dimensions in their original ratio

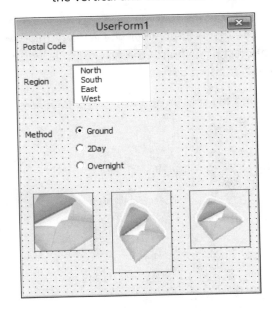

12

Adding spin buttons to UserForms

With Excel VBA UserForms, you and your colleagues can enter data quickly. Text boxes are flexible, but you can take more control over the numbers a user enters by linking a spin button to a text box. Clicking the spin button's up or down arrow changes the value in the attached control by an amount that you define.

To create a spin button, click the UserForm and then, in the Toolbox, click the SpinButton control and draw the spin button on the UserForm. Next, click the spin button and then, in the Properties panel, change the values of these properties:

- **Max** The largest value allowed in the spin button

- **Min** The smallest value allowed in the spin button

- **SmallChange** The amount that each click changes the spin button's value

Suppose you create a spin button with a *Min* value of *1*, *Max* value of *10*, and *SmallChange* value of *1*. Each click of the up button would increase the value by 1 (to a maximum of 10) and each click of the down button would decrease the value by 1 (to a minimum of 1).

After you create the spin button, create a text box to display the value assigned to the spin control. Write down the name of the text box, which you can discover by clicking the text box and observing the value of the *Name* property in the Properties panel.

Right-click the spin button and, from the shortcut menu that appears, click View Code. Doing so displays the outline of the event code that will run when the value of the spin button changes. To link the spin button with the text box, you set the text control's *Value* property so that it is equal to the same property of the spin button.

If the text box were named *PackageOunces* and the spin button were named *OuncesSpin*, your code would look like the following example.

```
Private Sub OuncesSpin_Change()
PackageOunces.Value = OuncesSpin.Value
End Sub
```

Writing UserForm data to a worksheet

After you've created your UserForm, you need to write VBA code to record the controls' values to a worksheet. You do that by adding a command button to your form and assigning code to the button's *On_Click* event that reads the controls' values and writes them to a worksheet.

The process to read and write these values identifies the first empty row in the target worksheet and then uses the *Value* property of the *Cells* object to write the data into the target cells. As an example, suppose you have a UserForm that collects four pieces of data for a shipment: the customer's name, origination postal code, destination postal code, and shipping method.

Next, create a command button to which you can attach code that writes the values to the worksheet. To create the command button, display a UserForm and then, in the Toolbox, click the CommandButton button. Draw the button on the UserForm and, if you want, change the button's Caption property so that the button's text describes its function.

Right-click the button and, from the shortcut menu that appears, click View Code to display the button's *On_Click* event handling code. You could use the following routine to find the first empty cell in column A of your worksheet, read the values in the four controls, and write values into the worksheet.

```
Private Sub CommandButton1_Click()
Dim lngFirstRow As Long

Worksheets("Sheet1").Activate
lngFirstRow = Worksheets("Sheet1").Range("A1048576").End(xlUp).Row + 1

Cells(lngFirstRow, 1) = txtCompName.Value
Cells(lngFirstRow, 2) = txtOrigPostCode.Value
Cells(lngFirstRow, 3) = txtDestPostCode.Value
Cells(lngFirstRow, 4) = lstMethod.Value
Cells(lngFirstRow, 4).Activate
End Sub
```

12

If two records were already in the target worksheet and you entered data from the UserForm, the result would be the following list.

	A	B	C	D
1	Company	Originating Postal Code	Destination Postal Code	Method
2	Contoso	22841	97220	Ground
3	Tailspin Toys	11210	54382	3Day
4	Northwind Traders	98013	33010	Overnight
5				

TIP On the Developer tab of the ribbon, you will also find buttons that you can use to add worksheet Form controls and ActiveX controls. You can use the skills learned in this section to create those controls and assign VBA code to them.

Displaying, loading, and hiding UserForms

After you create a UserForm, you must display it so that the user can interact with it. As an example, suppose you have a form named *frmShipmentEntry*. All you need to do to display the form is enter the name of the form followed by a period and the Show method. For example, the code to display *frmShipmentEntry* would be as follows.

```
frmShipmentEntry.Show
```

You can test a UserForm from within the Visual Basic Editor by displaying the UserForm and pressing the F5 key. You can also enter a UserForm into Excel's memory without displaying it by using the *Load* method. The command to load the same form into the Excel program's memory is as follows.

```
frmCustomerEntry.Load
```

When you want to display the UserForm in Excel, you can call the *Show* method as noted earlier.

Hiding a UserForm relies on the *Hide* method. The syntax follows the pattern used for the *Show* and *Load* methods.

```
frmCustomerEntry.Hide
```

The most common way to invoke the *Hide* method is to create a command button with the label Cancel and add the code including the *Hide* method in the command button's *On_Click* event handler. You can also hide a UserForm by clicking the Close box in the upper-right corner of the UserForm.

In this exercise, you'll create a UserForm, add a text box, add a list box, and then add a series of option buttons within a single group. You'll also add spin button controls to two text boxes, and use existing code to display the form and write its data to a worksheet.

→ SET UP You need the PackageWeight workbook located in the Chapter12 practice file folder to complete this exercise. Open the workbook, click the Enable Content button on the Message Bar (if necessary), and then follow the steps.

1 Press **Alt+F11** to open the Visual Basic Editor.

2 On the menu bar, click **Insert**, and then click **UserForm** to create a blank UserForm.

3 In the **Toolbox**, click the **Label** button and draw a label in the upper-left corner of the UserForm. Then, with the label still selected, in the **Caption** property box of the **Properties** panel, enter Pounds.

4 Click on the body of the UserForm and then, in the **Toolbox**, click the **Label** button and draw a label to the right of the **Pounds** label. Then, with the label still selected, in the **Caption** property box of the **Properties** panel, enter Ounces. Resize the label control so that the **Ounces** text fits within it.

5 Click on the body of the UserForm and then, in the **Toolbox**, click the **TextBox** button. Draw a text box below the **Pounds** label on the UserForm. Click the **TextBox** button again and, leaving some space for another control, draw a second text box below the **Ounces** label.

6 In the **Toolbox**, click the **SpinButton** button and then draw a spin button to the right of the text box beside the **Pounds** label.

7   With the new spin button still selected, in the **Properties** panel, enter 49 in the **Max** field. The spin button will now accept values from 0 to 49.

8   In the **Toolbox**, click the **SpinButton** button, and then draw a new spin button to the right of the text box beside the **Ounces** label.

9   With the new spin button still selected, in the **Properties** panel, enter 15 in the **Max** field. The spin button will now accept values from 0 to 15.

10   Click the spin button to the right of the text box below the **Pounds** label and make a note of its name (which is probably SpinButton1).

11   Right-click the spin button below the **Pounds** label and then click **View Code**. In the code window that appears, edit the code so it reads as follows.

```
Private Sub SpinButton1_Change()
TextBox1.Value = SpinButton1.Value
End Sub
```

TROUBLESHOOTING   The preceding code assumes the text box is named TextBox1 and the spin button is named SpinButton1. If they aren't, edit the code to reflect the controls' actual names.

12   Right-click the spin button below the **Ounces** label, and then click **View Code**. In the code window that appears, edit the code so it reads as follows.

```
Private Sub SpinButton2_Change()
TextBox2.Value = SpinButton2.Value
End Sub
```

13   In the **Project** window, double-click the **UserForm1** icon to return to the UserForm.

14   Click on the body of the UserForm and then, in the **Toolbox**, click the **ListBox** button. Draw a list box below the text boxes that display the **Pounds** and **Ounces** values. Your list box should be wide enough to display the text string **Priority Overnight**.

15   With the list box still selected, in the **RowSource** property box of the **Properties** panel, enter =ShipMethods and then press **Enter**. The methods appear in the list box.

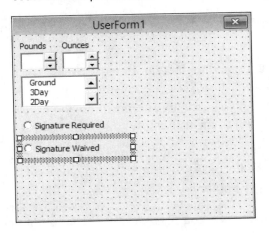

16 Click on the body of the UserForm and then, in the **Toolbox**, click the **OptionButton** button. Click in the body of the UserForm below the list box you just created. When you do, an option button appears.

17 With the option button still selected, in the **Caption** box of the **Properties** panel, enter Signature Required and press **Enter**. Then, in the **GroupName** box, enter Sig and press **Enter**.

18 Repeat step 16 to create an option button below the first option button you created. With the new option button still selected, in the **Caption** box, enter Signature Waived and press **Enter**. Then, in the **GroupName** box, enter Sig and press **Enter**.

19   Click on the body of the UserForm and then, in the **Toolbox**, click the
      CommandButton button. Draw a command button below the **Signature Waived**
      option button and then, with the command button still selected, in the **Caption** box,
      enter Submit and press **Enter**.

20   Right-click the **Submit** command button and click **View Code** to display the button's
      On_Click event handling routine. Edit the **Private Sub CommandButton1_Click()** sub-
      routine so it reads as follows.

```
Private Sub CommandButton1_Click()
Dim lngFirstRow As Long

Worksheets("Records").Activate
lngFirstRow = Worksheets("Records").Range("A1048576").End(xlUp).Row + 1

Cells(lngFirstRow, 1) = TextBox1.Value
Cells(lngFirstRow, 2) = TextBox2.Value
Cells(lngFirstRow, 3) = ListBox1.Value
Cells(lngFirstRow, 4) = OptionButton1.Value
Cells(lngFirstRow, 5) = OptionButton2.Value
Cells(lngFirstRow, 5).Activate

End Sub
```

21   In the **Project** pane, click **UserForm1** to display it and then press **F5** to run the
      UserForm.

22   Use the **Pounds** spin button to enter **4** in the **Pounds** text box; use the **Ounces** spin
      button to enter **8** in the **Ounces** text box; select **3Day** in the list box; and then select
      the **Signature Waived** option button. Click the **Submit** command button. When you
      do, the UserForm writes your data to the first empty row in the **Records** worksheet.

23   Click the UserForm's **Close** button to close it and then press **Alt+F11** to display the
      workbook. If necessary, click the **Records** sheet tab to display the worksheet of the
      same name to view the data you entered.

❌ CLEAN UP Close the PackageWeight workbook, saving your changes if you want to.

Key points

- Macros are handy tools that you can use to perform repetitive tasks quickly, such as inserting blocks of text.

- You don't have to be a programmer to use macros; you can record your actions and have Excel save them as a macro.

- Excel uses macro-enabled workbook types, which have the file extensions .xlsm (a macro-enabled workbook) and .xltm (a macro-enabled template workbook).

- If you're curious about what a macro looks like, you can display it in the Visual Basic Editor. If you know a little VBA, or if you just want to experiment, feel free to modify the macro code to find out what happens.

- You can create Quick Access Toolbar buttons and shapes that, when clicked, run a macro.

- If you want a macro to run whenever you open a workbook, create a macro named Auto_Open.

- UserForms provide a customizable interface for data entry.

12

Chapter at a glance

Link

Link to Office documents from workbooks, page 394

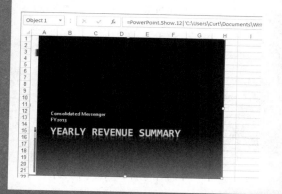

Embed

Embed workbooks into other Office documents, page 398

Create

Create hyperlinks, page 401

Paste

Paste charts into other Office documents, page 407

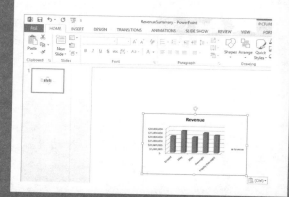

Working with other Office programs

IN THIS CHAPTER, YOU WILL LEARN HOW TO

- Link to Office documents from workbooks.

- Embed workbooks into other Office documents.

- Create hyperlinks.

- Paste charts into other Office documents.

By itself, Microsoft Excel 2013 provides a broad range of tools that you can use to store, present, and summarize your financial data. When you use other Microsoft Office 2013 programs, you can extend your capabilities even further, by creating databases, presentations, written reports, and custom webpages through which you can organize and communicate your data in print and over networks.

All the Office programs interact with each other in many useful ways. For example, you can include a file created with another Office program in an Excel workbook. If you use Microsoft Word 2013 to write a quick note about why a customer's shipping expenditures decreased significantly in January, you can include the report in your workbook. Similarly, you can include your Excel workbooks in documents created with other Office programs. If you want to copy only part of a workbook, such as a chart, into another Office document, you can do that as well.

Excel integrates well with the web. If you know of a web-based resource that would be useful to someone who is viewing a document, you can create a hyperlink to connect from a document to a place in the same file or to another file anywhere on a network or the Internet that the user's computer can reach.

In this chapter, you'll link to an Office document from a worksheet, embed an Excel workbook into another Office document, create hyperlinks, and paste an Excel chart into another document.

Linking to Office documents from workbooks

One benefit of working with Excel 2013 is that, because it is part of Office 2013, it is possible to combine data from Excel and other Office programs to create informative documents and presentations. Just as you can combine data from one Excel workbook into another, you can combine information from another Office document with an Excel workbook, either by pasting the other document into the Excel workbook or by creating a link between the two.

There are two advantages to creating a link between your Excel workbook and the other file. The first benefit is that linking to the other file, as opposed to copying the entire file into your workbook, keeps the file size of your Excel workbook small. If the workbook is copied to another drive or computer, you can maintain the link by copying the linked file along with the Excel workbook or by re-creating the link if the linked file is on the same network as the Excel workbook. The second benefit of linking to another file is that any changes in the file to which you link are reflected in your Excel workbook. If the linked file has been moved or isn't available over a network, then any changes to the linked file won't be reflected in your workbook.

You create a link between an Excel workbook and another Office document by clicking the cell in which you want the document to appear, clicking the Insert tab and then, in the Text group, clicking Object to display the Object dialog box. In the Object dialog box, click the Create From File tab.

When you click the Browse button on the Create From File page, the Browse dialog box opens. In this dialog box, you can browse to the folder that contains the file you want to link to. After you locate the file, double-clicking it closes the Browse dialog box and adds the file's name and path to the File Name box of the Object dialog box. To create a link to the file, select the Link To File check box, and click OK. When you do, a preview of the file appears in your workbook near the active cell.

If you want to link a file to your workbook but don't want the file image to take up much space on the screen, you can also select the Display As Icon check box. After you select the file and click OK, the file will be represented by the same program icon used to represent it in Windows. Double-clicking the icon opens the file.

13

After you have linked a file—for example, a Microsoft PowerPoint 2013 presentation—to your Excel workbook, you can edit the file by right-clicking its image or icon in your workbook and then, on the shortcut menu that appears, clicking the appropriate Object command and clicking Edit. For a PowerPoint file, you click Presentation Object. The file will open in its native program. When you finish editing the file, your changes appear in your workbook.

TIP The specific menu command you click changes to reflect the program used to create the file to which you want to link. For a Word 2013 document, for example, the menu command you click is Document Object.

In this exercise, you'll link a PowerPoint 2013 presentation to an Excel workbook and then edit the presentation after it opens in PowerPoint from within Excel.

IMPORTANT You must have PowerPoint 2013 installed on your computer to complete this exercise.

 SET UP You need the SummaryPresentation workbook and the 2013YearlyRevenue-Summary presentation located in the Chapter13 practice file folder to complete this exercise. Open the workbook, and then follow the steps.

1   In the **SummaryPresentation** workbook, on the **Insert** tab, in the **Text** group, click **Object** to open the **Object** dialog box.

2   Click the **Create from File** tab to display the **Create From File** page.

3   Click **Browse** to open the **Browse** dialog box.

4   Browse to the **2013YearlyRevenueSummary.pptx** presentation, and then click **Insert**. The **Browse** dialog box closes, and the full file path of the **2013YearlyRevenueSummary** presentation appears in the **File name** box.

5   Select the **Link to file** check box, and then click **OK** to create a link from your work-
    book to the presentation.

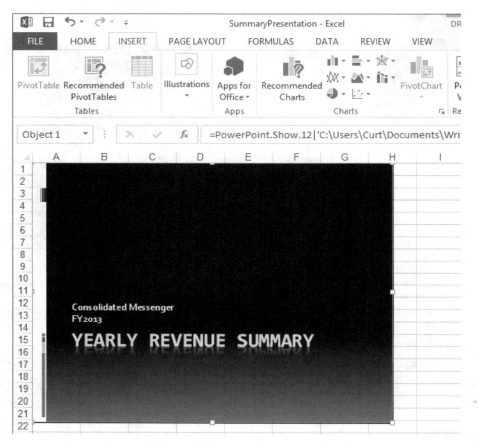

6   Right-click the presentation image in the workbook, click **Presentation Object**, and
    then click **Edit** to open the presentation in a PowerPoint 2013 window.

13

7   Click **Consolidated Messenger FY2013** to activate its text box.

8   Select the **FY2013** text, and then enter Calendar Year 2013.

9   In PowerPoint, on the **Quick Access Toolbar**, click the **Save** button. (You'll use this presentation again in the next exercise.) Because the presentation is linked to the workbook, Excel updates the linked object's appearance to reflect the new text.

❌ CLEAN UP Leave the 2013YearlyRevenueSummary presentation open for the next exercise. Close the SummaryPresentation workbook, saving your changes if you want to.

Embedding workbooks into other Office documents

In the preceding section, you linked to another file from within your Excel workbook. The advantages of linking to a second file are that the file size of your workbook is kept small and any changes in the second document will be reflected in your workbook. The

disadvantage is that the second document must be copied with the workbook—or at least be on a network-accessible computer. If Excel can't find or access the second file where the link says it is located, Excel can't display it. You can still open your workbook, but the linked file's contents won't be displayed.

If file size isn't an issue and you want to ensure that the second document is always available, you can embed the file in your workbook. Embedding another file in an Excel workbook means that the entirety of the other file is saved as part of your workbook. Wherever your workbook goes, the embedded file goes along with it. Of course, the embedded version of the file is no longer connected to the original file, so changes in one aren't reflected in the other.

IMPORTANT To view a linked or embedded file, you must have the program used to create it installed on the computer on which you open the workbook.

You can embed a file in an Excel workbook by following the procedure described in the preceding section but leaving the Link To File check box cleared.

It is also possible to embed your Excel workbooks in other Office documents. In PowerPoint, for example, you can embed an Excel file in a presentation by displaying the Insert tab in PowerPoint and then, in the Text group, clicking Object to display the Insert Object dialog box. Then in the Insert Object dialog box, select Create From File.

13

To identify the file that you want to embed, click the Browse button and then, in the Browse dialog box that opens, navigate to the folder in which the file is stored and double-click the file. The Browse dialog box closes, and the file path appears in the File box. Click OK to embed your workbook in the presentation.

If you want to embed a workbook in a file created with any other Office program but don't want the worksheet to take up much space on the screen, select the Display As Icon check box. After you select the file to embed and click OK, the file is represented by the same icon used to represent it in Windows. Double-clicking the icon opens the embedded document in its original application.

TROUBLESHOOTING If your Excel workbook's cells don't have a background fill color (that is, you have the No Fill option selected), PowerPoint treats the cells' backgrounds as if they were transparent. If you were to place cells with black text and no background fill over a dark background, the text would not be visible. To make your text visible, fill the cells with a very light gray color so that the presentation's background doesn't show through.

To open an embedded Excel workbook for editing, right-click the workbook (or the icon representing it) and then, on the shortcut menu that appears, click Worksheet Object and click Edit. After you finish making your changes, you can click anywhere outside the workbook to return to the presentation.

> **IMPORTANT** You must have PowerPoint 2013 installed on your computer to complete this exercise.

 SET UP You need the 2013YearlyRevenueSummary presentation you created in the previous exercise, and the RevenueByServiceLevel workbook located in the Chapter13 practice file folder to complete this exercise. If you did not complete the previous exercise, you should do so now. Open the workbook and, if necessary, open the presentation. Then follow the steps.

1   In the **Slides** pane of the presentation window, click the second slide to display it.

2   On the **Insert** tab, in the **Text** group, click **Object** to open the **Insert Object** dialog box.

3   Select **Create from file**. The **Insert Object** dialog box changes to allow you to enter a file name.

4   Click **Browse** to open the **Browse** dialog box.

5   Browse to the **RevenueByServiceLevel** workbook and double-click it. The **Browse** dialog box closes, and the file's full path appears in the **File** box of the **Insert Object** dialog box for PowerPoint.

6   Click **OK** to add the workbook to your presentation.

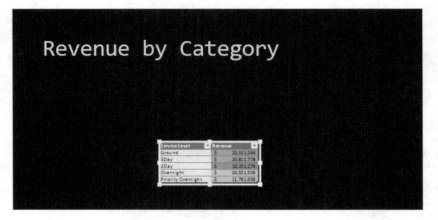

❌ CLEAN UP Close the RevenueByServiceLevel workbook and the 2013YearlyRevenue-Summary presentation, saving your changes if you want to.

Creating hyperlinks

One of the characteristics of the web is that documents published on webpages can have references, or *hyperlinks*, to locations in the same document or to other web documents. A hyperlink functions much like a link between two cells or between two files, but hyperlinks can reach any computer on the web, not just those on a corporate network. Hyperlinks that haven't been clicked usually appear as underlined blue text, and hyperlinks that have been followed appear as underlined purple text, but those settings can be changed.

	A	B	C	D
1				
2		Level	Note	
3		Ground	Revisit price structure at the start of the next quarter.	
4		Priority Overnight	Consider incentives to encourage use.	
5				
6		Consolidated Messenger	http://www.consolidatedmessenger.com	
7				

13

To create a hyperlink, click the cell in which you want to insert the hyperlink and then, on the Insert tab, click Hyperlink. The Insert Hyperlink dialog box opens.

KEYBOARD SHORTCUT Press Ctrl+K to open the Insert Hyperlink dialog box. For a complete list of keyboard shortcuts, see "Keyboard shortcuts" at the end of this book.

You can choose one of four types of targets, or destinations, for your hyperlink: an existing file or webpage, a place in the current document, a new document you create on the spot, or an email address. By default, the Insert Hyperlink dialog box displays the tools to connect to an existing file or webpage.

To create a hyperlink to another file or webpage, you can use the Look In navigation tool to locate the file. If you recently opened the file or webpage to which you want to link, you can click either the Browsed Pages or the Recent Files button to display the webpages or files in your History list.

If you want to create a hyperlink to another place in the current Excel workbook, you can click the Place In This Document button to display a list of available targets in the current workbook.

To select the worksheet to which you want to refer, you click the worksheet name in the Or Select A Place In This Document box. When you do, a reference with the name of the worksheet and cell A1 on that worksheet appears in the Text To Display box.

If you want to refer to a cell other than A1 on the selected worksheet, click the worksheet name in the Or Select A Place In This Document box, and then change the cell reference in the Type The Cell Reference box.

To have explanatory text appear when the user points to a hyperlink, click the ScreenTip button, enter the text you want in the ScreenTip Text box, and then click OK to close the Set Hyperlink ScreenTip dialog box.

You can also create a hyperlink that generates an email message to an address of your choice. To create this type of hyperlink, which is called a *mailto* hyperlink, click the E-mail Address button.

In the dialog box that opens, you can enter the recipient's email address in the E-mail Address box and the subject line for messages sent via this hyperlink in the Subject box.

TIP If you use Windows Mail, Microsoft Outlook, or Microsoft Outlook Express as your email program, a list of recently used addresses will appear in the Recently Used E-mail Addresses box. You can insert any of those addresses in the E-mail Address box by clicking the address.

Clicking a mailto hyperlink causes the user's default email program to open and create a new email message. The email message is addressed to the address you entered in the E-mail Address box, and the subject is set to the text you entered in the Subject box.

Regardless of the type of hyperlink you create, you can specify the text you want to represent the hyperlink in your worksheet. You enter that text in the Text To Display box. When you click OK, the text you enter there appears in your worksheet, formatted as a hyperlink.

TIP If you leave the Text To Display box empty, the actual link will appear in your worksheet.

To edit an existing hyperlink, right-click the cell that contains the hyperlink and then, on the shortcut menu that appears, click Edit Hyperlink. You can also click Open Hyperlink to go

to the target document or create a new email message, or click Remove Hyperlink to delete the hyperlink.

TIP If you delete a hyperlink from a cell, the text from the Text To Display box remains in the cell, but it no longer functions as a hyperlink.

In this exercise, you'll create a hyperlink to another document and then a second hyperlink to a different location in the current workbook.

 SET UP **You need the Hyperlink and LevelDescriptions workbooks located in the Chapter13 practice file folder to complete this exercise. Open the Hyperlink workbook, and then follow the steps.**

1   In the **Hyperlink** workbook, on the **Revenue by Level** worksheet, click cell **B9**.

2   On the **Insert** tab, in the **Links** group, click the **Hyperlink** button to open the **Insert Hyperlink** dialog box.

3   If necessary, click the **Existing File or Web Page** button.

4   If necessary, use the controls to the right of the **Look in** box to navigate to the **Chapter13** practice file folder and display the files in the **Insert Hyperlink** dialog box.

5   In the file list, click the **LevelDescriptions** workbook. The workbook's name appears in the **Text To Display** box and the **Address** box.

6   In the **Text to display** box, edit the value so that it reads **LevelDescriptions**.

Insert Hyperlink		? ×
Link to:	Text to display: LevelDescriptions	ScreenTip...
Existing File or Web Page	Look in: Chapter13	
	Current Folder	2013YearlyRevenueSummary	Bookmark...
		Hyperlink	
		LevelDescriptions	
Place in This Document	Browsed Pages	RevenueChart	
		RevenueSummary	
		SummaryPresentation	
Create New Document	Recent Files		
E-mail Address	Address: LevelDescriptions.xlsx	
		OK Cancel

7   Click **OK**.

8   Click the hyperlink in cell **B9** to open the **LevelDescriptions** workbook.

9   In the **LevelDescriptions** workbook, display the **Backstage** view, and then click **Close** to close the workbook.

10   Right-click cell **B11**, and then click **Hyperlink** to open the **Insert Hyperlink** dialog box.

11   In the **Link to** pane, click **Place in This Document**. The document elements to which you can link appear in the dialog box.

12   In the **Or select a place in this document** pane, click **Notes**.

13   Click **OK** to close the **Insert Hyperlink** dialog box and create a hyperlink in cell **B11**.

14   Right-click cell **B11**, and then click **Edit Hyperlink** to open the **Edit Hyperlink** dialog box.

15   Edit the **Text to display** box's value so that it reads Revenue Notes.

16   Click the **ScreenTip** button to display the **Set Hyperlink ScreenTip** dialog box.

17   In the **ScreenTip text** box, enter Link to Notes worksheet in this workbook and then click **OK** to close the **Hyperlink ScreenTip** dialog box.

18   Click **OK** to close the **Edit Hyperlink** dialog box and change the text in cell **B11** to **Revenue Notes**.

⁄	A	B	C	D	E
1					
2		Service Level ⏷	Revenue ⏷		
3		Ground	$ 20,101,264		
4		3Day	$ 26,811,778		
5		2Day	$ 19,251,279		
6		Overnight	$ 24,551,509		
7		Priority Overnight	$ 21,781,958		
8					
9		LevelDescriptions			
10					
11		Revenue Notes			
12					
13					

❌ **CLEAN UP** Close the Hyperlink and LevelDescriptions workbooks, saving your changes if you want to.

Pasting charts into other Office documents

One more way to include objects from one workbook in another Office document is to copy the object you want to share and then paste it into its new location. For example, you can copy Excel charts to Word documents and PowerPoint presentations to reuse your data without inserting a worksheet into the file and re-creating your chart in that new location.

Pasting a copied chart into another Office document by using Ctrl+V creates a link between the workbook and the other Office document. Whenever the original data changes, both copies of the chart will change as long as the files can connect on a computer or over a network. You can also select the Use Destination Theme & Link Data option or the Keep Source Formatting & Link Data option from the Paste Options list to create this link and control how the pasted chart should appear.

When you want to copy the current appearance of the chart to another document without creating a link back to the chart, you can right-click the chart and click Copy on the shortcut menu to copy the chart to the Microsoft Office Clipboard. Then, in the document into which you want to paste the chart's image, on the Home tab, in the Clipboard group, click the Paste button's arrow to display the menu of paste options that are available. The last option on the right, Picture, pastes an image of the chart in its current state.

13

In this exercise, you'll copy a chart to the Clipboard and paste an image of the chart into a PowerPoint presentation.

> **IMPORTANT** You must have PowerPoint 2013 installed on your computer to complete this exercise.

 SET UP You need the RevenueChart workbook and the RevenueSummary presentation located in the Chapter13 practice file folder to complete this exercise. Open the workbook and the presentation. Then follow the steps.

1   In the **RevenueChart** workbook, right-click the chart, and then click **Copy** to copy the chart to the Clipboard.

2   Display the **RevenueSummary** presentation, which contains a single, blank slide.

3   Right-click a blank spot in the visible slide, and then, in the **Paste Options** area of the shortcut menu, click the **Picture** icon to paste the chart as a static image.

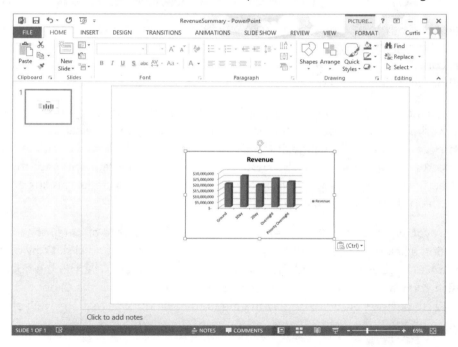

 CLEAN UP Close the RevenueChart workbook and the RevenueSummary presentation, saving your changes if you want to..

Key points

- Excel is a versatile program. You can exchange data between Excel and other Office programs in just a few steps.

- Because Excel is part of Office 2013, you can embed Excel worksheets into other Office documents and embed other Office documents into Excel workbooks.

- Excel works smoothly with the web You can add hyperlinks that go to webpages, other documents, or specific locations in the current workbook by using the options in the Insert Hyperlink dialog box.

- After you create a hyperlink, you can edit it to add a ScreenTip, change the text that appears in the link, or change the link's target.

- You can easily create charts in Excel. After you create a chart, you can paste it directly into another Office document.

13

Chapter at a glance

Manage

Manage comments,
page 418

Track

Track and manage colleagues' changes,
page 420

Protect

Protect workbooks and worksheets,
page 424

Save

Save workbooks as web content,
page 436

Collaborating with colleagues

IN THIS CHAPTER, YOU WILL LEARN HOW TO

- Share workbooks.

- Save workbooks for electronic distribution and as web content.

- Manage comments, and track and manage colleagues' changes.

- Protect workbooks and worksheets.

- Authenticate workbooks.

- Import and export XML data.

- Work with SkyDrive and Excel Web App.

Even though one individual might be responsible for managing an organization's financial data and related information, many people provide input about revenue projections. You and your colleagues can enhance the Microsoft Excel 2013 workbook data you share by adding comments that offer insight into the information the data represents, such as why revenue was so strong during a particular month or whether a service level might be discontinued. If the workbook in which those projections and comments will be stored is available on a network or an intranet site, you can allow more than one user to access the workbook at a time by turning on workbook sharing. When a workbook has been shared with your colleagues, you can have the workbook mark and record any changes made to it. You can then decide which changes to keep and which to reject.

If you prefer to limit the number of colleagues who can view and edit your workbooks, you can add password protection to a workbook, worksheet, cell range, or even an individual cell. By adding password protection, you can prevent changes to critical elements of your workbooks. You can also hide formulas used to calculate values.

If you work in an environment in which you and your colleagues, both inside and outside your organization, exchange files frequently, you can use a digital signature to help verify that your workbooks and any macros they contain are from a trusted source.

Finally, if you want to display information on a website, you can do so by saving a workbook as a webpage. Your colleagues won't be able to edit the workbook, but they will be able to view it and comment by email or phone.

In this chapter, you'll share a workbook, save a workbook for electronic distribution, manage comments in workbook cells, track and manage changes made by colleagues, protect workbooks and worksheets, digitally sign your workbooks, and save your workbooks as web content. You'll also experiment with Microsoft SkyDrive and Microsoft Excel Web App.

PRACTICE FILES To complete the exercises in this chapter, you need the practice files contained in the Chapter14 practice file folder. For more information, see "Download the practice files" in this book's Introduction.

Sharing workbooks

For several users to edit a workbook simultaneously, you must turn on workbook sharing. Workbook sharing is perfect for an enterprise such as Consolidated Messenger, whose employees need to look up customer information, shipment numbers, and details on mistaken deliveries.

To turn on workbook sharing, on the Review tab, in the Changes group, click Share Workbook. On the Editing page of the Share Workbook dialog box, turn on workbook sharing by selecting the Allow Changes By More Than One User At The Same Time check box. You can then set the sharing options for the active workbook by clicking the Advanced tab.

IMPORTANT You can't share a workbook that contains an Excel table. To share the workbook, convert the Excel table to a regular cell range by clicking the Excel table, clicking the Design tab and then, in the Tools group, clicking Convert To Range. Click Yes in the dialog box that opens to confirm the change.

On the Advanced page of the Share Workbook dialog box, two settings are of particular interest. The first determines whether Excel should maintain a history of changes made to the workbook and, if so, for how many days it should keep the history. The default setting is for the program to retain a record of all changes made in the past 30 days, but you can enter any number of days you want. If you revisit your workbook on a regular basis, maintaining a list of all changes for the past 180 days might not be unreasonable. For a workbook that changes less frequently, a history reaching back 365 days (one year) could meet your tracking and auditing needs. Excel deletes the record of any changes made earlier than the time you set.

14

The other important setting on this page deals with how Excel decides which of two conflicting changes in a cell should be applied. For example, a service level's price might change, and two of your colleagues might enter in what they think the new price should be. When Ask Me Which Changes Win is selected, you can decide whether to keep the original price or the changed price.

You can share a workbook with your colleagues in two main ways:

- You can make it available over your organization's network.
- You can send a copy of the file to your colleagues via email.

Every organization's network is different, so you should check with your network administrators to determine the best way to share a file. Similarly, although the specific command to attach a file to an email message is different in every email program, the most common method of attaching a file is to create a new email message and then click the Attach button, as you do in Microsoft Outlook 2013.

In this exercise, you'll turn on workbook sharing and then attach the file to an Outlook 2013 email message.

IMPORTANT You must have Outlook 2013 installed on your computer to follow this procedure exactly.

 SET UP You need the CostProjections workbook located in the Chapter14 practice file folder to complete this exercise. Open the workbook, and start Outlook. Then follow the steps.

1   In Excel, on the **Review** tab, in the **Changes** group, click **Share Workbook** to open the **Share Workbook** dialog box.

2   Select the **Allow changes by more than one user at the same time** check box.

    TIP Workbook merging is the process of bringing changes from several copies of a shared workbook into the source workbook. For more information about the topic, press F1 to display the Excel Help dialog box, search for *workbook merging*, and then click the Merge Copies Of A Shared Workbook link.

3   Click **OK**. When you do, a message box appears, indicating that you must save the workbook for the action to take effect.

4   Click **OK** to save and share the workbook.

5   Click the **File** tab, click **Share**, click **Email**, and then click **Send as Attachment** to create a new email message with the **CostProjections** workbook attached.

6   Enter an address in the **To** box.

7   Click **Send** to send the message. If Excel had to open your email program to send the message, the program would close at this point.

✖ CLEAN UP Exit Oulook and close the CostProjections workbook.

Saving workbooks for electronic distribution

You can create a more secure, read-only copy of a workbook for electronic distribution by saving it as a Portable Document Format (PDF) or XML Paper Specification (XPS) file. The controls you use to do so are available on the Export page of the Backstage view.

Book1 - Excel

Export

Create PDF/XPS Document

Change File Type

Create a PDF/XPS Document

- Preserves layout, formatting, fonts, and images
- Content can't be easily changed
- Free viewers are available on the web

Create PDF/XPS

Click the Create PDF/XPS button to open the Publish As PDF Or XPS dialog box. Enter a name for the destination file in the File Name box, select the file type you want from the Save As Type list, and then click Publish.

TIP You can also save a workbook as a PDF or XPS document by clicking Save As in the Backstage view. Then, in the Save As dialog box, in the Save As Type list, select either PDF or XPS to create the type of file you want.

In this exercise, you will save a workbook as a PDF file.

➡️ SET UP You need the ProjectionsDistro workbook located in the Chapter14 practice file folder to complete this exercise. Open the workbook, and then follow the steps.

1. Click the **File** tab to display the **Backstage** view, and then click **Export** to display the **Export** page.

2. Click **Create PDF/XPS Document**, and then click the **Create PDF/XPS** button.

3. In the **Publish As PDF Or XPS** dialog box, select the file format you want.

4. If you plan to distribute the file online but not print it, click **Minimum Size**.

5. If you want to specify what portion of the workbook or types of content to publish, click the **Options** button, make your selections, and then click **OK**.

6. Click **Publish**.

❌ CLEAN UP Close the ProjectionsDistro workbook.

14

Managing comments

Excel makes it easy for you and your colleagues to insert comments in workbook cells. Those comments can add insights that go beyond the cell data; for example, if a regional processing center's package volume is exceptionally high on a particular day, the center's manager can add a comment to the cell in which shipments are recorded for that day, and note that two very large bulk shipments accounted for the disparity.

When you add a comment to a cell, a flag appears in the upper-right corner of the cell. When you point to a cell that contains a comment, the comment appears in a box next to the cell, along with the user name of the person who was logged on to the computer on which the comment was created.

	A	B	C	D	E	F	G
1							
2			Department				
3		Year	Receiving	Sorting	Routing	Loading	Delivery
4		2013		Curtis Frye:			
5		2014		Very important that we make receiving more significant in the next three years.			
6		2015					
7							
8							

> **IMPORTANT** Note that the name attributed to a comment might not be the same as the name of the person who actually created it. Access controls, such as those that require users to enter account names and passwords when they access a computer, can help track the person who made a comment or change.

You can add a comment to a cell by clicking the cell, clicking the Review tab, and then clicking New Comment. When you do, the comment flag appears in the cell, and a comment box appears next to the cell. You can enter the comment in the box and, when you're done, click another cell to close the box.

If you want a comment to be shown the entire time the workbook is open, click the cell that contains the comment, click the Review tab and then, in the Comments group, click Show/Hide Comment. You can hide the comment by clicking the same button when the comment appears in the workbook, and delete the comment by clicking the Review tab and then, in the Comments group, clicking Delete. Or you can open the comment for editing by clicking Edit Comment in the Comments group.

TIP You can also manage comments by right-clicking a cell that contains a comment and then using the commands on the shortcut menu.

IMPORTANT When someone other than the original user edits a comment, that person's input is marked with the new user's name and is added to the original comment.

You can control whether a cell displays just the comment indicator or the indicator and the comment itself by clicking a cell that contains a comment and then, on the Review tab, clicking the Show/Hide Comment button. Clicking the Show/Hide Comment button again reverses your action. If you've just begun to review a worksheet and want to display all of the comments on the sheet, display the Review tab and click the Show All Comments button. To move through the worksheet's comments one at a time, click the Previous or Next button.

In this exercise, you'll add comments to two cells. You will then highlight the cells that contain comments, review a comment, and delete that comment.

→ **SET UP** You need the ProjectionsForComment workbook located in the Chapter14 practice file folder to complete this exercise. Open the workbook, and then follow the steps.

1   Click cell **E6**.

2   On the **Review** tab, in the **Comments** group, click **New Comment**. When you do, a red comment flag appears in cell **E6** and a comment box appears next to the cell.

3   In the comment box, enter **Seems optimistic; move some improvement to the next year?**

4   Click any cell outside the comment box to hide the comment box.

5   Click cell **G7**.

6   On the **Review** tab, in the **Comments** group, click **New Comment**.

7   In the comment box, enter **Should have more increases as we integrate new processes**.

8   Click any cell outside the comment box to hide the comment box.

9   Click cell **G7**.

10 On the **Review** tab, in the **Comments** group, click **Delete** to remove the comment.

❌ CLEAN UP **Close the ProjectionsForComment workbook, saving your changes if you want to.**

Tracking and managing colleagues' changes

Whenever you collaborate with your colleagues to produce or edit a document, you should consider tracking the changes each user makes. When you turn on change tracking, any changes made to the workbook are highlighted in a color assigned to the user who made the changes. One benefit of tracking changes is that if you have a question about a change, you can quickly identify who made the change and verify whether the change is correct. In Excel, you can turn on change tracking in a workbook by clicking the Review tab and then, in the Changes group, clicking Track Changes, and clicking Highlight Changes.

In the Highlight Changes dialog box that opens, select the Track Changes While Editing check box. Selecting this check box saves your workbook, turns on change tracking, and also shares your workbook, which enables more than one user to access the workbook simultaneously.

You can use the commands in the Highlight Changes dialog box to choose which changes to track. When the When, Who, and Where check boxes are selected, Excel will track all changes. By selecting a check box and using the commands to specify a time frame, users, or areas of the workbook, you can limit which changes are highlighted. Each user's changes are displayed in a unique color. When you point to a cell that contains a change, the date and time when the change was made and the name of the user who made it appear as a ScreenTip.

TIP Selecting the When check box and choosing the All option has the same effect as clearing the check box.

After you and your colleagues finish modifying a workbook, anyone with permission to open the workbook can decide which changes to accept and which changes to reject. To start the process, click the Review tab. In the Changes group, click Track Changes, and then click Accept Or Reject Changes. After you clear the message box that indicates Excel will save your workbook, the Select Changes To Accept Or Reject dialog box opens. From the When list, you can choose which changes to review. The default choice is Not Yet Reviewed, but you can also click Since Date to open a dialog box in which you can enter the starting date of changes you want to review. To review all changes in your workbook, clear the When, Who, and Where check boxes.

TIP After you and your colleagues have finished making changes, you should turn off workbook sharing to help ensure that you are the only person able to review the changes and decide which to accept.

14

When you are ready to accept or reject changes, click OK. The Accept Or Reject Changes dialog box opens and displays the first change, which is described in the body of the dialog box. Clicking the Accept button finalizes the change; clicking the Reject button removes the change, restores the cell to its previous value, and erases any record of the change. Clicking Accept All or Reject All finalizes all changes or restores all cells to their original values, but you should choose one of those options only if you are absolutely certain you are doing the right thing.

IMPORTANT Clicking the Undo button on the Quick Access Toolbar or pressing Ctrl+Z will not undo the operation.

You can create an itemized record of all changes made since the last time you saved the workbook by adding a History worksheet to your workbook. To add a History worksheet, click Track Changes in the Changes group, and then click Highlight Changes to open the Highlight Changes dialog box. Select the List Changes On A New Sheet check box. When you click OK, a new worksheet named History opens in your workbook. Excel will delete the History worksheet the next time you save your workbook.

In this exercise, you'll turn on change tracking in a workbook, make changes to the workbook, accept the changes, and create a History worksheet.

➡ SET UP You need the ProjectionChangeTracking workbook located in the Chapter14 practice file folder to complete this exercise. Open the workbook, and then follow the steps.

1   On the **Review** tab, in the **Changes** group, click **Track Changes**, and then click **Highlight Changes** to open the **Highlight Changes** dialog box.

2   Select the **Track changes while editing** check box to activate the **Highlight which changes** area, and then clear the **When** check box.

3   Click **OK**. When you do, a message box appears, indicating that Excel will save the workbook.

4   Click **OK** to close the message box. Excel saves the workbook and begins tracking changes.

5   In cell **E6**, enter **16%**, and then press **Enter**. A blue flag appears in the upper-left corner of cell **E6**, indicating that the cell was changed.

6   In cell **E7**, enter **14%**, and then press **Enter**.

	A	B	C	D	E	F	G	H
1								
2					Efficiency Improvement Projections			
3								
4			Department					
5		Year	Receiving	Sorting	Routing	Loading	Delivery	
6		2014	9%	8%	16%	13%	19%	
7		2015	9%	6%	14%	5%	5%	
8		2016	17%	11%	5%	5%	14%	
9								

7   On the **Quick Access Toolbar**, click the **Save** button to save your work.

8   On the **Review** tab, in the **Changes** group, click **Track Changes**, and then click **Highlight Changes** to open the **Highlight Changes** dialog box.

9   Select the **List changes on a new sheet** check box, clear the **When** check box, and then click **OK**. Excel creates and displays a worksheet named **History**, which contains a list of all changes made since the last time a user accepted or rejected changes.

	A	B	C	D	E	F	G	H	I	J	K	L
	Action							New	Old	Action	Losing	
1	Number ▾	Date ▾	Time ▾	Who ▾	Change ▾	Sheet ▾	Range ▾	Value ▾	Value ▾	Type ▾	Action ▾	
2	1	11/15/2012	11:09 PM	Curtis Frye	Cell Change	Sheet1	E6	16%	20%			
3	2	11/15/2012	11:09 PM	Curtis Frye	Cell Change	Sheet1	E7	14%	17%			
4												
5	The history ends with the changes saved on 11/15/2012 at 11:09 PM.											
6												

10   Click the **Sheet1** sheet tab to display the **Sheet1** worksheet.

11   On the **Review** tab, in the **Changes** group, click **Track Changes**, and then click **Accept/Reject Changes**. The **Select Changes to Accept or Reject** dialog box opens.

12   Click **OK** to display the first change in the **Accept or Reject Changes** dialog box.

14

Accept or Reject Changes

Change 1 of 2 made to this document:

Curtis Frye, 11/15/2012 11:09 PM:

Changed cell E6 from '20%' to '16%'.

Accept | Reject | Accept All | Reject All | Close

13 Click **Accept** to keep the change and display the next change.

14 Click **Accept** to keep the change and delete the **History** worksheet. The **Accept or Reject Changes** dialog box closes.

❌ CLEAN UP Close the ProjectionChangeTracking workbook, saving your changes if you want to.

Protecting workbooks and worksheets

Excel gives you the ability to share your workbooks over the web, over a corporate intranet, or by creating copies of files for other users to take on business trips. An important part of sharing files, however, is ensuring that only those users who you want to have access to the files can open or modify them. For example, Consolidated Messenger might have a series of computers available in a processing center so that supervisors can look up package volumes and handling efficiency information. Although those computers are vital tools for managing the business process, it doesn't help the company to have unauthorized personnel, even those with good intentions, accessing critical workbooks.

You can limit access to your workbooks or elements within workbooks by setting passwords. When you set a password for an Excel workbook, any users who want to access the protected workbook must enter the workbook's password in a dialog box that opens when they try to open the file. If users don't know the password, they cannot open the workbook.

To set a password for a workbook, open the workbook to be protected, and display the workbook in the Backstage view. On the Info page of the Backstage view, click the Protect Workbook button, and then click Encrypt With Password. The Encrypt Document dialog box opens, with a Password box in which you can enter your password. After you click OK, the Confirm Password dialog box opens, in which you can verify the password required to open the workbook. After you have confirmed the password, click OK. Now the Info page indicates that users must enter a password to open the file.

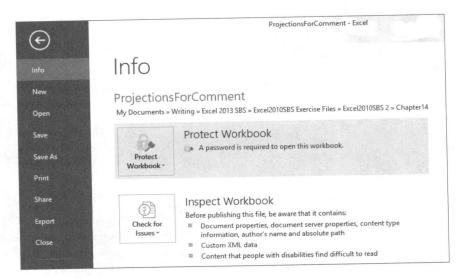

To remove the password from a workbook, repeat these steps, but delete the password from the Encrypt Document dialog box and save the file.

TIP The best passwords are long strings of random characters, but random characters are hard to remember. One good method of creating hard-to-guess passwords is to string two or more words and a number together. For example, the password *genuinestarcalibration302* is 24 characters long, combines letters and numbers, and is easy to remember. If you must create a shorter password to meet a system's constraints, avoid dictionary words and include uppercase letters, lowercase letters, numbers, and any special symbols such as ! or # if they are allowed.

14

If you want to allow anyone to open a workbook but want to prevent unauthorized users from editing a worksheet, you can protect a worksheet by displaying that worksheet, clicking the Review tab and then, in the Changes group, clicking Protect Sheet to open the Protect Sheet dialog box.

In the Protect Sheet dialog box, you can select the Protect Worksheet And Contents Of Locked Cells check box to protect the sheet. You can also set a password that a user must enter before protection can be turned off again, and choose which elements of the worksheet a user can change while protection is turned on. To allow a user to change a worksheet element without entering the password, select the check box next to that element's name.

The check box at the top of the worksheet mentions locked cells. A locked cell is a cell that can't be changed when worksheet protection is turned on. You can lock or unlock a cell by right-clicking the cell and then clicking Format Cells. In the Format Cells dialog box, you click the Protection tab and select the Locked check box.

When worksheet protection is turned on, selecting the Locked check box prevents unauthorized users from changing the contents or formatting of the locked cell, whereas selecting the Hidden check box hides the formulas in the cell. You might want to hide the formula in a cell if you draw sensitive data, such as customer contact information, from another workbook and don't want the name of the workbook in a formula to be viewed by casual users.

Finally, you can password-protect a cell range. For example, you might want to let users enter values in most worksheet cells but also want to protect the cells by using formulas that perform calculations based on those values. To password-protect a range of cells, select the cells to protect, click the Review tab and then, in the Changes group, click Allow Users To Edit Ranges. The Allow Users To Edit Ranges dialog box opens.

To create a protected range, click the New button to display the New Range dialog box. Enter a name for the range in the Title box, and then enter a password in the Range Password box. When you click OK, Excel asks you to confirm the password; after you do, click OK in the Confirm Password dialog box and again in the Allow Users To Edit Ranges dialog box to protect the range. Now, whenever users try to edit a cell in the protected range, they are prompted for a password.

TIP Remember that a range of cells can mean just one cell.

In this exercise, you'll password-protect a workbook, a worksheet, and a range of cells. You will also hide the formula in a cell.

 SET UP You need the SecureInfo workbook located in the Chapter14 practice file folder to complete this exercise. Open the workbook, and then follow the steps.

1   Display the **Backstage** view, and then, if necessary, click **Info** to display the **Info** page.

2   Click the **Protect Workbook** button, and then click **Encrypt with Password** to open the **Encrypt Document** dialog box.

Encrypt Document ? ×
Encrypt the contents of this file
Password:
Caution: If you lose or forget the password, it cannot be recovered. It is advisable to keep a list of passwords and their corresponding document names in a safe place. (Remember that passwords are case-sensitive.)
OK   Cancel

3   Enter work14pro in the **Password** box.

4   Click **OK**. When you do, the **Confirm Password** dialog box opens.

5   In the **Reenter password** box, enter work14pro.

6   Click **OK** to close the **Confirm Password** dialog box.

7   Click the **Go Back** button in the upper-left corner of the **Backstage** view.

8   Click the **Review** tab and, if necessary, click the **Performance** sheet tab to display the **Performance** worksheet.

9   Right-click cell **B8**, and then click **Format Cells** to open the **Format Cells** dialog box.

10   Click the **Protection** tab to display the **Protection** page of the dialog box.

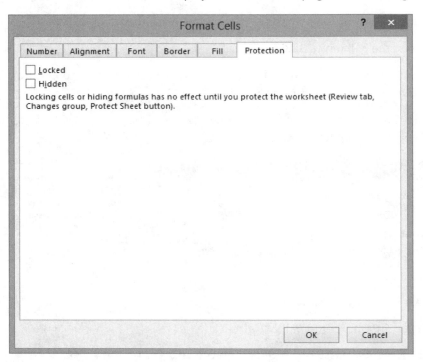

11   Select the **Hidden** and **Locked** check boxes, and then click **OK**. Excel formats cell **B8** so that it won't display its formula after you protect the worksheet.

12   On the **Review** tab, in the **Changes** group, click **Protect Sheet** to open the **Protect Sheet** dialog box.

13   In the **Password to unprotect sheet** box, enter prot300pswd.

14   Clear the **Select locked cells** and **Select unlocked cells** check boxes, and then click **OK**. When you do, the **Confirm Password** dialog box opens.

14

15   In the **Reenter password to proceed** box, enter prot300pswd, and then click **OK**.

16   Click the **Weights** sheet tab to display the **Weights** worksheet.

17   Select the cell range **B2:C7**.

18   On the **Review** tab, in the **Changes** group, click **Allow Users to Edit Ranges** to open the **Allow Users to Edit Ranges** dialog box.

19   Click **New**. When you do, the **New Range** dialog box opens, with the range **B2:C7** displayed in the **Refers to cells** box.

20   In the **Title** box, enter AllWeights.

21   In the **Range password** box, enter work14pro, and then click **OK**.

22   In the **Confirm Password** dialog box, reenter the password work14pro. The range appears in the **Allow Users to Edit Ranges** box.

23   Click **Protect Sheet** to open the **Protect Sheet** dialog box.

24   In the **Password to unprotect sheet** box, enter work14pro, and then click **OK**.

25   In the **Confirm Password** dialog box, reenter the password work14pro, and then click **OK**.

❌ CLEAN UP Close the SecureInfo workbook, saving your changes if you want to.

Finalizing workbooks

Distributing a workbook to other users carries many risks, not the least of which is the possibility that the workbook might contain private information you don't want to share with users outside your organization. With Excel, you can inspect a workbook for information you might not want to distribute to other people, and create a read-only final version that prevents other people from making changes to the workbook content.

Using the Document Inspector, you can quickly locate comments and annotations, document properties and personal information, custom XML data, headers and footers, hidden rows and columns, hidden worksheets, and invisible content. You can then easily remove any hidden or personal information that the Document Inspector finds.

To start the Document Inspector, save the file, and then display the Info page of the Backstage view. Click the Check For Issues button, and then click Inspect Document to open the Document Inspector dialog box.

The Document Inspector checks your document for every category of information that is selected in the list. Clear the check box of any type of information you want to remain in the workbook, and then click Inspect. In the inspection results dialog box that appears, click the Remove All button to the right of any data you want to remove.

When you're done making changes to a workbook, you can mark it as final. Marking a workbook as final sets the status property to Final and turns off data entry and editing commands. To mark a workbook as final, display the Info page of the Backstage view, click Protect Workbook, click Mark As Final, and then click OK to verify that you want to finalize the workbook.

To restore functionality to a workbook that has been marked as final, display the Info page of the Backstage view, click Protect Workbook, and then click Mark As Final to change its status.

To inspect and remove hidden or personal information, follow these steps:

1   Press **Ctrl+S** to save the file.
2   Display the **Info** page of the **Backstage** view, click **Check for Issues**, and then click **Inspect Document** to open the **Document Inspector** dialog box.
3   Clear the check box of any content type that you want to remain in the document, and click **Inspect**.
4   In the inspection results list, click the **Remove All** button to the right of any category of data that you want to remove.

Marking a workbook as final sets the status property to Final and turns off data entry, editing commands, and proofreading marks.

To mark a workbook as final, follow these steps:

1   Display the **Info** page of the **Backstage** view, click **Protect Workbook**, and then click **Mark as Final**.
2   In the message box that indicates that the file will be marked as final and then saved, click **OK**.
3   In the message box that indicates that the file has been marked as final, click **OK**.

Authenticating workbooks

The unfortunate reality of exchanging files over networks, especially over the Internet, is that you need to be sure you know the origin of the files you're working with. One way an organization can guard against files with viruses or substitute data is to authenticate every workbook by using a digital signature. A digital signature is a character string created by combining a user's unique secret digital signature file mathematically with the contents of the workbook, which programs such as Excel can recognize and use to verify the identity of the user who signed the file. A good analogy for a digital signature is a wax seal, which was used for thousands of years to verify the integrity and origin of a document.

TIP The technical details of and procedure for managing digital certificates are beyond the scope of this book, but your network administrator should be able to create a digital certificate for you. You can also directly purchase a digital signature from a third party, which can usually be renewed annually for a small fee. For the purposes of this book, you can use the selfcert.exe Microsoft Office accessory program to generate a certificate with which to perform the exercise in this topic. This type of certificate is useful for certifying a document as part of a demonstration, but other users will not accept it as a valid certificate.

To create a digital certificate that you can use as a demonstration, navigate to the folder that contains your Office 2013 program files. Whether you have the selfcert.exe file and the specific folder it's in if you do have it depends on your computer's configuration, the drive onto which you installed Office 2013, and whether you installed all available files when you installed Office 2013. One typical folder is C:\Program Files (x86)\Microsoft Office\Office15. In that folder, which contains a large number of files, you will find the selfcert.exe program. Double-click the program to run it.

In the Create Digital Certificate dialog box, enter a name for your certificate and click OK to have the program create your trial certificate. Then, in Excel, display the Info page of the Backstage view, click Protect Workbook, and click Add A Digital Signature. In the Sign dialog box, enter your purpose for signing the document, select the certificate you want to use, and then click Sign to sign your workbook.

IMPORTANT After you click Add A Digital Signature, Excel checks your computer for usable digital certificates. If it can't find one, Excel displays a dialog box that indicates that you can buy digital signatures from third-party providers. To get information about those services, click the Signature Services From The Office Marketplace button. You won't be able to add a digital signature to a file until you acquire a digital certificate, either by generating a test certificate using the included selfcert.exe program or by purchasing one through a third-party vendor.

14

If you have several certificates from which to choose, and the desired certificate doesn't appear in the Sign dialog box, you can click Change to display the Select Certificate dialog box. In the Select Certificate dialog box, click the certificate with which you want to sign the workbook, and then click OK. The Select Certificate dialog box closes, and the certificate with which you signed the workbook appears in the Sign dialog box. As before, click Sign to sign your document by using the digital certificate.

In this exercise, you'll create a digital certificate and digitally sign a workbook by using the certificate.

IMPORTANT You must have a digital certificate, such as one generated by selfcert.exe or purchased through a third-party vendor, to complete this exercise. If you don't have a third-party digital certificate and don't have selfcert.exe installed on your computer, read through the steps of the procedure to become familiar with the process.

 SET UP You need the ProjectionsSigned workbook located in the Chapter14 practice file folder to complete this exercise. Open the workbook, and then follow the steps.

1   On the drive where you installed Office 2013, navigate to the folder (such as *C:\Program Files (x86)\Microsoft Office\Office15*) that contains the Office 2013 program files, and then double-click **selfcert.exe**. The **Create Digital Certificate** dialog box opens.

Create Digital Certificate

This program creates a self-signed digital certificate that bears the name you type below. This type of certificate does not verify your identity.

Since a self-signed digital certificate might be a forgery, users will receive a security warning when they open a file that contains a macro project with a self-signed signature.

Office will only allow you to trust a self-signed certificate on the machine on which it was created.

A self-signed certificate is only for personal use. If you need an authenticated code signing certificate for signing commercial or broadly distributed macros, you will need to contact a certification authority.

Click here for a list of commercial certificate authorities

Your certificate's name:

OK   Cancel

2   In the **Your certificate's name** box, enter Excel2013SBS, and then click **OK**. When you do, a message box indicates that the program created your certificate successfully.

3   Click **OK** to close the message box.

4   Display the **Backstage** view, and then, if necessary, click **Info**. Click **Protect Workbook**, and then click **Add a Digital Signature** to open the **Sign** dialog box.

5   In the **Purpose for signing this document** box, enter Testing.

6   Verify that the name of your certificate appears in the **Signing as** area of the dialog box, and then click **Sign**. When you do, a dialog box opens, indicating that using a selfcert.exe certificate prevents users from validating the signature.

7   Click **OK** to acknowledge the message and display the **Signature Confirmation** dialog box.

8   Click **OK**. The **Signatures** pane opens and the workbook is marked as final. If you edit the workbook, it will invalidate the digital signature, which is based on the workbook's contents at the time you signed it.

✖ CLEAN UP Close the ProjectionsSigned workbook, saving your changes if you want to.

Saving workbooks as web content

With Excel, you can save your workbooks as web documents, so you and your colleagues can view workbooks over the Internet or an organization's intranet. For a document to be viewable on the web, it must be saved as an HTML file. These files, which end with either an *.htm* or an *.html* extension, include tags that tell a web browser such as Windows Internet Explorer how to display the contents of the file.

For example, you might want to set the data labels in a workbook apart from the rest of the data by using bold text for the labels. The coding that you use in an HTML file to indicate that text should be displayed as bold is *...*, where the ellipsis between the tags is replaced by the text to be displayed. So the following HTML fragment would be displayed as **Excel** in a webpage.

    Excel

You can create HTML files in Excel by displaying the Backstage view, and then clicking Save As to open the Save As dialog box. To save a workbook as an HTML file, click the Save As Type arrow, and then click Web Page. In the Save As dialog box, click Entire Workbook, enter a name for the file in the File Name box, and click Save to have Excel create an HTML document for each sheet in the workbook.

TIP If the only sheet in your workbook that contains data is the one displayed when you save the workbook as a webpage, Excel saves only that worksheet as a webpage.

After you save an Excel workbook as a set of HTML documents, you can open it in your web browser. To open the Excel file, start Internet Explorer, and then click Open in the Backstage view to open the Open dialog box. In the Open dialog box, click the Browse button to open the Windows Internet Explorer dialog box. You can use the commands in that dialog box to identify the file you want to open.

When you double-click the file you want to open, the Windows Internet Explorer dialog box closes and the file's name and path appear in the Open box. To display the Excel workbook, click OK, and the workbook appears in Internet Explorer. You can move among the workbook's worksheets by clicking the sheet tabs in the lower-left corner of the page.

When you save a workbook to an organization's intranet site, you can share data with your colleagues. For example, Consolidated Messenger's chief operating officer, Lori Penor, could save a daily report on package misdeliveries to her team's intranet site so that everyone could examine what happened, where the problem occurred, and how to fix the problem. It's also possible to save a workbook as a web file that retains a link to the original workbook. Whenever someone updates the workbook, Excel updates the web file to reflect the new content.

To publish a workbook to the web, display the Backstage view, click Save As and then, in the Save As Type list, click Web Page. When you do, Excel displays the Publish button; when you click the Publish button, the Publish As Web Page dialog box opens.

14

You can use the options in the Publish As Web Page dialog box to select which elements of your workbook you want to publish to the web. Clicking the Choose arrow displays a list of publishable items, including the option to publish the entire workbook, items on specific sheets, or a range of cells. To have Excel update the webpage whenever someone updates the source workbook, select the AutoRepublish Every Time This Workbook Is Saved check box. You can also specify what text appears on the web page's title bar. To do so, click the Change button, enter the page title in the Set Title dialog box, and click OK. When you save a workbook that has AutoRepublish turned on, Excel displays a dialog box that indicates that the changes will update the associated web file.

> **IMPORTANT** When you save a PivotTable to the web, the PivotTable doesn't retain its interactivity. Instead, Excel publishes a static image of the PivotTable's current configuration. For information about publishing a workbook with an interactive PivotTable to the web, see "Working with SkyDrive and Excel Web App" later in this chapter.

In this exercise, you'll save a workbook as a webpage and then publish a worksheet's PivotTable to the web.

➔ SET UP You need the ShipmentSummary workbook located in the Chapter14 practice file folder to complete this exercise. Open the workbook, and then follow the steps.

1   Display the **Backstage** view, and then click **Save As** to display the **Save As** page.

2   Click the **Browse** button to open the **Save As** dialog box.

3   In the **File name** box, enter **ShipmentSummaryWeb**.

4   In the **Save as type** list, click **Web Page**. The **Save As** dialog box changes to reflect the **Web Page** file type.

5 Click **Save**. When you do, a warning message box appears, indicating that the work-book might contain elements that can't be saved in a webpage.

6 Click **Yes** to save the workbook as a web file. The message box closes, and Excel saves the workbook as a webpage.

14

7   Display the **Backstage** view, and then click **Close**.

8   In the **Backstage** view, click **Open**, click **Recent Workbooks**, and then, in the list of recently viewed files, click **ShipmentSummary** to open the **ShipmentSummary** workbook.

9   In the **Backstage** view, click **Save As**, and then click **Browse** to open the **Save As** dialog box.

10   In the **File name** box, enter ShipmentSummaryPublish.

11   In the **Save as type** list, click **Web Page**. The **Save As** dialog box changes to reflect the **Web Page** file type.

12   Click **Publish** to open the **Publish as Web Page** dialog box.

13   In the **Choose** list, click **Items on Sheet2** to display the available items on **Sheet2**.

14   In the **Item to publish** list, click **PivotTable**.

15   Select the **AutoRepublish every time this workbook is saved** check box.

16   Click **Publish** to publish the PivotTable to a webpage. Excel will update the contents of the webpage whenever a user saves the **ShipmentSummary** workbook.

❌ CLEAN UP Close the ShipmentSummary workbook, saving your changes if you want to.

Importing and exporting XML data

By using HTML, you can determine how a document will be displayed in a web browser, such as by telling Internet Explorer to display certain text in bold type or to start a new paragraph. However, HTML doesn't tell you anything about the meaning of data in a document. Internet Explorer might "know" it should display a set of data in a table, but it wouldn't "know" that the data represented an Excel spreadsheet.

You can add metadata, or data about data, to web documents by using XML. Although a full discussion of XML is beyond the scope of this book, the following bit of XML code shows how you might identify two sets of three values (Month, Category, and Exceptions) by using XML.

```
<?xml version="1.0" encoding="UTF-8" standalone="yes"?>
<ns2:exceptions xmlns:ns2="http://www.w3schools.com">
<exception>
    <Month>January</Month>
    <Category>2Day</Category>
    <Exceptions>14</Exceptions>
</exception>
<exception>
    <Month>January</Month>
    <Category>3Day</Category>
    <Exceptions>3</Exceptions>
</exception>
</ns2:exceptions>
```

XML is meant to be a universal language, allowing data to move freely from one program to another. Excel might display those two sets of Exceptions data as rows of data in an Excel worksheet.

	A	B	C
1	Month	Category	Exceptions
2	January	2Day	14
3	January	3Day	3
4			

14

Other programs could display or process the XML file's contents in other ways, but you wouldn't have to change the underlying XML file. All of the work is done by the other programs' programmers.

To work with XML data in Excel, you must use the controls on the Developer tab. If the Developer tab doesn't appear on the ribbon in your copy of Excel 2013, display the Backstage view, and then click Options to open the Excel Options dialog box. Click Customize Ribbon to display that page of the dialog box and then, in the Main Tabs list in the panel on the right, select the Developer tab's check box.

When you click OK, the Developer tab appears on the ribbon.

To import XML data into an Excel worksheet, click the cell in which you want the first value to appear. Next, click the Developer tab and then, in the XML group, click the Import button to open the Import XML dialog box. Click the XML file you want to import and then click Open. When you do, Excel will display a dialog box that indicates that the XML source file doesn't refer to a schema, so the program will create one for you. Click OK, verify that the cell you selected appears in the XML Table In Existing Worksheet box of the next dialog box that opens, and click OK to import the data.

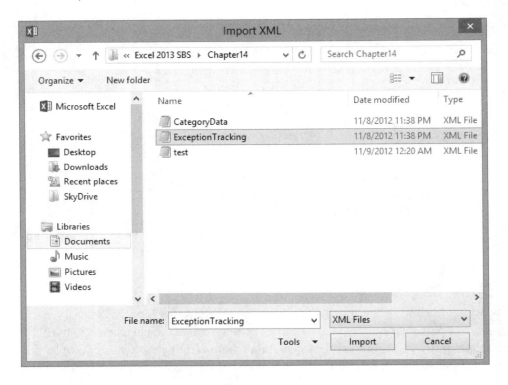

TIP If you think the XML data file has changed, click the Refresh Data button in the Developer tab's XML group to update your worksheet.

To export XML data, click any cell in an XML table and then, on the Developer tab, click the Export button to display the Export XML dialog box. Navigate to the folder in which you want to export your data, enter a name for the file, ensure that the Save As Type field's value is XML Files, and click Export.

For programs to process XML data properly, developers must create a formal model of the data's structure. That model is called a schema. The schema for the Exceptions data collection is as follows.

```xml
<?xml version="1.0"?>
<xs:schema xmlns:xs="http://www.w3.org/2001/XMLSchema"
           targetNamespace="http://www.w3schools.com"
           xmlns="http://www.w3schools.com"
          elementFormDefault="qualified">
 <xs:element name="exception">
  <xs:complexType>
    <xs:sequence>
      <xs:element name="Month"      type="xs:string"/>
      <xs:element name="Category"   type="xs:string"/>
      <xs:element name="Exceptions" type="xs:integer"/>
    </xs:sequence>
  </xs:complexType>
 </xs:element>
</xs:schema>
```

Toward the bottom of the schema's text are the elements for Month, Category, and Exceptions, plus their data types. Creating a schema is a technical challenge that's beyond the scope of this book, but Excel can create a schema from your XML data for all but the most complicated data sets.

In this exercise, you'll display the Developer tab of the ribbon, import XML data into a workbook, create a schema based on the structure of the data, and then export the data to another XML file.

⊕ SET UP You need the CategoryXML workbook and the ExceptionTracking.xml file located in your Chapter14 practice file folder to complete this exercise. Open the workbook, and then follow the steps.

1 If the **Developer** tab doesn't appear on the ribbon, display the **Backstage** view, and then click **Options** to open the **Excel Options** dialog box.

2 In the **Excel Options** dialog box, click **Customize the Ribbon** to display that page of the dialog box.

3 In the **Customize the Ribbon** list at the right side of the dialog box, select the **Developer** check box to indicate that you want Excel to display that tab on the ribbon.

4 Click **OK** to apply your changes.

5 Click the **Developer** tab, and then, in the **XML** group, click **Import** to open the **Import XML** dialog box.

6 Navigate to the **Chapter14** practice file folder, click **ExceptionTracking**, and then click **Open** to start the import process.

7 In the alert box that appears, click **OK** to have Excel create a schema for the imported data and display the **Import Data** dialog box.

8 Verify that cell **A1** appears in the **XML table in existing worksheet** box, and then click **OK** to import the data.

	A	B	C	D
1	Month	Category	Exceptions	
2	January	2Day	14	
3	January	3Day	3	
4	January	Ground	7	
5	January	Overnight	1	
6	January	PriorityOvernight	0	
7	February	2Day	9	
8	February	3Day	2	
9	February	Ground	20	
10	February	Overnight	10	
11	February	PriorityOvernight	0	
12				

9 With the active cell still in the imported data range, click the **Developer** tab and then, in the **XML** group, click **Export**. The **Export XML** dialog box opens.

14

10   In the **File name** field, enter ExceptionsExport, and then click the **Export** button to create your new XML file.

❌ CLEAN UP Close the CategoryXML workbook, saving your changes if you want to.

Working with SkyDrive and Excel Web App

As information workers become increasingly mobile, they need to access their data from anywhere and to have a single version of a file to which they can turn. Excel 2013 is integrated with SkyDrive, a Microsoft cloud service that stores your files remotely and lets you access them over the Internet.

To use SkyDrive, go to *www.skydrive.com.* You will need a Microsoft account to use SkyDrive.

☁ SkyDrive

Microsoft account What's this?

someone@example.com

Password

☐ Keep me signed in

Sign in

Can't access your account?

Sign in with a single-use code

Don't have a Microsoft account? **Sign up now**

Help Center   Feedback

If you don't have a Microsoft account, click the Sign Up Now link to create one. After you create your account, sign in by using those credentials. When you do, the Files page of your SkyDrive account is displayed.

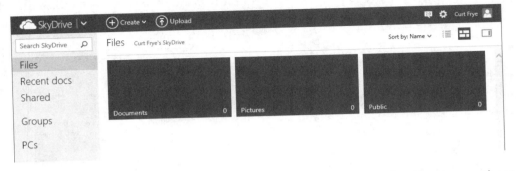

You can upload files to your SkyDrive account by clicking the Upload button on the menu bar at the top of the page and then clicking Select Them From Your Computer to display the Open dialog box. Select the files you want to upload, and click Open to add them to your account.

To open a folder, such as Documents, Pictures, or Public, click that folder in the Files pane. You can create a new folder anywhere in the SkyDrive site structure by clicking the Create button and then clicking Folder.

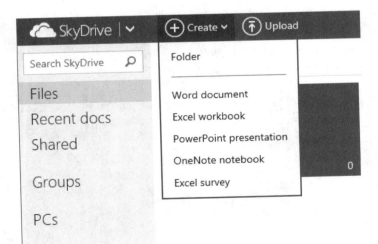

When you click Create, SkyDrive also displays options to create a Word document, an Excel workbook, a PowerPoint presentation, a OneNote notebook, or an Excel survey. If you click Create and then click Excel Workbook, SkyDrive displays the New Microsoft Excel Workbook dialog box. Enter a name for the new file, and then click Create to create it by using Excel Web App.

TIP Excel Web App saves your workbook every time you edit a cell, so there's no Save button on the Quick Access Toolbar.

Excel Web App provides a rich set of capabilities that you can use to create new workbooks and edit workbooks you created in the desktop version of the program. If you find you need some features that aren't available in Excel Web App, click Open In Excel on the ribbon to open the file in the Excel 2013 desktop program.

TROUBLESHOOTING You might encounter a series of dialog boxes that ask you to sign back in to your Microsoft account and to provide other information. These queries are normal and expected.

In this exercise, you'll upload an Excel workbook to your SkyDrive account, open the workbook in Excel Web App, and open the file in the Excel desktop program.

> **IMPORTANT** You need an active SkyDrive account and a working Internet connection to successfully complete the following exercise.

 SET UP You need the SkyDriveFile workbook located in the Chapter14 practice file folder to complete this exercise. Don't open the workbook yet; just follow the steps.

1   Start Internet Explorer, go to **http://www.skydrive.com**, and sign in to your SkyDrive account.

2   On the menu bar at the top of the SkyDrive **Files** page, click **Upload** to open the **Choose File to Upload** dialog box.

3   Navigate to the **Chapter14** practice file folder, click **SkyDriveFile**, and then click **Open** to upload your file.

4   When SkyDrive displays a dialog box that indicates that the file was uploaded successfully, click the **Close** button in the dialog box to dismiss it.

5   In SkyDrive, click the **SkyDriveFile** workbook's tile to open it in Excel Web App.

6   Click cell **A14**, enter April into the cell, and press **Tab**; enter Ground into cell **B14** and press **Tab**; then enter 102 in cell **C14** and press **Enter**.

7　On the Excel Web App ribbon, click **Open in Excel** to start the process of opening the file in the Excel desktop program.

8　Click **Yes** or **OK** as appropriate to clear the message boxes that appear. When you're done, the **SkyDriveFile** workbook opens in Excel.

9　Close Excel. Then, in Internet Explorer, click **Close the Excel Web App** to indicate that you opened the file successfully in the desktop program.

✖ CLEAN UP Exit Internet Explorer and, if necessary, Excel.

Key points

- When you share a workbook, more than one user can view and edit the data at one time, which is useful in group projects in which each member has a distinct area of responsibility.

- You can send files by email to efficiently collaborate with colleagues.

- You can add comments to cells to quickly let your colleagues know what you're thinking without taking up valuable space in a cell.

- Tracking changes is vital when you share responsibility for a workbook with several other people.

- When your workbook's data is too important to leave lying around in the open, use passwords to protect all or part of the file!

- Authenticating workbooks with digital signatures helps to identify the source of your files, so you won't have to guess about the origins of that next attachment in your email Inbox.

- Saving a workbook as a web-accessible HTML document is as easy as saving it as a regular Excel file, and opening a workbook saved for the web is just as easy as opening any other webpage.

- Use the AutoRepublish feature to update Excel files on the web. Whenever anyone changes the original workbook, Excel writes the edits to the HTML version of the file.

- You can import and export XML data in Excel 2013. When you import XML data, Excel creates the schema required to manage the data within the program.

- With SkyDrive and Excel Web App, you can work with data in the native Excel 2013 workbook format wherever you have web access. If you have Excel 2013 installed on your computer, you can open a file stored on SkyDrive and edit it by using the full power of the desktop program.

14

Glossary

3-D reference A pattern for referring to the workbook, worksheet, and cell from which a value should be read.

absolute reference A cell reference, such as $B$3, that doesn't change when you copy a formula that contains the reference to another cell. See also *relative reference*.

active cell The cell that is currently selected and open for editing.

add-in A supplemental program that can be used to extend functions in Excel.

alignment The manner in which a cell's contents are arranged within that cell (for example, centered).

arguments The specific data that a function requires to calculate a value.

aspect ratio The relationship between a graphic's height and its width.

auditing The process of examining a worksheet for errors.

AutoComplete The Excel functionality that completes data entry for a cell based on similar values in other cells in the same column.

AutoFill The Excel functionality that extends a series of values based on the contents of a single cell. See also *FillSeries, Flash Fill*.

AutoFilter An Excel tool that you can use to create filters.

AutoRepublish An Excel technology that maintains a link between a web document and the worksheet on which the web document is based, and updates the web document whenever the original worksheet is saved.

Backstage view A view introduced in Excel 2010, accessed by clicking the File tab, that gathers workbook management tasks into a single location.

browser A program with which users view web documents.

cell The box at the intersection of a row and a column.

cell range A group of cells.

cell reference The letter and number combination, such as C16, that identifies the row and column intersection of a cell.

chart A visual summary of worksheet data; also called a *graph*.

column Cells that are on the same vertical line in a worksheet.

conditional format A format that is applied only when cell contents meet specific criteria.

conditional formula A formula that calculates a value by using one of two different expressions, depending on whether a third expression is true or false.

data bar A horizontal line within a cell that indicates the relative magnitude of the cell's value.

data consolidation Summarizing data from a set of similar cell ranges.

dependent A cell with a formula that uses the value from a particular cell.

Document Inspector A utility with which you can inspect an Excel workbook for personal information, tracked changes, and other sensitive data.

embed To save a file as part of another file, as opposed to linking one file to another. See also *link*.

error code A brief message that appears in a worksheet cell, describing a problem with a formula or a function.

Excel table An Excel object with which you can store and refer to data based on the name of the table and the names of its columns and rows.

Excel Web App A browser-enabled version of the Excel desktop program.

field A column of data used to create a PivotTable.

fill handle The square at the lower-right corner of a cell that can be dragged to indicate other cells that should hold values in the series defined by the active cell.

FillSeries The ability to extend a series of values based on the contents of two cells, where the first cell has the starting value for the series and the second cell shows the increment. See also *AutoFill, Flash Fill*.

filter A rule that Excel uses to determine which worksheet rows to display.

Flash Fill A capability that senses patterns of data combination and separation and offers to continue the pattern for the remainder of the rows in a data list. See also *AutoFill, FillSeries*.

format A predefined set of characteristics that can be applied to cell contents.

formula An expression used to calculate a value.

Formula AutoComplete The Excel functionality with which you can enter a formula quickly by selecting functions, named ranges, and table references that appear when you begin to enter the formula into a cell.

formula bar The area just above the worksheet grid that displays the active cell's formula and within which you can edit the formula.

function A predefined formula.

Goal Seek An analysis tool that finds the value for a selected cell that would produce a given result from a calculation.

graph A visual summary of worksheet data; also called a *chart*.

header An area of the worksheet that appears above the contents of the worksheet grid when you print the worksheet or view it in Layout view.

HTML A document-formatting system that tells a web browser such as Windows Internet Explorer how to display the contents of a file.

hyperlink A connection from a hyperlink anchor such as text or a graphic that you can follow to display a link target such as a file, a location in a file, or a website. Text hyperlinks are usually formatted as colored or underlined text, but sometimes the only indication is that when you point to them, the pointer changes to a hand..

icon set A conditional format that uses distinct visual indicators to designate how a value compares to a set of criteria.

landscape mode A display and printing mode whereby columns run parallel to the short edge of a sheet of paper.

link A formula that has a cell show the value from another cell. See also *embed*.

Live Preview A feature of Excel that displays the result of an operation, such as pasting data or applying a cell style, without implementing the change until you complete the operation.

locked cell A cell that cannot be modified if its worksheet is protected.

macro A series of recorded automated actions that can be replayed.

mailto hyperlink A special type of hyperlink with which a user creates an email message to a particular email address.

map A correspondence between an XML schema and an Excel worksheet.

Merge And Center An operation that combines a contiguous group of cells into a single cell. Selecting a merged cell and clicking the Merge And Center button splits the merged cells into the original group of separate cells.

named range A group of related cells defined by a single name.

Paste Options A button that appears after you paste an item from the Microsoft Office Clipboard into your workbook, and which provides options for how the item appears in the workbook.

Pick From List The Excel functionality that you can use to enter a value into a cell by choosing the value from the set of values already entered into cells in the same column.

pivot To reorganize the contents of a PivotTable.

PivotChart A chart, which can be linked to a PivotTable, that can be reorganized dynamically to emphasize different aspects of the underlying data.

PivotTable A dynamic worksheet that can be reorganized by a user.

portrait mode A display and printing mode whereby columns run parallel to the long edge of a sheet of paper.

precedent A cell that is used in a formula.

primary key A field or group of fields with values that distinguish a row of data from all other rows.

property A file detail, such as an author name or project code, that helps identify the file.

Quick Access Toolbar A customizable toolbar that contains a set of commands that are independent of the ribbon.

Quick Analysis A selection of tools that a user can use to summarize data quickly by using formulas and charts.

range A group of related cells.

Recommended Chart A chart, designed by the Excel program, that summarizes a selected data range.

Recommended PivotTable A PivotTable, designed by the Excel program, that summarizes a selected data range.

refresh To update the contents of one document when the contents of another document are changed.

relative reference A cell reference in a formula, such as =B3, that refers to a cell that is a specific distance away from the cell that contains the formula. For example, if the formula =B3 were in cell C3, copying the formula to cell C4 would cause the formula to change to =B4. See also *absolute reference*.

ribbon The tab-based user interface introduced in Microsoft Office 2007.

row Cells that are on the same horizontal line in a worksheet.

scenario An alternative data set with which you view the impact of specific changes on your worksheet.

schema A defined structure that a program can use to interpret the contents of an XML file.

search filter A filter in which you enter a string of characters and have Excel display every value within an Excel table, data set, or PivotTable that contains that character string.

sharing Making a workbook available for more than one user to open and modify simultaneously.

sheet tab The indicator for selecting a worksheet, located at the bottom of the workbook window.

SkyDrive An online service, accessed through a Microsoft account, that a user can use to store data in the cloud.

slicer An Excel tool with which you can filter an Excel table, data list, or PivotTable while indicating which items are displayed and which are hidden.

Solver An Excel add-in that finds the optimal value for one cell by varying the results of other cells.

sort To reorder the contents of a worksheet based on a criterion.

sparkline A compact chart that summarizes data visually within a single worksheet cell.

subtotal A partial total for related data in a worksheet.

template A workbook used as a pattern for creating other workbooks.

theme A predefined format that can be applied to a worksheet.

tracer arrow An arrow that indicates the formulas to which a cell contributes its value (a dependent arrow) or the cells from which a formula derives its value (a precedent arrow).

trendline A projection of future data (such as sales) based on past performance.

validation rule A test that data must pass to be entered into a cell without generating a warning message.

watch Display of a cell's contents in a separate window even when the cell is not visible in the Excel workbook.

what-if analysis Analysis of the contents of a worksheet to determine the impact that specific changes have on your calculations.

workbook The basic Excel document, consisting of one or more worksheets.

worksheet A page in an Excel workbook.

XML A content-marking system with which you store data about the contents of a document in that document.

Keyboard shortcuts

This list of shortcuts is a comprehensive list derived from Microsoft Excel 2013 Help. Some of the shortcuts might not be available in every edition of Excel 2013.

Ctrl combination shortcut keys

Key	Description
Ctrl+Shift+(	Unhides any hidden rows within the selection.
Ctrl+Shift+&	Applies the outline border to the selected cells.
Ctrl+Shift+_	Removes the outline border from the selected cells.
Ctrl+Shift+~	Applies the General number format.
Ctrl+Shift+$	Applies the Currency format with two decimal places (negative numbers in parentheses).
Ctrl+Shift+%	Applies the Percentage format with no decimal places.
Ctrl+Shift+^	Applies the Scientific number format with two decimal places.
Ctrl+Shift+#	Applies the Date format with the day, month, and year.
Ctrl+Shift+@	Applies the Time format with the hour and minute, and A.M. or P.M.
Ctrl+Shift+!	Applies the Number format with two decimal places, thousands separator, and minus sign (-) for negative values.
Ctrl+Shift+*	Selects the current region around the active cell (the data area enclosed by blank rows and blank columns). In a PivotTable, it selects the entire PivotTable report.
Ctrl+Shift+:	Enters the current time.
Ctrl+Shift+"	Copies the value from the cell above the active cell into the cell or the formula bar.
Ctrl+Shift+Plus (+)	Opens the Insert dialog box to insert blank cells.
Ctrl+Minus (-)	Opens the Delete dialog box to delete the selected cells.
Ctrl+;	Enters the current date.
Ctrl+`	Toggles between displaying cell values and displaying formulas in the worksheet.
Ctrl+'	Copies a formula from the cell above the active cell into the cell or the formula bar.
Ctrl+1	Opens the Format Cells dialog box.

Key	Description
Ctrl+2	Toggles to apply or remove bold formatting.
Ctrl+3	Toggles to apply or remove italic formatting.
Ctrl+4	Toggles to apply or remove underlining.
Ctrl+5	Toggles to apply or remove strikethrough.
Ctrl+6	Toggles between hiding and displaying objects.
Ctrl+8	Toggles to display or hide the outline symbols.
Ctrl+9	Hides the selected rows.
Ctrl+0	Hides the selected columns.
Ctrl+A	Selects the entire worksheet. If the worksheet contains data, pressing Ctrl+A selects the current region. Pressing Ctrl+A a second time selects the entire worksheet. When the cursor is to the right of a function name in a formula, pressing Ctrl+A opens the Function Arguments dialog box.
Ctrl+Shift+A	Inserts the argument names and parentheses when the cursor is to the right of a function name in a formula.
Ctrl+B	Toggles to apply or remove bold formatting.
Ctrl+C	Copies the selected cells.
Ctrl+D	Uses the Fill Down command to copy the contents and format of the topmost cell of a selected range into the cells below.
Ctrl+F	Opens the Find And Replace dialog box, with the Find page active. Shift+F5 also displays this page, whereas Shift+F4 repeats the last Find action.
Ctrl+Shift+F	Opens the Format Cells dialog box, with the Font page active.
Ctrl+G	Opens the Go To dialog box. F5 also opens this dialog box.
Ctrl+H	Opens the Find And Replace dialog box, with the Replace page active.
Ctrl+I	Toggles to apply or remove italic formatting.
Ctrl+K	Opens the Insert Hyperlink dialog box for new hyperlinks or the Edit Hyperlink dialog box for selected existing hyperlinks.
Ctrl+L	Opens the Create Table dialog box.
Ctrl+N	Creates a new, blank workbook.
Ctrl+O	Opens the Open dialog box to open or find a file.
Ctrl+Shift+O	Selects all cells that contain comments.
Ctrl+P	Displays the Print page in the Backstage view.
Ctrl+Shift+P	Opens the Format Cells dialog box, with the Font page active.
Ctrl+R	Uses the Fill Right command to copy the contents and format of the leftmost cell of a selected range into the cells to the right.
Ctrl+S	Saves the active file with its current file name, location, and file format.
Ctrl+T	Opens the Create Table dialog box.

Key	Description
Ctrl+U	Toggles to apply or remove underlining.
Ctrl+Shift+U	Toggles between expanding and collapsing the formula bar.
Ctrl+V	Inserts the contents of the Microsoft Office Clipboard at the cursor and replaces any selection. Available only after you have cut or copied an object, text, or cell contents.
Ctrl+Alt+V	Opens the Paste Special dialog box. Available only after you have cut or copied an object, text, or cell contents on a worksheet or in another program.
Ctrl+W	Closes the selected workbook window.
Ctrl+X	Cuts the selected cells.
Ctrl+Y	Repeats the last command or action, if possible.
Ctrl+Z	Performs the Undo command to reverse the last command or to delete the last entry that you entered.

TIP The Ctrl combinations Ctrl+E, Ctrl+J, Ctrl+M, and Ctrl+Q are currently unassigned to any shortcuts.

Function keys

Key	Description
F1	Displays the Excel Help pane.
Ctrl+F1	Displays or hides the ribbon.
Alt+F1	Creates an embedded chart of the data in the current range.
Alt+Shift+F1	Inserts a new worksheet.
F2	Opens the active cell for editing and positions the cursor at the end of the cell contents. It also moves the cursor into the formula bar when editing in a cell is turned off.
Ctrl+F2	Displays the print preview area on the Print page in the Backstage view.
Shift+F2	Adds a cell comment or opens an existing comment for editing.
F3	Opens the Paste Name dialog box. Available only if names exist in the workbook.
Shift+F3	Opens the Insert Function dialog box.
F4	Repeats the last command or action, if possible.
Ctrl+F4	Closes the selected workbook window.
Alt+F4	Exits Excel.

Key	Description
F5	Opens the Go To dialog box.
Ctrl+F5	Restores the window size of the selected workbook window.
F6	Switches between the worksheet, ribbon, pane, and Zoom controls. In a worksheet that has been split, F6 includes the split panes when switching between panes and the ribbon area.
Ctrl+F6	Switches to the next workbook window when more than one workbook window is open.
Shift+F6	Switches between the worksheet, Zoom controls, pane, and ribbon.
F7	Opens the Spelling dialog box to check spelling in the active worksheet or selected range.
Ctrl+F7	Performs the Move command on the workbook window when it is not maximized. Use the arrow keys to move the window, and when finished press Enter or Esc to cancel.
F8	Turns extend mode on or off. In extend mode, *Extended Selection* appears in the status line, and the arrow keys extend the selection.
Ctrl+F8	Performs the Size command (on the Control menu for the workbook window) when a workbook is not maximized.
Alt+F8	Opens the Macro dialog box to create, run, edit, or delete a macro.
Shift+F8	Enables you to add a nonadjacent cell or range to a selection of cells by using the arrow keys.
F9	Calculates all worksheets in all open workbooks.
Ctrl+F9	Minimizes a workbook window to an icon.
Shift+F9	Calculates the active worksheet.
Ctrl+Alt+F9	Calculates all worksheets in all open workbooks, regardless of whether they have changed since the last calculation.
Ctrl+Alt+Shift+F9	Rechecks dependent formulas, and then calculates all cells in all open workbooks, including cells not marked as needing to be calculated.
F10	Turns key tips on or off. (Pressing Alt does the same thing.)
Ctrl+F10	Maximizes or restores the selected workbook window.
Shift+F10	Displays the shortcut menu for a selected item.
Alt+Shift+F10	Displays the menu or message for an Error Checking button.
F11	Creates a chart of the data in the current range in a separate Chart sheet.
Alt+F11	Opens the Microsoft Visual Basic Editor, in which you can create a macro by using Visual Basic for Applications (VBA).
Shift+F11	Inserts a new worksheet.
F12	Opens the Save As dialog box.

Other useful shortcut keys

Key	Description
Arrow keys	Moves one cell up, down, left, or right in a worksheet.
Ctrl+Arrow key	Moves to the edge of the current data region (range of cells that contains data and that is bounded by empty cells or datasheet borders) in a worksheet.
Shift+Arrow key	Extends the selection of cells by one cell.
Ctrl+Shift+Arrow key	Extends the selection of cells to the last nonblank cell in the same column or row as the active cell, or if the next cell is blank, extends the selection to the next nonblank cell.
Left Arrow or Right Arrow	Selects the tab to the left or right when the ribbon is selected. When a submenu is open or selected, these arrow keys switch between the main menu and the submenu.
Down Arrow or Up Arrow	Selects the next or previous command when a menu or submenu is open. When a ribbon tab is selected, these keys navigate up or down the tab group. In a dialog box, arrow keys move between options in an open drop-down list, or between options in a group of options.
Down Arrow or Alt+Down Arrow	Displays a selected drop-down list.
Backspace	Deletes one character to the left in the formula bar. Also clears the content of the active cell. In cell editing mode, deletes the character to the left of the cursor.
Delete	Removes the cell contents (data and formulas) from selected cells without affecting cell formats or comments. In cell editing mode, deletes the character to the right of the cursor.
End	Turns End mode on. In End mode, you can press an arrow key to move to the next nonblank cell in the same column or row as the active cell. If the cells are blank, pressing End followed by an arrow key moves to the last cell in the row or column. End also selects the last command on the menu when a menu or submenu is visible.
Ctrl+End	Moves to the last cell on a worksheet, to the lowest used row of the rightmost used column. If the cursor is in the formula bar, Ctrl+End moves the cursor to the end of the text.

Key	Description
Ctrl+Shift+End	Extends the selection of cells to the last used cell on the worksheet (lower-right corner). If the cursor is in the formula bar, Ctrl+Shift+End selects all text in the formula bar from the cursor position to the end—this does not affect the height of the formula bar.
Enter	Completes a cell entry from the cell or the formula bar, and selects the cell below (by default). In a data form, moves to the first field in the next record. Displays a selected menu (press F10 to activate the menu bar) or performs the action for a selected command. In a dialog box, performs the action for the default command button in the dialog box (the button with the bold outline, often the OK button).
Alt+Enter	Starts a new line in the same cell.
Ctrl+Enter	Fills the selected cell range with the current entry.
Shift+Enter	Completes a cell entry and selects the cell above it.
Esc	Cancels an entry in the cell or formula bar. Closes an open menu or submenu, dialog box, or message window. Also closes full screen mode when this mode has been applied, and returns to normal screen mode to display the ribbon and status bar again.
Home	Moves to the beginning of a row in a worksheet. Moves to the cell in the upper-left corner of the window when Scroll Lock is turned on. Selects the first command on the menu when a menu or submenu is visible.
Ctrl+Home	Moves to the beginning of a worksheet.
Ctrl+Shift+Home	Extends the selection of cells to the beginning of the worksheet.
Page Down	Moves one screen down in a worksheet.
Alt+Page Down	Moves one screen to the right in a worksheet.
Ctrl+Page Down	Moves to the next sheet in a workbook.
Ctrl+Shift+Page Down	Selects the current and next sheet in a workbook.
Page Up	Moves one screen up in a worksheet.
Alt+Page Up	Moves one screen to the left in a worksheet.
Ctrl+Page Up	Moves to the previous sheet in a workbook.
Ctrl+Shift+Page Up	Selects the current and previous sheet in a workbook.
Spacebar	In a dialog box, performs the action for the selected button, or selects or clears a check box.
Ctrl+Spacebar	Selects an entire column in a worksheet.
Shift+Spacebar	Selects an entire row in a worksheet.

Key	Description
Ctrl+Shift+Spacebar	Selects the entire worksheet. If the worksheet contains data, pressing Ctrl+Shift+Spacebar selects the current region. Pressing Ctrl+Shift+Spacebar a second time selects the current region and its summary rows. Pressing Ctrl+Shift+Spacebar a third time selects the entire worksheet. When an object is selected, pressing Ctrl+Shift+Spacebar selects all objects on a worksheet.
Alt+Spacebar	Displays the Control menu for the Excel window.
Tab	Moves one cell to the right in a worksheet. Moves between unlocked cells in a protected worksheet. Moves to the next option or option group in a dialog box.
Shift+Tab	Moves to the previous cell in a worksheet or the previous option in a dialog box.
Ctrl+Tab	Switches to the next page in a dialog box.
Ctrl+Shift+Tab	Switches to the previous page in a dialog box.

Index

Symbols

2DayScenario workbook, 221
3-D references, 205, 210, 213, 453
2013Q1ShipmentsByCategory, 57–58
2013YearlyRevenueSummary, 400
+ (addition), 80
& (concatenation), 80
{} (curly braces), 97
#DIV/0! error code, 99
/ (division), 80
= (equals), 80, 81, 204
(error code), 99
^ (exponentiation), 80
> (greater than), 80
>= (greater than or equal to), 80
< (less than), 80
<= (less than or equal to), 80
* (multiplication), 80
#N/A! error code, 99
#NAME? error code, 99
- (negation), 80
<> (not equal to), 80
% (percentage), 80
#REF! error code, 99, 205, 213
- (subtraction), 80
#VALUE! error code, 99

A

absolute references, 88, 105, 453
active cells, 54, 453
active filters, 153
ActiveX controls, 386
AdBuy workbook, 236–240
Add Constraint dialog box, 235
add-in, 453
Add-Ins dialog box, Solver Add-in, 233
addition (+), 80

addition operation, precedence of operators, 80
Add Level button, 176
Add Scenario dialog box, 220
Adjust group, 139
Advanced Filter dialog box, 163
Advanced page
 Cut, Copy, And Paste, 56
 General group, 179
advertising, adding logos to worksheets, 138–140
AGGREGATE function, 159–161
alert boxes, for broken links, 205
alignment, 453
Allow Users To Edit Ranges dialog box, 427
alphabetical sorting, 175, 179
alternative data sets
 defining, 219
 defining multiple, 223
 usefulness of, 215
alternative words, 63
amount loaned (pv), 83
Analysis group
 Data Analysis, 240
 Solver button, 233
 Trendline button, 264
Analysis ToolPak, 240, 243
arguments, 83, 190, 453
arithmetic operators, precedence of, 80
ARM processor, 5
Arrange group, 138, 281
array formulas, 96–98, 105
Ask Me Which Changes Win, 414
aspect ratio, 453
auditing, 99, 413, 453
authenticating workbooks, 433
AutoCalculate, 159
AutoComplete, 47, 72, 453
autocomplete, for formulas, 83
AutoCorrect Options, 68, 69
AutoExpansion, 68–69

X

Y

About the author

Curtis Frye is a writer, speaker, and performer who lives in Portland, Oregon. He is the author or coauthor of more than 20 books, including *Microsoft Excel 2010 Step by Step* and *Microsoft Excel 2010 Plain & Simple*. In addition to his writing, Curt presents keynote addresses on Excel and motivational topics.

How To Download Your eBook

Thank you for purchasing this Microsoft Press® title. Your companion PDF eBook is ready to download from O'Reilly Media, official distributor of Microsoft Press titles.

To download your eBook, go to
http://go.microsoft.com/FWLink/?Linkid=224345
and follow the instructions.

Please note: You will be asked to create a free online account and enter the access code below.

Your access code:

> ## TWLQPNM

Microsoft® Excel® 2013 Step by Step

Your PDF eBook allows you to:

- Search the full text
- Print
- Copy and paste

Best yet, you will be notified about free updates to your eBook.

If you ever lose your eBook file, you can download it again just by logging in to your account.

Need help? Please contact:
mspbooksupport@oreilly.com
or call 800-889-8969.

What do you think of this book?

We want to hear from you!
To participate in a brief online survey, please visit:

microsoft.com/learning/booksurvey

Tell us how well this book meets your needs—what works effectively, and what we can do better. Your feedback will help us continually improve our books and learning resources for you.

Thank you in advance for your input!

Learn Microsoft® Project the quick and easy way!

Microsoft Project can revolutionize the way a business works—if you know how to take advantage of all the features. This book's 18 lessons will systematically teach you how to plan, manage, and communicate project information in any business. The lessons are integrated with practice files in MICROSOFT PROJECT FOR WINDOWS® 95 STEP BY STEP and offer quick and easy training on the latest version of this popular and powerful project management software. The step-by-step method allows you to choose your best starting point, learn at your own pace, and build the skills you need. Each easy-to-follow lesson takes 20–50 minutes and includes real-world business examples and practice files on the accompanying disk.

With this book-and-disk self-training package, you'll learn how to:

- Develop, plan, schedule, and chart project information
- Break your project down into tasks and create a realistic timeline

Put Microsoft Project to work today—with MICROSOFT PROJECT FOR WINDOWS 95 STEP BY STEP.

U.S.A.	**$29.95**
U.K.	£27.99 [V.A.T. included]
Canada	$39.95
ISBN 1-55615-866-1	

"Look it up in Petzold!"

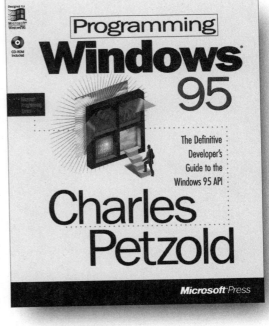